THE HIDDEN PLACES OF

SCOTLAND

By Jim Gracie

© Travel Publishing Ltd.

Regional Hidden Places

Cornwall
Devon
Dorset, Hants & Isle of Wight
East Anglia
Lake District & Cumbria
Northumberland & Durham
Peak District and Derbyshire
Yorkshire

National Hidden Places

England
Ireland
Scotland
Wales

Hidden Inns

East Anglia
Heart of England
South
South East
West Country

Country Pubs and Inns

Cornwall
Devon
Sussex
Wales
Yorkshire

Country Living Rural Guides

East Anglia
Heart of England
Ireland
North East of England
North West of England
Scotland
South
South East
Wales
West Country

Other Guides

Off the Motorway

Published by: Travel Publishing Ltd, 7a Apollo House, Calleva Park, Aldermaston, Berks, RG7 8TN

ISBN 1-904-434-53-3
EAN 9781904434535

© Travel Publishing Ltd

First published 1994, second edition 1997, third edition 1999, fourth edition 2002, fifth edition 2004, sixth edition 2007

Printing by: Scotprint, Haddington

Maps by: © Maps in Minutes ™ (2007)
© Crown Copyright, Ordnance Survey 2007

Editor: Jim Gracie

Cover Design: Lines and Words, Aldermaston

Cover Photograph: Glen Etive, Argyllshire
© www.picturesofbritain.co.uk

Text Photographs: © www.picturesofbritain.co.uk
and © Bob Brooks, Weston-super-Mare

Foreword

This is the 6th edition of *The Hidden Places of Scotland* and it has been fully updated. In this respect we would like to thank the Tourist Information Centres in Scotland for helping us update the editorial content. Regular readers will note that the pages of the guide have been extensively redesigned to allow more information to be presented on the many interesting places to visit in this very hospitable country. In addition, although you will still find details of places of interest and advertisers of places to stay, eat and drink included under each village, town or city, these are now cross referenced to more detailed information contained in a separate, easy-to-use section to the rear of the book.

Scotland has been inhabited for thousands of years and is rich in history and culture. It is blessed with some of the most impressive mountains in the British Isles and finest coastlines and offshore islands in the world. It is also full of "hidden places", which can enrich the visitor's knowledge of Scottish heritage and provide landscapes that astound the eye with their sheer beauty.

The Hidden Places of Scotland contains a wealth of interesting information on the history, the countryside, the towns and villages and the more established places of interest. But it also promotes the more secluded and little known visitor attractions and places to stay, eat and drink many of which are easy to miss unless you know exactly where you are going.

We include hotels, bed & breakfasts, restaurants, pubs, bars, teashops and cafes as well as historic houses, museums, gardens and many other attractions throughout Scotland, all of which are comprehensively indexed. Many places are accompanied by an attractive photograph and are easily located by using the map at the beginning of each chapter. We do not award merit marks or rankings but concentrate on describing the more interesting, unusual or unique features of each place with the aim of making the reader's stay in the local area an enjoyable and stimulating experience.

Whether you are travelling around Scotland on business or for pleasure we do hope that you enjoy reading and using this book. We are always interested in what readers think of places covered (or not covered) in our guides so please do not hesitate to use the reader reaction form provided to give us your considered comments. We also welcome any general comments which will help us improve the guides themselves. Finally if you are planning to visit any other corner of the British Isles we would like to refer you to the list of other *Hidden Places* titles to be found to the rear of the book and to the Travel Publishing website.

Travel Publishing

Did you know that you can also search our website for details of thousands of places to see, stay, eat or drink throughout Britain and Ireland? Our site has become increasingly popular and now receives over 160,000 hits per day. Try it!

website: **www.travelpublishing.co.uk**

The Borders

Of all the regions in Scotland, the Borders has the bloodiest history. It was here, from the 13th to the 16th centuries, that the constant bickering between Scotland and England boiled over into bloodshed and outright war. This was the land of the reivers, or "moss troopers" - men from both countries who regularly crossed the border and raped, pillaged, burnt, stole and rustled their way into the history books. People nowadays tend to romanticise them, and though some displayed great bravery, most were merciless thugs, with no one being safe from their activities - not even monks and churchmen. They gave the words "blackmail" and "bereave" to the English language, and were the first to practise what we nowadays call "protection rackets". An old legend states that when a male born in the Borders was baptised, his right hand was excluded from the ceremony so that he could use it to kill and maim.

Though it was a year-round activity, most reiving usually took place between autumn and late winter the following year, when there was plenty of darkness The Scots penetrated as far as Yorkshire on occasions, and the English

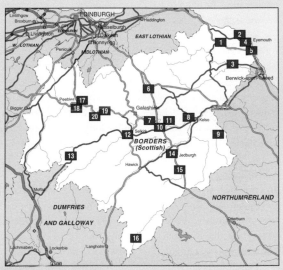

sometimes came as far north as the outskirts of Edinburgh. The great Borders families had branches on both sides of the border, and most took part, harrying each other even though they may have been related. It wasn't until James VI of Scotland also ascended the throne of England that reiving was finally brought to an end. Though it all took place over 400 years ago, you can still see reminders of the reivers in the area - notably in its fortified churches and old keeps, known as "peles".

But the Borders was also the land of romance, of ballads and tales of high chivalry. The literature of Sir Walter Scott, a Borders man to the core, is steeped in them. It was he who, almost single-handedly, invented Scotland's modern image, which depends not on the softer scenery of his native lands, but on the lofty mountains, clan chiefs, skirling bagpipes and kilts of the Highlands. This has not been lost on the hardy Borderers, who know there is more to Scotland than kitsch images. And there are, strictly speaking, no clans in the Scottish Borders at all. Instead there are families, such as the Armstrongs, the Kerrs, the Johnstones, the Maxwells, the Nixons and the Homes.

The Borders are sometimes dismissed by people who consider them to be "not the real Scotland". Certainly, in some areas the scenery has an English feel to it, but the Borders have more historical associations than anywhere else in Scotland, and it was here, and not the Highlands, that the nation as we know it today took the brunt of England's vain attempts to conquer it.

The area stretches from the North Sea in the east to the borders of Dumfriesshire in the west, and contains four former counties – Peeblesshire, Selkirkshire, Roxburghshire and Berwickshire. The scenery is gentler than the Highlands, and the hills are rounded and green, with fertile valleys, quiet villages and cosy market towns to explore. That flat area of Berwickshire known as the Merse, which lies roughly between the Lammermuir Hills and the English border, is one of the most intensely farmed areas in Britain.

There are castles and old houses aplenty, from Floors Castle just outside Kelso, home of the Duke of Roxburgh, to 10th century Traquair House in Peeblesshire, said to be the oldest continually inhabited house in Scotland. Mellerstain too, is worth visiting, as is Paxton, Manderston, Thirlestane and Abbotsford.

But perhaps the area's most beautiful and haunting buildings are its ruined abbeys. Again and again English soldiers attacked them, and again and again, as the Scots crossed the border hell bent on revenge, the monks quietly got on with rebuilding and repairing them. Now the ruins at Melrose, Kelso, Dryburgh and Jedburgh rest easy under the care of Historic Scotland, and they can be easily visited and appreciated.

The area's great icon is the 98-mile long River Tweed which, for part of its length, forms the boundary between Scotland and England. Just east of Kelso, the border turns south away from the river, and it becomes wholly Scottish. Its fame rests on salmon, and it is said that more salmon are caught from the Tweed than any other river within the EU. During summer and autumn, it also has some excellent sea trout. It is a river that in some ways defines the whole area, and most of its larger towns and villages, from Peebles to Coldstream, are to be found on its banks.

The Borders is also an area of woodland and forests, with plenty of woodland walks. The Tweed Valley Forest Park, between Peebles and Selkirk, is one of the best. At Glentress Forest, one mile east of Peebles, you can hire mountain bikes at the Hub car park. This is one of the most visited woodland areas in Scotland, and attracts over 130,000 visitors a year from both Scotland and England. But for all their leisure facilities, these are working forests, managed by the Forestry Commission, and form an integral part of the area's economy.

DUNS

Berwickshire is an unusual county, in that the town which gave it its name has been part of England since 1482. Therefore Greenlaw, and then in 1853 Duns, was chosen as the county town. It is a quiet, restful place with a wide and gracious market square. Up until the 18th century, it was known as "Dunse". Its motto, *Duns Dings A*, means "Duns overcomes everything".

The name itself comes from the word "dun", meaning a fort, and the first mention of it we have in history is in a charter dated before 1214, where we find a 'Hugo de Duns' signing it as a witness. Standing as it does on a main route in the Borders, it was a target for English armies. In 1377 the Earl of Northumberland invaded Scotland, and soon reached Duns. His army by this time was tired, and the Scots saw this. So they fashioned a contraption made of wood and dried skins which rattled in the wind. This so frightened the English horses that they bolted, closely followed by the English soldiers.

Then, in 1544/5, during the 'Rough Wooing', when Henry VIII tried to coerce the Scots into a marriage between his son and Mary Stuart, the town was again invaded and this time destroyed.

All this took place, not in the town as we know it today, but where it used to stand. This area is now known as The Bruntons, or 'burnt towns' on the western edge of Duns Law. A cairn marks the site.

On its outskirts is the 713 feet high **Duns Law**, with a pathway leading from the town's Castle Street to its summit. From the top there is a magnificent view of the surrounding countryside. The Cheviot Hills to the south and the Lammermuir Hills to the north can be seen on a clear day, as can the North Sea, 12 miles away to the east. In 1638 a Covenanting army of 12,000 men, which opposed the imposition of bishops on the Scottish church by Charles I, set up camp here under General Leslie, and a **Covenanter's Stone** commemorates this event. There are also the remains of an Iron Age fort, plus some defensive works built by the Covenanting army.

General Leslie was quartered in **Duns Castle**, built round the core of a pele tower built in about 1320 by the Earl of Moray, who had been given the surrounding lands by his uncle, Robert the Bruce. In 1696 it was bought by the Hay family, who enlarged it between 1818 and 1822, creating the Gothic Revival building we see today. It is still owned by the Hays, though not open to the public. It is now a venue for weddings and corporate hospitality.

Standing in the town square is the **Mercat Cross**, erected in 1792. The burgh of Duns received its charter in 1489, and it was around the cross that the town's market was held, though it is not now in its original position. It is one of the features on the **Duns Town Trail**,

In the grounds of Duns Castle is the quaintly named Hen Poo' (a shortening of the word 'pool'), which is the centrepiece of the Duns Castle Nature Reserve, owned and run by the Scottish Wildlife Trust. There is a bird hide on the northern shore, and from here you can see mallard ducks, tufted ducks, swans, and coots. Close by, the Mill Dam is also home to many bird species.

Within the town of Duns there is a memorial to a famous man who lived in more recent times: Jim Clark, the racing driver, was born on a farm near Kilmany in Fife in 1936, but from the age of six lived on Edington Mains, near Duns. The Jim Clark Memorial Trophy Room in Newtown Street is dedicated to his memory. His win at the 1965 Indianapolis Grand Prix astonished the Americans, who considered that no one but an American could cross the finishing line first. He was world champion in 1963 and 1965, and motor racing enthusiasts from all over the world now make the pilgrimage to view the trophies (including the two world championship trophies he won) and mementoes on display. He was killed at Hockenheim in Germany in 1968 aged 32, when a rear tyre burst during a Formula 2 race, and is buried in Chirnside Parish Church cemetery, about five miles east of Duns (see also Chirnside).

laid out by the local council.

It was in Duns that **John Duns Scotus**, known as "Doctor Subtilis", or the "subtle doctor"**,** was supposed to have been born in about 1266. He was a Franciscan monk who became one of the greatest theologians and philosophers of his time. His followers were known as Scotists, and his influence is still felt within the Catholic Church to this day, such as his championing of the doctrine of the immaculate conception. However, his opponents had another, less flattering, name for them - "Dunses" - from which we get the word "dunce". He entered the Franciscan Order in the friary at Dumfries (see also Dumfries), and eventually died at Cologne on November 8th 1308. On his tomb are the words "Scotland bore me, England adopted me, Cologne holds". In 1991 the Pope made him "Blessed", the first step on the ladder to sainthood (see also North Uist).

In Duns Public Park is a bronze statue of him, erected in 1996 and executed by Frank Tritchle. In the grounds of Duns Castle, close to where the cottage where he was born is supposed to have stood, the modern Franciscan Order erected a cairn to his memory in 1966. Near the cairn is the Gothic **Pavilion Lodge**, built in the 18th century.

Also born in Duns was **Robert Fortune**, in 1812. He was one of the most plant collectors of the 19th century. He was created Superintendent of the Hothouse Department of the Royal Horticultural Society in London, and then became the Society's Collector for China. Known in China as 'Sing Wa', he adopted Chinese dress while in that country, complete with shaved head and pigtail. The rose 'fortune's double yellow' is named after him.

On the west side of Market Square is the 19th century **Tolbooth House**, situated on the site of the town house of Sir James Cockburn, who owned most of the land surrounding Duns in the 17th century. The **Parish Church** dates from 1880, after its predecessor, built just six years before, was destroyed by fire.

Crumstane Farm Park lies a mile east of the town, off the A6105, and has over 60 breeds of animals on display, from llamas to donkeys and sheep.

Also east of the town is **Manderston House**, lying in 56 acres of formal gardens, and is open to the public. It was built between 1903 and 1905, and was the last great stately home built in Britain. It is a showpiece of Edwardian wealth and good taste, and was designed by architect John Kinross. It incorporates a silver staircase that is said to be the only one in the world, and was built for Sir James Miller and his wife, the Honorable Eveline Curzon, daughter of Lord Scarsdale, head of one of the oldest families in the country. Nowadays Manderston is the home of the Palmer family, of the famous Huntly and Palmer biscuit empire, which explains why it houses a large collection of biscuit tins. It was here that the Channel 4 series, *The Edwardian Country House*, was filmed

AROUND DUNS

COCKBURNSPATH

13 miles N of Duns just off the A1

The **Parish Church of St Helens** is partly 15th century, and close by is the ruined **Cockburnspath Tower**, dating from the 15th and 16th centuries. In its time it has been owned by the Dunbars, the Homes, the Sinclairs and the Douglases. The **Mercat Cross,** at the heart of the village, was erected in 1503 to celebrate the marriage of James IV to Margaret Tudor, sister of Henry VIII of England. It has as its motif a thistle and a rose, signifying Scotland and England. Just a few years later James was killed at Flodden fighting the English. At the same time, James presented lands around the village to his new wife. The village sits close to **Pease Dean**, a Scottish Wildlife Trust Reserve, where you can see butterflies, lichens and rare mosses. **Pease Bridge** was built in in 1783 and at the time was the highest stone bridge in Europe.

Though it lies inland from the North Sea, the Southern Upland Way terminates here, as the path reaches the sea east of the village and then turns west towards it.

East of the village, on the coastline, is the rocky **Siccar Point**, famous as the place where James Hutton (1726-1799), th father of geology, proved his theories about

the gradual decay and renewal of rocks. A prehistoric fort once stood on the point, but this has been destroyed by quarrying. At one time Siccar Point was within the parish of **Old Cambus**, but at some time in the past it was combined with Cockburnspath. The ruins of the old parish church can still be seen.

ABBEY ST BATHANS

5 miles N of Duns on a minor road off the B6355

The pretty village of Abbey St Bathans lies in the steep-sided valley of the Whiteadder Water, deep within the Lammermuir Hills. It is truly a hidden gem, and sits on the **Southern Upland Way**, the coast-to-coast footpath that transverses Southern Scotland from Portpatrick in the west to Cockburnspath in the east. The village's name is misleading, as there was never an abbey here. However, in 1170, Ada, Countess of Dunbar, founded the priory of St Mary in the village, and parts of the priory church have been incorporated into the present **Parish Church**. The village was chosen because, in about AD 500, St Bathan, a follower of St Columba, established a Celtic monastery here.

The tombstone of a former prioress, which touchingly shows her pet dog, is preserved within the church. To the south, at Cockburn Law, are the ruins of the 2nd century **Edins Hall Broch**, one of the few brochs (a round, fortified stone tower) to be found in Southern Scotland. It sits within the

| **I** CEDAR CAFÉ |

Grantshouse

Wholesome and appetising food in pleasant surroundings near layby on the A1.

¶ *see page 421*

5

Edins Hall Broch, Abbey St Bathans

2	DUNLAVEROCK

Coldingham Sands

Elegant Edwardian country house in superb beachside location offering quality D, B&B; also self-catering.

see page 418

ramparts and ditches of an even earlier fortification, and is named after Etin, a legendary giant with three heads who is said to have terrorised the area in olden times.

LONGFORMACUS

6 miles NW of Duns on an unmarked road off the B6355

This pretty, remote little village sits on the Southern Upland Way. **Longformacus Parish Church** dates from the early 1700s, and sits on the foundations of a much earlier building. **Longformacus House** (not open to the public) is an elegant Georgian building. To the south lies **Dirrington Great Law**, a hill which rises to 1,309 feet, and to the north, about five miles along a narrow road, are the **Mutiny Stones**, also called the "Mitten O' Stanes", a 5,000-year-old burial cairn.

COLDINGHAM

13 miles NE of Duns on the A1107

The village of Coldingham, a mile from the coast, is visited mainly for the remains of **Coldingham Priory**. It was founded in 1098 by King Edgar, son of Malcolm Canmore, and he gifted it to the monks of Durham. Originally it had been the site of a monastery founded by St Ebba, sister of King Oswy of Northumbria, in the seventh century. King Edgar's foundation suffered badly during the Scottish Wars of Independence, and was finally blown up by Cromwell in 1648 after he discovered Royalists hiding within it. Repairs to the ruins were carried out in about 1670. Between 1854 and 1855 the remains were restored, and today they are incorporated into the village's parish church.

Four miles northwest of the village, on the coast, are the ruins of **Fast Castle**, built on the site of an Iron Age fort. Once a stronghold of the Home family, it was held by the English for a while, but was subsequently taken again in 1410 by the Scots. In 1503 Margaret Tudor, sister of Henry VIII, stayed here overnight on her way north to marry James IV of Scotland. The ruins are perched 70 feet above the sea on a cliff top and can be reached via a minor road, though the last few hundred yards must be done on foot. Great care must be taken when visiting, however.

ST. ABB'S

12 miles NE of Duns, on the B6438

The picturesque fishing village of St Abb's is named after St Ebba (see Coldingham), who is said to have been shipwrecked here, and has a small, picturesque harbour. The whole coastline is rugged and spectacular, one of the most magnificent parts being **St Abb's Head** (National Trust for Scotland) to the north of the village. The cliffs are over 300 feet high, and are riddled with caves once haunted by smugglers. After her shipwreck, Ebba entered a monastery founded on the headland in the early 7th century, and eventually rose to become prioress.

St Abb's

An old legend recounts that the nuns, instead of living a life of austerity and prayer, eventually spent all their time eating, drinking and gossiping. This was because St Ebba had become too old and infirm to have control over them. The legend says the nuns also found time to bathe in the sea. The whole area is now a National Nature Reserve. Offshore there is one of the best diving sites in Scotland.

CHIRNSIDE

5 miles E of Duns on the B6355

Chirnside sits on the south side of a low hill with wonderful views over the surrounding countryside, and close to where the Blackadder Water and the Whiteadder Water meet. During World War I the peace of the village was shattered when a Zeppelin bombed it by accident. The **Parish Church** was founded by King Edgar of Scotland in the 12th century, possibly on a spot where Lindisfarne monks had already

erected a chapel in the 7th or 8th century. It is partly Norman, with an impressive Norman doorway and tympanum at its west end. The church was renovated and a substantial church tower built in memory of Fanny, Lady Tweedsmuir, who died in 1904 and was buried in the churchyard. She was an aunt of Sir Winston Churchill. Also within the cemetery is the grave of Jim Clark the racing driver (see also Duns). The **Jim Clark Memorial Clock**, with a silhouette of a Lotus racing car on it, stands in the middle of the village.

David Hulme, the 18th century philosopher, though born in Edinburgh, was educated at Chirnside School until he was 12 years old.

EDROM

3 miles E of Duns on a minor road off the A6105

The small village of Edrom has a fine **Parish Church** originally dedicated to St Mary. It was built in

3 CHIRNSIDE INN

Chirnside

Recently refurbished former coaching inn offering quality cuisine and en suite rooms, 2 with 4-poster beds.

see page 419

4   HOME ARMS HOTEL

Eyemouth

Overlooking the sea and offering en suite and dormitory accommodation, and honest-to-goodness pub food.

 see page 420

5   THE SHIP HOTEL

Eyemouth

Picturesque quayside hotel, refurbished in 2007, offering excellent seafood and comfortable en suite accommodation.

 see page 421

1732 on the site of a much earlier Norman church, and the present south aisle rests on foundations from this period.

Attached to it is the Blackadder Aisle, built for Archbishop Blackadder of Glasgow in 1499. It contains a tomb and effigy dating from 1553. A burial vault in the graveyard incorporates a Norman arch which was originally attached to the earlier Norman church

HUTTON

10 miles E of Duns on a minor road off the B6460

Close to the village stands **Hutton Castle**, one time home of Sir William Burrell, shipping magnate and art collector, who donated the Burrell Collection to the city of Glasgow in 1944 (see also Largs and Glasgow). It sits overlooking the River Whiteadder. Within the Burrell Collection in Glasgow are reproductions of the rooms in Hutton Castle - the hallway, the drawing room and the dining room. **Hutton Parish Church** dates from 1835 and has an old bell of 1661.

AYTON

10 miles E of Duns on the B6355

Ayton, a mile or so from the A1, is a pleasant village that sits on the north bank of the River Eye. Close by is **Ayton Castle**, built on the site of a much older, medieval structure which was burnt down in 1834. The ruin was bought by William Mitchell Innes, the governor of the Bank of Scotland. He commissioned James Gillespie Graham, a leading Gothic Revival

architect, to design a new castle, which was built between 1841 and 1846. It is reckoned to be one of the best examples in the country of that style of architecture called "Scottish Baronial", and is surrounded by a 6,000-acre estate. It is open from May - September, or by appointment, and houses fine paintings, furniture and porcelain.

Ayton Parish Church was built in 1864, and beside it are the ruins of its medieval predecessor.

EYEMOUTH

12 miles E of Duns on the A1107

Eyemouth is a picturesque little fishing town standing, as the name suggests, at the mouth of the River Eye, five miles north of the Scotland/England border. The monks of Coldingham Priory founded it as a small fishing port sometime in the 13th century.

At one time it was a smuggling centre, and some of the harbour-side houses still have old cellars and tunnels where contraband was stored. The centre of the trade was at **Gunsgreen House**, to the south of the harbour. It dates from 1755 and was designed by James and John Adam. It is said that it once contained a fireplace that opened like a gate, revealing a secret room behind.

The **World of Boats** at Gunsgreen, formerly housed in Exeter in Devon. is a collection of over 400 historic boats (one at least 4,000 years old) and 300 models from all over the world. Every year in July the **Herring Queen Festival** takes place, when the gaily be-decked fishing fleet escorts the "Herring Queen" into Eyemouth Harbour.

Eyemouth Museum, housed in the Auld Kirk built in 1812, records the history of the town and its fishing industry. Perhaps the most poignant exhibit is a 15-feet long by four feet wide tapestry sewn in 1981 that commemorates "Black Friday" - October 14, 1881. A great storm wrecked the whole of the town's fishing fleet, and 189 fishermen, 129 from Eyemouth alone, perished in sight of the shore.

An Eyemouth Town Trail has been laid out, and a leaflet is available from the museum.

LAMBERTON
11 miles E of Duns off the A1

Gretna Green was not the only place where runaway marriages took place. All along the border there were towns and villages only too willing to conduct a wedding ceremony in exchange for money. Lamberton, under a mile from the border, was one such place. At **Lamberton Bar** many ceremonies were conducted, and it is reckoned that at one time at least eight "priests", were involved in the business. Some of the records of these marriages still survive.

FOULDEN
9 miles E of Duns on the A6105

Foulden Parish Church, at the far end of the village, dates from 1786, and was built on the foundations of a medieval church. In 1587 commissioners appointed by Elizabeth I of England and James VI of Scotland met in the church to discuss the execution of James's mother, Mary Stuart. Nearby is an old two-storey **Tithe Barn** (Historic Scotland), dating from medieval times, though it was restored in the 18th and 19th centuries. "Tithe" means a tenth, and each farmer in the parish was supposed to donate a tenth of his crops to the church, which then stored it in the barn. It can only be viewed from the outside.

PAXTON
12 miles E of Duns just off the B6461 and close to the Tweed

Near the village, and close to the banks of the Tweed, stands **Paxton House**, the finest 18th century Palladian country house in Britain. It was built in 1758 by Patrick Home, Laird of Wedderburn, who, when he was 19, went to Leipzig University in Germany to study. He later went on to Berlin, where he was admitted to the court of Frederick the Great of Prussia. Here he fell in love with Sophie de Brandt, illegitimate daughter of Frederick and Lady-in-Waiting to Elizabeth Christina, Frederick's wife.

He returned home, and in anticipation of his marriage to Sophie, built Paxton House. Alas, the marriage never took place, though a pair of kid gloves given to Patrick by Sophie is on display. Also on display is a costume worn by Patrick at a great carnival held by Frederick in 1750.

The house was designed by John and James Adam, with

Close by Paxton is the Union Suspension Bridge across the Tweed, connecting Scotland and England. It was built between 1819 and 1820 by Sir Samuel Brown, who also invented the wrought-iron chain links used in its construction. It is 437 feet long and was Britain's first major suspension bridge to carry vehicular traffic as well as pedestrians. It is still in use today.

A priory for Cistercian nuns once stood in the town of Coldstream, but all trace of it has now disappeared. It was to the nunnery that some of the bodies of those slain at Flodden were brought in 1513 and given a Christian burial by the then prioress. However, some of the streets within the town, such as Penitent's Walk, Nun's Walk and Abbey Road, still remind us of the foundation.

plasterwork by their brother Robert. It houses the finest collection of Chippendale furniture in Scotland, and the art gallery (added to the house in 1811) is the largest private gallery in the country. It now houses paintings from the National Galleries of Scotland.

The house sits in 80 acres of grounds designed by Robert Robinson in the 18th century, and has nature trails, woodland walks and a "Paxton Ted" teddy bear trail. From the award-winning red squirrel hide you can catch glimpses of what is rapidly becoming one of Scotland's rarest mammals. There is also a tearoom and shop, and in the Victorian boathouse on the banks of the Tweed is a museum dedicated to salmon net fishing. Well behaved dogs are welcome if kept on a lead.

LADYKIRK

7 miles SE of Duns on a minor road off the B6470 and close to the Tweed

The **Parish Church of St Mary** dates from 1500, with a tower added in 1743. It is built entirely of

stone to prevent it being burnt down by the English. It is supposed to owe its origins to James IV, who had it built in thanksgiving for his rescue from drowning while trying to cross the Tweed in 1499. At the same time he changed the name of the village from Upsettington to Ladykirk.

COLDSTREAM

12 miles S of Duns on the A697

The town sits on the north bank of the Tweed at a point where the river forms the border between Scotland and England. **Coldstream Bridge**, joining the two countries, was built in 1766, and replaced a ford that had been a natural crossing point for centuries. On the bridge is a plaque that commemorates the fact that Robert Burns entered England by this route in 1787.

In the 18th and 19th centuries it rivalled, and then surpassed, Gretna Green as a place for runaway marriages. At the Scottish end of the bridge is the **Old Toll House**, where, in a 13-year period during the 19th century, 1,466 marriages were conducted.

General Monk founded the **Coldstream Guards** in 1659. It is the only regiment in Britain to take its name from a town, and within **Henderson Park** is a memorial stone which commemorates the regiment's foundation. The **Coldstream Museum** in Market Square houses extensive displays on its history. It also has a children's section and a courtyard with fountain and picnic area.

Old Toll House, Coldstream

A mile north of the town is **The Hirsel**, home of the Earls of Home since 1611. Sir Alec Douglas Home, the British prime minister for a short while in the 1960s, lived here. Though the house is not open to the public, the grounds can be explored. There is a small museum, a crafts centre, a gem display and a tearoom.

ECCLES

7 miles S of Duns on the B6461

In the mid-12th century, a Cistercian nunnery was founded here by the Earl of Dunbar. Remnants of it have been built into the wall surrounding the graveyard of the present **Eccles Parish Church**, built in 1774. The nunnery was badly damaged during English raids in 1545.

FOGO

3 miles S of Duns off the B6460

Fogo literally means the "foggage pit", foggage being the grass, or moss, that grows in a field after the hay has been cut. **Fogo Church** dates from the 17th and 18th centuries, though parts of it - especially the lower courses of its masonry - date from the 13th century or earlier. On the north wall are traces of built up arches. The church bell dates from 1644, and within the vestry is one of the oldest gravestones in Berwickshire, dating from the 14th century. On the outside wall of the church are stairs leading to private lofts, where the gentry once worshipped.

The picturesque lych gate is now a war memorial, and in the kirkyard are the war graves of 16 airmen from World War II. In the graveyard were also the graves of three German airmen from World War II, but these were exhumed in 1967 and reburied in Staffordshire.

GREENLAW

7 miles SW of Duns on the A697

Greenlaw was the county town of Berwickshire from 1696 to 1853, when Duns replaced it. It formerly stood near the "green law", or hill, a little to the southwest, and was given its burgh charter in 1596. The picturesque **Market Cross** dates from 1696, and the Parish Church dates from the 17th century, with a later tower that was once used as a jail. There are many fine buildings within the town, including a town hall built in 1829.

Marchmont House (not open to the public), three miles north east of the town, was built by Hugh Hume, third and last Earl of Marchmont, in the mid 18th century to the designs of Thomas Gibson. It is now a Sue Ryder home.

Three miles south of the town is the site of **Hume Castle**, ancient seat of the Hume family. The original castle was built in the 13th century, dismantled in 1515 and rebuilt in 1519. Over the years it was captured by the English and retaken by the Scots many times over. Eventually it was captured by Cromwell in 1650, and in 1651 it was demolished, the Hume family moving to the The Hirsel. What you see now is a folly built in 1770 on the castle's foundations. It sits

Three miles north of Coldstream, just off the A697, are the ruins of Castlelaw Castle, as well as a small hill known as a "mote". The former castle on the site was home to the Drienchester, or Darnchester, family, but was pulled down in the 16th century to make way for another building, the ruins of which we see today. From the mote there are some good views of the surrounding countryside.

6 THIRLESTANE CASTLE

Lauder

Thirlestane is one of the oldest castles in Scotland and superb details, including 17th century plasterwork, add to the splendour of the rooms.

 see page 421

Lauder Parish Church was built in 1673 to the designs of Sir William Bruce, and is in the form of a Greek cross. The medieval church stood in the grounds of Thirlestane Castle, and legend states that the Duke had it removed in the 17th century to improve his view. He instructed a bowman to fire an arrow westwards from the castle steps. Wherever the arrow landed the Duke would build a new church. That is why the church now stands within the town of Lauder itself.

600 feet above sea level, and makes an excellent viewpoint.

LAUDER

17 miles W of Duns on the A68

Lauder is a small royal burgh which sits on what was Dere Street - the foremost Roman road north into the land the Romans called Caledonia. To the east of the town is **Thirlestane Castle**, which is open to the public. It's a flamboyant place, with turrets, pinnacles and towers, giving it the appearance of a French château. It was originally built in the 13th century, but was extended and refurbished in the 16th century for the Maitland family, whose most famous member was John Maitland, second Earl and later first (and only) Duke of Lauderdale, who lived between 1616 and 1682. He was a close friend of Charles II and a member of the famous but unpopular "Cabal Cabinet". The word "cabal" comes from the initials of the five men who comprised it, Maitland's being "L" for Lauderdale. So powerful was he that he was soon regarded as the uncrowned king of Scotland. His ghost is said to haunt the castle.

The **Tolbooth** was once the administrative centre for the town, and dates from 1735. Here tolls were collected from market traders, and convicted felons (including witches) imprisoned in the vaulted rooms on the ground floor.

A **Lauder Town Trail** has been laid out, taking people on a tour of the towns' historical buildings and associations.

GALASHIELS

Galashiels (known locally as "Gala") derives its name from the "shiels" (dwellings) by the side of the Gala Water. It is a sizeable manufacturing town at one time noted for its tweed and woollen mills. As a reflection of this, the motto of the Galashiels Manufacturer's Corporation was "We dye to live and live to die".

The **Lochcarron Cashmere and Wool Centre** is located within the Waverley Mill in Huddersfield Street, and offers tours which explain the processes involved in the manufacture of woollens and tweeds. There is also a museum with a working Leffel water turbine wheel.

Old Gala House dates from the 15th century with later additions, and at one time was the town house of the Pringles, Lairds of Gala. It is now a museum and art gallery, and its gardens have recently been re-established, with a pond, spring bulbs and rhododendrons. Exhibitions of local art are sometimes held in the house. In Bank Street are the **Bank Street Gardens**, laid out shortly after World War II. In front of the town's war memorial (the work of local sculptor Thomas Clapperton, and described by H.V. Morton as "the most perfect town memorial in the British Isles") is a reminder of the area's bloody past - a bronze statue of a border reiver, armed and on horseback.

South of the town is part of an old earthworks known as the

Catrail, which is over 50 miles long

Also south of the town, on the banks of the Tweed, is **Abbotsford**, the home of **Sir Walter Scott**, writer and lawyer. Though born in Edinburgh in 1771, Scott was of good Borders stock, and was appointed sheriff depute (judge) at Selkirk Sheriff Court in 1799.

Scott had Abbotsford built between 1817 and 1822, and he lived in it until he died in 1832. Behind it is the Tweed, and here the monks of Melrose Abbey made a ford across the river, so Scott decided to call it Abbotsford. It is built in the Scottish Baronial style, and is crammed with mementoes and objects that reflected the great man's passion for Scottish history, such as a tumbler on which Burns had etched some verses, a lock of Charles Edward Stuart's hair, and a piece of oatcake found in the pocket of a Highlander killed at Culloden. There is more than a hint of Gothic about the interior, especially the panelled hallway, which contains a carriage clock - still keeping good time - once owned by Marie Antoinette.

The main focus of the house is Scott's austere study, where many of his later books were written. A gallery runs round the room, and in one corner is a door with a stairway behind it. Early each morning Scott descended these stairs from his dressing room to write for a few hours before heading for the courthouse in Selkirk.

Perhaps the most poignant room in the house is the dining room. Having returned from a trip abroad in September 1832, Scott knew that his end was near, and called for his bed to be set up at the window so that he could look out towards the Tweed. On September 21st he died. He had never got over the death of his French wife Margaret Charlotte (born in Lyon) in 1826, and at about the same time a publishing firm in which he was a partner went bankrupt. He decided to write his way out of debt, even though he still had his duties at Selkirk Sheriff Court to attend to. It eventually ruined his health, and he now lies beside his wife among the ruins of Dryburgh Abbey (see Dryburgh)

The Southern Upland Way passes through Galashiels, and you can also join the 89-mile-long **Tweed Cycle Way**, which passes close by. It starts at Biggar in Lanarkshire and ends up in Berwick-upon-Tweed.

AROUND GALASHIELS

CLOVENFORDS

3 miles W of Galashiels on the A72

Clovenfords sits about a mile north of the Tweed, and is home to the **School of Casting, Salmon and Trout Fishing**. It offers weekly courses throughout the season, with tuition taking place on the Tweed and local lochs. In 1803 William and Dorothy Wordsworth stayed in the local inn while touring the Scottish Borders.

The town of Galashiels is very old (the first mention of cloth mills was in 1588), and every year, in July, it holds the Braw Lads Gathering, which celebrates its long history. On the coat of arms of the old burgh appears the words "soor plooms" (sour plums), which refers to an incident in 1337, when some English troops were killed after crossing the border and found stealing plums in the town. In 1503, the betrothal of James IV to Margaret Tudor, Henry VII's daughter, took place at the town's old Mercat Cross. It's successor dates from 1695.

Our Lady's Well sits just south of the village pf Stow, and was rebuilt in the year 2000 by a local man. Legend says that King Arthur fought a bloody battle nearby against the Angles, and in gratitude for his victory had an image of the Virgin Mary brought to the village and put on display. Locals still insist that the battle is commemorated in the name of the village, as wedale means "dale of woe".

In the 19th century the village became famous for something you do not normally associate with Scotland - a vineyard. Grape growing was introduced into the village in 1869 by William Thomson, who grew the fruit under glass at his **Tweed Vineyards**. Soon the grapes became famous throughout Britain and Western Europe, and no less a person than the Emperor of France presented him with a gold medal for their quality. He died in 1895.

A statue of Sir Walter Scott stands outside the Clovenfords Hotel.

STOW

5 miles N of Galashiels on the A7

Stow (sometimes called Stow-of-Wedale) is a delightful village on the Gala Water. The imposing **St Mary of Wedale Parish Church** has a spire over 140 feet high. The ruins of an earlier, 14th century church can still be seen, and there are scant remains of a palace built for the Bishop of St Andrews.

To the west of the village are the lonely Moorfoot Hills, and to the east is some further moorland which separates it from Lauderdale. The B6362 leaves Stow and climbs up onto the moorland, reaching a height of 1,100 feet before descending through Lauder Common into the small town of Lauder.

The **Pack Bridge** across the Gala Water dates from 1655, and was the first bridge ever built across the river. Before that fords were used. It is said that it was built using stone from the old church.

GORDON

11 miles NE of Galashiels on the A6089

This pleasant village is the cradle of the Gordon clan, which moved north into Aberdeenshire in the 13th century, when Robert the Bruce granted them the lands of Strathbogie, which he had taken from the Earl of Atholl (see Huntly). The village sits on a crossroads, and to the north are the well-preserved ruins of **Greenknowe Tower**, built in 1581 by James Seton of Touch and his wife Janet Edmonstone. It is a typical L-shaped tower house, built originally as a fortified home. The Pringles, one of the great Borders families, later acquired it. Finally it came into the possession of the Fairholm family, and was abandoned by them in 1850

MELLERSTAIN

10 miles E of Galashiels, on an unmarked road between the A6089 and the B6397

Mellerstain is a grand mansion originally designed by William Adam in the 1720s, and completed by his son Robert in the 1790s. It is one of the grandest Georgian houses in Britain, and holds a collection of fine furniture, as well as paintings by Van Dyck, Naismith, Gainsborough and Ramsey. The Italian terraces were laid out in 1909 by Sir Reginald Blomfield, and give excellent views out over a small artificial loch towards the Cheviots.

Within the grounds is **Border Archery**, a small company making high quality bows.

MELROSE

3 miles SE of Galashiels just off the A6091

Melrose sits in the shadow of the triple peaks of the **Eildon Hills**, which have a waymarked path leading to their summits. Legend states that **King Arthur** and his knights lie buried beneath one of them, and indeed there is an old folk tale which tells of a horse trader called Canonbie Dick who actually found the cave, thanks to a mysterious stranger who bought a horse from him, and saw the knights slumbering. Before the slumbering King Arthur was a sword and a horn, and Dick was asked to choose one. If he chose correctly, he would become king of Britain. Dick, thinking that a horn would be a clarion call to waken up the knights, chose the horn and blew it. The stranger told him that he has chosen wrongly, for a horn was used to summon help during battle - therefore it was used by cowards. At that a great wind rose up and blew Dick out of the cave, and no one has ever been able to find it since.

Another legend says that the entrance to the Fairy Kingdom lies among the Eildon Hills, and that Thomas the Rhymer (see Earlston) used it to visit his lover, the Fairy Queen, for years at a time. The **Rhymer's Stone** is along a road to the cemetery, off the A6091. There are superb views from it, and there is easy access for wheelchairs.

At the summit of Eildon Hill North are the remains of the largest hill fort in Scotland, which dates to the 10th century BC. When the Romans came, they built a watch tower within it.

Melrose, which is on the Southern Upland Way, is mainly visited nowadays to view the ruins of **Melrose Abbey** (Historic Scotland), surely the loveliest of all the Borders abbeys. It was founded in 1136 by David I for the Cistercian monks of Rievaulx Abbey in Yorkshire, and rose to become one of the most important in Scotland. The ruins that the visitor sees nowadays date mainly from the late 14th and early 15th centuries, thanks to the English army of Richard II, which destroyed the earlier buildings.

It was here that the heart of Robert the Bruce, Scotland's great hero during the Wars of Independence, was buried. On his

7 KINGS ARMS HOTEL

Melrose

A traditional Scottish hotel that is famed for its food, its drink and its proximity to historic sites and big cities.

see page 422

River Tweed, Melrose

Catherine Helen Spense, who campaigned for social reform for women and children in Australia in the late 19th century, was born in Melrose in 1825. She emigrated to Australia when she was 14, and today a statue to her can be found in Adelaide. In 1975 a set of stamps depicting famous Australian women was issued, and Catherine Helen Spense featured in one of them.

death bed in 1329, the king had told Sir James Douglas (known as "Good Sir James" to the Scots, and "Black Douglas" to the English) to place his heart in a casket after his death and take it to the Holy Land. But in 1330, on his way to the Holy Land, Sir James was killed at Teba in Spain fighting the Moors. His friends did not want him buried on foreign soil, so they boiled his body in vinegar so that his flesh would fall from his bones. The flesh was buried in Spain and his bones, along with the casket, were brought back to Scotland (see also Cardross, Dunfermline and Threave Castle). In the late 1990s, during some

restoration work on the abbey, the lead casket containing his heart was rediscovered and subsequently reburied. A plaque in the grounds now marks its resting place.

At the Reformation in 1560, the monks of Melrose were allowed to stay on in Melrose Abbey, with the last one dying in about 1590. In order to preserve the abbey buildings, which were already in a bad state of repair, they had quietly accepted Protestantism, though they probably still continued saying mass in secret.

On a bend in the Tweed, two miles east of the town, is the site of **Old Melrose** (then called Mailros, meaning "bare moor"), where, in about AD 650, Celtic monks from Iona established a monastery. It was near here, in about AD 635, that a young shepherd, who was later to become **St Cuthbert**, was born. In AD 651, following a vision in which he saw the soul of St Aidan of Lindisfarne ascending to heaven, he entered the monastery to train as a monk. He eventually became Bishop of Lindisfarne, and died in AD 687. He now lies buried in Durham Cathedral. A 62-mile walking route called **St Cuthbert's Way** links Melrose and Lindisfarne.

Close to the abbey ruins is **Priorwood Gardens** (National Trust for Scotland). It specialises in plants which are suitable for drying and arranging, and classes are organised to teach the techniques involved. There is also a shop. **Harmony Garden**, also run by the Trust, is close by. It is set around a

Harmony Garden

19th century house which is not open to the public, and has excellent views of the Eildon Hills. There are herbaceous borders, well tended lawns and vegetable and fruit areas. It is renowned for its sense of peace and tranquillity. The house and small estate was built by Robert Waugh, a Melrose joiner, in the early 19th century after making his fortune from a Jamaica plantation called "Harmony". It was sold to the Pitman family in 1820, and was bequeathed to the NTS in 1996 by Mrs Christian Pitman.

The **100 Aker Wood Visitor Centre** is on the old Melrose to Newstead road, and has woodland walks, a children's play area, a coffee shop and car park.

The Scottish Borders is a rugby playing area, and at Melrose that version of the game known as "rugby sevens" was invented.

EARLSTON

8 miles E of Galashiels on the A68

The small town of Earlston is dominated by **Black Hill**, which gives a good view of the surrounding countryside. One of Scotland's earliest poets, **Thomas Learmont of Earlston,** was born here in about 1220. Also known as Thomas the Rhymer, Thomas of Erceldoune or True Thomas, he attained an almost supernatural status, as he was also a seer who could predict the future. Some ruins in the town are supposed to be of his home, **Rhymer's Tower**, though they are of a later date. However, they may have been built on the site of an earlier tower house.

It did not take much in those days for a man to gain a reputation for having mythical and prophetic powers, and no doubt Thomas's many trips abroad accounted for the stories of him going off to live with the Fairy Queen under the Eildon Hills for years at a time (see also Melrose). It may also be that Thomas had visitors from the Continent at his home in Earlston from time to time, and their strange, colourful dress and foreign tongues may have led the local people to conclude that they were fairies. Thomas is said to have eventually gone off to the land of the Fairy Queen and not returned.

His prophecies included Alexander III's death in 1285, the victory of Bruce over the English at Bannockburn in 1314 and Scotland's defeat by the English at Flodden in 1513. However, like most prophesies, they are all too easy to interpret after the event.

SMAILHOLM

10 miles E of Galashiels on the B6397

Smailholm Tower (Historic Scotland) lies west of the village, and seems to grow out of a low, rocky outcrop It is a four square 60 feet high tower which was once surrounded by a wall, and was originally a Pringle stronghold, though it was sold to the Scott family in 1645. Within it you can see a collection of costumed figures and tapestries connected with Scott's Minstrelsy of the Scottish Borders. Scott, as a child, spent a

A mile east of Melrose is Newstead, where there are the remains of Trimontium Roman Fort, covering 15 acres, and named after the three peaks of the Eildons. It was occupied between the late first century well into the second, and was the most important Roman settlement of the northern frontier, guarding as it did a crossing of the Tweed. At its height it housed 1,500 Roman soldiers, and supported a large town which covered a further 200 acres. The Three Hills Roman Heritage Centre, in the Ormiston Institute in Melrose's Market Square, has displays on what life was like within a Roman settlement, and has artefacts that were found there. On Thursday afternoons (and Tuesday afternoons in July and August) a guided five mile, four hour walk to the fort leaves from the Centre.

8 THE WAGGON INN

Kelso

Family friendly pub with excellent fresh food offerings for all tastes. Great value.

see page 423

In Kelso in July every year the Kelso Civic Week takes place, with many events that echo similar ceremonies in other Borders towns. On the banks of the Teviot, three miles southwest of the town, once stood the proud Royal Burgh of Roxburgh. This was probably founded about 1113, and was a thriving walled town in medieval times with no less than four churches, but nothing now survives above ground apart from a few mounds, thanks to the repeated attentions of succeeding English armies. It was one of Scotland's original "four burghs".

lot of time with his grandparents at the nearby farm of Sandyknowe, and knew the tower well.

Smailholm Parish Church is very picturesque, and though it has been altered over the years, there is plenty of medieval stonework still to be seen, as well as three Norman arched windows at the east end. St Cuthbert is supposed to have been born just outside the village in AD 634.

KELSO

16 miles E of Galashiels on the A698

Kelso is a gracious town with a large, cobbled **Market Square** (said to be the largest in Scotland) that would not look out of place in France or Belgium. Surrounding it are imposing 18th and 19th century buildings, with the supremely elegant **Town House** of 1816, which now houses the tourism information centre, as its centrepiece.

The town sits at the junction of the Tweed and the Teviot. **Kelso Abbey** (Historic Scotland) was founded in 1128, after David I, who had founded an abbey at Selkirk and brought over 13 monks from France, decided that Kelso was a much better place for it, as the strategically positioned Roxburgh Castle was already there to offer it protection. It was the biggest of the border abbeys, and is said to have two sets of transepts, with a tower built above each one - an arrangement which is unknown anywhere else in Scotland. During a siege by the English under the Earl of Hertford in 1545, it was almost

totally destroyed. Now all that remains are the transepts, part of the tower, two nave bays and part of the west end.

But the ruins are still dramatic and imposing, and are well worth a visit. A **Town Trail** has been laid out which takes you round the town's architectural gems.

The **War Memorial Garden** is in Bridge Street, and formed part of the former abbey grounds. It has helped Kelso to win the Beautiful Scotland and Britain in Bloom competitions on several occasions, and was gifted to the town by the Duke of Roxburgh in 1921.

Where the Teviot and the Tweed meet is a high defensive mound, the site up until 1550 of **Roxburgh Castle**. It was during a siege of the castle in 1460 that James II was killed outright when a cannon accidentally blew up in his face. The place has been suggested as yet another possible site for King Arthur's magnificent capital of **Camelot** (see also Ayr). To the west of Kelso, within parkland overlooking the Tweed, stands the magnificent **Floors Castle**, Scotland's largest inhabited castle. It was designed by William Adam in 1721, and is home to the Duke and Duchess of Roxburghe (with an "e" at the end), and has a huge collection of works of art and furniture.

The **Millenium Viewpoint**, on the other side of the Tweed and close to Maxwellheugh, was constructed in the year 2000, and is a vantage point for great views of the town and surrounding area.

Springfield Park is the venue, late in July every year, of the **Border Union Show**, which features not only agriculture, but fairground amusements, trade stands and sometimes parachutists.

Rennie's Bridge is a handsome, five-arched bridge spanning the Tweed - the first in the country to feature elliptical arches rather than round or pointed. It was designed by John Rennie the Scottish civil engineer, and was built in 1803 to replace an older bridge destroyed by floods. Rennie based his design for Waterloo Bridge in London on it (see also East Linton). The broad expanse of grass beside the river is known as **The Cobby**.

The bridge was the scene of a riot in 1854, when people objected to paying tolls to cross it, even though all the building costs had been met. So bad was it that the Riot Act was read. However, it took another three years before the tolls were withdrawn.

Horse racing in Kelso began in 1822, and **Kelso Race Course** (known as the "Friendly Course") hosts horse racing all year.

Market Square, Kelso

EDNAM

21 miles E of Galashiels on the B6461

The village stands on the Eden, a tributary of the Tweed, and was the birthplace of two famous men. The first was **James Thomson**, son of the local minister, who was born in September 1700 and who wrote the words to *Rule Britannia*. It was written about 1740 for a masque called *Alfred*, and was soon adopted as a patriotic song. The other was **Henry Francis Lyte**, born in June 1793, who wrote *Abide with Me* shortly before his death in 1847. A memorial to Thomson has been erected at Ferniehill, to the south of the village, and the bridge over the river has a plaque commemorating Lyte, who died in Nice in France in1847.

KIRK YETHOLM

25 miles E of Galashiels on the B6352

This village, lying within the Bowmont Valley, is at the northern end of the **Pennine Way**, with St Cuthbert's Way passing close by as well. It got its name from the Scottish word "yett", meaning a gate, as it was one of the gateways into England. It, and to a lesser extent its twin village of **Town Yetholm**, were famous at one time as being where the kings and queens of the Scottish gypsies lived, as it was more or less within a "no man's land" between England and Scotland. The most famous queen was Esther Faa Blyth, who

Town Yetholm

The ruins of the L-shaped Cessford Castle, which surrendered to the English in 1545, lie two miles to the southwest of Morebattle. It was built by the Kerrs in about 1450, and was once one of the most important castles in the Borders.

Just outside Morebattle lies Hoselaw Chapel. Although it looks old it dates only from 1905, and was built on the site of an earlier church as a memorial to Dr Thomas Leishman of Linton, who at one point had been the Moderator of the General Assembly of the Church of Scotland. It is said that the graveyard of the former church was where many of the dead from Flodden were buried.

ruled in the 19th century. In 1898 Charles Faa Blyth, her 73 year old son, was crowned king at Yetholm. The proceedings were spoiled somewhat when a letter was read out disputing Charles's right to be crowned. Though the title had lost much of its meaning by this time, the coronation was attended by an estimated 10,000 people, including churchmen and the gentry of the area, A small cottage is still pointed out as his "palace".

St Cuthbert's Way passes through the village, and the Pennine Way, which snakes over the Pennines in England, ends at **Yetholm Parish Church**, an elegant building with a small tower. It was built in 1836 and has a Burgerhuys bell cast in 1643.

MOREBATTLE

23 miles E of Galashiels on the B6401

This little village sits on the St Cuthbert's Way, close to the Kale Water. It's name comes from the "botl", or dwelling, beside the "mere", or small loch. In the 19th century the loch, which was located

between Morebattle and Linton, was drained to provide more agricultural land. Some of its banks can still be made out. The surrounding area was once a hiding place for Covenanters fleeing the persecution of Charles II's troops in the 17th century.

One of the streets in Morebattle has the unusual name of **Teapot Street**, said to be a corruption of "tip it street", as it led to the local dump at one time..

To the north of the village is **Linton Church**, which has Norman details, a fine Norman font and a belfry dated 1697. The finest Norman survival is the tympanum above the door, which commemorates the killing of the **Linton Worm** by John Somerville of Lariston in the 13th century. The Linton Worm was 12 feet long, and lived in a cave below the church. It terrorised the district, and the local people were powerless against it. John noticed that when it saw anything it wanted to eat, it opened its mouth wide. So he made a special spear that had inflammable materials of peat and tar instead of a point, and when he approached the worm on horseback with the spear blazing, it duly opened its mouth to devour him. John stuck the spear down the worm's throat, and the worm was killed. For this act the king granted him the lands of Linton.

The church sits on a low mound of fine sand, which is almost certainly a natural feature. However, a local legend tells a different story. It seems that a

Cessford Castle, Morebattle

young man was once condemned to death for murdering a priest. His two sisters pleaded for his life, saying they would carry out a specific task to atone for his crime. They would sieve tons of sand, removing all large grains, and from the small grains build a mound on which a church building could stand. The church authorities agreed to this, and the women set to work. Eventually, after many years, a mound of sand was created, and a church was indeed built on it.

MAXTON

8 miles SE of Galashiels on the A699

Maxton Parish Church was rebuilt in 1812, though it contains fragments of an earlier, medieval building. **Maxton Cross**, on the tiny village green, partially dates from the 14th century, though the main part was replaced in 1881.

Maxton was the birthplace, in 1874, of **Henry Grey Graham**, the only Scotsman to have been a Church of Scotland minister and a Catholic bishop. He was a son of the manse, and became a minister in Lanarkshire in 1901. Two years later he was inducted into the Roman Catholic Church at the Benedictine abbey in Fort Augustus, and in 1906 became a priest In 1930 he became the titular Bishop of Tipasa in Algeria. He died in 1959.

DRYBURGH

7 miles SE of Galashiels off the B6356

The ruins of **Dryburgh Abbey** (Historic Scotland) must be the most romantically situated in all of Scotland, sitting as it does on a loop of the Tweed, which surrounds it on three sides. .

Nothing much remains of the great abbey church, except for the west door and parts of the north and south transepts. However, the substantial ruins of the other abbey buildings (including a fine chapter house) can still be explored. Within the north transept is buried Sir Walter Scott and his wife Margaret Charlotte, as well as **Field Marshall Earl Haig of Bemersyde**. He was Commander-in-Chief of the British Expeditionary forces in France and Flanders during World War I.

The Premonstratensian abbey was founded in 1150 by Hugh de Moreville, Constable of Scotland, with monks being brought up from Alnwick in Northumberland to serve in it. The site had already been a sacred one, as it was here that **St Modan**, a Celtic monk, set up a monastery in about AD 600. In 1322, during the Wars of Independence, Edward II's army, after a successful invasion of Scotland, set fire to the place. This was the first of many sackings, including the one of 1544, when 700 English soldiers reduced it to ruins. It was abandoned soon after.

It now forms part of the 55-mile-long **Four Abbeys Cycle Route**, taking in the other three great Borders abbeys of Melrose, Kelso and Jedburgh. A short walk from the abbey is the 31 feet high (including pedestal) **William Wallace Statue**. He spent a lot of

North of Dryburgh is Scott's View, which gives an amazing panorama of the Eildon Hills. Sir Walter Scott used to ride up here to get inspiration, and when his funeral cortege was making its way to Dryburgh, the hearse stopped for a short while. It is best accessed from the A68, where it is signposted from the Leaderfoot Viaduct that spans the Tweed. Information plaques explain what can be seen from the viewpoint.

12   THE PLACE

Selkirk

A warm welcome and a good selection of drinks and freshly prepared food can be found at **The Place**.

❚❚ see page 425

•

In common with many Borders town, Selkirk has its Common Riding Ceremony, held annually in June, when over 500 riders regularly set out to patrol the marches, or boundaries, of the town lands. But the ceremony also commemorates the darkest day in the town's history. In 1513, Selkirk sent 80 of its bravest men to fight alongside James IV at Flodden, taking with them the town flag. The battle was a disaster for Scotland, with the flower of Scottish manhood, including the king himself, being killed. Only one Selkirk man, named Fletcher, returned, without the Selkirk flag but bearing a bloodstained English one, which can be seen in Halliwell's House. A memorial to the fallen can be found outside the Victoria Halls in the High Street.

•

time in the Borders hiding from the English in Ettrick Forest. The Earl of Buchan commissioned the statue in 1814.

ST. BOSWELLS

7 miles SE of Galashiels on the A68

This village is named after an old church that once stood nearby dedicated to **St Boisil**. who was an abbot of the Celtic monastery at Old Melrose in the 7th century. It's earlier name was Lessudden, meaning the "meadow by the sloping pasture". The centrepiece of the village is its green, which hosts a fair on July 18th (St Boisil's Day) each year. In past times, this fair was one of the largest in the country, and attracted people - especially gypsies - from all over the Borders and beyond. At one time over 1,000 horses were offered for sale at the fair.

In 1853 a great riot took place during the fair, when Irish workmen working on the new rail and locals drank too much and fought each other. The local police were powerless to intervene, and one man was actually killed. Eventually a party of dragoons was sent from Edinburgh to arrest everyone involved in the fight. One man was found to have blood stained clothing, and despite his protestations of innocence, was hanged for murder at Jedburgh. A few years later it was revealed that he was indeed innocent, and that the real culprit had managed to escape to America.

A mile or so to the east are **Mertoun House Gardens.**

Though the house is not open to the public, the 26-acre gardens can be visited between April and September. **Mertoun Kirk**, in the grounds of the house, was built in 1241, though the present building dates from 1658.

SELKIRK

5 miles S of Galashiels on the A7

Once the county town of Selkirkshire, Selkirk is now a quiet royal burgh on the edge of the Ettrick Forest. It was the site of the first abbey in the Borders, which was founded in 1113 by David I. However, 15 years later, before one stone was laid, David moved the monks to Kelso, where the abbey was finally built.

The Ettrick Water, a tributary of the Tweed, flows to the west of the town, and it is joined a couple of miles out of town by the Yarrow Water. The Vale of Yarrow is very scenic, with the hamlet of **Yarrow** itself, about eight miles west of Selkirk, being very picturesque. Scott's great-grandfather was once minister of **Yarrow Parish Church**. It was built about 1640. The **Ettrick Marshes** can be found at the head of the Ettrick Valley, and has a rich variety of wildlife. There are marked footpaths.

In Selkirk's High Street, outside the **Old Courthouse** where he presided, there is a statute of Sir Walter Scott, who was sheriff-depute here from 1804 until his death in 1832. Within the courtroom is an audiovisual display telling of his associations with the area. Another statue in the High Street commemorates **Mungo Park**, the explorer and surgeon, who was born in Yarrow in 1771. The oldest building in the town is **Halliwell's House and Robson Gallery**, housed in an ironmonger's shop and house just off the market square, where there is a small museum on the ground floor and art gallery on the upper floor. **Robert D. Clapperton Photographic** in Scotts Place is a working museum and photographic archive. It dates from 1867, and here, the good citizens of Selkirk posed stiffly in Victorian times while having their photograph taken. At the **Selkirk Glass Visitor Centre** at Dunsdalehaugh you can see glass paperweights being made.

Three miles west of the town is **Bowhill**, the Borders home of the Duke of Queensberry and Buccleuch. It is a fine mansion built in 1812, which is open to the public. It has many fine paintings, including works by Canaletto, Raeburn and Van Dyke. You can also see the Duke of Monmouth's saddle, as well as the shirt he wore at his execution (see also Hawick) and a restored Victorian kitchen. In its grounds is **Bowhill Little Theatre**, which presents many professional plays. There is also a visitors centre, rural walks and a display of fire engines. Within the Philiphaugh Estate, a mile from the town, is the **Philiphaugh Salmon Viewing Centre**, where you can watch salmon live underwater via underwater cameras. It is open from April to December.'

Countryside Overlooking Selkirk

The ruins of **Newark Castle** are also within its grounds, dating from about 1450. In 1645 the **Battle of Philiphaugh** took place nearby, when Leslie's Covenanting army met a royal army commanded by Montrose. Leslie's army was triumphant, and prisoners were taken to Newark Castle. it was here, on September 13th 1645, that several hundred soldiers and camp followers of the Montrose's army were savagely butchered. In 1810, when excavations were taking place beside the castle, bones were uncovered in a field known as "Slain Men's Lea". The tower can only be viewed from the outside.

Aikwood Tower, (not open to the public) is now the home of Sir David Steel. It is also associated with Michael Scott the legendary wizard. He lived from about 1175 to 1230, and was one of the cleverest men of his age. The story that he divided the Eildon Hills into three, however, came from the imagination of Sir Walter Scott,

•

The Scottish Borders Archive and Local History Centre is within St Mary's Mill in Selkirk, and offers research facilities on local history, geography and genealogy, including the records of the old counties of Berwickshire, Selkirkshire, Roxburghshire and Peeblesshire. Please note that from the spring of 2007 this facility will move to the Heritage Hub in Hawick.

•

•

To the east of Selkirk is the Whitlaw Mosses, four small wetland nature reserves that display a wide range of mosses, lichens, and butterflies.

13 GLEN CAFÉ AND BISTRO

St Mary's Loch

A real find - a café that serves tasty food and drink in the Scottish Borders, offers Internet access, and has superb views.

see page 425

who wrote about him in *The Lay of the Last Minstrel*.

There is no proof that he was born at Aikwood, nor, indeed, is there any proof that he was a Borders man at all. Some people claim that he was born in England, while others say Fife. To muddy the waters even further, there is no proof that his surname was even "Scott". We do know, however, that he was educated at Oxford, Paris and Bologna, where he studied mathematics, law and theology. In his day he was known as the "wonder of the world", and his reputation spread all over Europe as a man who had learned everything there was to know in the Christian world. He eventually came to the notice of Frederick II, the Holy Roman Emperor, and entered his service.

He is also said to have dabbled in alchemy, and some of the legends attached to him and his so-called "wizardry" (such as his "demon horse" and "demon ship") were no doubt borrowed from the story of Merlin the Magician. He probably died in Italy (some say after being hit by a piece of masonry that had fallen from a church) and was buried there. Another story, however, has him dying in Scotland and being buried within Melrose Abbey (see also Glenluce).

The lands of Aikwood were granted to a later Scott with the same name - Master Michael Scott - by the infant James V in 1517. He built the present tower around 1535.

ST. MARY'S LOCH

20 miles SW of Galashiels on the A708

The loch sits in a truly beautiful setting of rounded, green hills, and is the largest loch in the Borders. It was formed during the last Ice Age, when two glaciers scoured out a large hollow which was filled with water. Both Scott and William Wordsworth have sung its praises, but no words can adequately describe this delightful sheet of water. A narrow spit of land separates it from the smaller **Loch of the Lowes**, with **Tibbie Shiels Inn**, now an angling hostelry, situated between them. It was opened in 1824, and is named after Isabella Shiels, the woman who ran it until 1878. She was the wife of a mole catcher named Richardson, and they lived in what was then called St Mary's Cottage. When her husband died a year later. she resumed her maiden name and took in lodgers to support her six children. Gradually the cottage sprouted extensions and additions, and by the time of her death in 1878 had become well known for its hospitality. Her visitor's book is still in existence, and records such names as R.L. Stevenson, Gladstone and Thomas Carlyle. It is a favourite stopping point on the Southern Upland Way, which passes close by.

James Hogg, nicknamed "The Ettrick Shepherd", was also a frequent visitor. He was born at Altrive Lake (not a lake, but a farm) nearby in 1770, and wrote *Confessions of a Justified Sinner*, one of the great books of the 19th century (see also Selkirk).

HAWICK

Hawick is the largest town in the Borders, and is famous for the quality of its knitwear, with names like Pringle and Lyle and Scott being known worldwide.

The railway came to Hawick in 1849, which helped it develop into one of the powerhouses of textile manufacture In Scotland. In 1969 it closed again, making the Scottish Borders the only area in Scotland without a railway station. However, there are now plans to reopen the line and breath new confidence into it towns.

St Mary's Parish Church was built in 1763, and replaced an earlier, 13th century church. The town's oldest building is the 16th century **Drumlanrig's Tower**. In 1570 it survived a raid by English troops which destroyed the rest of Hawick, and was once a typical moated L-shaped Borders tower house before the area between the two "legs" was filled in to convert it into an elegant town house. At one time it belonged to the Douglas family of Drumlanrig, in Dumfriesshire, and it was here that Anna, Duchess of Buccleuch, and wife of the executed Duke of Monmouth, once stayed (see also Bowhill). The basement was later used as a prison, and finally a wine cellar when it became a hotel. Now the tower has been restored and houses the town's visitor information centre and an

exhibition explaining the history of the Borders.

The award-winning **Wilton Lodge Park** sits by the banks of the Teviot, and has 107 acres of riverside walks, gardens, a tropical glasshouse, recreational facilities and a café. Within it is the **Hawick Museum and Scott Art Gallery**, which explains the history of the town and its industries. The gallery has a collection of 19th and 20th century Scottish paintings, and regularly hosts exhibitions of works by local and national artists. Many of the mills in the town, such as **Peter Scott and Company** in Buccleuch Street and **Wrights of Trowmill** outside the town have visitor centres, shops and guided tours. The **Hawick Cashmere Company**, based in Trinity Mills in Duke Street, has a viewing gallery and shop. And if Duns has its Jim Clark Memorial Trophy Room, Hawick has its **Jimmy Guthrie Statue**. Andrew James Guthrie was a local TT rider who won six Tourist Trophy races on the Isle of Man. He was killed in 1937 while competing in the German Grand Prix at Chemnitz.

AROUND HAWICK

MINTO

5 miles NE of Hawick off the B6405

Minto was founded in the late 18th century as a planned village by the 2nd Earl of Minto, and laid out by the architect William Playfair. The **Parish Church** was completed in 1831, and replaced an earlier

The Hawick Common Riding takes place in June each year, and as well as continuing the tradition of patrolling the burgh boundaries, it commemorates yet another skirmish between the English and the Scots. This occurred in 1514, when some Hawick men beat off English soldiers camped near Hornshole, about two miles from Hawick, and captured their banner. A disagreement of a different kind took place in the mid-1990s, when two women riders tried to join what had traditionally been an all-male occasion. Their participation provoked hostile opposition, even from some women. It took a court case to establish that women had the right to join in, though even today some people still tolerate their presence rather than welcome it.

Eight miles southwest of Hawick, along the A7, is Teviothead. It was near here, at Carlanrig, that King James V met with Johnnie Armstrong before having him killed. Johnnie's grave can still be seen (see also Canonbie).

Fatlips Castle, Minto

Like most other Borders towns, Jedburgh has a riding ceremony. The Jedburgh Callants Festival takes place every year in June. It was inaugurated in 1947, and is based on the old common riding, when the boundaries of the burgh and its common land were patrolled once a year to ensure that no one had encroached. The festivities last a fortnight.

building dating from the 13th century.

On top of Minto Crags sits the curiously named **Fatlips Castle**, built in the 16th century for the Turnbull family. It was restored in 1857 and used as a shooting lodge and private museum, though it is now ruinous once more.

To the east of Fatlips are the ruins of **Barnhills Tower**, another Turnbull stronghold. It was built in the 16th century, but now only a few decayed walls are left standing.

DENHOLM
4 miles NE of Hawick on the A698

In 1775 this pleasant village, with its village green, was the birthplace of John Leyden, poet, doctor, linguist and friend of Sir Walter Scott. His birthplace, an 18th century thatched cottage on the village green, can still be seen. He was educated at the local school, and so gifted was he that he entered Edinburgh University when only 15 years old. The **John Leyden Memorial**, which stands on the green, commemorates the great man, who died in 1811 on the island of Java. He was the son of a local farmer, and in 1806 had settled in Calcutta, where he became assay master to the local mint. Here he wrote about the local languages. His name is a Scottish rendering of the university city of Leiden in the Netherlands, as his ancestor had been a servant from that city who came to Scotland.

Also born in the village was **Sir James Murray** (1837-1915), who undertook the tremendous task of editing the *New English Dictionary on Historical Principles*, forerunner of the *Oxford English Dictionary*.

A game called the **Denholm Hand Ba'** is played every year between the "doonies", or inhabitants of the village, and the "uppies", who are from outwith the village. In the 15th and 16th centuries, the ball was most probably the head of an Englishman.

BONCHESTER BRIDGE
5 miles SE of Hawick on the A6088

To the east of the village is the 1,059 feet high **Bonchester Hill**, topped by the remains of an Iron Age fort.

JEDBURGH
14 miles NE of Hawick on the A68

The present day A68 was at one

time the main route from Edinburgh down into England, so Jedburgh saw many armies passing along its streets when Scotland and England were constantly at war. The locals once called the town "Jethart", and it is still remembered in the expression "Jethart justice", meaning hang first and try later, a throwback to the bad old days of the reivers.

As in Denholm, every year at Candlemas (February 2nd) the **Fastern Even Handba'** game is played in the town, when the "Uppies" play the "Doonies" and chase beribboned balls through the streets of the town. Though the present game dates from the 18th century, it is thought that it had its origins in the 16th century, when the severed heads of English reivers were used instead of balls.

It is an attractive small town with gaily-painted houses, especially in the Market Place and the Canongate, and it regularly wins awards in "Beautiful Scotland in Bloom" competitions. **Jedburgh Abbey** (Historic Scotland), on the banks of the Jed Water, was founded in 1138 by David I for the Augustinians.

It was destroyed nine times by the invading English. Each time, save for the last one, the monks painstakingly rebuilt it. It is the most complete of all the Border abbeys, and a visitor centre explains its story, with one of its more intriguing exhibits being the "Jedburgh Comb", found during excavations. One story says that the comb, found in a ditch beside

a body, belonged to a Bishop of Durham called Eadwulf Rus who had fled to Jedburgh in the 11th century, but who was killed and thrown in a ditch. Part of the church building was used as a parish church up until 1875. The **Cloister Garden** was planted in 1986, and shows what a typical monastic garden would have looked like in the early 16th century.

Not far from the abbey is **Mary Queen of Scots Visitor Centre**, within an old house. Here, in October 1566, Mary Stuart stayed for four weeks when presiding at local courts in the Borders. While she was there she made an arduous journey to Hermitage Castle to visit her lover, the Earl of Bothwell, which nearly killed her. When Elizabeth I held her in captivity, she declared that she would have preferred to have died in Jedburgh than England. Now it is a museum and visitors centre with displays on the tragic queen's life (see also Hermitage Castle).

Jedburgh Castle Jail, in Castlegate, was a 19th century reform prison which now houses a display about the history of the town. Five miles northeast of Jedburgh, off the A698, are the **Teviot Water Gardens**, situated on three levels above the River Tweed. There are three riverside walks, a bird hide and a café.

Jedburgh was the birthplace of **David Brewster** (1781-1868), who invented the kaleidoscope in 1816. He was considered a child prodigy, and entered Edinburgh University

---

14 THE NIGHTJAR

Jedburgh

A friendly restaurant whose innovative cuisine is appreciated by locals and tourists alike

🍴 see page 425

---

15 JEDFOREST DEER AND FARM PARK

Camptown, Jedburgh

An interesting family day out where you cans see herds of deer as well as rare breeds of farm animals.

🏛 see page 426

The last Borders skirmish, known as the Redeswire Raid, took place near Jedburgh in 1575. It took the arrival of a contingent of Jedburgh men to turn what was going to be a Scots defeat into a victory.

16 BAILEY MILL ACCOMMODATION, TREKKING & RACE BREAK CENTRE

Newcastleton

A friendly farm holiday complex that lets you explore the beautiful Border Reiver country on horseback and at your own pace.

see page 426

Two miles east of the village of Ancrum, on Peniel Haugh, is the 150 feet high Waterloo Monument, erected by the Marquis of Lothian between 1817 and 1824 to commemorate the Battle of Waterloo. Though there are stairs within the tower, it is not open to the public. The best way to reach it is to walk from the Harestanes Countryside Visitor Centre, which is nearby. The Centre has countryside walks, activities and displays, all with a countryside theme, as well as a car park, gift shop and tearoom.

at the age of 12. He later became a minister of religion, but never pursued a career in the church. Instead he studied optics and developed several scientific instruments and lenses.

Jedforest Deer and Farm Park is five miles south of Jedburgh on the Mervinslaw Estate, just off the A68. It is a modern working farm with a deer herd and rare breeds. There are also birds of prey demonstrations using eagles, owls and hawks, and plenty of ranger-led activities.

Four miles beyond the Farm Park, the A68 reaches the English border at **Carter Bar**, which is 1370 feet above sea level in the Cheviots. From here there is a wonderful view northwards, and it almost seems that the whole of Southern Scotland is spread out before you. In the 18th century herds of sheep and cattle were driven over this route towards the markets in the south.

ANCRUM

10 miles NE of Hawick on the B6400

Ancrum is a typical Borders village, to the north of which was fought the **Battle of Ancrum Moor** in 1545. It was part of what was known as the "Rough Wooing", when Henry VIII tried to force the Scots into allowing the young Mary Queen of Scots to marry his son Edward. 3,000 English and Scottish horsemen under Sir Ralph Evers were ambushed by a hastily assembled army of Borderers. During the battle, the Scots horsemen changed sides when they

saw that the Borderers were gaining the upper hand, resulting in a total rout. Evers, who was said to be a particularly greedy and bloodthirsty man, was killed in the battle.

Ancrum Parish Church was built in 1890, though the ruins of the earlier 18th century church still survive in the graveyard. It is thought that the original Ancrum church was built in the 12th century. Ancrum, though in the Borders, was once within the diocese of Glasgow, and at the east of the village once stood a bishop's palace.

NEWCASTLETON

20 miles S of Hawick, on the B6357

Newcastleton, in Liddesdale, is a planned village, founded by the third Duke of Buccleuch in 1793 as a handloom-weaving centre. The **Liddesdale Heritage Centre Museum** is in the old Townfoot Kirk in South Hermitage Street, and has attractive displays about the history of the area and its people. A small exhibition is given over to railway memorabilia.

This is the heartland of the great Borders families of Kerr, Armstrong and Elliot, and was always a place of unrest before Scotland and England were united. The border with England follows the Liddel Water then, about three miles south of Newcastleton, strikes east along the Kershope Burn for a mile before turning northeast. At **Kershopefoot**, where the Kershope Burn meets the Liddel Water, the Wardens of the Western Marches of both Scotland and England met regularly to settle arguments and seek redress for crimes committed by both sides. A jury of 12 men settled the disputes, with the Scots choosing the six English, and the English choosing the six Scots. However, even these meetings were known to result in violence, and many a Scottish or English warden and his entourage were chased far into their own territory if redress was not forthcoming. It was at such a meeting in 1596 that the Scottish reiver William Armstrong of Kinmont, known as "Kinmont Willie", was illegally captured by English troops and taken off to be imprisoned in Carlisle Castle. Walter Scott of Buccleuch subsequently rescued him in a daring raid by scrambling up the castle walls. Armstrong was never recaptured, and eventually died in his bed.

Every year in July, the village holds the **Newcastleton Traditional Music Festival**, one of the oldest and largest such festivals in Scotland. It was founded in 1970, and has concerts, ceilidhs and competitions. There are many informal music sessions held throughout the village. On the last day of the festival is the "Grand Winners Concert".

A mile from the village, off the Canonbie road, is the **Millholm Cross**, It has the initials AA and MA carved on it. The AA is thought to be Alexander Armstrong, reiver from nearby Mangerton Tower.

The supposed site of the **Battle of Degsaston** lies about

eight miles north of Newcastleton, close to a minor road off the B6357 leading the Kielder Water. It was fought in AD 603 between an army of Angles led by King Aethelfrith from Bernicia, in what is now Northumberland, and an army of Scots under King Áedán mac Gabráin from Dalriada in modern day Argyll. It was a decisive victory for the Angles, and curtailed the Scot's expansionist plans.

Close by is **Riccarton Junction**, once a railway settlement that grew around where the railway line from Carlisle to Edinburgh met a line from Hexham. The settlement is now gone, though there is a small museum.

The **Dykescroft Information Centre and Newcastleton Historic Forest Walk** lies to the south of the village, off a minor road. It is closed in February and March each year. One walk ends at Priest Hill, where there is a 2000-year-old Iron Age hill fort.

A few miles north of the village is **Castleton**, the site of a lost village. All that remains of the medieval St Martin's Church is the kirkyard, and a series of earthworks marks where a castle belonging to the de Soulis family once stood. The village also had a green, and this is marked by a commemorative stone.

PEEBLES

The Royal Burgh of Peebles sits on the banks of the River Tweed, its name deriving from the old Welsh

Five miles north of Newcastleton is the massive bulk of Hermitage Castle (Historic Scotland). It dates from the 14th century, and its imposing walls and stout defences reflect the bloody warfare that was common in this area before the union of Scotland and England. It belonged to the de Soulis family, who built the original castle of wood in the mid-13th century. However, in 1320 William de Soulis was found guilty of plotting against Robert the Bruce, and his lands and property were confiscated by the crown. It later became a Douglas stronghold. While staying in Jedburgh, Mary Stuart covered the 50 miles between there and Hermitage and back again in one day to visit her lover, the Earl of Bothwell, whom she later married. During her journey, she lost a watch, which was recovered in the 19th century (see also Jedburgh).

17 HALCYON

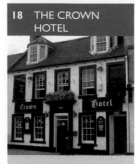

Peebles

Town centre restaurant providing exceptional cuisine in stylish surroundings.

⁋ see page 427

18 THE CROWN HOTEL

Peebles

Third generation family-owned and run town centre hotel offering good food and comfortable en suite accommodation.

⊨ ⁋ see page 428

Glentress Forest lies one mile east of Peebles off the A72. It is now the most visited tourist attraction in the Scottish Borders, and is said to have the country's best mountain biking course. There is live TV coverage of ospreys deep in the forest (see also Kailzie Gardens).

---

word "pebyl", meaning a camp site. Although it looks peaceful enough nowadays, its history is anything but. It was burnt to the ground by the English in 1549 during the "Rough Wooing", occupied by Cromwell in 1650 and 1651, and again by Charles Edward Stuart in 1745.

In June each year the Town holds its **Beltane Week**, with the crowning of the Beltane Queen. The ceremony's origins go right back to pagan times, though the present Beltane Week celebrations date only from the 19th century, when they were revived. The Chambers Institute, the core of which dates from the 16th century, was gifted to the town in 1859 by local man William Chambers. With his brother Robert, he went on to found the great Chambers publishing house in Edinburgh. Within it is the **Tweeddale Museum and Gallery**, where the history of the town is explained. Here you can also see the extraordinary classical frieze commissioned by William Chambers which is based on parts of the Parthenon Frieze in the British Museum and on the Alexander Frieze commissioned in 1812 by Napoleon Bonaparte.

On Innerleithen Road, opposite the Park Hotel, is the unusual **Cornice Museum of Ornamental Plasterwork**, dedicated to displaying and explaining ornate plasterwork. The **Cairns Gallery**, housed in a 1930s building in the High Street, showcases the work of modern artists working in a number of media. The **Eastgate Theatre and Arts Centre** was recently opened within an old church, and has a theatre, café, a studio and exhibition space.

The ruins of the **Cross Kirk** (Historic Scotland), founded in 1261 as the church of a Trinitarian Friary, are to the west of the town. The Trinitarians were a monastic order founded in 1198 by St John of Matha, a Frenchman, to redeem captives taken by the Saracens in the Holy Land during the Crusades. The tower of the former **St Andrews Church** still survives just off Neidpath Road. The present **Peebles Parish Church** is an imposing Victorian building at the west end of the High Street, a short distance from the quaintly named **Cuddy Bridge** over the Eddleston Water, a tributary of the Tweed. One of the hidden places of the town is to be found beyond an archway leading from the high street - the **Quadrangle**. Surrounding the town's war memorial are well laid out, colourful gardens.

AROUND PEEBLES

NEIDPATH CASTLE

1 mile W of Peebles on the A72

Neidpath Castle, with its eleven feet thick walls, stands on the banks of the Tweed. The previous castle that stood here was built by the Fraser family in the 14th century. It subsequently passed to the Hays when the daughter of Sir Simon Hay married Gilbert de Hay of Yester. It was probably Gilbert who built the present castle.

In 1685 William Douglas, the first Duke of Queensberry, bought it and it remained a Douglas property until 1810, when it passed to the Earl of Wemyss. Sir Walter Scott visited it frequently when his friend, Adam Ferguson, rented it at the end of the 18th century.

It is the epitome of a Scottish tower house, and originally consisted of three great vaulted halls, one above the other (though the top vault was subsequently removed and replaced by a timber roof), reached by winding stone staircases. There is a genuine dungeon below what was the guardroom which prisoners were sometimes lowered into and in many cases forgotten about. Mary Stuart and James VI both visited the castle, reflecting the importance of the Hay family in the 16th century. The castle is privately owned, and is open to the public. Wall hangings in the Great Hall depict the tragic life of Mary Stuart.

Neidpath Castle

KAILZIE GARDENS

3 miles E of Peebles on the B7062

Extending to 14 acres, Kailzie Gardens sit on the banks of the Tweed, surrounded by hills. The main part is contained in an old walled garden, plus there is a 15-acre wild garden and woodland walks among rhododendrons and azeleas. There is also a restaurant, gift shop and a viewing area for ospreys (see also Glentress Forest).

INNERLEITHEN

6 miles E of Peebles on the A72

Innerleithen is a small town which was the original for Sir Walter Scott's St Ronan's Well. It used to be a spa town, and the **St. Ronan's Well Interpretive Centre** at Well's Brae explains the history of the wells, whose waters were full of sulphur and other minerals. You can even sample the water if you're brave enough. In the High Street is **Robert Smail's Printing Works** (National Trust for Scotland). This was a genuine print works that still retained many of its original features and fittings when taken over by the Trust in 1987. Now you can see how things were printed at the turn of the century, and even have a go yourself.

The **St Ronan's Border Games** and the **Cleikum Ceremonies** take place each year in July. It is Scotland's oldest

At the beginning of August each year the Traquair Fair is held, with music, dance, theatre, puppetry and children's entertainment.

organised sports meeting. The Cleikum Ceremonies centre around St Ronan himself, an 8th century monk who settled in the area. A schoolboy is chosen from the local school to represent St Ronan, and in the Memorial Hall of the town is presented with his insignia of office - the Cleikum Crozier.

TRAQUAIR

6 miles SE of Peebles on the B709

Traquair is a small village visited mostly for the magnificent **Traquair House**. It is reputed to be the oldest continuously inhabited house in Scotland, and has its origins in a royal hunting lodge built on the banks of the Tweed in about AD 950. In its time, 27 kings and queens have visited the place, including Alexander I in the 11th century, Edward I of England (known as the "Hammer of the Scots") in the 13th, and Mary Stuart in the 16th (the bed where she slept is still on display). One laird of Traquair fell with his king at Flodden, and in the 18th century the then laird, the fifth Earl of Traquair, supported the Jacobite cause.

Charles Edward Stuart visited in 1745, and when he left, the laird closed the **Bear Gates** at the end of the long drive, vowing that they would never be opened until a Stuart ascended the British throne once more. They have remained closed ever since. Within the house itself are secret passages and priests' holes, as the owners reverted to Roman Catholicism in

the early 17th century. It is still the family home of the Maxwell Stuart family.

In 1965 the then laird renovated the brewhouse which lies beneath the private chapel, and the **Traquair House Brewery** now produces a fine range of ales which can be bought in the estate shop. It produces between 600 and 700 barrels of ale a year, which is sold throughout Britain.

DRUMELZIER

8 miles SW of Peebles, on the B712

It is reputed that Merlin the Magician lies buried where the Powsail Burn joins the Tweed, just north of the village. At Drumelzier Haugh is an old standing stone known as **Merlin's Stone**, and on Tinnis Hill there is a stone circle. At one time **Drumelzier Castle**, owned by the Tweedie family, stood close to the village, but now little remains above ground. In the graveyard of **Drumelzier Parish Church** is an old burial vault of the Tweedies.

LYNE

4 miles W of Peebles on the A72

Lyne Church, perched picturesquely on a hillside above the road, and at only 45 feet long and 15 feet wide, is said to be the smallest parish church in Scotland. A chapel has stood here since the 12th century at least, but the present church was built about 1645 by the first Earl of Tweeddale. It contains a pulpit and two pews reputed to be of Dutch workmanship.

STOBO

5 miles W of Peebles on the B712

Stobo Kirk, one of the oldest and most beautiful in the area, has a Norman tower, nave and chancel, with some later features and additions. The porch is especially fine, and has a barrelled stone roof. **Stobo Castle** is set in some lovely grounds, and is now one of Scotland's most luxurious health farms and spas. Two miles south, along the B712, is the **Dawyck Botanic Garden and Arboretum**, an outpost of the National Botanic Gardens in Edinburgh. It sits on the Scrape Burn, a tributary of the Tweed, and houses a unique collection of conifers, rhododendrons and other tree species within its 50 acres.

The original garden was laid out in the late 17th century by Sir James Naesmyth, who imported trees and shrubs from North America. In 1832 the garden was landscaped by Italian gardeners, who built bridges, terraces and steps.

There is a Scottish Rare Plants Trail and guided walks during the summer months.

BROUGHTON

10 miles W of Peebles, on the A701

Broughton is forever associated with the author and Governor-General of Canada, John Buchan, whose most famous work is *The Thirty Nine Steps*. Though born in Perth, his maternal grandparents farmed nearby, and his father, a Free Church minister, married his mother in the village. The old free kirk is now the **John Buchan Centre,** with displays about his life and writings. The village is also home to the famous **Broughton Ales**.

WEST LINTON

14 miles NW of Peebles, just off the A702

West Linton is a delightful village, and one of the hidden gems of Peeblesshire. The picturesque **St Andrews Parish Church** of 1781 stands in the middle of the village, and the surrounding gravestones testify to the craftsmanship of the many stone carvers who used to live in the area. The local **Whipman** ceremonies take place in June each year. They originated in 1803, when some local agricultural workers decided to form a benevolent society known as the "Whipmen of Linton". Now the week long festivities include honouring the Whipman (meaning a carter) and his Lass. In the centre of the village stands **Lady Gifford's Well**, with a stone carving of 1666 on one of its sides. A **West Linton Village Trail** takes you round many of the historical and architectural features of the village.

One of the many streets is quaintly called Teapot Lane, as a tap once stood here where the women of the village drew water into teapots to make tea.

> *The John Buchan Way is a footpath linking Broughton with Peebles. It is over 13 miles long, and has some steep sections.*

Dumfries & Galloway

People driving north along the M74 in search of the "real Scotland" rarely turn off at Gretna and head for Dumfries and Galloway. This is a pity, as it is a wonderful area that can match anything in Scotland for beautiful scenery, grandeur and history. There are over 200 miles of coastline with small coves, neat fishing ports, towering cliffs and wonderful sandy beaches. There also are beautiful villages, old abbeys and castles, vibrant towns and country roads that meander through soft, verdant scenery or climb up into bleak moorland landscapes that were made for walking. In the fields you will see herds of the region's own indigenous cattle - the Belted Galloways, so called because they have a wide white band running round their bodies.

Dumfries is the largest town in the area, and is a lovely place, full of old red sandstone buildings and great shopping facilities. It is also where Scotland's national poet, Robert Burns, is buried, and any trip to Scotland should include a visit to St Michael's Kirkyard to see his mausoleum. Kirkcudbright, because of the quality of light found there, has had an artist's colony since Victorian times, and is a gracious place, full of Regency and Georgian buildings. Wigtown is Scotland's official book town, Castle Douglas is Scotland's food town, and Stranraer, with its ferries, is a gateway to Northern Ireland. Then there's Lockerbie, forever associated with the disaster of 1988.

The area contains three former counties - Dumfriesshire, Kirkcudbrightshire and Wigtownshire, and each one has its own particular charm. You can explore beautiful Nithsdale in Dumfriesshire, for instance (absolutely beautiful in autumn), and visit Drumlanrig Castle, one of the homes of the Duke of Queensberry and Buccleuch. Kirkcudbrightshire was the birthplace of John Paul Jones, founder of the American navy, and Wigtownshire was where Christianity was introduced into Scotland by St Ninian.

Surrounding the fertile fields and picturesque towns of coastal Galloway are high hills and bleak moorland, which cut off Dumfries and Galloway from the rest of Scotland. Because of this, the area was almost independent of Scottish kings in medieval times, and was ruled by a succession of families, from the ancient Lords of Galloway to the mighty Douglases. All have left their mark in stone, such as Devorgilla's Bridge in Dumfries and the mighty Threave Castle, built on an island in the River Dee.

Then there are the abbeys. Like the Borders, this was an area much favoured by medieval monks, and at New Abbey are the ruins of a monastery that gave the word "sweetheart" to the English language. At Glenluce - a word which means "valley of light" - are the wonderful ruins of Glenluce Abbey; and south of Kirkcudbright is Dundrennan, where Mary Stuart - better known as Mary Queen of Scots - spent her last night on Scottish soil. The castles are equally as impressive. Drumlanrig - Threave - Cardoness - Caerlaverock; the names trip off the tongue, and go to the very heart of Scotland's history.

From the middle of August to the end of October each year the area holds its "Gaelforce Festival", bringing together musical events, literary festivals, traditional Scottish entertainment, concerts, drama and art.

This part of Scotland has a mild climate. At one time the coastline was nicknamed the "Scottish Riviera", and more recently "the Tuscany of Scotland" on account of the incomers and the people who have holiday homes here. First-time visitors are always surprised to see palm trees flourishing in cottage gardens near the coast or in the grand, formal gardens such as Logan Botanic Garden or Castle Kennedy Garden in Wigtownshire. But then, Dumfries and Galloway has always been full of surprises.

34

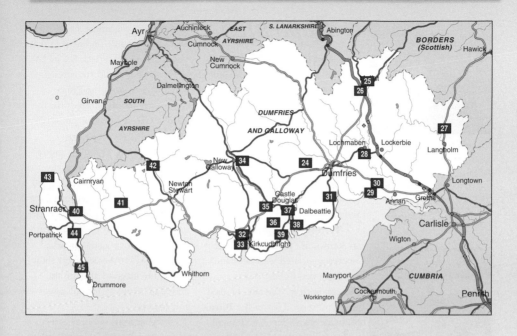

ACCOMMODATION

FOOD & DRINK

PLACES OF INTEREST

21 LAST POST

Dumfries

One of the friendliest pubs in Dumfries, with superb accommodation, that is just right for a quiet, relaxing drink.

🍴 🛏 *see page 430*

22 MARCHILLS RESTAURANT

Dumfries

A superb restaurant brasserie that is modern and stylish, and which sells the very best of food, all prepared from fresh local produce wherever possible.

🍴 *see page 430*

DUMFRIES

The Royal Burgh of Dumfries certainly lives up to its nickname of the "Queen of the South". It has a lovely location on the banks of the River Nith, and on more than one occasion was voted the town with the best quality of life in Britain. It has an illustrious history, having been granted its burgh charter in 1186 by William the Lion, king of Scotland.

The town, whose inhabitants are known as "Doonhamers", is forever associated with Scotland's national poet, Robert Burns. Though born in Ayrshire, he died in Dumfries, and lies in the **Burns Mausoleum** within the kirkyard that surrounds **St Michael's Parish Church**, built in the 1740s. Also buried there are his wife, Jean Armour, and five of their family. Burns had a family pew in St Michael's (marked by a plaque), and long after his death his wife was a regular attender.

When Burns died in 1796 his funeral in Dumfries was a grand affair. He had become a respected figure throughout Scotland, and the great and the good attended. Even the military attended as a solemn procession marched, to the strains of the *Dead March* by Handel, from the Midsteeple, where his body had lain overnight, to St Michael's Kirk. Here he was buried in a simple grave.

However, as the man's fame spread beyond Scotland, it was felt that something much grander was needed. Even the Wordsworths, who made a pilgrimage to his grave, had trouble finding it in the overcrowded graveyard. So, in 1813 it was decided to do something about it, with even the Prince Regent lending his support. In 1815, a Grecian mausoleum was built, and his remains were transferred to it. However, rather gruesomely, while the decaying coffin was being transferred, it fell open, revealing the great man's body. In 1834, when Jean Armour's body was placed in the mausoleum, his remains were again disturbed when a cast was taken of his skull.

In the kirkyard also are the graves of many of his colleagues and friends

Not far away is Burns Street (formerly called Mill Vennel), where **Burns' House** is situated. He lived here from 1793 until he died at the early age of 37. It is open to the public, and though not a grand house, it was nonetheless a substantial building for its day, showing that by the end of his life Burns had achieved some form of financial stability due to his work as an exciseman. On display are letters and manuscripts, copies of the Kilmarnock and Edinburgh editions of his works, the pistol he carried with him on his rounds and the chair in which he sat when he wrote his last poems.

The **Globe Inn** was the poet's "howff", or haunt, and it can still be visited. It was established in 1610, and is situated down a narrow passage off the main street. This was where Burns lodged when he found employment in Dumfries and before he moved his family from Ellisland. His seat is on display, and on one of the window panes are some verses he scratched on it with a diamond. Guided tours of the inn are available.

Maxwelltown sits on the west bank of the Nith, and though has been part of Dumfries since 1929, at one time it was a separate burgh. It wasn't even in Dumfriesshire, as the Nith at this point was the boundary between Dumfriesshire and Kirkcudbrightshire. In Maxwelltown is the **Robert Burns Centre**, within an old 18th century watermill. It tells the full story of the poet and his connections with the town. There are displays and exhibits, including a model of the Dumfries that Burns would have known in the late 18th century. There is also a cinema.

The history of Dumfries goes much further back than Robert Burns, however. It is an ancient town, and it was here, in 1306, that Robert the Bruce killed the Red Comyn, a rival contender for the throne of Scotland. The murder took place before the high altar of Greyfriar's Monastery, a deed for which he was excommunicated by the Pope. However, this did not seem to worry the man, as he immediately had himself crowned king of Scotland at Scone in Perthshire in the presence of Scottish bishops, who continued to give him communion. It is said that the Red Comyn was buried where he fell, and his grave is beneath some shops built on the site of the friary. Nothing now remains of the building, though the present **Greyfriar's Kirk**, a flamboyant building in red sandstone, is close to where it stood.

In the High Street stands the **Midsteeple**, built of red sandstone in 1707. It was formerly the town hall and jail, and on its south face is a carving of an ell, an old Scots cloth measurement of about 37 inches. There is also a table of distances from Dumfries to various important Scottish towns. One of the towns however, is in England - Huntingdon. Three successive Scottish kings in medieval times held the earldom of Huntingdon, a town that was one of the places where Scottish drovers took cattle to market in the 17th and 18th centuries.

Further down the High Street is the ornate **Fountain**, built in 1851 to commemorate the introduction of piped water into the town. Opposite is the façade of a building that once housed the County Hotel, where Charles Edward Stuart lodged in 1745. Dumfries, in common with most Lowland towns, was not sympathetic to the Jacobite cause.

In Shakespeare Street stands, rather appropriately, the famous **Theatre Royal**, one of the oldest theatres in Scotland, dating from 1792. Burns was one of the instigators in the building of the theatre, which saw actors of the calibre of Kean, McReady, Stan Laurel and Charlie Chaplin appearing there. In contrast, Dumfries's newest attraction is **Organised Chaos** on Lockerbie

23   THE LINEN ROOM

Dumfries

Outstanding and imaginative cuisine in one of the leading restaurants in the country.

🍴   *see page 431*

24   BARNSOUL FARM

Dumfries

A superb caravan and camping site with Wigwam mountain bothies that is ideally situated for exploring everything Dumfries and Galloway has to offer.

🛏   *see page 432*

Devorgilla's Bridge

On the northern outskirts of Dumfries, but now surrounded by modern housing, are the beautiful red sandstone remains of Lincluden College (Historic Scotland). Built originally in 1164 as a Benedictine nunnery by Uchtred, Lord of Galloway, it was suppressed in the late 14th century by Archibald the Grim, third Earl of Douglas, and replaced by a collegiate church. The present ruins date from that time. One of its main features is the elaborate canopied tomb of Princess Margaret, daughter of Robert III and widow of the fourth Earl of Douglas (see also Threave Castle). Adjoining the site is the Norman Lincluden Motte, which was later terraced and incorporated into a garden. The adjoining tower house was built in the late 16th century, after the Reformation, by the commendator, or lay provost of the college, William Stewart.

Road. This activity centre has a paint ball arena and a purpose-built, all terrain 800 metre track for off-road buggies.

Devorgilla's Bridge connects Dumfries with Maxwelltown, and was built in 1431. It is named after Devorgilla, Lady of Galloway, who built the original bridge in the 13th century. Her husband was John Balliol, who founded Balliol College in Oxford (see also New Abbey).

At the Maxwelltown end of the bridge is the **Old Bridge House Museum**, with exhibits and displays illustrating everyday life in the town. The museum building dates from 1660, and is built into the structure of the bridge. Also on the Maxwelltown side of the river is **Dumfries Museum**, housed in an 18th century windmill, and with a Camera Obscura that gives fascinating views of the town.

To the east of the town at Heathhall is the **Dumfries and Galloway Aviation Museum**, run by a group of amateur enthusiasts.

It has three floors of displays in what was the control tower of the old airfield of RAF Tinwald Downs, and holds a fascinating collection of military and civil aircraft, both propeller and jet powered, as well as engines, memorabilia and photographs.

Within what was Crichton Royal Hospital in Bankend Road, is the cathedralesque **Crichton Memorial Church**, designed by Sydney Mitchell and built between 1890-1897 as part of a mental hospital. The hospital grounds and buildings have now been turned into a campus for Glasgow and Paisley Universities, as well as two colleges.

Gracefield Arts Centre, on the Edinburgh Road, has a constantly changing programme of workshops, events and exhibitions throughout the year. For those interested in genealogy, the **Dumfries and Galloway Family History Research Centre** in Glasgow Street must be visited.

There are archives, fiches and books about local history and families, though there is a modest fee for the use of the facilities.

Another writer associated with Dumfries is J.M. Barrie (see also Kirriemuir). Though not born here, he attended **Dumfries Academy**, a handsome building in Academy Street. While at the school, he stayed in a house in George Street, and later admitted that the games of pirates he and his friends played in the garden sloping down to the Nith gave him the idea for Peter Pan and Captain Hook (see also Eliock).

Dumfries was the birthplace, in 1897, of **John Laurie**, who played Private Frazer in *Dad's Army*.

AROUND DUMFRIES

TERREGLES

3 miles NW of Dumfries on an unmarked road off the A76

This tiny village is visited mainly for the 18th century **Terregles Parish Church**, with its restored choir of 1583, where there are some ancient tombs.

DALSWINTON

6 miles N of Dumfries on a minor road off the A76

The hamlet of Dalswinton is no more than two rows of cottages on either side of the road. But it is an attractive place, built as an estate village. When Robert Burns was living locally at Ellisland Farm, Patrick Millar owned Dalswinton House, in the grounds of which (not open to the public) is

Dalswinton Loch. Patrick encouraged William Symington, originally from Leadhills, to experiment with his steam-driven boat on the waters of the loch in the late 18th century, and it is thought that Burns may have been a passenger on one of the sailings (see also Leadhills).

Patrick is said to have introduced turnips into Britain, when he was presented with seeds by King Gustav of Sweden. Hence the common name for a type of turnip - a swede.

ELLISLAND

6 miles N of Dumfries on the A76

Robert Burns brought his family south from Mauchline to Ellisland in June 1788. However, there was no farmhouse at the time, and he had to have one built, meaning that he could not move in properly until the following year. He leased the 170-acre farm from Patrick Millar of Dalswinton, but found the soil to be infertile and stony. So much so that by 1791 he gave up the unequal struggle to make a living from it, and moved with his family to Dumfries.

The farm sits in a beautiful spot beside the Nith, and it was this romantic location which had made Burns choose it in the first place. Here he wrote some of his best poetry, including *Auld Lang Syne* and his masterpiece of the comic/macabre, *Tam o' Shanter*. Burns used to recount that Tam o' Shanter was conceived while walking the banks of the Nith, laughing out loud as he thought up

The hamlet of Holywood sits just off the A76, two miles north of Dumfries. The present Holywood Parish Church of 1779 (with a tower dating to 1821) was partly built from the stones of a great medieval abbey which once stood here, of which nothing now remains above ground. To the west, on the other side of the A76, is a stone circle known as the Twelve Apostles, though one massive stone is now missing.

Three miles north of the village of Thornhill, and to the west of the A702, are the remains of 15th century Morton Castle, situated romantically on a tongue of land jutting out into Morton Loch. A castle of some kind has stood here since the 12th century, though the present castle was built by the Douglases, who were the Earls of Morton. In 1588 the castle was sacked by the troops of James VI, who were conducting a campaign against the Maxwells.

his hero's adventures with the witches. Now the farmhouse houses a lively museum. To the north is **Hermitage Cottage**, which Burns used as a place to muse and write poetry.

AE

8 miles N of Dumfries on a minor road off the A701

The small village of Ae is famous for having the shortest name of any town or village in Britain, and for having the only place name with no consonants in it. It takes its name from the Water of Ae, and was founded in 1947 to house forestry workers. It is set in a great conifer forest called the Forest of Ae, where there are many walks.

CLOSEBURN

11 miles N of Dumfries on the A76

Closeburn sits in one of the most beautiful parts of Dumfriesshire - Nithsdale. To the north of the village the wooded dale closes in on either side, with the River Nith tumbling through it. To the south, it gradually opens out into a wide, fertile strath, dotted with green fields and old, whitewashed farms. The **Parish Church of Closeburn** sits some distance away from the village, and is an attractive red sandstone Victorian building with a slim tower. Fragments of the older church, which date from 1741, can be seen in the kirkyard. **Closeburn Castle** (not open to the public) has been continuously inhabited since the 14th century, when it was built by the Kirkparticks, who were closely

associated with Robert I.

A small road winds up eastwards from just south of Closeburn into the moorland above the village. It makes an interesting drive, and takes you past the small but picturesque **Loch Ettrick**.

THORNHILL

13 miles N of Dumfries on the A76

This lovely village, with its wide main street and pollarded trees, has a French feel to it, and was laid out in 1714 by the Duke of Queensberry. At the crossroads in the middle of the village is a monument surmounted by a winged horse, a symbol of the Queensberry family. In a field to the west of the village, and close to the bridge over the Nith, is the 15th century **Boatford Cross**, associated with the ferry and ford that preceded the bridge.

It was at Wallacehall Academy, now within the town, that **Thomas Burns**, the nephew of the poet Robert, received part of his education. He was subsequently ordained a minister in the Church of Scotland, and emigrated to New Zealand, where he helped found the city of Dunedin (see also Haddington and Monkton).

Against the wall of a building in East Morton Street is the bust of Joseph Laing Waugh, Thornhill's own novelist and poet, who set some of his books, written in Lowland Scots, in and around the village.

Crichope Linn, which lies east of the village, is a waterfall on the Crichope Burn which has carved out a narrow passageway through the sandstone. It was a favourite hiding place for Covenanters in the 17th century, and is mentioned in Scott's *Old Mortality*.

DRUMLANRIG CASTLE

16 miles N of Dumfries on a minor road off the A76

Drumlanrig Castle is set in a 120,000-acre estate, and is the Dumfriesshire home of the Duke of Queensberry and Buccleuch. It was built by William Douglas, 1st Duke of Queensberry, and completed in 1691, though he is reputed to have spent only one night under its roof when the work was finished. It contains many fine paintings, including works by Gainsborough, Rembrandt and Hans Holbein. Its name comes from the word "drum", meaning a low hill, on a "lang", or long, "rig", or ridge. Therefore it is the low hill on the long ridge.

DURISDEER

19 miles N of Dumfries on a minor road off the A702

The tiny hamlet of Durisdeer sits at the end of a narrow road leading off the A702, in the shadow of the rolling Lowther Hills. It consists of a handful of cottages and a **Parish Church** built in 1699, and the church is unusual in that it has, attached to it, the former parish school. The church and schoolroom are surprisingly large for such a small hamlet, but this is due to the fact that it is the church for the Queensberry estates surrounding Drumlanrig Castle.

It also hides a secret which makes it special - the wonderful **Durisdeer Marbles**. They are, in fact, an elaborate funerary monument constructed in 1713 for the 2nd Duke of Queensberry and his wife, who lie buried in the crypt beneath. They were carved in marble by the Flemish sculptor Jan Nost, and are said to be the best of their kind in the country.

PENPONT

13 miles N of Dumfries on the A702

This small, attractive village is well worth a visit in the summer months to see the colourful gardens that surround some of the old picturesque cottages. The cathedralesque red sandstone **Parish Church** is Victorian, and seems far too large for such a small place.

Penpont was, in 1858, the birthplace of **Joseph Thomson** the African explorer, after whom Thomson's gazelle is named. The son of a quarry owner and stonemason, he studied at Edinburgh University and joined an

In the summer of 2003 Drumlanrig Castle was the scene of a daring burglary when a painting by Leonardo da Vinci worth millions of pounds was stolen from it in broad daylight. Within the estate is a country park and gardens, the ruins of Tibbers Castle, and some of the outbuildings have been converted into craft workshops. The Drumlanrig Sycamore is one of the largest sycamores in the country, and there is also the first Douglas fir ever planted in the United Kingdom.

Durisdeer Parish Church

Not far from Dunscore is Lochenhead Farm, birthplace in 1897 of Jane Haining, the only British person to have died at Auschwitz during World War II. While still young she joined the Church of Scotland's Jewish Mission Service, and was eventually appointed matron of the Jewish Mission in Budapest in 1932. In 1944 she was arrested, purportedly because she had been listening to BBC broadcasts, but actually because she had been working among the Jews. She was taken to Auschwitz, and on July 17th 1944 died there. Her death certificate gave the cause of death as cachexia, a wasting illness sometimes associated with cancer, but there is no doubt she was gassed. On the west wall of the parish church is a plaque to her memory.

expedition to Africa in 1878, thus starting a long association with that continent. He died at the young age of 37 in 1895, his body wasted by the many diseases he had contracted.

On a slight rise in a field between Thornhill and Penpont is a piece of sculpture shaped like a cone. This is the work of **Andy Goldsworthy,** the famous sculptor, who was born in Cheshire but now works in the village.

KEIR

12 miles N of Dumfries on a minor road off the A702

Keir is no more than a hamlet with a small **Parish Church** dating mainly from 1814. It was near here that **Kirkpatrick Macmillan**, inventor of the modern bicycle, was born in 1812, in Courthill Smithy, where there is a plaque commemorating the event. While his brothers all went on to become successful in their careers, Kirkpatrick was content to stay at home and ply the trade of a blacksmith.

Hobbyhorses, which relied on riders pushing themselves forward with their feet, had been around since the early part of the 19th century, but Kirkpatrick Macmillan's bicycle was the first to incorporate revolving pedals that powered the back wheels. On June 6th 1842 he set out on a 70-mile ride to Glasgow on his bicycle, and was greeted by crowds when he arrived there. However, while passing through the Gorbals, he knocked down a young girl, and

even though she was not badly injured, he was fined five shillings by a Glasgow magistrate, the first recorded case of a cyclist being fined for a traffic offence. However, rumour has it that the magistrate offered to pay the fine out of his own pocket if Kirkpatrick would allow him to have a ride on the bicycle.

Macmillan now lies buried in the churchyard at Keir.

TYRON

15 miles N of Dumfries on a minor road off the A702

This small, pretty conservation village has only one building dating after 1900. The **Parish Church**, which looks as if it is far too big for such a small place, was built in 1837, and was one of the last in Scotland to be lit by oil lamps. Early in the 20th century a distillery which had a contract to supply the Palace of Westminster was situated here.

At the summit of the 945 feet high **Tynron Doon** are the ramparts and ditches of an Iron Age fort.

DUNSCORE

8 miles NW of Dumfries on the B729

Dunscore (pronounced "Dunsker") is a small, attractive village with a neat, whitewashed **Parish Church** dating from 1823. When Robert Burns and his family stayed at Ellisland Farm, four miles to the east, they used to worship in its predecessor.

The isolated farm of **Craigenputtock**, where Thomas Carlyle lived while writing *Sartor*

Resartus, lies off an unmarked road five miles to the west (see also Ecclefechan). It was here that an unusual - not to say hilarious - event took place concerning a small religious sect known as the Buchanites, founded by Elspeth Buchan, known as Mother Buchan, in Irvine, Ayrshire, in the 18th century. She attracted a wide following, claiming she could bestow immortality on a person by breathing on them, and that she herself was immortal.

She also claimed that her followers would ascend to heaven in bodily form, without the inconvenience of death. The cult was eventually hounded from Irvine by the town magistrates, and it headed south towards Dumfries. In a large field near Craigenputtock she decided that it was time her followers went to heaven. So she had a wooden platform set up in a field at Craigenputtock, and she and her followers assembled on it, their heads shaved apart form a small tuft that the angels would grasp to lift them up into God's kingdom. However, in the middle of the service the platform collapsed, throwing her followers to the ground. The sect eventually broke up when Elspeth had the nerve to die a natural death (see also Irvine and Crocketford).

At **Glenkiln**, beside Glenkiln Reservoir, four miles (as the crow flies) south west of Dunscore, is a collection of sculptures by Henry Moore and Rodin. The land on which the statues stand was owned by Sir William Keswick, who first brought the sculptures here in 1951. Between then and 1976 they were added to.

MONIAIVE

16 miles NW of Dumfries on the A 702

Moniaive, caught in a fold of the hills at the head of Glencairn, through which the Cairn Water flows to join the Nith, must surely be one of the prettiest villages in Dumfriesshire. It is actually two villages, Moniaive itself and Dunreggan, on the east side of the river. Within the village is the **Renwick** Monument, which commemorates a local Covenater, the Reverend James Renwick who was executed in February 1688 at Edinburgh aged just 26. He is remembered as the last of the covenanting martyrs, for later in the same year the "Glorious Revolution" put an end to their persecution.

James Paterson was a painter who was a member of that group known as the "Glasgow Boys". In 1882 he settled in the village with his wife, and lived there until 1906, when he moved to Edinburgh. Several of his paintings show scenes in and around the village.

Every September the village hosts the **Scottish Comic Festival**, with displays and exhibitions, as well as talks by cartoonists and comic illustrators. There is also the yearly **Moniaive Folk Festival** in May.

CORSOCK

13 miles W of Dumfries on the A712

Close to the village is **Glenlair House**, the home of Edinburgh-born James Clerk Maxwell, a 19th

Three miles east is the great mansion of Maxwelton House (not open to the public), formerly known as Glencairn Castle. It was here that Anna (her real name) Laurie, of Bonnie Annie Laurie fame, was born in 1682. The song was written by William Douglas of Fingland (an estate west of Maxwelton) and later, in the 19th century, added to and put to music by Lady Scott. Douglas later jilted Anna and joined the Jacobite army. Anna herself went on to marry Alexander Fergusson, 14th Laird of Craigdarroch (see also Sanquhar).

Lead is not the only metal associated with Wanlockhead. In olden days, this whole area of the Lowther Hills was known as "God's Treasure House in Scotland" because of the gold found there. In fact, the Scottish crown was refashioned for James V in the 16th century from gold mined here. The largest nugget of gold ever discovered in the UK was found close to Wanlockhead. It weighed all of two pounds, and was the size of a cricket ball. Gold panning is still a popular activity in the local streams, and the UK National Gold Panning Championships are held here every May.

century scientist whose work on electro-magnetism led directly to the invention of the mobile phone, radio and TV, the microwave cooker, radiotherapy for cancer, the computer and so on. He also discovered the composition of Saturn's rings long before space probes proved him correct. He now lies in the nearby graveyard at Parton.

WANLOCKHEAD

25 miles N of Dumfries on the B797

People are usually surprised to discover that Scotland's highest village is not in the Highlands, but in the Lowlands. Wanlockhead, in the Lowther Hills, is 1,531 feet above sea level, and is a former lead mining village on the Southern Upland Way. It is best approached from the A76, passing through one of the most beautiful and majestic glens in southern Scotland - the **Mennock Pass**. As you drive up, keep your eyes open for a small cross laid flat into the grass on the north side of the road. It commemorates Kate Anderson, a nurse who was killed here in 1925 when she was returning to Sanquhar after attending a patient. She fell off her bicycle in a snowstorm and broke her neck.

In the middle of Wanlockhead, in what was the village smithy, you'll find the **Museum of Lead Mining,** which explains all about the industry, and gives you the opportunity to go down the **Lochnell Mine**, a former working mine. The **Miners' Library** is situated on a rise above the

museum, and was founded in 1756 by 35 men. At the height of its popularity it had 3,000 books on its shelves. Within the village you'll also find the **Beam Engine**, which has recently been restored. It used to pump water from one of the mines using, curiously enough, water to power it. **Straitsteps Cottages** shows the living conditions of the lead miners in the 18th and 19th centuries.

The **Leadhills and Wanlockhead Light Railway** is Britain's highest adhesion railway, reaching 1,498 feet above sea level. The line was originally built as a full gauge line to take refined lead to Scotland's central belt, but closed in 1938. Now a length of two-feet gauge track has been re-opened between Wanlockhead and its twin village of Leadhills in Lanarkshire, and trips are available at weekends during the summer.

SANQUHAR

28 miles N of Dumfries on the A76

Sanquhar (pronounced San-kar) is a small town in Upper Nithsdale that was created a royal burgh in 1598. The name comes from the language of the ancient Britons, and means "Old Fort". The site of this fort was on a small hill to the north of the town, close to **St Bride's Parish Church**, built in 1824 on the site of a much older church. Within the church is a small collection of stone carvings, including one of St Nicholas and a medieval cross.

The **Sanquhar Tolbooth** was built to the designs of William

Adam in 1735 as a town hall, schoolroom and jail, and now houses a small museum. It was in a house opposite the Tolbooth that William Boyd, 4th Earl of Kilmarnock, lodged while on his way south to be tried and executed for his part in the Jacobite uprising, and there is a plaque on the wall commemorating his stay. In Main Street is **Sanquhar Post Office**, dating from 1712, the oldest continuously used post office in the world. The Southern Upland Way passes through the burgh, and the **Sanquhar Historic Walk** takes you round many of the town's attractions and historic sites.

Sanquhar Castle

To the south of Sanquhar are the ruins of **Sanquhar Castle**, originally an old Crichton stronghold. It fell into the hands of the Douglases, and it was here that William Douglas, who wrote the original version of the song *Annie Laurie*, was born in 1672 (see Maxwelton House). The castle was founded in the 11th century by the Crichtons, though what you see now dates from much later.

In the 17th century, Sanquhar was a Covenanting stronghold. Charles II had imposed bishops on the Church of Scotland and declared himself its head, and the Covenanters took up arms, declaring that only Christ was head of the Church of Scotland, which they wanted to remain Presbyterian. These times were known as the "Killing Times", and many people were executed for following the dictates of their conscience. One of the most militant Covenanters

was **Richard Cameron**, who rode into Sanquhar in 1680 and attached what became known as the "**Sanquhar Declaration**" to the Market Cross. This disowned the king, which was effectively treason. Cameron was subsequently killed at the Battle of Airds Moss in the same year (see also Falkland).

Coalmining, up until the 1970s, was a major industry, though there were no mines within the town itself. One of the more unusual cottage industries during the 18th and 19th centuries was the hand knitting of gloves, and the intricate patterns soon made the gloves popular throughout the country. Up until the 1950s these patterns had never been published. Now it is possible once more to buy both hand and machine knitted gloves and garments made from the distinctive patterns.

A series of plaques on various buildings takes you on a historic walk round the town, with a leaflet being available in the local tourist office. One of the plaques recalls

The Riding of the Marches is an ancient ceremony, and takes place every August. The burgh boundaries are ridden by horse riders to ensure that adjoining landowners have not encroached onto burgh or common land - a common occurrence in olden times.

A few miles south of Sanquhar, on a bridge over the Nith off the A76, is a plaque commemorating an unusual event that took place in 1870. A stable boy had been told to lead a horse back to the stables, but instead he mounted it. As the horse and rider passed over the bridge, a train passed on the nearby line, scaring the horse. It immediately scaled the parapet of the bridge, and fell into the river, taking the boy with it. The horse was killed, but the boy mercifully survived. The grooves made by the horse's hooves as it mounted the parapet can still be seen. The plaque was placed there as a lesson for all boys who disobeyed their masters.

two French officers who were held as prisoners of war in the town during the Napoleonic Wars, and who fought a dual over a local woman. The loser, a Lieutenant Arnaud, now lies in Sanquhar kirkyard.

ELIOCK HOUSE

26 miles N of Dumfries on a side road running parallel to the A76

Set deep in the heart of Nithsdale off a minor road, Eliock House (not open to the public) was the birthplace in 1560 of **James Crichton**, better known as the "Admirable Crichton". He was the son of the then Lord Advocate of Scotland, and was educated at St Andrews University. He travelled extensively in Europe, where he followed careers in soldiering and lecturing at universities. Though a young man, he could speak 12 languages fluently, and was one of the best swordsmen of his day. However, this did not prevent him from being killed in Mantua in Italy in 1582 while a lecturer at the local university.

The story goes that he was returning from a party one evening when he was set upon by a gang of robbers. Being an excellent swordsman, he fought off the robbers easily. However, he then realised that one of the robbers was a pupil at the university, Vincentio di Gonzaga, son of the Duke of Mantua, ruler of the city. Realising what he had done, James handed Vincentio his sword and asked forgiveness. Vincentio, however, was a nasty piece of work. He took

the sword and stabbed the defenceless James through the heart, killing him outright.

J.M. Barrie, who had lived in Dumfries for a short while, later used James Crichton's nickname as the title of a play written in 1902. It was considered daring for its time, and was about a butler who assumes command of the family he once served after it had been shipwrecked.

KIRKCONNEL (UPPER NITHSDALE)

31 miles N of Dumfries on the A76

This former mining village in upper Nithsdale is not to be confused with Kirkconnell House near New Abbey or Kirkconnel graveyard in Annandale. **St Connel's Parish Church** dates from 1729, and is a fine looking building to the west of the village.

High on the hill, where a drove road used to run, are the scant remains of an even earlier church, which may date from before the 10th century. Near the present parish church is a monument to **Alexander Anderson**, a local poet who wrote under the name of "The Surfaceman". Though born in lowly circumstances, he rose to become chief librarian at Edinburgh University and subsequently the secretary of the Edinburgh Philosophical Union.

The **Kirkconnel Parish Heritage Society** has a small shop and office in the Main Street, and here you will find information on history and genealogy. The **Kirkconnel Miners Memorial** commemorates the men who lost their lives in the Upper Nithsdale mining industry between 1872 and 1968.

MOFFAT

20 miles NE of Dumfries on the A701

Sheep farming has always been important in Annandale, and this is illustrated by the ram that surmounts the **Colvin Fountain** in the middle of the wide High Street. The town is situated in a fertile bowl surrounded by low green hills, and at one time was a spa, thanks to a mineral spring discovered on its outskirts in the 17th century. By 1827 the sulphurous water was being pumped into the town, and by Victorian times it had become a fashionable place to visit and "take the waters".

Moffat was the birthplace, in 1882, of **Air Chief Marshal Lord Dowding**, architect of the Battle of Britain. A statue of him can be found in **Station Park**. Though he was not born in the town, **John Loudon McAdam**, the great road builder, is buried in the old kirkyard at the south end of the High Street. He lived at Dumcrieff House, outside the town, and died in 1836 (see also Ayr, Carsphairn and Muirkirk). Though born in Edinburgh, Dorothy Emily Stevenson, better known as the popular novelist **DE Stevenson**, lived in Moffat, and died there in 1973. She was a relative of Robert Louis Stevenson. She is buried in the local cemetery. The small **Moffat Museum** at The Neuk, Church Gate, charts the history of the town and the people associated with it, including Dowding, McAdam and Stevenson.

The **Black Bull Inn** is one of the oldest in Dumfriesshire, and dates from 1568. Burns was a regular visitor, and Graham of Claverhouse used it as his headquarters while hunting Covenanters in the district. Another hostelry in Moffat that has a claim to fame, albeit a more unusual one, is the **Star Hotel** in the High Street. It is only 20 feet wide, making it the narrowest hotel in Britain. On the other side of the road is the former **Moffat House**, designed by John Adam for the Earl of Hopetoun and dating from 1750s. It, too, is now a hotel.

GREY MARE'S TAIL

28 miles NE of Dumfries just off the A708

The A708 winds northeast from the town, and takes you past St Mary's Loch as you head for Selkirk. About eight miles along the road is a 300 feet waterfall called The Grey Mare's Tail (National Trust for Scotland), fed by the waters of tiny Loch Skeen, high in the hills. The surrounding area has changed little since the 17th century, when it was a hiding place for Covenanters. It is now a 2,150-acre nature reserve, and is rich in fauna and flora, including a herd of wild goats. During the summer months there is a programme of guided walks starting from the visitor centre. A live CCTV link at the visitor centre allows you to see a peregrine falcon nest in the Tail Burn gorge.

25 MORLICH HOUSE

Moffat

A four star B&B just off the M74 that is an ideal stopping off place for people travelling north or south.

see page 432

26 THE OLD STABLES

Beattock

A first class inn just off the M74 that offers great accommodation, good food and a relaxed atmosphere where you can enjoy a quiet drink.

see page 432

Two miles east of the town, on the A708, are Craiglochan Gardens, which are open during the summer months. They extend to four acres, and there is a small nursery. The nearby Craigieburn Forest has a waymarked woodland walk that takes you to a viewpoint with views over Moffat. There is a car park.

Close by Eskdalemuir is Eskdalemuir Geomagnetic Observatory, opened in 1908. It measures not only magnetism, but solar radiation and levels of atmospheric pollution. It was built at Eskdalemuir for an unusual reason. The observatory was originally at Kew in London, but the sensitive geomagnetic instruments used to measure the earth's magnetic field were affected by the overhead electricity lines used to power trams. It was at Eskdalemuir in June 1953 that the highest short-term rainfall for Scotland was recorded - 3.15 inches in half an hour. This represents about 15 per cent of Scotland's average annual rainfall.

27 BUSH OF EWES

Langholm

A wonderful B&B farmhouse and self-catering cottage right in the heart of the Scottish countryside, yet handy for the larger towns in the area.

▶ see page 433

TWEEDSWELL

26 miles NE of Dumfries, well off the A701

Tweedswell is the source of the Tweed, and sits 1,250 feet above sea level. It seems strange that within an area of no more than a few square miles, three rivers rise, all flowing in different directions. The Tweed flows east, the Annan flows south, and the Clyde flows north.

Here also is a great hollowed-out area among the hills known as the **Devil's Beef Tub**. Here, in olden times, border reivers used to hide their stolen cattle. The **John Hunter Monument** commemorates a Covenanter who was shot dead in the Devil's Beef Tub in 1685. To the east towers the 2,651 feet high **Hartfell**, supposedly the seat of Merlin the Magician in Arthurian days.

ESKDALEMUIR

23 miles NE of Dumfries on the B709

Eskdalemuir, high in the hills, holds one of Dumfriesshire's hidden gems. The **Samye Ling Centre**, founded in 1967 by two refugee Tibetan abbots, is the largest Tibetan Buddhist monastery in Western Europe. Not only is it a monastery, it is a place where Tibetan culture, customs and art is preserved. To see its colourful Eastern buildings, its flags flying and its prayer wheels revolving in a typical Scottish moorland setting comes as a great surprise. People of all religions, and none, are welcome to visit the monastery.

The **Eskdalemuir Prehistoric Trail**, which is suitable for walkers or bikers, takes you round nine sites in the Eskdale, from ancient farmsteads to forts and from stone circles to burial cairns.

LANGHOLM

24 miles NE of Dumfries on the A7

Though within Dumfriesshire, the "muckle toon" of Langholm, in Eskdale, owes more to the Borders than Dumfries and Galloway. It was here, in 1892, that Christopher Murray Grieve the poet - better known as **Hugh McDiarmid** - was born (see also Biggar), though it took many years for the people of the town to formally acknowledge him as Scotland's greatest 20th century poet. A memorial to him was erected on Whita Hill in 1998, and he now lies in the local graveyard. Also born in the town, but not a native, was **James Robertson Justice** the actor. His mother was passing through and was forced to stop at the Crown Hotel, where he was delivered.

This is Armstrong country, and when Neil Armstrong, the first man to set foot on the moon, came to Langholm in 1972. he was given the freedom of the burgh. The **Armstrong Clan Museum** at Lodge Walk in Castleholm traces the history of one of the greatest Borders family. **Langholm Castle**, which is ruinous (though there has been some restoration work done on it) dates from the 16th century, and stands at the confluence of the River Esk and the Ewes Water. It can be accessed from the car park beside the museum. On the last

Friday in July the annual **Common Riding Ceremony** is held in the town. Behind the town hall is the **Langholm Library**, containing many old books, and founded in 1843 by Thomas Telford the civil engineer. Opposite the library is a stone doorway built by Telford when he was an apprentice stone mason (see also Westerkirk).

The **Langholm Archive Centre** at 93 High Street has material on the history of the area, though it keeps no records on genealogy.

On a hillside to the east of the town is the **Malcolm Monument**, in memory of Sir John Malcolm, who died in 1833. He was born at Burnfoot, a farm near Langholm, in 1769, and became a major-general who distinguished himself in India.

WESTERKIRK

29 miles NE of Dumfries on the B709

The parish of Westerkirk lies a few miles north west of the Langholm, and it was here that **Thomas Telford** the great civil engineer was born in 1757. The son of a shepherd, he left school at 14 and was apprenticed to a stone mason in Langholm. However, he was destined for greater things, and rose to be the greatest civil engineer of his generation, building the Ellesmere Canal, the Caledonian Canal and the Menai Straits Bridge in Wales.

Within the parish is the unique **Bentpath Library**, founded in 1793 for the use of the antimony miners who used to work in the nearby Meggat Valley. It is still in use today, though only the people of the local parishes may borrow from its stock of 8,000 books. On his death in 1834, Thomas Telford bequeathed a sum of money to it, and it expanded rapidly. Between 1992 and 1997 both the stock and the building were completely restored.

LOCKERBIE

10 miles NE of Dumfries off the M74

This quiet market town in Annandale is remembered for one thing - the **Lockerbie Disaster** of 1988. On the evening of December 21st, Pan Am flight 103 exploded in mid air after a terrorist bomb was detonated within its hold. The cockpit crashed into a field at **Tundergarth**, two-and-a-half miles east of the town, and its fuselage crashed into the town itself, killing the passengers, the crew and 11 people on the ground. **Remembrance Garden** is situated within the town cemetery to the west of the motorway on the A709. It is a peaceful spot, though there is still an air of raw emotion about the place, and no one visits without developing a lump in the throat.

On December 6th, 1593 the **Battle of Dryfe Sands** took place on the banks of the Dryfe Water north of the town. The two great families in the area - the Maxwells and the Johnstones - were forever feuding, and eventually the Maxwells, under the Earl of Morton, brought things to a head by marching into Johnstone territory with 2,000 men, many of them mounted. The Johnstones, who called on help from

To the south of the town of Lockerbie is Burnswark. The Iron Age Fort on its summit contains, within its ramparts and ditches, 2nd century Roman forts. It is thought that the fort was the capital of the Novantae tribe, and that after an uprising of AD 155 the Romans destroyed it and built their own fortifications there.

28 ARDBEG COTTAGE

Lochmaben

A lovely B&B within an old cottage in the royal burgh of Lochmaben that draws people back again and again.

see page 434

the Grahams, Scotts and Armstongs, could only muster 1,000, and a Maxwell victory seemed inevitable. However, when they met in battle at Dryfe Sands, the Johnstones won the day, killing over 700 Maxwells. The Earl of Morton was eventually captured and slain.

HIGHTAE

8 miles E of Dumfries on a minor road off the B7020

Rammerscales House is an 18th century manor house with fine views from its grounds. There is a walled garden and a woodland walk.

LOCHMABEN

8 miles NE of Dumfries on the A709

Lochmaben is a small royal burgh in Annandale. In the vicinity are many small lochs in which is found the vendace, a rare species of fish. Near the Castle Loch stand the scant remains of **Lochmaben Castle** (Historic Scotland), which originally covered 16 acres. It can only be viewed from the outside. An earlier 12th century castle (now no more that a small earthwork on the local golf course) was the home of the Bruce family, Lords of Annandale, and is said to be the birthplace of Robert the Bruce (later Robert I), though Turnberry in Ayrshire lays a similar, and perhaps more likely, claim (see also Turnberry). A statue of Wallace stands outside the town hall.

About three miles to the southwest is Skipmyre, where **William Paterson** was born in 1658. He was the driving force behind the ill-fated Darien Scheme of 1698, which sought to establish a Scottish colony in modern day Panama. Many Scots who went to Central America perished there, and it almost bankrupted the country. He was more successful in another venture - he founded the Bank of England in 1694 (see also New Abbey).

TORTHORWALD

4 miles E of Dumfries on the A709

Within the village, on a narrow road off the A709, is the **Cruck Cottage**, an early 18th century example of a thatched cottage

Lochmaben Castle

made in the traditional way, with "crucks", or thick, curved wooden supports. Their bases were placed some yards apart within deep holes so that they leaned towards each other, forming the shape of an "A". The ruined 14th century **Torthorwald Castle** was once a stronghold of the Carlyle and Kirkpatrick families. In 1544 Lord Carlyle destroyed the castle during a dispute with his sister-in-law.

CAERLAVEROCK

7 miles S of Dumfries on the B725

Think of an old, romantic, turreted medieval castle surrounded by a water-filled moat, and you could be thinking of **Caerlaverock Castle** (Historic Scotland). An earlier castle was built as the main seat of the Maxwells to the southeast of the present castle, but this was soon abandoned The core of the present castle dates from the late 13th century, and was attacked by Edward I in 1300 during the Wars of Independence. It is triangular in shape, with a turret at two corners and a double turret at the other, where the entrance is located. It was attacked by Covenanters in 1640 and dismantled, though in the early 1600s the first Earl of Nithsdale had some fine courtyard buildings constructed within the walls in the Renaissance style.

ANNAN

14 miles E of Dumfries, on the A75

The picturesque old Royal Burgh of Annan, even though it is a mile from the coast, was once a thriving seaport, and had a boat-building

yard. The aptly named Port Street, running south from the High Street, still takes you to a partially-restored quay. The **Burns Cairn** stands nearby commemorating the fact that Robert Burns visited the port as an exciseman.

The predominant stone in the town is red sandstone, epitomised by the handsome **Town Hall** of 1878, which dominates the High Street.

Edward Irving, the founder of the Catholic Apostolic Church, which thrived on elaborate ceremony and a complicated hierarchy of ministers and priests, was born here in 1792. He entered Edinburgh University at he age of thirteen, and later became headmaster of a school in Haddington, East Lothian, where one of his pupils was Jane Welsh, later to become the wife of Thomas Carlyle. Later still, when he had become a clergyman, he became a minister in the Church of Scotland church in Regent Square, London. There he earned a great reputation as a preacher and what we would now call a "Pentecostal" scholar, for which he was ejected from the Church of Scotland in 1833 (see also Haddington).

Four years earlier, **Hugh Clapperton** the explorer had been born in the town. At the age of 13 he became a cabin boy on a ship sailing between Liverpool and North America, and later went to the Mediterranean after being press ganged into the Royal Navy. He was invited to join an expedition to find the source of the River Niger,

Caerlaverock Wildfowl and Wetlands Trust is about three miles west of the castle, and is situated in a 1,400-acre nature reserve. Here a wide variety of wildlife can be observed, including swans and barnacle geese. If you're lucky, you may also come across the extremely rare natterjack toad. A recent discovery at Caerlaverock are tadpole shrimps, which were previously thought to be extinct in Scotland. There are three observation towers, 20 hides and a wild swan observatory linked by nature trails and screen approaches. There are also picnic areas, a gift shop, refreshments and binocular hire. Some facilities are wheelchair friendly. The place is on the well-signposted Solway Coast Heritage Trail, which stretches from Gretna in the east to Stranraer in the west.

Haaf Net Fishing, a means of catching fish that stretches back to Viking times, is still carried out at the mouth of the River Annan from April to August each year. The fishermen stand chest deep in the water wielding large haaf nets, which are attached to long wooden frames. In 1538 James V granted the haaf net fishermen of Annan a royal charter. In 1992 the rights of the fishermen were challenged in court by the owners of a time-share development further up the river, but the judge took the view that the charter still held good today.

29 SAVINGS BANK MUSEUM

Ruthwell

A fascinating collection of early savings boxes, coins and bank notes.

 see page 434

and eventually reached Lake Chad, the source of one of the Niger's tributaries, in 1823. On a second expedition in 1827 he died at Sokoto, Nigeria. Another Annan man was **Thomas Blacklock**, born in 1721. He was the first blind man to be ordained a minister in the Church of Scotland. **Annan Parish Church** in the High Street, with its stumpy spire, dates from 1786. The place has associations with the Bruce family, who were Lords of Annandale. In Bank Street is the **Historic Resources Centre**, a small museum that puts on a programme of displays and exhibitions.

A plaque on a cottage opposite the public park marks where the Victorian painter William Ewart Lockhart was brought up (see also Kirkconnel/Kirtlebridge).

South of the town, at one time, was the **Solway Viaduct**, a railway bridge that connected Dumfriesshire to Cumbria across the Solway Firth. It opened for passenger trains in 1870, and at 1,940 yards long, was the longest railway bridge across water in Britain at the time. In 1875 and 1881 parts of the bridge were damaged when great ice flows from the Rivers Eden and Esk smashed into its stanchions. The 1881 damage was the most severe, and the then keeper of the bridge, John Welch, plus two colleagues, remained in their cabin on the bridge as the lumps of ice, some as big as 27 yards square, careered into the bridge's supports. At 3.30 in the morning, when disaster

seemed imminent, they were ordered to leave. Two lengths of the bridge, one 50 feet long, and one 300 feet long, collapsed into the firth, and 37 girders and 45 pillars were smashed. However, unlike the Tay Bridge disaster, there was no loss of life. By 1884 repairs were completed, and it once again opened. Finally, in 1934, the bridge was dismantled because, it is said, people living on the Scottish side used it as a shortcut to England every Sunday to take advantage of the more relaxed licensing hours. All that is left to see nowadays are the approaches on both shores, and a stump in the middle of the water.

To the northeast of the town is the outline of **Chapelcross Nuclear Power Station**, opened in 1959, making it one of the oldest in the country.

A booklet called *Walking In And Around Annan* is available.

RUTHWELL

10 miles SE of Dumfries off the B724

Within the **Parish Church** of 1800 is the famous 18-feet high **Ruthwell Cross**. It dates from about AD 800, when this part of Scotland was within the Anglian kingdom of Northumbria. The carvings show scenes from the Gospels, twining vines and verses from an old poem called *The Dream of the Rood*, which at one time was thought to have been written by Caedmon of Whitby.

The cross had been dismantled and defaced in 1642, with its pieces being either buried in the church-yard or laid as flooring in the nave of the church. In 1802 the **Reverend Henry Duncan**, the local minister, reconstructed the cross and placed it outside the church. In 1887 it was brought back into the church, and is now in the chancel. Duncan is also famous for having discovered fossil footprints in Corncockle Quarry near Lochmaben, and he wrote a paper on them for the Royal Society.

But perhaps he is most famous as the founder of the world's first savings bank, which he set up in the village. It was a simple concept. At the time, banks required an initial deposit of ten pounds before it would open an account. All Duncan required was sixpence. With the money given to him by his parishioners, he opened an account in a bank in nearby Dumfries, and shared the interest from the account between the subscribers. Within five years similar banks had been set up throughout Britain, Europe and America. The small **Savings Bank Museum** has displays and artefacts about the savings bank movement.

DALTON

9 miles SE of Dumfries on the B7020

This little village has picturesque cottages dating from the mid-18th century. The parish church dates from the late 19th century, though the remains of an earlier church, with some medieval fragments, stands in the kirkyard. Half a mile west, on a minor road, is **Dalton Pottery**, where young and old alike can have fun decorating pots and tiles using ceramic felt-tipped pens.

POWFOOT

13 miles SE of Dumfries on a minor road off the B724

Today Powfoot is a quiet village on the Solway coast. But in the late 19th and early 20th centuries plans were laid to make it a grand holiday resort, with hotels, formal gardens, woodland walks, a promenade, a pier, golf courses and bowling greens. The whole scheme eventually collapsed, though some of the attractions were actually built. Now the village is famous for its red brick housing and terraces, which look incongruous on the shores of the Solway, but would not look out of place in Lancashire.

EASTRIGGS

18 miles E of Dumfries on the A75

A huge government works manufacturing explosives and gunpowder was established in the area during the First World War. The **Devil's Porridge Exhibition**, in St John's Church on Dunedin Road, traces the lives of the 30,000 workers who manufactured what Sir Arthur Conan Doyle called "The Devil's Porridge". Within the nine miles between Dornock in Scotland and Longtown in England was the largest munitions factory in the world at the time. The exhibition also recalls the Quintinshill railway disaster (see also Gretna Green).

GRETNA GREEN

23 miles E of Dumfries off the M74

This small village, just across the border from England, is the

Near Gretna Green, at Quintinshill on the main Glasgow /London rail line, Britain's worst train disaster took place in 1915. Five separate trains were involved, and it is reckoned that 227 people (no one knows the real figure) were killed, most of them soldiers from the Royal Scots. Two signalmen were blamed, with one being sentenced to three years in jail for culpable homicide and the other 18 months (see also Eastriggs).

Gretna Green was within the Debatable Lands, a stretch of land which, as its name implies, was claimed by both Scotland and England. It was therefore a lawless area in the 15th and 16th centuries, as no country's laws were recognised, and no one could adequately police it. About a mile to the southwest is the Lochmaben Stone, a huge rock where representatives from the two countries met to air grievances and seek justice. It is also sometimes known as the "Clochmaben" Stone, Maben being a shadowy figure associated with King Arthur.

"romance" capital of Britain. In the 18th century it was the first stopping place in Scotland for coaches travelling north on the western route, so was the ideal place for English runaways to get married.

In 1754 irregular marriages in England were made illegal, and the legal age at which people could get married without parental consent was set at 21. However, this did not apply in Scotland, and soon a roaring trade in runaway marriages got underway in the village. The actual border between Scotland and England is the River Sark, and one of the places where marriages took place was the **Old Toll House** (now bypassed by the M74) on the Scottish side of the river. Another place was **Gretna Hall**. Dating from 1710, this is now a hotel.

But perhaps the most famous was the **Old Blacksmith's Shop**, built in about 1712. A wedding ceremony in front of the anvil became the popular means of tying the knot, and the Anvil Priests, as they became known, charged anything from a dram of whisky to a guinea to conduct what was a perfectly legal ceremony. By 1856, the number of weddings had dropped, due to what was called the "Lord Brougham Act", which required that at least one of the parties to the marriage had to have been resident in Scotland for the previous 21 days. This act was only repealed in 1979.

However, couples still come from all over the world to get married before the anvil in Gretna Green, though the ceremony is no more than a confirmation of vows taken earlier in the registry office. The Old Blacksmith's Shop is still open, and houses an exhibition on the irregular marriage trade. There are now even companies which will arrange Gretna weddings for lovestruck couples.

In the nearby village of **Gretna** is the **Gretna Gateway Outlet Village**, a complex of shops selling designer label fashions.

A recent claim to fame for the village of Gretna (population 2,000) is its football team. In 2006, four years after entering the Scottish League, this tiny club managed to reach the Scottish Cup Final, where it was beaten by mighty Hearts - but only after a penalty shoot out. The club even found itself playing in Europe.

ECCLEFECHAN

14 miles E of Dumfries on the B7076

This small village's rather curious name means the church of St Fechan or Fechin, a 7th century Irish saint. Within it you will find **Carlyle's Birthplace** (National Trust for Scotland), where Thomas Carlyle, the social historian and writer, was born in 1795. Called "The Arched House", it was built on the main street by Thomas's father and uncle, who were both master masons. Within it is a collection of memorabilia about the great man (see also Dunscore).

HODDOM BRIDGE

15 miles E of Dumfries on the B723

St Kentigern, patron saint of Glasgow, founded a monastery here in the 7th century. Recent excavations have revealed the site of the church within an old graveyard plus the boundary ramparts, or "rath" of the monastery itself.

KIRKCONNEL (KIRTLEBRIDGE)

17 mile E of Dumfries off the M74

In the kirkyard of the ruined Kirkconnel Church are said to be the graves of **Fair Helen of Kirkconnel Lee** and her lover **Adam Fleming** of Kirkpartick. The events are supposed to have taken place during the reign of Mary Stuart, and the story is a romantic one. Helen Irving was loved by two men, Adam Fleming and a man named Bell (whose first name is not known). Helen found herself drawn towards Adam, and Bell was consumed with jealousy. He therefore decided to kill his rival. He waylaid the couple close to the kirkyard, and pulled out a pistol. As he fired, Helen threw herself in front of her lover, and was shot dead.

There are two versions of the story after this. One says that Adam killed Bell where he stood, and another says he pursued him to Madrid, where he killed him. Either way, he was inconsolable, and joined the army. But he could never forget Helen, and one day he returned to Kirkconnel, lay on her tombstone, and died of a broken heart. He was buried beside her. It's a poignant tale, but, alas, there is no proof that the events actually took place, even though a famous ballad was written about it.

Bonshaw Tower (not open to the public) was built in the 1540s by the Irvings, and has a later mansion alongside it. The village of **Eaglesfield** lies north of Kirtlebridge, just off the M74, and it was here that **William Ewart Lockhart**, the famous Victorian painter, was born, though he was brought up in Annan (see also Annan).

KIRKPATRICK FLEMING

20 miles E of Dumfries off the M74

This pleasant little village is visited mainly to see **Robert the Bruce's Cave**, where the great man is supposed to have seen the spider, though similar claims are made for other caves in both Scotland and Ireland. Sir William Irving hid Robert the Bruce here for three months while he was being hunted by the English. In a field at Woodhouse Farm, a mile north of the village and close to the M74 motorway, is the **Merkland Cross**, a fine wayside cross dating from the 15th century.

CANONBIE

26 miles E of Dumfries on the B6357

Canonbie, only half a mile from the English border, means the "town of the canons", because an Augustinian priory

Hoddom Castle, now surrounded by a caravan park, dates from the 16th century, and was built by Sir John Maxwell of Terregles, though it was later sold by his grandson. Less than half a mile away is the early 16th century Repentance Tower, built by the same Sir John Maxwell. It gets its name from the word "repentance" carved above the doorway. This may refer to the fact that he demolished a church to provide building material for Hoddom Castle.

Robert the Bruce's Cave

31 THE CRIFFEL INN

New Abbey

A superb inn that is a Mecca for mountain bikers and tourists alike, and which serves good honest, pub food at reasonable prices and a wide selection of drinks.

🍴 🛏 see page 435

•

Shambellie House is a large mansion designed by David Bryce on the outskirts of New Abbey, which houses the Shambellie House Museum of Costume, part of the National Museums of Scotland. The house and its collection were given to the National Museums in 1977 by the then owner, Charles Stewart, and most of the costumes, which range from Victorian to the 1930s, are now displayed in appropriate settings.

•

once stood here. As it stood within the Debatable Lands, claimed by both Scotland and England, the English destroyed it in 1542 - the only instance of a Scottish religious house being destroyed during Henry VIII's Suppression of the Monasteries. Some of the stones may have been used in the building of **Hollows Bridge** across the River Esk, Scotland's second fastest flowing river. Being within the Debatable Lands, this area was a safe haven for reivers. Beyond the bridge, and marked by a stone and plaque, is the site of **Gilnockie Castle**, home of **Johnnie Armstrong**, one of the greatest reivers of them all. So much of a threat was he to the relationship between Scotland and England that James V hanged him in 1530. The story goes that Johnnie and his men were invited to a great gathering at Carlanrig, near Teviothead in Teviotdale, where they would meet the king, who promised them safe passage. Taking him at his word, Johnnie and a band of men set out. However, when they got there, James had them all strung up on the spot (see also Hawick). Perhaps the most amazing aspect of this tale is that the king was no world-weary warrior, but an 18-year-old lad at the time. Some of the castle's stones also went into building Hollows Bridge.

Gilnockie Tower, which dates from the 16th century, was a roofless ruin until 1980, but now it houses a small museum and Clan Armstrong library.

In 1551 the argument about who owned Debatable Lands - Scotland or England - was finally resolved when it was divided between the two countries. The **Scots Dyke**, two miles south of Canonbie, was built soon after to delineate the new boundary. It consists of a "dyke", or low, earthen wall and an accompanying ditch. Today's boundary still follows the dyke .

NEW ABBEY

6 miles S of Dumfries on the A710

This attractive little village sits in the shadow of **The Criffel**, a 1,866 feet high hill that can be seen from miles around. Within the village you'll find the beautiful red sandstone ruins of **Sweetheart Abbey** (Historic Scotland), which date from the 13th and 14th centuries. It was founded for the Cistercians in 1273 by Devorgilla, Lady of Galloway in her own right (see also Dumfries), and was one of the last abbeys ever built in Scotland.

Devorgilla's husband was John Balliol of Barnard Castle in County Durham, who founded Balliol College in Oxford. After his death she carried his embalmed heart around with her in a small casket, and when she herself died in 1289, she and the heart were buried in front of the abbey's high altar. The Cistercian monks gave the name "Dolce Cor" to the abbey, and thus was born the word "sweetheart". The last abbot of Sweetheart, Abbot Gilbert, continued to defy the Protestant authorities in Edinburgh, and was finally sent into exile in France in 1608. In its graveyard lies William Paterson, founder of the Bank of England and chief proponent of the Darien Scheme in 1698 (see also Lochmaben).

At the other end of the village is the **New Abbey Corn Mill** (Historic Scotland), dating from the late 18th century. It is in full working order, and there are regular demonstrations on how a water powered mill works. The original mill on the site is thought to have belonged to the monks of Sweetheart Abbey. The millpond behind the mill is thought to have been constructed by them.

The **Kirkconnell Flow**, a few miles north of the village, is a National Nature Reserve sited on a raised bog.

KIRKBEAN

6 miles SW of Dumfries, on the A710

About two miles south of the village is the estate of **Arbigland**, birthplace in 1747 of the founder of the American navy, **John Paul Jones** (see also Kirkcudbright). He was born John Paul, only adding the "Jones" when he emigrated to the American colonies, and was the son of an Arbigland gardener. He went to sea in the brig *Friendship* when he was about 13 years old, and by the age of 21 had his own ship. The cottage in which he was born is now a small museum, furnished in the way it would have been when he was born.

Kirkbean Parish Church was built in 1776, and inside is a font presented by the American Navy in

1945. To continue the American theme, **Dr James Craik**, Physician General of the United States Army during the American Revolution, and Washington's personal physician, was born on the estate in 1731. However, James was not born in the same humble circumstances as John Paul Jones. He was the illegitimate son of Robert Craik, owner of the estate and a Member of Parliament.

BEESWING

9 miles W of Dumfries, on the A711

This small village was laid out in the 19th century. The only remarkable thing about it is its name. It must be the only village in Scotland that is named after a horse. Beeswing was one of the most famous horses in the early 19th century, its finest performance being in the Doncaster Cup, which it won in 1840. A local man won so much money on the race that he opened an inn called The Beeswing, and the village grew up around it.

CROCKETFORD

9 miles W of Dumfries, on the A75

It was at Crocketford that the sorry tale of Elspeth Buchan, who founded a religious sect called the Buchanites, came to a macabre end. Part of the sect's beliefs was that Elspeth was immortal, and that she could bestow immortality on others by breathing on them. After having been driven out of Irvine, she and her followers headed south towards Dumfriesshire and settled there. Alas, Elspeth disappointed her

A few miles to the west is Drumcoltran Tower (Historic Scotland), now surrounded by the outbuildings of a farm. It was built by the Maxwells in the 1550s to guard the western approaches to Dumfries.

57

32 THE GORDON HOUSE HOTEL

Kirkcudbright

An elegant hotel with en suite accommodation, good food and a friendly, welcoming bar with plenty of authentic atmosphere.

⊨ ⫙ *see page 436*

33 THE CASTLE RESTAURANT

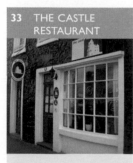

Kirkcudbright

A superb restaurant in Scotland's 'artists' town' that serves great food at remarkable prices.

⫙ *see page 437*

followers by dying a natural death, and the sect broke up.

But one man, Andrew Innes, who lived in Crocketford, still believed in her immortality, and that she would rise from the dead. He therefore acquired her body and kept it in a cupboard at the top of the stairs in his cottage, where it gradually mummified. Eventually he built an extension to the cottage, on the other side of the wall from the fireplace, and kept the corpse there. He even had a small opening cut through the wall so that he could examine the corpse every day to see if it had come alive again. Of course, it did not. though, this never shook his belief in her resurrection, and the body remained in the cottage with him until his own death in 1846. The cottage, called Newhouse, still stands. (see also Dunscore and Irvine).

KIRKCUDBRIGHT

Kirkcudbright (pronounced "Kirk-coo-bray") is one of the loveliest towns in Scotland, Its name simply means the kirk of St Cuthbert, as the original church built here was dedicated to that saint. It was an established town by the 11th century, and has been a royal burgh since at least 1455. It sits close to the mouth of the Dee, and is still a working port with a small fishing fleet.

Kirkcudbright was once the county town of Kirkcudbrightshire, also known as the "Stewartry of Kirkcudbright". It is a place of

brightly painted Georgian, Regency and Victorian houses, making it a colourful and interesting place to explore. This part of Galloway has a very mild climate, thanks to the Gulf Stream washing its shores, and this, as well as the quality of light to be found here, has earned it the nickname of "the artists' town", as an artist's colony has flourished here for many years. On a summer's morning, the edge between light and shadow can be as sharp as a knife, whereas during the day it becomes diffused and soft, and artists have been reaching for their paints and palettes for years to try and capture these two qualities. Even today, straw-hatted artists can still be seen at the harbour-side, committing paint to canvas or paper.

It is said that St Cuthbert himself founded the first church here, which was located within the cemetery to the east of the town. Down through the years, gravediggers have often turned up carved stones that belonged to it. Within the graveyard is **Billy Marshall's Grave**. Billy was known as the "King of Galloway Tinkers", and the gravestone states that he died in 1792 aged 120 years. During his 120 years, he married 17 times, joined the army and deserted seven times, and sired three children after his 100th birthday. Don't be surprised to see coins lying on top of the gravestone. It is supposed to be an old gypsy custom, whereby a passing gypsy or tinker without money could use the coins to buy food. The money nowadays is usually left by tourists, with the main beneficiaries being local children.

The present **Parish Church**, designed by William Burn, is a grand affair in red sandstone near the centre of the town, and dates from 1838. Parts of a much older church are to be found near the harbour. **Greyfriar's Kirk** is all that is left of a 16th century Franciscan friary that stood here, though it has been largely rebuilt over the years. Within it is the grand tomb of **Sir Thomas MacLellan of Bombie** and his wife Grizzell Maxwell, which was erected in 1597. But the tomb is not all it seems. The couple's son, in an effort to save money, used effigies from an earlier tomb within what is essentially a Renaissance canopy. The friary is thought to have been founded in 1224 by Alan, Lord of Galloway and father of Devorgilla, who founded Sweetheart Abbey. The kirk sits on a slight rise known as the **Moat Brae**, where Roland, Lord of Galloway in the 12th century, may have had a castle.

Nearby, in Castle Street, are the substantial ruins of **MacLellan's Castle** (Historic Scotland), built by the same Sir Thomas who lies in the Greyfriar's Kirk. He was a local magnate and favourite of the king who became Provost of Kirkcudbright. It is not really a castle, but a grand town house, and Sir Thomas, who was obviously his son's role model where thrift was concerned, used the stones from the friary as building material. Watch out for the small room behind the fireplace in the Great Hall. Sir Thomas used to hide himself there and listen to what was being said about him in the Great Hall through a small opening in the wall called the "Laird's Lug".

Walk up the side of the castle into Castle Bank, passing the whitewashed **Harbour Cottage Gallery**, where there are regular exhibitions of work by local artists, and you arrive at the **High Street**. This must be one of the most charming and colourful streets in Scotland. The elegant Georgian and Regency houses - some of them substantial buildings - are painted in bright, uncompromising colours, such as yellow, green and pink. **Auchingool House** is the oldest, having been built in 1617 for the McCullochs of Auchengool. **Broughton House**, dating from the 18th century, is now owned by the National Trust for Scotland, and was the home of E.A. Hornel the artist. Though born in Australia, he came from an old Kirkcudbright family, and was one of the Glasgow Boys, a band of painters that included James Paterson (see Moniaive), George Henry and James Guthrie, later knighted. He died in 1933. The house is very much as it was when he lived

> *Kirkcudbright was where the village scenes in the cult movie* **The Wicker Man** *were filmed, and indeed many locations in Dumfries and Galloway - and even Ayrshire - stood in for the fictional Summerisles, where the action is supposed to have taken place (see Dundrennan).*

The Tolbooth, Kirkcudbright

Kirkcudbright

The Galloway Wildlife Conservation Park is set within 27 acres of woodland one mile from the town of Kitkcudbright on the B727. Nearly 150 animals from all over the world can be seen.

---

there, though it has recently been renovated. Behind the house is the marvellous **Japanese Gardens**, influenced by trips that Hornel made to the Far East.

Further along the street is **Greengates Close**, (not open to the public) which was the home of Jessie M. King, another artist. A few yards further on the High Street takes a dog leg to the east, and here stands the **Tolbooth**, built in 1629, which has been refurbished and now houses a museum and art gallery telling the story of Kirkcudbright's artists' colony. The Queen opened it in 1993. This was the former town house and jail, and John Paul Jones, founder of the American navy, was imprisoned here at one time for murder. He got his revenge in later years when he returned to the town

aboard an American ship and shelled the nearby **St Mary's Isle**, where the seat of the Earl of Selkirk was located and a medieval priory of nuns once stood.

This "isle" is in fact a peninsula, and to confuse matters even further, one of the smaller bays in Kirkcudbright Bay (itself an inlet of the Solway Firth) is called **Manxman's Lake**, one of the few instances in Scotland of a natural stretch of water being called a lake rather than a loch (see also Lake of Menteith, Stenton and Ellon). A walk up St Mary's Wynd beside the Tolbooth and past the modern school takes you to **Castledykes**, where once stood a royal castle. Edward I stayed here, as did Henry VI and Queen Margaret after their defeat at the Battle of Towton in 1461 during the Wars of the Roses. James IV used it as a staging post on his many pilgrimages to Whithorn. In St Mary's Street is the **Stewartry Museum**, opened in 1893, which has many artefacts and displays on the history of the Stewartry of Kirkcudbright. There is an admission charge. On the opposite side of the street is the **Town Hall**, where themed painting exhibitions are held every year.

The town also has its literary associations. **Dorothy L. Sayers** set her Lord Peter Wimsey whodunit *Five Red Herrings,* written in 1931, among the artists' colony. It's not one of her best, as it over-relies on a detailed knowledge of train times between Kirkcudbrightshire and Ayrshire, and of the paints found on an artist's palette. **Ronald**

Searle also knew the town, staying with the artist William Miles Johnston. One day he drew a cartoon of the artist's daughters, who attended St Trinnean's School in Dalkeith Road in Edinburgh. In 1941 the magazine Lilliput published the cartoon. It showed a group of schoolgirls with torn stockings and gymslips looking at a notice board, and this was born the young ladies of St Trinian's School.

For a short while when he was a small boy **T.E. Lawrence** ("Lawrence of Arabia") lived in the town.

AROUND KIRKCUDBRIGHT

TONGLAND

2 miles N of Kirkcudbright on the A711

The small village of Tongland was once the site of the great **Tongland Abbey**, founded in 1218 by Fergus, Lord of Galloway, and the scant remains - no more than a medieval archway in a piece of preserved wall - can still be seen in the kirkyard. The abbey's most famous inmate was Abbot John Damien, known as the "Frenzied Friar of Tongland", who achieved fame by jumping off the ramparts of Stirling Castle in an attempt to fly like a bird (see also Stirling). Tours are available of **Tongland Power Station**, the largest generating station in the great Galloway hydroelectric scheme built in the 1930s. Close by is **Tongland Bridge**, a graceful structure across the Dee designed by Thomas Telford and built in 1805.

Though it is about two miles inland, there was once a thriving port close to the bridge, and in the village Arrol-Johnston, the Scottish car maker, once produced its Galloway model. .

LOCH KEN

9 miles N of Kirkcudbright between the A713 and the A762

Loch Ken is a narrow stretch of water almost nine miles long and nowhere wider than a mile. It was created in the 1930s as the result of the great Galloway hydroelectric scheme, with the turbines being housed in the power station at Tongland, further down the Dee. Other schemes were constructed at Clatteringshaws and Loch Doon.

Within Laurieston is a memorial to **R.S. Crockett** the writer, who was born at Little Duchrae Farm to the north of the village in 1860. His inspiration was the Galloway landscape, and at one time his books were very popular (see also New Galloway).

Details about using the loch are available from the **Loch Ken Marina,** off the A713 on the eastern shore. At the Marina you can also find the Loch Ken Water Ski School.

NEW GALLOWAY

17 miles N of Kirkcudbright on the A762

Though New Galloway is a small village with a population of about 300, it is still a proud royal burgh - the smallest in Scotland. Up until 1975 it had its own provost and council, and still boasts a town hall. It is a planned burgh, and gained its

---

Loch Ken is a favourite spot for bird watching and sports such as sailing, fishing and water skiing, and there is a small nature reserve on its west bank. The newly-established Galloway Kite Trail follows the shores of the loch, and highlights a bird that has recently been reintroduced into the area. There are six main viewing areas, one of them being a feeding station at Bellymack Hill Farm near Laurieston.

34 KENMURE ARMS HOTEL

New Galloway

A wonderful small hotel in a beautiful village with nine guest rooms, a great reputation for its food, and a cosy, inviting atmosphere.

see page 436

The road between New Galloway and Newton Stewart, the A712, was designated the Queens Way in 1977 to commemorate the Queen's Silver Jubilee. It passes the wonderfully named Clatteringshaws Loch, part of the Galloway hydroelectric scheme. Here you will find Bruce's Stone, which commemorates the spot where Bruce rested after defeating the English at Glen Trool. Across from the loch is the Clatteringshaws Forest and Wildlife Park. From the visitors centre the Loch View Trail climbs steeply to give views over the surrounding countryside. There is also an old, ten mile long drover's road called the Raider's Road, which featured in the novel of the same name by R.S. Crockett (see also Loch Ken). It takes you through Forestry commission land to the A726 near the banks of Loch Ken.

charter in 1630. It was laid out in the early 1600s by Viscount Kenmure, who wanted to encourage trade. This part of Kirkcudbrightshire is known as the **Glenkens**, an area combining the high drama of lonely moorland with fertile, wooded valleys. Within **Kells Churchyard**, north of the town, is the grave of a Covenanter, shot in 1685.

A mile to the south, near Loch Ken, are the ruins of **Kenmure Castle**, which belonged to the Gordon family. To say that the building is unlucky would be an understatement, as it has been burnt down three times and rebuilt twice. After the last burning in the 1880s, it was left as a shell.

Each year in early August New Galloway plays host to the **Scottish Alternative Games**. It is a refreshing antidote to all the traditional games held in Scotland, where tossing the caber, throwing the hammer, shot putting and Highland dancing are the preferred activities. At the Alternative Games, however, there are sports such as gird and cleek (hoop and stick) racing, hurlin' (throwing) the curlin' stane, snail racing, flingin' the herd's bunnet (throwing the herdsman's bonnet) and tossin' the sheaf. There are also pipe bands, side shows and craft stalls.

BALMACLELLAN

18 miles N of Kirkcudbright off the A712

This attractive little village is associated with **Robert Paterson**, a stonemason who was the model for Old Mortality in Scott's book of the same name. Probably born near Hawick in 1715, he travelled southern Scotland cleaning up the monuments and gravestones of the Covenanters, a group of men and women who fought the Stuart's attempts to have themselves declared head of the Church of Scotland and impose bishops on it.

He left home for good to concentrate on this work, leaving behind a no doubt angry wife and five children. Up to his death in 1801, he continued to travel the country, usually on an old grey pony. A statue of him and his horse sits outside the kirkyard of the whitewashed parish church.

Just outside the village you will find **The Balmaclellan Clog and Shoe Workshop**, where 20 styles of footwear are put together by hand. Visitors can look round the workshop and see shoes and clogs being made.

ST JOHN'S TOWN OF DALRY

19 miles N of Kirkcudbright on the A713

St John's Town of Dalry, sometimes known simply as Dalry, lies on the Southern Uplands Way and is a picturesque Glenkens village with many old cottages. It got its name from the Knights Hospitaller of the Order of St John of Jerusalem, an order of military monks which owned the surrounding lands in medieval times.

Within the village is a curious chair-shaped stone known as **St John's Stone**. Local tradition says that John the Baptist rested in it. In the kirkyard is the **Gordon Aisle**, part of the medieval church that stood here before the present church of 1832. When a reservoir was created at lonely **Lochinvar** near Dalry in 1968, the waters of the loch were raised, covering the scant ruins of a castle owned by the Gordons. This was the home of the famous Young Lochinvar, written about by Scott in his famous lines from Marmion:

"O, young Lochinvar is come
out of the west,
Through all the wide border his
steed was the best..."

A cairn by the loch side, which is reached by a narrow track from the A702, records the existence of the castle. It was built using stones from the castle ruins.

Dalry Motte was one of a string of mottes in the area, and at one time a castle stood atop it. As with many hills or mottes, there is a legend that a serpent once lived beneath it, and it was killed by a local blacksmith who had made special armour to defend himself.

Earlston Castle, overlooking Earlston Loch to the north of the village, was also a Gordon stronghold. It was the birthplace of Catherine Gordon, later Mrs Catherine Stewart, who befriended Burns and encouraged him to write poetry when she lived in Stair Castle in Ayrshire. She was buried, along with two daughters, in Stair kirkyard in Ayrshire (see also Stair).

CARSPHAIRN

27 miles N of Kirkcudbright on the A713

Close to this quiet village there used to be lead, copper and zinc

mines. John Loudon MacAdam the roads pioneer, whose father came from near the village, experimented on his revolutionary road surfaces on the A713 north of the village (see also Ayr and Moffat). The **Carsphairn Heritage Centre** has displays and exhibits on the history of the village.

CASTLE DOUGLAS

9 miles NE of Kirkcudbright off the A75

Castle Douglas is a pleasant town that grew out of what was a small village known as "Carlingwark". It was founded in the 18th century by William Douglas, a local merchant who earned his money trading with Virginia and the West Indies. He wanted to establish a thriving manufacturing town based on the woollen industry, and though he was only partly successful, he did lay the foundations for a charming town where some of his original 18th century buildings can still be seen. On the edge of the town is **Carlingwark Loch**, where crannogs (dwellings built on artificial islands) have been discovered. It covers 100 acres, though up until it was partially drained in 1765 for deposits of marl, a limey clay used as manure, on the loch bed, it covered over 180 acres. It was joined to the River Dee in 1765 by **Carlingwark Lane**, a narrow canal, and barges took the marl from the loch across to the River Dee, then on down to Kirkcudbright.

In Market Street is the **Castle Douglas Art Gallery**, gifted to the town in 1938 by the artist Ethel

35 DOUGLAS ARMS HOTEL

Castle Douglas

A former coaching inn that offers fine dining, good company, and superb, fully en suite accommodation.

⊨ ❙ *see page 438*

36 THE MAD HATTER

Castle Douglas

A charming café/restaurant at the heart of Castle Douglas, Scotland's food town, that offers the very best in home-cooked food.

❙ *see page 439*

Bristowe. Open between March and December, there is a continuing programme of painting, sculpture, photography and craft exhibitions.

Castle Douglas is Scotland's food town, and has over 50 businesses either selling or manufacturing high quality food and drink. Its small, specialised shops offer real Scottish produce, such as meat, fish, vegetables, baking and drinks, most if it produced locally. The **Sulwath Brewery** is in King Street, and here you can see the brewing process

from barley to beer, and enjoy a complimentary half pint of Criffel, Cuil Hill or Knockendoch real ale.

The **Ken Dee Marshes Nature Reserve** follows the woodland and marshes along the River Dee and Loch Ken, north west of the town.

THREAVE CASTLE
8 miles N of Kirkcudbright, close to the A75

On an island in the River Dee stand the magnificent ruins of Threave Castle (Historic Scotland), reached by a small ferry that answers the call of a brass bell on a jetty on the riverbank. The ferry is a ten to fifteen minute walk along a path starting at Kelton Mains Farm.

The castle was built on the site of an earlier castle by Archibald Douglas, 3rd Earl of Douglas - known as Archibald the Grim - soon after he became Lord of Galloway in 1369. It was Archibald's father, the "Good Sir James", who died while on his way to the Holy Land with the heart of Robert the Bruce (see also Melrose, Cardross and Dunfermline). When Archibald the Grim died at Threave in 1400, he was the most powerful man in southern Scotland, and almost independent of the king, Robert III. It was Archibald's son, also called Archibald, who married Princess Margaret, daughter of Robert III (see also Dumfries). When James II laid siege to the castle in 1455 to curtail the power of the Douglases, it took two months before the occupants finally surrendered.

Threave House & Gardens

THREAVE GARDENS

7 miles NE of Kirkcudbright, on the A75

Threave Gardens and Estate (National Trust for Scotland) surround a house built in 1872 by William Gordon, a Liverpool businessman. In 1948 the estate was given to the National Trust for Scotland by William's grandson, Major Alan Gordon. The gardens were created from scratch, and now house the Trust's School of Practical Gardening. The house itself is open to the public, with its interiors restored to how they would have looked when the place was owned by the Gordon family in the 1930s.

KIPPFORD

10 miles NE of Kirkcudbright off the A710

The tides in the Solway Firth are among the fastest in Britain, but this has not prevented the picturesque village of Kippford from becoming a great yachting centre. It was once a thriving port and fishing village, and it even had its own shipyard. Like its neighbour Rockcliffe, five miles away, it was also once a smuggling village.

PALNACKIE

10 miles NE of Kirkcudbright on the A711

This small, attractive village on the west bank of the Water of Urr is a mile from the sea, though at one time it was a thriving port. However, the meanderings of the river meant that ships were usually towed upstream by teams of horses. Each year, in summer, it hosts one of the most unusual

competitions in Great Britain - the annual **World Flounder Tramping Championships,** held at the end of July with all proceeds going to charity. People come from all over the world to compete, making it a truly international event. The object is to walk out onto the mud flats south of the village at low tide, feeling for flounders hiding beneath the mud with your toes as you go. The person who collects the largest weight of flounders wins the championship. It may seem a light hearted and eccentric competition, but it has a firm basis in local history, as this was a recognised way of catching fish in olden times.

The **North Glen Gallery** features glassblowing and interior and exterior design. It is also a good place to get advice on local walks and wildlife.

DALBEATTIE

11 miles NE of Kirkcudbright on the A711

This small town stands just east of the Water of Urr, which at one time was navigable as far up-river as here. Ships of up to 60 tons could make the six-mile trip from the open sea beyond Rough Island, pulled by teams of horses. Now the "Pool of Dalbeattie" (the name given to the port area) is derelict, and the river has silted up.

Dalbeattie was a planned town, founded in the 1793 as a textile and quarrying centre by two landowners - George Maxwell and Alexander Copland, who sold feus, or tenancies, to various people who wanted to build houses. Close by there were easily worked deposits

A mile south west of Palnackie is the 33 feet high Orchardton Tower, the only round tower house in Scotland. It dates from the middle of the 15th century, and was built by John Cairns as a home after his retirement. In the 17th century it passed to the Maxwells, who in turn sold the estate on which it stood to James Douglas, brother of William, who founded the town of Castle Douglas.

---

37   THE SHIP INN

Dalbeattie

A small, friendly inn in one of the most picturesque parts of Scotland that is just right for a quiet drink in the evening.

see page 440

On the west bank of the Urr, about a mile from the town of Dalbeattie, is all that remains of Buittle Castle and Bailey, home to John Balliol, son of Devorgilla, whom Edward I placed on the throne of Scotland as a puppet king. Robert I established a burgh here in 1325, and a recent archaeological dig has revealed that the castle's large bailey (an enclosed space in front of the castle) may have housed it. A later tower house, the Old Buittle Tower, stands close by. It has occasional displays of arms and armour.

of granite which also provided employment. The granite was of high quality, and was used in the building of Sydney Harbour Bridge, Liverpool Docks and the Thames Embankment.

In Southwick Road you will find the **Dalbeattie Museum**, and this has displays and exhibits about the history of the town. It has a particularly fine collection of Victoriana. Within Colliston Park is the **Granite Garden**, designed by Solway Heritage to celebrate the beauty of the stone and the workers and craftsmen who mined it.

The ruined **Buittle Parish Church** is to be found on the opposite side of the A745 from the castle. Dating from the 13th and 14th centuries, it was dedicated to St Colman.

On the wall of the former town hall is the Murdoch Memorial, which commemorates **Lieutenant William Murdoch**, who was the First Officer aboard the Titanic when it sank in 1912. History has not been kind to a man who acted heroically as the ship sank. He has been unfairly accused of being, among other things, a coward who shot passengers attempting to leave the ship. He was also accused of not allowing third class passengers near the lifeboats and of accepting bribes from first class passengers to let them board lifeboats to which they were not entitled.

The recent film also treated him unfairly, though witness statements presented at the later official Board of Trade Enquiry, which lasted 36 days, cleared him completely of all these charges. In 1996 his name was finally and officially cleared of any wrongdoing.

Three miles north of Dalbeattie is the **Motte of Urr**, a 12th century motte-hill and bailey that covers five acres, making it the largest non-industrial man-made hill in Scotland. At its summit at one time would have been a large, wooden castle, supposedly built by William de Berkeley. It stands close to the Water of Urr, and at one time the river flowed by on either side, creating an island that was easily defended. Tradition says that Robert the Bruce fought an English knight called Sir Walter Selby at the Motte of Urr. The wife of a man called Sprotte, who at that time lived within the motte, saw the fight, and observed that Selby was gaining the upper hand. So she rushed out and jumped on him, bringing him to his knees in front of the Scottish king.

However, Bruce chose to spare Selby, and both men retired to the woman's house. She produced one bowl of porridge and placed it before Robert, saying that she would not feed an Englishman. However, Robert told her to go outside and run as fast as she could. He would grant her and her husband all the land she could cover without stopping. The woman did so, and Robert and Walter finished off the porridge between them. Robert, however, kept his promise, and the Sprottes were granted 20 acres of land. They owned the land for over 500 years, with the condition that if a Scottish king were to pass by, they were to give him a bowl of porridge.

ROCKCLIFFE

10 miles E of Kirkcudbright on a minor road off the A710

Rockcliffe was at one time a great smuggling centre, but is now a quiet resort sitting on the **Rough Firth**, one of the smallest firths in Scotland. Off the coast is **Rough Island** (National Trust for Scotland), a bird sanctuary which can be accessed at low tide. However, due to nesting, you are not allowed to visit during May and June. Close to the village is the great **Mote of Mark** (National Trust for Scotland), the site of a 5th century fort. Legend says it is named after King Mark, of Tristan and Isolde fame. Isolde, Mark's wife, is supposed to have fallen in love with Tristan, and the story was later incorporated into the Arthurian legends. How the legend became associated with the Mote of Mark is not known. The earthwork is more likely to have been built by a powerful Dark Ages chief.

There are a number of footpaths connecting Rockcliffe with Kippford, the two-mile long **Jubilee Path** (National Trust for Scotland) being the main one. There is a programme of ranger-guided walks along it in the summer months. **Castlehill Point**, a mile south of the village on a clifftop, has the remains of an old hill fort. It can be reached by a pathway.

DUNDRENNAN

4 miles SE of Kirkcudbright on the A711

This quiet village is now visited mainly because of the ruins of the once substantial **Dundrennan Abbey** (Historic Scotland). It was founded in 1142 by David I and Fergus, Lord of Galloway, for the Cistercian monks of Rievaulx in Yorkshire, and was where, in 1568, Mary Stuart spent her last night on Scottish soil before sailing across the Solway to England and her eventual execution. Little of the grand abbey church now remains, though the chapter house and some of the other buildings are well worth seeing, as are some interesting grave slabs.

Near the village, at East Kirkcaswell, an annual **Wicker Man Festival**, based on the film, is held in July (see also Kirkcudbright).

TWYNHOLM

3 miles NW of Kirkcudbright on the A75

Twynholm is the home village of David Coulthard the racing driver, and within the **David Coulthard Museum** in Burnbrae you can learn about the man's life. There is also a gift shop and tearoom.

GATEHOUSE OF FLEET

6 miles NW of Kirkcudbright on the B727, off the A75

This neat little town was the original for the "Kippletringan" of Scott's *Guy Mannering*. It sits on the Water of Fleet, about a mile from

38 CLONYARD HOUSE HOTEL

Colvend

A superior, family-run hotel that offers great value-for-money in its accommodation, food and drink without compromising quality.

🛏 ❚ see page 439

39 BURNSIDE HOUSE

Auchencairn

A cosy and well-furnished B&B in a quiet village offering two rooms - one sleeping three and one sleeping four.

🛏 see page 440

●

The small hamlet of Anworth stands just off the A75 to the west of Gatehouse of Fleet. The ruins of the ancient Anworth Parish Church can be seen, set in a small kirkyard. The Reverend Samuael Rutherford was the minister here in the 17th century. He is best remembered for being exiled from his parish to Aberdeen because of his opposition to a Church of Scotland with bishops. After he was admitted back into the church, he became a professor of theology at St. Andrews University. Part of The Wicker Man was filmed in the interior of the church, and at the village's old schoolhouse.

●

Fleet Bay, and was at one time a port, thanks to the canalisation of the river in 1823 by a local landowner, Alexander Murray of Cally House. The port area was known as **Port MacAdam,** though the site has now been grassed over. Cally House is now a hotel, though next to it are the **Cally Gardens**, housed in a two-and-a-half acre walled garden.

Gatehouse of Fleet was laid out in the 1760s as a cotton-weaving centre by James Murray of Broughton, and today it remains more or less the way he planned it. He wished to create a great industrial town, though nowadays it is hard to imagine "dark satanic mills" in such an idyllic setting. Within one of the former cotton mills is a museum called the **Mill on the Fleet**, which tells the story of the town's former weaving industry.

It was supposedly in Gatehouse of Fleet, in the **Murray Arms**, that Burns set down the words to *Scots Wha Hae*. About a mile west of the

Cairnholy II

town stands the substantial ruins of 15th century **Cardoness Castle** (Historic Scotland), former home of the McCullochs of Galloway. It stands on a rocky platform above the A75, and is open to the public. The **Gatehouse Family and Local History Archive** at the YMCA in Digby Street has information on the town's history and genealogy.

CAIRNHOLY

11 miles W of Kirkcudbright off the A75

Cairn Holy (Historic Scotland) is a chambered cairn dating from between 2000 and 3000 BC, along with upright stones. The most remarkable thing about their construction is how our ancestors managed to raise such huge stones. The place is supposed to mark the grave of an ancient, mythical king of Scotland called Caldus. Another cairn, known as **Cairnholy II**, lies about 150 yards uphill. A mile west of the cairns, close to the A75, are the ruins of **Carsluith Castle**, dating from the 15th century. The castle was built by the Cairns of Orchardton, and then passed to the Broun family of London. Though now a ruin, a scattering of buildings surround it, as they would have done when it was occupied.

CREETOWN

14 miles NW of Kirkcudbright on the A75

Set at the mouth of the River Cree, the neat village of Creetown was once a centre for the mining of granite. Now it is visited chiefly because of the **Creetown Gem Rock Museum**, housed in a former school. It was established in 1971, and since then has amassed a remarkable collection of gemstones and minerals from all over the world. There are also exhibitions on geology and on the formation of our landscapes from earliest times. It even has an "erupting volcano"

At one time Creetown was the eastern terminus of a ferry that plied southwestwards across Wigtown Bay to the town of Wigtown itself, taking pilgrims to St Ninian's Shrine at Whithorn. The **Ferry Thorn**, said to be hundreds of years old, was where people waited for the ferry. At Spital Farm there was, before the Reformation, a Cistercian hospital that offered hospitality to pilgrims.

The **Creetown Exhibition Centre** in St John's Street has exhibits on local history and wildlife, as well as occasional exhibitions by local artists. Over a weekend in September each year, the **Creetown Country Music Weekend** takes place, featuring the best in country music. There is also a street fair, parades and children's activities.

STRANRAER

Sitting at the head of Loch Ryan, and on the edge of the **Rhinns of Galloway**, that hammer shaped peninsula that juts out into the Irish Sea, Stranraer is a royal burgh and was at one time the only Scottish port serving Northern Ireland. It was granted its burgh charter in 1595, and became a royal burgh in 1617. It is a town of narrow streets and old alleyways, with a picturesque town centre which belies the fact that there is a lot of unemployment in the area.

In the centre of the town is the **Castle of St John**, a tower house built by the Adair family in the 16th century. Claverhouse used it as a base while hunting down Covenanters in the area, and it was later used as the town jail. It is now a museum and interpretation centre. There is another museum in the **Old Town Hall**, which explains the history of the town and the county of Wigtownshire.

On the sea front is the **Princess Victoria Monument,** which commemorates the sinking of the car ferry Princess Victoria on January 31st, 1953. It had left Stranraer bound for Larne with 127 passengers and 49 crew, and on leaving the shelter of Loch Ryan encountered a horrific gale. Though lifeboats were launched, it eventually sank with the loss of 134 lives. One of the victims was the Deputy prime Minister and Finance Minister of the Northern Ireland government, Major JM Sinclair.

Three miles east of Stranraer are the magnificent **Castle Kennedy Gardens**. They cover 75 acres between two small lochs, and are laid out around the ivy-clad ruins of Castle Kennedy, destroyed by fire in 1710. The first owner of the estate, Sir James Dalrymple of Stair, was a lawyer who was appointed President of the Court of Session (which tries civil cases) in 1761. He codified the laws of

•

North West Castle is now a hotel in Stranraer, but at one time it was the home of Sir John Ross (1777-1856), who, in 1827, suggested to the British government that it ought to finance an expedition to find the North West Passage around North America to the Pacific. His suggestion was rejected, and one of his colleagues, Felix Booth, eventually put up the £18,000 for such an expedition. in May 1829 the expedition set out on the paddle steamer The Victory. *He eventually discovered the magnetic North Pole. Ross was born near Kirkcolm, son of a clergyman, and joined the navy at the age of nine, reaching the rank of commander by the time he was 35. On one of his many expeditions he discovered the Boothia Peninsula, mainland America's northernmost point. He later served as British consul in Stockholm.*

•

South of the A75 to the east of Stranraer is Soulseat Loch, where there is good fishing. A narrow peninsula with a few bumps and indentations on it juts out into the water - the site of Soulseat Abbey, of which not a stone now remains above ground. It was founded for the Premonstratensian Order of Canons by Fergus, Lord of Galloway, in 1148 and dedicated to St Mary and St John the Baptist.

Scotland, and his books still form the core of Scots Law today. It was his son who began creating the gardens in 1733, and being a field marshal under the Duke of Marlborough, he used some of his troops to construct some of it. Afterwards the gardens were neglected, and it was not until the building of **Lochinch Castle** in the 19th century that they were restored. The castle is still the home of the Earl and Countess of Stair, and is not open to the public.

Three miles beyond Castle Kennedy on the A75 is the village of Dunragit, where you'll find **Glenwhan Gardens**, overlooking beautiful Luce Bay. They were started from scratch in 1979, and now cover 12 acres. They are open from March to October.

AROUND STRANRAER

CAIRNRYAN

5 miles N of Stranraer on the A77

Cairnryan is strung out along the coast of Loch Ryan. Between the main road and the coast is a complex of car parks, piers, jetties and offices, as this small village is the Scottish terminus of P&O ferries to Larne in Northern Ireland. It was developed as a port during World War II, and had a breaker's yard. It was here that the famous aircraft carrier **HMS Ark Royal** was scrapped.

The Atlantic U boat fleet surrendered in Loch Ryan in 1945, and were berthed at Cairnryan before being taken out into the Atlantic and sunk.

GLENTROOL

20 miles NE of Stranraer on a minor road which leaves the A714 at Bargrennan

It was here, close to the lovely but lonely waters of Loch Trool, that Robert I, known as Robert the Bruce, defeated an English army in 1307, a year after his coronation. His soldiers had hidden themselves in the hills above the loch, and when the English troops went past, they rolled great boulders down on them before attacking. It was a turning point in the Wars of Independence, as up until then Robert had had little success. **Bruce's Stone** above the loch commemorates the event. The **Glentrool Visitor Centre**, three miles away, offers information about the surrounding forest walks, and has a small tearoom and gift shop. The **Glentrool Big Country Ride** is a waymarked 36 mile track for mountain bikers. Glentrool is within the Galloway Forest Park, home to Southern Scotland's highest mountain, 2.765 feet high **Merrick**.

Bruce's Stone, Glentrool

GLENLUCE

8 miles E of Stranraer off the A75

The attractive little village of Glenluce has been bypassed by the A75, one of the main routes from southern Scotland and Northern England to the Irish ferries at Stranraer and Cairnryan. At one time it was the home of **Alexander Agnew**, nicknamed the "Devil of Luce". He was a beggar who, in the mid 1600s, asked for alms from a weaver named Campbell in the village, but was refused. He thereupon cursed the family and its dwelling, and strange things began to happen. Stones were thrown at the doors and windows when there was no one about, and stones came down the chimney. The bedclothes were even ripped from the children's beds as they slept. If this was not bad enough, Andrews was heard to say that there was no God but salt, meal and water - a clear case of atheism. He was eventually hanged for blasphemy at Dumfries.

A mile to the northwest are the ruins of **Glenluce Abbey** (Historic Scotland), founded in 1190 by Roland, Lord of Galloway for Cistercian monks from Dundrennan Abbey. Its best preserved feature is the chapter house. The end of the abbey came in 1560, with the advent of the Reformation. However, the monks were allowed to live on within the abbey, the last one dying in 1602. Mary Stuart once visited, as did James 1V and Robert the Bruce. There is a small exhibition of finds discovered there over the years.

Castle of Park is an imposing tower house built in about 1590 by Thomas Hay, son of the last lay commendator, or lay abbot of Glenluce. A stone over the door commemorates the event. It is now owned by the Landmark Trust, and used as rented holiday accommodation.

Immediately after the Reformation, the then Earl of Cassillis (pronounced "Cassells"), head of the great Kennedy family, foiled a plot by Gordon of Lochinvar who tried to gain the property and lands of Glenluce by forging the abbot's signature. Cassillis then bought the land himself.

An old legend tells us that Michael Scott the wizard banished the plague from the area by confining it to one of the abbey's vaults (see also Aikwood).

NEWTON STEWART

22 miles E of Stranraer on the A75

The burgh of Newton Stewart sits on the River Cree, close to where it enters Wigtown Bay. It is a pleasant, clean town, founded in 1677 by William Stewart, son of the Earl of Galloway. A ford once stood where the present bridge crosses the Cree, and it was used by pilgrims to St Ninian's shrine at Whithorn. **Newton Stewart Museum** is within a former church in York Road, and has displays and exhibits about the history of the town and immediate area. In Queen Street you'll find an unusual but internationally known little museum called **Sophie's Puppenstube and**

---

41 TORWOOD COUNTRYSIDE

Glenluce

A superior development of holiday homes and cabins set among some of Scotland's loveliest scenery.

⊨ see page 440

42 HOUSE O' HILL HOTEL

Bargrennan

A superb small hotel in an unspoilt Scottish village that has the best of food, the best of drink and superior accommodation.

❙ ⊨ see page 442

71

The Wood of Cree Nature Reserve is owned and managed by the Royal Society for the Protection of Birds, and lies four miles north of the town on a minor road running parallel to the A714. It has the largest ancient woodland in Southern Scotland, and here you can see redstarts, pied flycatchers, wood warblers and so on. There is a picnic area and nature trails.

One mile west of Wigtown is Bladnoch Distillery, within the village of the same name. Scotland's most southerly whisky distillery is sited here, with a visitor centre and shop. Guided tours are available showing the distilling process.

Dolls House Museum, which has 50 beautifully made doll's houses and room settings. The scale is 1:12, and all the exhibits are behind glass. There is also a collection of over 200 exquisitely dressed dolls. Perhaps the most conspicuous building in the town is the white-washed **Town Hall** of 1800, with its distinctive tower.

Kirroughtree is an attractive part of the Galloway forest, and sits three miles east of the town. It is mixed deciduous woodland with a small visitor centre. And about two miles south of the town, at Carty Port, is the **Tropic House & Butterfly Farm**, where you can explore a rainforest in miniature and see colourful butterflies. Six miles west of Newton Stewart is the picturesque village of **Kirkcowan**, which has a church dating from 1834 with external stairs to the gallery.

WIGTOWN

23 miles E of Stranraer on the A714

This small royal burgh was granted its royal charter in 1457, and has achieved fame as being **Scotland's Book Town**, and has many bookshops and publishing houses. In fact, there are over 30 book-related businesses in the town, with about 250,000 books and related items for sale between them. The focus for book activity, apart from the shops, are the **County Buildings** of 1863, and during the two book fairs held here every year - one in May and one in September - many of the readings, talks and events take place within them.

Within **Wigtown Parish** Church is the stump of an old cross, said to date from the 10th century. In the churchyard are the remains of the medieval church, dedicated to St Machuto, who is known in France as St Malo, and gave his name to the French port. Also in the kirkyard are the **Martyrs' Graves**. In 1685, during the time of the Covenanters, two women - 18 year old Margaret Wilson and 63 year old Margaret McLachlan - were tied to stakes at the mouth of the River Bladnoch for adhering to the Covenant and renouncing Charles as the head of the church. Rather than give up their principles, they drowned as the tide rose over their heads. The shoreline has receded since the 17th century, and the spot where the martyrdom took place is now surrounded by salt marches. It is marked by the small **Martyrs Monument**, reached by a raised wooden footpath (see also Stirling). On Windy Hill behind the town is another **Covenanters' Monument**, this time a slender column.

Close to the village are the ruins of **Baldoon Castle**, said to be haunted by the blood-splattered ghost of a woman called Janet Dalrymple, who lived in the 17th century. She was the eldest daughter of Sir James Dalrymple, and her parents forced her to marry Sir David Dunbar of Baldoon, though she loved a penniless man called Archibald Rutherford. There are three versions of what happened next. The first version says that Sir David stabbed her on their wedding night and went insane, the second says that Janet stabbed her husband and went insane, and the third says that Archibald hid in the bridal chamber and stabbed Sir David. On hearing shrieks from the room, the door was broken down and Janet was found covered in blood and muttering insanely. Scott tells the tale in *The Bride of Lammermuir*, dating it to 1669.

CHAPEL FINIAN

16 miles SE of Stranraer on the A747

Beside the road that runs along the western shore of **The Machars**, the name given to that great peninsula that sticks out into the Irish Sea between Luce and Wigtown Bays, you'll find the foundations of a small church. The most interesting thing about them is their great age, as they probably date from the 10th century. Later, the chapel was probably used as a stopping off point for people landing on the shoreline from Ireland who were making a pilgrimage to St Ninian's Shrine at Whithorn, 12 miles to the southeast. The chapel was dedicated to St Finian of Moville who lived during the 6th century, and had founded a great monastic school in Northern Ireland where St Columba studied.

Four miles inland from the chapel, and reached by a minor road off the A7005, is the **Old Place of Mochrum**, on the northern edge of lonely Mochrum Loch. It was originally built in the 16th century by the Dunbar family, and was restored by the Marquis of Bute between 1876 and 1911. The gardens are particularly fine.

MONREITH

23 miles SE of Stranraer on the A746

This small village lies on Monreith Bay. The ruins of the old church of **Kirkmaiden-in-Fernis** can still be seen, the chancel now a burial place for the Maxwells of Monreith. It is one of the oldest churches in the area, and is said to have been founded by a young Irish princess called Medana. She had embraced Christianity, and to escape the attentions of a persistent suitor, she fled to Scotland and settled where the church now is. However, the suitor followed her to Scotland and Medana, on seeing him, threw herself into the sea and swam across to the Rhinns of Galloway. She settled there until her suitor once again found her, so this time she climbed a tree to escape him. "Why do you follow me?" she asked, and when the suitor replied

Four miles west of Wigtown, reached by the B733, is the Bronze Age Torhouse Stone Circle, built about 2000 BC to 1500 BC. It consists of 19 boulders forming a 62 feet diameter circle, with three other boulders in a line within it. It is of a type more commonly found in Aberdeenshire and north east Scotland.

The Animal World & Gavin Maxwell Museum at Monreith has displays about local wildlife. It is named after Gavin Maxwell, author of **Ring of Bright Water,** *who was born at nearby Elrig, which features in his book* **The House of Elrig** *(see also Skye).*

Old Place of Mochrum, Chapel Finian

•

*At Garlieston, four miles
north of Whithorn, are
the Galloway House
Gardens, laid out
informally at the ruined
Cruggleton Castle, and
with walks leading down
to the shores of
Cruggleton Bay. The
medieval Cruggleton
Church sits by itself in a
field, and was built as a
chapel for the castle. It
was restored in the 19th
century by the Marquis
of Bute, and a key for it
is available at nearby
Cruggleton Farm. It was
offshore at Cruggleton
that the massive
Mulberry Harbours were
tested before being used
in Normandy landings.
Part of one can still be
seen offshore today.*

•

•

*St Ninian's Cave is on
the shore three miles
southwest of Whithorn. It
has incised crosses on its
walls, and a legend states
that St Ninian himself
came to this cave to seek
solitude and pray.*

•

that he was captivated by her eyes, she plucked them out and threw them at his feet. The suitor then gave up and headed back to Ireland.

However, the story doesn't end there. Medana asked a maid servant to wash her face, and a stream magically appeared at her feet. As her face was bathed, she regained her sight.

WHITHORN

26 miles SE of Stranraer on the A746

This tiny royal burgh (no bigger than a village) is often called the "Cradle of Scottish Christianity". A century before Columba came to Iona, a monk and bishop called **St Ninian**, who is mentioned by Bede, established a monastery here. He also mentions Whithorn, and places it firmly in the kingdom of Bernicia, or modern day Northumberland, as the kingdom stretched right across the northern shores of the Solway in his day. Ninian, however, is a shadowy figure, and this is the only certain reference we have to him in history, apart from accounts which are more fable than fact. He may have been born in either Galloway or Cumbria, the son of a tribal chief. He almost certainly visited Rome, and stayed with St Martin of Tours, whom he greatly admired. On the death of St Martin in AD 397, Ninian dedicated the church at Whithorn to him. He died in AD 432, and was buried within the monastic church.

The monastery would have been a typical Celtic foundation, with a high circular bank, or "rath", enclosing an area of monks' cells, workshops and chapels. This monastery was different in one respect, however. The main church was made of stone, not the more common wood, and was painted white. For this reason it was called **Candida Casa**, or "White House". When this part of Scotland was part of the kingdom of Northumbria, the name was translated into Anglo Saxon as "Hwit Aerne", from which Whithorn is derived.

The place was subsequently an important ecclesiastical and trading centre. In the 12th century Fergus, Lord of Galloway, founded **Whithorn Priory** (Historic Scotland), and its church became the cathedral for the diocese of Galloway. All that is left of the priory church is its nave and crypt. To the east of the crypt may be seen some scant foundations which may be all that is left of Ninian's original whitewashed church. The saint's remains were transferred to the cathedral, and it eventually became a place of pilgrimage. Many Scottish monarchs, especially James IV, made pilgrimages to pray there.

The town's main street, George Street, is wide and spacious, with many small Georgian, Regency and Victorian houses. **The Pend**, dating from about 1500, is an archway leading to the priory ruins, and above it are the royal arms of Scotland. Close to the priory is the **Priory Museum** (Historic Scotland), with a collection of stones on which are carved early

Christian symbols. One of them, the **Latinus Stone**, dates from the 5th century, and may be the earliest carved Christian stone in Scotland. Some years ago, excavations were undertaken at Whithorn, and at the **Whithorn Visitors Centre**, owned by the Whithorn Trust, you can learn about the excavations and what was found there.

At Glasserton, two miles west of Whithorn, are the **Woodfall Gardens**, covering three acres within an old walled garden. They were laid out in the 18th century by Keith Stewart, second son of the Earl of Galloway. He was an admiral in the British navy when he was given the 2,000 acres of the Barony of Glasserton in 1767. He then built a new house and had the gardens and parkland laid out.

Three miles to the southeast is the tiny fishing village of **Isle of Whithorn.** On a headland are the 13th century ruins of the tiny **St Ninian's Chapel**. Though it sits on the mainland, the small area surrounding it was at one time an island, giving the village its name. It was probably built for pilgrims to Whithorn Priory who came by sea.

KIRKCOLM

5 miles N of Stranraer on the A718

The **Kilmorie Cross**, dating from the 10th century, originally stood at St Mary's Chapel, south of the village. It was moved to the grounds of Corsewall House and then to the churchyard of the Parish Church in 1989. **Corsewall Lighthouse**, northwest of the village, was built in 1815 to the designs of Robert Stevenson, father of RL Stevenson. It is now a hotel.

KIRKMADRINE

8 miles S of Stranraer on a minor road off the A716

Behind glass in the porch of what was the tiny parish church of Toskerton are the eight **Kirkmadrine Stones**, dating from the 5th to the 12th centuries. The earlier ones are thought to be the oldest inscribed stones in Scotland after those at Whithorn, with the oldest ones probably marking the graves of early priests. They were discovered when the church was being rebuilt and converted into a burial chamber by a local family, the McTaggarts of Ardwell. Parts of the former medieval church have been incorporated into it, though it is thought that there has been a church here since the 6th century.

ARDWELL

10 miles S of Stranraer on the A716

Ardwell Gardens are grouped around the 18th century Ardwell House (not open to the public). They feature azaleas, camellias and rhododendrons, and are a testimony to the mildness of the climate in these parts, and feature a woodland and a formal garden, as well as good views out over Luce Bay from the pond.

PORT LOGAN

12 miles S of Stranraer on the B7065

Port Logan is a small fishing village situated on Port Logan Bay. Close by is the **Logan Fish Pond**, a

43 CORSEWALL LIGHTHOUSE HOTEL

Kirkcolm

A unique, luxury hotel within an old lighthouse. Be pampered here, unwind, and sample the award-winning cuisine of one of Scotland's most unusual hotels!

⊨ ‖ see page 441

44 COUNTY HOTEL

Stoneykirk

A delightful, stone built hotel offering good food, good drink and superb accommodation.

⊨ ‖ see page 442

Ardwell Church is a handsome building built in 1902 to the designs of Glasgow architect P. MacGregor Chalmers, who was famous for his medieval church architecture and had restored Glenluce Abbey. It seems far too large for such a small village, but was actually paid for by the McTaggart family then gifted to the Church of Scotland.

45 LOGAN FISH POND

Port Logan

A unique historic attraction in the form of a 19th century fish larder, together with touch pools and an aquarium.

  see page 442

•

On a headland to the south of the village are the ruins of Dunskey Castle, built in the early 16th century by the Adair family. The recently re-established Dunskey Garden and Woodland Walk is well worth visiting. The restored MacKenzie and Moncur greenhouses cannot be missed. Within the village is the ruined Portpatrick Parish Church. It was built in the 17th century, and unusually, has a round tower.

•

---

remarkable tidal pond famous for its tame sea fish, which can be fed by hand. It was constructed in about 1800 by Colonel Andrew MacDougall as a source of fresh fish for the tables of nearby Logan House, his home. Now it is a marine centre.

If anywhere illustrates the mildness of the climate in this part of Scotland, it is **Logan Botanic Garden**, part of the National Botanic Gardens of Scotland. Here, growing quite freely, are exotic plants and trees such as the tree fern (which can normally only survive in glass houses in Britain), the eucalyptus, palm trees, magnolias and passionflowers. In fact, over 40 per cent of all the plants and trees at Logan come from the Southern hemisphere. Within the garden is the Discovery Centre, which gives an insight into the plants that grow here. From April until September, on every second Tuesday of the month at 10.30 am, there is a guided walk round the gardens.

The village achieved national fame when the TV series *2,000 Acres of Sky*, supposedly set on a Hebridean island, was filmed in and around Port Logan.

KIRKMAIDEN

15 miles S of Stranraer on the B7065

Kirkmaiden is Scotland's most southerly parish. Four miles south of the village is the **Mull of Galloway**, Scotland's most southerly point. It comes as a surprise to some people when they learn that places like Durham, Hartlepool and Sunderland in England are further north. The lighthouse was built in 1828 to the designs of Robert Stevenson, and sits on the massive cliffs, 270 feet above the sea. In Drummore, half a mile to the east of Kirkmaiden, is the **Kirkmaiden Information Centre**, which has displays and exhibitions about the area. There is also a family history section.

PORTPATRICK

6 miles SW of Stranraer on the A77

This lovely little village is at the western end of the Southern Upland Way. At one time it was the main Scottish port for Northern Ireland, 22 miles away, but was in such an exposed position that Stranraer eventually took over. It sits round a little harbour that is always busy, and, with its old cottages and craft shops, has become a small holiday resort.

Built as a hunting lodge in 1869 by lady Hunter Blair, **Knockinaam Lodge** stands to the south of the village. It is now a hotel, but it was here, during the closing stages of the Second World War, that Churchill and Eisenhower planned the Allied strategy.

Ayrshire & Arran

Ayrshire was at one time Scotland's largest Lowland county. Facing the Firth of Clyde, it is shaped like half a saucer, with moorland on its northern, western and southern edges sloping down to a central area of rich agricultural land bordered by the sea, with an intriguing patchwork of small fields, country lanes, woodland, and picturesque villages. The poet Keats, when he made his pilgrimage in 1818 to the birthplace of Robert Burns in Alloway, compared its scenery to that of Devon. Indeed, like Devon, this is dairying country, and in places you almost feel you are in an English rural landscape.

The county was formerly divided into three parts. Carrick is the most southerly, and owes a lot to neighbouring Galloway. It is separated from Kyle, a rich dairying area, by the River

Doon. Here you can see native Ayrshire cattle, with their brown and white mottling, dotting the

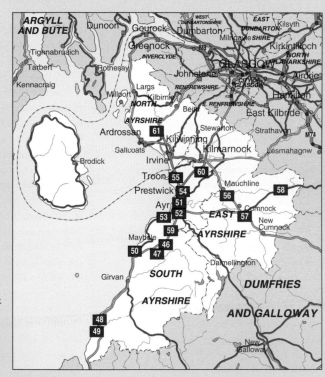

77

fields. To the north, beyond the River Irvine, is Cunninghame, which at one time was the most industrialised of the three, though it managed this without losing too much of its rural aspect.

Kyle itself was divided by the River Ayr into Kyle Regal and Kyle Stewart, reflecting the fact that one section was ruled directly by the king while the other was ruled by high stewards of Scotland, who eventually went on to be kings in their own right.

Ayrshire and Robert Burns, known to all Scottish people as "Rabbie" (never, ever *Robbie*!) are inextricably linked. Though his father was from Kincardineshire northeast Scotland, he was born in Alloway, which nowadays is a well-off suburb of Ayr, and spent the first 29 years of his life in the county, before moving south to Dumfriesshire. We know a lot about the man, and all the places in Ayrshire where he lived, drank, courted and caroused are well signposted. A full week could easily be spent meandering along the main roads and narrow lanes of the county, visiting such towns and villages as Tarbolton, Mauchline, Ayr, Kilmarnock, Irvine, Failford and Kirkoswald. Every year in May the Burns an' a' That Festival takes place throughout Ayrshire to celebrate his life and work. Venues include pubs, concert halls, theatres, museums and churches.

There are three main towns in the county - Ayr, Kilmarnock and Irvine. Ayr was the administrative and commercial capital before Ayrshire ceased to exist as a local government unit in the 1970s. Kilmarnock was traditionally the industrial centre, though it is an ancient town, and Irvine, in the 1960s, was designated a new town, taking an overspill population from Glasgow. Industrial estates were built, factories were opened and new housing established. However, its central core is still worth exploring.

Up until the 1960s, when more exotic places took over, the Ayrshire coast was Glasgow's holiday playground. Known as the "Costa del Clyde", it attracted thousands of people each year who flocked to such holiday resorts as Troon, Largs, Prestwick, Girvan and Ayr itself. These halcyon days are gone, though it is still a popular place for day trips and for people to retire to, giving it a new nickname - the "Costa Geriatrica". The coastline is also famous for golf. The first British Open Golf Championship was held at Prestwick in 1860, and both Troon and Turnberry have regularly hosted the tournament in modern times.

Ayrshire is also a county of castles, from the spectacular Culzean (pronounced "Cull- ane") perched on a cliff top above the sea, to Kelburn near Largs and Dean Castle in Kilmarnock, with its collection of rare musical instruments.

The Ayrshire coalfield used to employ thousands of people, though nowadays not a deep mine remains. But even at its height, the coal industry never scarred the environment as in, say, South Yorkshire or the Welsh valleys. Now you would never suspect that the industry ever existed at all, and a day just motoring round the quiet lanes is a relaxing experience in itself.

Twenty miles offshore is the island of Arran, at one time within the county of Bute, but now more associated with Ayrshire. It has been called "Scotland in Miniature", and is a wonderful blend of wild scenery, pastoral views and rocky coastlines. Its history stretches right back into the mists of time, as the many standing stones and ancient burial cairns testify. It is properly part of the Highlands, and Gaelic used to be the predominant language. A ferry connects it to Ardrossan on the Ayrshire coast.

Also within Bute, but now within Ayrshire, were two other islands - Great and Little Cumbrae. Little Cumbrae is largely uninhabited, apart from one or two houses, but Great Cumbrae boasts the town of Millport, a gem of a holiday resort. Within Millport is another gem - Cumbrae Cathedral, the smallest cathedral in Britain. A short ferry crossing from Largs takes you to the island.

MAYBOLE

This small, quiet town is the ancient capital of Carrick, and sits on a hillside about four miles inland from the coast. It was here that Burns's parents, William Burnes (he later changed the name to Burns) and Agnes Broun met in the 1750s and later married. A story is told of how William, when he met Agnes, had just written a letter to another young woman proposing marriage. However, because of his meeting with Agnes, the letter was never sent. Agnes was 27 years old at the time - almost on the shelf in those days - and William was 37.

In 1562, a famous meeting took place in Maybole between John Knox, the Scottish reformer, and Abbot Quentin Kennedy of nearby Crossraguel Abbey. The purpose of the meeting was to debate the significance and doctrine of the Mass, and it attracted a huge crowd of people, even though it was held in a small room of the house where the provost of the town's collegiate church lived. Forty people from each side were allowed in to hear the debate, which lasted for three days in late September. Knox and Kennedy were charismatic men, highly intelligent and sure of their own arguments. It only broke up - with no conclusion reached - when the town ran out of food to feed the thronging masses round the door. A plaque on a modern house marks where the debate took place. (see also Kirkoswald).

The ruins of **Maybole Collegiate Church** (Historic Scotland) can still be viewed, though they are not open to the public. The church, dedicated to St Mary, was founded by Sir John Kennedy of Dunure in 1371 for the saying of daily prayers for himself, his wife Mary and their children. The clergy consisted of a clerk, who was in charge, and three chaplains, who said the prayers daily. The present ruins date from a rebuilding in the 15th century, when it became a full collegiate church with a provost and a "college" of priests. The present **Parish Church** dates from 1808, and has an unusual stepped spire.

The artist **Robert MacBryde** was born in Maybole in 1913, and died as a result of a road accident in Dublin in 1966. He was a great friend of Robert Colquhoun, another Ayrshire artist (see Kilmarnock), and they attended Glasgow School of Art together before taking a studio in London.

At one time Maybole had no less that 28 lairds' town houses, each one referred to as a "castle". Now there are only two left, one at each end of the main street. The "upper" one is now part of the **Town Hall**, and was the 17th century town house of the lairds of Blairquhan Castle, about five miles to the east. The other is still referred to as **Maybole Castle.** though it too was a town house, this time for the Earls of Cassillis. It dates from the late 16th century, and there is a curious legend attached to the building.

It seems that Lady Jean Hamilton, daughter of the earl of

46   THE WELLTREES INN

Maybole

A lovely old inn set just off Maybole's main street that is perfect for a lunch, sumptuous dinner or just a relaxing drink.

see page 443

47   MAYBOLE CASTLE

Maybole

A 16th century town house with many fascinating features, built originally for the Earls of Cassillis

see page 444

A few miles west of Maybole, near the farm of Drumshang, is the curiously named Electric Brae, on the A719 road between Ayr and Turnberry. Stop your car on the convenient lay by at the side of the road, put it out of gear, let off the brake, and be amazed as it rolls uphill. Better still, lay a football on the lay by's surface, and watch it roll uphill as well. The phenomenon has nothing to do with lay lines, earth magic, the "unseen world" or the same power displayed by poltergeists when they move objects (as someone once declared). Instead it has everything to do with an optical illusion. The surrounding land makes you think that the road rises towards the west when it fact it descends. Another road with the same optical illusion can be found on the Isle of Man.

Haddington, was forced to marry John, 6th Earl of Cassillis, even though she was in love with Sir John Faa of Dunbar, the self-styled King of the Gypsies. After her marriage, she was taken off to Ayrshire, though she never forgot her first true love.

One day the Earl had to go away on business, leaving the countess on her own in Maybole Castle. Sir John saw his chance, and helped by 14 gypsies stormed the castle and took her away. However, the Earl returned unexpectedly, and set off in hot pursuit. He eventually caught the men, and had them all strung up from a tree - called the Dule Tree - at Cassillis Castle (pronounced "Castles castle"). He forced the Countess to watch Sir John's death throes, and then had her incarcerated in a small room in Maybole Castle, where she spent her lonely days working on tapestries.

The room is still pointed out to this day, and above its window are some carved heads, said to be of Sir John and the gypsies. But though it is a romantic story, it is completely untrue, and reflects other similar stories told throughout Europe. The 3rd Earl did indeed marry Lady Jean Hamilton, but letters sent between them show that they were a loving, close couple (see also Dalrymple).

AROUND MAYBOLE

KIRKMICHAEL

3 miles E of Maybole on the B7045

Like its neighbour Crosshill, Kirkmichael is a former weaving village. However, its roots go deep into Scottish history. The **Parish Church** dates from 1790, and the picturesque lych-gate from about 1700. Within the kirkyard is the grave of a Covenanter called Gilbert MacAdam, shot in 1686 by Archibald Kennedy.

Kirkmichael is the scene, every May, of the **Kirkmichael International Guitar Festival**, which draws musicians from all over the world. It covers everything from jazz to pop and country to classical. Huge marquees are erected, and local pubs host impromptu jamming sessions and folk concerts. It was founded by the internationally renowned jazz guitarist Martin Taylor, who, while born in England, lives locally. At the time of writing the guitar festival had been suspended, though it may resume.

DALMELLINGTON

11 miles E of Maybole on the A713

This former mining village sits on the banks of the Doon. Over the last few years, it has exploited its rich heritage, and created some visitor centres and museums that explain the village's industrial past. **Scottish Industrial Railway Centre** is located here, and steam trains run on a restored track. The **Cathcartson Centre** in the village is housed in weaving cottages dating from the 18th century, and shows how weavers lived long ago.

A couple of miles beyond Dalmellington is a minor road that takes you to lovely **Loch Doon**, surrounded by lonely hills and moorland, and the source of the river that Burns wrote about. It was here, during World War I, that a **School of Aerial Gunnery** was proposed. Millions of pounds were wasted on it before the plans were finally abandoned. When a hydroelectric scheme was built in the 1930s, the water level of the loch was raised. The eleven-sided **Loch Doon Castle**, which stood on an island in the loch, was dismantled stone by stone and reassembled on the shore, where it can still be seen.

In 1306 it was besieged by the English when Sir Christopher Seton, Robert the Bruce's brother-in-law, took refuge there after the Scottish army's defeat at the Battle of Methven. However, the governor of the castle, Sir Gilbert de Carrick, fearing that the Bruce's cause was lost, surrendered to the English troops. Seton was executed at Dumfries and Gilbert de Carrick was spared.

The castle was again besieged in 1446 by the Douglases, who were trying to usurp the Kennedys in Carrick. However, the siege failed, thanks to the McLellans of Dumfriesshire, who supported the Kennedys. It was again besieged in 1510, this time by the Crawfords, but the castle held firm.

In the late 1970s it was announced that 32 deep tunnels would be bored in the hills surrounding Loch Doon to store most of Britain's radioactive waste. After many protests by local people, the idea was abandoned.

Loch Doon Castle

CROSSHILL

3 miles SE of Maybole, on the B7023

Crosshill is a former handloom-weaving village established in about 1808, with many small, attractive cottages. Many of the weavers were Irish, attracted to the place by the prospect of work. There are no outstanding buildings, nor does it have much history or legend attached to it. But it is a conservation village with a quiet charm, and well worth visiting because of this alone. Some of the original cottages built by the Irish immigrants in the early 19th century can still be seen in Dalhowan Street.

STRAITON

6 miles SE of Maybole on the B741

A narrow road, called the **Nick o' the Balloch**, runs south from this lovely village. It does not go through the Carrick of gentle fields or verdant valleys, but over the wild hills and moorland that make the edges of this area so beautiful, and

Dalmellington is the starting point for the new Scottish Coal Cycle Route which will stretch between Dalmellington and Coalburn, 66km away in Lanarkshire. It will became part of the National Cycle Network.

Close to the village of Straiton is Blairquhan (pronounced "Blairwhan"), a Tudor-Gothic mansion built between 1821 and 1824 to the designs of the famous Scottish architect William Burn. Surrounding it is a 2,000 acre estate, 590 acres of which is parkland. It sits on the site of an earlier tower house dating to 1346 that was once a McWhirter stronghold before passing to the Kennedys. It is now owned by the Hunter Blair family, and is open to the public in summer. It has a fine collection of paintings by the Scottish Colourists.

finally drops down into Glentrool.

Straiton itself sits on the Water of Girvan, and has picturesque little cottages facing each other across a main street some with roses growing round the door. It was a planned village, laid out in 1760 by the Earl of Cassillis on the site of a small hamlet. The local pub, The Black Bull, dates from 1766, while parts of **St Cuthbert's Parish Church** date back to 1510.

On a hill above the village stands the **Hunter Blair Monument**, built in 1856 to commemorate James Hunter Blair, killed at the Battle of Inkerman two years previously.

Many of the scenes in the film *The Match* (also called *The Beautiful Game*) were shot in Straiton, which became the fictional Highland village of Inverdoune.

OLD DAILLY

9 miles S of Maybole on the B734

Old Dailly was originally called Dalmakerran, and is now a "lost village". It was once an important place, with many cottages, a manse for the minister and a mill. Now it is a row of unprepossing council houses and the ruins of 14th century **Old Dailly Parish Church**. Within the kirkyard are two hefty stones called the **Charter Stones**, which men tried to lift in bygone days during trials of strength.

Buried in the kirkyard is the pre-Raphaelite artist **William Bell Scott**, who was staying at nearby **Penkill Castle** (not open to the public) when he died. Many members of the pre-Raphaelite

Brotherhood visited the place, including **Dante Gabriel Rossetti**. Close by is the 17th century **Bargany House**, with its marvellous gardens. It was once a stronghold of one branch of the powerful Kennedy family, which was forever feuding with the other branch, the Kennedys of Dunure. In the 1601 the Kennedys of Bargany eventually lost the power struggle when Bargany himself was killed in Ayr during a skirmish. (see also Ballantrae and Dunure). The mining village of **New Dailly**, with its T-shaped **New Dailly Parish Church** of 1766 is three miles to the east. Close by, on the opposite side of the Girvan Water, are the substantial ruins of **Dalquharran Castle**. It was designed by Robert Adam and built between 1780 and 1791 for Kennedy of Dunure. Plans were announced in 2004 to turn it and its estate into a luxury hotel and golf resort, with Jack Nicklaus designing the golf course. The ruins of the 15th century **Old Dalquharran Castle** are close by.

BARR

11 miles S of Maybole on the B734

Tucked in a fold of the Carrick hills, Barr is an idyllic village that was once the site of the wonderfully named **Kirkdandie Fair**. It was the largest annual fair in Southern Scotland during the late 18th and early 19th centuries, and was held on a strip of land where stood the long gone Kirkdandie (or Kirkdominae) Church. Its main claim to fame was the fighting that took place there every year, and it soon became known as the "Donnybrook of Scotland". People even came over from Ireland to participate in the great pitched battles. So famous did it become that a ballad was written about it, describing at least 63 tents, the sound of pipes, and people socialising, dancing, drinking and eating.

Above Barr was once the estate of Changue (pronounced "Shang"), to which an old legend is attached. The cruel and wicked **Laird of Changue** was a smuggler and distiller of illicit whisky who enjoyed the fruits of his own still a bit too much and was therefore always penniless. One day, while walking through his estates, Satan appeared before him and offered a deal. If he handed over his soul when he died, he would become rich. The laird, who was a young man, agreed, and duly prospered. But as he grew older he began to regret his rashness, and when Satan at last appeared before him to claim his soul - at the same spot where he had appeared all these years before - the laird refused to keep his side of the bargain.

Instead he challenged the Devil to fight for it. Drawing a large circle on the ground round both of them, he said that the first person to be forced out of it would be the loser. After a bitter struggle, the laird cut off the end of Satan's tail with his sword, and he jumped out of the circle in pain. The laird had won.

Up until the end of the 19th century, a great bare circle on some grassland was shown as the place where all this took place. It's a wonderful story, but no one has ever managed to put a name or date to this mysterious laird. And it has often been pointed out that if Satan had bided his time and let the laird die in his bed, he would have had his soul anyway.

COLMONELL

19 Miles S of Maybole on the B734

The River Stinchar is the southernmost of Ayrshire's major rivers, and flows through a lovely glen bordered on both sides by high moorland and hills. In this valley, four miles from the sea, sits Colmonell. It's an attractive village of small cottages, with the romantic ruins of the old Kennedy stronghold of **Kirkhill Castle** close by. **Knockdolian Hill**, two miles west, was at one time called the "false Ailsa Craig" because of its resemblance to the volcanic island out in the Firth of Clyde.

BALLANTRAE

22 miles S of Maybole on the A77

Tradition tells us that Ballantrae, now a small fishing village, is where St Ninian first tried to set foot in Scotland again after spending time in Rome and on the Continent.

When on a walking tour of Carrick in 1876, R.L. Stevenson spent a night in Ballantrae. However, dour villagers took exception to his eccentric way of dressing, and almost ran him out of town. He got his revenge by writing "The Master of Ballantrae", which confused everyone by having

Knockdolian Castle is a mile west of the village of Colmonell. At one time it was owned by the Duchess of Wellington. An old legend tells of the wife of an owner of the castle ordering that a rock on the shore, a few miles west, be broken up to prevent a mermaid sitting on it and singing. The mermaid cursed the castle, saying that the castle owners would die without leaving an heir.

48 BUCHANAN'S VILLAGE SHOP

Ballantrae

A village shop as it should be - inviting and friendly, with a great range of local produce and goods, all at value-for-money prices.

 see page 445

49 KINGS ARMS HOTEL

Ballantrae

A delightful old inn on the Ayrshire coast that is handy for Ayrshire's golf courses as well as the ferry for Northern Ireland.

see page 445

Glenapp Castle, a few miles south of the village of Ballantrae just off the A77, was designed in 1870 by the noted Victorian architect David Bryce for James Hunter, the Deputy Lord Lieutenant of Ayrshire. It is now a luxury hotel within 30 acres of landscaped estate and garden.

Kirkoswald Parish Church dates from 1777, and was designed by Robert Adam while he was working on nearby Culzean Castle. Dwight D. Eisenhower worshipped here twice, and on one of these occasions he was still President of the United States (see also Culzean Castle). Another visitor is not so well known, though the airline he helped to found is. The late Randolph Fields, together with Richard Branson, founded Virgin Airlines. Randolph loved this part of Ayrshire, and when he died in 1997, he left some money for the restoration of the church. A year later his widow presented the church with a small table, on which is a plaque commemorating his donation.

no connection with the village whatsoever.

In the churchyard is the **Bargany Aisle**, containing the ornate tomb of Gilbert Kennedy, laird of Bargany and Ardstinchar, who was killed by the Earl of Cassillis (also a Kennedy) in 1601. A bitter feud between the Cassillis and Bargany branches of the Kennedy family had been going on right through the 16th century, with no quarter given or taken. Matters came to a head when the two branches met near Ayr, and Bargany was killed. The power of the Bargany branch was broken forever, and the feud fizzled out (see also Old Dailly).

The ruins of **Ardstinchar Castle**, Bargany's main stronghold, can still be seen beside the river to the south of the village. It was built in 1421, and in August 1566 Mary Stuart stayed here for one night.

LENDALFOOT

18 miles S of Maybole on the A77

Carleton Castle, now in ruins, was the home of Sir John Carleton, who, legend states, had an unusual way of earning a living. He married ladies of wealth then enticed them to **Gamesloup**, a nearby rocky eminence, where he pushed them to their deaths and inherited their wealth. Sir John went through seven or eight wives before meeting the daughter of Kennedy of Culzean. After marrying her, he took her to Gamesloup, but instead of him pushing her over, she pushed him over, and lived happily ever after on his accumulated

wealth. It is said that you can still occasionally hear the screams of the women as they were pushed to their death.

But if it's a gruesome tale you're after, then you should head for **Sawney Bean's Cave** a few miles south of the village, on the shoreline north of Bennane Head, and easily reached by a footpath from a layby on the A77. Here, in the 16th century, lived a family of cannibals led by Sawney Bean ("Sawny" being Scots for "Sandy"), which waylaid strangers, robbed them, and ate their flesh. They evaded capture for many years until a troop of men sent by James VI trapped them in their cave. They were taken to Edinburgh, tried and executed. It's a wonderful story, but there is no truth in it. No documentary evidence had ever been unearthed referring to the Bean family, and court records do not mention a trial.

KIRKOSWALD

4 miles SW of Maybole on the A77

The busy A77, carrying traffic from Glasgow to Stranraer, passes straight through Kirkoswald, which takes away from its attractiveness as a small rural village. However, there is a lot of history in the place. It was to Kirkoswald, in 1775, that Burns came for one term to learn surveying. Though his poem *Tam o' Shanter* is set in Alloway, all the characters in it have their origins in the parish of Kirkoswald, which was where his maternal grandparents came from.

The **Old Parish Church of St**

Oswald dates from the 13th century, though most of what you see nowadays is later. It lies at the heart of the village. It is a ruin now, but it was here, in 1562, that Abbot Quentin Kennedy of Crossraguel Abbey preached forcefully against the Reformation and in favour of the sacrifice of the mass. He challenged anyone to debate the matter with him, and John Knox, who was in the area, agreed to take him on. They met in nearby Maybole, where the two of them debated over three days without resolving the issue (see also Maybole). In its kirkyard are the graves of many people associated with Burns, including David Graham of Shanter Farm near Maidens, the real life "Tam o' Shanter".

Some say that a church has stood here for at least 1,400 years, the first church being built to commemorate Oswald's victory in a 7th century battle fought nearby. Others say it was built to commemorate Oswald's victory at the Battle of Heavenfield in AD 634 in Northumberland.

The church also contains one interesting relic - **Robert the Bruce's Baptismal Font.** Both Lochmaben in Dumfriesshire and Turnberry Castle, within the parish of Kirkoswald, claim to have been the birthplace of Robert the Bruce. Turnberry is the more likely, as it was the ancestral home of the Countess of Carrick, Bruce's mother, and it is known that she was living there at about the time of the birth. The story goes that the baby was premature, and that

he was rushed to **Crossraguel Abbey** for baptism in the abbey font in case he died. When Crossraguel was abandoned after the Reformation, the people of Kirkoswald rescued the font and put it in their own church (see also Lochmaben) .

CROSSRAGUEL ABBEY

2 miles SW of Maybole, on the A77

These romantic ruins (Historic Scotland) sit complacently beside the main Ayr-Stranraer road. They are very well preserved, and possibly give a better idea of the layout of a medieval abbey than anywhere else in Scotland. Some of the architecture and stone carving, such as that in the chapter house, is well worth seeking out. Duncan, Earl of Carrick, founded it in 1244 for Clunaic monks from Paisley Abbey, though most of what you see nowadays dates from after the 13th century. The name is supposed to come from an old cross which stood here before the abbey was built, and it may mean the regal, or royal cross, or the

Within the village of Kirkoswald you'll also find Souter Johnnie's Cottage (National Trust for Scotland), a thatched cottage dating from at least 1785. John Davidson was a "souter", or cobbler, and featured in Burns's poem Tam o' Shanter *as Tam's "ancient, trusty, drouthy crony", who drank with him in the tavern before Tam set out home. Behind the cottage, in an old outhouse (possibly an old alehouse), are life-size carvings of Johnnie, Tam, the innkeeper and his wife.*

Crossraguel Abbey

50 WILDINGS HOTEL & RESTAURANT

Maidens

One of the best coastal hotels and restaurants in SW Scotland, famed for its superb food and comfortable accommodation.

⊨ ‖ see page 445

•

Built onto the scant ruins of Turnberry castle is Turnberry Lighthouse, surrounded on three sides by the championship golf course. It was built between 1871 and 1873 on a particularly rocky and dangerous part of the Ayrshire coast, where the notorious Bristo Rock was situated, which claimed many ships.

•

•

Out in the Firth of Clyde the bulk of Ailsa Craig rises sheer from the water. It is the plug of an ancient volcano, and is now a bird sanctuary. Trips round it are available from Girvan harbour.

•

cross of Riaghail, either a local chief or a corrution of "Regulus".

To the north are the ruins of **Baltersan Castle**, an old fortified 16th century tower house built for John Kennedy of Pennyglen and his wife Margaret .

TURNBERRY

7 miles SW of Maybole on the A719

Very little now survives of the 12th century **Turnberry Castle,** where Robert the Bruce is supposed to have been born. The story of how his parents met is an unusual one. Marjorie, Countess of Carrick, the young widow of Adam de Kilconquhar, saw a knight passing by her castle at Turnberry. She immediately became infatuated with him, and had him kidnapped and brought into her presence. He turned out to be Robert de Brus, son of the Lord of Annandale, and she persuaded him to marry her. The result of the marriage was Robert the Bruce, who himself became Earl of Carrick on his mother's death (see also Kirkoswald). Because Robert ascended the throne of Scotland as Robert I, the earldom became a royal one, and the present Earl of Carrick is Prince Charles.

The elegant five star **Turnberry Hotel** is situated south east of the castle, just off the main road, and is one of the premier hotels in Scotland. It even has its own small runway for aircraft, and at one time had its own railway line from Ayr. During World Wars I and II, all this area was an airfield, and the runways can still be seen. There

is a **War Memorial** on the 12th green of the golf course dedicated to the men of the airfield who died in World War I. It is in the shape of a double Celtic cross, and was erected by the people of Kirkoswald parish in 1923. In 1990 the monument was altered so that the names of the airmen killed during World War II could be added.

GIRVAN

10 miles SW of Maybole on the A77

This pleasant little town is the main holiday resort in Carrick. It is also a thriving fishing port, with many boats in the harbour at the mouth of the Water of Girvan. Though there is a long, sandy beach, a boating pond and a small funfair in summer the town is a quiet place overlooked by the bulk of **Byne Hill** to the south. From the top there is a fine view of the Firth of Clyde, and on a clear day the coast of Northern Ireland can be seen. The small **Crauford Monument** above Ardmillan House, on the western side, commemorates Major A.C.B. Crauford, who took part in the capture of the Cape of Good Hope in 1795.

Within the town, in Knockcushan Street, is a small, curious building with a short spire which has been given the nickname **Auld Stumpy**. It dates from the 18th century, and at one time was attached to the later McMaster Hall, which burnt down in 1939. Behind Knockcushan House, near the harbour, are **Knockcushan Gardens**, the site of a court held by Robert the Bruce in 1328. At the **McKechnie Institute** in Dalrymple Street art exhibitions are sometimes held.

Alex Cubie, one of the illustrators of Rupert the Bear, regularly visited Girvan, and it is said that he based the seaside drawings, when Rupert was on holiday, on Girvan seascapes.

CULZEAN CASTLE

4 miles W of Maybole off the A719

Culzean Castle

Culzean Castle (National Trust for Scotland) perched on a cliff above the Firth of Clyde is possibly the most spectacularly sited castle in Scotland. It was designed by Robert Adam in 1777, and built round an old keep for the 10th Earl of Cassillis. It was presented to the National Trust for Scotland in 1945 by the then Marquis of Ailsa, his descendant, and the family moved out to Cassillis Castle. It has some wonderful features, such as the Oval Staircase and the Circular Saloon with its views out over the Firth. Surrounding the castle is **Culzean Country Park**, with such attractions as a Walled Garden, the Swan Pond, the Deer Park and the Fountain Court.

On the shoreline are the **Gasworks**, which produced coal gas to heat and light the castle. At one time a small boat-building yard stood on the shore immediately to the south of the castle, and many fine yachts were built there.

The caves beneath the castle are said to be haunted, and were at one time used by smugglers. A recent archaeological dig unearthed human bones dating form the Bronze Age, showing that the caves have been occupied for thousands of years. However, access to them is barred, as they can be dangerous.

DUNURE

5 miles NW of Maybole off the A719

This pretty little village would not look out of place in Cornwall. Arriving by car, you drop down towards it, giving excellent views of the cottages and pub, all grouped round a small harbour. It was developed in the early 1800s as a fishing village, though fishing has now gone.

To the south of the village are the ruins of **Dunure Castle**, perched on the coastline. This is the original castle of the Kennedys, and dates from the 14th century with later additions. It was here that the famous **Roasting of the Abbot** took place in 1570. The Kennedys were at the height of their powers, and Gilbert Kennedy, 4th Earl of Cassillis, owned most of the land in Carrick. He was, as his contemporaries observed, "ane very greedy man", and coveted the

In gratitude for his part in World War II, the National Trust for Scotland presented General Eisenhower with the life tenure of a flat in Culzean. Eisenhower accepted, and spent a few golfing holidays here. The Eisenhower Presentation, within the castle, explains his connections with the area, and has exhibits about D-Day (see also Kirkoswald).

Ayr was the starting off point for Tam o' Shanter's drunken and macabre ride home after spending the evening at an inn, as portrayed in Burns's poem of the same name. In the High Street is the thatched Tam o' Shanter Inn, where the ride was supposed to have started. Its association with the poem began in the mid 19th century, thanks to an enterprising landlord who wanted to increase business. At one time it was a small museum, but now it has thankfully reverted to its original purpose.

lands of Crossraguel Abbey, which, at the Reformation, had been placed in the hands of Allan Stewart, commendator, or lay abbot, of the abbey. Gilbert invited Allan to Dunure Castle for a huge feast, and when Allan accepted, had him incarcerated in the Black Vault. He then stripped him and placed him on a spit over a great open fire, turning him occasionally like a side of beef. Eventually Allan signed away the lands, and was released.

But he immediately protested to the Privy Council and the Regent (James VI was still a child at the time), which ordered Kennedy to pay for the lands. But such was Kennedy's power that he ignored the order.

AYR

Ayr is the major holiday resort on the Ayrshire coast, and has an air of history and prosperity to it. It stands at the mouth of the River Ayr, on the south bank, and was formerly the county town of Ayrshire. Always an important place, it was granted its royal charter in the early 1200s, and is the old capital of the Kyle district. At one

time it was walled, but all traces of the walls have disappeared. Its most distinctive feature is the tall, elegant steeple of the **Town Hall**, built between 1827 and 1832 to the designs of Thomas Hamilton. Seen from the north, it blends beautifully with a cluster of fine Georgian buildings beside the river.

After the Battle of Bannockburn, Bruce held his first parliament here, in the ancient kirk of St John the Baptist, to decide on the royal succession after he died. This kirk is no longer there save for the tower, now called **St John's Tower**, standing among Edwardian villas near the shore. At one time, before the land surrounding it was developed for housing, it was used as a lookout post to observe ships approaching Ayr harbour.

Oliver Cromwell dismantled the church and used the stone to build **Ayr Citadel**, which has now gone as well, save for a few feet of wall near the river and an arch in a side street. To compensate, he gave the burgh £600 to build a new church, which is now known as the **Auld Parish Kirk**, situated on the banks of the river where a friary once stood. It was built between 1652 and 1654, and is a mellow old T-plan building surrounded by tottering gravestones. Within the lych gate can be seen a couple of mortsafes, which were placed over fresh graves to prevent grave robbing in the early 19th century.

Robert Burns and Ayr are inseparable. He was born in Alloway, a village to the south of the town which has now become a

St John's Tower

well-heeled suburb, and his influences are everywhere. Off the High Street is the **Auld Brig o' Ayr**, which dates from the 14th century, and down river is the **New Bridge**, dating from 1878. In a poem called *The Twa Brigs* Burns accurately forecast that the Auld Brig would outlast the new one. He was right - the New Bridge of Burns's time was swept away in a flood, to be replaced by the present New Bridge, while the Auld Brig still survives. In the same poem he also mentions the **Wallace Tower**, which stands in the High Street. The present tower dates from 1833, and replaced the earlier one mentioned by Burns..

The second oldest building in the town is **Loudoun Hall,** in the Boat Vennel close to the New Bridge. It was built in the late 15th century as a fine town house for James Tait, a local merchant, and then passed to the Campbells of Loudoun, hereditary sheriffs of Ayr. It was due for demolition just after the war, but was saved when its importance was realised. South of Loudoun Hall, in the Sandgate, is **Lady Cathcart's House**, a tenement building which dates from the 17th century. Within it, in 1756, John Loudon McAdam, the roads engineer, was supposed to have been born (see also Muirkirk, Moffat and Carsphairn).

The bridges of Ayr take you to **Newton upon Ayr** on the north bank of the river, which was once a separate burgh with a charter dated to 1446. Part of its old tolbooth survives as **Newton Tower**, caught

in an island in the middle of the street.

The **Belleisle Estate and Gardens** are centred on a 19th century mansion which is now a hotel, and are to the south of the town, with parkland, deer park, aviary and pets corner. Nearby is **Rozelle House Galleries and Gardens**. There are art exhibitions within the mansion house, plus a tearoom and craft shop. Another estate well worth visiting is the **Craigie Estate**, on the banks of the River Ayr. It is centred on an elegant mansion built in the 1730s and designed by John Smith as a home for the Wallace family. It then passed to the Campbells, who sold it to the Burgh of Ayr in 1940.

South of the town, perched precariously on a cliff top and always seeming to be in imminent danger of collapsing into the sea, is **Greenan Castle**, a four storey tower house. It was built in 1603 for John Kennedy of Baltersan and his third wife Florence MacDowell, who owned the lands of Greenan. However, an earlier castle dating from the 13th century stood here, and it may also have been the site of an Iron Age fort. It is typical of many such tower houses in Ayrshire, but some experts believe it has one unique claim to fame - it may mark the real spot where King Arthur's **Camelot** stood (see also Kelso).

Ayr Racecourse is Scotland's leading racecourse, and is the venue for the Scottish Grand National in April and the Scottish Derby in July.

54 THE CAFÉ
    PRESTWICK

Prestwick

The café is renowned for its tasty snacks, wonderful teas and coffees, and a wide range of value-for-money, beautifully cooked meals.

🍴 see page 447

•

The very first British Open Golf Championship was held at Prestwick in 1860 (with eight competitors) and for 12 years after, and a cairn near the golf course, unveiled in 1977 by Henry Cotton, commemorates the event.

•

AROUND AYR

PRESTWICK

2 miles N of Ayr town centre, on the A79

Prestwick is one of the oldest burghs (it was never, as some people claim, a royal burgh) in Scotland, having been granted its original burgh charter in the late 12th century. However, some people put it even earlier than that, claiming it was founded in the late 10th century. It was also one of the most popular holiday resorts for Glaswegians until Spain and Florida took over, and has a long, sandy beach.

To the north of the town is **Prestwick International Airport**, at one time the main transatlantic airport for Glasgow. It is still a busy place, being a favourite starting point for those holidays in warmer climes that eventually saw off Prestwick as a holiday resort. On March 3rd 1960, the airport - or rather the American air force base (now gone) attached to it - had possibly its most famous visitor - **Elvis Presley**. Having been discharged from the American army, his plane touched down at the airport for refuelling when he was returning home from Germany. He stayed for just under an hour, phoned his 16 year old wife-to-be Priscilla in Frankfurt, and then re-boarded the flight. It was the only time that "The King" ever set foot in Britain. A plaque in the modern airport commemorates his visit, and people still turn up from all over Europe to pay their respects. In later life, someone asked Elvis what

country he would like to visit, and he replied that he would like to go back to Scotland, possibly because he also had Scottish ancestors.

The name Prestwick means "priest's burgh", and the ruins of the ancient **Parish Church of St Ninian** are near the coastline. At **Kingcase** was a lazar house where Robert the Bruce went to seek a cure for his leprosy. **Bruce's Well** can still be seen there.

MONKTON

4 miles N of Ayr on the A79

Traffic between Glasgow and Ayr used to thunder through Monkton, but now it is more or less bypassed. It sits on the edge of Prestwick Airport, and at one time the main road cut right across the main runway. This meant that traffic was held up every time an aircraft took off or landed - a magnificent site, but inconvenient for cars and buses.

The ruins of 13th century **St Cuthbert's Church** sit at the heart of the village, and at one time the Reverend Thomas Burns, Robert Burns's nephew, was minister here. His daughter lies in the old graveyard (see also Haddington and Thornhill). A church has certainly stood here since 1227, when it is mentioned in a charter of Walter, Bishop of Glasgow, as belonging to Paisley Abbey. In 1834 Monkton parish was united with Prestwick, and a new church was built in Prestwick to serve both communities.

William Wallace, it is said, once fell asleep in the church, and had a dream in which an old man presented him with a sword and a young woman presented him with a wand. He took it to mean that he must continue his struggle for Scotland's freedom. A plaque unveiled in 2005 commemorates the event.

The **Muckle Stane** is an "erratic" (a boulder brought by an ice flow towards the end of the last Ice Age), and previously stood in a field outside the village. In 1998 it was relocated within the village.

To the north of the village is a curious monument known as **MacRae's Monument**. It commemorates James MacRae, Governor of Madras in the early 18th century. He was born in 1670 in Ochiltree, a few miles inland from Monkton, in humble circumstances, his father having died before he was born. He was then brought up by a carpenter called Hugh McGuire, and when MacRae returned from India in 1731 a rich man he bought the Orangefield estate (which stood where part of Prestwick Airport now stands). He also found his old benefactor living in poverty. He bought him the estate of Drumdow at Stair, east of Monkton, and introduced his daughters into polite society, each of them making good marriages - one of them even becoming the Countess of Glencairn. MacRae was buried in the churchyard at Monkton, though no stone now marks his grave. A curious tale tells of a gravedigger who once inadvertently dug up MacRae's coffin in the 19th century,

and stripped it of its lead. However, the silver plaque on the coffin lid he gave to the authorities in Ayr.

TROON

6 miles N of Ayr, on the A759

This seaside resort is synonymous with golf, and the British Open has been held here many times. It's name derived from the Old Welsh word "trwyn", and indeed the local pronunciation of the name is "Trin". It is a young town, having been laid out in the early 1800s by the 4th Duke of Portland, who wished to create a harbour from which to export the coal from his Ayrshire coalfields. At one time the Duke wanted to construct a canal between Troon and Kilmarnock, eight miles inland, to carry the coal to the port. Instead he built a railway, and the town formed the western terminus of Scotland's earliest rail line, the **Troon/ Kilmarnock Railway**, which was opened in 1812. In 1816 the Duke introduced a steam locomotive onto the line, and it started pulling passenger trains (see also Kilmarnock). The town is now the Scottish terminal for the Scotland/ Ireland P&O express ferry service.

On the shoreline is the **Ballast Bank**, created over the years by ships which were allowed to discharge their ballast there before taking on coal for Ireland. The Duke himself encouraged the dumping of ballast, as the resultant hill protected the harbour from the prevailing southwest winds. Behind Troon a narrow road climbs up into

•

The estate of Ladykirk is to be found a few miles east of Monkton. It was here, in Ladykirk Chapel (which has all but vanished), that Robert II (the first Stewart king) married his first wife, Elizabeth Mure of Rowallan, in 1346. It was a marriage that some people considered unlawful, as the couple were related. They had also had many children before the wedding took place. But later in the year Pope Clement VI declared them lawfully married. Though Elizabeth was the wife of Robert II, she was never Queen of Scots, as she died before her husband ascended the throne. From the union came Robert III, Robert II's successor, and the long line of Stewart kings (see also Dundonald).

•

55	THE POSTAGE STAMP

Troon

A friendly pub in Troon with a golfing theme and serving good honest, pub food and a wide selection of drinks.

❦ see page 447

On a hillside to the west of the village of Symington, at a spot called Barnweil, is the Victorian Barnweil Monument, looking for all the world like a church tower without a church. This marks the spot where Wallace watched the "barns o' Ayr burn weel" after he set fire to them. Next to it are the scant ruins of Barnweil Church, where John Knox once preached. The parish of Barnweil was suppressed in 1673, and the church, which may have been one of the oldest in Ayrshire, gradually became ruinous.

the **Dundonald Hills**, from where a magnificent view of the Firth of Clyde can be obtained.

SYMINGTON

6 miles N of Ayr off the A77

Symington is a pleasant village of old cottages, though a large estate of council housing on its northern edge has somewhat marred the effect.. It is named after its Norman founder, Simon Lockhart, and at its heart is **Symington Parish Church**, Ayrshire's oldest church still in use. This Norman building, formerly dedicated to the Holy Trinity, was originally built about 1160, and has in its east wall a trio of delightful Norman windows. It has its original piscina in the south wall, and an ancient timbered roof. Over the years since

the Reformation the church had been altered and expanded, and it was only in 1919 that it was restored, as far as possible, to its original state. During the 1919 restoration, the supposed bones of Simon Lockhart were uncovered beneath the chancel, and reburied. A simple incised cross now marks the spot.

DUNDONALD

8 miles N of Ayr on the B730

Dundonald Castle (Historic Scotland) is one of Scotland's royal castles, and sits on a high hill overlooking the village. The hill has been occupied for at least 3,000 years, and has been the site of at least three medieval castles. What you see nowadays are the remains of the third castle, built in the 14th century by Robert II, grandson of Robert the Bruce and the first Stewart king of Scotland, to mark his accession to the throne in 1371. It was here, in his favourite residence, that Robert died in 1390. When Boswell and Dr Johnson visited the castle in 1773 during their Scottish journey, Johnson was much amused by the humble home of "Good King Bob". Though it may have looked humble to him in the 18th century when it was a crumbling ruin, in the 14th and 15th century it was anything but humble. All we see today is a single strong tower, but at its height it had outer defences, a surrounding wall with towers, stables, a brew house, quarters for troops, all surrounded by the humble dwellings of workmen and servants.

Dundonald Castle

When Robert II was in residence, it must have been even more imposing. The royal standard would have flown from its highest point, banners would have fluttered from the walls and troops would have been billeted in tents at the base of the hill. Scottish kings, unlike their English counterparts, constantly travelled throughout their realm accompanied by a huge entourage. One of the most important items carried about was the royal bed, which was dismantled and hauled up the castle walls and in through the window of the royal chamber when the king stopped anywhere. It would have been in this royal bed that Robert II died (see also Monkton).

Over the years, the castle has been owned by many families other than the Stewarts, including the Wallaces and the Cochranes, who later became Earls of Dundonald.

At the top, now reached by a metal staircase, are what would have been the royal apartments, and it is here that Robert II no doubt died. There are fine views northwards and eastwards over central Ayrshire.

TARBOLTON

6 miles NE of Ayr on the B744

When Burns stayed at nearby **Lochlee Farm** (not open to the public) both he and his brother Gilbert looked to the small village of Tarbolton for leisure activities. In 1779 they took dancing lessons (much to their father's disapproval) in a thatched 17th century house in Sandgate Street, and in 1780 founded a debating society within it as well. This house is now the **Bachelors' Club** (National Trust for Scotland). Round the fireplace in the upper room you'll see a helical pattern drawn in chalk - an old Ayrshire custom to prevent the Devil from entering the house by way of the chimney.

The farm of Lochlee (also known as Lochlea) sat beside a now drained loch to the west of the village, and had poor soil. When Burns's father died in 1784, the family moved to Mossgiel near Mauchline. In 1779 Burns wrote *The Tarbolton Lassies*, which praises the young women of the village.

Tarbolton Parish Church is an elegant, imposing building of 1821 standing on a low hill. It was designed by Robert Johnston

MAUCHLINE

10 miles NE of Ayr on the A76

When Burns's father died at Lochlee near Tarbolton, the Burns family moved to **Mossgiel Farm** to the north of the village of Mauchline. The farm that Burns knew is no more, but its successor still stands, with its farmhouse looking considerably more prosperous than the one Burns knew. It was in Mauchline that he met Jean Armour, his future wife, and it was here that they first settled down. Jean lived in a house (now gone) in the Cowgate, daughter to a prosperous stone mason who, not surprisingly, originally disapproved of Jean being courted by a penniless, failed farmer with a reputation for

The Parish Church you see today in Mauchline is not the one that Burns knew. The old Norman church of St Michael was pulled down and rebuilt in 1826, though the kirkyard still has many graves connected with the poet (including the graves of four of his children). A chart on the church wall explains where each one is. One to look out for is that of William Fisher of Montgarswood Farm (now East Montgarswood). William was an elder in Mauchline Kirk, and the butt of Burns's satirical poem Holy Willie's Prayer, in which he attacks the cant and hypocrisy of the church. Willie asks God's forgiveness for his own, understandable sins, while asking that he severely punish the sins of others. In 1790 William was called before the Mauchline minister to be rebuked for drunkenness, and in 1809 was found dead in a snow-filled ditch.

56   POOSIE NANSIE'S INN

Mauchline

One of Scotland's most historic inns, right in the heart of Mauchline, selling great food and drink.

❚   see page 448

•

To the north of the village of Mauchaline is the Burns Memorial, built in 1897. It is a tall, red sandstone tower with a small museum inside. From the top, you get good views of the rich agricultural lands of Ayrshire. Beside the memorial, and forming part of it, are some pleasant alms houses for old people.

•

womanising. So much so that Jean's mother packed Jean off to her uncle in Paisley, even though the couple had signed a marriage pact that was legal under Scots law of the time. Not only that - she was pregnant.

But eventually the Armours bowed to the inevitable, and Jean and Robert set up home in Castle Street (which at that time was the main street of the village and was called Back Causeway). Their home now houses the **Burns House Museum**. The red sandstone building actually had four families living in it in the 18th century, but it has now been converted so that various displays and exhibitions can be accommodated. Robert and Jean's apartment has been furnished in much the same way as it would have been in 1788 when they moved in. Across from it, but now a private house, was what is now called **Nance Tinnock's Inn**, but in Burns's day was the Sma' Inn. It was Burns's favourite drinking place, and was built in 1712.

Burns lived in Mauchline from 1784 until 1788, when he and his family moved to Dumfriesshire. The four years were the most productive in his life, and to his time in Mauchline we owe *To a Mountain Daisy, To a Mouse, Holy Willie's Prayer* and *The Holy Fair*. But it was also troubled times for him financially, and while trying to eke a living from the poor soil of Mossgiel, he contemplated emigrating to Jamaica. However, the success of his first book of verse, now called the

Kilmarnock Edition, made him change his mind. It also, to some extent, softened the Armours' opinion of him.

Opposite the parish church is **Poosie Nansy's Inn** (see panel). Though not a great frequenter of this inn, the poet still drank there occasionally, and Burns enthusiasts can still drink there today.

Gavin Hamilton was Burns's friend and landlord. His house can still be seen, attached to the 15th century **Abbot Hunter's Tower**. The tower looks like a small castle, but was in fact the monastic headquarters, or grange, of the Ayrshire estates owned by Melrose Abbey. Attached to it is the former home of Gavin Hamilton, Burns's friend and landlord (not open to the public).

The **Ballochmyle Viaduct**, to the south of the village, carries the Glasgow to Dumfries line across the River Ayr, and is considered to be one of the finest railway bridges in the world. Work started on it in 1843, and it is still Britain's highest stone and brick railway bridge, being 163 feet above the river. It has three smaller arches at either end, and one long, graceful arch in the middle that spans 181 feet. One of the main scenes from the film *Mission Impossible* was filmed there with Tom Cruise, though in the film it was supposed to be on the London to Paris line. During the First World War a pilot is supposed to have flown under the main arch.

The **Ballochmyle** estate, which stood to the south of the village, is no more. Up until recently it was the site of a hospital, but even that has been pulled down. When Burns first came to Mauchline it was owned by the Whitefoords, who lost everything when the Douglas Heron Bank of Ayr collapsed in 1773. They eventually sold it to Colonel Claud Alexander and his family to pay off their huge debts.

Burns had been used to wandering the Ballochmyle estates, which sit on the banks of the River Ayr, and one day in about 1786 when he was strolling along the banks, he saw Miss Wilhelmina Alexander, Claud's sister. He was so taken by her that he wrote *The Lass o' Ballochmyle*, one of his most famous works, in her honour. He sent it to her, but so angry was she that she never replied. However, the anger was more to do with the fact that she was in her 40s at the time, and thought that Burns was having a joke at her expense. In later years however, she cherished the poem, and died, unmarried, in 1843.

FAILFORD

7 miles E of Ayr on the B743

Near this little village, in 1786, Burns took his farewell of Highland Mary, who would die soon after in Greenock (see also Greenock and Dunoon). Burns, disillusioned by his treatment at the hands of Jean Armour's parents, had asked her to accompany him to Jamaica. They exchanged Bibles, which was seen as a marriage contract, and Mary set off home to Dunoon to prepare for the voyage. However, en route she died in Greenock. The **Failford**

Monument, on a slight rise, commemorates the meeting.

The guide centre for the **River Ayr Way,** a long-distance footpath that follows the course of the River Ayr from its source at Glenbuck to the sea for 41 miles, is within the village.

OCHILTREE

11 miles E of Ayr on the A70

Ochiltree was the birthplace of yet another Ayrshire writer, **George Douglas Brown**, who was born here in 1869, the illegitimate son of a local farmer and a serving girl. He attended both Glasgow and Oxford University and went on to write *The House with the Green Shutters*, a hard, unrelenting book about life in Scotland in the late 19th century. He wanted to banish the "kailyard school" of writing, which saw Scotland's countryside as being comfortable and innocent, full of couthy, happy people of unquestionable worth. He set his book in the fictional town of "Barbie", which is a thinly disguised Ochiltree, and not many characters in the book have redeeming features. Brown died in London in 1902 aged just 33, and was buried in Ayr.

One of the village's cottages (not open to the public) now has green shutters, and is itself known as the "House with the Green Shutters".

AUCHINLECK

13 miles E of Ayr off the A76

Though born in Edinburgh, **James Boswell** was the son of a Court of

A mile east of Failford, in a field, are the remains of a tumulus known as King Cole's Grave. Legend tells us that Old King Cole of nursery rhyme fame was a real person - a British king called Coel or Coilus, who ruled in Ayrshire. In the Dark Ages, he fought a great battle against the Scots under their king, Fergus. Cole's army was routed, and he fled the battlefield. Eventually he was captured and killed. His supporters later cremated his body and buried it with some pomp at the spot where he died (see also Coylton). The Kyle area of Ayrshire is supposed to be named after him. The tumulus was opened in 1837, and some cremated bones were discovered in two small urns. Up until not so long ago the nearby stream was referred to locally as the "Bloody Burn", and one field beside the stream was known as "Deadmen's Holm", as that is where those killed in the battle were supposedly buried. Tales were often told of bits of human bone and armour being turned up by men ploughing the field.

Alexander Peden was born at Auchincloich near Sorn in 1626. Known as Prophet Peden, he was a Covenanter who held secret conventicles, or prayer meetings, at lonely spots all over central Ayrshire. The whole area abounds with places that have been named after him, such as "Peden's Pulpit", "Peden's Cave" and "Peden's Table". There is even a field called "Preaching Peden". He died in 1686, and was buried in Auchinleck. However, the local military exhumed his body, intending to hang it from the local gallows in Cumnock. Common sense intervened in the guise of the Earl of Dumfries, and instead the body was buried at the foot of the gallows. A cemetery grew up around the grave, and a memorial, which can still be seen, was erected to his memory (see also Cumnock).

Session judge who lived in **Auchinleck House**, near what became the mining village of Auchinleck. He had the house built in about 1760 as his country seat, and Boswell brought the great Dr Johnson there to meet him when the pair were touring Scotland. They didn't hit it off.

The building is now owned by the Landmark Trust, and it is possible to book a short holiday in the house. Boswell himself died in 1795, and now lies in a small mausoleum attached to the old **Auchinleck Kirk**, which is no longer used for worship, but instead houses a museum dedicated to the writer and biographer.

SORN

14 miles E of Ayr on the B743

Sorn is one of the most picturesque villages in the county, and has won national and international awards for its tidiness and well kept gardens. It sits on the River Ayr, with an 18th century bridge spanning it, and has many delightful cottages. **Sorn Parish Church** dates from 1658, and the lofts, or galleries, are reached by stairs on the outside of the walls. **Sorn Castle** dates from the 14th century, with later additions. It was built by a branch of the Hamilton family, and James VI once visited on horseback in the depths of winter to attend the wedding of Isobel Hamilton, the daughter of his Treasurer, to Lord Seton. James VI's journey to Sorn so sickened him that he later said that if he were to play a trick on the devil, he would send him from

Glasgow to Sorn on a cold winter's day (see also Kilmarnock). It is open to the public in July and August between 2pm - 4pm.

CUMNOCK

15 miles E of Ayr off the A76

Cumnock is a small industrial town which was granted its burgh charter in 1509. In the middle of its square sits **Cumnock Old Parish Church**, built in the mid 1800s. It's a foursquare building that seems to sprout transepts, apses and porches in all directions. Two miles west of the town, at Lugar, is **Bello Mill** (not open to the public), birthplace in 1754 of William Murdoch, discoverer of gas lighting and, surprisingly, the man who invented the wooden top hat. He conducted his gas experiments in a cave on the banks of the Lugar Water, upstream from Bello.

Dumfries House (not open to the public), one mile west of Cumnock, was designed for the 4th Earl of Dumfries in the mid 1700s by John and Robert Adam. It is said that James Armour, Robert Burns's father-in-law, was one of the masons who worked on the building of the house.

At the north end of the town is the house that **James Keir Hardie**, the founder of the Scottish Labour Party, built for himself. Though born in Lanarkshire, he considered himself to be a Cumnock man. He was first of all MP for West Ham in London, and later for Merthyr Tydfil in Wales. His bust can be found outside the Town Hall.

Within the town cemetery is a

monument above the grave of the Covenanter Alexander Peden, known as "Prophet Peden" (see also Sorn).

MUIRKIRK

23 miles E of Ayr on the A70

This former mining and iron-working town is surrounded by bleak but still lovely moorland. It has many links with the Covenanters, and to the west is the site of the **Battle of Airds Moss**, fought in 1680 and marked by a memorial. Here a Covenanting army was heavily defeated by Government troops. The **Heritage Layby**, on the west side of the town on the A70, commemorates the battle and three Covenanters shot dead by Government troops - William Adam, John Smith and John Brown.

Just south of the town, and along an unmarked road, is a small monument to John Loudon McAdam the road builder, who owned a tar works in the vicinity. A mile-long canal was dug here in 1789, which served the former iron works (see also Ayr, Moffat and Carsphairn). The town claims to have been the first in Scotland to have gas lighting, and the last to have its own gas works.

Several walks have been laid out round the town, including the two mile **John Brown's Walk**, the two and a half mile **Old Railway Walk**, the 3 mile **Twa Brigs Walk**, the six and a quarter mile **Cairntable Walk** and the seventeen and a half mile **Sanquhar Walk**, which goes over moorland to

Sanqhar in Dumfriesshire.

Four miles east of the town is **Glenbuck**, a former mining village. It was here that Bill Shankly, possibly the greatest football manager of all time, was born in 1913. The local football team had possibly the most delightful name of any team in Britain - the Glenbuck Cherrypickers.

NEW CUMNOCK

18 miles E of Ayr on the A76

The parish of New Cumnock was carved from the much older parish of Cumnock in 1650, with a church being built on the site of Cumnock Castle, once owned by the Dunbars, and once visited by Edward II of England during his campaign to subjugate Scotland. The ruins of this church can still be seen. It was near the village that the **Knockshinnoch Mining Disaster** took place in 1950. 129 miners were trapped underground when a slurry of mud and peat filled some workings that were close to the surface. 116 were eventually brought out alive, and great bravery was shown by the rescuers. A feature film, *The Brave Don't Cry*, was made about the disaster in 1952, and starred John Gregson and Fulton MacKay. To the south of the village is **Glen Afton**, through which flows the Afton Water. A cairn marks the spot where Burns was inspired to write *Flow Gently Sweet Afton*.

DALRYMPLE

5 miles SE of Ayr on the B7034

In this quiet little village of

59 MINISHANT INN

Minishant

The Minishant Inn is a
traditional village pub that
offers the very best in
Scottish food and drink.

see page 451

•

*Two miles south of
Dalrymple, and straight
out of a fairy tale as
well, is Cassillis Castle
(not open to the public),
the home of the Marquis
of Ailsa, head of Clan
Kennedy, whose former
home, Culzean Castle,
was given to The
national Trust for
Scotland. It is a
wonderful concoction of
pepper pot turrets and
towers built originally in
the 15th century but
added to throughout the
years. It is here that the
hanging of Johnny Faa
from the Dule Tree is
supposed to have taken
place. (see also Maybole).*

•

weavers' cottages Burns first
received an education. While
staying at Mount Oliphant, he and
his brother Gilbert attended the
Parish School on alternate weeks.
The village sits on the Doon, and
has a small **Parish Church** built in
1849.

Some people say it was the
inspiration for the musical *Brigadoon*,
about a mysterious Scottish village
that only appears every 100 years.
Alan Jay Lerner, who wrote the
words, was looking for a way of
turning a German fairy tale about a
magical village called *Germelshausen*
into a musical, and one day while in
Scotland he suddenly happened
upon Dalrymple, which sits in a
small glen, hidden until you're
almost upon it. He immediately
thought of locating his musical in
Scotland, and called it Brigadoon
because of the bridge over the
River Doon in the village. He also
called one of the characters Charlie
Dalrymple.

ALLOWAY

2 miles S of Ayr town centre on the B7024

Robert Burns was not the
uneducated "ploughman poet"
from the peasant classes that his
more romantic admirers would
have us believe. His father was a
tenant farmer, and although not
well off, still managed to employ
workmen, dairymen, ploughmen
and serving girls on his farm.

Burns himself was a highly
educated man for his time, thanks
to his far-sighted father. He knew
his Classics, he could speak French
and some Latin, he could read and

write music, he took dancing
lessons, and he could play both the
fiddle and, surprisingly, the guitar.
When he went to Edinburgh in
later life, he was possibly better
educated than some of the gentry
who patronised him. Two of his
sons, James Glencairn Burns and
W. Nicol Burns, attained the ranks
of Lieutenant Colonel and Colonel
respectively in the British Army.

At one time, Alloway was a
small country village. Now it forms
part of Ayr, and is full of large,
impressive houses and villas which
illustrate the relative affluence of
this part of Ayrshire. It was here, in
1759, that Robert Burns was born
in a cottage that his father built
with his own hands. Now **Burns
Cottage** is a place of pilgrimage,
and people come from all over the
world to pay their respects. Within
the grounds of the cottage is the
Burns Museum, containing many
of his manuscripts, letters and
possessions.

The cottage was not always so
well maintained. When John Keats
made his pilgrimage to Burns's
birthplace in 1818 he found it had
been turned into an alehouse, and
was unimpressed by the
"mahogany-faced old jackass" who
showed him round.

Alloway Kirk is where Robert's
father, William Burns, lies buried,
and it was the main setting for the
poem *Tam o' Shanter*. It dates from
the early 16th century, but even in
Burns's day it was a ruin, though
part of its roof was still in place.
Across the road, within some
beautiful gardens, is the Grecian

Burns Monument, built in the 1820s. Inside is a small museum.

Across the road from Alloway Kirk is the **Tam o' Shanter Experience**, a visitor centre with two audiovisual shows within its large auditorium. One illustrates Burns's life and times, and the other re-creates what happened to Tam o' Shanter after he left the inn in Ayr and made his fateful ride south to his home in Turnberry.

East of Alloway is **Mount Oliphant Farm** (not open to the public) to which Burns and his family moved when he was seven years old.

ST QUIVOX

2 miles NE of Ayr just off the A77

The tiny **Parish Church** is a small gem of a building. Though altered beyond recognition over the years, its basic fabric is still medieval, and it takes its name from a shadowy Celtic saint called variously St Kevock, St Kennocha, St Kenochis, St Cavocks and St Evox. It was restored by Lord Cathcart of Auchincruive - and no doubt altered to suit Protestant services - in 1595.

To the east is **Oswald Hall**, designed by Robert Adam for James Oswald in 1767. It is now a conference centre. The surrounding Auchincruive estate is one of the campuses of the Scottish Agricultural College.

KILMARNOCK

Though it is largely an industrial town, Kilmarnock was granted its burgh charter in 1592, so its roots go deep into Scottish history. Legend says it grew up around a church founded by St Marnock, a Celtic saint, in the 7th century. The present **Laigh Kirk** (now called The Laigh West High Kirk) in Bank Street dates from 1802. It has a 17th century steeple (a date stone on it says 1410, but this is inaccurate), and is supposed to stand on the site of an earlier church. In 1801, during a service, 29 people were trampled to deaths when plasterwork started falling off the ceiling of this kirk, causing a mad rush for the doors. When it was rebuilt, it was given 13 exits in case it ever happened again. The town's other old church is the **Old High Kirk**, which dates from the early 1730s.

Kilmarnock has many Burns associations, and the first edition of his poems was published in the town, at Star Inn Close (now gone) in 1786. Now a copy is worth many thousands of pounds. A stone marking the spot can be found in the small shopping mall. Also in the mall is a stone marking the spot where Covenanting martyr **John Nesbit** was executed in 1683. His grave can be seen in the kirkyard of the Laigh and West High Kirk.

In truth, Kilmarnock's shopping centre, notably Kilmarnock Cross and King Street, is dull and unattractive, due to uninspired modern planning. But if you go down Cheapside towards Bank Street and the narrow streets round the Laigh and West High Kirk, you get an idea of what the

Spanning the Doon in Alloway is the graceful Brig o' Doon, a single arched bridge dating from the 15th century or possibly earlier. It was across the Brig o' Doon that Tam o' Shanter was chased by the witches he disturbed in Alloway Kirk. However, he managed to gain the keystone of the bridge and escaped unharmed, as witches cannot cross running water, even though his horse lost its tail. In Burn's day it lay on the main road south into Carrick, but a newer, wider bridge now carries traffic south.

Burns Statue, unveiled in the mid 1990s by the Princess Royal, stands at Kilmarnock Cross. It is the work of Sandy Stoddard, whose other works include the statue of David Hume on Edinburgh's Royal Mile and the sculptured friezes in the Queen's Gallery in Buckingham Palace.

Dean Castle

•

One place not to be missed in Kilmarnock is the Dick Institute, the town's museum, art gallery and library. It is housed in a grand classical building, and has large collections featuring geology, archaeology, biology and local history. The gallery is also impressive, with paintings by Corot, Constable, Turner and Kilmarnock's own painter, Robert Colquhoun. The area around the Dick Institute is particularly attractive, with a war memorial, Victorian houses, and the richly decorated façade of the old technical college, now converted into flats. Across from the Dick Institute is the statue of Kilmarnock's own Dick Whittington - James Shaw (known affectionately in the town as "Jimmy Shaw") who became Lord Mayor of London in 1805.

18th century town looked like.

It was in a shop in King Street that Johnnie Walker first started bottling and selling whisky in 1820. The man himself lies in the kirk yard of St Andrew's Glencairn Church (no longer used for worship) to the south of the town centre, and his statue can be found in the Strand.

To the north east of the town centre is the town's oldest building, **Dean Castle**. It was the home of the Boyd family, who became Earls of Kilmarnock, and is in fact two castles within a curtain wall - the 14th century Keep and the later Palace. Both are open to the public, and house wonderful collections of tapestries, musical instruments and armour. Surrounding it is **Dean Castle Country Park** with many walks and a small children's zoo.

The Boyd family rose to become the most important family in Scotland in the 1460s, when Sir Robert Boyd became Regent of Scotland. In 1746 the last earl was beheaded in London for fighting alongside Charles Edward Stuart at

Culloden, and all his lands and titles were forfeited, even though his son and heir fought for the Hanovarians in the same battle.

During his trial in London, his young wife, the Countess of Kilmarnock, stayed at the Boyd's other residence in the town - Kilmarnock House (now gone). Daily she walked its grounds, awaiting news of his fate. These grounds are now the **Howard Park**, which has a tree lined avenue known as **Lady's Walk**. The Countess herself died shortly after her husband, and some people say that her ghost still haunts the park (see also Falkirk).

Kilmarnock Academy, which stands on an eminence overlooking the town centre, is said to be one of the few schools in the world that has produced two Nobel Prize winners - Lord Boyd Orr (see also Kilmaurs) and Sir Alexander Fleming (see also Darvel).

Across from the new sheriff court building near the park is the **Old Sheriff Court** of 1852, an attractive building in neoclassical style. It sits on the site of one of the termini of Scotland's first railway, the Troon/Kilmarnock Railway, built by the Duke of Portland in 1812 (see also Troon). Two miles west of the town is the **Gatehead Viaduct**, built in 1807 to take the railway over the River Irvine. Though it no longer carries a railway line, it is still Scotland's oldest railway bridge.

Though Elderslie in Renfrewshire seems a likelier location, there are those who claim that **William Wallace** was born at Ellerslie, west of Riccarton, a suburb of Kilmarnock (and named after Sir Richard Wallace, a relation of William). There was certainly a Wallace castle in the area, and young William is known to have had his first skirmish with English troops on the banks of the River Irvine within the town. Definitely born in Kilmarnock in 1769, however, was Ensign Charles Ewart, who captured the eagle and standard of the French 45th Regiment of the Line at the Battle of Waterloo in June 1815. He now lies buried on the esplanade of Edinburgh Castle (see also Edinburgh).

Kilmarnock is the home town of **William McIlvanney** the novelist, **Stewart Conn** the playwright and poet, **Alexander Smith** the Victorian writer and **Kirsty Wark** the television political commentator.

In 1862, at Crosshouse, a mining village west of Kilmarnock, was born **Andrew Fisher**, who rose to become Prime Minister of Australia on three separate occasions.

A few miles north of Kilmarnock, on the A77 (now bypassed by a motorway) is the farm of Kingswell. It was here, in the late 16th century, that James VI stopped to drink the waters of the well that once stood here. He was on his way to Sorn Castle to attend a wedding in the middle of winter, and found the journey harrowing (see also Sorn).

AROUND KILMARNOCK

CRAIGIE

3 miles S of Kilmarnock on an unmarked road

This small village has a church dating from 1776. The ruins of the 15th century **Craigie Castle** lie to the south of the village, and has the remains of a fine vaulted hall. It was built for the Wallace family, of which William was the most notable member.

FENWICK

4 miles N of Kilmarnock off the A77

Fenwick (pronounced "Fennick") is really two villages - High Fenwick and Laigh ("Low") Fenwick. They lie on the edge of the Fenwick Moors, which separate the farmlands of Ayrshire from Glasgow and its suburbs, and were originally weaving villages. Some of the cottages still show their weaving origins, with two windows on one side of the door to allow plenty of light to enter the room containing the loom and one window on the other. **Fenwick Parish Church**, which dates from 1643, is an attractive whitewashed building with a Greek cross plan. On one wall hangs the original **jougs**, where wrongdoers were chained by their necks to the wall. It was from Fenwick that the ancestors of Edgar Allan Poe emigrated to America (see also Irvine and Saltcoats).

Fenwick was the birthplace, in 1803, of John Fulton, a shoemaker who gained considerable fame

60 CRAIGIE INN

Craigie

A real, olde worlde village inn that brings people from near and far to sample its marvellous cuisine and its well stocked bar.

see page 450

Two miles south east of Fenwick is the quaintly named, and often photographed, hamlet of Moscow (pronounced "Moss-cow" rather than "Moss-coe"), which actually has a burn called the Volga flowing through it.

St Maurs Glencairn Church in Kilmaurs dates from 1888, and replaced an earlier medieval collegiate church founded by the Cunningham family, Earls of Glencairn, who lived close by. Glencairn Aisle, the 16th century burial vault of the Earls of Glencairn, still stands to the rear of the church, however, and it has an ornate monument inside to the 7th Earl and his family. It dates from around 1600, and carries an inscription that reads nothing is surer than death, be therefore sober and watch in prayer.

It was in a farm near the village of Dunlop that the famous Dunlop cheese was first manufactured in the 17th century by a farmer's wife called Barbara Gilmour. It is made from the milk of Ayrshire cattle, and closely resembles a Cheddar. Barbara now lies buried in the kirkyard, and her grave can still be seen. Cheese making was recently revived in the village, and Dunlop cheese, which is harder than the original variety, is made by Dunlop Dairy.

throughout Scotland by making orreries - working models of the solar system where the planets revolve round the sun and satellites revolve round the planets, all synchronised by the use of gearing. Fulton built three such orreries, and one of them is still on show in the Kelvin Museum in Glasgow.

KILMAURS

2 miles NW of Kilmarnock, on the A735

Kilmaurs is a former weaving village, and though only a few fields separate it from Kilmarnock's suburbs, it is still a small, self-contained community with many small cottages. At its centre is the old 17th century **Tolbooth**, still with the jougs attached, which were placed round wrongdoers' necks as a punishment.

The village takes its name from St Maura, who died in AD 899, and was said to be the daughter of a Scottish chieftain on the island of Little Cumbrae in the Firth of Clyde. **John Boyd Orr**, first director of the United Nations Food and Agricultural Organisation and Nobel prize-winner, was born in Kilmaurs in 1880.

Kilmaurs Place (not open to the public) dates from the 17th century, and was built as a replacement for the earlier Kilmaurs Castle. It was the home of the Earls of Glencairn and later of the powerful Montgomery family.

STEWARTON

5 miles N of Kilmarnock on the A735

Stewarton is famous as being the home of bonnet making in

Ayrshire. It was the birthplace, in 1739, of **David Dale**, the industrialist and social reformer who founded New Lanark (see also Lanark). The **Parish Church of St Columba** dates originally from 1696, though it has been much altered.

DUNLOP

7 miles N of Kilmarnock on the A735

Dunlop is a delightful village of small weavers' cottages. The **Parish Church** dates from 1835, though it has fragments from the earlier church incorporated into the north aisle. In the kirkyard is the ornate early 17th century **Hans Hamilton Tomb**, contained within a small mausoleum. Hamilton was Dunlop's first Protestant minister, and was made Viscount Clandeboye by James VI. The small **Clandeboye Hall**, beside the mausoleum, dates from the 17th century, and was the village's first school.

It was in the farms surrounding the village that the now famous Ayrshire dairy cattle were first bred. Originally known as Dunlops, the name was later changed to Cunninghams and finally Ayrshires. The bye products of cheese making were fed to pigs, which then led to the production of the highly prized Ayrshire bacon.

GALSTON

4 miles E of Kilmarnock on the A71

This pleasant little town in the Irvine Valley has a splendid **Parish Church** dating from 1808. One of its ministers, Perthshire-born **Robert Stirling**, was the inventor of the Stirling Engine. He died in 1878.

Another church not to be missed is **St Sophia's RC Church**, modelled on the Hagia St Sophia in Istanbul. **Barr Castle** is a solid, 15th century tower house once owned by the Lockhart family. William Wallace is said to have taken refuge within the walls of a previous castle on the site in the 13th century, and when the English troops surrounded it he escaped by jumping from a window onto a tree. John Knox and George Wishart preached here in the 16th century. An ancient game of handball used to be played against its walls by the locals. The castle is now a small museum with many exhibits relating to local history.

To the north of the town are the impressive ruins of **Loudoun Castle**, ancestral home of the Campbells of Loudoun. It was burnt down in 1941, and in its time entertained so lavishly that it was called the "Windsor of Scotland". Three ghosts reputedly haunt it - a Grey Lady, a Phantom Piper and a Benevolent Monk. At one time the great sword of William Wallace was kept within the castle, but it was sold in 1930. Beside its walls is the **Auld Yew Tree**, under which Hugh, 3rd Earl of Loudoun, prepared the draft of the Treaty of Union between Scotland and England. Today the four-star **Loudoun Castle Theme Park** fills the grounds of the castle.

Loudoun Castle was the birthplace, in 1839, of **Lady Flora Hastings**, who shook the monarchy and government to its core. Flora was the daughter of the Countess of Loudoun and Sir Francis Rawdon. Queen Victoria was 20 years old at the time, and had been on the throne for just two years. Lady Flora was a Lady of the Bedchamber who contracted a disease which so swelled her abdomen that she appeared pregnant. Gossip raged through the court, and she was shunned, even though doctors whom she consulted confirmed that she was not pregnant but ill, and had an enlarged liver.

Neither the government nor the Queen did anything to dispel the rumours, and people began to sympathise with the young woman. Soon it was the Queen's turn to be shunned, and she was shocked when people turned their back on her as she proceeded through London by coach. It was not until Lady Flora was on her deathbed in 1833 in Buckingham Palace that a grudging reconciliation took place, though no apology was ever given. Members of Flora's immediate family were so incensed by Flora's treatment that when postage stamps were introduced bearing Victoria's image, they stuck them onto envelopes upside down, something which shocked the queen. They even printed their own stamps so that they would not have to look at the face of Queen Victoria. (see also Newmilns).

There is another side to this story, and a more intriguing one.

A mile or so away from Loudoun Castle are the ruins of the medieval Loudoun Kirk, at one time dedicated to St Michael. Flora now lies in the choir, which has been converted into a burial vault for the Campbells of Loudoun, and a slim monument stands in the kirkyard to her memory. Their coat-of-arms can still be seen on the choir walls, above the entrance to the vault. The church seems isolated today, but this was not always so. Up until just after the Second World War, a village stood here as well. However, the houses had no running water, electricity or sewage services, so were demolished, though the outlines of many gardens can still be seen. Attached to a wall of the ruined kirk is a plaque which commemorates the Belgian paratroopers who trained at Loudoun Castle during the Second World War.

During the American Civil War, the weavers of Newmilns sent a message of support to Abraham Lincoln, and he in turn sent back an American flag. This was subsequently lost, but in 1949 the American Embassy gave the town a replacement, which is now housed in the early 19th century Newmilns Parish Church in the main street.

To the east of the town of Darvel is the immense bulk of Loudoun Hill, the plug of a former volcano. A Roman fort was built here in about AD 60, and finally abandoned 100 years later. Nothing now remains of it due to sand and gravel excavations. Both William Wallace and Robert the Bruce fought battles at Loudoun Hill against the English, in 1297 and 1307 respectively.

For many centuries, rumours have circulated that Edward IV, who was born in France in 1442, the supposed son of Richard of York, was illegitimate, his mother Cecily having had what would now be called a "fling" with an English bowman. This meant that he had no right to the throne, and that the real heir was George, Duke of Clarence, a direct ancestor of Flora. In fact, even today some people claim that Flora's brother Lord Hastings should have been the rightful king of Great Britain.

Also in the graveyard is the grave of **Janet Little**, known as the "Scottish milkmaid". She was a poetess and friend of Burns, and died in 1813.

NEWMILNS

7 miles E of Kilmarnock on the A71

Newmilns is a small lace making and weaving town in the Irvine Valley, which was granted its charter in 1490, making it the oldest inland burgh in Ayrshire. The small crow stepped **Town House,** or Tolbooth, dates from 1739, and behind the Loudoun Arms, which itself dates from the 18th century, is **Newmilns Tower**, a tower house dating from 1530 and built by Sir Hugh Campbell, Earl of Loudoun. Sir Hugh was perhaps the most tragic member of the Campbell of Loudon family. After being involved in the murder of a member of the powerful Kennedy family during an ongoing feud, his wife and nine children were killed when the Kennedys besieged Loudoun Castle, now

focal point of the Loudoun Castle Theme Park.

The **Lady Flora Institute**, built in 1877 as a girl's school, commemorates the tragic Lady Flora Hastings, a lady-in-waiting to Queen Victoria (see also Galston). The institute has now been converted to private housing.

DARVEL

8 miles E of Kilmarnock, on the A71

Situated in the lovely Irvine Valley, Darvel is a small, attractive town which was laid out in the late 18th and early 19th centuries. Like its neighbour Newmilns, it is a lace making town, the skills having been brought here by the Dutch in the 17th century. It was in Lochfield, near Darvel, that **Sir Alexander Fleming**, the discoverer of penicillin, was born in 1881.

South of the town is the quaintly named **Distinkhorn**, at 1,266 feet the highest hill in the area.

IRVINE

7 miles W of Kilmarnock on the A71

Irvine is an ancient seaport and royal burgh which, in the 1960s, was designated as Britain's first seaside new town. It is a mixture of old and new, and has many unattractive industrial estates surrounding it. However, the historical core has been preserved, though a brutally modern shopping mall straddling the River Irvine dominates it., and cuts off what was once one of the best townscapes in Scotland. Robert Burns learned flax dressing in

Irvine in 1781, and lodged in a house in the cobbled **Glasgow Vennel**. A small museum has been created within both it and the heckling shop behind it.

Irvine has other, more unexpected, literary associations, however. In 1815 the American writer **Edgar Allan Poe** spent a couple of months in the town, attending the local school. It is said that part of his lessons was to copy the epitaphs from the tombstones in the kirkyard of the **Parish Kirk**, which may have prepared him for some of the macabre tales he wrote in later life (see also Saltcoats and Fenwick). Irvine was also the birthplace of the writer **John Galt**, a relative of the man who adopted Edgar Allan Poe in the United States. **Alexander MacMillan**, who, with his brother Daniel, founded the great publishing house in 1843, was also a native of the town.

The nearby village of **Dreghorn** can lay fair claim to be the oldest settlement in the United Kingdom, as a recent archaeological dig has discovered a continuous occupation of the site since at least 5500 BC. In it was born in 1840 yet another famous Ayrshireman - **John Boyd Dunlop**, who invented the pneumatic tyre. Born in 1840, he came from a farming background, and graduated from Edinburgh University as a veterinary surgeon, practising in Edinburgh and then Belfast. He found the roads of Ulster to be stony and rough, and eventually invented an inflatable tyre to overcome the discomfort of travelling along them. Unfortunately, unknown to him, another Scot, Robert William Thomson, had patented the idea before him, and only after a court case could he set up the Dunlop Rubber Company.

Dreghorn Parish Church, built in 1780, is unusual in that it is six-sided in plan. It was built by Archibald, the 11th Earl of Eglinton, and used to have the nickname of the "threepenny church", as its shape reminded people of the old threepenny bit.

The ruins of **Seagate Castle** date from the early 16th century, though a castle has stood on the site since at least the 12th century. It was a Montgomery stronghold, and it is said that Mary Stuart lodged here briefly in 1563. Every August the town has its **Marymass Week**, which supposedly commemorates her visit. However, the celebrations probably have more to do with a pre-Reformation religious festival, as the parish church was formerly dedicated to St Mary.

At the harbour side is the **Magnum Leisure Centre**, one of the biggest centres of its kind in Scotland. It has a theatre and concert hall, an indoor bowling green, an ice rink, swimming pool and fitness and coaching areas.

Near the Magnum Centre is one of the three sites of the **Scottish Maritime Museum** (see also Dumbarton and Glasgow). It houses a wide collection of ships and small craft. There's also the

In the 18th century, Irvine saw the founding of perhaps the most unusual religious cult ever seen in Scotland - the Buchanites. Elspet Buchan was the daughter of a publican, and claimed she could bestow immortality on a person by breathing on them, and that she herself was immortal. She attracted a wide following, including a gullible Irvine clergyman, but was hounded, along with her followers, from the town. She eventually died a natural death, and the cult broke up (see also Dunscore and Crocketford).

105

Linthouse Engine Works, which has a vast collection of maritime machinery, such as engines, winding gear and so on. In the Ship Worker's Tenement Flat, a typical "room and kitchen" flat dating from the 1920s has been re-created, showing how shipyard workers lived in those days. Visitors can also board the *Spartan*, one of the last puffers in Scotland. These small cargo boats, immortalised in the *Para Handy* tales by Neil Munro, sailed the west coast of Scotland for many years.

Irvine was the setting, in 1839, of the grand **Eglinton Tournament**, organised by the 13th Earl of Eglinton at his home,

Eglinton Castle, on the outskirts of the town. Here, a great medieval tournament was to be re-created, with jousting, horse riding and other knightly pursuits for the great and the good. They attended from all over Europe, but alas, the three-day event was a wash out due to colossal rainstorms. Little remains of the castle, but the grounds have been turned into **Eglinton Country Park**.

KILWINNING

9 miles NW of Kilmarnock on the A737

Though nowadays a continuation of Irvine, Kilwinning was, up until 1975, a separate burgh. Its former name was Segtoune, meaning the "saint's town", as it was founded in the 7th century by St Winnin, whom some people associate with St Finnan of Moville, who taught St Columba in Ireland. In the 12th century the great Tironensian **Kilwinning Abbey** was built on the site, and its ruins still dominate the town centre, though they are not as extensive as those of Ayrshire's other great abbey, Crossraguel. It was founded by Hugh de Morville, High Constable of Scotland and a relative of Richard de Morville, one of the murderers of Thomas à Becket at Canterbury. The tower you see nowadays was built in 1815, and replaced the original medieval one, which fell down the year before. The Ancient Society of Kilwinning Archers is one of the oldest archery organisations in the world, and each year in August it holds the **Papingo Shoot**, where archers shoot upwards at a target (the papingo) held from a window of the tower. The papingo

Kilwinning Abbey

is usually a wooden pigeon, and such shoots were once common throughout Britain. **Kilwinning Parish Church**, which sits within the ruins of the abbey, was built in 1775. The town is the home of Freemasonry in Scotland.

A few miles out of town, on the A737, is **Dalgarven Mill** (see panel), dating from about 1620. It is now a museum dedicated to country life in Ayrshire.

ARDROSSAN, SALTCOATS & STEVENSTON

11 miles W of Kilmarnock on the A78

These towns form a trio of holiday resorts on the Ayrshire coast. Ardrossan is the most industrialised, and is the ferry terminal for Arran. It is a planned town, with its core being laid out in the early 19th century by the 12th Earl of Eglinton. At one time it was also a ferry port for the Isle of Man, but as the Scots began to discover the delights of Spain as a holiday destination, the Isle of Man fell out of favour, and the sailings were suspended.

The ruins of 15th century **Ardrossan Castle**, once a stronghold of the Montgomeries, sit on Castle Hill overlooking the main streets. Cromwell is said to have plundered some of its masonry to build the Citadel at Ayr. The ruins and the land surrounding them were given to the town by the Earl of Eglinton as a public park. The **Obelisk** at the highest point on the hill commemorates a local doctor, Alexander McFadzean, who promoted piped water and gas

supplies in the town. At the foot of the hill stands **St Peter in Chains**, designed by Jack Coia, one of Scotland's best-known architects, and built in 1938. It is reckoned to be one of the finest modern churches in Ayrshire.

Just off the coast is **Horse Island**, an RSPB reserve. Though it looks peaceful enough, it has been the scene of many shipwrecks over the years, and many sailors have found themselves marooned on it after their ships struck its submerged reefs. At the **Clyde Marina** is a sculpture park featuring works by the Japanese artist Hideo Furuta, who lives and works in Scotland.

Ardrossan Docks, up until the 1930s, was one of the main supply ports for the Hudson Bay Company, and the harbour was crammed with ships loading supplies for North America and unloading furs, fish and sometimes animals.

Stevenston is a straggling town, with a **High Church** that dates from 1832. It has a good beach, though it is some way from the centre of the town. Nearby, at Ardeer, the British Dynamite Company, founded by the Swede Alfred Nobel of "Nobel Prizes" fame (and the inventor of dynamite), established a factory in 1873. It later became Nobel's Explosives Company, and in 1926 became part of ICI.

DALRY

11 miles NW of Kilmarnock on the A737

This small industrial town's square is dominated by the **Parish**

61   DALGARVEN MILL

Dalgarven

The mill offers an insight into 17th century flour production and historical displays of costumes and memorabilia add to the enjoyment.

 see page 451

At Saltcoats the North Ayrshire Museum, housed in a former church, has an interesting local history collection. A gravestone in the kirkyard may be that of an ancestor of Edgar Allan Poe (see also Irvine and Fenwick). The town has a fine beach, and its name is a reminder of the times when salt was produced here from seawater. The small harbour dates from the late 17th century with later alterations, and at low tide fossilised trees can be seen on the harbour floor. It was in Saltcoats, in 1793, that Betsy Miller, the only woman ever to have become a registered ship's captain, was born.

107

At the hamlet of Portencross, out on a headland beyond Seamill and West Kilbride, are the substantial ruins of 14th century Portencross Castle, another Boyd stronghold. Also on the headland is Hunterston Castle (not open to the public), ancestral home of Clan Hunter, and Hunterston Nuclear Power Station, opened in 1964 by Queen Elizabeth the Queen Mother. It has a visitor centre with displays on nuclear power.

Church of St Margaret, dating from the 1870s. The town's name comes from the Gaelic "Dal Righe", meaning the "King's Field", which shows that at one time it must have had royal connections. To the south east of the town is **Blair**, a large mansion centred on what was a typical Scottish tower house of the 12th century. The parkland, which surrounds it, was laid out by William Blair in the 1760s. It is the home of Clan Blair (the chief being known as "Blair of Blair"), who were supporters of both Bruce and Wallace. It was at one time the home of the daughter of the English King John, who had married William de Blare. Now the mansion, which has a five star rating from VisitScotland, can be hired as a venue for conferences and seminars.

BEITH

11 miles NW of Kilmarnock off the A737

Beith, whose name derives from the old Brythonic. or Welsh, word for "birch", is a small attractive town, and at 500 feet is the highest town in Ayrshire. The remains of the **Auld Kirk** date from the late 16th century, while the impressive **High Church** dates from the early 19th century. **Eglinton Street** is the most attractive part of the town, with small, neat two-storey buildings dating from the late 18th and 19th centuries.

KILBIRNIE

13 miles NW of Kilmarnock on the A760

Kilbirnie literally means the "kil" or "cell" of St Birinus or Birinie, a West Saxon monk who died at Dorchester in Dorset in AD 650. Within the town you'll find the **Barony Parish Church**, dating from the 15th century. Inside is some wonderfully exuberant woodwork from the 17th and 18th centuries, including the extravagant Crawford Loft and the Cunninghame Aisle. In the kirkyard is the **Crawford Mausoleum** of 1591, where, beneath recumbent carved images, lie the bodies of Captain Crawford and his wife. In medieval times the church was dedicated to St Brendan of Clonfert in Ireland. Standing next to the golf course are the ruins of the **Place of Kilbirnie**, a former castle of the Crawford family dating from the 15th century.

WEST KILBRIDE

16 miles NW of Kilmarnock off the A78

West Kilbride is a sedate village of Glasgow commuters, perched above its twin village of **Seamill**, on the coast. **Law Castle** was built in the 15th century for Princess Mary, sister of James III, on her marriage to Thomas Boyd of Kilmarnock, who became the Earl of Arran. However, the marriage was later annulled and he had to flee to the Continent, where he died in Antwerp. Mary eventually remarried, this time to James Hamilton, first Lord Hamilton, and the Earlship of Arran passed to their son.

Nicola Benedetti the young violinist was born in West Kilbride in 1987.

THE CUMBRAES

19 miles NW of Kilmarnock, in the Firth of Clyde

The two islands - **Little Cumbrae** and **Great Cumbrae** - were once in the county of Bute. Little Cumbrae is privately owned, but Great Cumbrae can be visited by a frequent ferry from Largs, the crossing taking only ten minutes.

The only town on the island is **Millport**, a small, attractive holiday resort with a unique feature - the **Cathedral of the Isles** (its proper name being the Cathedral of the Isles and Collegiate Church of the Holy Spirit), Britain's smallest cathedral. It is sometimes referred to as Europe's smallest, but this honour is held by an even smaller cathedral in Greece. Nevertheless it is a real gem, and was completed in 1851 as part of a theological complex funded by George Boyle, who later became the 6th Earl of Glasgow. In 1876 it became a cathedral. Its nave is 40 feet by 20 feet, and can only seat 100 people. It was designed by William Butterfield, who also designed Keble College, Oxford. The ceiling is painted with all the wild flowers found on the island.

On the eastern shore of the island, facing the mainland, is the **University Marine Biological Station**. It is an institution of both Glasgow and London Universities, and offers students research facilities, tuition in diving, and tuition in marine biology. It houses a museum, which is open to the public.

The **Museum of the Cumbraes** can be found at The Garrison, just off the seafront. There are exhibits and displays on Millport's heyday as one of the Clyde's most popular holiday resorts. In September of each year the **Millport Country and Western Festival** is held.

LARGS

19 miles NW of Kilmarnock on the A78

Largs is the epitome of the Ayrshire seaside town, though it has, surprisingly, no sandy beach. During the last fortnight in July, hordes of Glaswegians used to descend on places like this for their annual fortnight's holiday. These days are gone, but the towns themselves have adapted, and now cater for retired people and day-trippers. In fact, Largs is possibly the most popular retirement town in Scotland.

But it is still a lively, attractive place, and has the mainland terminal for the Cumbrae Ferry. It was south of here that the **Battle of Largs** took place in 1263, when the Scots defeated a force led by King Haakon IV of Norway and finally threw off the Norse yolk, at least on the western seaboard (see also Lerwick). A tall thin monument south of the town affectionately known as **The Pencil** commemorates the event.

Largs Museum, with its local history collection, is also worth a visit, as is the **Skelmorlie Aisle** (Historic Scotland). It was built in 1636, and sits in the old kirkyard in the centre of the town. It was built as a transept of the former medieval parish church. Within it is

Crocodile Rock is on the beach in Millport. It is, as the name suggests, a rock shaped like a crocodile's head, and it has been painted with eyes and teeth so that the crocodile features are even more evident. It is said that the rock got its name after a Millport town councillor, on leaving a pub where a council meeting had just finished, remarked that the rock on the foreshore resembled a crocodile.

Within the town of Largs you'll find the Vikingar Experience a museum and interpretation centre that explains the lifestyle and travels of the Vikings all these years ago. And each year in late June the town holds the Largs Viking Festival.

Skelmorlie Aisle, Largs

•

Kelburn Castle stands to the south of the townof Largs, overlooking the Firth of Clyde, of which it has spectacular views. It is the ancestral home of the Boyles, Earls of Glasgow, and parts of it date back to the 13th century. Its grounds are now a country park, with gardens, an adventure playground, woodland walks, a glen, a waterfall, a pet's corner and craft workshops.

•

the mausoleum of Sir Robert Montgomery of Skelmorlie and his wife, Dame Margaret Douglas. It is a Renaissance-style tomb with wonderful stone carving. **Sir Thomas Brisbane** (whose middle name was, unusually, Makdougall, with a "k"), was born in Largs in 1773. After a distinguished military career, he was appointed Governor of New South Wales in 1820, and gave his name to the city of Brisbane and the Brisbane River. There is also a crater on the moon named after him. He died in 1860, and lies in the Brisbane Vault next to Skelmorlie Aisle.

In the local cemetery is buried **Sir William Burrell**, shipping magnate and millionaire, who gave the Burrell Collection to the city of Glasgow in 1944 (see also Hutton).

ISLE OF ARRAN

Arran (13 miles and 55 minutes from Ardrossan by ferry) is called "Scotland in miniature", as it is mountainous in the north, low lying

in the middle and rises again towards the south. It is 19 miles long by about ten miles across at its widest, and within its 165 square miles it has history and spectacular scenery aplenty. This is an island of Celtic saints, mysterious standing stones, craft workshops, cairns and old castles. It was a Gaelic speaking island up until the early 19th century, though the place names owe as much to the language of the Norsemen who settled here in the 10th and 11th centuries as they do to Gaelic. In fact, **Brodick**, one of the main settlements, comes from the Norse for "broad bay".

The northern portion can be every bit as spectacular as the Highlands, and for those with the stamina, a climb to the summit of **Goat Fell**, at 2,866 feet the island's highest peak, is a must. There are two recognised routes to the top, with both routes eventually converging. Information on each can be had at the tourist office in Brodick.

Just north of Brodick is the **Arran Brewery**, which has a three-star visitor centre and shop. There are also viewing galleries where you can see the brewing processes. And at Home Farm, also near Brodick, is **Arran Aromatics**, Scotland's leading producer of body care products and scented candles. Again, you can watch the manufacturing processes from a viewing gallery.

Beneath Goat Fell, is **Brodick Castle** (National Trust for Scotland). This former Hamilton family stronghold (the Hamiltons became the Earls of Arran after the title was forfeited by the Boyds of Kilmarnock) sits in a wonderful location, surrounded by mature gardens and parkland reaching from the shoreline up into the hills behind the castle. During the summer months there are guided tours of the garden.

There has been a fortification of sorts here since the Dark Ages, and it is known that a Norse fort also stood on the site. The present building dates mainly from the 16th century and later, and inside there is a collection of paintings and furniture. In about 1844 the tenth Duke of Hamilton and his wife, Princess Marie of Baden, engaged on a building project that almost doubled the size of the castle.

North of Brodick, on the A841 is the beautiful village of **Corrie**, with its small harbour, whitewashed cottages and gardens aflame with colour in the summer months. It was here that the Scottish playwright Robert McLellan OBE lived from 1938 until his death in 1985 (see also Lanark).

The road from Corrie follows the coast north, then turns north west and goes through the bleak but extremely beautiful **Glen Chalmadale** before bringing you to **Lochranza** ("Loch of the rowan tree river"). On the shores of this small village are the imposing ruins of **Lochranza Castle** (Historic Scotland), built in the 16th century on the site of an earlier castle. It started life as a hunting lodge for the Scottish kings before passing first to the Campbells and then the

View to Goat Fell, Arran

Montgomeries, Earls of Eglinton. Surprisingly, the castle has associations with the Belgian writer and illustrator George Remi, who, as Hergé, wrote the Adventures of Tintin. The castle in *The Black Island* is supposed to be based on Lochranza Castle..

At the entrance to the village is the **Isle of Arran Whisky Distillery**, which has guided tours and a visitor centre which is open from March to October each year. In the summer months a small car ferry runs from Claonaig on the Mull of Kintyre to Lochranza, the crossing taking about 35 minutes.

Beyond Lochranza is the small village of **Catacol**, with a row of identical whitewashed cottages known as **The Twelve Apostles**. They were built in the 19th century to accommodate islanders cleared from Glen Catacol to make way for deer. From here you get a good view across to the Mull of Kintyre, which is only four miles away.

Further on, and inland from

On the northern outskirts of Brodick is the Isle of Arran Heritage Museum, which opens from April to October each year. It explains the history of the island and its people.

The Twelve Apostles, Arran

In Whiting bay sits the magnificent bulk of the 1,030 feet high Holy Island, so called because the Celtic St Molas lived a life of austerity here in the 6th and 7th centuries. The name Lamlash itself is a corruption of "Eilean Molaise", meaning Molas's Isle. Nowadays it has regained its religious significance, as it is home to a Tibetan Buddhist monastery and retreat. Boat trips to it leave from both Lamlash and Whiting Bay.

Machrie Bay, is the wonderful **Auchagallon Stone Circle**, a Bronze Age burial cairn with a circle of 15 upright slabs surrounding it. There are several ancient monuments in the area, including the **Machrie Moor Stone Circle** and the **Moss Farm Road Stone Circle**. It is said that this part of Arran has more stone circles per square mile than anywhere else in Scotland.

The magnificent cliffs at **Drumadoon** stand high above a raised beach, and are spectacular, with an old Iron Age fort atop them. Also here is the only 12-hole golf course in Scotland. The **King's Cave** is close to the shore, and is supposed to be the cave where Robert the Bruce saw his spider, (though many other places in Scotland and Ireland make a similar claim). Near the attractive village of **Blackwaterfoot**, south of Machrie Bay, a road called **The String** cuts across the centre of the

island towards Brodick. The village of **Shiskine**, on The String, has the lovely **St Molas Church**, with an ancient stone carving of the saint embedded in its wall. The **Balmichael Visitor Centre**, close to Shiskine, is within a converted mill complex, has speciality shops and facilities for various outdoor activities.

South of Blackwaterfoot the road continues on towards **Lagg**, and if you need convincing about the mildness of the climate hereabouts, the palm trees in the gardens of the Lagg Inn should do the trick. The **Torrylinn Creamery**, which makes traditional Dunlop cheese in the old fashioned way, has a viewing gallery and shop. The tiny island of **Pladda**, with its lighthouse of 1790, can be seen about a mile from the coast. The novel *Stargazing* by Peter Hill was inspired by the Pladda lighthouse. The road turns north once more towards **Whiting Bay**, another small village and holiday resort. At one time it was a fishing port, and it takes its name from the whiting that were caught in the bay. A splendid walk starts from south of the village towards **Glenashdale Falls** and the prehistoric burial cairns known as the **Giant's Graves. Lamlash** sits on Lamlash Bay.

Near Lamlash is **Arran Provisions**, the island's biggest employer. It makes a wide range of mustards, jams and preserves, and has a visitor centre and shop.

Glasgow & West Central Scotland

Glasgow and West Central Scotland was at one time the country's industrial hub. Heavy engineering, shipbuilding, coal mining and steelworks predominated, providing work for thousands and fortunes for the favoured few. As well as the city of Glasgow, the area takes in the former counties of Dunbartonshire, Renfrewshire and Lanarkshire, which all played their part in Scotland's rich industrial history. But while it is still Scotland's most populous area, where the bulk of its industry and commerce was once located, it is now clean and attractive, with much to do and see.

The scenery can be outstanding, from the upper reaches of the Clyde, with its quiet pastoral scenery and cosy villages surrounded by high, lonely moorland, to the hills above Greenock and of course, the bonnie banks of Loch Lomond. Then there is Glasgow. Once a gritty working class city with a huge image problem, it has burgeoned into a sophisticated, cosmopolitan city with a lively café society (at least once during a visit, do what the locals do - sit at a pavement café sipping coffee while people watch you watching them). There are art galleries and museums galore, bars, shops and shopping malls, (it is the second largest shopping centre in Britain after London), award-winning restaurants,

glitzy hotels, theatres, concert halls and nightclubs.

It is home to Scottish Opera, The Royal Scottish National Orchestra, Scottish Ballet, and a string of theatres where you can see anything from serious drama to variety shows. It is also one of Britain's best dressed cities, and it is reckoned that there are more Armani and Versace outfits worn here than anywhere else in Britain outside London.

That area of the West End known as Kelvinside is the city's wealthiest area. It is not just a place of trendy flats and apartments,

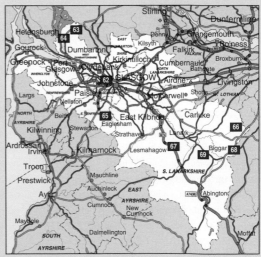

though these abound. It also has some seriously large mansions - once the homes of wealthy industrialists - in the streets north and south of Great Western Road. These are occupied by professional people such as TV personalities, doctors, writers and lawyers, who appreciate the leafy elegance of the district. Cutting from north to south through the area is Byres Road, with its trendy restaurants, cafés, pubs and shops.

And in the centre of Glasgow is the Merchant City, once run down and seedy, but now home to the city's café society. New apartment blocks have recently been built and older properties have been converted into flats to create a fashionable area where there seem to be more bars and cafés than people to fill them.

But there is still, thank goodness, the quirky, working class Glasgow - the city of fish and chips shops, betting shops, working men's pubs, raucous laughter and street markets, including the famous Barras, held every Saturday and Sunday in the east end. The city is ringed by enormous council estates that took the families who used to live in the teeming tenements of the Gorbals and other areas. It may not be the image of Glasgow that some people would like to project, but they are still there, and in their own way they have as much to do with the city's character as its new, chic additions.

Glasgow has always been an easy place to get out of. Within half an hour of the city centre you can be admiring the grandeur of bens, glens and lochs, taking it easy in some wonderfully bucolic pastoral scenery, or strolling along a lonely beach with a backdrop of magnificent hills.

Loch Lomond is renowned the world over. A train can take you straight to its bonnie banks in under an hour, and it's a journey thousands of Glaswegians make. We're on the edge of the Highlands here, and indeed the Highland Boundary Fault, which separates the Highlands from the Lowlands, passes through the loch.

The River Clyde has traditionally been a working river, its banks once ringing to the sound of shipbuilding. But there is another Clyde, one that is not so well known. The upper reaches of the river, in rural Lanarkshire, present an altogether different picture. Within the verdant Clyde Valley, you will find quiet orchards, green fields, woodland, small attractive villages and cosy pubs. The area around the historic town of Lanark is particularly green and pleasant. And the lonely moorland where the river rises has a gaunt but compelling beauty.

The settlements also have their attractions. Do not be put off by hackneyed descriptions of weary industrial towns surrounded by bleak council estates. Yes - they do exist, but they are being cleaned up, and some places - previously thought of as grim and bleak - have now become desirable commuting towns.

Helensburgh, Gourock and Dumbarton (once the capital of the Kingdom of Strathclyde) sit on the shores of the Firth of Clyde, with the first two always having a reputation as well-to-do. Hamilton, Paisley, Motherwell and the new town of East Kilbride are inland towns, and each has its attractions, such as the magnificent Paisley Abbey or the marvellous shopping malls (the largest in Scotland) in East Kilbride. In some towns close to Glasgow, such as Motherwell, Airdrie or Coatbridge, the excesses of industry (which made the area prosperous in the first place) are being cleaned up, and some places, such as Summerlee at Coatbridge, have taken this industrial heritage and turned it into a tourist attraction.

This whole area was once the powerhouse of Scotland. It is not ashamed of the fact, nor should it be. Coal was mined here, steel was produced, heavy industry sent smoke pluming into the sky, ships were built, deals were struck and money made. Money is still being made in the area, but now it comes from electronics, banking, tourism, broadcasting and publishing. But the people haven't changed. They are as resilient as ever, adapting to the changes that are being made yet staying the same.

GLASGOW

Glasgow has worked hard on its image over the last few years. Gone are the constant references to gang fights, organised crime, drunkenness, ugly industrial townscapes and bad housing. Now people talk of trendy nightspots, theatres, restaurants, pavement cafés and art galleries.

The city has changed its image more than once over the years. It was founded in the 7th century by St Kentigern, also known as St Mungo, and started life as a small religious community. When the first cathedral was built in early medieval times, a city grew up around it, and it became an important ecclesiastical centre - more so when it was made the seat of an archbishop in 1492, with Robert Blackadder becoming its first archbishop. At this time its population was no more than two or three thousand, and it was not until the 17th and 18th century that it began to expand rapidly.

In these centuries, after the Reformation had robbed it of its importance, it turned to trade, dealing with the American colonies in such commodities as tobacco and cotton, making many people very rich indeed. In the 19th century it became a city of industry, with shipyards and heavy engineering works. Now it relies mostly on tourism, the media, service industries and the arts for employment.

The area round the **Cathedral of St Mungo** (Historic Scotland) is where it all started. This was where St Kentigern, or Mungo, established a small church in the 6th century. The present cathedral was founded in the 12th century by David I, and the building shows work from this period onwards. It is the only Scottish mainland cathedral that escaped the Reformation of 1560 more or less intact. In its crypt is the **Tomb of St Mungo**, once a place of pilgrimage, but now visited by pilgrims of a different sort -

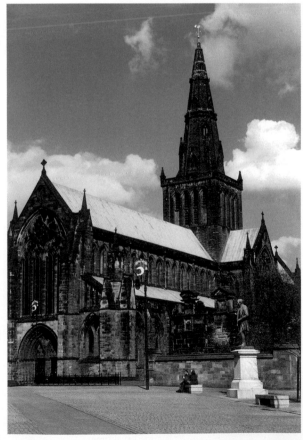

Cathedral of St Mungo

115

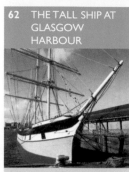

Glasgow

Explore the beautifully restored Glenlee and learn about the conditions aboard and the cargo she carried.

 see page 451

•

Close to the Tall Ship is the Scottish Exhibition and Conference Centre, a mammoth complex of halls and auditoriums, including what Glaswegians now refer to as the Armadillo, a metal and glass creation whose design owes more than a little to Sydney Opera House. And across the river from it is the city's newest attraction, the Glasgow Science Centre. Built on the site of the Glasgow Garden Festival, it is a combination of museum, laboratory and hands-on exhibition area that explores science and discovery, and has four floors featuring over 300 exhibits. The accompanying Glasgow Tower is Scotland's tallest freestanding structure at 412 feet, and there's also an IMAX Theatre.

•

tourists. The **Blackadder Aisle** is a wonderful piece of architecture added by Archbishop Robert Blackadder in about 1500, soon after he was raised from bishop to archbishop.

Behind the Cathedral, on a hill, is the **Necropolis** (meaning "city of the dead"), Glasgow's ancient burial ground, reached by a bridge over Wishart Street called the "Bridge of Sighs". It was originally modelled on the Père-Lachaise Cemetery in Paris, and contains tombs that range in style from the restrained and dignified to the wildly outrageous and quirky.

At the top of the hill is a monument to John Knox. Over 50,000 burials have taken place here over the years within 3500 tombs and mausoleums. From September 2006 there will be monthly guided tours of the cemetery, run by the Friends of Glasgow Necropolis.

In front of the cathedral, on the site of the original bishop's palace, is the modern (but looking anything but modern) **St Mungo Museum of Religious Life and Art**, which examines the main religions of the world and our relationships with them. Across from it is Glasgow's oldest house, **Provand's Lordship**, built in 1471 as a manse for the former St Nicholas Hospital. The interior re-creates a fine town house of the 17th century, complete with genuine furniture of the period. Behind the house is a herb garden, laid out as it would have been in late medieval times.

"The Clyde made Glasgow, and Glasgow made the Clyde", runs an old, but true, saying. In the 17th century, the city was seen as being wholly inland, with a river so shallow that people could wade across it. In those days, the city's ports were further down the Clyde, in Irvine of Port Glasgow. But in 1768 a man called John Golborne began canalising and deepening it to allow large ships to sail right up into the city. Telford completed the task in 1805, and the city became a leading port. The **Tall Ship at Glasgow Harbour** at Stobcross Road tells the story of the river and the industries it spawned. The centrepiece is the tall ship itself, the S.V. Glenlee, built in 1896. At Braehead, on the south side of the river, and a few miles downstream, is another museum, which celebrates the Clyde - the award-winning **Clydebuilt**. It is part of the Scottish Maritime Museum (see also Irvine and Dumbarton), and tells the river's story from the 1700s up to the present day.

The **Clyde Waterbus Service** takes you on a 30 minute boat trip on the "Pride o' the Clyde" along the river from the city centre to Braehead, with a commentary on the history of the river as you go.

Glasgow has always been a city of museums and art galleries, even when it relied on industry for its employment. Like most large cities, its West End is where the well off built their mansions, as the prevailing south westerly winds carried the smells of the city away from them. Here you'll find the

Kelvingrove Art Gallery and Museum, newly refurbished and housed in a grand red sandstone building. It has internationally important collections on archaeology, botany, zoology, geology and all the other ologies you can think of. There are Egyptian mummies, fossils, stuffed animals, dinosaur skeletons, clothing and uniforms from all over the world, weapons, and a host of other material. The art collection is stunning, and is possibly the most comprehensive civic collection in Europe.

River Kelvin, Glasgow

The **Glasgow Museum of Transport**, with trains, carriages, motorcars and a marvellous collection of model ships, sits opposite the Kelvingrove Art Gallery and Museum. Perhaps the most striking display is the one on Glasgow's "underground" system. The system forms a simple loop round the city centre and West End, and in the late '70s was upgraded, with orange trains taking the place of the much-loved wood and metal ones. The Glaswegians immediately dubbed it the "Clockwork Orange" and the name has stuck. More properly, it is known as the **Glasgow Subway**, rather than "underground" or "metro". There are now plans to extend the system.

Also in the West End, just off Byres Road are the **Hunterian Museum** and the **Hunterian Art Gallery**, which form part of Glasgow University. The museum has fine collections covering geology and numismatics, while the gallery has paintings, furniture and interior design by Mackintosh and Whistler. At the top of Byres Road is the **Glasgow Botanic Gardens**, with at its centre the **Kibble Palace**, a huge greenhouse with plants from all over the world. It is named after its builder John Kibble, who erected it beside his house on the banks of Loch Long. It was rebuilt here in 1873, after being dismantled and sailed up the Clyde.

The heart of Glasgow nowadays is **George Square,** a huge open space in front of the Victorian **City Chambers** (conducted tours available). There are statues galore, and it is a favourite place for city workers to relax in the sun. The City Chambers themselves reflect Glasgow's wealth and confidence in Victorian times, and so opulent are the interiors that they stood in for the Vatican in the film *Heavenly Pursuits*. Round the corner you'll find **Hutcheson's Hall** (National

Within Victoria Park, a few miles to the west, is the Fossil Grove (open between April and September only), undoubtedly the city's most ancient attraction. It consists of fragments of an ancient forest over 300 million years old, which was discovered in 1887 while digging a pathway through an old quarry. They are housed within a small building to protect them.

117

Glasgow Green, a huge area of parkland in the city's east end, is "Glasgow's lung". It has been common land for centuries, and it was here that Charles Edward Stuart mustered his troops during the Jacobite Uprising when he occupied the city. Now it is the city's largest park, with its centrepiece being the People's Palace and Winter Gardens, a museum and glasshouse complex which tells the city's own story. Close to it is the Doulton Fountain, at 46 feet high and 70 feet wide the world's largest terracotta fountain. It was recently refurbished at a cost of £3.75m.

Trust for Scotland), founded in 1641 as a hospice, though the building itself is 18th century. It was designed by David Hamilton, and has a small exhibition about the **Merchant City**, that area that housed the homes and offices of the rich 17th and 18th century slave-owning merchants who traded with America. Nowadays it is an area of expensive apartment blocks, smart bars, restaurants and pubs.

Not far away, in Queen Street, is the **Gallery of Modern Art**, with four floors of work by modern artists such as Christine Borland and Toby Paterson. In Buccleuch Street near Charing Cross, is the **Tenement House** (National Trust for Scotland). Built in the late 19th century, it re-creates the genteel tenement living conditions that were common among Glasgow's lower middle classes in the early 20th century. It is open between March and October. The **Centre for Contemporary Arts** (CCA) is at 320 Sauchiehall Street, and has a changing programme of events, performances and exhibitions. There are six galleries, small cinema, bookshop and bar/restaurant. The **Glasgow Film Theatre**, in Rose Street (just off Sauchiehall Street), has a programme of art films. The **Collins Gallery** is located within the University of Strathclyde, and has a full programme of art exhibitions and events throughout the year, ranging from the traditional to the modern.

The **Mitchell Library** is an imposing domed building in North Street, not far from Charing Cross. It is Britain's largest municipal library, and has collections covering Scottish and local history, genealogy, and Robert Burns.

The **Glasgow Police Museum** is in St Andrews Square (to the south of Glasgow Cross). There are two exhibitions within it - one centred on the City of Glasgow Police (the world's first city police force) between 1779 and 1975, and one on international policing. And at the Cross itself is the old **Glasgow Tolbooth Steeple**, dating from the 1620s. At one time it provided offices for the City Council, and had a jail incorporated into it.

On the eastern edge of Glasgow Green is one of the city's most colourful buildings - **Templeton's Carpet Factory** (now a business centre), built between 1888 and 1892. It is based on a Venetian design, with walls that incorporate multi-coloured bricks.

Glasgow is synonymous with football, and at Hampden Park, Scotland's national football stadium on the south side of the Clyde, is the **Scottish Football Museum**. It reveals the sights, sounds and stories of the world's most popular game, and tells how it almost shaped the history of Glasgow in the late 19th and 20th centuries. You can see such things as the oldest football ticket in the world, the Scottish Cup trophy and Kenny Dalglish's 100th Scottish cap.

At Celtic Park in the Parkhead area of the city is the **Celtic**

Visitor Centre, which traces the history of Celtic Football Club, one of Glasgow's "big two" football clubs. There are exhibits, a stadium tour and a shop selling Celtic memorabilia. Rangers Football Club is Glasgow's other major team. It plays at Ibrox in Govan (once a separate burgh outside the city boundaries), to the south of the river. The **Rangers Tour Experience** takes you on a guided tour of the stadium, including the Trophy Room.

If you want to immerse yourself in something typically Scottish, then the **National Piping Centre** in Otago Street has a small museum and interpretation centre dedicated to Scotland's national instrument.

Charles Rennie Mackintosh is the most famous of Glasgow's architects, and was born in 1868. He designed a number of buildings in Glasgow, and there are organised tours taking you to the best of them arranged by the Charles Rennie Mackintosh Society. His most famous building is the **Glasgow School of Art** in Renfrew Street. It is still a working college, though tours are only available by appointment. On the south side of the river is the **Scotland Street School**, now a museum dedicated to education in Scotland in the 20th century. Another building is the **Martyr's Public School** in Parson Street, (no longer used as a school) and it

Pollock House

is open to the public. The **Willow Tea Rooms** in Sauchiehall Street still sells traditional Scottish "high teas" amid Mackintosh's designs, and the **Queen's Cross Church** on Garscube Road is now the headquarters of the Charles Rennie Mackintosh Society. At Bellahouston Park, on the south side, is the **House for an Art Lover**, which interprets some of the incomplete designs Mackintosh submitted to a competition in a German magazine. **The Lighthouse**, Scotland's centre for architecture, design and the city, is in Mitchell Lane just off Argyle Street, and has a Mackintosh interpretation centre. It is housed in a six-floored Mackintosh building that was once the home of one of Glasgow's daily newspapers, the Herald. In the Hunterian Art Gallery there is also the **Mackintosh House**, featuring the

•

Perhaps Glasgow's most famous modern attraction is the Burrell Collection, housed in a purpose built complex of galleries in Pollok Country Park, south of the river. William Burrell (see also Largs and Hutton Castle) gifted a huge collection of art and historical objects to the city of Glasgow, and now over 8,000 of them are on display. A whole day could be spent going round the collection. Also in the park is Pollok House (National Trust for Scotland), a Georgian mansion that houses the Stirling Maxwell collection of decorative arts.

•

Glasgow is Britain's second largest shopping centre, the three main shopping streets being Argyle Street, Sauchiehall Street and Buchanan Street. There are also enormous shopping malls. The St Enoch Centre is just off Argyle Street, the Buchanan Galleries are at the corner of Buchanan Street and Sauchiehall Street, while the Braehead Shopping Centre is south of the river on the city's western fringes, near Renfrew. There's also the Forge at Parkhead, in the east end. Within the city centre there are two exclusive retail developments. Princes Square, off Buchanan Street, is a mix of upmarket shops and cafés, while the Italian Centre in John Street is where you'll find the designer labels.

principal rooms from Mackintosh's own house, together with a collection of designs and watercolours.

Another Glasgow architect, formerly overshadowed by Mackintosh but now more widely known, was Alexander Thomson, known as "Greek" Thomson because of the Greek influences in his work (see also Balfron). He lived in the 19th century, and designed **St Vincent Street Church**, as well as **Holmwood House** (National Trust for Scotland) in Netherlee Road, in the southern suburbs.

In Sauchiehall Street is the **Regimental Museum of the Royal Highland Fusiliers**. It was Scotland's second oldest infantry regiment (all regiments in the Scottish Division have now been amalgamated into one single regiment), and was formed in the 1960s when the Highland Light Infantry amalgamated with the Royal Scottish Fusiliers.

AROUND GLASGOW

KIRKINTILLOCH

7 miles NE of Glasgow city centre on the A803

The old burgh of Kirkintilloch sits on the **Forth and Clyde Canal**. It connects the Firth of Clyde and the Firth of Forth, with a further canal, the Union Canal, connecting it to Edinburgh. The **Auld Kirk Museum** in the Cowgate is housed in the former parish church, which dates from 1644. In **Pecl Park** are some Roman remains from the Antonine Wall, a turf wall that

stretched from Scotland's east to west coast (see Bo'ness).

Craft Daft (On a Raft) is a craft studio on a canal boat moored in the Forth and Clyde Canal at Glasgow Bridge.

CUMBERNAULD

12 miles NE of Glasgow off the A80

Cumbernauld is one of Scotland's new towns, and the setting for the 1981 film *Gregory's Girl*. It sits on a hill above the A80, and was originally a weaving centre, as was its neighbouring village of Condorrat. It has an indoor shopping centre that has courted controversy ever since it was built in the 1960s. It has been named "Britain's ugliest building", the "shopping centre from hell" and "top of the ugly league". Raised up on concrete stilts, some people see it as an eyesore, while others see it as an example of forward thinking architecture that should be more appreciated.

Cumbernauld Museum is in Allander walk, within the town library, and had displays and artefacts about the history of the town.

Palacerigg Country Park covers 750 acres, and is to the southeast of the town. The town was established in the 1950s partly on what was an old country estate. Though it sits to the north east of Glasgow, Cumbernauld, like Kirkintilloch, was once in a detached part of Dunbartonshire.

KILSYTH

11 miles NE of Glasgow on the A809

The **Battle of Kilsyth** was fought

on the 15th August 1645, when the 1st Marquis of Montrose routed a Covenanting army led by William Baillie of Letham. A reservoir is now located where Montrose's army camped, and a cairn marks the spot where the battle took place. The defeat was due in no small measure to the interference of inexperienced members of the Scottish aristocracy with Covenanting sympathies plus Calvinist clergymen, known collectively as the "Committee of the Estates", who countermanded Baillie's orders (see also Dunbar). These were for the Covenanting army to hold its superior position and see what Montrose would do next, which was tactically sound. Instead, the committee ordered the troops to move in columns round the flank of the Royalist army and take up a new position. Montrose, seeing his opportunity, attacked the column, bringing it to a halt. It was now exposed, and Montrose attacked its flank, killing over three quarters of the Covenanting troops.

RUTHERGLEN

2 miles SE of Glasgow city centre on the A749

This royal burgh is one of the oldest in Scotland, having been granted its royal charter by David I in the 12th century. For a short while the burgh was incorporated into the city of Glasgow, something that was greatly resented by some of its citizens, but since 1997 has formed part of the local authority area of South Lanarkshire. A gable of its medieval **Parish Church** survives in the kirkyard of its more modern successor. Robbie Coltrane (Hagrid in the Harry potter films) was born here, and for a short while Stan Laurel lived in the town and went to a local school. Cambuslang, two miles away, was the birthplace of Midge Ure, lead singer of the group Ultravox.

Rutherglen Town Hall is now an arts venue, with theatre, meeting rooms, performance spaces and galleries.

NEWTON MEARNS

7 miles S of Glasgow on the A77

Newton Mearns is a commuter town of smart bungalows and substantial houses. The foursquare Parish Church dates from 1755, and close by is **Greenbank House** (National Trust for Scotland) surrounded by beautiful gardens. It was built in 1764 for a Glasgow merchant, and is not open to the public.

Mearns Castle was built by the Maxwells in about 1499, and is possibly the only castle in Scotland that is incorporated into the fabric of a modern church.

CLYDEBANK

7 miles W of Glasgow city centre on the A814

Clydebank is a former shipbuilding town, and it was here that the *Queen Mary*, the *Queen Elizabeth* and the *Queen Elizabeth II* were built. The town suffered more damage from air raids in proportion to its size than any other British town in World War II. In March 1941, during the Clydebank Blitz, the centre of the town was flattened and many people were killed. Of

To the north of the town of Cumbernauld is Castlecary, with its viaduct carrying the main Glasgow Edinburgh line over the A80. In December 1935, during a blizzard, a railway accident at the local station killed 35 people, including an eight year old girl. People say that her ghost still haunts the area.

Paisley was the birthplace of many famous people. Tom Conti the actor was born here, as was John Byrne the artist and writer (whose most famous work is undoubtedly the TV series Tutti Frutti), Andrew Neill, now editor of the Scotsman, Gerry Rafferty the singer, Fulton Mackay of Porridge fame, Kenneth McKellar the singer and David Tennant, the actor who played Dr Who.

the 12,000 dwellings in the town, only seven were undamaged. The effects of the bombing are still being felt today. The **Clydebank Museum** at the Town Hall in Dumbarton Road has exhibits devoted to the Blitz, as well as to the famous Singer sewing machine factory which once stood in the town.

A well laid out **Clydebank Heritage Trail**, with its accompanying leaflet, takes you round the town. The **Auchentoshan Distillery** is at Dalmuir, to the west of Clydebank, and has a visitor centre and shop.

PAISLEY

5 miles W of Glasgow city centre on the A761

The large town of Paisley is centred on the great Abbey Church of Saints Mary the Virgin, James the Greater of Compostella, Mirin and Milburga, otherwise known as **Paisley Abbey**. It was founded in 1163 by Walter FitzAlan, first High Steward of Scotland and progenitor of the Stewart dynasty. Thirteen monks from Much Wenlock in

Paisley Abbey

Shropshire came to oversee the founding of what was then a priory. Only in 1245 did it become an abbey, answerable only to the Pope. William Wallace is believed to have been educated here.

Within its walls are the tombs of most of the non-royal High Stewards, as well as that of Princess Marjory, daughter of Robert the Bruce, who married Walter, the sixth High Steward, and their grandson Robert III. It can legitimately claim to be the birthplace of the Stewart dynasty, because Robert II, the first Stewart king, was born here in 1316. Marjory had been seriously injured in a riding accident at Knock, a nearby hill, and she was brought to the abbey, where she died soon after giving birth to her son.

The building as you see it now was built from the 15th century though there are earlier fragments. After the reformation, the church was allowed to fall into ruin, with only the nave being preserved as the parish church. Finally, in the early 1900s, the choir was rebuilt and the abbey became one of the most important medieval churches in Scotland. Within the abbey is a memorial to **John Witherspoon**, a former minister of the Laigh Kirk in Paisley, who signed the American Declaration of Independence. A statue of him can also be found in front of **Paisley University** (see also Gifford).

Another famous Paisley church is the Baptist **Thomas Coats Memorial Church**, sometimes known as the "Baptist Cathedral" because of its size. It was built in 1894 in memory of Thomas Coats of the Coats and Clark thread making firm. The same Thomas Coats gifted the **Coats Observatory** to the town's Philosophical Institution in 1883. It is now open to the public. Adjacent is **Paisley Museum and Art Galleries**, with displays of Paisley shawls and other memorabilia. One of its prized possessions is the Missal of Arbuthnott (see also Arbuthnott)

At the Corner of Shuttle Street and George Place are the 18th and 19th century weaving cottages known as **Sma' Shot Cottages**, housing an interpretation centre which gives an insight into the living conditions of Paisley weaving families and mill workers in the past. Nearby, in New Street, is **Paisley Arts Centre**, housed in the former Laigh Kirk of 1738. It has a theatre, performance areas and a gallery.

In the 18th century, the town was famed for its poets, the most famous being Robert Tannahill, who was born in **Tannahill Cottage** in Queen Street in 1774. He was a silk weaver who wrote the words to such beautiful songs as *Jessie the Flower o' Dunblane* and *The Braes o' Gleniffer*. The actual braes themselves now form part of the 1,300 acre **Gleniffer Braes Country Park**, to the south of the town. There are spectacular views from the Robertson Car Park, and guided tours are available.

To the north of Paisley, on the other side of the M8, is **Glasgow International Airport**.

The village of Elderslie, a mile west of the town, is the supposed birthplace of William Wallace, and the **Wallace Memorial,** built in 1912, explains his exploits.

LOCHWINNOCH

16 miles SW of Glasgow on the B786

The **Clyde Muirshiel Regional Park** covers 106 square miles of magnificent countryside from Greenock to Inverkip and down into Ayrshire. It is ideal for walking, cycling, fishing and observing wildlife. The **Castle Semple Visitor** Centre is on Lochlip Road. Castle Semple Loch itself has sailing and fishing. Near its shores are the ruins of **Castle Semple Church**, founded in the early 16th century by John Semple. He was later killed at the Battle of Flodden in 1513, and his tomb can be seen at the east end of the church.

All that remains of the former parish church, built in 1729, is the west gable. It is now known as **Auld Simon**.

KILBARCHAN

11 miles SW of Glasgow, off the A761

This is undoubtedly the most picturesque village in Renfrewshire, and is a huddle of old 18th century weaving cottages. **The Weaver's Cottage** (National Trust for Scotland) dates from 1723, and shows what a typical weaver's cottage (complete with working loom) was like.

In a niche on the wall of the Steeple Hall of 1755 is a statute to **Habbie Simpson**, the village's famous 17th century piper. It is a bronze reproduction of one made

Jenny's Well Local Nature Reserve, on the south bank of the White Cart Water, is less than a mile from the centre of the town, and is locked between a council estate and a chemicals factory. For all that, it is a haven for wildlife with some pleasant walks.

The Lochwinnoch Nature Reserve is run by the RSPB, and has nature trails through woodland, with viewing areas and a visitor centre.

•

The Renfrew Community Museum in the Brown Institute in Canal Street was opened in 1997. It has displays of local history, including exhibits to do with Renfrew Airport, the forerunner of the present Glasgow International Airport .

•

from wood by Archibald Simpson in 1822. The **Clochoderick Stone** is a famous landmark, and is what is known as an "erratic" - a huge boulder slowly moved by ice during the last Ice Age, with Argyllshire being its likely starting point. According to legend, is was visited by Merlin during the Dark Ages. Its dimensions are 22 feet long by 17 feet wide by 12 feet high.

RENFREW

5 miles W of Glasgow on the A8

The ancient royal burgh of Renfrew was granted its charter in 1143, making it one of the oldest in Scotland. It was here, in 1164, that one of the lesser-known, but still important, Scottish battles took place - the **Battle of Renfrew**. It was fought between Somerled, Lord of the Isles, and the royal army of Malcolm IV led by Walter FitzAlan, founder of Paisley Abbey and first High Steward of Scotland, who had been granted the lands of Renfrew by the king. This battle brought the Western Isles fully under the control of the Scottish monarchy. The story of the battle is an intriguing one. Somerled had sailed up the Clyde the previous year with 15,000 troops carried in over 160 great warships. One version of the story says that the king had bribed Somerled's nephew to murder him, and this was duly carried out, causing the troops to return home. Another version - probably the true one - says that Somerled was killed during the battle along with his heir, and they

were carried off to be buried in Saddell Abbey on the Mull of Kintyre (see also Saddell). A cairn marks the supposed site of the battle.

BEARSDEN AND MILNGAVIE

6 miles NW of Glasgow city centre on the A810 and A81

These two prosperous towns are firmly within Glasgow's inner commuting belt, and are full of large Victorian and Edwardian mansions as well as the more modest bungalows of the 1930s. The **Antonine Wall** (named after Roman Emperor Antoninus Pius) passes close by (see also Falkirk). It was built of turf in the 2nd century to keep out the warring tribesmen of the north, and stretched for 37 miles between the Clyde and the Forth. In Bearsden there are the remains of a **Roman Bathhouse.**

Mugdock Country Park sits off the A81 north of Milngavie (pronounced "Mull-guy"), which is the starting point for the 95-mile long **West Highland Way**, which connects the Glasgow conurbation with Fort William. **Mugdock Castle**, which is now ruined, dates originally from the 13th century, and was a Graham stronghold.

The Lillie Art Gallery, in Station Road, Milngavie, was founded by banker and amateur artist Robert Lillie, and opened in 1962. It has a collection of 20th century Scottish paintings, including works by the Scottish Colourists, Joan Eardley and Philip Reves.

DUMBARTON

The town sits where the River Leven, fed by Loch Lomond, enters the Clyde. It is dominated by **Dumbarton Castle** (Historic Scotland), which sits high on a volcanic plug 240 feet above the Firth of Clyde. Known in olden times as Alcluith, it is one of the oldest fortified sites in Britain, and from the 8th to the early 11th centuries was the capital of the ancient kingdom of Strathclyde. The kingdom was incorporated into Scotland in 1034, when its king, Duncan, also assumed the throne of Scotland.

The name of the town means "Fort of the Britons", and though the town is called Dumbarton, the former county is Dunbartonshire, with an "n". The castle now mainly consists of modern barracks, but there is still plenty to see, including a 12th century gateway, a dungeon and a museum. From the top there is a splendid view out over the Firth of Clyde. It was from Dumbarton in 1548 that Mary Queen of Scots set sail for France and her eventual marriage to Francis, the Dauphin. This was considered to be much safer than leaving from an east coast port, as Henry VIII's ships were patrolling the North Sea. The English king had wanted Mary to marry his son Henry, and when the Scottish parliament refused to ratify such an agreement, Henry tried unsuccessfully to force the marriage, a period known as the "Rough Wooing".

The **Denny Tank Museum** in Castle Street forms part of the Scottish Maritime Museum (see also Glasgow and Irvine). It is the oldest experimental water tank in the world, and is the length of a football pitch. It was built in 1882 as part of Denny's shipyard (whose most famous ship was undoubtedly the tea clipper the "Cutty Sark"), and it was here that hull shapes were tested in water using carefully crafted models before the ships themselves were built. On display

College Bow, Dumbarton

63 GREYSTONELEA LODGE

Gartocharn

Charming self-catering cottage which is also an eco-friendly showhouse for renewable energy.

see page 452

64 ANCHORAGE TEAROOM & GUEST HOUSE

Balloch

A splendid guest house and tearoom sitting close to the 'bonny, bonny, banks of Loch Lomond' that offers comfort and value for money.

see page 452

are many of the models built by Denny craftsmen.

Though Denny was famous for its ships, it also has a place in aircraft history, as it built the world's first hovercraft, and, in 1909, the world first helicopter that was capable of flight.

A **Dumbarton Heritage Trail** has been laid out, and takes you round the town centre. In Church Street is an old archway called the **College Bow**, once part of the long gone Collegiate Church of St Mary. On the hillside above the town is the beautiful **Overtoun Estate**, with wonderful views over the Firth. It was bequeathed to the people of Dumbarton by Douglas White, a London doctor, in 1939.

Old Kilpatrick, to the west of the town, is supposed to be the birthplace of St Patrick, who was captured by raiders and taken to Ireland in the 4th century. The village sits in the shadow of the **Erskine Bridge**, the lowest crossing point of the Clyde, opened in 1971.

AROUND DUMBARTON

BALLOCH

4 miles N of Dumbarton on the A811

This pleasant town sits at the point where the River Leven (at five miles long, Scotland's shortest river) leaves **Loch Lomond** on its way to Dumbarton and the Clyde. The loch is recognised as Scotland's largest and most beautiful sheet of water, covering over 27 square

miles. The **Loch Lomond and the Trossachs National Park** was Scotland's first national park, opened in 2002, and **Lomond Shores** at Balloch includes the National Park Gateway Centre.

The loch is at its widest to the south. It gradually narrows and gets deeper as it goes north, and at some points it reaches a depth of over 600 feet, making it the third deepest loch in Scotland. Many songs have been written about this stretch of water, the most famous being the *Bonnie, Bonnie Banks o' Loch Lomond*. It was written by a Jacobite prisoner held in Carlisle Castle who was due to be executed. He is telling a fellow prisoner whose life had been spared that he (the condemned man) will be in Scotland before him because he will take the "low road", i.e., the road of death, while his colleague will take the "high road", or the road of life.

At the nearby village of Gartocharn is **Duncryne Hill** (nicknamed "The Dumpling" by locals), where you get a marvellous view, not just of the loch, but also of the surrounding countryside. The **Highland Boundary Fault**, which separates the Lowlands of Scotland from the Highlands, passes through Loch Lomond from Glen Fruin on the west to Balmaha on the east. The **Balloch Castle Country Park**, north east of Balloch, has lochside walks, gardens and a visitor centre. South from the town you can follow the **Leven Valley Heritage Trail**, taking you down the valley of the Leven to

Dumbarton, passing such small industrial towns as **Alexandria** and **Renton**. A small leaflet about the trail is available. Renton, with a population of just over 2,000, was once home to Renton Football Club, which won the world football championships in 1888. It did this by winning first the Scottish Cup, and then playing, and winning against West Bromwich Albion of England at Hampden Park. It had been agreed that the winner would be called "world champions".

The author **Tobias Smollett** was born in Renton in 1721.He wrote such books as *The Adventures of Peregrine Pickle*, *The Adventures of Roderick Random* and *The Expedition of Humphry Clinker*. There is a small memorial to him near the local school.

CARDROSS

4 miles W of Dumbarton on the A814

Geilston Gardens (National Trust for Scotland) surround a late 17th century house (not open to the public) to the east of the town. Its most prominent feature is a huge Wellingtonia tree. Also at Cardross, in Darleith Road, is **St Mahew's Chapel**, dating from 1467, though a church of some kind has stood here since the 7th century. It was restored in 1955, and is still in use today as a Roman Catholic church. It was at Cardross Castle (now gone) that Robert the Bruce died of leprosy in 1329 (see also Dunfermline and Melrose).

Cardross Parish Church is housed in what was the Free Church for the village. The former parish church was destroyed by bombing in May 1941, and rather than rebuild it completely, the tower was refurbished as a war memorial.

A.J. Cronin the novelist, who wrote the Doctor Finlay stories which were later adapted for television, was born in Cardross in July 1896.

GREENOCK

Situated on the south bank of the Firth of Clyde, at a point known as **The Tail of the Bank**, Greenock is a bustling industrial town and port. It was the birthplace, in 1736, of **James Watt**, who perfected the steam engine. Hills pile up behind the town, and on the slopes of Lyle Hill is a huge **Cross of Lorraine** mounted on an anchor, which was built in 1946. It commemorates the Free French sailors who sailed from Greenock and lost their lives on the Atlantic during World War II. There are excellent views out over the Firth of Clyde and as far north as Ben Lomond.

Customhouse Quay was the departure point for thousands of Scottish emigrants sailing away to America in the 19th and early 20th centuries. The magnificent **Custom House**, built in 1810, reflects the port's importance in bygone days, and it now houses a museum dedicated to the work of HM Customs and Excise. Another museum is the **McLean Museum and Art Gallery** on Kelly Street, which features exhibits on local history as well as paintings by

In Alexandria, on the Lomond Industrial Estate, is the Antartex Village Visitor Centre. It incorporates a factory making sheepskin coats (with factory tours available), a mill shop and a small craft village. Close by is the Loch Lomond Factory Outlets and Motoring Memories Museum, housed in a magnificent building where one of Scotland's former makes of car, the "Argyll", was manufactured.

In Greenock cemetery is the grave of Highland Mary, whose real name was Mary Campbell (see also Failford and Dunoon). Burns had met her at a low point in his life in Mauchline, and had asked her to accompany him to the West Indies when he thought of emigrating. However, on a trip home to Dunoon to make arrangements for her departure, she died. She was previously buried in the kirkyard of the former Old West Kirk, but was exhumed and reburied in 1920. When the Old West Kirk, which dated from the late 16th century, was dismantled in 1926, some of its stones were used to build the new Old West Kirk, on the Esplanade. It has some wonderful stained glass and woodcarving.

Courbin, Boudin and the Scottish Colourists. The **Watt Library** in union street is named after the town's most famous son, and is the place to go for genealogical information.

The **Greenock Cut** was, in its day, one of the greatest feats of engineering in Scotland, and there are now plans to turn it into a tourist attraction. In the early 19th century, the town was short of water to power its industries, so between 1825 and 1827 the engineer Robert Thom cut a five and a half mile long aqueduct from Loch Thom in the hills down into the town. It is still largely intact, though it was eventually superseded by tunnels.

William Kidd, better known as **Captain Kidd** the pirate, was born in Greenock in 1645. Also born in Greenock, in 1936, was **Richard Wilson**, better known as Victor Meldrew of *One Foot in the Grave*. Another famous son is **Hector MacCunn** the composer, born here in 1868.

AROUND GREENOCK

PORT GLASGOW

4 miles E of Greenock on the A8

Before the Clyde at Glasgow was canalised and deepened, this town was Glasgow's main port. Around 1667 Glasgow merchants, aided by Glasgow Town Council, had bought some land here and built a small harbour which soon expanded. Shipbuilding developed, and in 1812 the world's first commercial steamship, the **Comet**, was built here.

Newark Castle (Historic Scotland) lies close to the riverbank, and dates from the 16th and 17th centuries. Up until the 1980s the castle was completely surrounded by shipyards. It was originally built by George Maxwell in the late 15th century, and upgraded in 1597 to what you see today by its most notorious owner, Sir Patrick Maxwell. He was an unsavoury man who was always quarrelling with other families, most notably the Montgomerys of Skelmorlie near Largs. In fact he murdered two of them - Montgomery himself and his eldest son - in the one day. He also treated his wife Margaret abominably. In 1632, in front of the local minister during dinner in the castle, he struck her on the face so hard that she had to take to her bed for six months. As soon as she had recovered, he attacked her again, this time with a sword.

Many times Margaret had resorted to the law to have her husband restrained. Patrick even had his son ejected from the castle when he tried to intervene. Eventually, after 44 years of marriage and 16 children, Margaret left him, choosing a life of abject poverty rather than suffer any more. This caused the authorities to take an interest in his conduct, but before he could be brought to trial in Edinburgh he died of natural causes.

Two miles west of Port Glasgow is the **Finlaystone Estate**, where the present head of the Clan Macmillan lives. It is open to the public, and features gardens and 140 acres of woodland, which can be explored. Finlaystone House, at the heart of the estate, dates back to the 14th century, though it has been extended over the centuries. It can be visited by special arrangement.

GOUROCK

2 miles W of Greenock town centre on the A770

This little holiday resort is now more or less a suburb of Greenock, though at one time it was a separate burgh. It is on a most attractive part of the Clyde, opposite Kilcreggan, the Gareloch and the entrance to Loch Long, where the mountains tumble down towards the sea. The Firth of Clyde is a famous yachting area, and the town is the home of the **Royal Gourock Yacht Club**, which is situated near the Promenade.

At Cloch Point, four miles to the southwest, is the much-photographed **Cloch Lighthouse** of 1797, a famous landmark for ships sailing on the Clyde. Between Castle Gardens and Kempock Street in the town is the curiously named **Granny Kempock's Stone**, which dates from prehistoric times. It is shaped like a cloaked figure, and to walk round it is said to bring good luck. However, it also has associations with witchcraft. In 1662 a young woman was burnt to death after she admitted that she was going to use supernatural powers to throw the stone into the waters of the Firth of Clyde and cause shipwrecks

HAMILTON

Hamilton was once the county town of Lanarkshire, Scotland's most populous and industrialised county. It became a royal burgh in 1548, though it lost this status in 1669. It is very much connected with one of the most important families in Scotland, the Dukes of Hamilton, Scotland's premier ducal family. Up until medieval times, the town was known as Cadzow, but gradually Hamilton took over as the family grew in importance. By the 1920s, when it was demolished, the immense **Hamilton Palace**, home

Granny Kempock's Stone, Gourock

129

A two-mile long Grand Avenue once stretched from Hamilton Palace all the way to Chatelherault, pronounced "Shattly-row"), a Hamilton family hunting lodge east of the town. Most of the avenue is gone, but Chatelherault survives, having been refurbished in the 1980s in the largest project of its time in Britain, and then officially opened in September 1987 by the Duke of Gloucester. It was originally designed by William Adam and dates from the 1730s. The lodge once also housed the Duke's hunting dogs, and was therefore known as the "Dog Kennels". Now it houses a museum and interpretation centre.

to the dukes, was the grandest non-royal residence in Britain. More than one royal visitor to the palace admitted to being overawed by the opulence and splendour of the place.

Not a stone now remains of it above ground, though the Hamilton's burial place, the grandiose **Hamilton Mausoleum**, still remains. It is a curious building with an immense dome, and is full of Masonic symbolism. It consists of a chapel above and a crypt below, and was built in the mid 19th century for Alexander, the 10th Duke (nicknamed "Il Magnifico"), who had his ancestors removed from the ruins (now gone completely) of the old Collegiate Church of Hamilton and re-interred in the crypt. When he himself died, he was laid to rest in the sarcophagus of an Egyptian princess, and this was placed in the upper chapel. A curious tale tells of how the duke was found to be too tall to fit into the sarcophagus when he died. Therefore his legs were broken and folded over. However, that's all it is - a tale. The duke was indeed too big for the sarcophagus, but he knew this long before he died, as he used to lie within it. So he had stonemasons enlarge the space that took the body.

The crypt is entered through the middle arch of three arches. Above each arch is a carved head, representing life, death and immortality. One thing to note is that the crypt doors lock from the inside. The reason is simple - once a month a servant was sent from the palace to dust and clean the

huge coffins. To prevent ghoulish sightseers, a policeman was stationed outside and she locked herself in.

The bodies were all removed from the mausoleum in 1921, and the place can now be visited. The upper chamber was never used as a chapel, however, as it is reckoned to have the longest echo of any building in Britain.

The lodge got its name because the Dukes of Hamilton were also the Dukes of Châtellerault (the French spelling of the name) near Poitou in France. The title was bestowed in 1548 by Henry II of France in recognition of the part the family played in arranging the marriage of Mary Stuart to his son Francis, the Dauphin. The spelling of the name changed over the years, and Châtellerault gradually became Chatelherault. Surrounding the lodge is **Chatelherault Country Park**, with over ten miles of woodland walks. The ruins of **Cadzow Castle**, the original home of the Hamiltons, and where Mary Stuart once stayed, can be see within the park. There are also the remains of an old **Iron Age Fort** and the **Cadzow Oaks**, which are very old. In a field in front of Chatelherault is a small but famous herd of **White Cattle**.

Hamilton Parish Church, within the town, was designed by William Adam in the early 1730s at the same time as he was designing Chatelherault. It is an elegant building in the shape of a Greek cross, with a cupola over the crossing. The pre-Norman

Netherton Cross stands at the church entrance, and in the kirkyard is the **Heads Monument**, commemorating four Covenanters beheaded in Edinburgh after the Pentland Rising of 1666.

In Almada Street you'll find the town's most prominent landmark - the **County Buildings**. They were built in the 1960s for the then Lanarkshire County Council, and were modelled on the United Nations building in New York. It is one of the few 1960s buildings in Scotland to be listed.

In the Bent Cemetery is the simple grave of one of Scotland's best-known entertainers, **Sir Harry Lauder**. Born in Portobello near Edinburgh in 1870, he at one time worked in the coalmines in Quarter, a village near Hamilton. He died in 1950 (see also Strathaven). Nearby is the plot where the members of the Hamilton family who formerly lay in the mausoleum are now buried. The 10th Duke, who had the mausoleum built, still lies in his Egyptian sarcophagus.

Hamilton is the start of one of Scotland's ten national tourist routes, the **Clyde Valley Tourist Route**. It follows the Clyde Valley all the way south to Abington on the M74.

AROUND HAMILTON

AIRDRIE AND COATBRIDGE

7 miles N of Hamilton on the A89

The twin towns of Airdrie and Coatbridge are industrial in character. In Coatbridge, in 1889, was born **John Reith**, first general manager of what was then the British Broadcasting Company. Single-handedly he shaped the character of the organisation. The late **Ian Bannen**, who played Dr Findlay in the TV series, was born in Airdrie in 1928

Coatbridge at one time was known as the "Iron Burgh", due to the iron works situated within its boundaries. It is now home to the **Summerlee Heritage Centre**, built on the site of the old Summerlee Ironworks, which traces the history of the area's old industries - steel making, coalmining and the manufacture of heavy plant. Tramlines have been laid out in it, and there is a small collection of trams from all over Europe. There is also a short section of the Summerlee branch of the **Monklands Canal** (now closed), which ran from Glasgow to the Lanarkshire coalfields. The canal was built between 1770 and 1794, and at one time was the most profitable in Scotland. **The North Calder Heritage Trail** runs from Summerlee to Hillend Reservoir, and passes many sites connected with the past industry of the area.

The **Time Capsule** is one of the largest leisure centres in the area. In the **Drumpellier Country Park** there is a visitor centre, butterfly house, formal gardens, golf course and pets' corner.

MOTHERWELL AND WISHAW

3 miles E of Hamilton on the A721

The twin towns of Motherwell and Wishaw were, up until 1975,

Based in an old 17th century coaching inn once known as the Hamilton Arms is the Low Parks Museum, which has displays and memorabilia on local history. It also houses a large display on Lanarkshire's own regiment - the Cameronians (Scottish Rifles). Raised as a Covenanting force in 1689, it took its name from Richard Cameron, a Covenanting minister who opposed bishops in the Church of Scotland and the king being its head. The regiment chose to disband itself in 1968 rather than amalgamate with another regiment (see also Douglas). Most of the Low Parks, which at one time formed some of Hamilton Palace's parkland, has been given over to a huge retail development that includes a multi-screen cinema and supermarket.

131

A mile north east of Motherwell is the small industrial village of Carfin, where you will find the Lourdes-inspired Carfin Pilgrimage Centre and Grotto, created in the 1920s by the local priest Fr. Thomas Nimmo Taylor, helped by out-of-work miners. There are displays and exhibits that help explain the notion of pilgrimage, not just in the Roman Catholic religion, but also in all major religions.

included in the one burgh. They were steel making towns, though the steelworks at Ravenscraig have now gone. The award-winning **Motherwell Heritage Centre** on High Road has a number of exhibitions, and hosts varied activities with a heritage theme. To the west of Motherwell, adjoining the M74, is the 1,100 acres of **Strathclyde Country Park**, built on waste ground in the early '70s. Within it there is an international-sized rowing lake where the rowing events of the 1986 Commonwealth Games were held. On its banks are the remains of a **Roman Bathhouse**. There are guided walks throughout the year, as well as nature trails and a camping and caravanning site. **M&D's Theme Park**, with carousels, big dipper, bowling alley and other amusements, is located near the north banks of the loch. **Amazonia** claims to be Scotland's largest rain forest attraction, and houses reptiles, insects and animals connected with the Amazon rain forest.

The **Shotts Heritage Centre** is in Benhar Road in Shotts, eight miles to the west of Motherwell and Wishaw. There are displays on the history of this former mining town.

DALSERF

7 miles SE of Hamilton town centre off the A72

Once a sizeable village with inns and a ferry across the Clyde, Dalserf has now shrunk to no more than a few cottages and a church. **Dalserf Parish Church**,

with its whitewashed walls, looks more like a doll's house than a place of worship, and dates from 1655, though an ancient chapel dedicated to St Serf stood here before that. The building is a rare survivor of a mid-17th century Scottish church. Most churches from that period were simply built, with earth floors and a thatched roof. In the 18th and 19th centuries they were usually demolished to make way for something more imposing. Dalserf has lasted because the parish was a poor one, and could not afford to rebuild, preferring instead to upgrade whenever it could. In the kirkyard is a pre-Norman "hogs back" grave slab, which was dug up in 1897, and also a memorial to the **Reverend John Macmillan**, sometimes called "the last of the Covenanters". He died in 1753.

STONEHOUSE

6 miles S of Hamilton on the A71

This former weaving village sits in the valley of the Avon, and still has rows of 18th and 19th century weaving cottages. On one side of the main door is a large window, which allows plenty of light into the room which housed the loom, and on the other is a small window, which allowed light to enter the main living quarters.

Patrick Hamilton, Scotland's first Protestant martyr, was born in Stonehouse in about 1503. He was burned at the stake in St Andrews in 1527 When aged just 13, he was appointed abbot of Fearn Abbey in present day Ross and Cromarty, and at 16 went to the University of

Paris, where he was exposed to the work of Martin Luther and other reformers. On his return to Scotland he studied at St Andrews, and there began practising the reformed religion in earnest. He was burnt at the stake for heresy in 1527 at the behest of Archbishop James Beaton (see also St Andrews).

The **Alexander Hamilton Memorial Park** was opened in 1925, the gift of a local man. It has a bandstand, which was originally made for the Great Glasgow Exhibition of 1911.

The remains of the medieval **Old St Ninian's Parish Church** (a gable and a bell cote) are to the north of the village, surrounded by an old kirkyard. A prehistoric burial kist was once dug up in the kirkyard, showing that the site may have had a religious significance long before Christianity came to the area.

STRATHAVEN

7 miles S of Hamilton on the A723

Strathaven (pronounced "Strayven") is a real gem of a small town that sits at the heart of Avondale. The ruins of **Strathaven Castle** (also known as Avondale Castle) are all that is left of a once large and powerful 14th century stronghold. It was built by the Douglas family, then passed to the Stewarts, who became Earls of Avondale, and eventually came into the hands of the Hamiltons. A legend says that before the Reformation, a wife of one of the owners was walled up alive in the castle, and when parts

of a wall fell down in the 19th century, human bones were found among the rubble. On the edge of the **John Hastie Park** is the **John Hastie Museum**, which has local history collections.

Close to the cemetery is the **James Wilson Monument** of 1846. James Pearle Wilson (known as "Pearly") was born in Strathaven in 1760, his father being a weaver. He was a free thinker on the matter of religion, and was also a radical reformer, something of which the local landowners, including the Duke of Hamilton, did not approve. In 1820 a band of reformers, of which he was a member, posted a bill on the streets of Glasgow that was held to be treasonable. He was arrested near Falkirk and executed in 1820.

EAST KILBRIDE

5 miles W of Hamilton on the A726

East Kilbride is the largest and undoubtedly the most successful of Scotland's new towns. Work started on laying it out in 1947 round an old village, and now it has a population of about 70,000. It is renowned for its shopping facilities, and has four shopping malls, **Princes Mall**, the **Plaza**, the **Olympia Centre** and **Centre West**, which together make up the largest undercover shopping area in Scotland. Another one is now planned, which should make it one of the largest undercover shopping centres in Britain.

In the Calderwood area of the town is **Hunter House**, birthplace in the 18th century of the Hunter

To the west of Strathaven, at Drumclog, was fought the Battle of Drumclog, where an army of Covenanters overcame government troops in 1679. A memorial on a minor road off the A71 commemorates the event. At the small village of Sandford, two miles to the south of Strathaven, are the lovely 50-feet high Spectacle E'e Falls on the Kype Water, a tributary of the Avon.

133

•

It was in a field near Eaglesham in 1941 that Rudolph Hess, Hitler's deputy, landed after he parachuted from an ME 110. He was found by a local farmer called David McLean, who took him home where he was treated firmly but politely. Hess gave his name as Alfred Horn, but it was soon established that he was Hitler's deputy. He said he was on a secret mission to speak to the Duke of Hamilton, and a map he possessed showed that he had been trying to reach Dungavel House, one of the Duke's hunting lodges on the road between Strathaven and Muirkirk. The then Duke of Hamilton declared that he had no idea why anyone from Germany would want to get in touch with him. He was then taken to Maryhill Barracks in Glasgow, where he was sometimes in the custody of Corporal William Ross, who went on to become the Secretary of State for Scotland in the Wilson government of the 1960s. Hess was later moved to Buchanan Castle near Drymen in Stirlingshire, where he was interrogated (see also Drymen).

•

brothers, John and William, pioneering surgeons and anatomists who worked in Glasgow and London. The house has a small display and museum about the men and their lives. The Hunterian Museum in Glasgow is one of their legacies. The newly built Hairmyres Hospital was where George Orwell spent some time recuperating from tuberculosis after being diagnosed with the illness when he lived on Jura. He polished and rewrote some of *1984* while convalescing there. A plaque near the entrance commemorates him (see also Jura).

On the outskirts of the town is **Calderglen Country Park**, based around Torrance House, bought by a branch of the Stuart family in 1650 (not open to the public). It has play areas, nature trails and a children's zoo. To the north of the town is the **James Hamilton Heritage Park**, with a 16-acre boating loch. Behind it is the restored **Mains Castle** (not open to the public), which was built by the Lindsay family in the early 15th century and subsequently sold to the Stuarts of Torrance. Up until the 1970s it was a ruin.

Close by the **Scottish Museum of Country Life** is based around Wester Kittochside Farm, which had been home to the Reid family since the 16th century. In 1992, the last of the family, Margaret Reid, gifted it to the National Trust for Scotland. Run jointly by the National Museums of Scotland and the National Trust, it explains rural life in Scotland throughout the ages, and has a huge

collection of farm implements and machinery. The elegant Georgian farmhouse of Wester Kittochside, which dates from 1783, is also open to the public.

In Albion Way, in Kelvin Industrial Estate, is **The Ceramic Experience**, where you can throw and decorate your own pots.

EAGLESHAM

9 miles W of Hamilton on the B764

The conservation village of Eaglesham is yet another hidden gem of a place. It was planned and built by the Earl of Eglinton in the mid 1700s. It is shaped like a huge "A", with the point facing the moorland to the west of the village. Between the two arms of the "A" is a large village green area known as the "Orry", on which once stood a cotton mill. The lovely period cottages and houses in the village make a perfect picture of Scottish rural life, though the village has largely been colonised by commuters from Glasgow and Lanarkshire. The **Parish Church**, which dates from 1788, has the look of an Alpine church about it, and it is reckoned that while planning Eaglesham the 10th Earl was influenced by villages he had admired in northern Italy. However, a church probably stood on the site for many years before the present one was built, as the name Eaglesham has nothing to do with eagles - it simply means "church village". In the kirkyard are the graves of two Covenanting martyrs - Gabriel Thomson and Robert Lockhart.

BOTHWELL

2 miles NW of Hamilton off the M74

In the centre of this small town is **Bothwell Parish Church**, with a chancel dating from 1398. It was built as part of a collegiate church by Archibald the Grim, 3rd Earl of Douglas, and has a roof made entirely of stone. Inside it is a monument to William, the third Duke of Hamilton, who died in 1694. It was removed from the old collegiate church of Hamilton when it was finally pulled down in the 1730s and then erected here. William was the son of the Marquis of Douglas, and married Ann, Duchess of Hamilton in her own right, in 1656. Though not born into the Hamilton family, he was declared Duke of Hamilton by Charles ll.

A year after the church was built, it was the scene of a royal wedding when David, son of Robert III, married Archibald the Grim's daughter Marjory. Outside the west end of the Victorian nave is a monument to **Joanna Baillie**, a playwright and poetess born at Bothwell manse in 1762. She was praised by Scott as being one of the finest writers of the 18th century. Her work, though at times filled with humour, is dark and sometimes violent, with murderous, paranoid characters, and more than one critic has wondered where a seemingly prim daughter of a minister found the material to write such stuff.

On the banks of the Clyde, some distance from the town, are the massive and impressive remains of **Bothwell Castle** (Historic Scotland), which historians have rated as one of the most important secular medieval buildings in Scotland. It was most likely built in the 13th century by Walter de Moravia, who was granted the lands of Bothwell by Alexander II. It later passed to the Douglas family, who rebuilt and strengthened most of it. In the 15th century, when James II overthrew the Douglases, it passed to the crown. It was never the home of the Earl of Bothwell, Mary Stuart's lover. His surname was Hepburn, and he had no connection with the area, apart from his title.

BLANTYRE

3 miles NW of Hamilton on the A724

Blantyre is a former mining town, which nowadays is visited because of the **David Livingstone Centre** (National Trust for Scotland). Here, at Shuttle Row, was born in 1813 the African explorer and missionary David Livingstone. A great cotton mill once stood here, and Shuttle Row was a tenement block that housed some of the workers. The great man was born in a one-room flat, though the whole tenement has now been given over to housing displays and mementos about his life and work.

Within the centre there is also an art gallery, social history museum, African play park, tearoom and gift shop.

---

65   THE WISHING WELL

Eaglesham

A well-known tearoom and restaurant, in a beautiful conservation village, offering everything from teas and coffees to lunches, light snacks and dinners.

¶ *see page 453*

Upstream is Bothwell Bridge, scene, in 1679, of the Battle of Bothwell Bridge between the Royalist forces under the Duke of Monmouth (illegitimate son of Charles ll) and a Covenanting army. The Covenanters were heavily defeated, with between 200 and 300 killed and 1,200 taken prisoner. The bridge you see today is basically the same bridge, though much altered and widened. A memorial on the Bothwell side of the bridge commemorates the event.

LANARK

In St Kentigern's kirkyard in Lanark is buried William Smellie (pronounced Smillie), the father of modern midwifery. He was born in Lanark in 1697, and was the first obstetrician to teach midwifery on a formal basis as a branch of medicine. He also pioneered the use of forceps. He began life as a doctor in Lanark, but then studied in Glasgow and Paris before establishing a practise in London, where he also lectured. He was a kindly man, and frequently delivered the babies of the poor of London free of charge. He died in 1763.

Set above the Clyde Valley near the upper reaches of the Clyde, the ancient royal burgh of Lanark received its royal charter in about 1140, making it one of the oldest towns in Scotland. But even before this it was an important place, because in AD 978 Kenneth II of Scotland held the very first recorded meeting of a Scottish parliament there.

Every year, in June, the town celebrates **Lanimer Day**, which originated as a ceremony of riding the boundaries of the burgh. And on March 1 each year is held the **Whuppity Scoorie** celebrations, when the children of the town race round **St Nicholas's Church** of 1774, waving paper balls above their head, and then scrambling for coins thrown at them. Nowadays it is the opening event in the Whuppity Scoorie Storytelling Festival, but it may have had its origins in pagan times, when it celebrated the arrival of Spring. The church replaced a medieval chapel that stood here since the 12th century. It's steeple contains the town bell, cast in 1130 and recast in1659 and 1983.

The cathedralesque **St Mary's RC Church** was built between 1856 and 1859, and rebuilt in 1907 after a fire. With its tall spire, it can be seen from all over the town, and is a superb example of a Gothic revival church.

Another custom is the **Het Pint**, held on January 1st each year. Citizens of the town meet at 10am and are given a glass of mulled wine. Anyone wishing to do so can also claim a pound. The tradition goes back to the 17th century, when Lord Hyndford gave money to the town to be used each year for pious or educational purposes.

High on a wall of St Nicholas's Church is a statue of William Wallace the Scottish freedom fighter. It recalls an event which took place when the town's royal castle (now gone) was garrisoned by English troops. Wallace committed some misdemeanour that brought him to the attention of the English sheriff of Lanark, Sir William Hesselrig. He fled, and when Wallace's wife Marion Braidfute (some versions refer to her as his "lemman", or girlfriend) refused to divulge where he was, Hesselrig killed her and her household. Wallace later returned and killed the sheriff in revenge. The supposed site of **Wallace's House** is now marked by a plaque near the church, and the site of the castle is marked by a memorial stone.

In the Westport you'll find the **Royal Burgh of Lanark Museum**, which explains the incident, as well as the town's history. Near the centre of the town are the ruins of the original place of worship, **St Kentigern's Church**. It is said that William married Marion Braidfute within the church, though there is no proof of this. However, there certainly was a real Marion Braidfute living in the area at the time, referred to as the "heiress of

Lamington", a village to the south of Lanark.

The **Lanark Heritage Trail**, with an accompanying leaflet, takes you round the burgh, highlighting its most historic features and buildings.

On the banks of the Clyde below Lanark lies the village and UNESCO World Heritage Site of **New Lanark**. It was here, in 1785, that David Dale (see also Stewarton) founded a cotton mill and village of 2,500 people that became a model for social reform Under Dale's son-in-law **Robert Owen**, who was manager, there were good working conditions, decent homes, fair wages, schools and health care in the village.

The mills were still in production up to 1968. Under the care of the New Lanark Conservation Trust, it has become one of the most popular tourist destinations in Scotland, even though people still live in some of the original tenements and cottages.

Attractions include a **Visitors Centre** (including a Textile Machinery Exhibition and the New Millennium Ride that introduces you to Robert Owen's original vision), the **Millworker's House**, the **Village Store Exhibition** and **Robert Owen's House**. Other buildings have been converted into craft workshops, and there is also a hotel housed in a former mill. A presentation called **Annie McLeod's Story** is shown in what was **Robert Owen's School**, and uses the latest in 3-D technology. The "ghost" of 19th century mill

girl Annie Macleod returns to tell the story of her life in the days of Robert Owen. The **New Millennium Experience** takes you in the opposite direction - into the future, accompanied by a young lady called Harmony. Also in the village is a **Scottish Wildlife Trust Visitors Centre**.

The mills were at one time powered by the Clyde, and close by are the **Falls of Clyde** waterfalls, the most famous being Cora Linn and Bonnington. A hydroelectric scheme now harnesses the power of the water, and the falls are only seen at their most spectacular at certain times of the year.

A few miles north of Lanark is Carluke, which stands above the Clyde Valley. It is said to be Scotland's fastest growing community, and has a memorial to three men from the town who won a Victoria Cross during the Second World War, as well as to General Roy, born in Carluke in 1726, and founder of the Ordnance Survey. The area surrounding the town is

66 DUNSYRE MAINS

Dunsyre

One of the best B&Bs in Lanarkshire, offering three comfortable rooms, hearty breakfasts and evening meals by prior arrangement.

see page 453

67 THE STAR INN

Lesmahagow

One of the best stopping places on the M74 Glasgow to Carlisle motorway for a quiet drink or beautifully cooked meal.

see page 454

Lesmahagow Priory, Lanark

68 COFFEE SPOT

Biggar
A warm welcome and
delicious home baking are
served in the Coffee Spot.

❚❚ *see page 453*

*At Brownsbank Cottage,
a mile-and-a-half from
Biggar, lived the Scottish
poet Christopher Grieve,
better known as Hugh
McDiarmid (see also
Langholm). He died in
1978, and his wife Valda
continued to live there
until her death in 1989.
Now it has been restored
to exactly how it looked
when the poet lived
there, and it is home to a
writer-in-residence. It
can be visited by
appointment only.*

noted for its orchards, introduced in medieval times by the monks of Lesmahagow Priory, and a company making jam still survives here. The bell tower of the former parish church, built in 1715, still stands.

The small, pleasant village of **Kirkfieldbank** stands northwest of the town, and is said to be haunted by a motor car. In 1912 a young girl - sister to Robert MacLellan the playwright - was killed by a car, and it is said that the ghostly sound of a car door slamming can still sometimes be heard on the main road through the village when there are no cars on the road (see also Corrie in Arran). It was said to be Scotland's first fatal car accident. To the west of the village is **Black Hill** (National Trust for Scotland), rich in Iron Age, Bronze Age and medieval remains. There are good views from it.

AROUND LANARK

BIGGAR

10 miles SE of Lanark on the A702

Biggar is a small, attractive market town that still has its original medieval layout. It sits among the rich agricultural lands of South Lanarkshire, and was granted its burgh charter in 1451.

It must have more museums per head of population than any other place in Britain. The **Biggar Gas Works Museum**, housed in the town's former gas works dating from 1839, explains how gas was produced from coal in former times, and the **Moat Park Heritage Centre** has exhibits and

displays about the town and its immediate area from the time the landscape was formed millions of years ago right up until the present day. **Greenhill Covenanter's House** used to stand at Wiston, 10 miles away, but was transported to Biggar stone by stone, and is now dedicated to the memory of the Covenanters. These were men and women who, in the 17th century, resisted the Stuart monarchs' attempts to impose bishops on the Church of Scotland, and place themselves as head of it, sometimes paying with their lives. The **Gladstone Court Museum** has re-created a Victorian street, with a dressmaker's shop, boot maker's shop and even a schoolroom.

The Albion Building houses the **Albion Motors Archives**, which are the records of the Albion Motor Company, started up locally in 1899 by Norman Fulton and T.B. Murray before moving production to Glasgow. It soon grew to be the largest manufacturer of commercial vehicles in the British Empire.

In Broughton Road is the professionally run **Biggar Puppet Theatre**, which has a Victorian-style theatre seating up to 100 people, plus a museum. Purves Puppets, which owns it, is Scotland's largest puppet company, and regularly presents shows all over Britain. The **Biggar Corn Exchange Theatre** is housed in, appropriately enough, the former Corn Exchange, and has a full programme of drama and music.

St Mary's Church was founded in 1546 by Malcolm, Lord

Fleming, Chancellor of Scotland. It was formerly collegiate, and is a graceful, cruciform building. It was the last full church to be built in Scotland before the Reformation. In the kirkyard is a gravestone commemorating the Gladstone family, forebears of William Ewart Gladstone, British Liberal prime minister during Victorian times.

To the west of the town, just off the M74, are the twin settlements of **Abington** and **Crawford**, which have a number of services, and make ideal stopping off places when heading north or south along the motorway.

The **Biggar Little Festival** takes place each year in October, and features arts, crafts and music.

LEADHILLS

18 miles S of Lanark on the B797

Like its neighbour Wanlockhead (which is in Dumfriesshire), Leadhills is a former lead mining village. It has the highest golf course in Scotland, and is full of old 18th and 19th century lead miners' cottages. It forms one terminus for the Leadhills and Wanlockhead Light Railway (see also Wanlockhead). The **Leadhills Miners Library** was founded in 1741, and is the oldest subscription Library in Scotland. At one time it was called the Allan Ramsay Library, after the famous poet (and wigmaker!) born here in 1686 (see also Penicuik). In the graveyard is the grave of **John Taylor**, a lead miner who lived to be 137 years old. Next to the cemetery is a monument to **William Symington**,

who was born in the village in 1764. He worked as an engineer in the mines, and was a pioneer of steam propulsion in ships. His paddleboat the *Charlotte Dundas* was launched at Grangemouth in 1802 (see also Dalswinton).

CARMICHAEL

4 miles S of Lanark on a minor road west of the A73

The small **Carmichael Parish Church** dates from 1750, and has an interesting laird's loft. One of the past lairds, the Earl of Hyndford, left a sum of money called the Hyndford Mortification to provide the local schoolmasters with a yearly pair of trousers and a supply of whisky. The **Carmichael Visitor Centre** is situated on the Carmichael Estate, and has a display of waxwork models (formerly housed in Edinburgh) that illustrate Scotland's history from the year AD 1000 to the present day. There are also displays about the history of the Carmichael family, which has owned the lands of Carmichael since the 13th century, and about wind energy.

DOUGLAS

8 miles SW of Lanark on the A70

It was in Douglas, in 1968, that the Cameronians (Scottish Rifles), a proud Scottish regiment, was disbanded (see also Hamilton) rather than amalgamate with another regiment. The ceremony took place in the grounds of **Castle Dangerous**, ancestral home of the Douglases, of which only a tower now survives. It was here, in

69 FARMHOUSE KITCHEN

Carmichael Estate

A superb eating place with reasonable prices that uses fresh, local produce wherever possible.

❙❙ *see page 455*

139

A monument to James Gavin, a tailor and Covenanter, stands on the site of his former home in Douglas. He had his ears cut off in 1684 by Claverhouse using his own shears, then he was deported to the West Indies. He returned four years later, and in 1695 carved a stone commemorating the outrage, inserted it above the door of his home. The stone now forms part of a cairn on the site where his house once stood.

1689, that the regiment was raised by **James, Earl of Angus**. His statue now stands in the village.

The centre of Douglas is a conservation area, with many old cottages and houses. **The Sun Inn** of 1621 was once the village's Tolbooth, where justice was meted out. **Old St Bride's** is the choir of the former parish church dating from the 14th century. Within it are memorials to members of the Douglas family, including Archibald, the 5th Earl of Angus. He was killed at Flodden in 1513, and had the curious nickname of "**Bell the Cat**". There is also a memorial to "the Good Sir James of Douglas", killed by the Moors in Spain while taking Robert the Bruce's heart to the Holy Land for burial. The clock in the clock tower was gifted to the church by Mary Stuart in 1565, and is the oldest working public clock in Scotland.

Douglas Heritage Museum, in Bell's Wynd, is situated in the former dower house of the castle. It is open on Saturdays and Sundays by prior appointment. It has displays on the Douglas family and on the Cameroonians (Scottish Rifles).

CROSSFORD

4 miles NW of Lanark on the A72

This lovely little village sits in the heart of the Clyde Valley, on the banks of the river, and is pronounced with the emphasis on the "ford" component of the name. Above it you'll find the substantial ruins of **Craignethan Castle** (Historic Scotland), where Mary Stuart once stayed. It was built in the 1530s by Sir James Hamilton of Finnart, illegitimate son of James Hamilton, 1st Earl of Arran and ancestor of the present Dukes of Hamilton. He was Master of Works to James V, who gave him the lands of Draffan on which the castle was built. However, the king later suspected that Hamilton had been plotting against him (which was probably not true), and had him executed.

The castle then passed to the crown, and subsequently given to the 2nd Earl of Arran, Sir James's half-brother and the Regent of Scotland.

Sir Walter Scott is reputed to have used the castle as a model for his "Tillietudlem Castle" in *Old Mortality*, though he later denied any link.

Craignethan Castle

Edinburgh & The Lothians

The Lothians consist of the three former counties of East Lothian, Midlothian and West Lothian. The land is generally low lying to the north, rising to moorland and hills in the south, with areas of industry to the west and areas of good farmland to the east. Being close to Edinburgh, this area is at the heart of Scottish history, full of castles, grand houses and churches. It is also a place of quiet, pastoral villages and marvellous scenery, and in East Lothian at least it has a distinctly English feel to it. The only towns that could possibly be said to be industrial are Dalkeith in Midlothian and Bo'ness, Armadale and Bathgate in West Lothian, and even here industry has not done the kind of damage it did to the countryside surrounding Glasgow.

Dominating it all is the city of Edinburgh, Scotland's capital, which probably has more history per square mile than any other

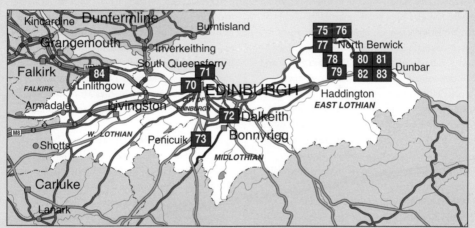

comparable place in the world. But it's a compact city, and its suburbs haven't yet gobbled up too much countryside. Behind the city are the Pentland Hills, a lonely area of high moorland stretching southwest towards the Lanarkshire boundary, and to the south and southeast are the Moorfoot and Lammermuir Hills respectively, which thrust down into the Borders.

East Lothian (formerly "Haddingtonshire") is a farming county, and is a patchwork of fields and woodland dotted all over with small, neat villages. The quiet country lanes cry out to be explored by car, and though there is none of the grandeur of the Highlands here, it is still a beautiful area. The county rises to the south, where it meets the Lammermuir Hills, and here the landscape changes, though it never loses its gentle aspect. Haddington is the county town, and is full of old buildings. The main Edinburgh-London railway line passed it by, so it never developed as a place of industry. The town's main building is the cathedralesque St Mary's Church, the tower of which is sometimes called the "Lamp of the Lothians". A succession of small resorts and golfing centres ring the coastline, though none have been commercialised to any great extent.

Mid Lothian was at one time called "Edinburghshire". Towards the south it meets the Moorfoot Hills, and has a string of small towns sitting like satellites round Edinburgh itself. Coalmining was once important here, though all vestiges of the industry have now gone. It is home to such places as Dalkeith and Bonnyrigg, which have never been overwhelmed by industry. Plus, of course, it has the world famous Rosslyn Chapel, which, people claim (as does Dan Brown in his book *The Da Vinci Code*), conceals a mystery that goes right to the heart of Christianity.

Before 1975, the county town of West Lothian was Linlithgow. It is an ancient burgh with a royal palace where Mary Stuart, better known as Mary Queen of Scots, was born. West Lothian is more industrial in character than the other two Lothians, and at one time had coal and shale mines, the latter being used to produce shale for oil production. Both industries have gone, though the occasional red shale spoil heap (called a "bing" hereabouts) can still be seen.

But there are still plenty of tranquil places to be visited, such as Torphichen, with its preceptory of St John, and South Queensferry, in the shadow of the two Forth bridges. A full day could be taken up exploring Linlithgow itself, with its royal palace, medieval church, canal basin and old, stone buildings. Then there are the county's grand houses, such as Hopetoun and The Binns, which deserve to be visited and explored.

The Lothians were absorbed into Scotland after the Battle of Carham in 1018, when Malcolm ll defeated the Northumbrians. Before that they had been either part of the Anglian kingdom of Bernicia, or had at times amalgamated to form a separate kingdom. One of these kingdoms was called Gododdin, and the events in the poem known as *Y Goddodin,* written by the poet Aneirin, took place in the Lothians and not in Wales, even though it was written in Old Welsh. It tells of the exploits of the Goddodin king Mynyddog Mwynfawr, who gathered men from all over Britain to fight on his behalf.

EDINBURGH

Edinburgh, the cultural and administrative capital of Scotland, is one of the great cities of the world. It used to be called the "Athens of the North", and a full month would not be enough to see everything it has to offer the tourist. Whereas Glasgow has worked hard at building a new image, Edinburgh has never needed to do so, though this has led to a certain amount of complacency at times.

With the advent of the Scottish Parliament, the world has rediscovered Edinburgh, and it now has all the feel and buzz of a great capital city once more. It has a population of 450,000, and is the sixth most important financial centre in Europe, and both the Church of Scotland and the Scottish law courts have their headquarters here.

The name "Edinburgh" has two possible origins. It either comes from the old Brithonic "eiden burg", meaning "fortress on the hill slope", (and indeed this describes its situation perfectly) or "Edwin's Burgh", from a 7th century Anglo Saxon king of Northumbria who built a fort where the castle now stands, though there was no doubt a fort here even before this.

Whatever the explanation, there's no denying that **Edinburgh Castle** (Historic Scotland) is where it all began. It sits on a volcanic plug (the solidified core of a volcano), with a narrow ridge running east from it on which sits the old town. There has been a fortification of some kind on the site for thousands of years, though the first stone castle was probably built by Malcolm III in the 11th century.

Edinburgh Castle has never been a thing of beauty, though age has mellowed it and given it a certain character. Neither has it been one single building, as some castles are. Rather, it is a series of buildings perched on a hilltop and surrounded by an enclosing wall. The castle as you see it now, dates from all periods, with the oldest part being **St Margaret's Chapel**, which dates from the 12th century. St Margaret was the wife of Malcolm III, and it was thanks to her that the Scottish Church came under the jurisdiction of Rome and swept away the last vestiges of Celtic monasticism (see also Dunfermline). Her son David may have built the chapel in her memory.

Every year in August the Castle Esplanade hosts the Edinburgh Military Tattoo, an extravaganza of military uniforms, marching, music and spectacle that is known the world over. Open all year, the Spirit of the Tattoo is a new tourist attraction housed in a former enclosed Victrian reservoir at the top of the Royal Mile, and tells the story of Scotland's greatest military event. There are exhibits, displays and a movie theatre.

Edinburgh Skyline

From the castle every day except Sunday is fired the One o' Clock Gun. It booms out over the city, frightening tourists who are visiting the castle at the time. There is a joke that the favourite question posed by tourists within the castle is "at what time is the one o' clock gun fired?". The custom was introduced in 1861 to give an accurate time check for ships in Leith harbour, two miles away. The first firing descended into farce when it took three attempts before the gun went off. Another gun associated with the castle is Mons Meg. It is one of two huge siege guns presented to James II in 1457 by the Duke of Burgundy, his wife's uncle. Some people imagine that it is Mons Meg which is fired at one o' clock. However, up until its replacement in 2001 with a 105 mm light gun, it was a 25lb gun manufactured in 1939 situated on Hill Mount Battery. When the changeover to the new gun took place on November 30, the two guns were fired simultaneously - the first and last time that the one o' clock gun was in fact two guns.

Not only did she introduce Roman Catholicism as a state religion, It is also likely that she was the first person to introduce buttons onto the sleeves of gentlemen's jackets and coats. When she first arrived at the Scottish court, she was distressed to see that courtiers blew their noses on their sleeves. To counteract this, she popularised buttons so that it became uncomfortab[l]el for men to do so.

The **Ensign Ewart Tomb** on the esplanade contains the body of Charles Ewart of the 2nd (Scots Greys), who captured the eagle and standard of the French 45th Regiment of the Line at the Battle of Waterloo on 18th June 1815. A famous pub in the Royal Mile is named after him (see also Kilmarnock).

A curious story once circulated that the Castle Esplanade was made part of the Scottish colony of Nova Scotia, now in Canada, in the 17th century. This was so that the newly created barons of Nova Scotia could set foot in the colony and legally claim their titles. The story was completely untrue, though there is a plaque on the esplanade which states that in 1625 Sir William Alexander took possession of the colony of Nova Scotia "by the ancient and symbolic ceremony of delivery of earth and stone" (see also Menstrie and Stirling).

Overlooking the Esplanade and the entrance to the castle is the **Half Moon Battery**, built by Regent Morton in the 16th century after what was known as the "lang

siege" of 1571 to 1573, when troops within the castle supporting Mary Stuart held out against him. Behind it is the **National War Memorial**, designed by Sir Robert Lorimer and converted from an old barracks block between 1924 and 1927. The **King's Lodging** opposite dates from the 15th century, and it was here that the monarch had his personal apartments. The Lodging was extensively refurbished by William Wallace, Master Mason to James VI when he revisited Edinburgh in 1617. One of the rooms, **Queen Mary's Room**, is where, in June 1566, Mary Stuart gave birth to James VI. There are two curious stories about this birth. One says that the Earl of Bothwell, and not Lord Darnley, Mary's husband, was the father of the baby, which would have made him illegitimate. The other says that Mary's baby was stillborn, and that another baby - the son of the Earl of Mar - was substituted in its place, while the stillborn child was entombed within a wall of the room. In 1830, when the room was being refurbished, workmen are supposed to have found a tiny coffin in the walls near the door, in which was the mummified body of a baby, wrapped in silk (see also Alloa).

In the **Crown Chamber** can be seen the Scottish crown jewels, known as the **Honours of Scotland**, and the **Stone of Destiny** (see also Dunadd and Scone), supposed to be the pillow on which Jacob slept, and on which the ancient kings of Ireland and

Scotland were crowned. It was taken from Scone near Perth by Edward I in 1297, and lay in Westminster Abbey for 700 years. Some people claim, however, that it is merely a copy, and that the monks of Scone gave Edward a worthless drain cover and hid the real one. Others claim that, when the Stone was "liberated" from Westminster Abbey in 1953 by Scottish Nationalists, the perpetrators substituted another stone in its place when it was returned. Whatever is the truth of the matter, there is no doubt that it is a potent symbol of Scottish nationhood. The **National War Museum of Scotland** is also within the castle, and explores military service over the last 400 years. Another museum within the castle is the regimental **Museum of the Royal Scots Dragoon Guards**, Scotland's only cavalry regiment.

Leading from Edinburgh Castle down to the **Palace of Holyroodhouse** is the **Royal Mile**, one of the most famous streets in the world. It follows the crest of a ridge that slopes down from the castle, and was the heart of the old Edinburgh. It is actually four streets - Castlehill, Lawnmarket, the High Street and the Canongate, and each one had tall tenements on either side. The city was surprisingly egalitarian in olden days, and the gentry and the poor lived in the same tenement blocks, the rich at the top, the professional classes in the middle, and the poor at the bottom.

Palace of Holyrood

The **Tolbooth Church** was built in 1844, and was for a time the annual meeting place of the General Assembly of the Church of Scotland, the kirk's governing body. It was designed by James Gillespie Graham and Augustus Welby Pugin, and has a 240-feet spire, which is the highest point in the city centre. Now it is "The Hub" - the administrative centre for the Edinburgh International Festival.

The **Scotch Whisky Heritage Centre** on Castlehill tells the story of Scotch, and brings three hundred years of its history to life. You'll learn about how it's made, and every Sunday afternoon there is a tasting session.

Edinburgh has often been called the "medieval Manhattan", as the 16th and 17th century tenement blocks on the Royal Mile, which look no more than four of five storeys high, are in fact up to 12 storeys high, due to the steep slope on which they were built.

Gladstone's Land (National Trust for Scotland), in the

Between July and September, Edinburgh plays host to many festivals, the most important being the Edinburgh International Festival (with its attendant Fringe Festival) in August. The Royal Mile then becomes a colourful open-air theatre, where Fringe performers and buskers take over every inch of pavement to present drama, juggling, classical music, comedy, magicians, jazz, piping, folk music and a host of other activities. It has often been observed that someone could spend four weeks in Edinburgh in August without spending a penny on festival tickets and still be regally entertained.

Across from Edinburgh Cathedral are the Edinburgh City Chambers, home to the city council. It started life as a royal exchange, and was built between 1753 and 1761 to designs by John Adam, brother of the better-known Robert. Though it appears to have only two or three storeys if seen from the Royal Mile, it actually has 12 storeys, which tumble down the slope at the back. Under the Chambers is the Real Mary King's Close, a warren of old, narrow Edinburgh streets which were closed off and built over after the bubonic plague visited the city in 1645. Conducted tours of this most moving of places are available, though participants are advised to seek out a pub afterwards to steady the nerves, as the place is suppose to be haunted. The most moving ghost is said to be that of a young girl, and visitors still leave gifts for her, such as sweets, flowers and dolls.

Lawnmarket, belonged to Thomas Gladstone, a rich merchant. It was built about 1620, has painted ceilings, and is furnished in the way it would have been in the 17th century. In Lady Stair's House, off the Lawnmarket, you'll find the **Writer's Museum**, with displays on Scotland's trio of great writers, Burns, Scott and Stevenson. The house is named after Lady Stair, who owned the house in the 18th century.

The glory of the Royal Mile is undoubtedly **St Giles Cathedral**. Originally the High Kirk of Edinburgh, it was only a cathedral for a short while in the 17th century when the Church of Scotland embraced bishops. It is now the spiritual home of Presbyterianism in the country. The first church in Edinburgh was built in the 9th century by monks from Lindisfarne, and St Giles is its direct descendant. It dates mainly from the 15th century, with a magnificent crown steeple, which is, along with the castle, one of Edinburgh's icons. At one time, in the Preston Aisle, an arm bone of St Giles was kept as a holy relic.

Attached to the cathedral is the ornate **Thistle Chapel**, designed by Sir Robert Lorimer and built in 1911. It is the home of the **Most Ancient and Noble Order of the Thistle**, which is said (erroneously, some people claim) to have been founded by Alexander II when he came to the throne in 1249. Another story puts its founding even further back, to AD 809, when King Achaius founded it to commemorate an alliance he had with Charlemagne. We do know, however, that James VII instituted the modern order in 1687, and it consists of 16 knights (who may be female) and the sovereign. There is provision also for certain "extra" knights, who may be members of the British or foreign royal families. Its motto is *nemo me impune lacissit*, which means "no one provokes me with impunity". However, it is usually expressed in Lowland Scots as "wha daur meddle wi me?", meaning "who dares meddle with me?" One of the delights of the chapel is a woodcarving of an angel playing the bagpipes.

Behind St Giles is **Parliament House**, where Scotland's parliament met up until the Treaty of Union in 1707. The building itself dates from 1639, though the façade was added in 1829 to give it a more Classical appearance. When the Scottish Parliament dissolved itself, it had 314 members. The Great Hall, where Parliament actually sat, has a magnificent hammer beam roof of oak. Now the whole building is home to the Scottish legal system, and the Court of Session - where civil cases are heard - meets within the buildings. It is also home to the Advocate's Library, founded in 1682. Alongside Parliament House is the **Signet's Library**, belonging to the Society of Writers to her Majesty's Signet. This is an exclusive society of Scottish solicitors (rather than advocates, who are the Scottish equivalent of barristers). It is the oldest such society in the world, and gets its name from the "signet", or private seal, of the Scottish monarch. The earliest mention of this seal dates to 1369, and the society originally safeguarded it and authorised its use in court. There is still a "signet" in use today, and it was struck in 1954 by the Royal Mint.

The old **Tron Church**, built in 1648, was in use as a church up until 1952. It is now a visitor information centre. An archaeological dig inside the church in 1974 revealed the foundations of shops and cellars from a medieval street called Marlin's Wynd, and these can now be seen. Up until the 1980s, the church was where revellers would gather to bring in the New Year, known in Scotland as **Hogmanay**. Now the celebrations take place all over the city centre, and have become what is claimed to be the best New Year celebrations in the world, lasting over four days.

Further along the Royal Mile, at 42 High Street, is the **Museum of Childhood**, opened in 1955, a nostalgic trip down memory lane for most adults. It features toys, games and books, and even medicines such as castor oil. It prides itself in being the "world's noisiest museum", and was the first museum in the world to concentrate on children's toys, games and activities. **John Knox House** is almost opposite. It dates from about 1470, and was the home of James Mossman, who was Mary Stuart's goldsmith. There is no real evidence that John Knox

lived in the house, though he may well have died there. There are exhibitions over three floors on Scottish history.

Eastwards from John Knox's House the Royal Mile becomes the **Canongate**, so called because it was the "gate" or street, that led to Holyrood Abbey and its canons. Up until 1865 Canongate was a separate burgh with its own provost (the Scottish equivalent of mayor) and councillors, and the **Canongate Tolbooth** of 1591, which held the council chamber, courtroom and burgh jail, is a curious building with a clock that projects out over the pavement. It now contains the **Museum of Edinburgh,** which gives an insight into the history of the city itself, and is packed with exhibits from its colourful past.

The **Canongate Church**, built between 1688 and 1691, has Dutch influences. Thomas Moodie had left a substantial sum of money for the building of a parish church for Canongate, and James Vll gave the go ahead for the Canongate Church, using this money. However, by the time it was finished in 1691 James had been deposed, and William lll was on the throne in London. At the time of building, Scottish churches were simple affairs suited to the Presbyterian form of worship. The Canongate Church's layout, however, resembles that of a Catholic or Episcopalian church, with chancel, transepts and nave, which have led some historians to believe that James was building a

The Scottish Storytelling Centre seeks to promote the art of storytelling, something which has been popular in Scotland for many years. It offers training, is involved in the Scottish education system, studies storytelling traditions in Scotland, and has regular storytelling sessions for both children and adults.

147

Close to Holyrood is the new Scottish Parliament Building, designed by the late Catalan architect Enric Miralles. Officially opened in October 2004 by HM the Queen, it is a controversial building, as it's completion date was surpassed by four years, and its cost was ten times over the original estimate. It's appearance has also divided the nation, with some people loving it and others loathing it. Guided tours are available, and while Parliament is in session you can sit in the public galleries and watch the proceedings. The building incorporates Queensberry House, built in 1667 for Margaret Douglas of Balmakellie. It got its name because, in 1689, it was bought by William Douglas, the first Duke of Queensberry, and used as a town house up until 1801 by subsequent dukes.

church that could accommodate Catholic ritual once he had re-established Catholicism in Scotland.

In the kirkyard is buried **Adam Smith** the famous economist, **Agnes McLehose** for whom Burns wrote *Ae Fond Kiss*, and **Robert Fergusson** the poet. He was Burns's hero, and died aged 24 in a madhouse. When Burns visited his grave, he was disgusted to see that there was no grave marker, so he paid for the tombstone over the grave that we see now. **White Horse Close**, beyond the church, is the most picturesque of Edinburgh's closes (though it is more modern than it looks), and it was from the White Horse Inn that the horse-drawn coaches left for London and York. It may stand on the site of the Royal stables for the Palace of Holyroodhouse.

The **Palace of Holyroodhouse** is the Queen's official residence in Scotland. It grew out of the Abbey of Holyrood, of which only the ruined nave remains. Legend says that while out hunting, David I was injured by a stag, and while he fought with it he found himself grasping, not the stag's antlers, but a holy cross or "rood". As an act of thanksgiving he founded the abbey in 1128 for Augustinian canons. It became a favourite residence for Scottish kings, being much less draughty than the castle up the hill. After the Reformation and the ejection of the monks, the abbey buildings were gradually converted and expanded for the royal court. It was here that Mary

Stuart set up court on her return from France in the 16th century, and it was here that the murder of Rizzio, her Italian secretary took place (see also Seton).The picture gallery contains portraits of over 100 Scottish kings.

The **Queen's Gallery**, next to the entrance to the grounds of the palace, is the first permanent exhibition space in Scotland for the royal collection of paintings and sculpture. It was designed by Benjamin Tindall Architects, and is housed in the former Holyrood Free Church and Duchess of Gordon's School.

To the south of the palace is **Arthur's Seat**, Edinburgh's mini mountain. Like the hill on which the castle stands, it is the plug of an old volcano, and rises to a height of 823 feet. To the south of the hill are the **Salisbury Crags**, a series of spectacular cliffs. In 1836, within a small cave, seventeen miniature coffins were discovered, each one having a miniature figure within it. No one has adequately explained their existence, though one theory suggests that they were a memorial to the corpses dug up by Burke and Hare. The coffins are now within the Museum of Scotland.

In Holyrood Road is **Our Dynamic Earth**, an exhibition and visitors centre that takes you on a journey through the history of the universe, from the beginning of time and on into the future. It features dinosaurs, earthquakes, lava flows and tropical rainstorms.

To the south of the Royal Mile, in Chambers Street behind

Edinburgh University, are the **Royal Museum** and the new **Museum of Scotland**. They house internationally important collections relating to natural history, science, the arts and history. On Nicolson Street is the **Surgeon's Hall Museum**, owned and run by the Royal College of Surgeons of Edinburgh.

One of Edinburgh's hidden gems can be found in the Cowgate - the **Magdalen Chapel** of 1547. It was built by Michael McQueen and his wife Janet Rynd, who are buried within it. It then passed to the Guild of Hammermen. The chapel contains pre-Reformation stained glass, and was where the very first General Assembly of the Church of Scotland was held in 1560, with 42 churchmen attending.

Another famous church south of the Royal Mile is **Greyfriars**. Built in 1612, it was here that the National Covenant rejecting bishops in the Church of Scotland was signed in 1638. From this, the adherents of Presbyterianism in the 17th century got the name "Covenanters". In nearby Candlemaker Row is the famous **Greyfriars Bobby** statue. It commemorates a terrier that faithfully kept guard over the grave of John Gray, his former master, who died in 1858 of tuberculosis. He did this for 14 years, until he too died in 1872. Bobby became famous after an American author, Eleanor Stackhouse Atkinson, wrote a book about it. But the story told in the book and film is not altogether true. For a start,

Atkinson made John Gray a simple farmer and shepherd, an occupation he would have found difficult in Victorian Edinburgh. And Bobby did not spend all his time at his master's grave. He left frequently to be fed, and during the winter months stayed in houses surrounding the graveyard. Disney turned Atkinson's story into a film in 1961, but what is not so well known is that Bobby also featured in a Boris Karlof film of 1945 called *The Bodysnatchers*. Boris was a grave robber, supplying corpses to hospitals for money. He chose to dig up John Gray's corpse, and Bobby tried to stop him. For his pains, he was killed by a blow from a spade.

The **City Art Centre** is in Market Street, immediately behind Waverley Station. Since its opening in 1980, it has mounted temporary exhibitions about everything from rare Egyptian antiquities to comic-book art, Michelangelo and Star Trek. It also has a fine collection of Scottish paintings, prints, photographs, sculpture and tapestries. Also in Market Street is

70 MUSEUM OF SCOTLAND

Edinburgh

A superb museum tracing the story of Scotland from the dawn of time to the present day.

 see page 455

Greyfriars

149

At the west end of the New Town is one of Edinburgh's most spectacular churches - St Mary's Cathedral. It was built as the cathedral for the Episcopalian diocese of Edinburgh, and is as large and grand as a medieval cathedral, with three soaring spires (the central one rising to 270 feet) that have become Edinburgh landmarks. It was designed by the eminent architect Sir George Glibert Scott and built in the 1870s, though the spires were added in the early 20th century. Beside the cathedral is the much altered 17th century manor house of Easter Coates House, now part of the choir school.

The Edinburgh Dungeon, which brings Scotland's bloody past to life.

North of the Royal Mile is Edinburgh's **New Town**. In the late 18th and early 19th centuries the medieval city was overcrowded and unhealthy, so the New Town was laid out in a series of elegant streets and squares to a plan by James Craig. **Princes Street** was one of these streets, and is now the city's main shopping area. It faces **Princes Street Gardens**, created from the drained bed of the old Nor' Loch.

As with today, the latest trends in architecture was not appreciated by some citizens of Edinburgh when the New Town was being built, and what we see today as a gracious, classical development was looked on with disquiet in some quarters. Henry Cockburn, a high court judge, especially disliked the whole thing, particularly its "mathematical" plan.

Within the new town's Charlotte Square you will find the **Georgian House** (National Trust for Scotland), which re-creates the interiors found in the New Town when it was built in 1796. The first occupant was John Lamont, 18th Chief of Clan Lamont. At **No. 28 Charlotte Square** is the National Trust for Scotland's headquarters with its accompanying art gallery, bookshop and small restaurant. And within the gardens at the centre of the square each August is held the **Edinburgh Book Festival**.

The **National Gallery of Scotland** on the Mound, the **Scottish National Portrait Gallery** (combined with the **Scottish National Photography Collection**) in Queen Street, the **Dean Gallery** and the **Scottish National Gallery of Modern Art** in Belford Road are all part of the National Galleries of Scotland, and are all within, or close to, the New Town. A bus service runs between all four. The **Talbot Rice Gallery**, part of Edinburgh University, is in the Old College on South Bridge.

The **Scottish Genealogy Society Library and Family History Centre** is in Victoria Terrace off George IV Bridge, and has collections of materials tracing Scottish families both high and low and their members, including old parish registers. There is also material relating to Scottish families abroad. At the east end of Princes Street you will find **Register House**, where the National Archives of Scotland are stored. It

The Georgian House

was designed by Robert Adam, with the foundation stone being laid in 1774. In front of it is an equestrian statue of the Duke of Wellington by Sir John Steell.

Also in Princes Street is Scotland's official memorial to one of its greatest writers, Sir Walter Scott. The Gothic **Scott Monument**, which soars to over 200 feet, and offers a marvellous view from the top, was designed by George Meikle Kemp, with work beginning in 1840. In August 1846 it opened to the public. The statue of Scott was done by the same Sir John Steell who did the equestrian statue of Wellington at Register House.

Further north, off Inverleith Row, are the **Royal Botanic Gardens**, 70 acres of greenery and colour surrounded by the bustle of the city. They were founded in 1670 as a "physic garden" at Holyrood, but were transferred here in 1823. And at Leith you'll find the **Royal Yacht Britannia** (see panel) moored at the **Ocean Terminal**, a leisure, shopping and entertainment complex. The ship is open to the public.

Leith was, up until 1920, a separate burgh. In fact it was a royal burgh -the only one in Scotland to be absorbed into another burgh. Other royal burghs either became cities, or, like Roxburgh, were abandoned.

In Pier Place in Newhaven, to the west of Leith, is the **Newhaven Heritage Museum** explaining the history of this former fishing village. It was in

Newhaven that the largest fighting ship of its day, the Great Michael was built between 1507 and 1513 for James IV's Scottish navy. It is said that the whole fleet which sailed to America with Columbus in 1492 could fit comfortably into her hull. She was the envy of Europe, and Henry VIII even demanded that she be handed over to him, as he considered her far too good for the Scots. In charge of the building project was Scotland's Admiral of the Fleet Sir Andrew Wood (see also Largo).

She may have been the largest ship of her day, but her short life was inglorious. Soon after she was built, she was sold to the French and, some people claim, was allowed to rot in Brest harbour.

Granton sits further west, and at one time was a busy harbour and industrial area developed by the local landowner, the Duke of Buccleuch. It had a huge gas works, but is now undergoing a major redevelopment, though one of the gas work's huge gasometers has been preserved. At its centre is **Caroline Park**, an elegant mansion dating from the 17th century (not open to the public).

Further to the west, at Corstorphine, are the **Edinburgh Zoological Gardens**, set in 80 acres. The zoo is famous for its penguins, and the daily "penguin parade" when the penguins march round part of the zoo. However, whether the parade takes place or not depends on the weather and the whim of the penguins themselves, who sometimes choose

•

On Calton Hill, to the east of Princes Street is the 106-feet high Nelson Monument, from the top of which are views out over the city. It commemorates Nelson's death at the Battle of Trafalgar in 1805, and was designed by the architect Robert Burn. A time signal is installed at the top, consisting of a ball which drops at 12 noon in winter and 1pm in summer. It allowed ship's captains on the Forth to set their watches accurately. However, it could not be seen when conditions were bad, so the firing of the one o' clock gun from Edinburgh Castle was introduced in its place.

•

71 THE ROYAL YACHT BRITANNIA

Edinburgh

Experience the splendour of the yacht used by Her Majesty the Queen and the Royal Family for over forty years.

  see page 456

151

The Battle of Pinkie, the last battle fought between Scottish and English national armies, took place near Musselburgh in 1547 during the "Rough Wooing", when Henry VIII was trying to force the Scottish parliament to agree to a marriage between his son and the infant Mary Stuart. The Scots were defeated due to the incompetence of the Earl of Arran, Scotland's commander, though Mary herself eventually married the Dauphin of France, heir to the French throne.

not to hold it.

Craigmillar Castle (Historic Scotland) is on the southeast outskirts of the city. The extensive ruins date from the 14th century, with many later additions. Mary Stuart stayed here for a short while after her Italian secretary Rizzio was murdered. **Lauriston Castle**, near Davidson's Mains, is also worth visiting. It is set in 30 acres of parkland, and is the home of the Edinburgh Croquet Club. One of its owners was the father of **John Napier**, who invented logarithms. It now has a collection of furniture and decorative arts.

Napier's own home, **Merchiston Tower**, is now part of Napier University. John lived between 1550 and 1610, and was known as "Marvellous Merchiston". Not only did he invent logarithms, his simple invention to aid multiplication, known as "Napier's Bones", plus his invention of a system of metal plates to ease calculations, makes him the father of the modern calculator. Curiously, he also invented a walled chariot with openings through which guns could be fired in times of war - the precursor of the modern tank.

The **Royal Observatory** sits on Blackford Hill, south of the city centre, and has displays and exhibits relating to astronomy. At one time it sat atop Calton Hill in the city centre, but moved to its present site in 1896. There is a visitor centre.

AROUND EDINBURGH

MUSSELBURGH

6 miles E of Edinburgh on the A199

Musselburgh got its name from the beds of mussels that once lay at the mouth of the River Esk, on which the town stands. Now it is a dormitory town for Edinburgh. The **Tolbooth** dates from the 1590s, and was built of stones from the former Chapel of Our Lady of Loretto, which in pre-Reformation times was served by a hermit. The tolbooth now has regular exhibitions and displays about Musselburgh's history. **Inveresk Lodge Gardens** (National Trust for Scotland), with their terraces and walled garden, illustrates methods and plants that can be used in a home garden. The statue at the west end of the High Street is to **David Macbeth Moir**, a local doctor, writer and benefactor. It was erected in 1853. Also in the High Street is the 18th century **Mercat Cross**, erected on the site of its medieval predecessor. In the former St Thomas's Church is a small **Doll Museum**.

The **Roman Bridge** across the Esk originally dates from the 13th century (with many alterations), though it is claimed that it was built on the foundations of a Roman Bridge. It is still in use today as a footbridge.

Musselburgh Racecourse is situated on the town's links, and has been there since 1818, when it was moved from Leith Sands. It is one of only two racecourses in Scotland that has races on the flat and over obstacles. Flat racing usually takes place in the summer and autumn, with jumps in the winter.

PRESTONPANS

7 miles E of Edinburgh on the B1348

The town takes its name from the pans that were built here in medieval times by monks to produce salt from sea water. At the **Battle of Prestonpans** on 21 September 1745, the Jacobite army of Charles Edward Stuart defeated a Hanoverian army under Sir John Cope. The whole battle only took 15 minutes, with many of the Hanoverian troops being trapped against a high wall (which can still be seen) surrounding **Prestongrange House**. Contemporary accounts tell of terrified Hanoverian troops trying to scale the wall and dropping into the comparative safety of the house's grounds. Even though it took place in the early 18th century, the site was largely an industrial one, with even a primitive tramway for hauling coal crossing the battle field. The Jacobite song *Hey Johnnie Cope* lampoons the English commander, though he was not wholly to blame for the Hanoverian defeat, and was in fact exonerated of any blame by a court martial. A small memorial to the battle can be found at Meadowhill.

Prestonpans Mercat Cross is unique in that it is the only one in Scotland that has stayed in the same position since being built. **Prestongrange Industrial**

Heritage and Museum is at Morrison's Haven, and tells the story of the local industries through the ages. It has an old beam engine. **Preston Tower and Gardens** are to be found in some parkland. Built in the 15th century by the Hamiltons, the tower was first burnt by the English troops of the Earl of Hertford during the Rough Wooing and then attacked and left in ruins by Oliver Cromwell in the 17th century.

PORT SETON AND COCKENZIE

9 miles E of Edinburgh on the B1348

Port Seton Collegiate Church (Historic Scotland) was built, but never completed, in the 14th century as a collegiate church served by a college of priests. It is dedicated to St Mary and the Holy Cross, and has some tombs of the Seton family, as well as fine vaulting. In 1544 it was looted and stripped by the Earl of Hertford and his English army. **Seton Castle** dates from 1790, and was designed by Robert Adam. It replaces the former Seton Palace, one of the grandest Scottish buildings of its time. Mary Stuart visited the Palace after the murder of Rizzio by her second

Prestonpans Parish Church dates from the early 17th century, and was built at the behest of the Reverend John Davidson, a fiery minister who would have nothing to do with James VI, bishops or the Scottish Parliament. For a short while he was imprisoned in Edinburgh Castle, and on his release in 1601 was forbidden to leave his parish.

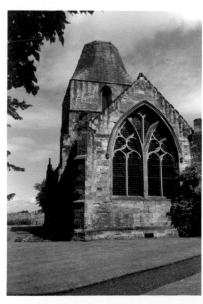

Port Seton Collegiate Church

153

Fa'side Castle stands two miles southwest of Tranent, and was built in the 14th century by the de Quincey family. Due to its support for Edward l during the Wars of Independence in the early 14th century, Bruce stripped them of their lands after the Battle of Bannockburn. The castle was sacked by English troops during the Rough Wooing, and though rebuilt was allowed to become ruinous again in the 19th century. It has now been completely restored.

---

72 SAM'S

Dalkeith

Popular hostelry with beer garden; regular music sessions and weekly pub quiz.

see page 456

---

husband, Lord Darnley (see also Edinburgh).

Cockenzie House (not open to the public) dates from the 17th century, and was the home of John Cadell, who did much to bring industry to the area in the 18th century. Overshadowing the village is **Cockenzie Power Station**, which was opened in 1968 to make use of the coal that was mined here at one time. Both its chimneys rise to over 500 feet.

TRANENT

9 miles E of Edinburgh on the A199

Tranent claims to be one of the oldest towns in East Lothian. Coal was worked here since at least the 12th century, though all mine working has long disappeared. In the Civic Square stands the **Jackie Crookston Statue**, commemorating a woman who, along with eleven others, was shot dead by government troops in 1797 during a protest against compulsory conscription into the British Army. The protest was known as the "Tranent Militia Riot", and a cover-up ensured that no one in the army was ever brought to justice for the atrocity.

ORMISTON

10 miles E of Edinburgh on the B6371

This small pleasant village sits on the banks of the Tyne Water, and has an interesting **Mercat Cross** set into modern steps. For all the great age of the cross, the village itself dates to 1735, when it was laid out by James Cockburn, one of the agricultural reformers of the

time. Ormiston was the birthplace, in 1795, of **Robert Moffat** the missionary, and there is a monument to his memory. His daughter Mary was wife to David Livingstone.

The **Pencaitland and Ormiston Community Path Network,** on the old Winton estate, connects the village with its neighbour a few miles to the east.

DALKEITH

7 miles SE of Edinburgh on the A68

This pleasant town is nowadays a dormitory for Edinburgh, and indeed it recently earned the dubious distinction of having the most expensive housing in Scotland. At one time it was an important market and industrial town on the main road south from Edinburgh to England, and indeed high-tech industry still flourishes here. **Dalkeith Palace** was built around the medieval Dalkeith Castle for Anne, Duchess of Monmouth and Buccleuch in the early 18th century. It became known as the "grandest of all classical houses in Scotland". Its 2,500 acre grounds are now a country park.

Anne's husband James Scott, Duke of Monmouth, was an illegitimate son of Charles II who had defeated a Covenanting army at Bothwell Bridge. However, he later plotted to usurp his father, and had himself declared king on 20 June 1685. He was defeated at the Battle of Sedgemoor (the last battle fought on English, rather than British soil) on July 6th, and was executed on Tower Hill in London nine days later. Anne had been Countess of Buccleuch in her own right, and was allowed to keep her title, though the Monmouth title was suppressed. The heir to the Dukedom of Buccleuch and Queensberry now carried the title of Earl of Dalkeith, though he lives in Drumlanrig Castle in Dumfriesshire (see also Drumlanrig).

NEWTONGRANGE

8 miles SE of Edinburgh on the A7

The monks of Newbattle Abbey started coal mining in the Lothians in the 13th century, so the industry has a long history in the area. The Lady Victoria Colliery in Newtongrange houses the **Scottish Mining Museum**, which tells the story of coal mining in Scotland from those days right up until the present. There is a re-created coalface, as well as the original winding engines and a visitor's centre. The Lady Victoria is one of the finest surviving Victorian collieries in Europe. It opened in the 1890s and closed in 1981. At its peak, it employed over 2,000 men.

The oldest part of **Dalhousie Castle**, in nearby Bonnyrigg, is the round tower, which dates from the 15th century. The rest dates from the 17th century. The first castle on the site was built by Simundus de Ramasie a Norman knight from what is now Cambridgeshire, in the 13thcentury. The Ramsays, the Earls of Dalhousie, became the chiefs of Clan Ramsay. They now

live in Brechin Castle. The castle is now a luxury hotel.

ARNISTON

9 miles SE of Edinburgh off the A7

Arniston House has been the home of the Dundas family for over 400 years. It was built between 1726 and the 1750s to the designs of William and John Adam on the site of an old tower house. The interior detail is wonderful, and there is also a fine collection of paintings by artists such as Raeburn and Ramsay. In the 17th century the Dundas family was one of the most powerful in Scotland, and held many important posts in the Scottish legal system. The house is open to the public, though dates and times should be checked, as they vary throughout the summer.

BORTHWICK

11 miles SE of Edinburgh off the A7

Borthwick Castle, now a hotel, is a massive twin-towered castle built by Sir William Borthwick in about 1430 on the site of an earlier tower house. It was to this castle that Mary Stuart and Bothwell came after their marriage in 1567. It was a marriage which displeased the Scottish people, and over 1,000 Scottish nobles cornered the couple there. They demanded that Mary hand over Bothwell for his part in the murder of Lord Darnley, Mary's second husband. However, Bothwell escaped and fled to Dunbar.

On hearing of his escape, they immediately retired from the

St Nicholas Buccleuch Church in Dalkeith is a large building, formerly a collegiate church, dating mainly from an extensive rebuilding in the mid 19th century. The ruined apse, however, is 14th and 15th century, and the boy of Duchess Anne, who died in 1732, lies here. Also buried here are the first Earl of Morton (a Douglas, and original owner of Dalkeith Castle) and his wife Joanna, daughter to James I of Scotland.

Soutra Aisle in Soutra is all that remains of a medieval hospital. It was dedicated to the Holy Trinity, and it was here that Augustinian monks looked after travellers, pilgrims and the sick and wounded. A recent archaeological dig uncovered evidence of surgery and the treatment of patients by herbal remedies. Even some pieces of bandage with human tissue still attached to them were recovered.

Queen's presence, thinking that she had seen through his treachery. However, no sooner had they left her, she tore off her fine gowns and put on breeches and a pageboy's shirt, and made her escape so that she could rejoin her husband. The Red Room is said to be haunted by her ghost.

The Borthwicks were a powerful family, and when they took prisoners one of the games they played was to tie the prisoners' hands behind their backs and make them jump the 12 feet from the top of one tower to the other. If they succeeded they were set free.

In 1650 the castle was attacked by Oliver Cromwell's Parliamentarian army, and it was abandoned not long after. In the early 20th century it was restored, and during World War II it was secretly used to store national treasures.

The modern **Borthwick Parish Church** has a 15th century aisle with effigies of the first Lord and Lady Borthwick.

CRICHTON
11 miles SE of Edinburgh on the B6367

Crichton Castle (Historic Scotland) was probably built in the late 14th century by John de Crichton. It consisted of a simple tower house typical of the period, but was added to by his son William, an ambitious and unscrupulous man who became Lord Chancellor of Scotland. During the minority of James II, Archibald the 5th Earl of Douglas was appointed regent, but he died

two years after James ascended the throne. Both Crichton and Sir Alexander Livingstone competed to take Archibald's place, fearing that a Douglas might be appointed again.

They invited the 6th Earl of Douglas, who was only 16, to a banquet at Edinburgh Castle in 1440, along with his brother and a friend. The head of a black bull was brought to the table, and at this sign the Earl, his brother and their friend were murdered. The affair became known as the *Black Dinner*.

Crichton Collegiate Church was built in 1449 by William Crichton. It consists of a chancel and transepts, and at one time had a nave, which is now gone. **Vogrie Country Park** lies to the north of the castle, and is centred on Vogrie House. It has woodland walks, picnic areas and a golf course.

SOUTRA
15 miles SE of Edinburgh off the A68

From Soutra, high in the Lammermuir Hills, it is reckoned that you get the best view in Central Scotland. On a clear day you can see the full sweep of the Firth of Forth with Fife beyond, and at least 60 Highland peaks.

ROSSLYN CHAPEL
7 miles S of Edinburgh on the B7006

The village of Roslin has gained world renown through *The Da Vinci Code*, by Dan Brown. **Rosslyn Chapel** (the village is Roslin, the chapel is Rosslyn), even without its *Da Vinci Code* associations, would still be worth visiting, however. It is an extravaganza of a building on which work began in 1446. Its founder was Sir William St Clair, third and last Prince of Orkney, who lived at nearby **Rosslyn Castle**. In the choir of this unfinished church (still in use) are carvings with both Masonic and Knights Templar associations (see also Kirkwall).

Dan Brown, however, got the derivation of the name wrong. Rosslyn has nothing to do with the Rose Line. It comes from the two Scottish words "ross" meaning a promontory, and "lyn" meaning a stream, and indeed the chapel sits on a promontory above a stream. Nor is there a Star of David pathway on the floor, caused by the countless feet of pilgrims as they move between the six main features of the chapel. There is seating for the congregation, which makes this impossible.

The carving in the interior is spectacular, and shows plants that only grow in the New World, even though Columbus had not yet sailed across the Atlantic when it was built. There are also pagan carvings of "The Green Man", as well as the famous **Apprentice Pillar**. This was said to have been carved by an apprentice when the master mason working on the church was on the Continent seeking inspiration. When he returned and saw the workmanship, the mason is supposed to have murdered the apprentice in a fit of jealousy.

Legends abound about the church. One theory says that the writings of Christ lie in its unopened vaults. Another says that the bodies of Knights Templar lie in the unopened crypt, fully dressed in armour. A third says that the **Holy Grail** is embedded in one of the pillars. And yet another says it is a re-creation of **Solomon's Temple** in Jerusalem.

There's even a theory that the body of Christ himself lies in the vaults. Whatever the truth of the matter, and the theories seem to get wilder and wilder with every new book written about it, there's no denying that it is one of the most beautiful buildings in Britain (see also Kilmartin).

Nearby is the **Roslin Glen Country Park**, with woodland walks that go past old gunpowder works. **The Battle of Roslin** took place in 1303, during the Wars of Independence. An army of 8,000 Scots, led by John Comyn, faced an English army of over 30,000 and soundly defeated them. While not an important strategic battle in its own right, it did give the people of Scotland renewed courage when they saw that the English could be defeated.

Hawthornden Castle lies a mile east of the chapel, and was built by the poet William Drummond in 1638 round an old tower house. It is owned by the widow of the chairman of the Heinz food company, and is now a retreat for professional writers. Ian Rankin has stayed there.

PENICUIK

9 miles S of Edinburgh on the A701

Penicuik was once a mining and

A few miles southeast of Roslin is the small village of Temple. While there is no proof that Rosslyn Chapel had any real connection with the Knights Templar, there is no doubt that Temple did. The Order had its Scottish base here until it was suppressed in 1307. The ruined Temple Church supposedly dates from the 12th century, but it may be later. When the Knights Templar were suppressed, the Knights of St John inherited all its properties, and this order may have built the church (see also Torphichen).

To the west of Penicuik, beyond the A702, is the Pentland Hills Regional Park, with Scald Law being the highest peak in the range at 1,898 feet. Castlelaw is an old souterrain, or underground dwelling dating from the Iron Age.

paper making town, founded in 1770 by its laird, Sir James Clerk of Penicuik. In the grounds of Penicuik House stands the **Allan Ramsay Obelisk**, dedicated to the memory of Allan Ramsay, who was born in Leadhills in Lanarkshire in 1685. Ramsay visited the town often, as he was a friend of Sir James Clerk, who raised the obelisk, and had a house nearby (see also Leadhills). **St Mungo's Parish Church** dates from 1771, and has a 12th century detached belfry.

CRAMOND

5 miles W of Edinburgh on a minor road off the A90

Cramond is a charming village of old whitewashed cottages on the banks of the River Almond where it enters the Firth of Forth. The **Parish Church** of 1656, with its medieval tower, sits within the ruins of a **Roman Fort** built about AD 142. The Reverend Robert Walker, who was painted by Raeburn skating on Duddingston Loch in the 18th century, was minister here. **Cramond Tower** (not open to

the public) dates from the 15th century, And **Cramond House** (not open to the public) dates from 1680. At one time, the village was famous for the manufacture of nails. **Cramond Island** sits one mile offshore, and it is possible to walk to it via a causeway at low tide, though walkers should heed the notices about tide times before setting off.

INGLISTON

7 miles W of Edinburgh off the A8

Almost in the shadow of Edinburgh International Airport at Turnhouse is the **Royal Showground**, home each year of the Royal Highland Show, Scotland's premier country and farming fair.

BALERNO

7 miles SW of Edinburgh off the A70

Malleny Garden (National Trust for Scotland) is a walled garden beside the 17th century Malleny House (not open to the public) extending to three acres and dominated by 400-year-old clipped yew trees. There are herbaceous borders, a fine collection of old-fashioned roses, and it houses the National Bonsai Collection for Scotland. The house was built for Sir James Murray of Kilbaberton in 1635.

RATHO

8 miles W of Edinburgh on a minor road off the A8

Ratho sits on the Union Canal, and from the **Edinburgh Canal Centre**, opened in 1989, canal

Cramond Roman Fort

cruises are available. Parts of **Ratho Parish Church**, dedicated to St Mary, date from the 12th century, though little of this can now be seen due to restorations over the years.

The **Adventure Centre** is billed as the "gateway to adventure", with the National Rock Climbing Centre having 2,400 square metres of artificial wall surfaces, the largest climbing arena in the world. One other feature is the Airpark, Europe's largest suspended aerial adventure ropes ride.

At Ratho you will find a branch of the **Seagull Trust**, which offers trips on the canal to disabled people. The first cruise took place in 1979, long before the canal was restored. Now 5,000 disabled people a year cruise on the canal.

SOUTH QUEENSFERRY

9 miles W of Edinburgh city centre off the A90

South Queensferry is named after St Margaret, Malcolm III's queen, who founded a ferry here in the 11th century to carry pilgrims across the Forth to Dunfermline Abbey and St Andrew's Cathedral. When she herself died she was buried in the abbey and later canonised, with her shrine becoming a place of pilgrimage as well. Now the ferry has been replaced by the **Forth Rail Bridge** and the **Forth Road Bridge**, two mammoth pieces of civil engineering. The rail bridge was built between 1883 and 1890 to link Edinburgh and Aberdeen, and the road bridge was completed in 1964. In the shadow of the Rail Bridge is the historic **Hawes Inn** of 1683, which features in R.L. Stevenson's *Kidnapped*. Opposite is the slipway from which the former ferry sailed.

The town has a glorious mix of cottages and houses dating from the 16th century onwards. **Plewlands House** (National Trust for Scotland) dates from 1643, and has been converted into private flats. The **Queensferry Museum**, in the High Street, has exhibits and displays on local history. There are also wonderful views of the two bridges from it. The church of the former **Carmelite Friary** in Rose Lane dates from the 15th century, and is now an Episcopalian church, St Mary's. The whitewashed **Tolbooth** dates from the 1600s, with a clock tower that was added in 1720. **Black Castle** dates from 1626, and was built by a sea captain. He was, however, lost at sea and his maidservant was accused of paying a witch to cast a spell on him to make this happen. Both were burnt at the stake.

Dalmeny House, to the east of the town, overlooks the Firth of Forth. It is the home of the Primrose family, who are Earls of Roseberry, and was built in the 1820s. There is an excellent collection of tapestries and furniture. On the shoreline is the **Eagle Rock** (Historic Scotland), with a carving of an eagle on it. **Dalmeny Church**, dedicated to St Cuthbert, is one of the best-preserved Norman churches in Britain. The south doorway is richly carved, as is the chancel and apse.

Each year in early August the quaint custom of the Burry Man takes place. Dressed from head to toe in plant burrs, he spends nine hours walking about the town on a Friday. While everyone agrees it is an ancient custom, no on knows how it originated or what purpose it served. A more recent custom is the Looney Dook, when swimmers jump into the Firth of Forth on New year's Day, some dressed in funny costume. The words literally mean "lunatic dip" (see also Broughty Ferry).

It was in the 12th century St Martin's Church in Haddington (now roofless, and all that is left of an old Cistercian nunnery that stood in Nungate, outside the then burgh boundaries) that the Scottish and French parliaments met in 1548 to sanction Mary Stuart's marriage to the Dauphin of France. Members of both the French and Scottish nobility attended, and put an end to Henry VIII's plans to have Mary marry his son Edward. The 16th century Nungate Bridge over the Tyne is named after the nunnery.

Another stately home near South Queensferry is **Hopetoun House**, possibly the grandest "big house" in Scotland, and certainly the best example of a Georgian house in the country. It sits almost on the banks of the Forth, and is home to the Marquis of Linlithgow. It was started in 1699 by the 1st Earl of Hopetoun, ancestor of the present Marquis, and designed by Sir William Bruce with enlargements by William Adam, who introduced the sweeping curves. The inside is spectacular and opulent, with ornate plasterwork, tapestries, furnishings and paintings. Surrounding the house is magnificent parkland extending to 150 acres, with a deer park and spring garden. The main approach to the house is by the Royal Drive, which can only be used by royalty. George IV used it when he visited Scotland in 1822, and Elizabeth II also used it in 1988.

HADDINGTON

The royal burgh of Haddington received its royal charter in the 12th century from David I, and is thought to be the birthplace in 1505 of **John Knox**. It sits on the River Tyne (but not the one that flows through Newcastle), and at one time it was the fourth largest town in Scotland. The **Town House**, in the High Street, dates from 1748, and was designed by William Adam.

It is a quiet town of old buildings, including the quite superb cathedralesque **Parish Church of St Mary.** It was formerly collegiate, and dates from the 15th century. It stood outside the burgh boundaries at that time, and when the parliament was meeting at St Martin's, the Scots were laying siege to the town, as it was occupied by the English. Mary of Guise (Mary Stuart's mother) attended the parliament, and when she climbed to the top of St Mary's tower to view the English defences she was shot at. The ruined choir was restored in the 1970s, and such is the church's size and beauty (it is the longest parish church in Scotland) that some people erroneously think it is the church of a former abbey. In the choir is the burial place of **Jane Welsh** (Thomas Carlyle's wife), who was born in the town. **Jane Welsh Carlyle Museum,** within the early 18th century house where she was born, can be visited.

The **Lauderdale Aisle**, owned by the Earls of Lauderdale, is unique in that it is a small Episcopalian chapel within a Presbyterian Church. This

Nungate Bridge, Haddington

ecumenicalism continues every year in May with the **Whitekirk and Haddington Pilgrimage**, when people from all the main Christian religions in Scotland walk between the two towns (see also Whitekirk).

St Mary's is one of the few Church of Scotland churches to have a full peel of bells, which were installed in 1999. There are eight bells, the last peel (three bells) having been taken by Henry VIII's troops in 1548.

The writer **Samuel Smiles** was born in Haddington in 1812. Though he wrote many books, he is best known for *Self Help*. Alexander II and William the Lion may also have been born here, in a royal castle that has long gone.

About four miles east of Haddington is **Traprain Law**, from the top of which there are superb views. The summit was occupied from Neolithic times right up until the Dark Ages, and the outline of a fort can clearly be seen. It was the capital of a tribe the Romans called the Votadini, which roughly translated means "the farmers". More Roman finds have been made here, including a horde of Roman silver, than anywhere else in Scotland.

The village of **Bolton** lies a few miles south of the town, and in the churchyard are the graves of Robert Burn's brother Gilbert, his mother Agnes and his sister Annabella. One of Gilbert's sons, the Reverend Thomas Burns, helped found the city of Dunedin in New Zealand (see also Thornhill and Monkton).

AROUND HADDINGTON

GULLANE

6 miles N of Haddington on the A198

This village sits inland from the Firth of Forth, but has fine views north towards Fife. Nowadays it is a small golfing resort (it has three courses) with many large, imposing villas. The British Open is held here regularly, and the course at **Muirfield** is home to the Honourable Company of Edinburgh Golfers. The **Heritage of Golf** exhibition on the West Links Road traces the golfing history of the area.

The ruins of the **St Andrew's Church** can be seen at the west end of the main street. They date from the 12th century, and were abandoned in 1612 due to sand blowing in from the beach and threatening to cover it. On Gullane Bay, and signposted from the main street, is **Gullane Bents**, one of the best beaches on the Firth of Forth.

South of Gullane, in the village of Drem, is the **RAF Drem Museum**. The Royal Air Force station here was one of the busiest in Scotland during World War II, and some of the old buildings still survive, though the runway is long gone. However, there is still a small exhibition and display in what was the WAAF accommodation.

Greywalls is an imposing house designed by Sir Edwin Landseer Lutyens and built about 1901 as a holiday home for the

•

Close to Haddington is Lennoxlove, home to the Dukes of Hamilton since 1946. It houses the death mask of Mary Stuart, which shows her to have been, as many contemporaries observed, an extremely beautiful woman. The origins of the house go back to at least the 13th century, when it was called Lethington Hall, and the home of the Maitland family. Within the house is the Nigel Tranter Centre, dedicated to the famous writer of historical novels. There are original manuscripts and other artefacts and objects connected with the great man. Tranter's father was a minister in the Catholic Apostolic Church, better known as the "Irvingites" (see also Aberlady and Annan).

•

Archerfield House sits to the west of the village of Dirleton, and was built in 1733 for the Nisbet family. In the late 19th century it was rented by Herbert Asquith, the then prime minister, and during World War ll a meeting took place here between Winston Churchill and Franklin D. Roosevelt. It was later allowed to decay, and was due for demolition until saved in the late 20th century. Now it is the centrepiece of an exclusive golfing resort. The house and estate got its name from the bowmen of Edward l of England, who practised here during the Wars of Independence in the 12th and 13th centuries.

Hon Alfred Lyttleton. Lutyens was most famous for designing and laying out New Delhi. The gardens were designed by the famous Gertrude Jekyll. In later years, Edward Vll was a regular visitor to Greywalls. It is now a hotel.

DIRLETON

6 miles N of Haddington off the A198

The impressive ruins of **Dirleton Castle** (Historic Scotland) dominate this pleasant village, whose main buildings are grouped round a village green. The oldest parts of the castle date to the end of the 13th century, though there have been extensive additions and alterations over the years. The castle was taken by Edward I of England in 1298, but was back in Scottish hands by 1311. It was built by the Norman family of de Vaux, though it has also been owned by the Halyburtons and the Ruthvens. The third Lord Ruthven was implicated in the murder of Mary Stuart's Italian secretary Rizzio in Holyroodhouse. To the west of the castle are some formal terraced gardens, which were in the Guinness Book of Records as having the longest herbaceous border in the world.

Dirleton Parish Church dates from 1612, and was built to replace the church at Gullane.

ABERLADY

6 miles N of Haddington on the A198

This pleasant village was the port for Haddington until the bay silted up. The **Aberlady Bay Nature Reserve** covers 1,439 acres of foreshore and dunes, and is popular with bird watchers. The village was home to one of Scotland's most popular historical novelists, **Nigel Tranter**, who died in the year 2000. There is a small cairn to his memory close to Quarry House, where he used to live. In addition to his Scottish novels, he also wrote eleven Westerns under the pseudonym Nye Tredgold.

On the Longniddry road, west of the village, is **Gosford House,** built in the 1790s to the designs of Robert Adam. It is the residence of the Earls of Wemyss and March, and is open to the public during the summer months.

Myreton Motor Museum contains displays of motorcars, cycles and military vehicles. **Aberlady Parish Church** was remodelled in the 19th century, though an interesting 16th century tower still stands. In the High Street is the old **Mercat Cross** of 1780. To the east of the village is **Luffness Castle**, once the ancestral home of the Hepburns, and now a hotel.

ATHELSTANEFORD

2 miles NE of Haddington on the B1343

Athelstaneford has a special place in Scottish history. It was here that the Scottish flag, the **Saltire**, or St Andrew's Cross, was first adopted. Athelstan was a king of Northumbria who fought a combined army of Picts and Scots at Athelstaneford in AD 832. The Pictish leader, Angus mac Fergus, on the day before the battle, saw a huge white cross made of clouds in the sky, and took it as an omen. Athelstane was duly defeated, and a white cross on a blue background was adopted as the flag of Scotland, making it the oldest national flag in Europe.

This is why the Saltire on its own should be white and sky blue, whereas when it is incorporated into the Union Jack the blue darkens. The **Saltire Flag Heritage Centre** in an old doocot (dovecot) in the village explains the story of the battle and the flag. There is also a memorial within the kirkyard of the fine **Parish Church**, which dates from 1780.

To the north of the village is **Chesters**, an Iron Age fort with ditches and banks.

NORTH BERWICK

7 miles NE of Haddington on the A198

North Berwick is one of Scotland's best-known holiday and golfing resorts. It is a clean, attractive town which was granted a royal charter by Robert II in 1373. **North Berwick Law**, a volcanic plug, rises to a height of 613 feet behind the town, and makes a wonderful viewpoint. It is topped by the ruins of a Napoleonic watchtower. Two miles off the coast lies the **Bass Rock**, another volcanic plug that broods over the waters of the Firth of Forth. Over 150,000 sea birds nest each year on the 350-feet high cliffs and on smaller islands such as Fidra and Craigleith.

From the **Scottish Seabird Centre** on a promontory near the old harbour you can use remote controlled cameras which are situated on the islands to study them without disturbing the colonies. There are also powerful telescopes on a viewing deck, a film about Scotland's sea birds, and a café restaurant.

In the 8th century the Bass Rock was home to the hermit **St Baldred**, who evangelised this part of Scotland (though he is not to be confused with another St Baldred who succeeded St Mungo as Bishop of Glasgow, and who lived a century earlier). In later times it also served as a prison for Jacobites and Covenanters, and there are traces of old fortifications on it.

Also on the promontory are the scant ruins of the **St Andrew's Auld Kirk**, which date from the 12th century onwards, though there was probably a wooden chapel here since at least the 7th century. It was finally abandoned in 1656 when the chancel collapsed due to coastal erosion, and when the Seabird Centre was being built, over 30 well-preserved skeletons from the old graveyard were uncovered, the earliest one dating back to the 7th century.

74 THE COUNTY HOTEL

North Berwick

Handsome town centre hotel offering immaculate en suite accommodation and restaurant.

see page 457

75 12 QUALITY STREET

North Berwick

High standard en suite rooms and great hospitality can be found at **12 Quality Street**. Fully licensed ground floor Bistro.

see page 457

North Berwick Law

163

76 NETHER ABBEY HOTEL

North Berwick

With 13 rooms and a restaurant serving fresh local produce, this is a popular choice for visitors to the area.

see page 457

77 THE WESTGATE GALLERY

North Berwick

The Westgate Gallery has a wide selection of artwork and gifts and has a licensed café serving refreshments.

see page 457

78 FENTON TOWER

Kingston

Unique and unforgettable luxury accommodation in fully restored 16th century tower house.

see page 458

In the 16th century the town was supposed to have been the home of a notorious **Witches' Coven**, and a well-publicised trial took place in 1595. One of the accusations made was that the witches had caused a terrible storm to rise up when James VI's ship was returning from Denmark with his new bride.

It all started when a poor serving girl called Gelie Duncan was found to have remarkable healing powers, which aroused suspicion. Her master, David Seaton, tried to extract a confession of witchcraft from her using thumbscrews, and when this failed he had her body examined for the "marks of the devil". These were duly found on her throat, and she confessed and was thrown in jail.

On being tortured further, Gelie claimed to be one of 200 witches and warlocks in the town who, at the behest of David Seaton's sworn enemy the Earl of Bothwell, were trying to harm the king. At Hallowe'en in 1590, Gelie told them, the witches convened at the Auld Kirk, where Satan appeared and preached a sermon from the pulpit. King James had all the women who were identified by Gelie put to death, including one Agnes Sampson and a schoolmaster from Prestonpans called John Fian. Gelie herself was burnt on the Castle Esplanade in Edinburgh.

Though people have subsequently claimed that the Earl of Bothwell dressed up as Satan to take part in the Hallowe'en coven in the kirk, there's little doubt that Gelie made up the stories to save herself from further torture, and many innocent people were executed because of this. There is also no doubt that David Seaton was not interested in whether the women were witches or not - he merely wanted to harm the Earl of Bothwell.

Robert Louis Stevenson holidayed at North Berwick when he was a child, and an annual **Robert Louis Stevenson Festival** is held here every June.

East of North Berwick is **Tantallon Castle** (Historic Scotland). Its substantial and romantic ruins stand on a cliff top above the Firth of Forth, almost opposite the Bass Rock. It was a Douglas stronghold, built in the 14th century by William, 1st Earl of Douglas. Cromwell ordered General Monk to take the castle, and in 1651, after a 12-day siege, he destroyed it.

WHITEKIRK

7 miles NE of Haddington off the A198

St Mary's Parish Church dates from the 15th century, and is the eastern end of the annual Whitekirk to Haddington Pilgrimage (see also Haddington). However, Whitekirk had been a place of pilgrimage long before this. In pre Reformation times, people came to the village to seek cures at the Well of Our Lady, which used to be located nearby, but which dried up due to farming improvements and drainage in the 19th century. An account of 1413 relates that over 15,000 people of all nationalities visited yearly. In 1914 suffragettes set fire to the church, which was subsequently repaired at the expense of Sir Robert Lorimer. Close to the church is the 16th century **Tithe Barn**, built to store the "tithes" (a tithe being a tenth part) given to the church as offerings from the parishioners' agricultural produce.

The place's most famous pilgrim - but one who did not come seeking a cure - was a young Italian nobleman called **Aeneas Sylvius Piccolomini**. He had set out from Rome in the winter of 1435 as an envoy to the court of James I, and during the sea crossing he was blown off course by a raging gale. Aeneas vowed that if he made it to dry land he would offer thanksgiving at the nearest church dedicated to Our Lady. The boat was eventually shipwrecked between North Berwick and Dunbar, and Aeneas survived. He therefore set out on a ten-mile pilgrimage in a snowstorm to Whitekirk, where he duly offered prayers of thanks. While in Scotland, he fell in love with a young woman, and made a pledge of love to her. However, he was ambitious, and soon gave her up. Twenty years later, Aeneas became Pope Pious II.

EAST LINTON

6 miles E of Haddington off the A1

Anyone travelling along the A1 should make a small detour to view this picturesque village. To the east is **Phantassie**, the mansion where **John Rennie** the civil engineer was

born. He designed Waterloo, London and Southwark bridges over the Thames, and Rennie's Bridge at Kelso (see also Kelso).

Preston Mill (National Trust for Scotland) is an old, quaint water mill that has been restored to full working order. It sits in an idyllic rural spot, and dates from the 18th century, though a mill has stood on the spot for centuries. With its conical roofed kiln and red pantiles, it is a favourite subject for painters and photographers. Close by is **Phantassie Doocot** (National Trust for Scotland), which belonged to Phantassie House, and could hold 500 birds. Also close by

Preston Mill, East Linton

•

The ruins of Hailes Castle lie to the west of East Linton. Its earliest masonry dates from the 13th century, when it was built by the de Gourleys, who supported Edward l against Robert the Bruce. Bruce subsequently siezed the castle and granted it, and the accompanying lands, to the Hepburns, who much altered it in later years. James Hepburn, 4th Earl of Bothwell, brought Mary Stuart to Dunbar and then Hailes after seizing her at Fountainbridge in 1567. He was later to become her third husband.

•

79 MUSEUM OF FLIGHT

East Fortune Airfield

A fascinating museum, housed in original hangars, telling the story of this famous airfield.

 see page 459

---

is **Prestonkirk**, a small, attractive church. It was built in 1770, though the 13th century early Gothic chancel still stands, as it was used as a mausoleum for the Hepburn family. The original church to stand here is said to have been founded by St Baldred, who lived as a hermit on the Bass Rock.

The **Scottish Museum of Flight** (see panel) is situated at East Fortune, to the north east of the village. Formerly a World War II airfield, it now houses a collection of aircraft, rockets, models and memorabilia. The most famous exhibit is Concorde, brought to the museum in 2004. The aircraft in the museum was the first one in BA's fleet to fly commercially. Another is a Prestwick Pioneer, the only aircraft ever to have been wholly designed and built in Scotland. Also on display are a Soviet MIG, a Blue Streak rocket and a Lightning.

STENTON

7 miles E of Haddington on the B6370

This small conservation village still retains its old **Tron**, on which wool brought to the Stenton Fair by local sheep farmers was weighed. To the south of the village is **Pressmennan Lake**, one of the few lakes, as opposed to lochs, in Scotland (see also Lake of Menteith, Ellon and Kirkcudbright). This one, however, is artificial, created in 1819 by the local landowner. The **Pressmennan Forest Trail** runs along its southern shore, and from the highest point you can see Arthur's Seat in Edinburgh and the Bass Rock in the Firth of Forth.

Stenton Kirk is a handsome building designed by the noted architect William Burn in 1829. In the kirkyard are the remains of the **Old Kirk**, dating probably from the 14th century.

TYNINGHAME

7 miles E of Haddington on the B1407

Originally the lands of Tyninghame belonged to the Archbishops of St Andrews, but in 1628 they were acquired by the Earls of Haddington. Tyninghame itself is a small conservation village which formerly stood in what are now the grounds of **Tyninghame House**, which has been divided up into private flats. In 1761 it was moved to its present position by the then Earl of Haddington to improve the view from his house, though the remains of the former parish kirk, dedicated to St Baldred, still stand there.

DUNBAR

11 miles E of Haddington on the A1087

The Royal Burgh of Dunbar received its royal charter in 1445. It is a former fishing and whaling port, though its main industries are now brewing and tourism. It was to the south of here, in 1650, that the **Battle of Dunbar** took place between the troops of Cromwell and a Covenanting army under General Leslie. The Covenanters were resoundingly beaten when General Leslie's advice not to confront Cromwell was ignored by Scottish ministers. A similar interference in military matters by the clergy resulted in a defeat at the

Battle Kilsyth as well (see also Kilsyth). A stone commemorates the event.

The ruins of **Dunbar Castle** overlook the harbour, and date back to the 12th century. The castle was originally built for the Cospatrick family, which later changed its name to Dunbar. It was to Dunbar Castle that Edward II fled after his defeat at Bannockburn. He then boarded a boat for Berwick-upon-Tweed. In 1338 the Countess of Dunbar, known as "Black Agnes", held the castle for five months against an English army while her husband was away fighting in the north.

The siege commander was the Earl of Salisbury, and he began by catapulting huge rocks at the walls. Between attacks, much to his annoyance, she sent her maids out onto the ramparts to clean up the debris left by the assault, using dainty cloths to wipe away the dust. When the rocks were unsuccessful, he rolled up a huge battering ram that started battering at the gates. It had a wooden roof over it to protect the soldiers from attack from above, but Agnes had huge boulders hurled down on it, shattering the roof and killing the men below.

She was finally relieved by a small contingent of Scots with supplies who entered the castle by a secret gate on the seaward side. Salisbury by now was sensing victory, as he reckoned food supplies within the castle had dwindled to nothing. However, Black Agnes put some of the supplies to good use. She sent out a bottle of wine and some loaves to Salisbury as a gift.

Finally, Salisbury brought Anne's brother, an English prisoner, to the castle, and announced that if Anne did not surrender, he would kill him. Anne told him to go ahead, as she was next in line to inherit, and she would be a rich woman. At that, Salisbury gave up and marched his troops away. On the orders of the Scottish Parliament, the castle was dismantled after Mary Stuart abdicated.

The old **Town House** in the High Street dates from about 1620 and houses a small museum on local history and archaeology. A much newer "attraction" is situated south of the town, near the shore. **Torness Nuclear Power Station** was built in the early '80s, and has a visitor centre that explains how electricity is produced from nuclear power.

John Muir, founder of the American national parks system, was born in Dunbar in 1838. His birthplace in the High Street is now the four star **John Muir Centre**, with displays on his travels and his work. The **John Muir Country Park** is to the north west of the town. Established in 1976, this was the first park of its kind in Scotland, and covers 1,760 acres.

Two miles south of the town, off the A1, is **Doonhill Homestead** (Historic Scotland), where once an Anglian hall dating from the 7th - 8th century stood. It is marked out on the grass, and

Southeast of the village of Gifford is Yester House, designed by James Smith and dating from 1745. It was here, beside the house, that the original village stood before being moved to its present position.. The interiors were later re-styled by Robert Adam in 1789. The Italian composer Gian Carlo Menotti, who wrote the opera Amahl and the Night Visitors, *which was shown on TV every Christmas at one time, lives in Yester House. Beyond it are the ruins of Yester Castle, built by Hugo de Gifford in the late 13th century. He was known as the "Wizard of Yester", and beneath the castle is a chamber known as Goblin Ha' where he is supposed to have practised magic and called up goblins and demons. Scott mentions him in* Marmion. *The narrow road from Gifford up into the Lammermuir Hills is a fine drive, and takes you past Whiteadder reservoir and down into Berwickshire.*

shows that this area of Scotland was once part of the mighty Anglian kingdom of Northumbria.

GARVALD

6 miles SE of Haddington off the B6370

This tiny red sandstone village lies on the northern slopes of the Lammermuir Hills. **Garvald Parish Church** dates mostly from a rebuild of 1829, though there are fragments of the earlier, 12th century church incorporated into it. It has a sundial dated 1633, and is surprisingly light and modern inside. South east of the village is the mansion of **Nunraw,** in whose grounds Cistercian monks, who arrived here in 1946, began building the Abbey of Sancta Maria. It was the first Cistercian monastery in Scotland since the Reformation, and was colonised by monks form Tipperary in Ireland. A Cistercian nunnery, founded by nuns from Haddington, had previously been founded here in about 1158.

GIFFORD

4 miles S of Haddington on the B6369

Gifford was laid out in the 18th century on the site of an earlier village, and is a pretty village with views of the Lammermuir Hills to the south. The whitewashed **Yester Parish Church**, which has Dutch influences, was built in 1708, and has a medieval bell. It was in Gifford that John Witherspoon, the only clergyman to sign the American Declaration of Independence, was born in 1723 (see also Paisley).

PENCAITLAND

6 miles SW of Haddington on the A6093

The oldest part of **Pencaitland Parish Church** is the Winton Aisle, which dates from the 13th century. Close to the village is the 500-year-old **Winton House**. It was built for the Seton family by James VI's master mason William Wallace, and is famous for its "twisted chimneys". It overlooks the Tyne, and has lovely terraced gardens. **Glenkinchie Distillery**, to the south of the village, was opened in 1837, and has a small exhibition. It offers tours showing how whisky is distilled.

The three-arched **Pencaitland Bridge**, which crosses the River Tyne and joins East Pencaitland to West Pencaitland, dates from the 16th century.

LINLITHGOW

This ancient royal burgh was granted its royal charter in 1138. It is a lovely place, with many historic buildings in its old High Street, and has played a central role in Scotland's history. **Linlithgow Palace** (Historic Scotland), situated on the banks of **Linlithgow Loch**, dates originally from the reign of James I, who ruled in the early 15th century, with additions by succeeding monarchs. It replaced an older castle where Edward I once stayed when he invaded Scotland in support of John Balliol's claim to the Scottish throne.

It was a favourite of many Scottish kings and queens, and it was here, in 1512, that James V was born. It was also the birthplace, in 1542, of his daughter, the tragic Mary Stuart. The birth room was most probably the **Queen's Bedchamber** in the northwest tower. Her association with Linlithgow Palace lasted only seven months, as her mother, Mary of Guise, took her to the more secure Stirling Castle. When Mary Stuart returned from France in 1561 after the death of her husband King Francis II, she only stayed briefly at the castle, and it was allowed to decay.

Cromwell stayed here briefly in 1650 when he invaded Scotland after its parliament had declared Charles II king of Britain. Then, in 1745, Charles Edward Stuart stayed in the Palace. A year later the troops of the Duke of Cumberland moved in, and when they moved out they left their straw bedding too close to the fires. The whole place caught fire, and soon the building was ablaze, leaving it roofless and uninhabitable.

In the castle courtyard is the **King's Fountain**, built between 1536 and 1538 for James V and now restored to full working order. It is the oldest fountain in Britain, and is in three tiers, with elaborate carvings that symbolise his reign. It was badly damaged during the fire. A restoration scheme of the 1930s used concrete to replace some of the carvings, and this introduced salts into the structure, which began its decay.

The **Outer Gateway** to the palace still stands, and on it are the coats of arms of the four orders of chivalry to which James V belonged - the Garter of England, the Thistle of Scotland, the Golden Fleece of Burgundy and St Michael of France.

Opposite the Palace is **St Michael's Parish Church**, one of the most important medieval churches in Scotland. It dates from the 15th century, though a church had stood here long before that. Within the church one of the most unusual incidents in Scottish history took place. The church was especially dear to James IV, who worshipped there regularly. In 1514, he had decided to take a large army into England in support of France, which had been invaded by Henry VIII's troops. Most of the Scottish court was against the idea, as was James's wife Margaret, Henry's sister.

But James held firm, and a few

84 LIVINGSTON'S RESTAURANT

Linlithgow

A superb restaurant serving a tempting range of fresh Scottish food, 'with a French flavour'.

see page 461

Linlithgow Loch

169

Muiravonside Country Park lies a few miles west of the town of Linlithgow, and covers 170 acres of woods, parkland and gardens. There are nature trails, woodland walks and a visitor centre.

At the Linlithgow Canal Centre in Manse Road is a small museum dedicated to the 31 mile long Union Canal, which links the Forth and Clyde Canal at Falkirk with Edinburgh. Trips along the canal are also available at weekends between Easter and October, with weekday trips in July and August. One of the favourite trips is over the 810 feet long Avon Aqueduct, 86 feet above the river and the second longest aqueduct in Britain.

days before he and his army set out, he was at mass in St Michael's Church with his courtiers. A strange man with long, fair hair suddenly appeared in the church dressed in a blue gown tied with a white band and carrying a staff. Pushing aside the courtiers, he approached James and spoke to him. He had been sent "by his mother", he said, to tell James that no good would come of the invasion of England. Furthermore, he was not to meddle with other women.

Some of the courtiers tried to grab him, but before they could the old man made good his escape. Confusion reigned, and people immediately took the man to be a ghost. The reference to his mother, they said, meant that he had been sent by Our Lady (of whom James was especially fond). James took no heed, and marched into England. He, and all the flower of Scottish manhood, were wiped out on the field at Flodden. The "ghost's" prophecy came true.

People nowadays discount the ghost theory, and say that the whole thing had been orchestrated by James's wife with the help of some of the court. The reference to the king's meddling with other women was the Queen's own contribution to the event, as James was renowned for his philandering.

One of the courtiers was Sir David Lyndsay, Lord Lyon and playwright, who knew all the tricks of the stage, and he may have been involved as well. There is a theory that says that Margaret had been

put up to it by her brother Henry VIII, who was totally unprepared for a Scottish invasion, though this is now discounted.

The **Town House**, in the centre of the town, dates from 1668, and replaces an earlier building destroyed by Oliver Cromwell in 1650. The **Cross Well** dates from 1807, and replaces an earlier structure.

It was in Linlithgow that the Earl of Moray, Regent of Scotland, was assassinated in the street by James Hamilton of Bothwellhaugh, who later escaped to France. A plaque on the old **County Buildings** commemorates the event. In Annet House in the High Street is the **Linlithgow Story**, with displays, exhibits and audio visual programmes explaining the history of the town. There is also a terraced garden. There are also herb, fruit tree and flower gardens.

Beecraigs Country Park, to the south of the town, is set in 913 acres of land near the Bathgate Hills. It has a loch where you can fish, a deer farm and a camping and caravan park.

To the north of the town is the **House of the Binns** (National Trust for Scotland), ancestral home of the Dalyell family, the best known member of which is Tam Dalyell the former MP. In 1601 the Edinburgh butter merchant Thomas Dalyell married Janet, daughter of the first Baron Kinloss, and bought the lands of Binns. Between 1621 and 1630 he enlarged the house, and the present building has at its core that 17th century structure. It represents possibly the best example of the transition from a fortified castle to a comfortable home in Scotland.

His son was also Thomas, though he earned an unsavoury reputation as "Bluidy Tam Dalyel", scourge of the Covenanters. He was every inch a king's man, and when Charles I was executed in 1649, he vowed never to cut his hair until there was a king on the throne once more. And indeed, Bloody Tam's portrait in The Binns shows a man with hair flowing down past his shoulders. Tam also helped the Tsar of Russia reorganise the Russian army, and was made a nobleman of Russia. For that reason he also had another nickname - "The Bluidy Muscovite". He also made time to found a troop of the Royal Scots Greys. One legend about him tells of a card game with Satan, and the actual table at which the card game took place can be seen.

House of the Binns

AROUND LINLITHGOW

BO'NESS

3 miles N of Linlithgow on the A904

The town's real name is Borrowstoneness, though it is always referred to nowadays by its shortened name. It is an industrial town, and was formerly one of Scotland's leading whaling ports. It was near here that the eastern end of the 39 mile long **Antonine Wall** terminated.

Near Bo'ness town is the Kinneil Estate, with, at its centre,

Kinneil House. It was built by the Hamilton family as a simple keep, but expanded into a fine House by Duchess Ann in the 17th century. It is not open to the public, though it can be viewed from the outside. A ghost known as the "White lady" is said to haunt the house and grounds. She is said to be the wife of a Cromwellian general called Lilbourne. She had been brought north by her husband, and he had tired of her attempts to flee south to her home in England. He therefore locked her within a room in the House, but she threw herself to her death from a window in the house.

Within the 17th century stable block is the **Kinneil Museum**, which tells the story of Bo'ness over the last 2,000 years. There is also an exhibition called "Rome's Northern Frontier", which highlights the Antonine Wall and the Roman soldiers who manned it. The ruins of **Kinneil Church** lie near the house, and probably date from the 13th century with later additions. It was abandoned as a

Bo'ness's main attraction is the Bo'ness and Kinneil Railway, which has been developed since 1979 by the Scottish Railway Preservation Society. There is a Scottish railway exhibition as well as workshops and a working station. Trips on the steam trains, which run between Bo'ness and Birkhill Station are popular with the public, and trains can also be chartered for special occasions. At Birkhill are the caverns of the former Birkhill Fireclay Mine, which can be explored. It is hoped that a Scottish Railway Museum can be established here. Part of it, the Scottish Railway Exhibition, has already opened.

place of worship in 1669, when a new parish church was built at Corbiehall. It was accidentally destroyed by fire in 1745 by a troop of dragoons stationed at the house.

BLACKNESS

4 miles NE of Linlithgow on the B903

Blackness Castle (Historic Scotland) must be the most unusually shaped castle in Scotland. It sits on a promontory jutting out into the Firth of Forth, and from the air looks like a huge ship. It was a Crichton stronghold, with the first castle on the site being built in about 1449 by Sir George Crichton, Sheriff of Linlithgow and Admiral of Scotland. However, there is an intriguing but untrue story about how the castle eventually came to look like a ship.

By the early 16th century the castle had passed to the Douglases. James V appointed Archibald Douglas as Lord High Admiral of the Scottish fleet, but soon discovered that he had made a mistake, as every time Archibald went to sea he became sea sick.

The young James was enraged, and threatened to dismiss him. Archibald, who was making a fortune out of selling commissions in the navy, wanted to retain his position. So he promised his king that if he was allowed to keep his job, he would build him a ship that the English could not sink and on which he would never be sick. Mollified, the king agreed, and Douglas built Blackness Castle. However, a more mundane

explanation of its shape is the restricted shape of the site on which it was built.

The castle was subsequently besieged by Cromwell's army in 1650, and was later used as a prison for Covenanters. During the Napoleonic wars, it was again used as a prison, this time for French prisoners-of-war. After that it was used as an ammunition dump, and was finally restored and opened to the public.

TORPHICHEN

3 miles S of Linlithgow on the B792

The unusual name of this picturesque village comes from Gaelic "Torr Phigheainn", meaning the "hill of the magpies", and is pronounced "Tor-fichen". It is an ancient place, with its history going back to the founding of a church dedicated to St Ninian in the 6th century.

The Knights of the Order of St John of Jerusalem, or the Knights Hospitallers as they were more commonly called, was a monastic order of soldier monks formed in the 11th century to look after St John's Hospital in Jerusalem, and to offer hospitality and protection to pilgrims travelling to the Holy Land. **Torphichen Preceptory** (Historic Scotland) was one of only two such establishments in Britain, the other one being in London. It was founded in about 1124, when the lands of Torphichen were given to the monks by David I. The head of a Knights Hospitaller monastery was called a "preceptor", and for this reason a monastery was always known as a "preceptory". During the Wars of Independence, the then preceptor supported Edward I of England, and after Bannockburn the monks had to flee. However, they later returned. When the Knights Templar were suppressed by the Pope in 1307 the Knights Hospitaller assumed many of their properties and duties (see also Rosslyn).

The only parts left standing of the original preceptory are the transepts and crossing of the monastic church. Above the crossing is a tower, which, no doubt because of the Knights' military role, looks more like a castle than a church tower. Within a small room is a display about the modern Order of St John, which was refounded in 1947 as a separate order in Scotland by George VI. Nowadays it runs old folks homes, mountain rescue units and hospitals. Where the nave once stood is now **Torphichen Parish Church**, which dates from 1756, though it incorporates masonry from the earlier building. One further relic of the preceptory is to be found in the churchyard. This is the **Sanctuary Stone**, which stood at the centre of the preceptory's sanctuary land, which roughly extended for one mile in each direction. Within it, people hunted by the law could claim sanctuary for a while. The stones that marked the eastern and western boundaries of the sanctuary land are still in place.

LIVINGSTON

6 miles S of Linlithgow off the M8

Livingston is one of Scotland's new towns, built round an historic village which has the **Livingston Parish Church** of 1732. At the 20-acre **Almond Valley Heritage Centre** in Millfield the visitor can find out about local history and the environment, including the Scottish shale oil industry, which once thrived in West Lothian. There is also an 18th century water mill, a small railway line, a farm, a picnic area and teahouse.

MID CALDER

8 miles SE of Linlithgow off the A71

The Kirk of Mid Calder (St John's) has an apse built in the 16th century. One of the 17th century ministers of the church was Hew Kennedy, who was zealous in his persecution of witches. In 1644 several of them were burnt at the stake.

While staying at **Calder House** (not open to the public) in 1556 (four years before the Scottish Reformation) John Knox first administered Holy Communion using the new reformed liturgy. In 1848 the Polish pianist Chopin also stayed here. Originally an L-shaped tower house, it was added to and extended by the Sandilands family, the owners, over the years.

BATHGATE

6 miles S of Linlithgow on the A89

Bathgate is a substantial industrial town, and was formerly a centre for the shale oil industry. **Sir James**

The Almondell and Calderwood Country Park is three miles east of Livingston, and has woodland and riverside walks. Almondell was originally a private estate, which belonged to the Erskine family, and many items from Kirkhill House, with which it was associated, have been relocated within the park, such as the entrance gates and the astronomical pillar. The visitor centre is within an old stable block. Calderwood was also a private estate, and belonged to the barons of Torphichen. This area has been deliberately left undeveloped to encourage wildlife. The Oakbank Shale Bings are a reminder of the shale industry, and have been landscaped. A good view of the surrounding countryside, and even up into Fife, is available from the top.

Young Simpson, who introduced chloroform into midwifery, was the son of a Bathgate baker, and he was born here in 1811. In 1851, **James "Paraffin" Young**, a Glasgow man, established the world's first oil refinery at Whiteside near Bathgate, which produced naphtha and extracted paraffin from "cannel", a form of coal. Later he began extracting oil from shale.

Cairnpapple Hill (Historic Scotland), to the north of the town, is 1,017 feet high, and has at its summit a ceremonial site built about 2000 - 2500 BC. Fragments of bone and pottery have been found. One of the burial cairns has been re-created in concrete which covers a burial cist. The view from the top is magnificent, and on a clear day both the Bass Rock in the Firth of Forth and the mountains of Arran in the Firth of Clyde can be seen.

In Mansefield Street is the **Bennie Museum**, housed within two cottages, the earliest of which is 18th century. It contains collections relating to local history. **Polkemmet Country Park** is four miles west of the town, and has a golf course, a driving range, bowling green and picnic areas. The whole area was owned at one time by the Baillie family, and a mausoleum built by Robert Baillie, 4th Lord Polkemmet, in 1907, can still be seen within it.

Fife

The county of Fife consists of a long peninsula bounded on the south by the Firth of Forth and on the north by the Firth of Tay. It is steeped in history, with a long association with Scottish kings, and for that reason is sometimes referred to as the "Kingdom of Fife". James II, who ruled from 1437 to 1460, once called it a "fringe of gold on a beggar's mantle", meaning that, in his day, it had prosperous coastal towns and a barren interior. It is no longer like that. The interior is excellent faming country, and while it may not have the grandeur of the Highlands, it has a quiet pastoral charm and small, picturesque villages. Plus, for many years, there was a coal mining industry (first started by monks) that employed thousands of people.

Also, in the late 20th century, it contained a secret. During the Cold War years, Fife was where Scotland was to be governed from in the event of a nuclear attack. The underground Secret Bunker, as it is now known, was located on a farm near St Andrews.

Dunfermline, still an important town, was

Scotland's capital before Edinburgh took over. On the coast are small seaports which once traded with Europe - especially the Low Countries and the Baltic states. You can still see the European influence today. Some of the older buildings in the coastal towns have a distinctly European feel to them, with their red pantile roofs, the pantiles being brought in as ballast from abroad. These ports, with names such as Crail, Pittenweem and Anstruther, are still there, though now they rely on tourism rather than trade.

Of all the towns on the county's east coast the most famous is surely St Andrews. Seen from a distance, it shimmers with spires and towers,

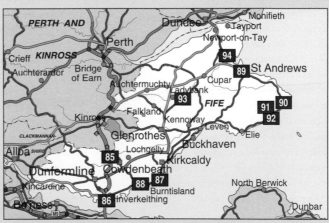

and is crammed with old buildings and historical associations. Like Dunfermline, it formerly a place of pilgrimage because of its great cathedral, the impressive ruins of which still overlook the shore. In it were kept the relics of St Andrew, Scotland's national saint, and this made it the country's ecclesiastical capital in pre-Reformation days.

It was also the seat of an archbishop, and was where Scotland's first university was founded in 1413 at the behest of the church. Before that, Scottish students studied on the Continent, with hardly any going to Oxford or Cambridge. Even today, students can be seen dressed in their traditional red gowns as they scurry to lectures during term time. And the place still attracts pilgrims, though now they come in the name of sport, for the town - or perhaps we should call it a small city - is the recognised home of golf.

The county's largest town is Kirkcaldy, famous for the manufacture of linoleum. So much so that people used to say that you could always tell when you were approaching the town by its "queer-like smell". But this royal burgh, which was granted its charter in 1644, is much more that a manufacturing centre, and has many historical associations. At one time it was known as the "Lang Toun", because it appeared to consist of one long street, though it has now spread inland. And it can lay fair claim to being the birthplace of economics, because, in 1728, Adam Smith was born here.

To the west of the county another industry held sway - coal mining. The Fife coalfields have all but gone, leaving in its wake many small mining villages that are proud and fiercely independent. Dunfermline is the largest town in this area - another Fife royal burgh whose roots go deep into Scotland's history, having been granted its royal charter in 1124. It's abbey, like the cathedral at St Andrews, was once a place of pilgrimage due to the tomb of St Margaret, and is now the resting place of one of Scotland's great heroes, Robert the Bruce. And, like Kirkcaldy, it too has its famous sons. Charles I was born here in 1600, three years before his father James VI assumed the British throne. So too was, in 1835, Andrew Carnegie the millionaire philanthropist.

Mining has given way to electronics as an employer, and this part of Fife is well and truly part of "silicon glen". But the area has not lost its attractiveness, and one of the places that must be visited is Culross, surely one of the loveliest and most historic small towns in Scotland.

Since the opening of the Tay Road Bridge in 1966, the towns and villages of northern Fife, such as Newport-on-Tay, Tayport, Leuchars and Wormit, looked to Dundee, across the river, for work asnd play. Now they are dormitory towns for the city thanks to the Tay Road Bridge. Even before this, people were commuting because of the Tay Rail Bridge, opened in 1887 after the first bridge collapsed into the firth in 1879 with much loss of life.

DUNFERMLINE

Now an important industrial town, Dunfermline was at one time the capital of Scotland, and still has many reminders of its past glories. It was here that **Malcolm III** (known as "Malcolm Canmore", meaning "big head, or chief") and his second queen, later to become **St Margaret of Scotland**, held court in the 11th century.

Malcolm was the son of Duncan l, killed in 1040 by Macbeth. His first wife was Ingebjørg, daughter of the Norwegian Earl of Orkney, and when she died in 1069, he waited a year before marrying Margaret. Their reign was a turning point in Scotland's history. Margaret was the daughter of Edgar Aetheling, heir-apparent to the English throne, and was half-Saxon and half-Hungarian. When she came to the Scottish court in about 1067, she was shocked at what she found, and, after marrying Malcolm three years later, set about changing things. The Scottish church, though nominally subservient to Rome, was still observing the old Celtic rites during Mass, which she found abhorrent. So the church was the first thing she changed.

A Culdee (from the Irish céli dé, meaning "servants of God") monastery manned by Celtic/Irish priests had been established in Dunfermline for many years, and she suppressed it, inviting monks from Durham to found a Benedictine priory (later to become Dunfermline Abbey) in its place.

She died in 1093, soon after her husband and son were killed at the Battle of Alnwick in Northumberland.

In 1250 she was canonised by Pope Innocent IV, and her body was transferred to an ornate shrine. The remains of the shrine, largely destroyed during the Reformation, can still be seen. Some of her body parts were removed as religious relics, and it is said that Mary Queen of Scots owned her skull. It later passed to the monks of Douai in France, and was lost during the French Revolution

Scotland in the 11th century was a small kingdom, perched precariously on the edge of the known world. It was Margaret who brought refinement to the court and made the country think of itself as an integral part of Europe. Under Margaret and Malcolm, who was also a driving force, trade with the continent flourished. Malcolm revelled in this, as though he could neither read nor write, he hankered after refinement and culture, and only a few years before had moved Scotland's capital from Perthshire

One other innovation is attributed to St Margaret - buttons on the sleeves of men's jackets. She had been disgusted to see that Scottish courtiers - in common with courtiers throughout Europe - wiped their noses on their sleeves, so set about making this habit as uncomfortable as possible. The buttons eventually became fashionable, and the fashion spread throughout Europe (see also Edinburgh).

Dunfermline Abbey

Andrew Carnegie was, in the 19th century, the richest man in the world. He was born in Dunfermline in 1835, and emigrated with his parents to the United States in 1848. By the 1880s, he had amassed a fortune through iron and steel making, and retired from business in 1901 to distribute his wealth. His humble birthplace in Moodie Street, a former weaver's cottage, is now the central feature of the Andrew Carnegie Birthplace Museum. It tells the story of the great man from his humble origins to his death in 1919. In 1895 Louise Carnegie, his wife, bought it for him as a 60th birthday present. In Pittencrief Park, close to the Louise Carnegie Gates is a statue of the great man.

to Dunfermline to be nearer the Fife ports that traded with Europe. Under Margaret, the centre of power shifted once more - this time to Edinburgh, which later became the nation's capital.

Dunfermline Abbey as we see it today is a mixture of dates. The original building was commissioned by David l, Margaret's son, in 1072. He went on to found many more abbeys, and eventually earned the nickname "a sair sanct for the croon" (a sore saint for the crown). The present heavily buttressed nave is Norman, and is reminiscent of Durham Cathedral. Beneath it lie the remains of the original church. The choir was rebuilt in the early 19th century as the parish church, and it was during its construction that workmen came across the skeleton of a man lying within a stone coffin, wrapped with gold cloth. It was immediately recognised as that of Robert the Bruce, King of Scots, as the breastbone and ribs had been sawn away. After he died, Bruce's heart had been removed from his body so that it could be taken to the Holy Land (see also Melrose, Cardross and Threave Castle). It was re-interred with due reverence, and now a brass plate beneath the pulpit marks the spot. Around the battlements of the abbey tower are the words "King Robert the Bruce".

The **Dunfermline Abbey and Palace Visitors Centre** (Historic Scotland) tells of the history of the abbey and of the later palace that was built on the site of the monastic buildings. A magnificent 200-feet-long buttressed wall is all

that now remains of the palace where Charles I was born.

To the west of the abbey is a great mound known as **Malcolm's Tower**, all that remains of Malcolm's fortress. The town takes part of its name from the mound, as *Dunfermline* literally means "fort on the hill by the crooked stream".

It sits within **Pittencrieff Park** (famous for its peacocks), which was gifted to the town by Andrew Carnegie in 1908. The park had always fascinated him as a boy, and as it was privately owned at the time, he was always denied access. So when he had the money, he bought it and threw it open to the people of the town. Also in the park is **Pittencrieff House Museum**, based in a 17th century mansion, which has an art gallery and displays on local history.

The **Abbot House Heritage Centre** is housed in a 14th - 16th century house to the north of the abbey in Maygate. It was formerly the Abbot's Lodgings for the great Benedictine monastery, as well as its administrative centre. Poets, kings and bishops visited, and it played its part in some of the great events in Scottish history. During World War ll, it was used as a training centre for fighter pilots.

St Margaret's Shrine has been reconstructed within its walls, showing just how rich the interior of the abbey was when it was at the height of its powers. In all, over 1,000 years of history can be seen, from the Picts right up until the present day.

Near Chalmers Street Car Park,

about a quarter of a mile north of Abbot House, can be found St Margaret's Cave, where the pious queen prayed in solitude. A legend has it that Malcolm, who was deeply in love with his wife, became suspicious of her unexplained absences from court, and fearing that she had a lover, followed her to the cave one day, where he found her kneeling in prayer. It's fortunate that the cave still exists, as in the 1960s the local council wanted to cover it in concrete as part of a car park.

It is not only New York that has a **Carnegie Hall** - Dunfermline has one as well, housing a theatre and concert hall. It can be found in East Port, near the **Dunfermline Museum and Small Gallery** in Viewfield. Here the history of the town is explained, including its time as a centre of manufacture for linen and silk, which continued right up until the 20th century. There are special displays from the Dunfermline Linen Damask Collection.

To the north of the town, at Lathalmond, is the **Scottish Vintage Bus Museum**, housed in a former Royal Navy Stores depot. It is possibly the largest collection of vintage buses in Britain, and has been open since 1995.

AROUND DUNFERMLINE

COWDENBEATH

5 miles NE of Dunfermline, off the A909

This small town at one time had a population of over 25,000, and was at the centre of the Fife coalfields. Though the mines have long gone, it still has the feel of a mining community about it. Its football team, which plays in the Scottish league, has perhaps the most unusual nickname of any senior team in Scotland - the **Blue Brazil**. **Racewall Cowdenbeath** has stock car racing every Saturday evening from February to November.

LOCHGELLY

7 miles NE of Dunfermline on the B981

Lochgelly is a small mining town, famous throughout Scotland at one time for the manufacture of the "Lochgelly", the leather strap, or "tawse", used to punish children in school. So popular did they become that small companies all over Scotland started to make them.

Loch Gelly itself, after which the town was named, has water sports facilities, and at one time was famous for the quality of its leeches, used by doctors for bloodletting.

Ian Rankin, the famous crime writer, was born at nearby Cardenden in 1960, and educated at Beath High School in Cowdenbeath, six miles away.

SALINE

6 miles NW of Dunfermline on the B913

To the east of Saline is the **Knockhill Racing Circuit**, Scotland's national motor sports centre for cars and motorbikes. It has meetings on most Sundays from April to October.

---

85   THE CLIPPIE'S FAYRE

Kelty

A huge variety of dishes are available at the The Clippie's Fayre, popular with both visitors and locals.

see page 461

Near the town of Lochgelly is the Lochore Meadows Country Park, set in 1,200 acres of reclaimed industrial land. The last pits closed here in 1966, with the park being created on the site in the early '70s. The area is now a haven for wildlife, and at the west end of the loch is a bird hide with disabled access. The 260-acre Loch Ore, created as a result of mining subsidence, is stocked with brown trout. It can also be used for water sports.

Aberdour Castle (Historic Scotland), close to the church, dates originally from the 13th century, when a simple tower house was built by the de Mortimer family, with later additions being made in the 16th and 17th century. It was later owned by James Douglas, 4th Earl of Morton and Regent of Scotland between 1572 and 1578. In 1580 he was executed for his part in the murder of Mary Stuart's second husband, Lord Darnley.

On Bandrum Hill is the **Bandrum Standing Stone**, which is over eight feet high. It may have marked a boundary of some kind in olden times.

ABERDOUR

6 miles E of Dunfermline on the A921

Aberdour is a small coastal burgh that received its charter in 1500. The restored **St Fillan's Church** is partly Norman, with fragments that may date back to at least 1123, and has what is known as a "leper window". This was a window looking on to the altar through which lepers could see the mass being celebrated from a private room. It is said that Robert the Bruce, himself suffering from leprosy, used the window after his victory at Bannockburn in 1314.

In 1790 the church was abandoned, and gradually became a ruin. However, in 1925 work began on restoring it, and it now open for services once more. The town has two beaches, one of which, **Silver Sands**, has won a European blue flag for its cleanliness. The **Aberdour Festival** is held every year at the end of July.

DALGETY BAY

4 miles SE of Dunfermline off the A921

The ivy-clad ruins of **St Bridget's Church**, once the burial place of the Earls of Dunfermline, date from the 12th century, and were first mentioned in a Papal Bull of 1178. It is quiet and undisturbed today, but in medieval times a small village surrounded it.

DONIBRISTLE

4 miles E of Dunfermline on the B925

It was near Donibristle that the murder of James Stewart, the **Earl of Moray**, took place, an event which is remembered in one of the best known of Scottish songs, *The Bonnie Earl o' Moray*. Moray was the grandson of Regent Morton, regent of Scotland when Mary Stuart abdicated in favour of her infant son, later to be James VI, and was a popular nobleman, dashing and handsome. But he was a staunch Protestant, and was always feuding with the Earls of Huntly, one of the great Catholic families of the time. He was rumoured to be implicated in a coup to overthrow James VI, though he probably had no involvement.

But Huntly saw the rumours as his chance, and armed with a king's warrant and a troop of soldiers, set out to seize the young earl. He eventually found him at his mother's castle at Donibristle and demanded that he give himself up. Moray refused.

The troops therefore set fire to the building. Some men ran out from the front of the castle to distract Huntly's men while Moray ran out the back way, hoping to hide in some undegrowth. Unfortunately, unknown to Moray, his bonnet had caught fire, and the smoke gave him away. He was hacked to death, with Huntly, it is said, striking the fatal blow. When James VI found out about the murder, he feigned outrage, though when the crowds later discovered that Huntly had been armed with a king's warrant, James had to flee to Glasgow to escape their wrath.

It was a death that touched the pulse of the common people of Scotland at a time when the country was in turmoil, not knowing if the Reformation would take hold or whether Roman Catholicism would make a return. Huntly spent a few weeks in Blackness Castle as a punishment, and was then released.

INCHCOLM

6 miles SE of Dunfermline, in the Firth of Forth

This small island was at one time known as the "Iona of the East". On it are the substantial ruins of **Inchcolm Abbey** (Historic Scotland), dedicated to St Columba. The story goes that Alexander I, son of Malcolm III and Queen Margaret, was crossing the Forth in 1123 when a storm blew up and the royal party had to seek refuge on the island, which had, for many years, supported a succession of hermits. The hermit of the time shared his meagre provisions with his guests for three days until the storm subsided. When Alexander reached the Fife shore he vowed to build a monastery dedicated to St Columba on the island in thanksgiving for his safe passage, but before he could put his plans into effect he died. His younger brother David I, who succeeded him, founded a priory, which eventually became the Abbey of Inchcolm in 1223.

A small stone building to the west of the abbey may have been the original monks' cell, though it has been much restored over the years. The abbey buildings as we see them now date mainly from the 15th century, and represent the most complete medieval abbey in Scotland, with most of the buildings remaining intact.

The Romans named the island Emonia, and at the time it may have had some connection with the pagan worship of a sea-god called Mannawydan.

In the late 18th century, a military hospital was set up on the island to look after wounded sailors from the Russian fleet, which was using the Firth of Forth as a base. In the 20th century it was fortified as part of the United Kingdom's sea defences, and some of these can still be seen. Over 500 troops were stationed on the island, and the first air raid of World War II took place close by, when German bombers, in 1939, dropped bombs not far from the Forth Rail Bridge.

INVERKEITHING

3 miles S of Dunfermline off the A90

Inverkeithing is truly one of Scotland's "hidden places". This charming ancient royal burgh received its royal charter from William the Lion in about 1193. In medieval times it was a walled town with four "ports", or gates, though the walls were pulled down in the 16th century. It sits close to the Forth Road and Rail Bridges, and has many old buildings. The **Mercat Cross** is 16th century, and the **Old Town Hall** opposite, with its outside staircase, dates from

The Inchcolm Antiphoner dates from the 14th century, and is a document containing musical notation and chants dedicated to St Columba. The music may have echoes of the plainchant sung in the pre-Catholic Celtic church, as practised by St Columba. The document is now within Edinburgh University library.

Mercat Cross, Inverkeithing

**86   INVERKEITHING
MUSEUM**

Inverkeithing

A small but interesting
museum housed in a 14th
century Friary guest house.

 see page 461

1770. Of the 15th
century **St Peter's
Church**, only the
tower remains, as
the rest dates from
1826. Two other old
buildings are
**Thomsoun's
House** dating from
1617 and **Fordell's
Lodging** dating
from 1670.
**Inverkeithing
Museum** (see
panel), housed in
the hospitum of an
old friary, tells the
story of
Inverkeithing and
of **Admiral Sir
Samuel Greig**, a
local man born in 1735 in what is
now the Royal Hotel in the High
Street, and who entered the service
of Tsarina Catherine of Russia in
1764, having been sent to Russia by
the British government to help the
then Czarina, Catherine the Great.
He largely created the modern
Russian navy, manning it initially
with Scottish officers. He died in
1788 aged only 53, and was given a
huge state funeral.

Near the town, in 1651, was
fought the **Battle of
Inverkeithing** between a Royalist
force under Sir Hector MacLean of
Duart and the Parliamentarian
forces under John Lambert. The
result was a victory for the
Parliamentarians, and the death of
MacLean. As a result of the battle
the towns of Inverkeithing and
Dunfermline were plundered, and

the long-term result was the
ascendancy of Cromwell in
Scotland. A small cairn by the
roadside opposite **Pitreavie Castle**
(not open to the public), erected by
the Clan MacLean, commemorates
the event.

In the 14th century Pitreavie
Castle was owned by Christina
Bruce, Robert the Bruce's sister. It
later passed to the Kellock family,
which later sold it to the Wardlaws.
The family effectively rebuilt the
castle, and what you see today dates
from the early 17th century. From
World War II until 1996 a bunker
beneath the castle was the naval
operations HQ for Scotland. Both
George VI and Churchill visited it,
and it was from here that the Battle
of the Atlantic was masterminded.

It is reputedly haunted by three
ghosts: the Grey Lady, the Green
Lady and a headless Highlander
who is said to moan in anguish.

NORTH QUEENSFERRY
4 miles S of Dunfermline off the A90

This small town was the northern
terminus for the ferry that plied
across the Forth from South
Queensferry in West Lothian,
originally founded by Queen
Margaret (hence the town's name)
in the 11th century. It sits on a
small peninsula which juts out into
the Forth where the river has its
narrowest point between
Kincardine, further upstream, and
the sea. The **Forth Bridges
Visitors Centre** is housed within
the Queensferry Lodge Hotel, and
tells the story of the two bridges
spanning the Forth. There is a

magnificent scale model of the Firth of Forth, as well as photographs, documents and artefacts. Entrance is free.

Deep Sea World is billed as "Scotland's Aquarium", and takes you on a walk along the "ocean floor", thanks to the world's longest underwater tunnel made of specially toughened glass. Fish swim above and beside you in a specially made sea containing a million gallons of water. As you stand within it you can see sharks, stingrays and electric eels. A special touch pool allows you to touch sharks, sea urchins and anemones. One of the most popular experiences on offer at the aquarium is the chance to dive with sharks.

The town's oldest building is the ruined **Chapel of St James**, dating from the 14th century. It was founded by Robert the Bruce and looked after by the monks of Dunfermline. Here pilgrims would stop and pray on their way to Dunfermline or on their way back before crossing on the ferry.

CHARLESTOWN

3 miles SW of Dunfermline on a minor road off the A985

This small village was established in 1756 by Charles Bruce, 5th Earl of Elgin, to exploit the large deposits of limestone in the area, including an easily worked crag facing the sea. It was Scotland's first planned industrial village, though Bruce died before the work was finished. It was finally completed by the 7th Earl (of Elgin Marbles fame).

There were nine kilns here at one time producing lime for building, agriculture and the making of iron and glass. At its height, it produced one third of all the lime used in Scotland's building industry. It was a self-sufficient community, with its own harbour, shops and school, and the houses were arranged in the shape of the founder's initials - CE, meaning Charles Elgin.

The works closed in 1956, having produced in their 200 years of existence over 11 million tons of quicklime. Now guided walks round the complex are available in the summer months thanks to the **Scottish Lime Centre** in the Granary Building in Rocks Road. The centre's main purpose is to offer courses on the use of lime in the traditionally based building and construction industries. Nearby is the village of **Limekilns**, which was once a port for the monks of Dunfermline Abbey.

CULROSS

7 miles W of Dunfermline on a minor road off the A985

If you wish to see what a Scottish burgh looked like in the 16th, 17th and 18th centuries, then the royal burgh of Culross is the place to go. It was granted its royal charter in 1592, and though having a population of no more than a few hundred, it had its own town council and provost up until local government reorganisation in 1975.

It is undoubtedly the most picturesque of Fife's old burghs - a situation that owes a lot to the town's relative poverty in the 18th,

North Queensferry is the start of the Fife Coastal Path, a 78-mile long path-way that eventually takes you through most of the small picturesque towns and villages on the Fife coast, ending at the Tay Bridge on the Firth of Tay.

Culross Palace

Culross is a thriving and lively community with most of the quaint crow-step gabled houses occupied. The streets are cobbled, and those around the old Mercat Cross (dating from 1588) have a feature known as the "crown o' the causie", a raised portion in the middle where only the wealthy were allowed to walk, while the rest of the townsfolk had to walk on the edges where water and dirt accumulated.

19th and early 20th centuries when there was no money for modernisation. In the 16th century it was a prosperous port that traded with the Low Countries, but when this trade dried up it sunk into poverty. Now it is largely owned by the National Trust for Scotland, and has reinvented itself as a must-see place on the tourist trail.

The town's main industries were coalmining, salt panning and the making of baking girdles. Coal mining had been introduced by the monks of Culross Abbey at a time when coal was little known about, and wondrous tales spread round Scotland about the "stones that could burn". After the Reformation, the mines were taken over by Sir George Bruce, a descendant of Robert the Bruce. Between 1575 and his death 50 years later he revolutionised the industry. He was the first man to extend a coal mine beneath the sea, something which is taken for granted today. One of his mines had a tunnel out under the waters of the Firth of Forth for over a

mile. It eventually came up to sea level, surrounded by a stone wall to keep the water out. James VI was fascinated by Culross's industry, and paid a visit. Sir George took him on a tour of the mine, and led the unsuspecting king along the tunnel. When he emerged and found himself surrounded on all four sides by water, he panicked, shouting "treason!"

As an offshoot of the mining industry, salt panning became another major occupation in the town. It is reckoned that at one time there were 50 saltpans along the coast, all using inferior coal to heat salt water from the sea. Another industry was the making of iron girdles for cooking. Culross blacksmiths are said to have invented these round, flat utensils for frying and cooking after Robert the Bruce, in the 14th century, ordered that each one of his troops be given a flat pan for cooking oatcakes.

Nothing remains of Sir George's mining ventures. However, his home, now called **Culross Palace**, still stands, and is open to the public. Work started on it in 1597, and is a typical residence of its time for someone of Sir George's standing. It has splendid kitchen gardens. Along from it is the **Town House**, built in 1625 and gifted to the National Trust for Scotland in 1975 when Culross Town Council was wound up. At one time the ground floor was a debtors' prison, while the attic was used as a prison for witches. It now houses the local tourist information centre.

Beside the Mercat Cross is **The Study**. It was built about 1610, and after the Palace, is Culross's grandest house. When the Church of Scotland was Episcopalian, the town formed part of the diocese of Dunblane, and it was here that Bishop Robert Leighton stayed on his visits. The quaint Outlook Tower housed his actual study, hence the name of the house. If you continue past The Study, along Tanhouse Brae and into Kirk Street, you will eventually reach **Culross Abbey**, dedicated to St Serf and St Mary. The choir of the church (restored in 1633) still stands, and is used as the parish church, though the other buildings have either completely disappeared or are in ruins. It was founded in 1217 by Malcolm, Earl of Fife, and housed a Cistercian order of monks who left Kinloss Abbey. It is likely that the site of the abbey is where St Serf founded a monastery in the 6th century. Off the north transept is the Bruce Vault, where there is an impressive monument to Sir George Bruce of Carnock, his wife and their eight children.

Culross Harbour was built by the monks of the local abbey to ship locally quarried stone across the Forth to Edinburgh. It later traded with the Low Countries and the Baltic. However, over the years the harbour fell into decay, and it is now being restored.

Culross's attractions aren't all historical. Close to the town is **Longannet Power Station**, one of Scotland's largest. There are organised tours (which have to be pre-booked), and you can see the huge turbine hall from a viewing platform, as well as tour the visitors centre, which shows how coal produces electricity.

Stretching from Longannet past Culross to Combie Point on the shores of the Firth of Forth is the **Torry Bay Local Nature Reserve**, where there is series of artificial lagoons built from the waste ash from Longannet. Here you can see many species of birds, such as shelduck, greenshank and great crested grebe.

KINCARDINE-ON-FORTH

10 miles W of Dunfermline, on the A985

This small burgh, which received its charter in 1663, sits at the north end of the **Kincardine Bridge**. Up until the Forth Road Bridge opened in 1964, this was the only road crossing of the Forth downstream from Stirling. Opened in 1936, the middle section used to swivel to allow ships to pass up the river. It was controlled from a control room above the swivel section, and was, at the time, the largest swivel bridge in Europe. It allowed ships to sail up to Alloa, but has not opened since the 1980s, when Alloa declined as a port.

There are now plans to build yet another Kincardine Bridge, west of the existing one, to take traffic away from the streets of the town.

The town is full of small, old-fashioned cottages with red pantiled roofs, and there are the ruins of the 17th century **Tulliallan Church**. The burgh's **Mercat Cross** dates from the 17th century, and it was in

Culross was the birthplace, in AD 514, of St Kentigern, patron saint of Glasgow. In 1503 Archbishop Blackadder of Glasgow erected a small Chapel of St Kentigern on the spot where the birth is supposed to have taken place, and its ruins can still be seen to the east of the village. The story goes that he was the son of Thenew (also known as Enoch), a princess of the kingdom of the Lothians. When her father Loth (after whom the Lothians was supposedly named) discovered that she was pregnant, he banished her from his kingdom, and she set sail in a boat across the Firth of Forth. She landed at Culross, and here gave birth to her son, who was taken into care by a monk called Serf (later St Serf), who had established a monastic school there. It is now known that St Serf lived in the century following Kentigern's birth, so the story is doubtful.

•

Anyone who follows the adventures of the comic character "Oor Wullie" in the Sunday Post, published in Dundee, will have heard of PC Murdoch, who tries to thwart some of Wullie's adventures. The characters were created by Dudley D. Watkins, and he based Murdoch on a real policeman, Constable Sandy Marnoch, who was a policeman working in Kincardine-on-Forth when Watkins was a special constable there. The Oor Wullie cartoons, plus their stable mate, the "Broons" cartoons, were - and still are - the embodiment of couthy, Scottish humour. However, Watkins himself was English.

the town, in 1842, that Sir James Dewar, inventor of the vacuum flask and co-inventor of cordite was born. It was not until 1904, however, that the vacuum, or Thermos, flask was produced commercially by a firm in Germany. The term "Thermos" was coined in Munich, and comes from the Greek word *therme*, which means "hot". To the west of the town is **Tulliallan Castle**, now the main police training college in Scotland. During World War ll, it was the home of the Polish Free Forces, under the command of General Wladislaw Sikorski, who was eventually killed in an air crash in Gibraltar in 1943.

At Overton is an old churchyard surrounding the ruins of a 17th century church. Within a mausoleum is the burial place of **Admiral Lord Keith**, who died in 1823. He was the son of Lord Elphinstone, and fought during the Napoleonic Wars.

Up until 1891, Kincardine-on-Forth and the adjoining parish or Tullieallan was in a detached part of Perthshire. In that year it was transferred into Fife, a move that was opposed by many people. In 1994 it was proposed to take the town out of Fife, and this was again opposed - succcessfully - by many people.

KIRKCALDY

Kirkcaldy is the largest town in Fife, and is famous for the manufacture of linoleum. At one time it was known as the "Lang Toun", due to the fact that it

appeared to stretch out along one main street. It was created a royal burgh in 1644, and one of the famous events held here every year in April is the **Links Market**, reckoned to be the longest street fair in Europe. The town's Esplanade is cordoned off from traffic and taken over by swings, roundabouts, dodgems, carousels, hoopla stalls and all the other attractions of a modern funfair. The very first Links Market took place in 1306 in Links Street in the town, hence its name.

Within **Kirkcaldy Museum and Art Gallery** at the War Memorial Gardens is an exhibition devoted to Wemyss Ware, a form of earthenware pottery that was produced in the town by the firm of Robert Heron and Son between 1882 and 1930. It is now much collected, and is possibly the most sought after pottery ever to have been made in Scotland. Its most distinctive feature was its decoration, which was bold, simple and direct. The firing methods caused a lot of waste, which meant that the pottery was always expensive. The museum also houses a local history collection, plus an extensive collection of Scottish paintings.

The ruins of **Ravenscraig Castle** sit on a promontory to the east of the town centre. It was built in the 15th century by James II for his queen, Mary of Gueldres, who died there in 1463. James had a passion for weaponry - especially guns - and had it built so that it could withstand the latest artillery.

In 1470 it passed to William Sinclair, Earl of Orkney, who had to give up his earldom and Kirkwall Castle to acquire it. Overlooking the town harbour is the 15th century **Sailor's Walk**, the town's oldest house. The **Old Parish Church** sits at the top of Kirk Wynd, and dates from 1808. However, its tower is medieval.

Beyond Ravenscraig Castle is **Dysart**, which, up until 1930, was a separate burgh. Its harbour area is very picturesque, with whitewashed cottages and houses dating from the 16th, 17th and 18th centuries. At one time this was a salt panning area, and **Pan Ha'** (meaning "Pan Haugh") is a group of particularly fine 17th century buildings with red pantiled roofs (not open to the public). **St Serf's Tower** is the tower of the former parish church, and dates from the 15th century. It looks more like a castle than a tower, and reflects the area's troubled times when English ships prowled the Forth. In Rectory Lane is the **John McDouall Stuart Museum**, dedicated to the life of a locally born explorer who, in 1861-62, made the first return journey across the Australian continent.

A series of plaques have been put up all over the town, and there is a "walkabout" guide available.

Thomas Carlyle taught in the town in the early 19th century, and the novelist John Buchan spent part of his youth here.

In the town's Abbotshall Kirkyard stands a statue to another person born in Kirkcaldy, but an unusual one. **Marjory Fleming**

Sailor's Walk

was a child author, born in 1803, whose writings have intrigued and delighted people down through the ages, and whose nickname was "Pet Marjory". She was a distant relative of Sir Walter Scott, and died in 1811. She kept a journal, in which she jotted down thoughts, poems and biographical scraps. She was, by all accounts, a "handful", and when her mother gave birth to another girl in 1809, Marjory was sent to live with her aunt in Edinburgh. This is where her writing began, encouraged by her cousin Isa.

She eventually filled three notebooks. Nobody knows what she might have achieved in adulthood, because, one month short of her ninth birthday, after she had returned to Kirkcaldy, she tragically died of meningitis. Her last piece of writing was a touching poem addressed to her beloved cousin. Her writings were

Adam Smith, the founder of the science of economics, was born in Kirkcaldy in 1723. He went on to occupy the chair of moral philosophy at Glasgow University, and his famous book, **The Wealth of Nations,** *was partly written in his mother's house (now gone) in the town's High Street. Also born in the town were William Adam the architect, and his son, Robert Adam.*

Falkland burgh's Town Hall, which dates from 1805, houses an exhibition about the town. Close to it, in the square, is a house with a plaque which commemorates Richard Cameron, a local schoolmaster and Covenanter, who was killed at the Battle of Airds Moss in Ayrshire in 1680 (see also Sanquhar).

subsequently published, and found great favour with the Victorians, though some frowned on the absolute honesty she displayed when it came to describing her tantrums and innermost thoughts.

AROUND KIRKCALDY

GLENROTHES

5 miles N of Kirkcaldy on the A92

Glenrothes was one of the new towns established in Scotland in the late 1940s. In **Balbirnie Park**, which extends to 416 acres, is a late Neolithic stone circle dating from about 3000 BC. It was moved to its present site in 1971-1972 when the A92 was widened. The park was created in the estate of Balbirnie House, once owned by the Balfours. There is a caravan site.

FALKLAND

10 miles N of Kirkcaldy on the A912

This little royal burgh sits in the shadow of the **Lomond Hills**. There are two distinct peaks - East Lomond, at 1,471 feet, and West

Lomond at 1,713 feet, the highest point in Fife. It has quaint old cobbled streets lined with 17th and 18th century cottages, and was the first conservation area in Scotland. It was a favourite place of the Scottish kings, and **Falkland Palace** (National Trust for Scotland) was built in the 15th century by the Duke of Albany on the site of an earlier castle owned by the Earls of Fife. James V later employed stonemasons to turn it into a magnificent Renaissance palace.

It was never an important castle like Edinburgh or Stirling. Rather it was a country retreat for Stuart kings to hunt deer and boar and get away from the affairs of state. James V died in Falkland Palace in 1542, and his daughter Mary Stuart, it is said, spent the best years of her tragic life at Falkland.

Mary was born a few days before James V died, and the story is told that when he was on his deathbed, aged only 30, and told about the birth of a daughter and heir, he exclaimed: "It cam' wi' a lass, and it'll gang wi' a lass!", meaning that the House of Stuart had started with Marjory, daughter of Robert the Bruce, and it would die out with another woman, his own daughter. He was both right and wrong. It did die out "wi' a lass", but not Mary Stuart. The last Stuart monarch was Queen Ann, who died in 1715. The Palace is still nominally the property of the monarch, and its chapel, housed in what was the banqueting hall in the South Range, is the only Roman Catholic Church in Britain within

Falkland Palace

royal property. In 1654 Cromwell burnt the Great Hall to the ground, and it was never rebuilt.

Both Charles I and Charles II visited Falkland, and it was in the Palace, in 1650, that Charles II founded the Scots Guards. His father Charles I had founded a regiment in 1642 called "Argyll's Regiment" to act as his personal bodyguard in Ireland, and this had later merged with nine small regiments to form the Irish Companies. While at Falkland Charles II renamed this regiment The King's Lyteguard of Foot, and proclaimed it to be his bodyguard. It was later renamed the Scots Guards.

In the East Range can be seen the King's Bedchamber and the Queen's Room, and within the Gatehouse are the Keeper's Apartments. The gardens were laid out in the mid-20th century, and have magnificent herbaceous borders. Within the gardens is the **Royal Tennis Court**, which dates from the early 16th century, and the oldest in the country still in use. Here "real tennis" is played, with the roofs of the "lean tos" on either side of the court playing an integral part in the game. Tennis is still played here today, and there is a thriving club. The word "real" simply means royal, and it was a favourite sport of kings throughout Europe at one time. It is said that it dates back to at least the 11th century, when monks played it in the cloisters of their abbeys and priories. In the 14th century the Pope banned the playing of the game, but by this time it had

become popular among the nobility.

The **Falkland Fountain** was designed by Alexander Ross and built in 1856. **Moncrieff House**, in the High Street, is the only thatched building left in the town, and is named after Nicol Moncreiff and his bride, who, according to a marriage stone, lived there.

WEMYSS

4 miles NE of Kirkcaldy on the A955

Below the substantial ruins of **MacDuff Castle**, near the shoreline, are some caves in the sandstone cliffs with old carvings on the walls. They date mainly from between AD 400 to 800, though some may go back to before Christ. It has been claimed that there are more carvings within these caves than in all the other caves in Britain put together. However, due to erosion and subsidence, most of the caves can no longer be entered, though they may be viewed from the shore.

The ruins of MacDuff Castle itself date from the 14th century, and formed part of a tower built by the Wemyss family. It is reputed to be haunted by a ghost known as the "Grey Lady", said to be Mary Sibbald, who died as the result of her punishment. A previous castle that stood on the site was built by the MacDuffs, Earls of Fife, in the 12th century,

BUCKHAVEN AND METHIL

7 miles NE of Kirkcaldy on the B931

Buckhaven and Methil constituted one burgh which was created in

At the beginning of the 19th century the Keepership of the Palace in Falkland was in the hands of Professor John Bruce of Edinburgh University. For six years he spent a lot of his own money on rebuilding and refurbishment, and when he died in 1826 he left the Keepership to his niece Margaret and to an Indian lady. In 1828 Margaret married a Bristol lawyer with the delightful name of Onesiphorus Tyndall, who added Bruce to his name to become Onesiphorus Tyndall-Bruce, whose statue stands in the town. The Keepership later passed to John Crichton Stuart, Marquis of Bute., and his descendants still hold it.

189

Wemyss Castle dates from the 15th century and was built by Sir John Wemyss on the site of an earlier fortification to replace a castle at Kilconquhar (pronounced "Kon-ucker"). It was here that Mary Stuart first met Lord Darnley, her second husband, in 1565.

1891 when Buckhaven, Innerleven and Methil came together. Its motto was Carbone Carbasoque, which means "By Coal and by Sail", reflecting the fact that it used to export local coal from its harbours. As with other Fife ports, it also had saltpans, and by 1677 three pans were in operation, fuelled by the local coal.

The Methil docks were opened in 1887. In Lower Methil's High Street is the **Methil Heritage Centre**, a lively community museum that explains the history of the area.

Buckhaven, to the west, was never as industrialised as Methil. It was once a fishing port and ferry terminal, and has some old, quaint cottages. In College Street there is the **Buckhaven Museum**, which has displays about the town's industries, including fishing.

LARGO

11 miles NE of Kirkcaldy on the A915

There are two Largos - Lower Largo on the shores of the Forth and Upper Largo about half a mile inland, where the **Parish Church**, some parts of which date from the early 17th century, stands. It was here that Scotland's greatest seafarer and one time Admiral of the Fleet, **Sir Andrew Wood**, had his home. He oversaw the building in Newhaven of the largest and most magnificent fighting ship of its day, the **Great Michael**, flagship of the Scottish fleet (see also Edinburgh). He died in 1515, and was buried in the kirkyard. So enamoured of sailing was he that he built a canal between his home and the parish church so that he could attend Mass on a boat rowed by English prisoners. His last journey to the church was for interment in the churchyard, and prisoners again manned the boat. Nothing now remains of Wood's castle but a tower.

Alexander Selkirk was another seafaring man who came from Largo. He was born in 1676, and was the seventh son of a shoemaker. At the age of 19 the Kirk Session ordered him to appear before it after fighting with his brother, but instead of appearing he fled to sea, where he eventually became a privateer, or legalised pirate working for the British king.

By all accounts he was a short-tempered, unpleasant man, and while sailing on a ship called the *Cinque Ports* in 1704, quarrelled with the captain, who put him ashore (at Selkirks's request) on the uninhabited island of Juan Fernandez in the Pacific Ocean. He immediately regretted his decision,

Lower Largo

but was unable to recall the ship. He remained there until 1709, when he was rescued. Daniel Defoe, though he never met Selkirk, based his novel *Robinson Crusoe* on his adventures. A statue of Selkirk can be found near the harbour.

KINGHORN

4 miles SW of Kirkcaldy on the A921

This quiet little royal burgh saw one of the most decisive events in Scottish history. At the **Pettycur Crags** to the west of the town Alexander III was killed, throwing Scotland into turmoil.

He was the last of the country's Celtic kings, and had previously married Princess Margaret, daughter of Henry III of England, who had borne him two sons. But Margaret and the sons died; so, at the age of 45, Alexander married again, this time Yolande, daughter of the Count of Dreux in France, in the hope of continuing the direct royal line.

After a meeting of his nobles at Edinburgh in 1286, Alexander was anxious to return to his queen, whom he thought was pregnant, and who was staying at Kinghorn Castle (now gone). The weather was stormy, and some of his men tried to dissuade him from crossing the Forth. However, he was adamant, and was taken across to Fife. But while riding along the Pettycur Crags, almost in sight of the castle where his wife awaited him, his horse stumbled, sending him over the cliffs to his death. It is said that the spot is haunted by the ghost of Yolande, still waiting for her husband to return to her arms.

The heir to the Scottish throne was now three-year-old Margaret, known as the "Maid of Norway". She was the daughter of Alexander's own daughter, who had married Eric II of Norway. But while crossing from Norway to Scotland, Margaret also died, leaving the country without an heir. In the resultant vacuum, noblemen jockeyed for position, putting forward many claimants to the throne. Edward I of England was asked to intercede, and he saw his chance. He tried to incorporate Scotland into his own kingdom by installing a puppet king, and thus began the Wars of Independence.

A tall monument at the side of the road, erected in 1886, marks the spot where Alexander was killed.

Kinghorn Parish Church dates from 1774, though there are partial remains of an earlier church dating from 1243 in the kirkyard.

BURNTISLAND

6 miles SW of Kirkcaldy on the A921

This small royal burgh, called Portus Gratiae, or "Port of Grace" by the Romans, is overlooked by a 632-feet high hill called **The Binn**. In medieval times it was the second most important port on the Forth after Leith, and in Victorian times exported coal from the Fife coalfields. **St Columba's Parish Church** is a four square building dating from 1592, and is possibly based on a Dutch design. It was the first church built in Scotland after

87 THE SHIP TAVERN BAR & RESTAURANT

Kinghorn

The Ship Tavern serves a good selection of freshly prepared meals in the newly refurbished surroundings.

see page 461

Earthship Fife, at Kinghorn Loch, is an unusual building made of used car tyres and soft drink cans. It has its own heating, lighting, water supply and sewage works, and explains all about eco-buildings and sustainable lifestyles. It share the site with Craigencalt Ecology Centre, which offers displays about the environment and how we can make better use of it.

191

88 MILTON HOUSE

Burntisland

A small, friendly pub with a great atmosphere that sells a good range of drinks, including real ales and malt whiskies.

🍴 *see page 461*

•

The Burntisland Heritage Centre in the Kirkgate organises a series of heritage walks each year in the summer. Off the coast of the town, in 1633, Charles I lost most of his treasure, estimated to be worth over £20m in today's money. A small barge, the **Blessing of Burntisland,** *was carrying the money out to a seafaring vessel when it foundered and sank within reach of the shore. Nineteen witches, who, it was claimed, put a curse on the ship, were executed. The wreckage was discovered in 1999 lying under feet of silt, and plans are afoot to explore it and recover the money.*

•

the Reformation which is still in use today, and has a wealth of detail inside, including elaborate lofts and pews. The chancel sits at the centre of the church, with the altar, or "Holy Table", sitting in the middle. The pews face it on four sides, emphasising the "equality of all believers". It is the birthplace of the **Authorised Version of the Bible,** as James VI attended a General Assembly of the Church of Scotland here in May 1601, and put forward the proposal for a translation of the Bible into English. The suggestion was enthusiastically received, but it was not until James had assumed the throne of Britain that work began.

The **Burntisland Edwardian Fair Museum** is in the High Street, and features displays about Edwardian fairgrounds and local history.

The restored **Rossend Castle,** at the western end of the town, was once owned by the Durie family. It was the scene of a bizarre incident concerning Mary Stuart and a love struck French poet called Pierre de Châtelard, who broke into her room to declare his undying love for her. As he had attempted it once before at Holyrood, he was later executed at St Andrews (see also St Andrews).

ST ANDREWS

St Andrews is one of the most important and historic towns in Britain. Perhaps one should call it a city, as it was Scotland's ecclesiastical capital up until the

Reformation on account of its huge cathedral, which was Scotland's largest building in medieval times. It is also a university town, and the home of golf.

St Andrews Cathedral (Historic Scotland) was begun by Bishop Arnold in 1160, though the magnificent ruins you see nowadays date from many periods. The choir was the first part to be built, and shows both Norman and Gothic details. The nave was completed in the late 13th century, though the great west front was blown down in a gale and had to be rebuilt. The whole building was finally consecrated in July 1318 in the presence of Robert the Bruce. As well as being a cathedral, it was also a priory served by Augustinian canons.

This was not the first cathedral on the site. In about 1127 a more modest church was built, a remnant of which still remains. This is the 108 feet high **St Rule's Tower** and its attached chancel, to the south of the ruins. From its top, there's a magnificent view of the town.

Legend tells us that St Rule (or Regulus) came from Patras in Greece in the 4th century, carrying with him the bones of St Andrew. He set up a shrine for them on the Fife coast, at what was then called Kilrimont - present day St Andrews. A more likely story is that the bones were brought here by Bishop Acca of Hexham in AD 732. The relics were eventually transferred to the later building, housed in a shrine behind the high altar. St Andrews soon became a place of pilgrimage, with people coming from all over Europe to pray at the shrine. However, in 1559 John Knox preached a sermon in the town, which resulted in reformers sacking the cathedral and destroying the fittings and altars. Though there were plans to restore the building, by 1600 it was being used as a quarry for building material.

To the east of the cathedral and outside its precincts are the scant ruins of another church, **St Mary on the Rock**. When the cathedral was being built, there were still Culdee monks of the old Celtic church at St Andrews, and they refused to join the cathedral priory. In the 13th century they built this church for themselves, which became the first collegiate church in Scotland. However, the monks gradually adopted the rites of the Catholic Church, and its priests were soon allowed a place in the cathedral chapter.

St Andrews Castle was the archbishop's residence. It too sits on the coast, and its ruins are sturdy yet picturesque. The first castle on the site was probably built in the early 13th century, though this has been rebuilt and altered over the years. It was here, in 1546, that **Cardinal David Beaton**, Archbishop of St Andrews, was murdered. In March of that year, George Wishart the Protestant reformer had been burnt at the stake in front of the castle on Beaton's authority, which made him many enemies (see also Dundee and Montrose). In May a group of

Coastline at St Andrews

Fife lairds broke into the castle and murdered him in his bedroom, hanging the corpse from the window. There then followed a long siege of the castle, during which sappers working for the Earl of Arran dug a tunnel beneath the fortifications to gain entry. These tunnels can still be seen today.

Beaton was not the only Archbishop of St Andrews to have been murdered. The other one was **Archbishop James Sharp**, the Protestant archbishop when the Church of Scotland was Episcopalian. He had embarked upon a savage and bloody persecution of Covenanters (Presbyterians who objected to bishops in the Church of Scotland and denied that the King was the head of the church), and so was a hated man. In May 1679 he was returning to St Andrews from Edinburgh in a coach with his daughter. At Magus Muir, near the city, he was waylaid by Covenanters. Not averse to acts of unspeakable

---

89   THE NEW INN

St Andrews

A traditional pub serving a good range of food and drink.

¶   see page 462

cruelty themselves when it suited them, they stabbed the archbishop to death in front of his daughter. This was not the first attempt on his life. In 1668 a man called James Mitchell attempted to murder him, and he was captured six years later and executed. Perhaps the most amazing thing about James Sharp was that he himself had once been sympathetic to the Covenanting cause.

Wishart was not the only Protestant to have been executed in the town. There were others, including **Patrick Hamilton**, who was burnt at the stake in 1528 (see also Stonehouse). The spot is marked by his initials incorporated into the cobbles outside **St Salvator's Church** in North Street, part of **St Salvator's College**. The church was founded in 1450 by Bishop James Kennedy, not only to serve the college, but as a place of worship for the people of the town. Bishop Kennedy's tomb can be seen within it, though at the Reformation his body was removed by a mob which was "cleansing" the church of Catholic symbolism.

Also in North Street is the imposing **Younger Hall**, built in 1929 using money donated by an Edinburgh brewer. Here the university graduation ceremonies take place. It is also St Andrews University's musical centre, where concerts and musical performances take place.

It was on August 28th 1413 that Pope Benedict XIII issued six papal bulls authorising the founding of the university. At first the classes

were held in the cathedral, but this was found to be unsatisfactory. In 1450 Bishop Kennedy founded St Salvator's College, and classes moved there. In the 16th century two others were founded, **St Leonard's College** and **St Mary's College**. St Leonard's was eventually incorporated into St Salvator's, and a girl's school now stands on the site where it once stood. **St Leonard's Chapel** still exists, however, and the earliest parts date from the 12th century, showing it had been built long before the college came into being.

St Mary's College is undoubtedly the loveliest of today's colleges. Step through the arch from South Street and you are in a grassed quadrangle surrounded by old, mellow buildings from the 16th century onwards. At the foot of the Stair Tower is **Queen Mary's Thorn**, said to have been planted by Mary Stuart in 1565. She visited the town five times, and possibly lodged at what is now known as **Queen Mary's House** in South Street. It dates from about 1525, and was built by one of the cathedral's canons. Charles II also stayed in it in 1650.

Further along South Street, in front of **Madras College**, one of the town's schools, is all that remains of the **Dominican Friary**. This is the 16th century north transept of the friary church, with some wonderful tracery in its windows. The friary was originally founded in the 13th century by Bishop William Wishart.

Almost across from it is **Holy**

Trinity Parish Church. It was founded in the 15th century, though the building as we see it today dates largely from a rebuilding early in the 20th century. The only surviving parts of the medieval building are to be found in the west wall, some pillars and the tower. It contains a memorial to Archbishop Sharp, slain in 1679, though his body no longer rests under it. No doubt it had been removed and disposed of as soon as the Scottish church reverted to Presbyterianism.

At the west end of South Street can be found the **West Port**, one of the original gates into the town. It was built about 1589 on the site of an earlier port. In North Street is the **St Andrews Preservation Trust Museum and Garden**, housed in a charming building dating from the 16th century. It has displays and artefacts illustrating the town's history. The **St Andrews Museum** at Kinburn Park also celebrates the town's heritage.

At the Scores, near the shore, you'll find the **St Andrews Aquarium**, which lets you see and sometimes touch lots of fish and animals from sea horses to seals and piranha to sharks. Also on the Scores is the **Martyr's Monument**, which commemorates the Protestant martyrs who were executed in St Andrews. It is a tall, needle-like monument, erected in 1842. Close by is the **British Golf Museum**, which illustrates the history of a game that Scotland gave to the world, with a particular focus on St Andrews. It has an array of exhibits from over 500 years of golfing history, and gives an insight into "surprising facts and striking feats".

St Andrews and golf are inseparable. The town is still a place of pilgrimage, only today the pilgrims come wearing Pringle sweaters and weighed down by golf bags. **The Royal and Ancient Golf Club** is the world's ruling body on the game (with the exception of the United States), and formulates its rules as well as organising the yearly British Open Championship. The most famous of the town's courses is the **Old Course**, and it is here, in the clubhouse, that the Royal and Ancient has its headquarters.

Two of the greatest names in golf were born in St Andrews - **Tom Morris** and his son, also called Tom. Old Tom was made green keeper at the Old Course in 1865, and was one of the best golfers of his day. His son, however, was even better, and won the Open Championship three times in a row while still a teenager. He eventually died in 1875, aged only 24, some say of a broken heart after his wife died in childbirth. Memorials to both men can be seen in the cathedral graveyard.

The **Crawford Arts Centre**, originally part of the university, is in North Street, and has regular exhibitions of art and craftwork by living artists.

St Andrews is the eastern terminus for the 128 mile **Scottish**

Craigton Country Park sits about a mile outside the town to the southwest. It has a small boating loch, miniature railway, aviary, pet's corner, glasshouses, restaurant and café. Cambo Gardens is a two-and-a-half acre walled garden within the Cambo estate at Kingsbarns. Cambo has been the home of the Erskine family since 1688, though the present mansion dates from 1881. There is also 70 acres of woodland, which is famous for its snowdrops.

90 MARINE HOTEL

Crail

Situated on the coastline of Fife, **The Marine Hotel** boasts 10 en suite rooms.

see page 462

At Troywood, three miles west of the town, off the B9131, is perhaps the most unusual visitor attraction in Scotland. The Secret Bunker was Scotland's underground command centre in event of a nuclear attack. It has an amazing 24,000 square feet of accommodation on two levels, 100 feet underground and encased in 15 feet thick concrete walls. It was from here that the country was to have been run in the event of war with the Soviet Union. It is entered by an innocent looking farmhouse, and guarded by three tons of blast proof doors. As well as operations rooms, living quarters and six dormitories, it also contains two cinemas, a café and a BBC sound studio. Several similar bunkers were built around the country, and this is one of the largest. It came off the Official Secrets list in 1993 at the end of the Cold War.

Coast to Coast Walk that snakes across Scotland to Oban, taking in such places as Taynuilt, Balquidder, Comrie and Abernethy (see also Oban).

AROUND ST ANDREWS

CRAIL

8 miles SE of St Andrews on the A917

The royal burgh of Crail is one of the oldest ports in the East Neuk ("East Corner"), as this area of Fife is known. It is also possibly the most picturesque, and the small harbour has featured on countless calendars and post cards. Artists flock to the place because of the light and the quaint buildings. The **Tolbooth** dates from the early 16th century with a tower dated 1776, and has Dutch influences. In the Marketgate is the **Crail Museum and Heritage Centre**, which traces the history of the town and its industries.

The **Blue Stane** sits at the entrance to the parish church. It is said that the Devil took exception to the building of the original Crail church in the 12th century, and threw the stone from the Isle of May - out in the Firth of Forth - to demolish it, but missed. The blue markings on the stone are said to be the Devil's thumbprints.

The **Crail Raceway** is situated in an old 350 acre naval airbase known as HMS Jackdaw. Drag racing and other events take place here throughout the year. The airbase also includes an old hangar

which is used as a sound studio by filmmakers.

The four star **Jerdan Gallery,** in Marketgate South, has a wide variety of paintings and craftwork from the 19th and 20th centuries, with exhibits changing on a monthly basis. There is a sculpture garden to the rear.

ANSTRUTHER

9 miles S of St Andrews off the A917

Anstruther (sometimes pronounced "(Ainster)" is a former herring fishing port, and the largest of the East Neuk fishing villages. It comprises two ancient royal burghs, Anstruther Easter and Anstruther Wester, and is a picturesque place full of old white washed cottages with red pantiled roofs and crow stepped gables.

There is a story that, after the English defeated the Spanish Armada in 1588, one of the ships of the Spanish fleet put in at Anstruther and was civilly received by the people of the town. The ship's commander was one Jan Gomez de Midini, and he and his crew were offered hospitality (this at a time when Scotland and England were still independent countries). A few years later the Spaniard repaid his debt when he discovered fishermen from Anstruther marooned in a foreign port after their boat had been wrecked. He re-equipped them and sent them homewards once more.

Located in 16th century St Ayles House, once a lodging house for the monks from Balmerino Abbey, is the **Scottish Fisheries**

Museum, which was opened in 1969. Here you can follow the fleet with the "herring lassies", explore a typical fishing family's cottage and see skilled craftsmen at work. Also on display are two boats - a 78-feet long "Zulu" built in the early 1900s and based on an original African design, and the *Reaper*, a "fifie" herring drifter built in 1901. In a small private chapel is the poignant Memorial to Scottish Fishermen Lost at Sea.

Buckie House was covered in shells by a man called Alex Batchelor. It is said that he covered his coffin with shells as well, and charged people a penny to enter the House and look at it.

Six miles southeast of Anstruther, in the Firth of Forth, is the **Isle of May**, measuring just over a mile long by a quarter of a mile wide at its widest. There are the scant remains of an old Augustinian priory, dedicated to St Oran and St Colman, which was founded by David I and colonised from Reading Abbey in England. In 1996 an archaeological investigation uncovered the remains of a 9th century church - one of the oldest on Scotland's east coast. The whole place is now a national nature reserve managed by Scottish Natural Heritage. It was on this island that Scotland's first lighthouse was built in 1635. It was no more than a small stone tower with a brazier atop it, which burnt coal. Trips to the island are available from the pier at Anstruther.

The so-called **Battle of May Island** took place on the evening of 31 January and the morning of 1 February 1918. Forty Royal Navy ships set out for Scapa Flow in the Orkneys from Rosyth to take part in some exercises. They were sailing in a single column past the Isle of May, when some of the ships collided, killing over 100 sailors and sinking three submarines. It was the largest loss of life in the services during the First World War that didn't involve enemy action.

KILRENNY

9 miles S of St Andrews on the A917

The name Kilrenny comes from the Gaelic for the "Church of the Bracken". The present **Kilrenny Parish Church** has a tower dating from the 15th century, though the rest is early 19th century. In the Kirk yard is a mausoleum to the Scotts of Balcomie. There are many picturesque 18th and 19th century cottages, formerly the homes of fishermen. The adjacent village of **Cellardyke**, coupled with Kilrenny, was once a royal burgh.

91   THE SMUGGLER'S INN

Anstruther

The Smuggler's Inn is a welcoming establishment serving traditional Scottish fare. Six rooms are available for B&B.

❙❙   ➤   see page 462

92   SCOTTISH FISHERIES MUSEUM

Anstruther

Numerous displays and reconstructions illustrating the fishing industry, make for a fascinating day out.

🏛   see page 462

Isle of May, Anstruther

Kellie Castle (National Trust for Scotland), stands to the west of Pittenweem, and dates from the 14th century. It is one of the best examples in the Lowlands of the secular architecture of the time. It contains superb plaster ceilings, murals, painted panelling and furniture designed by Sir Robert Lorimer, who refurbished the place in the late 19th century. There are fine gardens with old roses and herbaceous borders.

Salt panning was once an important industry in St Monans, and the 18th century St Monans Windmill at one time formed part of a small industrial complex, which produced salt from seawater. The windmill pumped the water up from the sea into the saltpans, where it was heated, eventually leaving only salt.

PITTENWEEM

9 miles S of St Andrews on the A917

The older houses in this small royal burgh crowd around the picturesque fishing harbour, which is now the busiest of all the fishing harbours in the area. Like most of the houses in the East Neuk, they are whitewashed, and have red pantiled roofs and crow step gables. An Augustinian Priory was founded here in the 12th century by monks from the Isle of May, though very little of it now remains. The **Parish Church** has a substantial tower (which looks more like a small castle than a piece of ecclesiastical architecture) dating from the 16th century, while the rest is Victorian. **Pittenweem Priory**, of which there are now only scant remains, was founded in the 13th century by Augustinian monks from the Isle of May. **Kellie's Lodging** in the High Street was the town house of the Earls of Kellie, and it was where, in 1651, the townspeople of Pittenweem entertained Charles ll.

Pittenweem means "the place of the cave", and the cave in question is **St Fillan's Cave** in Cave Wynd, which is supposed to be where St Fillan, an 8th century missionary to the Picts, used to go for private prayer (see also Tyndrum, Madderty and St Fillans). It was renovated and re-dedicated in 1935. There are also many art galleries and antique shops, a testimony to the popularity of this area with artists and retired people.

ST MONANS

10 miles S of St Andrews on the A917

This little fishing port's motto is Mare Vivimus, meaning "From the Sea we Have Life". It is famous for the **Parish Church of St Monans**, built by David II, son of Robert the Bruce, in thanksgiving after he survived a shipwreck on the Forth. It stands almost on the shoreline, and is a substantial building consisting of a nave, transepts and stumpy spire atop a tower. The chancel was never built. One unusual internal feature is the model ship that hangs above the crossing.

St Monan himself is a shadowy figure. Some say he was a monk from St Andrews, further north, who evangelised the Firth of Forth coastline, while others say he was an Irish monk called St Moinenn, who who was bishop of Clonfert.

The ruins of 15th century **Newark Castle** can also be seen near the shore. It originally belonged to the Newark family, but perhaps its most famous owner was General David Leslie, who fought for Cromwell in the 17th century.

EARLSFERRY AND ELIE

10 miles S of St Andrews off the A917

These two villages are small holiday resorts surrounding a sandy bay. The older of the two is Earlsferry, which was created a royal burgh in 1373 by Robert ll. In 1929 the two towns were united as a single burgh. Earlsferry was once the northern terminal for ferries which plied between it and ports on the south bank of the Forth. The "earl" in its name comes from an incident concerning Macduff, who was the Earl of Fife. In 1054 he escaped from King Macbeth, took refuge in a cave at Kincraig Point near the town, and was then ferried across the Forth to Dunbar.

Gillespie House, in Elie, dates from 1689, and has a fine carved doorway. **Elie Parish Church** dates from 1639, though the unusual tower was added in 1729. There are clock faces on only three sides of the tower, as, when they were added, there were no houses on the north side, so a clock was unnecessary. At Ruby Bay are the scant remains of **Lady's Tower**, built in the late 18th century as a changing room for Lady Janet Anstruther, who bathed in the sea here. A bell ringer went round the town warning people to stay away when she did so. The building known as **The Castle** dates from the 16th century. However, it was never a castle. Instead it was a fine town house for the Gourley family of Kincraig.

At one time an old track called the "Cadgers Road" led from Earlsferry to Falkland, and it was along this that supplies of fresh fish were taken to feed the king when he stayed there.

CUPAR

8 miles W of St Andrews on the A91

This small town, sitting on the River Eden, was, up until 1974, the county town of Fife, as can be seen from its many fine buildings. It is an imposing, prosperous place, and well worth strolling round just to see and appreciate its many old buildings. The **Mercat Cross**, topped with a unicorn, was moved from Tarvit Hill to its present location in 1897 to commemorate Queen Victoria's Diamond Jubilee. In Duffus Park is the **Douglas Bader Garden**, designed with the disabled in mind. The **Old Parish Church**, more properly known as the Parish Church of Cupar Old and St Michael of Tarvit, dates from 1785, though the tower is medieval.

The **Battle of Cupar Muir** took place here, and is the only recognised battle in Britain where no shots were ever fired and no one was killed.

Hill of Tarvit Mansion House (National Trust for Scotland) is a fine Edwardian mansion that lies two miles south of the town, and was refurbished by Sir Robert Lorimer in 1906 for Frederick Sharp, a Dundee jute factory owner. It has French, Scottish and Chippendale furniture, a collection of paintings, an Edwardian laundry and fine gardens. Close by is **Scotstarvit Tower** (Historic Scotland). It was built by the Inglis family around 1487 when they were granted the lands of Tarvit. In 1612 it was bought by Sir John Scott. He was an advocate who was deprived of his twin positions in the Scottish judiciary as judge and director of chancery by Cromwell in the 17th century, and retired to Scotstarvit, where he was visited by many

A few miles west of Cupar, at Rankeilor Park, is the Scottish Deer Centre and Raptor World. At the Deer Centre you can see - and even feed - both species of deer native to Scotland, the roe and the red deer, plus other species from around the world. At the Raptor Centre there are exhibitions about birds of prey such as owls, hawks and falcons, plus there are spectacular flying demonstrations. There is also a small shopping court, an indoor adventure play area and picnic areas.

93 THE VILLAGE INN

Pitlessie

The Village Inn is a popular place serving a good range of traditional Scottish fare in its spacious restaurant.

❦ see page 463

eminent men of the time.

To the north of the town is a 95 feet high column known as **The Mount**, which commemorates the 4th Earl of Hopetoun, Sir John Hope. It was near here that the famous Scottish Renaissance writer and playwright **Sir David Lyndsay** was born in about 1490. His most famous work was the satirical play *Ane Pleasant Satyre of the Three Estates* (more commonly just referred to as *The Three Estates*). He was also appointed Lord Lyon, who presided over the armorial bearings of the Scottish nobility.

CERES

7 miles W of St Andrews on the B939

Ceres gets its name from the family which once owned the lands surrounding the village - the de Syras family. It is a small picturesque place with a village green and the hump-backed, medieval **Bishop's Bridge**. In the **Fife Folk Museum** you can find out about what everyday life was like in Fife in bygone days.

Two miles southwest of Ceres are the ruins of 14th century **Struthers Castle**. It has been owned by the de Ochters, the Keiths, the Lindsays and the Crawfords. At one time the lands belonging to the castle were called "Outhirothistrodyr", from which the word "Struther" comes.

The village's **Bannockburn Monument** is close by the Bishop's Bridge (named after Archbishop Sharpe of St Andrews), who was killed in 1679, and was erected in 1914, 600 years after the Battle of Bannockburn took place, to commemorate the archers of Ceres who fell in it. The **Parish Church** was built in 1806 on the site of a much older church. It also contains a medieval tomb of an Earl of Crawford which stood in the previous medieval church. Built into a wall on the main street is a curious carving known as **The Provost**, said to have been the Revd Thomas Buchanan, the last holder of the title in 1578.

NEWBURGH

16 miles W of St Andrews on the A913

This small royal burgh stands on the banks of the Tay. To the east are the red sandstone ruins of **Lindores Abbey**, founded by David I in 1178 for Tironenisan monks.

In 1559 Protestant sympathisers, worked up by the rhetoric of Kohn Knox, sacked the place and destroyed altars and religious statues. And the very first mention of whisky production in Scotland is contained in a document of 1494, when James IV commissioned John Cor, a monk at the abbey, to make the equivalent of 400 bottles of "aquavitae" for the king's table.

The **Laing Museum** in the High Street has displays on Newburgh's history from medieval burgh to industrial town.

AUCHTERMUCHTY

16 miles W of St Andrews on the A91

The royal burgh of Auchtermuchty (or "'Muchty", as it is known by the locals) is a typical inland Fife town.

It is small and compact, and sits in a fertile area known as the Howe of Fife ("Hollow of Fife"). The **Tolbooth** dates from 1728, and it was here that the TV series *Dr Finlay* was filmed, its town centre being turned into a typical Scottish townscape of the 1930s. The **Town House**, with its tower and stumpy spire, dates from 1728.

Though born in East Wemyss, **Jimmy Shand**, the well known Scottish dance band leader, lived in the town for many years. There is a statue of him, complete with kilt, at Upper Glens in the town.

LEUCHARS
4 miles NW of St Andrews, on the A919

Every September, the Royal Air Force puts on the **Leuchars Air Show**, held in one of Scotland's biggest RAF bases. The village is also famous for it's **Parish Church of St Athernase**, said by some to be the second finest Norman church in Britain. It was built in the late 12th century by Robert de Quinci, who lived in Leuchars Castle. The best parts are the finely carved chancel and apse, with the rather plain nave being Victorian. A bell tower was added to the apse in the 17th century. St Athernase is also known as St Ethernesc, and he was a companion of St Columba who travelled and preached throughout Fife.

Earlshall Castle (not open to the public) was started in 1546 by Sir William Bruce, and completed by his descendant of the same name in 1617. It subsequently fell into disrepair, but was rebuilt in 1891 under the direction of Sir Robert Lorimer. **Tentsmuir Forest**, to the north of Leuchars, is a 3,700-acre pine forest planted on sand dunes on the shores of the North Sea and the Firth of Tay. The whole area is rich in wildlife.

NEWPORT-ON-TAY
9 miles NW of St Andrews on the A92

This little town sits at the southern end of the Tay Road Bridge, and at **Wormit**, about a mile to the west, is the start of the Tay Rail Bridge. The ruins of **Balmerino Abbey** (National Trust for Scotland) sit five miles to the west. It was founded in 1229 by Queen Ermengarde, widow of William the Lion, king of Scotland, and colonised by Cistercian monks from Melrose. When the queen died, she was buried in front of the high altar. The ruins are not open to the public, but can be viewed from close by. A Spanish chestnut tree stands in the abbey grounds, and it is one of the oldest in the country.

TAYPORT
8 miles N of St Andrews on the B945

This small town, thanks to the Tay Road Bridge, which opened in 1966, is now a dormitory town for the city of Dundee across the Firth of Tay. The **Auld Kirk** of Tayport, which dates mainly from the 1794, is no longer used for worship. It has an unusual leaning clock tower.

---

94 HILLPARK HOUSE

Leuchars, St Andrews

Five comfortable rooms and a delicious breakfast are on offer at **Hillpark House**.

⊨ see page 463

Stirlingshire & Clackmannanshire

That area of Scotland between the Firths of Clyde and Forth has always been strategically important. It is often referred to as Scotland's "waist", and before the Kincardine Bridge was built in 1936, the bridge at Stirling was the lowest crossing point of the River Forth. To the west of the town are the Campsie and the Kilsyth Hills, and these, along with marshy bogland such as Flanders Moss, formed another natural barrier, so the bridge at Stirling became the gateway to Perthshire and the Highlands.

That's why so many battles have been fought in and around Stirling and

Falkirk, including Scotland's most important, the Battle of Bannockburn, which secured Scotland's future as an independent nation. It is also the reason why Stirling Castle was built. This royal

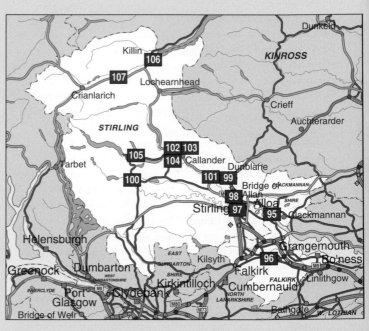

castle sits sentinel on a great rocky outcrop, with the town of Stirling laid out below on its western side. In medieval times it was almost impregnable, and from its top an approaching army could easily be seen from miles away.

This is an area which has witnessed great changes over the years due to local government reorganisations. The cathedral city of Dunblane, to the north of Stirling, was at one time in Perthshire, as was Callander and Port of Menteith. For a while, the county of Clackmannanshire ceased to exist (though it remained alive in the hearts of all those born there). Now it has returned, and still proudly proclaims itself to be Scotland's smallest county, with an area of only 30,400 acres. It sits in the shelter of the Ochil Hills , which rise to well over 2,000 feet in places, and was a centre for woollens and textiles. The string of "hillfoot villages" at the foot of the Ochils are all picturesque and well worth visiting.

Around Falkirk and Grangemouth, Stirlingshire is unashamedly industrial. This is the heart of Scotland's petrochemical industry, with great refineries lining the shores of the Forth, which is still tidal at this point. It was also at one time a coal mining area, though the mines have long gone.

Travel northwest from Stirling however, and you enter another world - the Trossachs, one of Scotland's most beautiful areas. Though its hills are not as high as those of the Grampians or the Cairngorms, and don't have that brooding majesty we tend to associate with Highland scenery, it is still Highland in character. The hills slip down to the wooded banks of lochs such as Loch Katrine, Loch Venachar and the wonderfully named Loch Drunkie, which are among the most picturesque in Scotland, and the skies seem endless and sweeping. The Loch Lomond and Trossachs National Park (see also Balloch) takes in most of the Trossachs in its 720 square miles. It was the country's first national park, opened in 2002.

The town of Stirling is one of the most historic in Scotland, and has played a leading role in shaping the country's destiny. The castle has been fought over countless times by the Scottish and the English, and eventually became a favourite royal residence. Mary Queen of Scots stayed there, and her son, who became James VI, had his coronation in the town's Church of the Holy Rood. Falkirk, though more industrial in character, is also an ancient town, and has witnessed two important battles as Scotland's history unfolded. Alloa, Clackmannanshire's largest town, is also industrial in character, though it too has history aplenty. At one time it was a thriving port and Scotland's brewing capital, though only one brewery now remains.

For those interested in architecture, the whole area offers some memorable buildings. Stirling Castle itself was given a Renaissance makeover by James IV. Dunblane Cathedral, Alloa Tower, the ruins of Camubuskenneth Priory, the Wallace Monument, Doune Castle and Castle Campbell are also well worth visiting.

CLACKMANNAN

This small town was granted its burgh charter in 1550, and up until 1822, when Alloa replaced it, it was the county town of Clackmannanshire. It was once a small port on the Black Devon, a tributary of the Forth, but the river silted up years ago, leaving it high and dry. In the centre of the town is the belfry of the old **Tolbooth**, built by William Menteith in 1592. He was the sheriff of the town, and objected strongly to holding felons in his own home, so he built the Tolbooth to hold them instead.

Beside it stands the **Mannau Stone**. Legend states that when St Serf came to this part of Scotland in the 6th century to convert it to Christianity, he found the locals worshipping the sea god Mannau, or Mannan, in the form of the stone (known as the "clach mannau"). From this, the town supposedly got its name. Another legend states that the name derives from an incident in the life of Robert the Bruce. It seems that he once rested close to the stone, and on remounting his horse, left his glove lying on it. He ordered one of his servants to return to the "clach" (stone) and retrieve his "mannan" (glove). The stone can still be seen on top of a column close to the Tolbooth and the **Mercat Cross**, which dates from the 1600s.

Clackmannan Tower, on King's Seat Hill, where once a royal hunting lodge built by David Il stood, dates from the 14th century, with later alterations. Though in the care of Historic Scotland, it can only be viewed from the outside at present. Robert Burns visited the area in 1787, and was "knighted" by a direct descendant of Robert the Bruce, a Mrs Bruce, who lived in a mansion house (demolished in 1791) near the castle. She was in her nineties at the time, and a woman of "hospitality and urbanity". She still possessed her ancestor's helmet and two-handed sword, and she used the sword to

Mannan Stone

carry out the ceremony, declaring that she had a better right to confer knighthoods than "some people" (meaning the Hanovarian kings who were on the throne in London).

Clackmannan's **Parish Church** dates from 1815, and replaced a 12th century church. St Serf may have founded the original church in the 6th century. Inside the present church is the beautiful Coronation Window, gifted to the church by its congregation to mark the coronation of Elizabeth II in 1953. It is the only such window in the whole of Britain. The Queen visited the church specially to view it in 1997.

Two miles north of the town is the **Gartmorn Dam Country Park**. It is centred on the 170-acre Gartmorn Dam, the oldest man-made reservoir in Scotland. It was constructed in the early 1700s by John Erskine, 6th Earl of Mar, to power the pumps which pumped water out of his coal mines at nearby Sauchie. Now a nature reserve, the park is popular with walkers and nature lovers, and the reservoir itself is stocked with brown trout.

AROUND CLACKMANNAN

TILLICOULTRY

4 miles N of Clackmannan on the A91

Tillicoultry is one of the "hillfoot villages" which relied on water tumbling down from the Ochils to power the mills in which most people were employed. It became a burgh in 1634, and behind it is the picturesque **Tillicoultry Glen**, whose waters once powered eight mills in the town.

Robert Burns, along with his friend Dr James Adair, visited Harvieston, near the town, in October 1787, and there met the mother and half-sister of his landlord in Mauchline, Gavin Hamilton. Burns fell for Charlotte, Gavin's half-sister, though it was Adair she eventually married in 1789. While in Harvieston he wrote two poems - *The Fairest Maid on Devon Bank* and *Banks of the Devon*.

DOLLAR

5 miles NE of Clackmannan on the A91

Dollar is another "hillfoot village", famous as the home of **Dollar Academy**. This private school (the equivalent of an English public school) was founded in 1818 thanks to a bequest by Captain John McNabb, a local herd boy born in 1732 who amassed a fortune in London as a merchant before his death in 1802. When he died he was worth £60,000, which was a huge sum -the equivalent of several million today. By 1820 the academy had been built, though if McNabb came back today he might be puzzled to see it, for he had intended it to be a school, not only for the children of the wealthy (who would have to pay), but for the children of the poor in Dollar parish, whose education would be free, and who would receive clothing and medical care.

The elegant, colonnaded building was designed by the

An old story says that Tillicoultry got its unusual name from a Highlander who was driving some cattle along a road where the town now stands. He stopped at a stream to allow the cattle to drink. However, none of the cattle did so, and he exclaimed, "there's tiel a coo try", meaning "devil a cow is thirsty!" However, a more prosaic explanation of the name is that it comes from the Gaelic, and means "hill in the back land".

Above the town of Dollar, and reached through the wooded Dollar Glen (National Trust for Scotland), is Castle Campbell (National Trust for Scotland). It was one of Clan Campbell's Lowland homes, and was formerly known as "Castle Gloom". Close by are two burns called Care and Sorrow, and even the name Dollar itself is said to derive from "dolour", meaning sadness. It seems strange that such a beautiful spot should have such names. The castle dates essentially from the 15th century, with some later additions. In 1654 the castle was destroyed by a Scottish army in retaliation for the Campbell's support of Oliver Cromwell. Both John Knox and Mary Stuart stayed in the castle, Knox in 1556 and Mary in 1563.

eminent architect William Playfair, and was opened in 1819. In the 1930s McNabb's coffin was rediscovered in a London crypt. The remains were cremated, and the ashes now rest in a niche above the bronze doors of the school.

Within an old, white-washed woollen mill now called Castle Campbell Hall in Dollar is the small **Dollar Museum**, which has displays on the history of the village and on the Devon Valley railway.

The **Battle of Dollar** took place in AD 877 between an army of Scots led by Constantine l (son of Scotland's first king, Kenneth McAlpine) and an army of Vikings. The Vikings won a crushing victory, and Constantine himself was killed as he fled from the battlefield.

Though the town lies six miles north of the Forth, James Watt the engineer once proposed deepening the Devon Water and creating a small port in the town.

ALVA

3 miles NW of Clackmannan on the A91

Alva sits at the foot of the Ochils, and is yet another of the "hillfoot villages" where weaving and spinning were the main industries. It's name means "rocky plain", as does that of its near neighbour Alloa. To the northeast is the Ochil Hills' highest peak, the 2,363-feet **Ben Cleuch**. At the **Mill Trail Visitor Centre**, housed in the former Glentana Mill building of 1887, there are displays and exhibits that explain what life was

like in mill factories over the last 150 years. There is also a shop and a café. **The Mill Trail** itself is a signposted route taking you to many mills with retail outlets. **The Ochil Hills Woodland Park** has attractive walks and a visitor centre. It is centred on what were the grounds of the long gone Alva House, home of the Johnstone family. It was used for target practise during World War ll.

At one time Alva formed a small enclave of Stirlingshire, but in 1832 became part of Clackmannanshire.

Alva Glen, also called the "Silver Glen", is very picturesque. Silver was once mined here in the 18th century, and **St Serf's Parish Church** in Stirling Street, which dates from 1815, has some communion vessels made from local silver. It was the Erskine family that mined the silver, and according to them it was a hit or miss affair. A story is told of one member of the family, Sir John Erskine, showing two of the mines to a friend. "Out of that hole there I earned £50,000," he told him. "And in that hole there I lost it all again."

Sir John also exploited the coal reserves in the area, and dug a short canal between the coal mine and the River Devon to take the coal down to the Fiirth of Forth.

BLAIRLOGIE

6 miles NW of Clackmannan on the A91

Blairlogie is possibly the most beautiful of the "hillfoot villages", and was the first conservation village in Scotland. It sits in the shadow of the 1,373-feet **Dumyat**, which has two distinct summits, a west and an east. There are the remains of a hilltop fort on its western summit, known as Castle Law. The name derives from Dun Maetae, meaning the fort of the Maetae, a Pictish tribe. At the summit there is also a memorial to the Argyll and Sutherland Highlanders, and superb views as far as Edinburgh.

MENSTRIE

4 miles NW of Clackmannan on the A91

Sir William Alexander, 1st Earl of Stirling, was born in **Menstrie Castle** in 1567. He was the founder of Nova Scotia ("New Scotland"), Scotland's only lasting colony in North America. The only part of the castle open to the public is the Nova Scotia Commemoration Room, which has displays about the colony. There are also the armorial bearings of the Nova Scotia baronetcies created in Scotland at the beginning of the 17th century. The baronetcies had nothing to do with nobility, chivalry or valour, but everything to do with money, as they were offered for sale at 3,000 Scots merks each.

In 1621 Sir William persuaded James VI to create the baronetcies, and when James realised how much money he could make from it, he readily agreed. In 1624, while at Windsor, he began the money making scheme. A year later he was dead, and his son Charles I, not unnaturally, continued the practise. By the end of 1625 the first 22

titles had been conferred. Even today there are 109 titles still in existence. Sir William died penniless in London in 1644, and now lies buried in the Church of the Holy Rood in Stirling. There is a monument to him in Halifax, Nova Scotia (see also Edinburgh and Stirling).

The castle itself was built in the late 16th century, and was a stronghold of Clan McAllister, a family that changed its name to Alexander as it adopted English customs. It gradually fell into a state of disrepair, but was refurbished in the 1950s as a private housing complex.

ALLOA

2 miles W of Clackmannan on the A907

With a population of about 15,000, Alloa is the largest town in Scotland's smallest county. Though an inland town, it sits on the River Forth at a point where it is still tidal, and its name is supposed to mean "rocky plain" or "seaway". It was traditionally an engineering, brewing and glass-making town, though today these industries are less important than they once were.

The rather grand **St Mungo's Parish Church** dates from 1817, though there is the 17th century tower of an earlier church. **Alloa Tower** (National Trust for Scotland) is Scotland's earliest surviving keep, and dates from the 14th century. It was the ancestral home of the Erskines, one of the most important families in Scotland. They eventually became the Earls of Mar, and as such were (and still

Sir Ralph Abercromby, who commanded the British troops at the Battle of Alexandria in 1801, was born in Menstrie in 1734, the son of a lawyer. He died at Alexandria in 1801 of wounds received during the battle. During his lifetime, he was considered to be Britain's greatest general.

95 THE ROYAL OAK HOTEL

Alloa

The Royal Oak Hotel is a comfortable hotel with en suite rooms and a restaurant serving superb food, whilst drinks are available from the Oak Pub.

🛏 ‖ *see page 463*

are as the Earls of Mar and Kellie) Hereditary Keepers of Stirling Castle. The tower was built for Alexander Erskine, the 3rd Lord Erskine, in the late 15th century, and later remodelled by the 6th Earl of Mar in the 18th century. It has the original oak roof beams, medieval vaulting and a dungeon. There is also a grand, sweeping early 18th century staircase.

The Erskines were custodians of Mary Stuart during her infancy, and she lived in the tower for a time. An old story says that when Mary gave birth to James VI in Edinburgh Castle in 1566, the baby was stillborn, and the Earl of Mar's infant son was substituted (see also Edinburgh). Certainly, while still a boy, James stayed here, as did his mother. Mary and her estranged husband, Lord Darnley, were reconciled while on a visit to the tower. However, the reconciliation did not last.

The 6th Earl was an ardent Jacobite, and after the 1715 Uprising he was sent into exile. The story of the Erskines is told within the tower, and the present Earl has loaned a superb collection of paintings, including works by Raeburn and Kneller.

Alloa's rail link with Stirling was closed in 1968, but it is now being reinstated, and is expected to open in 2007. The noted Canadian newspaper owner and politician **George Brown** was born in Alloa in 1818.

Alloa Museum and Gallery, in the Speirs Centre in Primrose Street, has exhibits tracing the history of the town.

TULLIBODY

4 miles W of Clackmannan on the B9140

Legend says that Tullibody was founded by King Kenneth McAlpine, first king of Scotland. He was the king of the Dalriadan Scots, and on the eve of a battle with the Picts in AD 834 he and his knights swore an oath that they would never stop fighting until the Picts were defeated or they themselves were killed. The battle duly took place, and Kenneth was victorious.

He had a stone erected on the spot where they had taken the oath, and called the place "Tirlbothy", meaning the "oath of the crofts". The stone still stood at Baingle Brae until it was moved in 1805. In

Alloa Tower

AD 843 Kenneth also succeeded to the throne of the Picts through intermarriage on his mother's side, and united the Picts and Scots into an embryonic Kingdom of Scotland (see also Dunadd).

Robert Dick, the eminent, but self taught, botanist was born in Tullibody in 1811. He was a baker, and worked in various Scottish towns. In 1839, at the behest of his father, who was living there, he moved to Thurso, and remained there for the rest of his life. In his spare time he studied the fauna of the area, moving on to fossils a few years later (see also Thurso).

FALKIRK

With a population of 32,300, Falkirk is Stirlingshire's largest town, and received its burgh charter in 1600. It sits at an important point on the road from Edinburgh to Stirling, and nearby **Stenhousemuir** was once the meeting place of various drove roads coming down from the Highlands. Here great herds of cattle were kept before being sold at "trysts" and taken further south to the markets of Northern England. It has been estimated that over 24,000 head of cattle were sold annually at the three trysts held each year.

Falkirk is located in an important part of Scotland. Here the country narrows, with the Firth of Forth to the east and the Campsie and Kilsyth Hills to the west. This meant that any army trying to march north from the Lowlands or south from the Highlands had to pass close to the town. For that reason, there have been two battles fought at Falkirk. One was in 1298, when William Wallace and his Scottish army were defeated by the English army of Edward I.

The second **Battle of Falkirk** was fought in 1746, when a Jacobite army defeated a Hanovarian army led by Lieutenant General Henry Hawley, who, it was rumoured, was a natural son of George II. The story goes that Hawley, before the battle, was being entertained by Lady Ann Livingstone, wife of the Jacobite Earl of Kilmarnock, at Callendar House, her Falkirk home. On hearing that the battle was about to begin, Hawley hastily rose from the table and rode to take command. The site of the battle is now marked by a memorial unveiled by the Duke of Atholl in 1927.

The name of the town means the "kirk of mottled stone", a reference to its first stone built medieval church. The present **Old Parish Church** dates from 1810, and incorporates fragments of an earlier church. Its tower dates from 1734. The church was the burial place for many prominent local families, and buried in the churchyard is said to be Sir John de Graeme, who was killed at the Battle of Falkirk fighting in William Wallace's army.

The **Town Steeple** was built in 1814, and was designed by the famous architect David Hamilton. It replaced an earlier building,

Tullibody Auld Brig, which spans the River Devon, was built about 1535 by James Spittal, tailor to the royal family (see also Doune). In January 1560 the easternmost arch of the bridge was dismantled by Kirkcaldy of Grange to impede a French army, which was in Scotland in support of Mary of Guise, mother of Mary Stuart and widow of James V. However, the French army dismantled the roof of Tullibody Auld Kirk, which dated from the early 16th century, and made a new bridge from the rafters. In 1697, Thomas Bauchop, a local mason, was commissioned by John, 6th Earl of Mar, to build a new eastern arch.

Centred on the village of Bonnybridge, two miles west of Falkirk, is the Bonnybridge Triangle, so called because there have been more sightings of UFOs and unexplained phenomena in this area than anywhere else in the UK. It all started in 1992 when a cross shaped cluster of lights was seen hovering above a road, and it has continued up until the present day, with mysterious football-sized lights, delta shaped craft and even spaceships with opening doors being seen as well. At one time, there were even plans to build a theme park around the flying saucer sightings.

which dated from the 17th century, and has traditionally been a meeting place for the people of the town. In 1927 the upper portion of the steeple was struck by lightning and had to be rebuilt. Tolbooth Street, behind the steeple, is, at 58 feet long, Britain's shortest street.

Near Falkirk the two great Lowland canals - the Forth and Clyde and the Union Canal - meet. Thanks to the £84.5 million Millennium Link Project, they have recently been restored, and the magnificent new 120-feet high **Falkirk Wheel** at Rough Castle, which has become a tourist attraction in its own right, carries boats between one canal and the other (which are on different levels), within water filled "gondolas". It can carry eight boats at a time, with the "trip" taking 15 minutes, and is the world's first (and as yet only) rotating lift for boats. Special trip boats are available so that visitors can experience being taken up or down on the gondolas. The wheel replaced a series of locks built in

the early 19th century but which had been abandoned when the canals fell into disuse. Not only has the wheel been hailed as a feat of engineering, it is being looked on a piece of modern sculpture, so beautiful are its lines and curves.

Falkirk sits on the line of the Antonine Wall, a massive turf wall on a stone base, built on the orders of the Roman emperor Antonius Pius just after AD 138 (see also Bearsden and Milngavie). It stretched the 39 miles from the Firth of Clyde at Bowling to the Firth of Forth west of Bo'ness. **Rough Castle** (National Trust for Scotland) five miles from the town, is one of the best preserved of the wall's fortifications. Parts of the wall can be seen in the town's **Callendar Park**, in which you will also find **Callendar House**. This magnificent building, modelled on a French château, has played a major role in Scotland's history. In 1293 Alexander II granted land to one Malcolm de Kalynter, and he may have built a wooden castle. A descendant of Malcolm became involved in plots against David II in 1345, and the estates were forfeited and given to Sir William Livingstone, whose descendants lived there until the 18th century.

The Livingstones were close to Mary Stuart, and the queen visited the estate many times. In 1600 James VI rewarded the family by making them Earls of Linlithgow. But with the rise of the Jacobites, the family's fortunes went into decline. The 5th Earl was forced into exile for siding with the Old

Rough Castle

Pretender in 1715, and his daughter, Lady Anne married the ill-fated Earl of Kilmarnock, who was beheaded in London for his part in the 1745 Uprising (see also Kilmarnock).

In 1783 the house and estate were bought by the businessman William Forbes, whose descendants lived there for almost 200 years. It has now been restored by the local council as a heritage centre and museum, with a working Georgian kitchen, printer's and clockmaker's workrooms and a general store. In the Victorian library is an extensive archive of books, documents and photographs on the history of the area, and the Major William Forbes Falkirk exhibition traces the history of the town. The **Park Gallery**, which runs a series of art exhibitions and workshop activities, is also located in Callendar Park.

AROUND FALKIRK

AIRTH

5 miles N of Falkirk on the A905

It is hard to imagine that a huge royal dockyard founded by James IV once stood close to this small village in the 15th and 16th centuries. A small harbour still operated in the 1700s, but now it too has gone. The present day Shore street once led to it.

Parts of the nearby **Airth Castle** (now a hotel) date from the 14th century. An earlier castle stood on the site, and it was here that William Wallace's uncle, a priest, was held prisoner by the English before Wallace rescued him. The castle frontage as seen today dates from 1810, and was designed by David Hamilton.

Airth Parish Church dates from around 1820, but the ruins of the earlier church, mainly 17th century but with some 12th century features, can still be seen. The **Mercat Cross** dates from 1697, and was built to replace an earlier one which now stands near Airth Castle.

GRANGEMOUTH

3 miles E of Falkirk on the A904

Grangemouth is a modern town, and the centre of Scotland's petrochemical industry. It was one of the country's first planned towns, having been established by Sir Laurence Dundas in the late 18th century to be the eastern terminus of the Forth and Clyde Canal. His son Thomas continued the work.

On Bo'ness Road, above the library, is the **Grangemouth Museum**, which traces the history of the town up to the present day. The **Jupiter Urban Wildlife Garden** is off Wood Street, and was established in 1990 by Zeneca (formerly ICI) and the Scottish Wildlife Trust on a piece of land that was once a railway marshalling yard. Surrounded by industrial buildings and smokestacks, this oasis of green shows how derelict industrial land can be cleaned up and reclaimed for nature. It has four ponds, an area of scrub birch known as The Wilderness, a wildlife plant nursery and a formal wildlife garden, as well as meadows,

Airth is visited mainly because of one of the most unusual buildings in Scotland - The Pineapple (National Trust for Scotland) in Dunmore Park. It is a summerhouse, built in 1761, and on top of it is a huge, 45-feet high pineapple made of stone. It is heated using an early form of central heating, as passages and cavities within the stone walls carry hot air through them. It can be rented as a holiday home. Also at Dunmore are 16 acres of gardens. The Pineapple was built by John Murray, 4th Earl of Dunmore, governor of New York in 1760 and then the last governor of the colony of Virginia before independence between 1771 and 1776. As governor, he led a war against the Indians, now remembered as Lord Dunmore's War. He later went on to become the governor of the Bahamas.

96 FORMULE I HOTEL

Polmont

The Formule 1 Hotel is an ideal base for visitors to the region. Comfortable rooms with a continental breakfast available at a cost of £2.50 per person.

see page 463

97 CASTLE CROFT

Stirling

Comfortable B&B with six en suite rooms, in an historic area of Stirling.

see page 465

marshland and reed beds. **Zetland Park** is the town's main open area, and offers putting, crazy golf, an adventure playground, a boating pond and tennis courts.

STIRLING

Stirling is one of the most strategically placed towns in Scotland, and was granted its royal charter in 1226. It sits astride the main route north from the Lowlands at Scotland's narrowest point, and guards the route to the Highlands. On the craggy plug of an ancient volcano a fort was built in prehistoric times, which evolved over the years to become a castle and royal residence. At the same time, a settlement grew to the east to cater for its needs. It is Scotland's newest city, as in 2002 it was granted city status as part of the Queen's Golden Jubilee celebrations.

Stirling Castle (Historic Scotland) is a mixture of styles and dates, and like Edinburgh is not one building, but a series of buildings on top of a rocky outcrop. Some form of fortification has stood here from at least pre-Christian times, and it is one of the many sites in Scotland associated with King Arthur. Someone has even suggested that there were two Camelots in Britain - one at Carlisle and one at Stirling. It entered recorded history in the early 12th century, when Alexander I dedicated a chapel. There must also have been a palace of some kind, as Alexander died here in 1124. We

next hear of it in 1174, when William the Lion was compelled to hand over various Scottish castles to Henry II of England, Stirling included.

During the Wars of Independence in the 13th and 14th centuries, Stirling Castle played a leading role. By this time it was back in Scottish hands, and Edward I was outraged by the fact that it was the last Lowland castle to hold out against his conquest of the country, and a barrier to further conquest in the north. So, in 1304, he set out to besiege it, and it eventually fell. For the next ten years the English garrisoned it. In 1313 Edward Bruce, brother of Robert I, laid siege to it, and its commander, Sir Philip Mowbray, agreed to surrender on 24th June 1314 if it was not relieved by an English army.

By this time Edward I was dead, and his son Edward II, a much weaker man, was on the throne. He did not want to lose Stirling, so he came north with a great army to relieve it. The Scots met this army at Bannockburn, and secured a great victory - one that sealed Scotland's independence.

All traces of the castle as it was at the time of Bannockburn have long gone. Most of the buildings now date from the 15th century and later. James III was the first of the Scottish kings to take an interest in its architecture, and built the Great Hall as a meeting place of the Scottish parliament and for great ceremonial occasions. James IV then began building a new palace in the Renaissance style, with his son James V finishing the work. In 1594 James VI had the Chapel Royal built, and these three buildings represent the most important architectural elements in the castle. It was within the Chapel Royal, on 9th September 1543, when she was barely nine months old, that Mary Stuart, later known as Mary, Queen of Scots, was crowned in a ceremony that was curiously lacking in pomp or majesty.

A curious tale is told of Stirling Castle. It concerns James IV and John Damien, the Abbot of Tongland in Kirkcudbrightshire, who earned the nickname of the **Frenzied Friar of Tongland** (see also Tongland). He was an Italian, and a learned man who spent a lot of time at court. In 1507 he convinced James IV that man could fly, and to prove it, he told him that he would jump from the walls of the castle and fly all the way to France.

A date was set for the flight to take place, and a bemused James IV and his court assembled on the battlements. Meanwhile, Abbot Damien had told his servants to amass a large collection of feathers from flying birds and construct a large pair of wings from them. However, his servants could not collect enough feathers of the right kind in time, so incorporated some chicken feathers as well. The Abbot duly presented himself on the battlements of the castle with the wings strapped to his back and wrists. No mention is made in contemporary accounts of how the king and the court viewed this unusual sight, but there must have been a few suppressed sniggers.

Damien stood on the battlements, made a short speech, and began flapping his wings. He then jumped - and fell like a stone, landing in the castle midden, on which more than the castle's kitchen scraps were deposited. His fall could not have been that far, as all he succeeded in doing was breaking a leg. When he later discovered that his servants had incorporated chicken feathers in the wings, he blamed this for the failure of his flight. The court poet William Dunbar was present at this attempt at the world's first manned flight, and wrote some verses about it.

The **Church of the Holy Rude** on St John Street is Stirling's parish church. The word "rude" in this context means "cross", and is also found in Holyrood Abbey in Edinburgh. Originally founded in 1129, the present building dates from the 15th century, and was built at the command of James IV, who, tradition says, worked alongside the masons during its construction. It is one of the finest medieval churches in Scotland, and has its original oak roof. Within the church, in 1567, the infant James VI was crowned king of Scotland in a Protestant ceremony at which John Knox preached a sermon and which Mary Stuart, his mother, did not attend as she was being held prisoner in Loch Leven Castle. Just over a year before, James had been

The Old Town Jail, down the slope in the city itself, was opened in 1847 to take the prisoners that were formerly held in the Tolbooth. From 1888 until 1935 it was used as a military prison. Now it has been reopened as a tourist attraction, and shows what life was like for prisoners and wardens in the 19th century. You'll also meet a character called Jock Rankin, who was the town's hangman. If, during your visit, a prisoner should try to escape, you should remain calm and follow the advice of the warden! There is an audio tour in five languages.

The Church of the Holy Rude is one of only two still functioning churches in Great Britain to have witnessed a coronation, the other one being Westminster Abbey. From just after the Reformation until the 1930s a wall divided the church in two, with two independent congregations worshipping at the same time.

baptised into the Roman Catholic Church in Stirling Castle's Chapel Royal, and this Protestant coronation sealed the ascendancy of the Protestant church in Scotland. What is not generally known is that James (who later became James VI and I of England and Great Britain) had been christened Charles. James was chosen as his "royal" name to continue the tradition of having a "James" on the Scottish throne.

The kirkyard was once the castle's tilting ground, where great tournaments of jousting and horsemanship were held. One of the monuments in the kirkyard is the **Martyr's Monument**, commemorating two women who were drowned for their religious beliefs at Wigtown in 1685 (see also Wigtown). The **Star Pyramid** also commemorates the Covenanting martyrs of the 17th century. A local legend says that a man was interred within it, sitting at a table laden with food. **Lady's Rock** is next to the kirkyard, and was where the ladies of the court sat and watched

staged events take place on the fields below.

Close by is **Cowane's Hospital**, built between 1637 and 1649. It is named after John Cowane, a Stirling merchant and Dean of Guild (the body that oversaw the development of the town), who bequeathed funds to establish an almshouse for 12 unsuccessful merchants, or "decayed guildsmen" of the town. It was later used as a school and an epidemic hospital, and is now a venue for ceilidhs and concerts. Above the door is a statue of Cowane himself.

The **King's Knot** sits beneath the castle and church, on the south side, and is all that is left of a formal garden, originally planted in the 1490s, though the knot itself is much older - possibly early 14th century. It is in the shape of an octagonal stepped mound nine feet high, now grassed over. Near it used to be the **King's Park** (where houses now stand), once a favourite hunting ground for the Scottish kings.

Below the north east slope of the outcrop on which the castle stands was a croft known as Ballangeich, with a pathway leading down the slope towards it. It was down this path that James V used to come dressed as a commoner to talk to the ordinary people of his kingdom. When in disguise, he called himself the **Guidman of Ballangeich** (see also Arnprior).

The old town is a mixture of buildings dating from the 15th century onwards, and a day could

Argyll's Lodging

be spent walking about and admiring them.

The intriguingly named **Mar's Wark** is in Broad Street, close to the parish church. It was the "wark" (meaning work, or building) of John Erskine, the sixth Earl of Mar, Regent of Scotland and guardian of the young James VI. In 1570 he began building a new Renaissance palace using French masons that would reflect his status and power, and Mar's Wark was the result. In the 18th century it became a military hospital, but soon after fell into disrepair. Now all that is left of the building is a façade along the street front.

On the opposite side of the street is **Argyll's Lodging** (Historic Scotland), a Renaissance-style mansion built about 1630 by Sir William Alexander, the founder of Nova Scotia (see also Edinburgh and Menstrie). It was further enlarged by the 9th Earl of Argyll in the 1670s, and is possibly the best example of a 17th century town house in Scotland. Most of the rooms have been restored, showing what life would have been like when the Earl lived there.

Stirling is one of the few Scottish towns with parts of its **Town Wall** still standing. It was built in 1547 as a defence against the English armies of Henry VIII when he was trying to force a marriage between his son Edward and Mary Stuart (a time known as the "Rough Wooing"). It was only built along the town's southern approaches, as that was where the main threat came from. People living on the northern edge of the town were compelled to build and maintain walls at the edge of their gardens to act as a defence if anyone attacked from the north. The remaining parts of the wall stretch from near the Old Town Jail to Dumbarton Road. Incorporated into the Thistle Shopping Mall is the 16th century **Bastion**, one of the wall's defensive towers. It contains a vaulted guardroom above an underground chamber, and has a small display about the history of the town.

The **Tolbooth** sits at the heart of the old town. It was built in 1704 by Sir William Bruce, and was where the town council met and looked after the affairs of the burgh. A courthouse and jail were added in 1809. It is now used as a venue for concerts and rehearsals. The **Mercat Cross**, close to the Tolbooth, has the figure of a unicorn on top, and this is known locally as the "puggy". Close to it is **Norrie's House** (not open to the public), which was built by James Norrie, a town clerk of Stirling in the 17th century.

Two famous battles have been fought near Stirling. The **Battle of Stirling Bridge** took place in 1297, when William Wallace defeated an English army under John de Warenne, Earl of Surrey, and Hugh de Cressingham. Wallace, who was a guerrilla fighter and a master tactician, used the bridge to divide the English forces - leaving one contingent on each bank - before launching his attack. It was a major set back for Edward I, and he more

One bloody association with Scotland's past is to be found at the Beheading Stone, well to the north of the castle. It was here, in 1425, that James I took his revenge on Murdoch, Duke of Albany, his two sons and the Earl of Lennox and his father-in-law by having them beheaded. The Duke's father had controlled Scotland for 18 years while the English held James captive, and he and his cronies had brought the country to its knees by their greed and cruelty. Their lands were forfeited to the crown, and James gave them to his supporters (see also Doune and Perth).

215

Another of Scotland's national heros, of course, is William Wallace, and on Abbey Craig, to the east of the town and across the river, is the National Wallace Monument. Built in 1869 to the designs of architect John Rochhead, this spectacular tower is 220 feet high, with 246 steps, and from the top you get a panoramic view that takes in the Forth Bridges to the east and Ben Lomond to the west. Here you can learn about the Battle of Stirling Bridge, plus see a re-creation of Wallace's travesty of a trial at Westminster, when he was charged with treason, even though he was not English. You can even gaze on his great two-handed broadsword, which is five feet six inches long. Within the Hall of Heroes other famous Scottish people are commemorated, including Sir Walter Scott, Robert Burns, George Buchanan and Adam Smith *(see also Killearn).

or less had to start his conquest of the country all over again. The bridge in those days was a wooden one, and the present **Old Stirling Bridge**, which stands upstream from the original, was built in the late 15th century. It was only a few years ago that the site of the original old bridge was rediscovered. Up until 1831, when **Stirling New Bridge** was built downstream, this was the lowest crossing point of the Forth, which made it one of the most important bridges in Scotland.

The other famous battle was the **Battle of Bannockburn**, fought over two days to the south of the town in 1314. The actual site of the battle still arouses much debate, but there is no doubt that it was a defining moment in Scotland's history. Even today, nearly 700 years after the event, the battle is still remembered and revered by most Scots. Edward I had died by this time, and his son Edward II, a much weaker man, was in charge of the English army, which was trying to reach Stirling Castle to relieve it. Robert the Bruce, one of Scotland's great heroes, achieved a stunning victory – one that secured the country's status as an independent nation. An old legend says that Bruce was aided in his victory by no less than the Knights Templar, a band of monastic soldiers that had been disbanded by the Pope under mysterious circumstances in 1307, with members being killed and tortured. The story relates how they fled to Scotland, where Robert

the Bruce gave them shelter, as he had been excommunicated by the Pope and so Papal authority didn't reach this far north. There are certainly stories of a great wave of knights on horseback joining in the battle as it raged, but other sources say these were gleeful Scottish camp followers (on foot, and not mounted) who saw that the Scots were gaining the upper hand.

The Bannockburn Heritage Centre (National Trust for Scotland), on the A872 two miles south of the town, commemorates this victory. There are exhibitions, an audiovisual display and a huge statue of Bruce on his warhorse.

At St Ninians, to the south of the town, are the remains of **St Ninian's Old Parish Church**. It was blown up in 1746 by Jacobite soldiers who had used it as a munitions dump. Only the tower, which had been added to the medieval building three years before, survived. The present parish church was built to take its place, and was built in 1751.

The scant ruins of **Cambuskenneth Abbey** (Historic Scotland) also lie on the eastern banks of the Forth. David I founded it as an abbey in 1140 for Augustinian monks, and in 1326 Robert the Bruce held an important parliament here. It suffered greatly at the hands of various English armies, and by 1378 was in ruins. It was rebuilt in the early 15th century through royal patronage. The detached bell tower of the abbey is more or less complete, though only the foundations of the rest of the buildings survive. James III and his queen, Margaret of Denmark, are buried before the high altar, and a monument marks the spot. In 1488 the king had been assassinated near Bannockburn after his defeat at the Battle of Sauchieburn, where his son, the future James IV, was on the opposing side.

His marriage to his wife Margaret of Denmark brought the Orkney Islands into Scotland. On their betrothal, the King of Denmark and Norway pledged 60,000 guilders as a dowry, with the proviso that if he failed to pay, Orkney and Shetland would become Scottish. The king did fail to pay, so the Scots Parliament passed an act annexing the islands and placing them within the Kingdom of Scotland.

Margaret was a popular queen, and when she died in 1488 rumours began to spread that she had been poisoned by her husband, who was disliked by the aristocracy and commoners alike.

AROUND STIRLING

BRIDGE OF ALLAN

2 miles N of Stirling off the M9

Bridge of Allan, which is a suburb of Stirling nowadays, was once a small spa town and watering place with a pump room and baths. Now it is chiefly known for being the home of Stirling University, based in the grounds of the **Airthrie Estate**, with its picturesque loch. In fact, the university campus has often been described as the most beautiful in the world. In 1617,

James VI wanted to establish a college or university at Stirling, but it was not until 1967 that his wish came true, when the first 180 students enrolled. Now it has over 9.000 students, and is one of the premier universities in Scotland.

Airthrie was owned by Sir Robert Abercrombie, who was instrumental in setting up the village as a spa, having had the waters of a local spring analysed. In 1844 the estate was bought by a Major Henderson, who developed the town even further. The **Fountain of Nineveh** on Fountain Road was built by him in 1851 to honour Sir Austin Latyard, who was conducting archaeological excavations at Nineveh in what is now Iraq. Though healing waters are no longer taken, other, equally interesting, liquids are most certainly consumed. **The Bridge of Allan Brewery**, a microbrewery in Queens Lane, has tours showing how beer is produced.

Bridge of Allan Parish Church (formerly known as Holy Trinity Church) was built in 1860, and inside it are some furnishings designed by the Glasgow architect Charles Rennie Mackintosh. It is open on Saturdays between June and September. The **Inverallan Watermill** was built in 1710 to grind flower from the local grain.

DUNBLANE

5 miles N of Stirling off the M9

Before local government reorganisation, Dunblane (and most of the area north and northwest of Stirling) was in Perthshire. This

The Smith Art Gallery and Museum in Albert Place chronicles Stirling's long history through displays, exhibitions and artefacts. It has a fine collection of paintings, including ones by Naysmith and Sir George Harvey, who painted great works depicting Scottish history. One of the more unusual exhibits in the museum is the world's oldest football, found in Mary Stuart's bedchamber in Stirling Castle and dated to the late 16th century. The world's oldest curling stone is also exhibited.

98   THE ALLANWATER CAFÉ

Bridge of Allan

A bright and spacious cafe offering a good selection of freshly made dishes and a variety of ice-creams.

see page 465

217

Dunblane

99 CHIMES HOUSE

Dunblane

Overlooking the cathedral, Chimes Guest House offers comfortable B&B accommodation.

see page 465

small town, or more properly city, is famous for two things. The first is the horrific shooting that took place here in 1996 when 16 schoolchildren and their teacher were killed in a local school. The **Dunblane Memorial Garden**, built in 1998, commemorates the victims, and is within Dunblane Cemetery.

The second is the **Cathedral Church of St Blane and St Lawrence** (Historic Scotland) which sits on the site of a Celtic monastery founded by St Blane in about AD 602. He had been born on Bute, and had founded a great monastery there as well (see also Bute). Dunblane monastery would have been a cleared space surrounded by a low wall, or "rath", within which would have

been wooden churches, monks' cells, school rooms, brewhouses and workshops.

The Church of Scotland is Presbyterian, so there are, strictly speaking, no cathedrals within it. However former cathedral churches are still referred to as cathedrals to honour their pre-Reformation purpose. What you see nowadays at Dunblane dates mainly from the 13th century, and was built by Bishop Clement, who was elected bishop in 1233. He decided that the only part of the previous 12th century Norman church which would be left standing was the tower, though two extra storeys were added to it in the 15th century. It is not a great cathedral in the style of Elgin, St Andrews or any of the great English establishments but rather it is an intimate church with no side aisles or transepts - just right for Presbyterian worship.

The diocese was established in about 1150 by the Earl of Strathearn, and a simple stone cathedral was built. However, the diocese was a poor one, and the Pope eventually authorised the bishops of Dunkeld and Glasgow to give a fourth of their income to help establish it properly. With this income, Clement managed to build most of the cathedral we see today before his death in 1258.

In the 16th century, with the arrival of Protestantism, only the choir was used for worship, and the nave fell into decay, with the roof collapsing about 1600. The city, having lost its role as an ecclesiastical centre, also fell into decay, its only industry being weaving. In 1898 the whole building was restored under the direction of Sir Rowand Anderson, a noted Scottish architect, and in 1914 Sir Robert Lorimer did further work on the choir, designing, among other things, one of the glories of the cathedral - the choir stalls.

Within the **Dean's House**, built in 1624 by Dean James Pearson during the time the Church of Scotland was episcopal, is a small museum, which explains the history of the city and its cathedral. Within it are genealogical records taken from the burial ground of the cathedral. **Bishop Leighton's Library** is housed in a building that dates from 1681 and contains over 4,000 books, some of them priceless. Bishop Robert Leighton, who was Protestant bishop between 1661 and 1669, left his large collection of books to the diocese, plus £100 so that the collection could be expanded and preserved.

With the coming of the railways, Dunblane became a popular place in which to holiday, and it regained some of its former prosperity. **Dunblane Hydro** was built in 1875 to cash in on the tourist boom, and it is still a luxury hotel to this day.

FINTRY

12 miles SW of Stirling on the B818

This charming village sits on the northern slopes of the **Campsies**, that great range of hills that forms a northern backdrop for the city of Glasgow. There are some fine walks on the hills, which are popular with Glaswegians at weekends and holidays. The **Loup of Fintry**, east of the village, is a fine series of waterfalls caused by the Endrick Water tumbling down a 94-feet high slope.

Culcreuch Castle (now a country house hotel) is a 700-year-old tower house within a large estate that was once owned by the Galbraiths. The last Galbraith chieftain to live there was Robert Galbraith, who fled to Ireland in 1630 after killing a guest in his home. It is said to house three ghosts, one of them being a phantom clarsach (or harp) player. **Carron Valley Reservoir**, to the east of the village, was built in the 19th century to supply Falkirk and Grangemouth with a water supply. It now offers trout fishing (permit required).

Fintry Parish Church dates from 1823, and its method of building was unusual. The former church was too small for the growing congregation, so the present church was built around it. Only when it was complete was the earlier church, which had continued in use, demolished.

KIPPEN

9 miles W of Stirling on the B822

This attractive little village sits to the south of that expanse of flat land called **Flanders Moss**. At one time it was peat bog; then, in the 18th century, Henry Home (who sat on the bench as Lord Kames), began removing the peat to get at

---

About three miles northeast of Dunblane is the site of the Battle of Sheriffmuir (see also Callander), one of the deciding battles in the 1715 Jacobite Uprising. It took place on 13th November 1715, and was an unusual battle in that the outcome was a stalemate, with both sides claiming victory. However, the Jacobites had superior numbers on the field of battle, and they were demoralised by not having won the battle decisively. The Jacobite forces were led by John Erskine, 6th Earl of Mar, and the Government forces were led by John Campbell, 2nd Duke of Argyll.

219

In 1891, a man called Duncan Buchanan planted a vineyard in Kippen within a glasshouse, and one of the vines, later to be called the Kippen Vine, grew to be the largest in the world. When fully grown, it had an annual crop of over 2,000 bunches of table grapes, and in 1958 created a record by producing 2,956 bunches. By this time it was enormous, covering an area of 5,000 square feet and stretching for 300 feet within four large greenhouses. It became a tourist attraction, and people came from all over Scotland and abroad to see it. But alas, the vinery closed down in 1964 (when it could also boast the second and third largest vines in the world) and the Kippen Vine was unceremoniously chopped down by Selby Buchanan, Duncan's son. The land was later used for housing.

the fertile bands of clay beneath (see also Blair Drummond). There are still a few remnants of the original peat bog left, and they have been declared Areas of Special Scientific Interest.

It has, in the 1825 **Kippen Parish Church**, one of the finest post Reformation churches in Scotland. Between 1924 and 1936 the building was transformed by Sir David Cameron, who was an elder of the kirk, and who had tired of the austere Presbyterian interior. He was the King's Painter and Limner in Scotland, and was the ideal man to carry out the work. The building's glory is its collection of stained glass windows. The best is the Carmichael Memorial Window, which was installed in 1985, and is the work of John Clark. Herbert Hendrie of Edinburgh, who designed windows for Liverpool Anglican cathedral, is also represented. The ruins of the old church, built in 1691, still survive, surrounded by an old graveyard.

To the east of Kippen, and off the A811, is the village of **Gargunnock**, with a picturesque parish church built in 1774.

ARNPRIOR

10 miles W of Sterling on the A811

In the early 16th century, a man called John Buchanan, who had styled himself the **King of Kippen**, lived in this small village. One day a party of hunters was returning to Stirling Castle with some venison for James V's court, and passed John's castle. John

captured them and confiscated the venison. The hunters told him that the meat was for the king, but John merely replied that if James was King of Scotland, then he was King of Kippen.

The king was duly informed of this, and instead of being angry, found the incident amusing. He and some courtiers rode out from Stirling one day to pay the King of Kippen a visit. He approached John's castle, and demanded that he be allowed to enter. His demand was refused by a guard, who told the king that John Buchanan was at dinner, and could not be disturbed.

James V had a habit of dressing up in peasant's clothes and slipping out of his palaces alone to meet and speak to his subjects and gauge their opinions of their king and country. When he did this, he assumed the guise of the "Guidman of Ballengeich" (meaning "The Goodman of Ballengeich"), Ballengeich being the name of a croft at the foot of a pathway he always took down from Stirling Castle when in disguise.

He therefore told the guard to tell Buchanan that the Guidman of Ballengeich was at his door, and he humbly requested an audience with the King of Kippen. When informed, John Buchanan knew who his visitor was, and rushed out in trepidation. But James greeted him cordially, and laughed at the escapade of the venison. Buchanan invited the king into his home to dine, and the king agreed. Soon the company was merry, and the king told Buchanan that he could take as much venison as he liked from the royal hunters that passed his door. He also invited the King of Kippen to visit his brother monarch at Stirling any time he liked. The "king" was later killed at the Battle of Pinkie in 1547 (see also Stirling).

PORT OF MENTEITH

14 miles W of Stirling on the B8034

This little village sits on the shore of the **Lake of Menteith**, sometimes erroneously called the only lake (as opposed to loch) in Scotland. However, there are several bodies of water in Scotland - some natural, some man made - which are called lakes (see also Kirkcudbright, Stenton and Ellon). It is also on the eastern extremities of the Loch Lomond and Trossachs National Park.

There is no doubting that the Lake of Menteith is one of Scotland's most beautiful stretches of water. It is only a mile wide by a mile-and-a-half long, with low hills sloping down towards its northern shores. Its name is probably a corruption of Laigh (meaning a flat piece of land) and of Menteith, as the land to the south of the lake, Flanders Moss, is flat.

On the island of Inchmahome are the beautiful ruins of **Inchmahome Priory** (Historic Scotland), within which Mary Stuart was kept after the Battle of Pinkie in 1547. Within the re-roofed chapter house are many carved effigies and tombstones. The priory was founded in 1238 by Walter Comyn, Earl of Menteith, for Augustinian canons. In 1306, 1308

and 1310, Robert the Bruce visited the place, as the then prior had sworn allegiance to Edward I of England. No doubt Robert was pressurising him to change his mind. The island can be reached by a ferry that leaves the pier in Port of Menteith.

On the nearby **Inchtulla** the Menteiths had their castle, and on **Dog Island** the Earl kept his hunting

Inchmahome Priory

dogs. If the weather is particularly cold, the loch can freeze over, and a grand curling match called a bonspiel is held. However, the loch hasn't frozen over for many years.

ABERFOYLE

17 miles W of Stirling on the A821

Aberfoyle has been called the Gateway to the Trossachs (see also Callander), and sits on the River Forth after it emerges from beautiful Loch Ard. The six-mile long **Duke's Road** (named after a Duke of Montrose who laid out the road in 1886) goes north from the village to the Trossachs proper, and has some good views over Lochs Drunkie and Venachar.

Standing close to the village's main road is a gnarled oak known as the **Poker Tree**. In Scott's novel *Rob Roy*, Baillie Nicol Jarvie, a

100 THE COACH HOUSE

Aberfoyle

The Coach House offers a good selection of food and drink as well as three comfortable rooms for B&B.

❚ ▭ see page 465

•

South of Aberfoyle, near the conservation village of Gartmore, is the Cunninghame Graham Memorial (National Trust for Scotland). Robert Cunninghame Graham of Ardoch (born Robert Bontine) was a Scottish author and politician who died in 1936 in Argentina and was buried within Inchmahome Priory. For many years he lived in Argentina, where he was known as "Don Roberto", and was a close friend of Buffalo Bill (William Cody). In his time, he sat in Parliament as a Liberal, Socialist and finally Scottish Nationalist. He was married to Gabriela de la Balmondiere, a Chilean poet, who later turned out to be a woman called Caroline Horsfall from Ripon, Yorkshire. She had invented the new personna to impress Cunninghame Graham's mother. The memorial once stood at Castlehill in Dumbarton, but was moved here in 1980.

•

Glasgow magistrate and cousin of Rob Roy, gets involved in a fight with a Highlander at a local inn, and draws a red hot poker from the fire to defend himself. A poker was later hung from the tree to remind people of the escapade.

The **Scottish Wool Centre** is situated within the village, and tells the story of Scottish wool. You can visit the Spinner's Cottage, and have a go at spinning wool into yarn. There are also occasional visits from local shepherds, who put on sheepdog demonstrations. There is also a shop where woollen items - from coats to blankets - can be bought.

It was in Aberfoyle that the famous and mysterious disappearance of the **Reverend Robert Kirk**, minister at Aberfoyle Parish Church, took place. He was born in 1644, and had an abiding interest in fairies, even writing a book called *The Secret Commonwealth of Elves, Fauns and Fairies.*

Legend states that the fairies were none too pleased that Robert had revealed their secrets. In 1692, while walking on Doon Hill, well known in the area as one of the entrances to the fairy realm, Robert disappeared. People claimed that he had been taken to the fairy kingdom, and that one day he would come back, looking no older than he did when he disappeared. To this day, he has not returned.

Another legend states that Robert's wife was given the chance of getting her husband back. He would appear, she was told, during Sunday service in the kirk, and she

had to throw a knife at him, which should penetrate his flesh. Robert did appear during the service, but his wife could not bring herself to throw the knife, so he disappeared once more.

Robert Kirk was indeed a minister in Aberfoyle in the 17th century, and he did indeed disappear one day while out walking. Another version of the story tells of how he collapsed and died on the hill, his body being subsequently discovered. However, his apparition appeared to members of his family, and it told than that, he, Robert, was not dead, but merely in a swoon. His unearthly body had been carried off to fairyland. Robert's son was due to be baptised, and the apparition said that it would be there in the church while the baptism was taking place. Again, someone would have to throw a knife at him, but no one did, so he remained with the fairies. No one will ever know what really happened - unless Robert Kirk turns up again to give his account!

On the eastern edges of the village the ruins of **Old Aberfoyle Parish Church** can be seen, as can mortsafes, which were placed over fresh graves to prevent the bodies being dug up again and sold for dissection. It was within the church that Robert Kirk once preached, and there is a small memorial to him

KILLEARN

18 miles W of Stirling on the A875

Killearn Glen is a picturesque area of deciduous woodland over 250 years old with narrow footpaths.

The village was the birthplace, in 1506, of George Buchanan, Protestant reformer and tutor to James VI, who greatly admired him. He was a noted linguist, and could speak Latin, Greek, French, Gaelic, Spanish, Hebrew and Italian. He also wrote plays, mostly in Latin, and now lies buried in the Greyfriars kirkyard in Edinburgh. The **Buchanan Monument**, built in 1788, commemorates him (see also Stirling).

Glengoyne Distillery is at Dumgoyne, south of the village. It distils a single Highland malt, and has a visitor centre.

DRYMEN

20 miles W of Stirling off the A811

Drymen is within the Loch Lomond and Trossachs National Park, and being a picturesque village, can get very busy in the summer. The West Highland Way passes close by as well.

Loch Lomond lies three miles to the west. The small village of **Balmaha** (also on the West Highland Way) sits on the shore of the loch, and should be visited for the wonderful views it gives of Britain's largest sheet of water. A small ferry leaves the boatyard at Balmaha for **Inchailloch**, an island in the loch that has a small nature reserve. **Balfron**, four miles east of Drymen, is an attractive village with a parish church that dates from 1832. Alexander "Greek" Thomson, the noted architect whose work can bee seen in Glasgow, was born in Balfron in 1817.

The village of **Gartocharn** lies south west of Drymen, only a mile from Loch Lomond. **Duncryne Hill** rises to a height of only 462 feet, though it looks much bigger. It is nicknamed "The Dumpling", and there are good views of the loch from the summit. Further west, at Loch Lomond, is **Ross Priory**, a large house. It was never a monastic establishment, and was given its name when it was built in the 17th century. Now owned by Strahclyde University, it is a residential and conference centre. Though the house is not open to the public, the gardens occasionally are. Within the priory Sir Walter Scott wrote part of *Rob Roy*.

BLAIR DRUMMOND

6 miles NW of Stirling on the A84

Blair Drummond Safari and Leisure Park is one of the most visited tourist attractions in Scotland. You can tour the 1,500-acre park by car or coach, and see animals such as elephants, lions, zebras, giraffes, white rhino and ostriches in conditions that allow them plenty of freedom. You can take a boat trip round Chimp Island, watch the sea lion show or glide above the lake on the "Flying Fox".

In the 18th century Blair Drummond was the home of Henry Home, a law lord who sat in the High Court as Lord Kames (see also Kippen). In 1916 it was bought by Sir John Kay, a Glasgow merchant, and then passed to Sir John Muir, father of the present owner. The present House dates from Victorian times.

During World War II, Buchanan Castle in Drymen was a military hospital. Its most famous patient was Rudolph Hess, Hitler's deputy, who was kept here after he parachuted into Scotland in 1941 on a secret mission to see the Duke of Hamilton (see also Eaglesham). The castle itself dates from 1855, and was built by the 4th Duke of Montrose after a former castle was destroyed by fire three years previously. In 1925 the castle was sold to the Grahams, and for a short while in the 1930s was a hotel. The roof was removed in 1955 to prevent the paying of taxes on it, and it is now partly ruinous, though it can be viewed from the outside.

101 RED LION HOTEL

Doune

A superb village inn that encapsulates all that is good about Scottish hospitality - great accommodation, great drink, good company and superb food!

¶ ⊫ *see page 464*

On the B824 between Doune and Dunblane is the Sir David Stirling Memorial Statue, commemorating the founder member of the Special Air Services (better known as the SAS) during World War II. He died in London in 1990.

DOUNE

6 miles NW of Stirling on the A820

The bridge across the River Teith in this picturesque village was built by James Spittal, tailor to James IV (see also Tullibody). Legend has it that he arrived at the ferry that once operated where the bridge now stands without any money, and the ferryman refused to take him across. So, out of spite, he had the bridge built in 1535 to deprive the ferryman of a livelihood. In 1715 the Jacobite Earl of Mar partly dismantled the bridge to delay the movement of Government troops north.

Doune Castle (Historic Scotland) is one of the best preserved 14th century castles in Scotland, and was built for the first Duke of Albany, Robert Stewart, brother of Robert lll, King of Scotland. He was the unofficial regent for his infirm brother, and regarded the kingdom as a means of enriching himself at the expense of others. Because of this Robert once more took over, but soon afterwards handed over the running of the kingdom to another of his brothers, David. In compensation for not being appointed regent again, Robert was given the title Duke of Albany ("Albany" being another word for Scotland). During the minority of James l, and during the king's exile in England, Robert's son Murdoch acted as regent until he was executed by James l when the king returned to Scotland (see also Stirling and Perth).

In 1570 the castle later passed to Sir James Stewart, whose descendants became the Earls of Moray through marriage. It has two main towers connected by a Great Hall with a high wooden ceiling. In 1883 the 14th Earl of Moray restored the castle. It is visited each year by many fans of Monty Python, as some of the scenes in *Monty Python and the Holy Grail* were filmed here. To the east of the castle is the small tower known as **Newton Doune** (not open to the public), home of the Edmonstone family, hereditary keepers of Doune Castle on behalf of the Morays.

The village itself gained its burgh charter in 1611, and originally stood close to the castle. In the early 1700s, however, it and the 17th century **Mercat Cross** were moved to their present position. The village was, at one time, famous as a centre of pistol making. The industry was started in about 1646 by a man called Thomas Cadell, and so accurate and well made were his guns that they soon became prized possessions. By the 18th century Cadell's descendants were all involved in making guns, and began exporting them to the Continent. It is said that the first pistol fired in the American War of Independence was made in Doune.

DEANSTON

8 miles NW of Stirling on the B8032

Deanston is a village on the banks of the River Teith, built round the Adephi Cotton Mill, founded in 1785 and designed by Sir Richard Arkwright. It passed through several hands before finally closing in 1965. Now the mill houses the **Deanston Distillery**, which makes a range of whiskies, using the same water that once powered the weaving machines. It is not open to the public.

CALLANDER

13 miles NW of Stirling on the A84

This pleasant holiday town stands to the east of the Trossachs, and has some wonderful walking country on its doorstep. It is a planned town, laid out in the 1770s, though its plan dates back to a plan prepared by the Duke of Perth in 1735. Being an ardent Jacobite, the Duke forfeited his lands after 1745. It is home to the **Rob Roy and Trossachs Visitor Centre**, housed in a former church in Ancaster Square, and, as the name suggests, tells the story of both the Trossachs and its most famous son, Rob Roy MacGregor (see also Balquhidder). His real name was Robert MacGregor (1671-1734) and even today people still cannot agree on whether he was a crook, a freedom fighter or the Scottish Robin Hood.

The Duke of Montrose confiscated his lands in 1712, and he was imprisoned by the English in the 1720s. He was made famous by two books - Daniel Defoe's *Highland Rogue* and Sir Walter Scott's *Rob Roy*, as well as by the recent film starring Liam Neeson and Jessica Lange. An earlier film, *Rob Roy the Highland Rogue*, was made in 1953, starring Richard Todd and Glynis Johns.

There's no denying that the man was an outstanding leader who could read and write in English and Gaelic, and possessed a large library. It was Sir Walter Scott who made him behave dishonourably at the Battle of Sheriffmuir (see Dunblane), when in fact he acquitted himself with courage and honour fighting for the Jacobites. At his funeral on New Year's Day 1735, people came from all over Scotland to pay their respects.

Also in Callander is the **Hamilton Toy Museum**, five rooms of model cars, planes, dolls, teddy bears and such TV collectables as Thunderbird, Star Trek and Star Wars figures.

The **Kilmahog Woollen Mill**, to the west of the town, is over 250 years old, and has its original water wheel. A shop sells a wide range of Tweed and woollen garments.

LOCH KATRINE

23 miles NW of Stirling close to the A821

There is no doubt that Loch Katrine is one of the most beautiful lochs in Scotland. It is surrounded by craggy hills, which in autumn blaze with orange and gold. But the loch as you see it today has more to do with man than nature. In the mid-19th century, the loch became a huge reservoir for the city of Glasgow, and the depth of the water was increased considerably until it could store over 5,623 million gallons. In 1859 Queen Victoria opened the new reservoir, and 90 million gallons of water a day flowed towards Glasgow over 30 miles away.

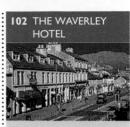

102 THE WAVERLEY HOTEL

Callander

Recently totally-renovated hotel with award-winning bar, regular live music sessions, and quality accommodation

🛏 🍴 *see page 466*

103 DALGAIR HOUSE HOTEL

Callander

A superb town centre hotel with eight fully en suite rooms, a delightful bar and a restaurant selling the finest food.

🛏 🍴 *see page 465*

104 MYRTLE INN

Callander

A delightful, white-washed roadside inn that is just right for a tasty, beautifully cooked meal or a quiet drink in convivial surroundings.

🍴 *see page 467*

105 THE BYRE INN

Brig o' Turk

A picturesque old Scottish inn that sells good food and drink as well as offering a self catering cottage to discerning tourists.

¶ ⊨ see page 467

Loch Katrine is the heart of the Trossachs (the name translates as "bristly" or "prickly"), and there are other equally as attractive lochs nearby. Loch Lubnaig, to the east, is the largest. Loch Venachar, Loch Achray and Loch Drunkie (which can only be reached by a footpath through the forest) are well worth visiting. At the southern end of Loch Lubnaig are the spectacular Falls of Leny.

The engineering that made this happen was well ahead of its time, and consisted of tunnels and aqueducts that relied purely on gravity to carry the water towards the city. The civil engineering work on the loch was equally as spectacular. The water from **Loch Arklet**, high in the hills between Lochs Katrine and Lomond, used to flow west into Loch Lomond. By the use of dams, this was changed so that it flowed east into Loch Katrine. The whole scheme was the largest of its kind in the world for many years, and even today, Glasgow still gets its water from the same source.

The loch's name comes from the early Welsh "cethern", meaning "furious", a reference to the many mountain torrents found in the area. It was made famous by Sir Walter Scott, who set his poem *The Lady of the Lake* here. And at **Glengyle**, at the western end of the loch, Rob Roy MacGregor was born. Glengyle is still a remote place, and cannot be reached by car.

Sir Walter Scott was not the only writer inspired by Loch Katrine. In 1859 the French writer **Jules Verne** visited, and was inspired to write *The Underground City*, about a coal mine beneath the loch.

The steamer **Sir Walter Scott** has been sailing the waters of the loch from the beginning of the 20th century, and it still docs so today. It was built in Dumbarton, and people have long wondered how it got from there to the loch,

The answer is simple. It was transported by barge up the river Leven onto Loch Lomond, then dragged overland by horses from Inversnaid. When it reached Loch Katrine, the engines were fitted.

The steamship takes you from the pier at the east end of the loch towards **Stronachlachar,** six miles away. The small islet at Stronachlachan is known as the **Factor's Island**, and recalls one of Rob Roy's exploits. He captured the Duke of Montrose's factor, who was collecting rents in the area, and imprisoned him on the island. He then sent a ransom note to the Duke, but none came. So Rob Roy calmly relieved the man of the £3,000 he was carrying and sent him on his way.

BALQUHIDDER

24 miles NW of Stirling on a minor road off the A84

This small village sits to the east of the picturesque **Loch Voil**. It lies in that area of Scotland known as **Breadalbane** ("uplands of Alban", as Alban is the ancient name for Scotland), and in the heart of Clan MacGregor country. In the kirkyard of the roofless kirk is **Rob Roy MacGregor's Grave** (see also Callander), plus those of some of his family, including his wife.

Rob's real name was Robert McGregor, the "Roy" coming from the Gaelic *ruadh*, meaning red-haired. He died in 1734 a free man, having received a royal pardon for his misdeeds (if indeed they were misdeeds) in 1726.

Above the village is **Creag na**

Loch Voil, Balquhdder

Tuirc ("Boar's Rock"), from where you can get some fine views. At its top is a cairn dedicated to Clan MacLaren, as this was where the clansmen assembled before setting off in support of Charles Edward Stuart. Behind the present church is **Tom nan Angeael**, the "Hill of Fire".. Up until the 19th century this was where fires were lit twice a year, at Beltane (May 1) and Samhain (Novem,ber 1), to encourage the return of warmth to the land..

KILLIN

30 miles NW of Stirling on the A827

Killin sits close to the western end of **Loch Tay**, which stretches for 15 miles north eastwards into Perthshire. The best views of the loch are from the wooded south shore road, though the northern road is wider and straighter.

The **Falls of Dochart**, a series of cascades on the River Dochart as it enters Loch Tay, are within the village, and next to them is the

106 THE COACH HOUSE

Killin

A superb hotel in a picturesque village that offers great food, excellent accommodation, good drink and entertainment.

see page 468

The ruins of Finlarig Castle, which date from the late 16th century, are to the north of the village of Killin. The castle was once a Campbell stronghold, and was built by Black Duncan, one of the most notorious members of the clan. Within its grounds are the remains of a beheading pit and a Campbell mausoleum built in 1829.

Breadalbane Folklore Centre, housed in an old mill, which gives an insight into life and legends of the area. The five Healing Stones of St Fillan can be seen at the mill. Each one resembles the part of the body it is supposed to influence - the lungs, heart, kidneys, eyes and liver (see also Tyndrum). Three miles north on a minor road are the **Falls of Lochay** on the River Lochay, though care should be taken when approaching them. The **Moirlanich Longhouse** (National Trust for Scotland) on the Glen Lochay road dates from the 19th century, and is a rare surviving example of a cruck-frame Scottish longhouse, where a family and their livestock lived under the one roof. In an adjacent shed is a display of working clothes found in the longhouse, along with displays, which explain the building's history and restoration.

West of Killin, and towering above Loch Tay, is **Ben Lawers** (National Trust for Scotland), at 3,984 feet the highest mountain in the area. There is a visitor centre just off the minor road that heads north from the A827 heading for Bridge of Balgie. From there you can climb to the summit. The **Ben Lawers Historic Landscape Project** is an archaeological dig that started in 2002 and is due to finish in March 2007. The Project is looking at the landscapes to the north of Loch Tay, and the uses to which they have been put over the last 1,000 years. At Kinnell, to the east of the village, is the **Kinnell Stone Circle**, consisting of six upright stones, each one about six feet high. Kinnell is the ancestral home of Clan McNab. Though some of the clan followed Charles Edward Stewart, the then clan chief, John McNab, fought on the government side. An ancient McNab burial ground can be found on the island of Inchbuie in the River Dochart.

LOCHEARNHEAD

21 miles NW of Stirling on the A84

This small, attractive village is at the western end of Loch Earn, and is a centre for sailing, fishing, water skiing and diving. East of the village is **Edinample Castle** (not open to the public), owned by Black Duncan Campbell of Glenorchy in the 16th century. It was originally a McGregor stronghold, and is associated with tales of black deeds, doom and gloom. It is said that in the 6th century St Blane cursed the lands around the castle. Another tale says that the castle was doomed as it was built using old gravestones. Another tale says that Black Duncan instructed the builder to put a parapet around the tower where he could walk and survey his lands, but the builder forgot. To curry favour, the builder then walked on the roof to show that it was still possible to survey the Campbell lands. Rather that pay the builder, Black Duncan pushed him off, and he perished. It is said that his ghost still walks the roof to this day.

Ben Vorlich, four miles south east of the village, rises to a height of 3,230 feet. From its peak there are marvellous views.

CRIANLARICH

32 miles NW of Stirling on the A82

The name of this small village comes from the Gaelic for "low pass", and sits on the southern edge of Breadalbane, where the A82 meets the A85. Surrounding it is some marvellous walking and climbing country, with the West Highland Way passing close to the village. The twin peaks of **Ben More** (3,843 feet) and **Stobinian** (3,821 feet) are to the south east, while the picturesque **Falls of Falloch** (with a small car park close by) lie four miles to the southwest on the A82.

TYNDRUM

40 miles NW of Stirling on the A82

This little village has a population of no more than 100 people, and yet has two railway stations - one on the line from Glasgow to Oban and the other on the line from Glasgow to Fort William. It sits at the head of **Strath Fillan**, which snakes southeast towards

Crianlarich. At **Dalrigh** (meaning "the field of the king"), in 1306, Robert the Bruce was defeated in battle. Nearby is the site of **St Fillan's Priory**, founded by Bruce in 1318. St Fillan was an Irish monk who lived during the 8th century and founded a Celtic monastery in the vicinity (see also Killin, Pittenweem, Madderty and St Fillans). It is said that while building the monastery, a wolf attacked and killed one of the oxen used to bring materials to the site. St Fillan then prayed, and a miracle occurred - the wolf took the place of the ox. It is merely a coincidence that the name "Fillan" comes from the Irish Gaelic for "Little Wolf". St Fillan's relics - his crozier, bell and left armbone and hand - were paraded before the Scottish army at the Battle of Bannockburn, and the subsequent victory endeared the saint to the Scottish king. Before this time, there had been five relics, but his psalter and a portable altar were lost. The head of his crozier can still be seen in the Museum of Scotland in Edinburgh.

107 SUIE LODGE HOTEL

Crianlarich

A small, friendly family-run hotel with comfortable accommodation, standing in its own grounds between Crianlarich and Killin.

see page 469

Argyll

Argyll (sometimes also called Argyllshire) is one of the most diverse and beautiful counties in Scotland. It sits on the country's western seaboard, where long sea lochs penetrate deep into the interior, and mountains tumble down towards fertile glens. The name "Argyll" comes from the Gaelic *Earraghaidheal*, meaning the "coastline of the Gaels". It can truly claim to be the cradle of Scotland, for this was, at one time, the kingdom of Dalriada, founded by the "Scott" who came from a kingdom of the same name in Ireland in about AD 502.

The founders were three brothers, whose names were Fergus, Lorne and Angus, sons of Erc, king of the Irish Dalriada. They divided the colony into three tribal areas. Cineal Gabran, or sons of Fergus, settled in Kintyre, Cineal Loth settled around Oban, and Cineal Angus settled on Jura and Islay. Fergus gradually gained the ascendancy over the other two tribes, and became king of this new colony, establishing his fort and capital at Dunadd, a rocky outcrop near Lochgilphead. With them, the brothers brought "Jacob's Pillow", which we now know as the Stone of Destiny.

Kenneth's father had been Alpin Mac Eochaid and his mother a daughter of a Pictish king. When her father died in AD 843, Kenneth ascended the throne of the Pictish kingdom, uniting it with Dalriada to form an embryonic Scotland.

He abandoned Dunadd, and established his capital at a more central location - Scone in Perthshire. When he left Argyll, he took with him the Stone of Destiny. However, Scotland at that time was largely above a line drawn between the Rivers Clyde and Forth. In the 11th century, the Lothians (centred on Edinburgh) and Strathclyde (centred on Dumbarton) were absorbed into Scotland, and the country as we know it today,

with the exception of the Orkneys and Shetlands, was formed.

The other great Dalriadan centre was at what is now Dunstaffnage, north of Oban, and indeed it may have been the capital for a while. Today the site is occupied by Dunstaffnage Castle, one of the most spectacular fortifications on Scotland's western seaboard.

Though it has attractive towns such as Oban, Lochgilphead, Inveraray and Campbeltown, Argyll is sparsely populated. There are few clogged highways, (though Oban can get very busy in the summer months), and driving is a pleasure. New vistas are constantly being opened up as you drive along roads such as the one from Lochgilphead to Oban, and even on overcast days they are a constant source of wonder and delight. The climate is mild, thanks to the Gulf Stream, and the county has many fine gardens to explore, such as Ardkinglas, Crarae and Arduaine. Some have palm trees and other species you would not expect to thrive so far north.

Argyll lies north of the Highland Boundary Fault, which means that it comes within the Scottish Highlands, though not within the local government area now known as the Highlands. Man has lived in Argyll for centuries, and around Kilmartin there are cairns and standing stones built long before the ancient Egyptians built the pyramids. A museum in the village of Kilmartin itself explains the history of the area, and explains the many cairns, standing stones, stone circles, graves and henges that abound in the area.

The Argyll coastline is rugged and rocky, though there are some marvellous, glistening beaches which are invariably empty. Diving is popular, and there is even a diving centre south of Oban. So too is fishing, water skiing and yachting, and in many of the lochs and inlets small (and not so small) yachts and boats can be found at anchor.

And, while the landscapes are rugged and romantic, there are also lush meadows and farmlands where heavily-horned Highland cattle can be seen.

That great peninsula known as the Mull of Kintyre, which hangs down into the Atlantic like an arm, is also in Argyll. This is a remote part of Scotland. It forms part of the mainland yet is as isolated as any island. Though Glasgow is only 60 miles from Campbeltown as the crow flies, it takes the average driver three or four hours over twisting, loch-girt roads to make the journey between the two. This is the area made famous by Sir Paul McCartney's song *Mull of Kintyre*, where he sings of "mists rolling in from the sea".

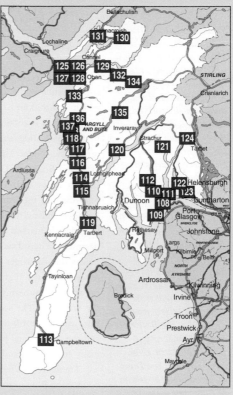

ACCOMMODATION

FOOD & DRINK

PLACES OF INTEREST

Rothesay Castle (Historic Scotland) is one of the oldest in Scotland. It is a royal castle, and indeed the Dukedom of Rothesay is the oldest dukedom in Scotland, The title was reserved for the heir to the Scottish throne, and is now held by Prince Charles. The castle has an unusual circular curtain wall and a water-filled moat, and was probably built in the 13th century by Walter, third steward of the royal household. Not long after, the Vikings besieged it. King Haakon of Norway took it in 1263, but afterwards was defeated at the Battle of Largs. The Treaty of Perth, signed in 1266, gave Scotland the Inner Hebrides and the island of Bute, and it became a favourite residence of the first Stewart king Robert II, and his son, Robert III, who may have died there. The courtyard contains the remains of a royal chapel, dedicated to St Michael the Archangel. At one time the castle stood guard over Rothesay Bay, but succeeding reclamations of land from the sea has pushed it inland. The whole building was in a ruinous state until 1816, when it was partly rebuilt by the 2nd Marquis of Bute.

BUTE

The island of Bute is the second largest of the islands in the Firth of Clyde, and used to be part of the small county of the same name, which also took in Arran and the Cumbraes. It is about 15 miles long by five miles wide, and though it now comes under Argyll, the Highland Boundary Fault (an old fracture in the earth's crust) passes right through the island's capital, Rothesay. Inland from the town, the boundary is marked by the long, narrow, 175 acre **Loch Fad**. This means that the larger northern portion is in the Highlands while the smaller southern portion is in the Lowlands. The scenery reflects this, with the north being rugged, and the south being pastoral, with many small farms and settlements.

There are two ferries connecting Bute to the mainland. The main one is from Wemyss Bay in Renfrewshire to Rothesay, while another, smaller one, runs between Ardentraive on the Cowal Peninsula and Rhubodach on the north east tip of the island. The latter crossing takes only about five minutes, with the distance being only a third of a mile. At one time cattle, instead of being transported between the Bute and the mainland, were made to swim across.

The main town is **Rothesay**, an ancient royal burgh that was given its charter in 1401. It was recently voted one of the top ten holiday resorts in Britain by Holiday Which readers, though it has always been one of the most famous holiday resorts on the Firth of Clyde. At one time it attracted thousands of Glasgow tourists in the "Glasgow Fair", which was always the last two weeks in July. During that fortnight the workers of Glasgow, and the middle classes, took their annual fortnight's holiday, and the city and all its industries closed down. The "Ferr" (as Glaswegians pronounced it) died out in the 70s and 80s of the last century, and nowadays Glaswegians fly abroad rather than spend two weeks in a town which is no more than 35 miles from their home city.

Fine Victorian mansions line the front, built to take Glasgow merchants who would descend on the town, complete with family and servants, for weeks at a time. There were also more modest B&Bs and guest houses that took in the working classes. It eventually earned the nickname of "Scotland's Madeira", not just because it was on an island, but also because palm trees flourish here due to the influence of the Gulf Stream.

The gentleness of the climate can best be appreciated at **Ardencraig Gardens** in Ardencraig Lane, which were bought by Rothesay Town Council in 1970. They formed part of the original gardens designed by Percy Cane for the owners of Ardencraig House. Every summer it shimmers with colour, and is a popular spot with holidaymakers. Another popular spot is **Canada Hill**, to the south of the town, where there are spectacular views of the Firth of Clyde. From here, people used to watch ships sailing down the Clyde taking Scottish emigrants to a new life in North America, hence its name. It can be reached by driving up **Serpentine Hill**, which, as its name suggests, wriggles uphill, with no less than eight curves where the road turns back on itself as it climbs.

On the sea front is the **Men of Bute Memorial Stone**, which commemorates other people who left Rothesay but never returned, only this time in the 13th century - the Bute bowmen who fought alongside William Wallace at the Battle of Falkirk in 1298.

In Stuart Street, close to the castle, is the **Bute Museum**, which has displays and artefacts about Rothesay, the Firth of Clyde, pleasure steamers and the island of Bute itself. The ruins of **Church of St Mary** (Historic Scotland), on the southern outskirts of the town, are next to the present High Kirk, built in 1796. The ruins date mainly from the 13th and 14th centuries and have two canopied tombs. One contains the effigy of a man, and the other the effigy of a woman with a baby, possibly the man's wife. There is also the grave slab of an unknown Norman knight on the floor. The church has been recently re-roofed to protect them.

Rothesay has more unusual attractions, such as the **Victorian Toilets** at the end of the pier, which date from 1899. They still work perfectly, and are full of ornate design. They were recently voted the second best place in the

Rothesay Castle

world to spend a penny. If you want the best place, you'll have to go to Hong Kong. Women can view the toilets at "quiet times".

Scotland's first long distance island footpath, the 30-mile long **West Island Way**, starts at Kilchattan Bay and finishes at Port Bannatyne. Full details of the trail are available from the Isle of Bute Discovery Centre.

Close to Kilchattan Bay, at **Kingarth**, is **St Blane's Chapel**. The ruins of this Norman structure sit within what was a Celtic

The Isle of Bute Discovery Centre is housed in the town's Esplanade Gardens, on the front. It houses an exhibition highlighting life on the island through interactive displays and plasma screens, as well as a cinema/theatre. There is also a new Genealogy Centre.

Off the west coast of Bute is the small privately owned island of Inchmarnock, no more than two miles long by half a mile wide. Its name means "Marnock's island", the Marnock in question being a Celtic saint whose name is also found in other Scottish place names. There are the ruins of an ancient chapel.

monastery, founded by St Blane in the sixth century (see also Dunblane). The whole area shows how such a monastery would have been laid out. The "rath", a low wall surrounding the monastery, can still be seen, as can the foundations of various beehive cells in which the monks lived. There are two old graveyards - one for men, and one for women. Close by is the **Dunagoil Vitrified Fort**, which dates from the Iron Age. Vitrified forts are so called because at one time they were exposed to great heat, turning the surface of the stone used in their construction to a glass-like substance.

There are lots of other religious sites on Bute, some dating from the Dark Ages. At **Straad** (a name which tells you that the island once belonged to the Vikings) there are the scant remains of **St Ninian's Chapel**, which may go back at least 1,500 years, and at **Kilmichael** there are the ruins of the old **St Macaille Chapel**.

The village of **Kerrycroy**, south of Rothesay, was modelled on a typical English village. The half-timbered houses do look rather incongruous on a Scottish island, but the overall effect is pleasing. **Mount Stuart House**, close to the village, is the ancestral home of the Marquis of Bute. In 1877 a fire destroyed most of the old house, built during the reign of Queen Anne, and the third Marquis employed Robert Rowand Anderson to design the present Victorian Gothic one. It is an immense house, full of treasures,

and reflects the history and importance of the family who owned it. When built, it was full of technological wonders. It was the first house in Scotland to be lit by electricity, and the first private house to have a heated indoor swimming pool. Surrounding the house are 300 acres of delightful gardens. The house achieved international fame in 2003 when Stella McCartney, daughter of Paul, got married here.

Near Port Bannatyne, north of Rothesay, is **Kames Castle**, dating from the 14th century. It is a typical Scottish tower House, and was once the home of the Bannatyne family. Neither it nor its beautiful gardens are open to the public, but they can be viewed from the road. One place which can be visited, however, is **Ascog Victorian Fernery and Garden**, three miles south of Rothesay. It was built about 1870, and has a sunken fern house which houses over 80 sub-tropical fern species. It had been allowed to decay over the years, and was brought back to its former glory in 1997. It was awarded the first ever Scottish prize by the Historic Gardens Foundation, which promotes historic gardens and parks throughout the world.

Bute is the home of **Sir Richard Attenborough,** the film actor and producer. In Victorian times it had another thespian connection, as the Shakespearian actor Edmund Kean also made his home on the island for a while.

The late singer **Lena Zavaroni** was born in Rothesay. After a meteoric rise to stardom, she tragically died in 1999, aged just 35. Another singer who came from Rothesay was **Emyr Griffith**, who, with his wife Barbara Salisbury, were known as Miki and Griff.

DUNOON

Dunoon is one of the best-known Clyde holiday resorts. It sits across from the Renfrewshire coast, and an all year ferry connects it to Gourock, with a further ferry going from Hunter's Quay, north of the town, to the mainland. Each year in August the town hosts the **Cowal Highland Gathering**, where competitors take part in tossing the caber, throwing the hammer, Highland dancing and other Scottish events. The first gathering took place in August 1894, and since then it has grown to become the largest such gathering in the world, attracting over 3,500 competitors each year.

The **Castle House Museum** is in the Castle Gardens, and has an exhibition entitled "Dunoon and Cowal Past and Present". There are models, artefacts and photographs, which bring the Dunoon of yesteryear to life. There are also furnished Victorian rooms and a shop. The "castle" in which it is housed was the holiday home of a Lord Provost of Glasgow. The statue of **Highland Mary**, erected in 1896, is close by (see also Failford and Greenock). She was a native of Dunoon, and worked as a maid in a large house near Mauchline in Ayrshire. Burns met

her there, and asked her to accompany him to the West Indies when he was thinking of emigrating. She agreed, but on a trip home to Dunoon to make arrangements, she died and was buried in Greenock. In 1920, during development of the graveyard, her lair was opened, and beside her bones were the remains of an infant's coffin.

Little now remains of **Dunoon Castle** apart from a few crumbling foundations. It was built in the 12th century, and Mary Stuart is said to have stayed in it for a short while. It belonged to the Campbells, who abandoned it in the 17th century. The modern castle is partly built of stones from the old Dunoon Castle. On Tom-a-Mhoid Road, in West Bay, is the **Lamont Memorial**, erected in 1906 to commemorate the massacre of the Lamonts by the Campbells in 1646 (see also Toward).

In the **Dunoon Ceramics Visitor Centre** you can see how mugs, tableware and cups and saucers are made. Dunoon Ceramics was established in 1973, and since then has expanded rapidly. **Morag's Fairy Glen** is a beauty spot lying south of the town, and was recently reopened after a major refurbishment costing in excess of a quarter of a million pounds.,

Three miles north of Dunoon, on the A815, is **Adam's Grave**, the popular name for a 3,500-year-old neolithic burial cairn, which still has two portals and a capstone intact at its entrance. It sits close to the **Holy Loch**, chosen in 1961 as the

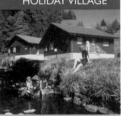

111 ENMORE HOTEL

Dunoon

An elegant family-run hotel, famed for the quality of its accommodation and its fine dining.

 see page 472

112 BENMORE BOTANIC GARDEN

Dunoon

Set amid dramatic scenery, Benmore Botanic Garden is famous for its collection of trees and shrubs.

 see page 474

site for an American nuclear submarine base. It was chosen not just because of its deep water, but because this part of Argyll has a cloud covering for most of the year, thwarting satellite and aerial photography. The Americans left in 1992, taking with them their American cars and their accents, which were once common in the streets of Dunoon. At Sandbank, on the shores of the loch, is the two-mile long **Ardnadam Heritage Trail**, with a climb up to a viewpoint at Dunan. The **Cowal Bird Garden** at Sandbank is open from Easter to November every year, and has parrots, exotic birds, donkeys, rabbits and other birds and animals. Details of the 47-mile long **Cowal Way**, a footpath which runs from Portavadie to Artgartan, can be had at the local tourist office.

George Robertson, former MP, Secretary General of NATO and now Baron Robertson of Port Ellen, attended Dunoon Grammar School, as did the late Labour leader John Smith (see also Islay, Iona and Lochgilphead).

AROUND DUNOON

KILMUN

3 miles N of Dunoon on the A880

Kilmun Church, dedicated to St Munn or Mund, was a collegiate church founded in 1442 by Sir Duncan Campbell of Lochawe, ancestor of the present Dukes of Argyll. All that remains is the tower, now roofless. In 1794 a Campbell mausoleum was built close to the present church of St Munn, built in 1841 to designs by Thomas Burns, and in the kirkyard is the grave of **Elizabeth Blackwell**, who, in 1849, was the first woman to graduate in medicine. Born in Bristol in 1821, she studied in Geneva (where she graduated), in the United States and at Paris and London. After returning to the United States, she opened (despite intense opposition) the first hospital staffed entirely by women. She died in 1910, and was buried in the churchyard as she regularly holidayed in the area. Close by is the grave of the **Reverend Alexander Robinson**, a former minister who was deposed after publishing, in 1898, *The Saviour in the Newer Light*, a book that put forward opinions which brought accusations of heresy. The Douglas Mausoleum, also in the graveyard, contains the body of **General Sir John Douglas**, who died in 1888.

On a hillside is the **Kilmun Arboretum**, extending to 180 acres. First planted in 1930, it has a wide range of trees - some rare - from all over the world, and is maintained by the Forestry Commission, which does research work here.

BENMORE

6 miles N of Dunoon off the A815

The **Younger Botanic Garden** is a specialist section of the Royal Botanic Garden in Edinburgh. The land was gifted to the nation in 1925, and in 1929 the gardens were given to the Royal Botanic Garden. In its 140 acres you can see a wide collection of trees and shrubs from all over the world. There are 250 species of rhododendron, an avenue of giant redwoods from America and a formal garden. Within the Glen Massan Arboretum are some of the tallest trees in Scotland, including a Douglas fir over 178 feet high. From the top of Benmore Hill there is a magnificent view across the Holy Loch to the Firth of Clyde and the Renfrewshire coast. **Puck's Glen** was once part of the Benmore Estate, but is now a delightful walk with great views and picnic areas.

To the north of Benmore is the seven mile long **Loch Eck**, with the A815 following its eastern shores towards Strachur on Loch Fyne. Near the head of the loch is **Tom-a-Chorachasich**, a low hill where, legend says, a Viking prince was once slain.

ARDENTINNY

7 miles N of Dunoon on a minor road

Ardentinny sits on the shores of Loch Long, and is a small, attractive village made famous by the Sir Harry Lauder song *O'er the Hill to Ardentinny*. It is one of the few places in the area to have a sandy beach. There are two forest walks near the village - **Birchwood Walk** and **Clunie Walk**.

TOWARD

6 miles S of Dunoon on the A815

The ruins of **Toward Castle** date mainly from the 15th century. It was a stronghold of the Lamonts,

Toward Castle

who supported Charles II in his attempts to impose bishops on the Church of Scotland.

An episode in 1646 shows just how the Scottish clans took matters into their own hands when dispensing justice. The Campbells, who opposed the imposition of bishops, laid siege to Lamont Castle, and after unsuccessfully trying to blow it up, offered safe passage as far as Dunoon to the

113 SEAFIELD HOTEL

Campbeltown

A truly outstanding small hotel close to the heart of Campbeltown that has an award-winning restaurant.

⊨ ‖ *see page 473*

•

The town sits on Campbeltown Loch, which is guarded by the small island of Davaar. Within a cave on the island is a famous painting of the Crucifixion by local artist David MacKinnon from 1887. The island can be reached on foot at low tide by a long shingle beach known as The Doirlinn.

•

Lamonts sheltering within. The Lamonts duly left the castle, and were immediately rounded up and taken to Tom-a-Mhoid ("Hill of Justice") in Dunoon, where 36 clansmen were hung (see also Dunoon).

It was not just political or religious differences that prompted the massacre. Previously, the Lamonts themselves had slaughtered Campbells at Strachur and attacked and slaughtered the villagers of Kilmun, who were hiding in their church.

CAMPBELTOWN

Campbeltown has the reputation of being the most isolated town on the British mainland. It sits on the Mull of Kintyre, that great peninsula hanging down from the main body of Argyll. It received its royal charter in 1700, making it the second youngest royal burgh in Scotland. Though 140 miles from Glasgow by road, it is only 30 miles from Ballycastle in Northern Ireland. It also has the distinction of being the most southerly town in the Scottish Highlands, and is 20 miles further south than Berwick-upon-Tweed.

At one time the main industries were fishing and distilling, but the fishing fleet has gone now, and only three distilleries remain of the 30 or so that once produced over two million gallons of whisky a year. There are conducted tours, by appointment only, round **Springbank Distillery**, established in 1828. It is one of the few

Scottish distilleries where every stage in the process is contained within one site, including bottling. At the **Campbeltown Heritage Centre**, in an old kirk, there are displays and exhibits about South Kintyre, including photos of the light railway that once connected the town with Machrihanish on the peninsula's west coast, where the town's airport now stands. The airport has one of the longest runways in Europe, though only one flight uses it - a Loganair flight to Glasgow. The **Campbeltown Museum** in Hall Street has exhibits on the geology, wildlife and archaeology of the Kintyre Peninsula. It also has a working model of the former Machrihanish to Campbeltown Light Railway, closed in 1931.

Campbeltown Cross, erected near the harbour, dates from the 14th century. It was used as the mercat cross after the town became a royal burgh. In the grounds of Campbeltown Library are the **Lady Linda McCartney Memorial Gardens**, named after the late wife of Sir Paul McCartney, who has a holiday home on Kintyre. It features a statue of her. Campbeltown Picture House was built in 1913, and is the oldest purpose-built cinema still functioning in Scotland.

Five miles to the west, on the Atlantic coastline, is the village **Machrihanish** and its airport, once an RAF base. It has the longest runway of any commercial airport in Scotland, and has daily flights to Glasgow.

AROUND CAMPBELTOWN

SOUTHEND

8 miles S of Campbeltown on the B842

This is the most southerly village in Argyll. It was near here, at **Keil**, that St Columba is supposed to have first set foot on Scottish soil before sailing north towards Iona. In the ancient churchyard at Keil are footprints which are said to mark the spot. Further north is **St Kiaran's Cave**, which has a rudimentary stone altar and a carved water basin.

It was near Southend that a massacre by the Campbells of 300 MacDonald clansmen under Sir Alasdair MacDonald took place in 1647. **Dunaverty Rock**, also known as the Rock of Blood, is supposed to mark the spot. The nine feet tall **Knockstapple Standing Stone** can be seen from the Campbeltown - Southend Road.

SADDELL

9 miles N of Campbeltown on the B842

Saddell Abbey (Historic Scotland) was founded by Somerled, Lord of the Isles in 1148 for Cistercian monks, and completed by his son Reginald, who also founded Iona Abbey and its nearby Nunnery. Only scant remains can now be seen, most notably the presbytery and the north transept. As at other places in Argyll, stone carving once flourished here, and no fewer than 11 beautiful grave slabs, each one showing either a knight in full armour, a monk or animals and

fish, can be seen. After the Battle of Renfrew in 1164, the bodies of Somerled and his heir were brought to Saddell for burial (see also Renfrew). **Saddell Castle** (not open to the public) was built in 1508 for David Hamilton, the Bishop of Argyll, from stones taken from the abbey. It has been converted into self-catering holiday accommodation. A small footpath takes you from the castle gates down to the beach.

CARRADALE

12 miles N of Campbeltown on the B879

This quiet fishing village lies opposite Arran, on the east coast of the Mull of Kintyre. The **Network Carradale Heritage Centre**, in an old school, has displays about fishing, farming and forestry in the area, as well as hands-on activities for children. **Carradale House** dates from the 18th century, but was extended in 1804 for the then owner Richard Campbell. In its grounds are gardens noted for their rhododendrons, of which there are over 100 varieties. Until her death in 1999, it was the home of the Scottish writer **Naomi Mitchison CBE**.

Torrisdale Castle, which has been converted into holiday accommodation, was built in 1815, and has an organic tannery which uses natural methods of tanning.

GLENBARR

10 miles N of Campbeltown on the A83

At the **Clan Macalister Centre** in Glenbarr Abbey (not an abbey but

The remote Sanda Island, two miles south of the village of Southend, can be reached by boat from Campbeltown. Though it is remote, it still has a pub - the one-man Byron Darnton Tavern, named after a ship that ran aground off the island in 1946. Sanda Island Bird Observatory was set up in 1995.

The 50-acre Achamore Gardens, near the ferry port at Ardminish, are open to the public. They were founded by Sir James Horlick, of bedtime drink fame, after he bought the island in 1944. They are famous for their rhododendrons and camellias. In 2001 the inhabitants of Gigha bought the island, and it is now managed by a trust.

114 EMPIRE TRAVEL LODGE

Lochgilphead

Superb value-for-money accommodation, right in the heart of Lochgilphead, that offers nine well-equipped, en suite rooms.

⊨ see page 474

115 ARGYLL TRAIL RIDING & CASTLE RIDING CENTRE

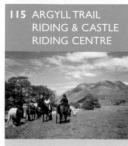

Ardrishaig

The UK's leading equestrian centre, offering holidays and short breaks to beginners and experts.

🏛 see page 475

a mansion house) are exhibits tracing the history of Clan Macalister as far back as Somerled, Lord of the Isles, nearly 900 years ago. The castle was presented to the clan in 1984 by Angus C. Macalister, 5th Laird of Glenbarr. The mansion house itself is open to the public between Easter and mid October each year.

GIGHA

17 miles NW of Campbeltown off the west coast of Kintyre

This small island, no more than six miles long by two miles wide at its widest is reached by ferry from Tayinloan. It is best to see the island on foot, and the **Gigha Path Network** makes this easy. The name Gigha (pronounced gee-yah, with a hard "g") was given to the island by the Norse king Hakon, and means "God's island". It is reputed to have a climate of its own, and while the rest of Argyll is enveloped in cloud, Gigha is sometimes bathed in sunshine due to the Gulf Stream washing its shores. Its highest peak, at 330 feet, is **Creag Bhan**, where you can see a 4th century inscribed stone.

The scanty ruins of **Kilchattan Church**, behind the hotel, date from medieval times. In the kirkyard are some old grave slabs showing knights in armour. One is possibly of Malcolm MacNeill, Laird of Gigha, who died in 1493.

And behind the church, atop the Cnoc A'Charraidh (Hill of the Pillar) is the **Ogham Stone** dating from the time the island formed part of the kingdom of Dalriada. It

carries a carving that reads *Fiacal son of Coemgen*, and probably marks a burial.

LOCHGILPHEAD

Lochgilphead, as the name suggests, stands at the head of Loch Gilp, a small inlet of Loch Fyne. It is a planned town, laid out in about 1790, and is the main shopping centre for a wide area known as Knapdale, that portion of Argyll from which the long "arm" of the Mull of Kintyre descends. Knapdale is steeped in history, and though it now seems to be on the edge of things, at one time it was at the crossroads of a great communications network. Ireland was to the southwest, the Isle of Man was to the south, the Hebrides were to the north, the bulk of Scotland itself was to the east, and all could be easily reached by boat.

Kilmory Woodland Park, off the A83, surrounds Kilmory Castle, which has been turned into local government offices. The park contains many rare trees, plus a garden and woodland walks.

The **Crinan Canal** (known as "Scotland's most beautiful shortcut") starts at **Ardrishaig**, a couple of miles south of Lochgilphead, and skirts the town as it heads across the peninsula towards the village of Crinan on the west coast. Designed by civil engineer John Rennie, work started on the canal in 1794. However, it was beset with problems, and finally opened, albeit in an incomplete form, in 1801. By 1804 it was still incomplete and had debts of £140,000. Then, in 1805, some of the canal banks collapsed and had to be rebuilt. It was finally opened in 1809, though in 1815 Thomas Telford, the civil engineer, inspected it and declared that even more work needed doing. In 1817 it reopened, this time to everyone's satisfaction.

It is nine miles long, has a mean depth of nine feet six inches (though Rennie's recommended depth throughout was fifteen feet) and rises to 65 feet above sea level. it has, in this short length, 15 locks. In 1847 it got the royal seal of approval when Queen Victoria sailed its full length as she was making a tour of the Highlands. Perhaps the most unusual craft to have used it were midget submarines during World War II.

Ardrishaig was the birthplace, in 1938, of the late **John Smith**, the Labour leader who died in 1994. He is buried on Iona (see also Iona and Dunoon).

Barnluasgan lies 5 miles west of the town, on the B8025. Here there is a visitor centre and a forest trail. Close by, on a rocky outcrop, there are also the scant remains of an old dun, or fort, and enclosure. A few miles south along the same road is the **Taynish National Nature Reserve**, which contains one of the largest natural deciduous woodlands in Britain.

Achahoish Parish Church has no great artistic merit, though it is curious in that it looks like a small, square-windowed cottage with a tower at one end.

AROUND LOCHGILPHEAD

DUNADD

4 miles N of Lochgilphead off the A816

Dunadd (Historic Scotland) is one of the most important historical sites in Scotland. This great rocky outcrop rises to a height of 175 feet from a flat area of land called **Moine Mhor** ("Great Moss"), which is now a national nature reserve. It is where the ancient kings of **Dalriada** had their royal fort and capital. From here, they ruled a kingdom that took in all of modern day Argyll. It was founded by immigrants from Antrim in present day Northern Ireland in the 5th century, and gradually grew in importance. With them from Ireland they brought that great icon of Scottish nationhood, the Stone of Destiny (see also Scone and Edinburgh).

A climb to the top of Dunadd gives a wonderful view over the surrounding countryside, which is the reason the fort was established here in the first place. Parts of the

At Achahoish, eight miles southwest of Lochgilphead on the B8024, is St Columba's Cave, on the shores of Loch Caolisport. It is said that St Columba stopped here to pray on his way north from Ulster to Iona. A footpath, which starts beside the ruins of an old chapel, leads down to the cave. Care should be taken when visiting it.

Dunadd

Though it may now look austere and lonely, Dunadd, in its heyday, would have been a busy place, as excavations have shown that it traded with the kingdoms of present day England, Ireland, Wales and the Continent. When the king was in residence, great flags would have fluttered from the wooden buildings, colourful banners and pennants would have hung from the ramparts and soldiers would have stood guard at its entrance. The River Add, no more than a couple of feet deep nowadays, winds its way round the base of the rock before entering the sea at Loch Crinan. In olden days, before the Moine Mhor was partly drained for agriculture, it would have been navigable right up to the rock itself. Boats would have been tied up at its banks, and there would have been a small township to house the king's retainers and attend to their needs. There would also have been storerooms, stables and workshops where jewellery and weapons were crafted, cloth woven and pots made.

ramparts can still be seen, and near the top, on a flat outcrop of rock, are some carvings of a boar, a footprint, a bowl and some ogham writing, which may have been connected to the inauguration of the Dalriadan kings.

The kings of Dalriada were special. Before this time, kings were looked upon more as great tribal leaders and warriors than men set apart to rule a kingdom. One man changed all that - St Columba. His monastery on Iona was within Dalriada, and on that island he conducted the first Christian "coronation" in Britain. In AD 574 he anointed Aidan king of the Dalriadans in a ceremony that relied on Biblical precedents. Though nowadays kings are crowned, anointing also takes place. It also contained an element that is still used in today's coronations, when the assembled crowds shouted out "God Save the King!" in unison. There is no doubt that Aidan sat on the Stone of Destiny during the ceremony.

The other great kingdom north of the Forth and Clyde was the kingdom of the Picts, with its capital at Inverness, and for years it and Dalriada traded, fought, mingled and intermarried. Eventually, in AD 843, through this intermarriage, Kenneth MacAlpin, king of Dalriada, inherited the throne of the Picts. By this time the centres of power had moved west because of constant Norse raids, so Kenneth set off for Scone in present day Perthshire (taking the Stone of Destiny with him) and

established his capital there. Thus was born the kingdom of Scotland, or Alba as it was known then, with Kenneth becoming Kenneth 1 of Scotland. It would be another 200 years before the kingdoms of the Lowlands - the Angles of the Lothians and the British of Strathclyde - were incorporated as well.

Dunadd survived for a few years after Kenneth left, but it was no longer an important place, and by the 12th century was largely abandoned.

KILMICHAEL GLASSARY

4 miles N of Lochgilphead on a minor road off the A816

In common with many other kirkyards in this part of Argyll, the kirkyard of the attractive 19th century **Parish Church** has a fine collection of carved, medieval and later, grave slabs.

The **Cup and Ring Rock** (Historic Scotland) lies within a small fenced-off area in the village, and has some ancient cup and ring markings carved into it. No one knows the significance of such carvings, though there are many throughout Scotland.

KILMARTIN

8 miles N of Lochgilphead on the A816

The area surrounding Kilmartin is said to be Scotland's richest prehistoric landscape. Within a six-mile radius of the village over 150 prehistoric and 200 later monuments are to be found. The whole place is awash with standing stones, stone circles, cairns, henges, burial mounds, forts, crannogs, cup and ring markings, castles, chapels, carved grave slabs and crosses.

A church has stood in the village for centuries, though the present **Parish Church** was only built in 1835. Its former dedication to St Martin shows that a church has stood here since at least the Dark Ages, as St Martin was a favourite saint of Celtic monks. Within it is a decorated cross that dates from about the 9th century, and within the kirkyard are three further crosses, dating also from the 9th century. Also in the kirkyard is the finest collection of carved medieval grave slabs in Western Scotland. Most date from the 14th or 15th century, though there are some, which might be older. They might come as a surprise to people who imagine Scottish warriors to be wild Highlanders in kilts who brandish broadswords as they dash across the heather. These warriors are dressed in the kind of sophisticated armour found all over Europe at the time. Only the well-off could have afforded it, and the other carvings on the slabs, such as swords, coats-of-arms and crosses, bear out their aristocratic lineage.

Some people have suggested that the carvings show Knights Templar, those warrior monks suppressed by Pope Clement V in 1307, egged on by Philip le Bel, king of France, who wanted his hands on the order's fabled treasure.

A great Templar fleet left La Rochelle in France soon after the order was suppressed - supposedly carrying the Templar's treasure - and was never heard of again. Not long before, the Pope had excommunicated Robert the Bruce for his murder of the Red Comyn in a friary in Dumfries, and people believed the Templars were heading for Scotland. The Pope's influence in the country was minimal - indeed the clergy was ignoring the Pope and still giving communion to Bruce. So it would certainly have made sense for the Templars to make for Scotland, bringing their treasure with them. Edward I was forever bemoaning the fact that the Scots seemed to have unlimited funds to defend themselves.

Dan Brown's book *The Da Vinci Code* claims that the treasure was not money, jewels or gold, but a great secret about Jesus and Mary Magdalen. However, this theory has been around for many years, and there is no hard evidence for it. Some people now even claim that the Stuart dynasty is directly descended from Jesus (see also Rosslyn).

Behind the church is the **Glebe Cairn**, a circular mound of stones dating from 1500-2000 BC. It forms part of what is known as the linear cemetery, a collection of such cairns, which stretches for a mile along the floor of Kilmartin Glen. The others are **Nether Largie North Cairn**, **Nether Largie Mid Cairn**, **Nether Largie South Cairn** and **Ri Cruin Cairn**. All are accessible by foot. In addition, there is the **Dunchraigaig Cairn**, just off the A816, which doesn't

243

118 THE CRAFTY KITCHEN

Ardfern

A wonderful eating place, with a small craft shop attached, that uses locally sourced produce wherever possible in its imaginative dishes.

see page 477

form part of the linear cemetery.

The **Temple Wood Circles**, south of Kilmartin, date from about 3500 BC. There are two of them, with the northern one possibly being used as a solar observatory when agriculture was introduced into the area. Burials were introduced at a later date. The **Nether Largie Standing Stones** are close to the Temple Wood Circle, and the **Ballymeanoch Standing Stones** are to the south of them. Of the seven stones, only six now survive in their original positions.

To the north of Kilmartin are the substantial ruins of **Carnassarie Castle** (Historic Scotland), dating from the 16th century. It was built for John Carswell, Protestant Bishop of the Isles and the man who translated Knox's Book of Common Order (the liturgy for the reformed church) into Gaelic. It was the first book ever to be printed in that language. **Kilmartin Castle**, which dates from the 16th century, was built by Neil Campbell, rector of Kilmartin and later Bishop of Argyll. It has recently been restored, and sits on a terrace overlooking Kiklmartin Glen. It is privately owned, and not open to the public.

If you find all these stone circles, cairns, castles, carvings and burial mounds hard to comprehend, then you should visit the award winning **Kilmartin House Museum** next to the church in the village. Using maps, photographs, displays and artefacts it explains the

chronology of the area from about 7000 BC right up until AD 1100.

KILMARIE

On the B8002 10 miles NW of Lochgilphead

If you drive south along the B8002, which leaves the A816 a few miles north of Kilmartin, you will find yourself on the Craignish Peninsula. Beyond the attractive village of **Ardfern**, a popular haven for yachtsmen is **Kilmarie Old Parish Church**. This roofless ruin, dedicated to St Maelrubha, dates from the 13th century, and contains a wonderful collection of carved grave slabs dating from the 14th and 15th centuries. There was once a small settlement called Kirkton which surrounded the church.

KILMORY

13 miles SW of Lochgilphead on a minor road off the B8025

Three miles north of Kilmory, on the shores of Loch Sween, stands the bulky ruins of **Castle Sween**, mainland Scotland's oldest surviving stone castle. Four massive, thick walls surround a courtyard where originally wood and thatch lean-tos would have housed stables, workshops and a brewery. It was originally built by one Suibhne (pronounced "Sween"), ancestor of the MacSweens, in about 1100, and in later years became a centre of craftsmanship and artistry. This is shown by the **Kilmory Sculptured Stones**, at the 700-year-old Kilmory Knap chapel, a few miles south west of the castle. There was a thriving settlement here in medieval times, and within the ruins of the chapel is a remarkable collection of carved stones collected from the kirkyard, some going back at least 1,000 years. The symbols on them include men in armour, blacksmiths' and woodworkers' tools, swords and crosses. They probably all marked the graves of craftsmen and warriors associated with Castle Sween over the years.

The most spectacular stone is **MacMillan's Cross**, which dates from the 15th century. On one side it shows the Crucifixion, and on the other a hunting scene. There is a Latin inscription that translates, "This is the cross of Alexander MacMillan". Across Loch Sween, at the end of the B8025, is **Keills Chapel**, which has another fine collection of grave slabs. On Eilean Mor ("Great Island"), a couple of miles offshore from Kilmory, are the ruins of **St Cormac's Chapel** dating from the 12th century. The chancel is still roofed.

KILBERRY

10 miles SW of Lochgilphead on the B8024

At Kilberry Castle are some late medieval sculptured stones (Historic Scotland), which were gathered from the Kilberry estate and placed under cover.

TARBERT

12 miles S of Lochgilphead on the A83

This small fishing port sits at a point where Kintyre is no more than a mile wide, and is the gateway to the peninsula. To the east is the small East Loch Tarbert, and to the

west is the eight-mile long West Loch Tarbert, where, at **Kennacraig**, ferries leave for Islay and Jura. In 1093 King Magnus Barelegs of Norway is said to have been dragged in his galley across the narrow isthmus, proving to his own satisfaction that the Mull of Kintyre was an island, and he was entitled to add it to his empire. **An Tairbeart**, to the south of the village, is a heritage centre that tells of the place's history and people. **Tarbert Castle**, which is now ruinous, dates originally from the 13th century. Robert the Bruce later added further defences. The ruins as we see them today date from the late 15th century. It can be reached along a footpath from Harbour Street.

North of the village is Stonefield Castle, built in 1837 and now a hotel. Attached is **Stonefield Castle Garden**, which is open to the public. As with so many gardens in the area, it is famous for its rhododendrons. There are also plants from Chile and New Zealand, and conifers such as the sierra redwood.

Seven miles south of Tarbert is **Skipness Castle** (Historic Scotland), which dates originally from the 13th century. The first

Medieval Sculptured Stones, Kilberry

119 ANCHOR HOTEL

Tarbert

A superb hotel, pub and restaurant on the quayside that is renowned throughout the country for its food - especially its seafood.

see page 478

Being the main town for a large area, Inveraray was the place where justice was meted out. Inveraray Jail takes you on a trip through Scotland's penal system in the 1800s, and here you can see what the living conditions were like in cells that housed murderers and thieves. There are two prison blocks, one built in 1820 and one in 1848, the latter having more "enlightened" conditions. You can also see the branding irons, thumb screws and whips that passed for justice in the early 19th century, and see what life is like in prison today. There is also a courtroom where a tableau, complete with sound, shows how a trial was conducted before a High Court judge.

historical mention of it is in 1261 when the McSweens owned it, though it later came into the possession of Walter Stewart, Earl of Menteith. It finally came into the possession of the Campbells, and was abandoned in the late 17th century, when a newer, more comfortable house was built close by. The ruins of **Kilbrannan Chapel**, near the foreshore, dates from the 13th century, and were dedicated to St Brendan. Five medieval grave slabs are to be found inside the chapel walls and in the kirkyard. The church replaced an earlier building dedicated to St Columba.

INVERARAY

Standing on the western shores of Loch Fyne, Inveraray is a perfect example of a planned Scottish town. It was built between 1753 and 1776 by the 3rd Duke of Argyll, who had pulled down his decaying castle and replaced it with a grander one, which would reflect his important position in society. At that time the small clachan, or township, of Inveraray stood in front of the castle, and as the duke wanted to improve the castle's view out over Loch Fyne, he had it demolished. He then built a new town to the immediate south, which became a royal burgh thanks to a charter of 1648 granted by Charles I. The result is an elegant place with wide streets and well-proportioned, whitewashed houses. It is actually no bigger than a village, but so well-planned is it that

it has all the feel of a bustling town, and indeed in the summer months tourists flock to it, making it extremely busy.

Inveraray Castle sits to the north, and is an elegant, foursquare stately home. With its four turrets - one at each corner of the building - it looks more like a grand French château than a Highland castle, but this was the intention. It was designed to tell the world that the Campbells, Dukes of Argyll, belonged to one of the most powerful families in the land - one which had always supported the Presbyterian cause and the Hanovarians against the Jacobites. It was designed by Roger Morris and Robert Mylne, and contains a famous armoury, French tapestries, Scottish and European furniture, and a genealogy room that traces the history of Clan Campbell.

There are important branches of the clan throughout Scotland, though the Argyll branch is undoubtedly the most famous. There are many theories as to how the name "Campbell" came about. One states that it comes from a Norman knight called "Campo Bello", though no family of that name has ever been found in contemporary records of the Norman conquest of England. The most likely derivation is from the Gaelic "cam beul", meaning "twisted mouth", a nickname that was given to one Gillespie O'Duithne, who lived in the early 13th century.

There are two churches within the town - the rather plain **Parish Church,** which dates from 1794, and the Episcopalian **Church of All Saints**. The Parish Church was designed by Robert Mylne, and is divided in two so that services can be held in both English and Gaelic, though this is seldom done nowadays. All Saints Church, which dates from 1886, has a bell tower with the second heaviest ring of ten bells in the world. Each bell is named after a saint, and has the name inscribed on it. Ringers can sometimes be watched in action, and visiting ringers can practise by appointment.

Within the Arctic Penguin, a three-masted iron-hulled schooner built in 1911, is the **Inveraray Maritime Museum**. Here the maritime history of Scotland's western seaboard is vividly brought to life. There's an on-board cinema with an archive of old film, and people can see what conditions were like aboard a ship taking them to a new life in America. The latest addition to the museum is the *Eilean Eisdeal,* a typical puffer built in Hull in 1944. In 2006 it was re-registered as the *Vital Spark* in honour of the *Para Handy* books, written by **Neil Munro**, the writer and journalist, who was born locally. On the A819 through Glen Aray towards Loch Awe is a monument that commemorates him. It stands close to his birthplace at Carnus.

The **Argyll Wildlife Park** lies south of the town, off the A83. Within its 55 acres there are albino wallabies, badgers, racoons, foxes and monkeys.

AROUND INVERARAY

CAIRNDOW

6 miles NE of Inveraray across Loch Fyne on the A83

This small village stands at the western end of Glen Kinglas, on the shores of Loch Fyne. Within the Ardkinglas Estate is the 25-acre **Ardkinglas Woodland Garden**. High annual rainfall, a mild climate and light, sandy soils have created the right conditions for a collection of coniferous trees. The Callander family established the collection in about 1875, and it has seven "champion trees" (as attested by the Tree Register of the British Isles) that are either the tallest or widest in Britain. There is also one of the best collections of rhododendrons in the country. Ardkinglas House itself, designed by Robert Lorimer in 1907, is not open to the public, though interested groups can be taken round by prior appointment.

The award-winning **Fyne Ales** lies south of the village, and was founded in 2001. The beers can be bought locally.

STRACHUR

4 miles S of Inveraray across the loch on the A815

Strachur sits on the shores of Long Fyne, on the opposite bank from Inveraray. **Strachur Smiddy** (meaning "smithy") dates from 1791, and finally closed in the 1950s. It has now been restored as a small museum and craft shop, and has some original tools and

At Clachan Farm near Arkinglas you'll find the Clachan Farm Woodland Walks, which allow you to see many species of native tree, such as oak, hazel and birch. The walks vary from a few hundred yards in length to two-and-a-half miles, and even take in the old burial ground of Kilmorich.

121 THE SHORE HOUSE INN

Lochgoilhead

A lochside inn that offers the best accommodation, food and drink in the area. A place that cannot be missed!

see page 480

Some of Argyll's finest mountains are to be found close by Arrochar, such as Ben Narnain (3,036 feet) and Ben Ime (3,318 feet). This area could fairly claim to be the homeland of Scottish mountaineering, as the first mountaineering club in the country, the Cobbler Club, was established here in 1865. The road westwards towards Inveraray climbs up past the 2,891 feet Ben Arthur, better known as The Cobbler, and over the wonderfully named Rest and Be Thankful until it drops down again through Glen Kinglas to the shores of Loch Fyne. It is a wonderful drive, with the floor of Glen Croe several hundred feet below the road at some points.

122 BEN ARTHUR'S BOTHY

Arrochar

Undoubtedly one of the best value-for-money eating places in Arrochar that sells great food and a wide range of drinks to suit all tastes.

see page 479

implements used by blacksmiths and farriers. **Glenbranter**, which was once owned by Sir Harry Lauder, has three short walks through mature woodlands. In the kirkyard at Strachur is buried **Sir Fitzroy Maclean**, diplomat and spy, who died in 1996, and was said to be the inspiration for Ian Fleming's James Bond. He stayed in Strachur House (not open to the public).

Lachlan Castle (not open to the public, though it can be rented as holiday accommodation), is the ancestral home of the MacLachlans, and lies six miles south of Strachur on the B8000. The family, which is descended from the kings of Ulster, came from Ulster in the 13th century and settled in the area. The older 15th century castle, which is in ruins, is close by. Nine miles south of the castle, still on the B8000, is **Otter Ferry**. As the name implies, this village was once the eastern terminal of a ferry that crossed Loch Fyne, but it is long gone. The word "otter" comes from the Gaelic "oitir", meaning a gravel bank, and has nothing to do with the animal.

A single lane track, the **Ballochandrain**, leaves Otter Ferry and rises to over 1,000 feet before descending to Glendaruel. It has some wonderful views towards the Inner Hebrides.

South of Otter Ferry is the small, peaceful clachan of Kilfinan. The ruined **St Finan's Chapel**, dedicated to St Finian, a 6th century Irish saint, dates from about the 12th century and has

some old burial stones. Five miles further on at Millhouse is a turn off to the right along an unmarked road for **Portavadie**, where the Portavadie-Tarbert ferry will take you onto the Mull of Kintyre (summer only). If you turn left at the same junction and head north again, you pass through **Tighnabruaich** on the Kyles of Bute, and eventually arrive at **Glendaruel**, the site of a battle in about 1110 between Norsemen led by Mekan, son of Magnis Barefoot, and native Gaels, in which the Vikings were defeated. The name translates from the Gaelic as the "glen of red blood", as the defeated Norsemen were thrown into a local burn whose water turned red with their blood. The road hugs the shoreline most of the way, and gives some wonderful views of sea and hill. At Glendaruel are the **Kilmodan Sculptured Stones**, within the graveyard of Kilmodan Parish Church

ARROCHAR

13 miles E of Inveraray on the A83

Arrochar sits at the head of Loch Long, a sea loch. Two miles to the west is the small village of **Tarbet**, which sits on the shores of Loch Lomond, a fresh water loch. It surprises many people that Britain's largest sheet of fresh water is so close to the sea. The name "Tarbet" comes from the Gaelic. From the jetty at Tarbet small ships offer cruises on the loch. **Arrochar Parish Church** is a whitewashed building dating from 1847, and it was recently saved from demolition by the concerted effort of the villagers.

Near the Jubilee Well in Arrochar are the **Cruach Tairbeirt Walks**. These footpaths (totalling just over a mile and a half in length) give some wonderful views over Loch Lomond and Loch Long. Though well surfaced, they are quite steep in some places.

LUSS

24 miles SE of Inveraray off the A82

This beautiful little village - one of the loveliest in Scotland - was once the setting for Scottish Television's soap opera *High Road*, where it was called Glendarroch. It is an estate village built by the Colquhoun family of nearby Rossdhu Castle, and sits on the banks of Loch Lomond. On the opposite shore, the mighty bulk of **Ben Lomond** can be seen. It is the most southerly of Scotland's "Munros", or mountains over 3,000 feet, and is a comfortable climb if you are reasonably fit and active. The **Parish Church of St MacKessog,** built in 1875 on the site of a much older church, is well worth a visit. St MacKessog, or Kessog, was an Irish saint who lived in the 6th century, and who founded a monastery on Inchtavannach, one of the islands in loch Lomond, the name of which comes from the Gaelic "island of the monk's house".

GARELOCHHEAD

22 miles SE of Inveraray off the A814

This old village at the head of the beautiful **Gare Loch** now finds

itself in Argyll for administrative purposes. However, along with the picturesque **Rosneath Peninsula**, it was once part of the old county of Dunbartonshire, and it is to Dumbarton that it still looks for shopping and other services. It makes a fine centre for hill walking, bird watching and yachting. At **Cove**, on the Rosneath Peninsula, are the **Linn Botanical Gardens**, extending to three acres.

RHU

28 miles SE of Inveraray on the A814

Rhu (pronounced "roo") is a small, attractive village at the entrance to the Gair Loch. It was originally called Row, and in the 18th century was one of the ports for the Rhu - Roseneath ferry. **Glenarn Gardens** off Glenarn Road is a sheltered woodland garden famous for its rhododendrons.

HELENSBURGH

30 miles SE of Inveraray on the A814

Helensburgh was founded in the 18th century by Sir James Colquhoun of Luss, and named after his wife Helen. It is one of the ports of call in July and August for the **PS Waverley**, the world's last ocean-going paddle steamer. At one time it was a popular, if genteel, holiday resort, thanks to its rail connections to Glasgow. **John Logie Baird**, the inventor of television, was born here in 1888. What is not so well known is that he also invented colour television and, believe it or not, stereoscopic television.

123 THE UPPER CRUST

Helensburgh

A charming seafront restaurant that serves home-cooked Scottish cuisine at realistic prices.

☐ see page 479

124 THE HILL HOUSE

Helensburgh

A superb example of a Charles Rennie Mackintosh deisgn, built for the publisher, Walter Blackie .

☐ see page 481

In Upper Colquhoun Street in Helensburgh you'll find one of Charles Rennie Mackintosh's masterpieces - the Hill House. It was commissioned by Walter Blackie, the Glasgow publisher, in 1902, and contains some of Mackintosh's finest work. For not only did he design the building, he also designed the interior decoration, the fittings and most of the furniture. There are also gardens surrounding the house.

North of Helensburgh is **Glen Fruin**, which has a narrow road that connects Garelochhead with Loch Lomond. It was the scene of a battle in 1603 when the MacGregors defeated the Colquhouns with much loss of life. The story goes that two members of Clan McGregor were returning to Loch Rannoch from Glasgow in early winter in 1602, and stopped near the Loch Lomond end of Glen Fruin to ask for hospitality from the Colquhouns. This was refused, a blatant breach of the rules of Highland hospitality, so the two McGregors killed, cooked and ate a sheep. On finding out, the Colquhoun chief ordered that the two men be executed, even though they had offered to pay for the animal.

The execution was duly carried out, and when word reached the McGregor chief, Alasdair of Glenstrae, he decided to seek revenge. A party of 80 men set out for Glen Fruin, where they killed two Colquhouns and drove off over 300 cattle and the same number of sheep and goats. The Colquhoun chief, bent on revenge, sent some men off to Stirling disguised as widows, each one carrying what was claimed to be the bloodied shirt of her murdered husband. James Vl was appalled by what he thought was the cruelty of the MacGregors, and granted Colquhoun the right to hunt down the 80 MacGregor clansmen. However, MacGregor led over three hundred of his best men into Glen Fruin, which belonged to the Colquhouns, intent on battle. Meanwhile, Colquhoun got to hear of it, and set off with 300 mounted troops and 500 infantry to confront them. In February 1603 the armies met, and despite their superior manpower, the Colquhouns were heavily defeated.

When James Vl got to hear of the battle, he was outraged, and the MacGregors were declared outlaws, and were harried and hunted throughout Scotland.

CRARAE

10 miles S of Inveraray on the A83

The 50 acre **Crarae Garden** was started by Lady Campbell in 1912, and includes the national collection of southern beech, as well as eucalyptus and Eucryphia. It is one of the finest woodland gardens in

Crarae Garden

Scotland, with rare trees and exotic shrubs thriving in the mild climate, and over 400 species of rhododendron and azaleas providing a colourful display in spring and summer. A fine collection of deciduous trees adds colour and fire to autumn. There are sheltered woodland walks and a spectacular gorge. The Scottish Clan Garden features a selection of plants associated with various clans.

AUCHINDRAIN

5 miles S of Inveraray on the A83

Auchindrain Township is an original West Highland village which has been brought back to life as an outdoor museum and interpretation centre. Once common throughout the Highlands, many of these settlements were abandoned at the time of the Clearances, while others were abandoned as people headed for cities such as Glasgow and Edinburgh to find work. Queen Victoria visited Auchindrain in 1875 when it was inhabited, and you can now see what she saw. Most of the cottages, barns and byres have been restored and furnished to explain the living conditions of the Highlanders in past centuries. The visitor centre also has displays on West Highland life, showing many farming and household implements.

OBAN

Seeing Oban nowadays, it is hard to imagine that in the 18th century this bustling holiday resort was no more than a handful of cottages built round a small bay. It got its original burgh charter in 1811, but even then it was an unimportant place. With the coming of the railway in 1880, the town blossomed as people discovered its charms. Great Victorian and Edwardian villas were built by prosperous Glasgow merchants, and local people began to open hotels, guest houses and B&Bs.

Now it is the capital of the Western Highlands, and known as the "Gateway to the Western Isles". It has two cathedrals, the Roman Catholic **Cathedral of St Columba,** built in 1930 of granite and the town's largest church, and the Episcopalian **Cathedral Church of St John the Divine** in George Street, built in the 19th century but never fully completed.

Dominating the town is **McCaig's Folly**, a vast coliseum of a building that was begun in 1897 and cost £5,000. To call it a folly is a misnomer, because the man who built it, wealthy Oban banker John Stuart McCaig, wanted to establish a museum and art gallery inside it, but he died before it was completed. As the town had a lot of unemployed people at the time, he also wanted to create work for them. In his will he left money for a series of large statues of himself and his family to be erected around the parapet, but these were never erected.

The oldest building in Oban is **Dunollie Castle**, the ruins of which can be seen on the northern outskirts of the town beyond the

125 THE BARRIEMORE

Oban

A delightful guest house overlooking Oban Bay which offers eleven individually furnished and decorated rooms at realistic prices.

⊨ see page 481

126 CORRIEMAR GUEST HOUSE

Oban

A delightful guest house right on the seafront with an international décor and a warm, friendly atmosphere.

⊨ see page 482

127 GLENARA

Oban

A truly wonderful small guest house that places great emphasis on friendly, efficient service, comfort and great value for money.

⊨ see page 482

128 SOROBA HOUSE HOTEL

Oban

A friendly, welcoming hotel that provides great value for money and a warm, friendly atmosphere.

⊨ ∥ see page 482

Dunollie Castle

•

The pier at Oban is where most of the ferries leave for the Western Isles. From here you can sail for Lismore, Mull, Coll, Tiree, Colonsay, Barra and South Uist, and one of the joys of Oban is sitting on the pier watching the graceful ferries entering and leaving Oban Bay.

•

Corran Esplanade. It was built on a site that has been fortified since the Dark Ages, and was a MacDougall stronghold. It was finally abandoned as a dwelling house in the early 1700s, when a new McDougall mansion was built. It soon became a quarry for the people of the area. A pathway takes you up to it, but care should be taken. From the ruins there are fine views out over Oban Harbour. North of the castle, near the beach at Ganavan, is the *Clach a' Choin*, or **Dog's Stone**, where, legend has it, the giant Fingal tied up his dog Bran. The groove at the base is supposed to be where the leash wore away the stone.

The **Rare Breeds Farm Park** at Glencruitten was established in 1987, and covers 35 acres. It is part of a working farm, and has, among others, Tamworth pigs, Shetland sheep, Castlemilk moorits (a type of sheep) and belted Galloway cattle.

Ardmaddy Castle Garden, eight miles south of Oban off the

B844 road for Seil Island, is another of the local gardens that benefit from the area's mild climate. The castle itself dates from the 15th century, and was once the home of the Marquis of Breadalbane.

The **Oban Distillery** in Stafford Street produces a whisky that is one of the six "classic malts" of Scotland, and has tours showing the distillery at work. The whisky is a lightly peated malt, and the tour includes a free dram. On the Corran Esplanade is the **Oban War and Peace Museum**, which has photographs and military memorabilia. There is also a model of a flying boat with a 14 feet wingspan.

And at Upper Soroba is the **Oban Zoological World**, a small family-run zoo specialising in small mammals and reptiles. The **Puffin Dive Centre** at Port Gallanach is an award winning activity centre where you can learn to scuba dive in some remarkably clear water.

Offshore from Oban is the small rocky island of **Kerrera**, which can be reached by passenger ferry from a point about two miles south of the town. At the south end of the island are the ruins of 16th century **Gylen Castle**, another former MacDougall stronghold. It was built by Duncan MacDougall, brother (or son) of the clan chief, Dougal McDougall. It was sacked by a Covenanting army under General Leslie in 1647 and all the inhabitants were slaughtered.

Oban is one terminal of the Scottish Coast to Coast Walk,

stretching the 128 miles across Scotland to St Andrews (see also St Andrews).

AROUND OBAN

CONNEL BRIDGE

4 miles NE of Oban off the A828

Connel Bridge was at one-time a railway bridge which now carries the A828 over the narrow entrance to Loch Etive, a sea loch that reaches 16 miles into the heart of Argyllshire. This entrance is very shallow, and when the tide ebbs, the water pours out of the loch into the Firth of Lorne over the shallow **Falls of Lora**. Three miles west of the bridge, off the A85, is **Achnacloich Garden**, which is open from April to October.

DUNSTAFFNAGE

3 miles N of Oban off the A85

On a promontory sticking out into Ardmuchnish Bay, in the Firth of Lorne, is the substantial **Dunstaffnage Castle** (Historic Scotland). Seen from the east, it has a glorious setting, with the island of Lismore and the hills of Morvern behind it. And the setting is not just beautiful. This must be one of the most strategic places in Argyll as far as sea travel is concerned, as many important sea routes converge here. The castle was originally built in the 13th century by either Ewan or Duncan MacDougall, Lords of Lorne, on the site of a Dalriadan royal fort and settlement, though the castle as seen today dates from all periods up to the 19th century. In 1309 the castle fell into the

hands of Robert the Bruce, and he gave it to the Stewarts. In 1470 Colin Campbell, the first Earl of Argyll, was created hereditary captain, or keeper of Dunstaffnage.

In 1363 a dark deed was carried out here. The then Stewart owner was set upon outside the castle and murdered by a troop of MacDougalls, who still considered the castle theirs. The troop then attacked the castle, and it fell into their hands once more. A few months later a force of men sent by David II, Robert the Bruce's son, retook it. In 1746, Flora MacDonald was held captive here for a short while.

The castle's resident ghost is called the **Ell Maid**, who is dressed all in green. Sometimes on stormy nights she can be heard wandering through the ruins, her footsteps clanging off the stone as if shod in iron. If she is heard laughing, it means that there will be good news for the castle. If she shrieks and sobs, it means the opposite.

It was at Dunstaffnage that the Dalriada kings were supposed to have kept the Stone of Destiny, bringing it to Iona and Dunadd for coronations.

BENDERLOCH

8 miles N of Oban on the A828

The **Oban Seal and Marine Centre** is Scotland's leading marine animal rescue centre, and it looks after dozens of injured or orphaned seal pups before returning them back into the wild.

Barcaldine Castle, which is located down a side road off the

129 OYSTER INN & FERRYMAN'S OF CONNEL

Connel Bridge

A superb traditional Scottish inn and eating place, famed for the quality of its food and its warm welcome to visitors.

❚❙ ⊨ see page 483

•

Dunstaffnage Chapel sits outside the castle, and also dates from the 13th century. It is unusual in that chapels were usually within the defensive walls of a castle. A small burial aisle built in 1740 for the Campbells of Dunstaffnage forms an eastern extension.

•

130 APPIN HOLIDAY HOMES

Appin

A wide choice of self catering accommodation that is stunningly beautiful and packed full of history and things to do.

see page 483

131 THE PIERHOUSE HOTEL & SEAFOOD RESTAURANT

Port Appin

Comfortable, stylish accommodation and one of the best seafood restaurants in the country.

see page 484

132 AIRDENY CHALETS

Glen Lonan, Taynuilt

Well-equipped, three and four star self-catering chalets, in a beautiful location near Taynuilt.

see page 484

A828 leading to Eriska, has associations with the Appin murder and the Massacre of Glencoe. It was built by Sir Duncan Campbell of Glenorchy, known as Black Duncan, in the late 16th century. There are secret passages and a bottle dungeon, and the castle is said to be haunted by a Blue Lady. Though not open to the public, it offers B&B accommodation. **Tralee Beech** is one of the best beeches in the area, and it too can be reached using the Eriska road.

The **Kintaline Farm Plant and Poultry Centre** is centred on an old farm and water mill, and offers advice and equipment for the keeping of poultry. There is a small garden with a G scale narrow gauge model railway in it.

ARDCHATTAN

8 miles NE of Oban on a minor road on the north shore of Loch Etive

Ardchattan Priory (Historic Scotland) was built in about 1230 by Duncan McDougall, Lord of Lorne, for the Valliscaulian order of monks. In 1308 Robert the Bruce held a parliament here, the last Scottish parliament to be conducted solely in Gaelic. The ruins of the church can still be seen, though the rest of the priory, including the nave and cloisters, was incorporated into Ardchattan House in the early 17th century by John Campbell, who took over the priory at the Reformation. There are some old grave slabs which mark McDougall graves. **Ardchattan Priory Garden** is open to the public, and has

herbaceous borders, roses, a rockery and a wild flower meadow.

KINLOCHLAICH GARDENS

11 miles N of Oban on the A828

This old walled garden was created in 1790 by John Campbell. It sits on the shores of Loch Linnhe, in an area known as Appin, and it has one of Scotland's largest plant and nursery centres. Kinlochlaich House was built in the 17th and 18th centuries, and is not open to the public.

DRUIMNEIL HOUSE GARDEN

10 miles N of Oban on a minor road off the A828

This ten acre garden has a fine display of rhododendrons, shrubs and trees, plus a garden centre. It is open from Easter to October each year under the Scottish Gardens Scheme. Teas and coffees are available. To the east of the A828, on a minor road, is **Glasdrum Wood**, a national nature reserve. It sits on the shores of Loch Creran, and climbs up the slopes of Ben Churalain.

TAYNUILT

9 miles E of Oban on the A85

Taynuilt lies close to the shores of Loch Etiven and is on the 128-mile long Coast to Coast Walk from Oban to St Andrews. Nearby, at Inverawe, is the **Bonawe Furnace**, which dates from 1753. Ironworking was carried out here for over 100 years, and the furnace made many of the cannonballs used by Nelson's navy. In 1805 the workers erected a statue to Nelson, the first in Britain, and it can still be seen today near **Muckairn Parish Church**, which dates from 1829. The nearby ruined **Killespickerill Church**, which dates from the 13th century, was chosen to be the first cathedral of the new Diocese of Argyll and the Isles, but before it could be enlarged the bishop moved his seat to Lismore.

LOCH AWE

16 miles E of Oban on the A85

If you take the road east from Dunstaffnage Castle, passing near the shores of Loch Etive and going through the Pass of Brander, you will come to Scotland's longest loch, Loch Awe. This is its northern shore, and it snakes southwest for a distance of nearly 25½ miles until it almost reaches Kilmartin. Twenty crannogs, or artificial islands, have been discovered in the loch. On them defensive houses were built of wood, with a causeway connecting them to the mainland. They were in use in the Highlands from about 3000 BC right up until the 16th century. Near the village of Lochawe are the impressive ruins of **Kilchurn Castle** (Historic Scotland), right on the shores of the loch. It was built by Sir Colin Campbell, who came from a cadet branch of the great Campbell family, in about 1450. The family was eventually elevated to the peerage as the Earls of Breadalbane. In the 1680s Sir John Campbell converted the castle into

a barracks to house troops fighting the Jacobites. However, it was never used as such.

Care should be taken when accessing the castle from the A85, as the pathway crosses the rail link between Glasgow and Oban.

St Conan's Kirk, also on the banks of the loch, is reckoned to be one of the most beautiful churches in Scotland, though it dates only from the 1880s, with later additions. It was built by Walter Douglas Campbell, who had built a mansion house nearby. The story goes that his mother disliked the long drive to the parish church at Dalmally, so in 1881 Walter decided to built a church on the shores of Loch Awe. Not only did he commission it, he designed it and also carved some of the woodwork. The church was completed in 1887, but it proved too small for him, so in 1907 he began extending it. He died in 1914 before he could complete the work, and it was finally finished in its present state in 1930 by his sister and later his trustees. It has a superb chancel, an ambulatory, a nave with a south aisle, various chapels and, curiously for a small church, cloisters. The Bruce Chapel commemorates a skirmish near the church, when a small force of men loyal to Robert the Bruce defeated John of Lorne, who had sworn allegiance to Edward I of England. The chapel contains a small fragment of bone from Bruce's tomb in Dunfermline Abbey. On the outside, watch out for the drainpipes with, at the top, the

• *At Barguillean Farm near Taynuilt you will find the nine-acre Angus's Garden, established in 1957 on the shores of Loch Angus. It extends to nine acres, and was created by Betty Macdonald in 1957 in memory of her son Angus Macdonald, a journalist who was killed in Cyprus in 1956.* •

133 CRUACHAN VISITOR CENTRE

Dalmally

Visit a working power station deep within the mountains and see the enormous turbines that convert water into electricity.

 see page 485

134 BLARGHOUR FARM COTTAGES

Dalmally

Four superb self-catering cottages with spectacular views over Loch Awe, each one being well-equipped and appointed for a great holiday.

see page 486

135 RAERA FARM

Kilninver

Superb, peaceful, self-catering accommodation on a farm that can be used as a base from which to explore Argyll.

see page 485

faces of floppy-eared rabbits.

The waters of Loch Cruachan, high above Loch Awe, have been harnessed for one of the most ambitious hydroelectric schemes in Scotland. Not only does the **Cruachan Power Station** produce electricity from the waters of the loch as they tumble down through pipes into its turbines and then into Loch Awe, it can actually pump 120 tons of water a second back up the pipes from Loch Awe by putting the turbines into reverse. This it does during the night, using the excess electricity produced by conventional power stations. In this way, power is stored so that it can be released when demand is high. It was the first station in the world to use the technology, though nowadays it is commonplace.

The turbine halls are in huge artificial caves beneath the mountain, and there is an exhibition explaining the technology. Tours are also available taking you round one of the wonders of Scottish civil engineering - one that can produce enough electricity to supply a city the size of Edinburgh.

ARDANAISEIG GARDEN

14 miles E of Oban on a minor road off the B845 on the banks of Loch Awe

Ardanaiseig is a large, 100-acre woodland garden with a large herbaceous border. It is open from April to October.

DALMALLY

19 miles E of Oban on the A85

The whitewashed, early 19th century **Dalmally Parish Church** was designed by James Eliot, and is unusual in that it is octagonal in shape, with a small tower tacked on to one of its sides. Up a small track way (formerly a military road connecting Dalmally and Inveraray), is a monument to **Duncan Ban MacIntyre** ("ban" meaning "fair"), born near Loch Tulla in Glenorchy in 1724. He was a Gaelic poet who, in protest at the Highland Clearances, wrote a famous poem in praise of the fox as it hunted the sheep. In 1746 he fought on the Hanovarian side against Charles Edward Stuart at the Battle of Falkirk, and later wrote a humorous poem about it.

KILMELFORD

11 miles S of Oban on the A816

To the west of this little village, near the shores of Loch Melfort, there was once a gunpowder mill, one of the many small industries that dotted Argyll. In the kirkyard of the small **Kilmelford Parish Church** of 1785 are some gravestones marking the burial places of people killed while making the "black porridge".

It was at Loch Melfort, in 1821, that one of Scotland's most unusual weather phenomenons took place, when it rained herrings. The likeliest explanation is that the brisk south westerly which was blowing at the time lifted the herring from the loch and deposited them on dry land.

ARDUAINE

15 miles S of Oban on the A816

The 50-acre **Arduaine Gardens** (National Trust for Scotland) are situated on a south-facing slope overlooking Asknish Bay. They are another testimony to the mildness of the climate on Argyll's coast, and have a wonderful collection of rhododendrons. There are also great trees, herbaceous borders and a diversity of plants from all over the world. They were laid out by James Arthur Campbell, who built a home here in 1898 and called it

Arduaine, which means "green point". It was acquired by the NTS in 1992.

DALAVICH

13 miles SE of Oban on a minor road off the B845 on the banks of Loch Awe

If you follow the B845 south from Taynuilt along Glen Nant, then turn south west onto a minor road near Kilchrenan, you will eventually reach the **Dalavich Oakwood Trail**. It is a two-mile long walk laid out by the Forestry Commission, with not only oaks, but also alder, hazel, downy birch and juniper. There are also small sites where 18th and 19th century charcoal burners produced charcoal for the Bonawe Iron Furnace near Taynuilt. Other woodland trails are the **Timber Walk** and the **Loch Avich**.

136 CUILFAIL HOTEL

Kilmelford

A traditional Highland inn that offers a great Scottish welcome, an informal atmosphere and great food and drink

see page 485

137 CRAOBH HARBOUR COTTAGES

Craobh Haven

Six beautifully equipped self-catering cottages, right on the shoreline, in a picturesque, modern village with a marina.

see page 488

138 LUNGA ESTATE

Craobh Haven

A traditional Highland estate, on Scotland's western seaboard, that offers the very best in B&B and self-catering accommodation.

see page 487

Inner Hebrides

The Inner Hebrides, unlike the Western Isles, is not a compact geographical unit. Rather it is a collection of disparate islands lying off the Argyll coast, and forming part of that county (apart from Skye, which is part of the Highlands). Each island has its own distinct character, with sizes ranging from the 87,800 hectares of Mull (the third largest of Scotland's islands) to the 33 hectares of Staffa and the 877 hectares of Iona.

Not all the islands are inhabited, and of those that are, most have seen a substantial drop in population since the 19th century. Some of the uninhabited ones had people living on them at one time, and the remains of cottages and even old chapels, are still to be found. The names trip off the tongue like a litany, and some, to English ears, are decidedly unusual. Mull; Muck; Rum; Eigg; Coll; Canna; Tiree; Islay; Jura; Colonsay. All have their origins in the Gaelic, and in some cases, the Norse tongue.

And each island is different. Lismore, for instance, is flat and fertile, while Jura is mountainous. Mull is easily accessible from the mainland, while Canna, beyond Rum, is remote. Islay (pronounced "Eyelah") and Jura are the most southerly, and lie off the western coast of the Mull of Kintyre, from where they are reached by ferry. Islay is where you will find, at Finlagan, the capital of the ancient Lordship of the Isles. It is also an island famous for its distilleries, which make a peaty, dark malt. Tiree is said to be the sunniest spot in Britain, though it is also one of the windiest. It is low lying, and its name in Gaelic, "Tir an Eorna" actually means "the land below the sea". It is now famous for its surfing beaches, and many championships are held there.

Even though most of the islands lie well away from the mainland, they have still been influenced by Lowland Scots and English sensibilities. Rum has changed its name three times over the last century. Originally it was Rum, then, when the Bullough family bought it in the late 19th century, they changed it to Rhum in deference to their teetotal beliefs. In 1957 the island was bought by Scottish Natural Heritage and the name changed back to Rum.

Places like Mull and Skye are proving to be popular retirement spots, and the islanders have a name for Lowland Scots and English people who settle there - "white settlers". Though there has been some grumbling in the past about incomers seeking to impose English values on what is essentially a Gaelic culture, they are generally welcomed.

The Inner Hebrides can also claim to have the most sacred place in Scotland, if not Britain. Iona, off the west coast of Mull, was where St Columba established his great monastery, and from where missionaries set out to convert the northern lands. St Columba was not the first man to bring Christianity to Scotland - that honour goes to St Ninian - but he was the most influential, and we know a lot about his life, thanks to a biography written by St Adamnan, ninth abbot of Iona, almost a 100 years after he died. Though some of it is an uncritical hagiography, there is enough to see the man behind the venerated saint. He tells of someone who was all too human - vengeful yet forgiving, impetuous yet thoughtful, arrogant yet unassuming and boastful yet modest. Today Iona is still a place of pilgrimage, though most people now come as tourists to see and admire the later abbey buildings and experience that feeling of calm for which the island is famous.

In the Dark Ages, Irish missionaries sailed the waters between the islands, establishing preaching stations, chapels, crosses, monasteries and abbeys. So much so that their names are remembered today, with churches still being dedicated to them.

There are other sacred sights in the Inner Hebrides, such as the ruins of Oronsay Priory, the Columban remains on Eileach an Naoimh, part of the Garvelloch group of islands, and the remains of the cathedral on Lismore, built on the site of a Celtic monastery. All have an air of calm about them, and all are well worth visiting.

On islands in Loch Finlaggan, west of Port Askaig (where there is a ferry to Feolin Ferry on Jura and West Loch Tarbert on the Mull of Kintyre) you will find the ruins of the medieval centre of the Lordship of the Isles, with a visitor centre close by. This is the heartland of the MacDonalds, who were descended from Somerled, the first Lord of the Isles, who died in 1164. Their territory stretched from the Outer Hebrides in the north to the Mull of Kintyre in the south. The important remains are to be found on two of the islands in the loch, Eilean Mor (the Great Island) and Eilean na Comhairle (the Council Island) Ancient burial slabs are thought to mark the graves of important women and children, as the chiefs themselves would have been buried on Iona.

ISLAY

35 miles SW of Inveraray in the Atlantic Ocean

Islay's relatively mild, wet climate has meant that the island has been inhabited for thousands of years. Clan Donald, which claims descent from Somerled, made the island the centre of their vast Lordship of the Isles, which at one time was almost a separate kingdom beyond the reach of Scottish monarchs. It is a truly beautiful island, with a range of hills to the east rising to 1,500 feet, and low, fertile farmland. It is famous for its distilleries, with over four million gallons of whisky being produced each year. Most of them have tours explaining the distilling process, and offer a dram at the end of it. An Islay malt has a peaty taste all of its own, due to the grain being dried over peat fires.

Close to Port Askaig itself are the **Bunnahabhain** and the **Caol Ila** (pronounced "Cul Eela", meaning "Sound of Islay") distilleries. To the east of **Port Ellen** (which also has a ferry to Tarbert) are the distilleries of **Lagavulin, Laphroaig** and **Ardbeg**.

The ruins of **Dunyveg Castle**, a MacDonald stronghold, sit near Lagavulin. At one time it was owned by a man called Coll Ciotach, or "left handed Coll". While he was away on business, the castle was captured by his enemies the Campbells, and his men taken prisoner. They then waited for Coll to return so that they could overpower him. But one of the prisoners was Coll's personal piper,

and when he saw his master approach the castle, he alerted him by playing a warning tune. Coll escaped, but the piper had his right hand cut off, and never again could play the pipes. It's a wonderful story, though whether it is true or not is another matter, as the legend is also associated with other castles in Argyll, notably Duntroon.

Near Ardmore Point on the eastern side of the island is the **Kildalton Cross and Chapel**. The incised cross - the most complete cross of its kind in Scotland - dates from the 9th century. **Bowmore**, on the A874 beside the shores of Loch Indaal, has one of only two round churches in Scotland. It was built in 1767 by Daniel Campbell, who reckoned that, having no corners, the devil could not hide anywhere within it. The **Islay Columba Centre**, on the site of an old hospital at Bowmore, is a college that offers qualifications in Gaelic language and heritage, and is linked to the University of the Highland and Islands.

Bowmore Distillery - the oldest (founded in 1779) and one of the most famous on the island - can be visited. North of Bowmore, near Bridgend, is an Iron Age fort with the wonderful name of **Dun Nose Bridge**, and to the southwest of the village, at the tip of the Mull of Oa (pronounced "oh"), is the **American Monument**, which commemorates the 431 American sailors lost when HMS Otranto, which was carrying American troops to Glasgow and Liverpool, was in collision with HMS Kashmir in October 1918. Many of the bodies were washed up at the foot of the cliff. In February 1918 another disaster had taken place, when HMS Tuscania was torpedoed by a German U-boat, with the loss of 266 lives. This took place seven miles off the Mull of Oa, and many of the deaths took place when the lifeboats foundered at the foot of the cliffs at the Mull of Oa. Many of the dead from both sinkings were buried at **Kilchoman,** on the west side of the island, in a military cemetery.

On the opposite side of the loch is a peninsula called the Rhinns of Islay, and it is here that you will find the **Bruichladdich Distillery**, which, in 2003, found itself under surveillance by American intelligence agents, as the whisky distilling process is similar to the one used in making certain kinds of chemical weapons. At **Port Charlotte** is the **Islay Natural History Trust**, housed in a former whisky bond. It has a wildlife information centre, and provides information on the natural history and wildlife of Islay. Also in the village is the **Museum of Islay Life**, which tells of everyday life on the island through the ages, and has a special display on the many shipwrecks that have taken place off Islay's rugged coastline. Continue past Port Charlotte on the A874 and you will come to **Portnahaven**. About four miles from the village, and situated on the west side of the Portnahaven to Kilchiaran road, is the **Cultoon**

Stone Circle. Not all the stones have survived, but three are still standing and 12 have either fallen over at the point where they once stood or been removed. The site was excavated in 1974/75

Loch Gruinart, a sea loch on the northwest of the island, is famous for its many birds. The **Loch Gruinart Nature Reserve**, run by the Royal Society for the Protection of Birds, has a visitor centre which gives an insight into the lives of the many birds that can be seen here. For underwater life, there is the **Islay Dive Centre** in Charlotte street, Port Ellen, which organises dives at various points around the coastline.

Further north is the **Kilchoman Church and Cross**, accessed by another narrow track, which leaves the B8018 and goes past Loch Gorm. The cross dates from the 15th century, and was erected by "Thomas, son of Patrick". The church replaces a

The ruins of Kilchiaran Chapel, on the west coast of the Rhinns of Islay at Kilchiaran Bay, can be reached by car via a narrow track. Though its fabric is basically medieval, its origins go right back to the time of St Columba, who founded it in honour of his friend St Ciaran. There is an old baptismal font and some carved gravestones. The nearby beach is a favourite place for seals to sun themselves.

Ruined Croft on Islay

Near the northern coast of the island of Jura is the farmhouse of Barnhill, where George Orwell (real name, Eric Blair) wrote most of 1984. He moved into the farmhouse in April 1946. It was while he was there that he was diagnosed with tuberculosis. He died in 1950 (see also East Kilbride).

Just under a mile off Jura's north cost is the small island of Scarba. It has been uninhabited since the 1960s, though in the late 18th century it managed to support 50 people. It rises to a height of 1,473 feet, and has many Iron Age sites on its west coast. On the east coast are the ruins of Cille Mhoire an Caibel ("St Mary's Church of the Graveyard"). Many miracles were supposed to have taken place within the kirk in early medieval times.

medieval building which once stood here, but has been boarded up, and is in a bad state of repair.

Lord Robertson of Port Ellen, formerly George Robertson MP and Secretary General of NATO, was born on Islay in 1946.

JURA

24 miles W of Inveraray in the Atlantic Ocean

Jura is a sizeable island, and yet has no direct ferry link to the Scottish mainland. People wishing to travel to it must take the ferry from West Tarbert to Port Ellen on Islay, drive north to Port Askaig, and then take the short ferry crossing to Feolin Ferry on Jura.

It is an island of peat bogs, mists and mountains, its name coming from the Norse for "deer", which are plentiful here. The highest mountain, at over 2,500 feet, is **Ben an Oir** ("Mountain of Gold"), one of that range of three mountains known as the **Paps of Jura**.

The island's only road, the A846, takes you from **Feolin Ferry**, north along the east coast, where most of the island's population lives. You will pass **Jura House Garden** at Cabrach, with its collection of Australian and New Zealand plants, the seeds for which were specially brought over to Scotland. They thrive in this mild and virtually frost and snow free environment. There is also a cliff top walk. **Craighouse** is the island's capital, and here you will find the **Isle of Jura Distillery**, which you can visit by prior appointment. Behind the parish

church of 1776 is a room with some old photographs and artefacts of life on Jura through the ages. On the small island of Am Fraoch Eilean, in the Sound of Islay, are the ruins of **Claig Castle**, an old MacDonald stronghold. Ships passing through the Sound of Islay had to pay tolls to the MacDonalds.

A mile or so north of Craighouse is the ruined **Chapel of St Earnadail** ("Earnan's Dale"). St Earnan was St Columba's uncle, and the story goes that he wanted to be buried on Jura when he died. When asked where on the island, he replied that a cloud of mist would guide the mourners to the right spot. On his death, a cloud of mist duly appeared and settled where the ruins now stand.

The road then takes you north to **Ardlussa**, where it peters out. Within the old burial ground there is the tombstone of **Mary MacCrain**, who died in 1856, aged 128. They seem to have been long-lived on Jura, for the stone goes on to say that she was a descendant of Gillouir MacCrain,

"who kept one hundred and eighty Christmases in his own house, and died during the reign of Charles I".

At Glengarrisdale Bay, on the western coast, which can only be reached on foot, is the gruesome **Maclean's Skull Cave**. Up until the 1980s it contained a human skull and bones surmounting a small cairn. They were said to have belonged to a Maclean clansman who perished during a battle with the Campbells in the 17th century.

Between Jura and Scarba, in the Gulf of Corryvreckan, is the notorious **Corryvreckan** whirlpool. The name comes from the Gaelic Coire Bhreacain, meaning "speckled cauldron", and it is best viewed from the safety of the cliff tops on Jura (even though you have to walk about five miles from just beyond Ardlussa to get there) as it has sent many boats to the bottom. It is caused by the combination of an immense pillar of rock rising from the seabed and a tidal race, and the best time to see it is when a spring tide is running westward against a west wind. The sound of it can sometimes be heard at Ardfern on the mainland, over seven miles away. George Orwell nearly perished in it, and he later wrote an account.

Legend tells us that the whirlpool's name has a different derivation. A Norwegian prince called Breachkan was visiting the Scottish islands, and fell in love with a beautiful princess, a daughter of the Lord of the Isles. Her father disapproved of the young man, but declared that he could marry his daughter providing he could moor his galley in the whirlpool for three days.

Breachkan agreed to the challenge, and had three cables made - one of hemp, one of wool and one from the hair of virgins. He then sailed into the Gulf of Corryvreckan, and while there was a slack tide, moored his boat in the whirlpool. The tides changed, and the whirlpool became a raging monster. The hemp cable snapped on the first day and the wool one snapped on the second. But Breachkan wasn't worried, for he knew that the one made from virgins' hair would keep him safe.

But on the third day it too snapped, sending the prince to his death. It seems that some of the virgins from whom the hair had come were not as innocent as they had made out.

COLONSAY AND ORONSAY

40 miles W of Inveraray in the Atlantic Ocean

The twin islands of Colonsay and Oronsay are separated by an expanse of sand called **The Strand** which can be walked across at low tide. Half way across the strand are the remains of the **Sanctuary Cross**. In medieval times, any law-breaker from Colonsay who passed beyond it and stayed on Oronsay for a year and a day could claim sanctuary.

Oronsay is famous for the substantial ruins of **Oronsay Priory** (Historic Scoland), perhaps the most important monastic ruins in the west of Scotland after Iona. Tradition gives us two founders. The first is St Oran, companion to St Columba, who is said to have founded it in AD 563. The second is St Columba himself. When he left Ireland, the story goes, he alighted on Colonsay, and then crossed over to Oronsay, where he established a small monastery. However, he had made a vow that he would never settle where he could still see the coastline of Ireland. He could from Oronsay, so eventually moved on to Iona.

Colonsay, to the north, is the bigger of the two islands, and has a ferry service connecting its main village of Scalasaig to Oban.

It is a beautiful place, full of rocky or sandy coves and areas of fertile ground. Perhaps the most beautiful part is Kiloran Valley, which is sheltered and warm. So warm that palm trees and bamboo grow quite happily here. It is where Colonsay House, stands. It is said that the builder, Malcolm MacNeil, used stones from an old chapel which stood close by when building it in 1722. Its gardens are open to the public. At the north end of the island are the remains of Kilcatrin ("Catherine's Church").

On Seil's southern tip is the small ferry port of Cuan, where a ferry plies backwards and forwards to Luing. This is a larger island than Seil, though is more sparsely populated. Here too slate quarrying was the main industry. It is a quiet, restful place where seals can be seen basking on the rocks, as well as eagles and otters. Above the clachan of Toberonochy are the ruins of Kilchattan Chapel, with slate gravestones. One commemorates a Covenanter called Alex Campbell.

John, Lord of the Isles, founded the present priory in the early 14th century, inviting Augustinian canons from Holyrood Abbey in Edinburgh to live within it.

However, when the Lordship of the Isles collapsed in the 15th century, the MacDuffie's came to prominence on the island, and many of the priors and canons came from that clan. The church is 15th century, and the well-preserved cloisters date from the 16th century. A series of large carved grave slabs can be seen within the Prior's House, and in the graveyard is the early 16th century **Oronsay Cross**, intricately carved, and carrying the words *Colinus, son of Christinus MacDuffie*. Another cross can be found east of the Prior's Chapel, with a carving of St John the Evangelist at its head.

EILEACH AN NAOIMH
29 miles W of Inveraray in the Atlantic Ocean

This small island is part of the Garvellochs, and is famous for its ancient ecclesiastical remains

(Historic Scotland) dating from the Dark Ages, which include chapels, beehive cells and an ancient graveyard. A monastery was founded here in about AD 542 by St Brendan, better known as Brendan The Navigator. This was before St Columba founded the monastery on Iona. In the 10th century the monastery was destroyed by Norsemen, and the island remained uninhabited. It is reputed to be the burial place of both Brendan and Columba's mother, **Eithne**, a princess of Leinster. There is no ferry service to the island, though boats can be hired to take you there.

SEIL AND LUING
9 miles S of Oban on the B844

These two islands are known as the "slate isles" due to the amount of slate that was quarried here at one time. Seil is a genuine island, but is connected to the mainland by the **Bridge Across the Atlantic**, designed by Thomas Telford and built in 1792. It is more properly called the Clachan Bridge, with the channel below being no more than a few yards wide. It is a high, hump-back bridge to allow fishing boats to pass beneath.

It got its nickname because at one time it was the only bridge in Scotland to connect an island with the mainland. Now the more recent Skye Bridge dwarfs it. On the west side of the bridge, on the island itself, is a late-17th century inn called the Tigh na Truish, or "House of Trousers". This recalls the aftermath of the Jacobite

Bridge Across the Atlantic

Uprising, when the wearing of the kilt was forbidden. The islanders, before crossing onto the mainland by a ferry which preceded the bridge, would change out of their kilts here and into trousers.

On the west coast of the island is the village of **Ellenabeich**, with, facing it, the small island of Easdale. Ellenabeich was itself an island at one time, but the narrow channel separating it from the mainland was gradually filled up with waste from the local slate quarries. One of the biggest quarries was right on the shoreline, with its floor 80 feet below the water line A huge wall of rock separated it from the sea. During a great storm one night, the wall was breached, and the quarry filled with water. Now it is used as a harbour for small craft.

An Cala Garden dates from the 1930s, and is behind a row of cottages that was turned into one home. There are meandering streams, terracing built from the local slate, and wide lawns. A 15-feet high wall of grey brick protects the garden from the worst of the gales that occasionally blow in from the Atlantic.

One of the former quarries' cottages in the village has been turned into the **Ellenabeich Heritage Centre** with a number of displays connected with the slate industry.

Kilbarndon Parish Church, south of Balvicar, dates from 1866, and while looking unprepossessing from the outside, has a collection of five suberb stained glass windows, the most striking being the one showing Jesus quelling the storm on the Sea of Galilee.

LISMORE

7 miles N of Oban, in Loch Linnhe

Lismore is a small island, no more than a mile-and-a-half wide at its widest and ten miles long. It's name means "great garden", and is a low-lying, fertile island connected to Oban by a daily ferry. The main village and ferry terminal is **Achnacroish,** though a smaller pedestrian ferry plies between Port Appin on the mainland and the north of the island in summer. In the village is the **Commann Eachdraidh Lios Mor** (Lismore Historical Society), situated in an old cottage that re-creates the living conditions in the Lismore of yesteryear.

Lismore, before the Reformation, was the centre of the diocese of Argyll. When the diocese was first established, the cathedral was to be at Taynuilt, but it was felt that Lismore would provide a much safet site. (see also Taynuilt). **Lismore Cathedral** stood at **Kilmoluaig**, near the small village of Clachan. It was destroyed just after the Reformation, but the choir walls were lowered and incorporated into the present church in 1749. The site had been a Christian one for centuries, and was where St Moluag set up a small monastery in AD 564.

Lismore was a prized island even in those days, and it seems that St Moluag and another Celtic saint, St Mulhac, had a quarrel

Offshore from Seil lies the small island of Easdale, connected to Ellenabeich by a small passenger ferry. This too was a centre of slate quarrying, and in the Easdale Island Folk Museum you can see what life was like when the industry flourished. It was founded in 1980 by the then owner of the island, Christopher Nicolson.

On the west coast of Lismore, facing the tiny Bernera Island, are the ruins of the 13th century Achadun Castle, where the Bishops of Argyll lived up until the 16th century, and further up the coast are the ruins of Coeffin Castle, built by the MacDougalls in the 13th century. A legend says that it is named after a Norse prince called Caifen, whose sister died there, and haunted the place until her remains were taken back to Norway to be buried beside her lover.

139 TOROSAY CASTLE & GARDENS

Craignure

A fine example of a Scottish Baronial style house built in 1858 by David Bryce, with superb gardens.

 see page 488

about who should found a monastery there. They finally agreed to a race across from the mainland in separate boats, with the first one touching the soil of Lismore being allowed to establish a monastery. As the boats were approaching the shore Moluag realised that he was going to lose, so took a dagger, cut off one of his fingers and threw it onto the beach. As he was the first to touch the soil of the island, he was allowed to build his monastery. This was supposed to have taken place at Tirefour, where there are the remains of a broch now called **Tirefour Castle**, whose walls still stand to a height of 16 feet.

The highest point on the island, at a mere 412 feet, is **Barr Morr** (meaning "big tip"). For all its lack of height, there is a wonderful panoramic view in all directions from the top.

MULL

8 miles W of Oban, in the Atlantic Ocean

The island of Mull, with over 300 miles of coastline and 120 miles of roads, is the third largest island in Scotland (only Lewis/Harris and Skye are bigger). Within its 216,308 acres is a wild divergence of scenery, from rugged coastline to pasture and high mountains. The soils are, unlike some other rugged islands off Scotland's west coast, very fertile, so there is very little heather in the late summer and early autumn. However, it is still one of the most beautiful islands in the country, and it has the added advantage of being easy to reach, as

a car ferry plies all day between the pier at **Craignure** and Oban.

On its northeast side Mull is separated from Morvern on the mainland by the **Sound of Mull**, a deep sea trench that offers some of the best diving in Scotland. One of the favourite dives is to the Hispania, sunk in 1954 and now sitting at a depth of 30 metres. She was sailing to Sweden from Liverpool with a cargo of steel and asbestos when she hit Sgeir Mor ("Big Rock") reef. A story is told that the captain refused to leave the sinking ship, thinking that he might be blamed for the accident. As the crew were rowing to safety in high seas, the last they saw of him was a figure standing on the ship saluting as it slowly submerged.

Another, unusual, wreck is of the Rondo, which sunk in 1935. It sits vertically beneath the water, and though it is in two parts, it's bow is 50 metres below the surface, embedded in the sea bed, and its stern six metres below the surface of the water.

"Mull" comes from the Gaelic *Meall*, meaning a rounded hill. It is steeped in history, and was known to the Romans and Greeks. Even Ptolemy wrote about it, calling it *Maleus*. The highest peak, at 3,140 feet, is **Ben More**, the island's only Munro (a Scottish mountain above 3,000 feet).

It is home to 816 species of plants and trees, including 56 varieties of ferns, 247 varieties of seaweed, 22 species of orchid and 1,787 species of fungi. This diversity has made it popular with botanists, who visit the island throughout the year. In April many parts of Mull are carpeted with bluebells (known as harebells in England), with Grasspoint, a few miles south of Craignure, being a favourite place to see them.

The wildlife is just as diverse. You can see birds of prey such as golden eagles, sea eagles and buzzards (UK's commonest bird of prey), as well as polecats, mountain hares, badgers, pine martens, adders, slow worms, otters, mink (which escaped from captivity) and red squirrels. And the lonely coastal cliffs are home to wild goats. Take a sea trip and you can see bottlenose dolphins, porpoises, seals and even Minke whales.

Close to Craignure is **Torosay Castle**, with its fine gardens. The castle sits in 12 acres of grounds, and is a fine Victorian mansion completed in 1858 to the designs of David Bryce in the Scottish Baronial style. It was a favourite place of Winston Churchill in his younger days, and on display are photographs of him in the grounds. It is open to the public from April to October, while the gardens are open all year round. There is also a farm, which can be visited.

The walls of the front hall are crowded with red deer antlers. Though it is open to the public, it is still the family home of the Guthrie Jones family, who live on the upper floors. **Wings Over Mull** is at Auchnacroish House, close to the castle, and brooded over by the island's second highest mountain, Dun da Ghaoithe. It is a conservation centre for birds of prey, with owls being especially well represented, though you can also see hawks, kites, eagles and even vultures. There are flying displays every day during the season, and a display on the history of falconry.

To the east of Torosay Castle, on a small promontory, is **Duart Castle**, perched on the cliffs above Duart Point, and looking exactly like a Scottish castle should look. It is the ancestral home of the Macleans, and the clan chief still lives there. Parts of it go back to the 13th century, though it is such a well defended position that there was certainly a fort here long before that. The keep was dated from the 14th century, and was built by Lachlan Lubanach Maclean, who had married Elizabeth, a daughter of the Lord of the Isles and granddaughter of Robert ll of Scotland.

The buildings in the courtyard were added in the 16th century by Lachlan Mor ("Great Lachlan"). In 1688 the castle was sacked by the Campbells. It was confiscated after Culloden, as the Macleans fought alongside Charles Edward Stuart, but in 1911 the 26th MacLean chief, Sir Fitzroy MacLean, bought it back and restored it. "Maclean" means "son of Gillean", who is better remembered as "Gillean of the Battleaxe", "Gillean" means "follower, or servant, of John", and he was said to have descended from the ancient kings of Dalriada. The Macleans of Duart had the world's first recorded tartan - the Hunting Duart, first mentioned and described in 1587.

The Mull and West Highland Railway, a one-and-a-quarter mile long narrow gauge line, connects the castle with the pier. It has a gauge of 26 cm, and was opened in 1984 specifically to link the castle with the pier. In 1975 Torosay and its gardens had opened to the public, and there were fears that most ferry passengers would arrive on the island without cars. To make it easier to get to the castle, the line was built. It passes through woodland and coastal scenery, and at one point it even crosses over a peat bog, which brought special drainage problems when it was being built. The tiny engines that pull the carriages are a mixture of steam and diesel, with possibly the Lady of the Isles being the prettiest of the lot. It was the first engine on the line, though there are now six operating.

Duart Castle

Near Duart Point is the William Black Memorial, erected in memory of the 19th century writer William Black, who died in 1898. It is in the shape of a small, castellated lighthouse. Black wrote such books as Macleod of Dare, A Princess of Thule *and* Prince Fortunatus. *They were extremely popular in their day, though they are hardly ever read now. However a new version of* Macleod of Dare *was recently published.*

Some Maclean chieftains were unsavoury characters. The 11th chief, Lachlan Cattanach, was one such man. He detested his wife, as she could not provide him with an heir. Unfortunately for him, she was a sister of the Earl of Argyll, the most powerful man in the Western Highlands. Maclean hatched a plot. In 1497, he had her tied up and marooned on a rocky island below the castle that flooded at each high tide. He left her there for a whole night, and next morning noted that she had gone. Seemingly distraught, he later reported her sad death to the Earl, saying that she had been washed out to sea and drowned.

The Earl was sympathetic and overcome with emotion. He immediately invited him to his castle in Inveraray, and when the chief got there, he discovered his wife alive and well and seated at the top of the table beside her brother. A passing fisherman had rescued her. Nothing was said during the chief's visit, and the meal passed pleasantly, with much small talk and smiles all round. Lachlan and his wife eventually went home together, and still nothing was said. Terrified for his life, he treated his wife with the greatest respect, as he knew that retribution would eventually come, However. the event was never mentioned, even by Maclean's wife, and when she eventually died of natural causes, the chief heaved a great sigh of relief. He married again, and his second wife also died of natural causes, again without bearing him an heir. So he married a third time, his new wife eventually giving birth to a son. After the birth, in 1527, Maclean had to go to Edinburgh on business. While there, he was murdered in bed in mysterious circumstances and for no apparent reason. A rumour spread that the deed was carried out by a Campbell of Cawder. Retribution had come 30 years after the event.

A single track road leaves the A849 at Strathcoil, and heads south and then east towards Lochbuie. The 15th century **Moy Castle** sits on the shores of Loch Buie, and was the family seat of the Macleans of Lochbuie. Inside is a dungeon that floods twice a day with the incoming tide. In the middle of the dungeon is a stone platform where the prisoners had to huddle to keep dry. A small island a few miles south has possibly the most unusual name of any island in the Western Isles - **Frank Lockwood's Island**. It was named after the brother-in-law of a Maclean of Duart in the 19th century.

During the Jacobite Uprising in 1745 it was garrisoned by a troop of Campbells. In 1752 it was finally abandoned, and though it is still in a fine state of preservation, it is not open to the public. Close to the castle is one of the very few stone circles on Mull. There are nine stones, with the circle having a diameter of 35 feet.

To the west of Craignure, on the A849, is **Fishnish Pier**, where a ferry connects the island to Lochaline on the mainland, across the Sound of Mull. At **Salen** the road becomes the A848, and a couple of miles north of the village are the ruins of **Aros Castle, an** old MacDonald stronghold dating from the 13th century. **Pennygown Chapel**, now in ruins, has some carved grave slabs in its churchyard, though its most famous graves are found outside the graveyard. These are of a Maclean chief and his wife who were considered to be worshippers of the devil and were therefore buried as near to the chapel as possibly without actually being within the churchyard.

If you turn southwest along the B8035 you can visit the **Macquarie Mausoleum** at Gruline, where lies Major General Lachlan Macquarie, Governor General of New South Wales between 1809 and 1820, and sometimes called the "Father of Australia". It is a square, cottage-like building of local stone surrounded by a high wall. Also buried there is his wife Elizabeth and their son, also called Lachlan. Born on the island of Ulva in 1762, he was related to

the 16th and last MacQuarrie clan chief, and his mother was the sister of Murdoch Maclaine, chief of Lochbuie. He joined the army at the age of 14, and quickly rose through the ranks, serving in America, Egypt, Nova Scotia and India. In April 1809 he was appointed Governor of New South Wales. However, he suffered frequent bouts of ill health, and in 1820 he resigned, having turned New South Wales from a penal colony into a prosperous state.

He died in London in 1824, and his wife built the memorial above his grave in 1834. Now it is owned by the National Trust of Australia and maintained by the National Trust for Scotland. In the year 2000 the Australian government spent $A70,000 on its refurbishment. So famous is he in Australia that there are many towns, schools, universities, streets and even teashops named after him.

At this point Mull is no more that three miles wide, thanks to **Loch na Keal**, which drives deep into the island in a north easterly direction. Its shores are famous for their birdlife, which includes wigeon, Slavonian grebe, teal, golden eye, mallard, black-throated diver and shelduck. At the entrance to the sea loch is the 130-acre island of **Inch Kenneth**. Curiously enough, its geology is unlike that of Mull, and it is flat and fertile. The "Kenneth" in question is supposed to be St Cannoch, a contemporary of St Columba. The ruins of **St Kenneth's Chapel** date from the 13th century, and in the kirkyard

Mackinnon's Cave, on the Ardmeanach Peninsula near Balnahard, can only be reached at low tide, and great care should be taken if you visit. The cave goes hundreds of feet into the cliff face, and you'll need a torch if you want to explore it. It was visited by Dr Johnson, and is said to be the largest cave in the Hebrides, being over 90 feet high. A legend tells of a piper and his dog entering the cave in days gone by. The piper was killed by a witch who lived there, while his dog escaped. At the back of the cave is Fingal's Table, a flat rock used as an altar by early Celtic saints. Also on the Ardmeanach Peninsula is McCulloch's Tree, a huge fossil over 36 feet high and three feet in diameter. It is reckoned to be over 50 million years old. There is another fossil in a nearby cave. Part of the land here, including the fossils, is owned by the National Trust for Scotland. The cave can be reached by a track which branches off the B8035. To the south of the Ardmeanach Peninsula is Loch Scridain, the largest of the island's sea lochs. Like other locations on Mull, it is famous for its bird life.

Mull only has two large fresh water lochs. One is the wonderfully named Loch Ba, close to Gruline (not to be confused with Loch Ba on Rannoch Moor on the mainland), which has the remains of a crannog. The other, Loch Frisa, sits in inaccessible country in the north west of the island, and is famous for its bird life. Like Loch Ba, it has some good fishing.

are many wonderfully carved grave slabs. A tradition says that ancient Scottish kings were buried here if the weather was too rough for the royal barges to travel to Iona, but this is doubtful. One of the best grave slabs is that of an armed man lying with his head on a cushion and his feet on an unnamed animal of some kind. In one hand is a cannonball and in the other is a shield. The shield once had a coat of arms on it, but it has long since been weathered away.

Inch Kenneth was a favourite haunt of Diana Mitford, whose father Lord Redesdale owned the island. She married the infamous Oswald Mosley, the British Nazi. When her sister Unity was recovering from a suicide bid (she had tried to shoot herself in the head), she stayed on the island until she died in 1948 in an Oban hospital of meningitis brought on by the shooting.

Another owner at one time was Sir Harold Boulton, who wrote perhaps the most famous Jacobite song ever- *The Skye Boat Song*. Many people believe it is traditional, but in fact it was written in 1884.

When Johnson and Boswell were making their Highland tour in the 18th century, they were entertained on the island by Sir Alan Maclean, chief of the Macleans of Duart. Johnson described it as a "pretty little island" - praise indeed from a man who disliked most things Scottish.

Tobermory, Mull's capital, sits on the A848 to the north west of the island. Its name means "Mary's Well", and it is an attractive small burgh with many brightly painted houses and buildings fronting Tobermory Bay. Up until 1788 it was no more than a village, but in that year a small fishing station was established which changed its fortunes forever. The brightly painted houses date from that time, though they were not painted until many years later. **St Mary's Well**, which gave its name to the town, can be found in Dervaig Road. At one time its waters were thought to have healing qualities.

Tobermory was the setting for the popular children's TV programme **Balamory**, though the houses you see on the programme are even more brightly painted than the real ones thanks to the magic of television. **Mull Museum** is situated in the Columba building in Main Street, and has displays explaining the history of the island. It is open from Easter to October. There is also a small exhibition explaining Boswell and Dr Johnson's visit in 1773. Also in

Tobermorey

Main Street is the headquarters of the **Hebridean Whale and Dolphin Trust**, a research, education and conservation charity. There is a small visitors centre with displays on whales, dolphins and porpoises. Here you can watch videos of these animals in the Hebrides, as well as, in some cases, listening to their "songs".

At the bottom of Tobermory Bay lies the famous wreck of the 800-ton **San Juan de Sicilia**, (though some say it was the Florencia, or Florida) part of the Spanish Armada fleet. Fleeing in September 1588 from the English ships, she anchored in the bay to repair her hull and take on provisions. Being part of the Spanish fleet which had tried to attack Scotland's old enemy England, the local people made her welcome. Donald Maclean of Duart Castle agreed to supply the ship with provisions if its captain agreed to pay for them and give him 100 soldiers to attack his enemies on Coll.

The Spanish captain agreed, and provisions were taken on board while repairs were carried out. However, Maclean suspected that the captain would try to sail from the harbour without honouring his part of the bargain. He therefore boarded the ship and blew it up, making good his own escape. She sank in 60 feet of water, taking 350 Spaniards with her. Stories started circulating that she had 30 million gold ducats aboard her, and though some items were recovered (which can now be seen in the local museum), successive dives to locate the ducats failed. The first dive was in the early 17th century, when the Earl of Argyll sent men down to the wreck. Successive dives, including one by the Royal Navy, have recovered small items such as a skull, cannon shot, pieces of wood and even a gold coin. A rumour started circulating that the ducats had actually been recovered in secret, and lay hidden at Aros Castle. Sir Walter Scott owned a writing case made of wood from the wreck, and it is said that the Queen owns a snuff box made from the wood, The ship now lies completely covered in silt, and it is unlikely that anything will ever be recovered from her again (see also Fort William). Protecting Tobermory Bay is **Calve Island**, close to which there is plenty of good diving. Tobermory has one of the island's three ferry links with the mainland, this one plying to Kilchoan on the Ardnamurchan Peninsula.

Glengorm Castle lies a few miles west of Tobermory, at the end of a single track road. It was built in 1860 for local landowner James Forsyth, who instigated the Clearances in the area, removing crofters from their land and replacing them with the more profitable sheep. It is not open to the public, though there is a flower garden and a market garden here where you can buy plants and vegetables. There is also a coffee shop. At **Bloody Bay** about a mile east of the castle a battle was fought in 1480 between the last

The Tobermory Distillery is the only distillery on the island, and is one of the oldest in Scotland. It dates from 1798, when a local merchant called John Sinclair was granted a license to distil spirit from the local grain. It now makes five distinct single malts, and there is a visitor centre and shop.

The ruins of Aros Castle lie a mile or so north west of the village of Salen, south east of Tobermory. They date mainly from the 13th and 14th centuries. Originally built by the MacDougalls, the castle later became the Mull base for the Lords of the Isles, and was the most important place on the island up until the mid 18th century. In 1608 clan chiefs were invited to the castle by Lord Ochiltree, lieutenant to James VI. The chiefs, suspecting nothing, boarded Ochiltree's ship, The Moon, and sat down to dine. However, Ochiltree had an ulterior motive. He calmly stood up and announced that they were all prisoners of the king, as they had plotted against James VI and were rebellious and disloyal. The chiefs tried to leave the ship, but it was too late. It had weighed anchor and was now sailing south. The chiefs were later imprisoned in Blackness, Stirling and Dumbarton castles until they agreed to swear undying loyalty to their king. The castle later passed to the Campbells, and after 1690 it was allowed to become ruinous.

Lord of the Isles and his son Angus, who was aided by the mighty Crawford and Huntly families.

The narrow B8073 rises up from Tobermory and passes through **Dervaig,** reckoned to be the loveliest village on the island. It is home to the 38-seat **Mull Little Theatre**. According to the Guinness Book of Records, it is the smallest professional working theatre in the world, and puts on a season of plays every year to packed audiences. It was founded in 1966, in the converted coach house of a Free Church manse by Barrie and Marianne Hesketh, professional actors who had settled on Mull to bring up their children. Now it not only presents plays within the tiny theatre, it tours the Highlands and Islands as well. At the end of 2006 it may have to relocate, and plans are being made to build an entirely new theatre two miles outside Tobermory at Aros Park, which will open some time in 2007. At the **Old Byre Heritage Centre** in Glen Belart, Mull's visitors can learn about the island's history and heritage. There are also displays on natural history, and a half hour video.

The B8073 continues on to the small village of **Calgary**, on Calgary Bay. The name in Gaelic means the "harbour by the dyke", the dyke being a natural basalt formation. Here you will find what is possibly the best beach on the island, with vast stretches of white sand. In 1883 Colonel J.F. Macleod of the Royal North West Mounted

Police holidayed in Calgary, and was so impressed by the scenery that he named the Canadian city after it. The **Calgary Art in Nature**, a woodland walk, has many outdoor sculptures on display. There is also a gallery and tearoom, as well as workshops in summer.

The road continues in a south easterly direction along the shores of **Loch Tuath**, giving views across to the islands of **Ulva**, visited by Boswell and Johnson in 1773, and **Gometra**. The ancestors of David Livingstone, the African explorer and missionary, came from Ulva (see also Blantyre). From the 10th century until the 19th century, when it was sold to pay off debts, the island was owned by the MacQuarries. In 1773 Boswell and Johnson visited Ulva, and was entertained by the then MacQuarrie chief. Though they found their host to be a charming, intelligent man, Boswell wrote that the house was "mean", and that the chief was burdened with debts. At one time there was a great piping school on the island.

To summon the privately-owned ferry to Ulva, visitors slide back a small white panel to uncover a red panel which can be seen from the island. At the ferry point on the island is the small **Ulva Heritage Centre**, housed in a restored thatched cottage, with attached tearoom. To the west of Ulva is the smaller island of Gometra, connected to Ulva by a causeway over **Am Bru**, a narrow channel. It has been uninhabited since 1983, though Gometra House can still be seen. Since early times, Gometra was owned by the monastery of Iona, and indeed was known as "Iona's granary" on account of the crops grown there. Later it was acquired by the Campbells when James VI abolished the title of Lord of the Isles.

The B8073 then swings east along the northern shores of Loch na Keal before joining the B8035, which, if you turn right, takes you along the southern shore of Loch na Keal and eventually on to the A849.

Pennyghael, gateway to the Ross of Mull, sits just off the A849, on the way to Fionnphort and the ferry for Iona. Nearby is the **Beaton Cairn and Cross**, which commemorates the hereditary doctors of the Lord of the Isles, known as the "Ollamnh Muileach", or Mull doctors. A narrow road branches south at Pennyghael, taking you to the southern shore of the Ross of Mull at Carsaig. If you walk westwards along the beach you will reach the **Nun's Cave**, which has Celtic Christian carvings. The cave got its name because the nuns of Iona Nunnery are supposed to have hidden here during the Reformation. The spectacular **Carsaig Arches** is further on, at Malcolm's Point. They were once caves, but the sea has eroded the 600-feet high cliffs behind them and left the arches standing. Part of the 1945 film *I Know Where I'm Going*, set in the Scottish islands, was filmed here and at other places on Mull.

Bunessan, nine miles west of Pennyghael, sits on the small Loch na Lathaich, which is a favourite anchorage for small boats and yachts. Next to the village hall, in a Portacabin, is the **Ross of Mull Historical Centre**, which gives information about the history, wildlife and people of the area. One mile east of the village is a simple memorial to **Mary MacDonald**, who died in 1872. She spoke Gaelic, and in that tongue wrote the words to the famous hymn *Child in a Manger*. She set it to an old Highland tune which is now called "Bunessan". Nowdays it is more recognisable as the melody for *Morning Has Broken*.

At the end of the A849 is **Fionnphort** (pronounced "Finnafort", meaning "fair port"), the ferry terminal for Iona. Before crossing, a visit to the four-star **Columba Centre** (Historic Scotland) should prepare you for what you'll find on the island. On the shore stands **Fingal's Rock**, supposedly thrown by the giant Fingal while in a bad temper as he travelled from Ireland to Staffa.

IONA

36 miles W of Oban off the coast of Mull

No tourists' cars are allowed on Iona (National Trust for Scotland), though it is so small (no more than three miles long by a mile and a half wide) that everything on it can easily be visited on foot. It is one of the most sacred spots in Europe (and unfortunately, during the summer months, one of the busiest), and was where **St**

The Treshnish Islands is a small chain of islands well to the west of Gometra. The main islands are Lunga, Fladda, Bac Mor, Cairn na Burgh Mor and Cairn na Burgh Beg. Now uninhabited, they are a haven for wildlife, with Lunga especially being a favourite nesting site for puffins, shags, guillemots, razorbills and kittiwakes. On Cairn na Burgh are early Viking and Iron Age fortifications. Autumn is the breeding season for grey Atlantic seals, and many can be seen on all the islands' beaches at that time. Boat trips to the Treshnish Islands leave from various ports on Mull and from Iona.

273

Reilig Odhrain, Iona

Just west of the cathedral is the Tor Ab, a low mound on which St Columba's cell may have been situated. Of the many crosses on the island, the best are the 10th century St Martin's Cross, outside the main abbey door, and the 16th century MacLean's Cross.

Columba set up his monastery in AD 563. An old prophesy states that, seven years before Judgement Day, both Ireland and Islay will disappear under the waves during a great flood, but that Iona will float on the water.

From Iona, Columba evangelised the Highlands, converting the Picts to Christianity using a mixture of saintliness, righteous anger and perseverance. His monastery would have been built of wood and wattle, and little now survives of it apart from some of the cashel, or surrounding wall. The present **Iona Abbey** (Historic Scotland), on the site of the original monastery, was founded in 1203 by Reginald, son of Somerled, Lord of the Isles, though the present building is early 16th century. It was a Benedictine foundation, and later became a cathedral. By the 18th century it was roofless, and the cloisters and other buildings were in ruins. In the 20th century they were restored by the Reverend George MacLeod, a Church of Scotland minister who went on to found the **Iona Community** in 1938. It runs a small shop that sells a range of crafts and gifts.

Beside the cathedral is the **Reilig Odhrain**, or St Oran's Cemetery. Within it is the **Ridge of the Chiefs**, which is supposed to contain the bodies of many West Highland chiefs who were buried here in medieval times. Close by is the **Ridge of the Kings**, where, it is claimed, no less than 48 Scottish, eight Norwegian and four Irish kings lie buried, including Macbeth. However, modern historians now doubt if any kings are buried there at all apart from some from ancient Dalriada. They say that the supposed burials were a "marketing exercise" by monks wishing to enhance the status of their abbey.

One man who does lie within the cemetery is **John Smith** the politician, who was buried there in 1994 (see also Ardrishaig and Dunoon). **St Oran's Chapel**, near the cemetery, was built as a funeral chapel in the 12th century by one of the Lords of the Isles. The ruins of **St Mary's Nunnery** are near the jetty, and date from the 13th century. It too was founded by Reginald, and he placed his sister Beatrice in charge as prioress. A small museum has been established in the **Chapel of St Ronan** close to the ruins.

In the former parish church manse (designed by Telford) is the **Iona Heritage Centre**, which traces the history of the people who have lived on the island throughout the years.

STAFFA

34 miles W of Oban in the Atlantic Ocean

The most remarkable feature of this small uninhabited island is **Fingal's Cave**, which was visited in August 1829 by the composer Felix Mendelssohn. Though he found Edinburgh delightful, he was less enamoured of the Highlands, which he declared to be full of "fog and foul weather". When he made the boat trip to see the cave, he was violently seasick and called the cave "odious". However, it later inspired one of his most famous works, the **Hebrides Overture**.

Other visitors have included Queen Victoria, Keats, Wordsworth and the painter Turner, who afterwards painted *Staffa: Fingal's Cave*. The cliffs are formed from hexagonal columns of basalt that look like wooden staves, some over 50 feet high. The Vikings therefore named the island *Stafi Øy* (Stave Island) from which it got its modern name.

Boat trips to the island are available from Mull and Iona.

COLL AND TIREE

50 miles W of Oban in the Atlantic Ocean

These two islands, lying beyond Mull, can be reached by ferry from Oban. They are generally low lying, and can be explored by car in a few hours. The ferry first stops at **Arinagiour**, Coll's main village before going on south to **Scarinish** on Tiree.

Robert the Bruce granted Coll to Angus Og of Islay, and it was Angus who was responsible for building **Breachacha Castle** (not open to the public) to the south of the island. Later it was owned by the Macleans of Coll, the MacNeils and the MacDonalds. The 13th chief of the Macleans of Coll, Lachlan, employed a personal harpist to serenade him when he stayed in the castle. He was an astute man, and refused to send his clansmen to support the Jacobite Uprising, not because he disagreed with it, but because he saw from the outset that it was a lost cause. The present castle, which is largely 15th century, was restored in 1965.

Cille Ionnaig is a ruined chapel standing off the B8072 to the north of the island. It contains the grave of Donald Maclean, who was drowned in 1774. He was the young man who shared a bed with Boswell when he and Johnston visited the island the previous year.

Tiree means the "land of corn", as it is one of the most fertile of the Inner Hebridean islands. It is sometimes called "Tir fo Thuinn", meaning the "land beneath the waves", because of its relative flatness. Its highest peaks are **Ben Hynish** (460 feet) and **Ben Hough** (387 feet). In the south eastern corner of the island is the spectacular headland of **Ceann a'Marra**, with its massive sea cliffs. They are home to thousands of sea birds, and on the shoreline you can see seals basking in the sun.

Tiree has the reputation of being the sunniest place in Britain, though this is tempered by the fact that it is also the windiest. This has

It was in Coll that an incident called the Great Exodus took place. In 1856 the southern part of the island, which was the most fertile, was sold to one John Lorne Stewart. In spite of protests from the crofters who farmed there, he raised their rents to a level they could not afford. So, in 1861, the tenants took matters into their own hands. Overnight, they all left their crofts and moved north to the less hospitable lands owned by the Campbells, where the rents were reasonable. Lorne Stewart was powerless to stop them leaving, though in truth this may have been what he wanted, as, soon after, he introduced Ayrshire dairy cattle onto his lands, which proved more profitable.

Skye

The remains of a stone broch called **Dun Mor Vaul** lie west of Vaul Bay. It dates from the 1st century BC, and still has the remains of 12 feet thick walls.

SKYE

50 miles NW of Oban in the Atlantic Ocean

The new **Skye Road Bridge** opened in 1995 amid controversy over its tolls, although it is now toll-free. Skye is one of the most beautiful and haunting of the Inner Hebrides, and the place has beauty and history aplenty.

On average, it has more sunshine than the Scottish mainland, though it also has a lot more rain. In fact, in some of the more mountainous areas the average rainfall is 118 inches a year, compared to a UK national average of just over 39 inches. However, rainfall is much less on the lower, coastal areas.

Its name may come from the Norse word *skuy* meaning misty, and it is an apt description of an island that seems to get more beautiful the cloudier and mistier it becomes. Another possible derivation of the name is from the Gaelic *sgiath*, meaning "winged", and a glance at a map will show you that the island does indeed look as if it has wings. Nowadays Gaelic speakers know it as *Eileen à Cheo*, meaning the "Misty Isle". It is one of the few Inner Hebridean islands that has seen an increase in population over the last few years, due to people from the mainland settling there to find a better quality of life.

---

140 THE MACKINNON COUNTRY HOUSE HOTEL

Kyleakin

A wonderful hotel offering a relaxed, friendly atmosphere, great Scottish hospitality and fine food.

🛏 ❙❙ *see page 489*

---

made the island the windsurfing capital of Scotland. Near Vaul to the northeast of the island is a curious marked stone called the **Ringing Stone**, which, when struck, makes a clanging noise. Legend says if it is ever broken the island will disappear beneath the Atlantic. At Sandaig is the tiny **Sandaig Island Life Museum**, housed in a row of restored thatched cottages.

The **Skerryvore Lighthouse Museum** at Hynish, opened in 1987, tells the story of the Skerryvore lighthouse, ten miles to the south on rocks surrounded by open sea. It was designed by Alan Stevenson, uncle of Robert Louis Stevenson, and completed in 1842. The museum is within houses built for the Skerryvore workers.

The island has been inhabited for thousands of years, and has many ancient cairns, standing stones, stone circles and burial mounds. St Columba is said to have visited and baptised a Pict there by the name of Artbranan. He was an old man - a chieftain of a Geona tribe - and Columba had to talk to him through an interpreter. Later the Vikings raided the island, and then settled, bringing many Norse place names with them.

At **Kyleakin**, near the bridge, is the **Bright Water Visitor Centre**, with tours to the island nature reserve of *Eilean Ban* ("White Island") beneath the bridge. This was where Gavin Maxwell, author of *Ring of Bright Water,* lived between 1968 and his death in 1969 (se also Monreith). Nearby are the ruins of **Castle Moil**, which was a stronghold of Clan Mackinnon. Legend says it was built by a Norse princess called "Saucy Mary" who had married a Mackinnon chief, and who laid a chain from the castle to the mainland, demanding payment from passing ships. It is totally untrue, as the Mackinnons only settled there in the 15th century. In the 17th century they abandoned the castle, and it gradually fell into disrepair.

Perhaps the most famous features on the island are the **Cuillin** (never "Cuillins" in the plural), a range of mountains in the south east of the island. They are divided into the Black Cuillin and the Red Cuillin. The former are made from hard rock that has been shaped into jagged peaks and ridges by the last Ice Age, while the latter are of soft granite which has been weathered by wind and rain into softer, more rounded peaks. Though not the highest, they are perhaps the most spectacular mountains in Scotland, and a challenge to any climber. The highest peak is **Sgurr Alasdair**, at 3,257 feet.

The A87 leaves the Skye Bridge and heads westwards, hugging the north coast and passing through **Broadford**, one of its main settlements. At Harrapool is the **Skye Serpentarium Reptile World**, an award winning reptile and snake exhibition. There are regular handling sessions (if you are up to it). The road then passes through Sconser, the southern terminus of a ferry linking Skye to the smaller island of **Raasay** (once visited by Boswell and Johnson), before reaching the island's main settlement of **Portree**.

Its name (*port an righ*, meaning "king's harbour") comes from a visit made to the place in 1540 by James V. Before that it was called Kiltaragleann, which in Gaelic means the "Church of St Talicarin in the Glen". Across the bay is **Ben Tianavaig**, which gives good views out towards the island of Raasay. The **Aros Experience** is on Viewfield Road on the south side of the town, and it incorporates a theatre, cinema, shops and exhibition area. **An Tuireann Art Centre**, on Struan Road off the A87 to Uig, is a gallery that presents exhibitions of contemporary art and crafts

277

144 CAFÉ ARRIBA

Portree

A fabulous, modern establishment that is a café by day and a smart, intimate restaurant in the evening.

| see page 491

145 URQUHART CALEDONIAN HOTEL

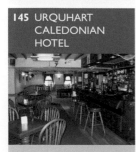

Portree

A child-friendly hotel, right in the heart of Portree, offering comfortable accommodation and great food at competitive prices.

⊨ | see page 491

146 GLENVIEW HOTEL

Staffin

A wonderful small hotel, best known for its superb cuisine as well as its five comfortable guest rooms.

⊨ | see page 492

The town is the gateway to the Trotternish Peninsula, which juts out for 20 miles into the Minch, that sea channel separating the Outer Hebrides from the mainland. A road from Portree follows its coastline right round until it arrives back at the town. **Dun Gerashader**, an Iron Age hill fort, lies about a mile north of Portree just off the A855. The fort still has some of its stone ramparts intact, and sits on a hilltop that gives good views. Also off the A855, about seven miles north of Portree is the 160 feet high pinnacle of rock known as the **Old Man of Storr**, which sits proud of a rocky hill, called simply The Storr.

To the north, the **Lealt Falls** are possibly the most spectacular on the island. Though not visible from the road, there is a lay-by where you can park your car then walk the hundred yards or so to the gorge and the falls themselves. A few miles away is **Kilt Rock**, a formation of basalt rocks above the shore that resembles the folds of a kilt. **Kilt Rock Waterfall**, which plunges down some cliffs into the sea, can also be seen. Across from the Kilt Rock viewpoint, but not within the village of Staffin, is the **Staffin Museum**, famous for its collection of dinosaur bones, the first ever discovered in Scotland. It is housed within an old schoolhouse. At **An Corran,** close to Staffin Bay, is a prehistoric rock shelter dating from 8,000 years ago.

North of Staffin, within the grounds of the Flodigarry Country House Hotel, is **Flodigarry House**, where Flora MacDonald and her husband Allan MacDonald settled in 1751. Some people imagine Flora was a simple, Highland lass who helped Charles Edward Stuart - disguised as her Irish maid Betty Burke - cross from the Western Isles to Skye by boat. She came, in fact, from a wealthy family who were tenant farmers on South Uist, though she herself was brought up on Skye and went to school in Edinburgh. Her husband, Allan MacDonald of Kingsburgh, was an officer in the Hanovarian army who later fought on the British side in the American War of Independence.

The sea crossing from Benbecula to Skye is remembered in the famous **Skye Boat Song**. However, it is not, as some people imagine, a traditional Jacobite song. It was written in 1884 by Englishman Sir Harold Boulton.

The ruins of **Duntulm Castle** date from the 15th century. It is an old MacDonald stronghold, and was abandoned in 1732 . An old legend tells of why it was abandoned. It seems that a nurse was looking after the child of the castle owner, and while she was cradling it in her arms and looking from a window, it fell to its death. From then on, the owner could not bear to live there. Another says that the castle was haunted, and the ghosts were making the owner's life unbearable. The likeliest reason for it being abandoned is that it fell into decay, so the chief moved out rather than repair it.

The **Skye Museum of Island**

Life at Kilmuir is near the northern tip of the Trotternish Peninsula, and is a group of seven thatched cottages furnished very much as they would have been in times long past. Here you can also learn about the crofter rebellions of the 19th century, plus exhibits connected with Charles Edward Stuart and Flora MacDonald. Also at Kilmuir is the grave of **Flora MacDonald**. She died in 1790, aged 65. After the Battle of Culloden, she was arrested and imprisoned first in Dunstaffnage Castle and then the Tower of London, but later released. Johnston met her on his Scottish tour and, though he was anything but a Jacobite, said that she would be long remembered by anyone who valued honour.

Loch Chaluim Chille was at one time one of Skye's largest lochs, being over two miles long. It was drained in 1829 to create grazing land, and now you can walk across the old loch bed (which in places is reverting to marshland, so take care) to what used to be islands to see the remains of an old Celtic monastery. It is a favourite place for birdwatchers.

The B886 heads north from the A850 onto the Waternish Peninsula before becoming a minor road. At its head are the ruins of **Trumpan Church**. In the churchyard is a stone with a hole through it. In olden times people on trial were blindfolded before being led to the stone, where they had to stick their arm through the hole. If they did it unaided they were declared innocent.

Fifteen miles west of Portree along the A850 is Dunvegan, famous for **Dunvegan Castle**, perched above the waters of Loch Dunvegan. It has been the home of Clan MacLeod for eight hundred years, and though much of it is Victorian, parts date back to the 13th century. In the drawing room is the famous Fairy Flag, revered by members of Clan MacLeod, which was supposed to bring success in battle. It is one of Clan MacLeod's most important possessions, and legends abound about its origins. Experts have examined the flag and say that the cloth is Middle East silk from either Rhodes or Syria. For this reason, some people have connected it to the Crusades. But the fabric dates from about AD 400 to AD 800, many years before the Crusades took place. Another theory says it was the battle flag of King Harold Hardrada of Norway, who was killed in 1066. But how did he get hold of a flag from the Mediterranean?

Others are content to put a fairy origin on it, citing the old legend about a MacLeod who fell in love with a fairy princess. He asked the fairy king for his daughter's hand in marriage, but the king refused, declaring that he would eventually bring her great sorrow when he died, as he was mortal and fairies lived forever. His daughter openly wept, and the father relented, saying that they could be married, but only for a year and a day. Nine months after the marriage, a son was born to the couple, and there was great rejoicing.

147 LODGE HOTEL

Edinbane

A historic old inn that offers superb food, comfortable accommodation, good drink and even the odd ghost or two!

🛏 ‖ *see page 493*

The Fairy Flag

Knock Bay

A magnificent, small luxury hotel on the Isle of Skye with an informal atmosphere where you will feel pampered and cosseted.

see page 494

However, a year and a day after the marriage, the fairy princess returned to her people, leaving behind her husband and son. Their farewells took place on the **Fairy Bridge** near Dunvegan, and the princess made the heartbroken chief promise that he would never give their son cause to cry, as she could hear him from Fairyland and would grieve.

After she had gone, the chief was inconsolable, and his clansmen decided to organise a great party to cheer him up. The chief took part, leaving his son in the care of a nurse. However, when she heard the laughter and music, she stole out of the nursery to take part, leaving the child alone. He began to cry, and no one could hear him apart from the fairy princess. She came back to the castle and lifted the child from his cradle, soothing him and singing fairy songs. When the nurse returned to the nursery, she heard the magical singing, and knew at once who it was. She burst into the room and found the child wrapped in a silk shawl.

She told the chief about the shawl, and he placed it in a locked case, vowing to take it with him wherever he went. Years later the son told his father that he miraculously remembered his mother returning. He told him that if Clan MacLeod ever needed help, he was to wave the shawl three times and a fairy army would rush to its aid.

Within the village of **Dunvegan** itself is the **Giant MacAskill Museum**, housed in the former thatched smithy belonging to Angus Mor Macaskill, who died in 1863 aged only 38. He was seven feet nine inches tall. He was born on Berneray in the Western Isles and died in Canada.

Across the loch, and reached by the B884, is the **Colbost Croft Museum**, based on a "black house" (a small traditional cottage of turf or stone, topped with a thatched roof). It shows the living conditions of islanders in the past, and features an illicit still. Black houses got their name, not because they were blackened inside by the peat fire, but to differentiate them from the "white houses" which were built in Victorian and later times, and which were more modern and usually painted white.

Travelling north from **Colbost** along a minor road takes you to Boreraig, and the **MacCrimmon Piping Heritage Centre**. The Macrimmons were the hereditary pipers to the MacLeods, and reckoned to be the finest pipers in the country. West of Colbost is the **Glendale Toy Museum**. Destroyed by fire in 2002, it has since reopened and claims to be better than ever. As well as old toys, it features modern ones from such films as Star Wars, as well as Barbie and Action Man.

Glendale was the scene of the famous **Battle of the Braes** of 1882, when crofters rose up against a tyrannical estate factor. The government had to send a gunboat to deal with the insurrection, and the ringleaders were subsequently imprisoned. The incident led, four years later, to the Crofters Holding Act, which gave them a more secure tenure on their land.

To the southeast of the island, on the **Sleat** (pronounced "Slate") Peninsula at Armadale, is the **Armadale Castle Gardens and Museum of the Isles**. It sits within a 20,000 acre Highland estate, once owned by the MacDonalds of Sleat, and was purchased by the Clan Donald Land Trust in 1971. The earliest parts of the castle date from the 1790s, when it was built by the first Lord MacDonald on the site of a farm and gardens where Flora MacDonald married in 1750. North of **Armadale**, is **Sabhal Mór Ostaig**, where short courses in Gaelic are offered.

Dunscaith Castle, the ruins of which lie on the western side of the peninsula near Tokavaig, was abandoned by the MacDonalds in the 18th century. Legend says that the castle was built by fairies in one night, and subsequently protected by a pit full of snakes. It was the home, the legend continues, of Scathath, the Queen of Skye, who taught the arts of war.

EIGG

42 miles NW of Oban in the Atlantic Ocean

In 1997 the island of Eigg was bought on behalf of its inhabitants by the Isle of Eigg Heritage Trust from the German artist who called himself "Maruma". Its most famous feature is the 1,277 feet high **An Sgurr**, which slopes gently up to a peak on one side, and dramatically plunges on the other.

Southwest of the main pier is St Francis's Cave, also known as the **Massacre Cave**. It got its name from a gruesome event in 1577, when nearly 400 MacDonalds took refuge there when pursued by a force of MacLeods. The MacLeods lit fires at the entrance to drive them out, and every one of the MacDonalds was suffocated to death. The story was given some credence when human bones were removed from the cave in the 19th century and buried. A nearby cave, MacDonald's Cave, is also known as the **Cathedral Cave**, as it was used for secret Catholic church services following 1745.

MUCK

39 miles NW of Oban in the Atlantic Ocean

The tiny island of Muck's improbable name comes from "eilean nam muc", meaning "island of pigs", though in this case the pigs may be porpoises, which are called "sea pigs" in Gaelic. It is reached by ferry from Mallaig, and is a low-lying island with good beaches. **Port Mor** is the main settlement and harbour, with, above it, an ancient graveyard and ruined

149 MORAR

Ardvasar

A superior, modern B&B establishment, with its own swimming pool, that is one of the most popular on the island of Skye.

see page 493

150 THE SHED

Armadale

A superb small restaurant that has a reputation that goes far beyond its immediate area for fine local produce beautifully cooked.

see page 495

At Kildonnan, on the west coast of Eigg, are the ruins of a 14th century church, built on the site of an ancient Celtic monastery founded by St Donan. The saint and his 52 monks were massacred in AD 617 by a band of Norsemen. The monks had just completed Mass and were in the refectory, which the Norsemen set alight. A legend says that a local woman, who felt aggrieved by the actions of the monks for some reason, bribed the Norsemen to commit the atrocity.

The Bullough Mausoleum in Glen Harris on Rum, to the south of the island, was built to take the bodies of Sir George, his father John and his wife Monica. It is in the form of a Greek temple.

church. On the south side of the Port Mor inlet are the scant remains of **Dun Ban**, a prehistoric fort. The highest point at 445 feet, is **Beinn Airein**, and from the top there is a good view of the whole of the island.

RUM

47 miles W of Fort William

When Sir John Bullough bought the island of Rum in 1888 he arrogantly changed its name to "Rhum", as he disliked the associations it had with alcoholic drinks. However, when the Nature Conservancy Council (now Scottish Natural Heritage) took over the island in 1957 they changed the name back to the more correct "Rum", meaning "wide island", and it has been that ever since. Nowadays it is a Special Site of Scientific Interest and a Specially Protected Area, as its plant life has remained almost unchanged since the Ice Age.

The main settlement is Kinloch, on the east coast. **Kinloch Castle**, overlooking Loch Scresort, was built by Sir George Bullough, John's son, as his main home on the island between 1901 and 1902. The sandstone for its building was brought all the way from Dumfriesshire and the soil for the garden from Ayrshire. Sir George was eccentric, and paid the builders two pence a day to wear kilts as they worked.

Kilmory, on the north coast of the island, has a fine beach and an old burial ground.

CANNA

60 miles NW of Oban in the Atlantic Ocean

Canna has been owned by the National Trust for Scotland since 1981, when it was given to them by Gaelic scholar John Lorne Campbell. It is about five miles long by just over a mile wide at its widest, and is usually sunny and mild. The remains of **St Columba's Chapel**, dating from the 7th or 8th centuries, with an accompanying Celtic cross, stand opposite the small island of Sanday, and have been excavated. **An Corghan**, on the east coast, is all that is left of a small tower house where a Clanranald chief imprisoned his wife, who was having an affair with a MacLeod clansman. At **Uaigh Righ Lochlain** can be seen remnants of Viking occupation, and at **Camas Tairbearnais**, a bay on the western side of the island, a Viking ship burial was uncovered. **Sanday** is a small island which lies off the southeast coast, and is joined to it by a bridge, and, at low tide, a sand bar. Canna is predominantly Catholic, with the Church of St Edward being on the smaller island. In 2001 it became the **St Edward's Centre**, opened by Princess Ann. Leased by the Hebridean Trust from the National Trust for Scotland, it can accommodate 12 students, and is affiliated to the University of the Highlands and Islands.

Canna is reached by ferry from Mallaig.

Perthshire, Angus & Kinross

The two counties of Perthshire and Angus straddle the Highland Boundary Fault, which separates the Highlands from the Lowlands, while Kinross, once Scotland's second smallest county, is wholly Lowland in character. So there is a wide variety of scenery within this area, from mountains, glens and lochs to quiet, intensely cultivated fields and picturesque villages.

Perthshire is a wholly inland county, a place of agriculture, high hills and Highland lochs. It is the county of Loch Rannoch and Loch Tummel, and of possibly the loneliest railway station in Britain, Rannoch, deep within the bleak expanse of Rannoch Moor. It is connected to Scotland's road network by the B846, which snakes west from Aberfeldy for many miles, but goes no further than the station. It is also the county of the Gleneagles Hotel, one of Britain's most luxurious, and of rich farmland surrounding Perth itself.

Blairgowrie is the centre of Scotland's fruit growing industry - fruit that once went to the Dundee jam makers.

The A9 from Perth heads north towards the Drumochter Pass, which reaches its highest point of 1,505 feet at the Perthshire - Inverness-shire border, overlooked by four Munros. On the way, it passes deeply wooded glens, and skirts such historic towns and villages as Dunkeld, Pitlochry and Blair Atholl. In fact, Perthshire likes to call

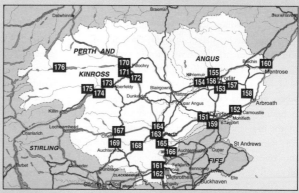

itself the "Big Tree Country", as it has some of the most remarkable woodlands anywhere in Europe.

Perth is a city, and before local government reorganisation in the '70s, had a lord provost, one of only six places in Scotland that could claim that distinction, the others being Edinburgh, Glasgow, Dundee, Aberdeen and Elgin. No one has ever specifically taken that honour away from it, so it remains a city still. It is often referred to as the "Fair City of Perth", and this is no idle description. It may be in the Lowlands, but it was never scarred by the industrial developments of the 19th century, as other places in the Lowlands were. It remains a confident, attractive place with many fine buildings and a good quality of life.

Angus has a coastline that takes in high cliffs and sandy beaches. The coastal towns are famous. Carnoustie, where the British Open is sometimes held; Montrose and its almost land-locked basin where wildfowl can be seen; and of course Arbroath, with the ruins of an abbey where one of the momentous documents in Scottish history was signed - the Declaration of Arbroath. Inland, the countryside is gentle and pastoral, with the glens of Angus, such as Glen Prosen, Glen Clova and Glen Doll, being particularly beautiful as they wind their way into the hills.

Dundee is the area's largest settlement, and the fourth largest city in Scotland. It is a place of industry, and sits on the north bank of the Firth of Tay. At one time it was one of the powerhouses of Scotland, relying on its three traditional industries of jute, jam and journalism. But it is an ancient place as well, and its roots go deep into Scottish history. One of Scotland's famous historical characters, John Graham of Claverhouse, adopted its name when he became 1st Viscount Dundee.

He was a man with an ambiguous reputation, being loved by some and loathed by others. To admirers of the Covenanters he is Bloody Clavers, a ruthless and cruel persecutor of those opposed to the introduction of bishops into the Church of Scotland. To admirers of the Jacobites he is Bonnie Dundee, a dashing and gallant supporter of the Stuarts who was killed fighting for his king at Killiecrankie in 1689.

Kinross, to the south east of Perthshire, sits in a great saucer shaped depression with, at its heart, Loch Leven. The main industry is farming, and the gentle countryside, ringed by hills, is well worth exploring if only for the sense of "getting away from it all". Loch Leven is famous for its fishing, and Vane Farm Nature Reserve was the first educational nature reserve in Europe.

Everywhere in Perthshire, Angus and Kinross there is history. The medieval cathedrals at Dunkeld and Brechin are well worth exploring. In AD 685, at Nechtansmere, a Pictish army under King Nechtan defeated the Northumbrians and secured independence from Anglian rule. The Battle of Killiecrankie in 1689 was the first of the Jacobite battles in Scotland.

Scone, outside Perth, was where the medieval Scottish kings were crowned as they sat on the Stone of Destiny; at Blair Atholl the Duke of Atholl keeps the only private army in Britain; Glamis Castle was the childhood home of the late Queen Mother; and Mary Stuart was held captive in a castle on an island in Loch Leven, later making a daring escape from it.

At Crook of Devon in Kinross a coven was discovered in 1662, with the witches being put on trial and subsequently executed. At Scotlandwell we have yet another place of pilgrimage. A friary once stood here, along with a holy well, and people came from all over Scotland seeking cures for their ailments. The well is still there, and the waters may still be drunk.

Then there are the literary associations. J.M. Barrie was born at Kirriemuir, and Violet Jacob was born near Montrose. Beatrix Potter regularly holidayed at Dalguise, near Dunkeld, and was influenced by its scenery. The Dundee publisher D.C. Thomson has given us a host of comic characters that have delighted children (and adults) for years, such as Desperate Dan, Beryl the Peril, Dennis the Menace, Lord Snooty, The Bash Street Kids and Oor Wullie. And no one can ever forget the contribution that Dundee's favourite poet, William Topaz McGonagall, has made to literature.

DUNDEE

Dundee is Scotland's fourth largest city, and sits on the banks of the Firth of Tay. It is a manufacturing town, at one time famous for the "three Js" of jam, jute and journalism. It also brims with history and heritage, and was granted royal burgh status in the 12th century, when it was one of the largest and wealthiest towns in Scotland. **Dundee Law** (571 feet) looms over the city, and from its summit there is a superb view south towards the Tay Bridges and Fife. A road and separate footpath (with a series of steps) take you to the summit, where there is a war memorial, an observation point and "fact panels". At one time a tunnel was bored through the flank of the hill to take a railway.

Dundee is joined to Fife by two bridges across the Tay, the **Tay Road Bridge**, opened in 1966, and the **Tay Rail Bridge**, opened in 1887. The road bridge (which replaced a ferry) opened up a huge area of north Fife to commuters wishing to work in Dundee, and also making it the main shopping centre for the area . The rail bridge replaced an earlier bridge, built in 1878. On the evening of 28 December 1879, during a violent westerly gale, the bridge collapsed while a train was crossing it. The 75 train passengers perished.

Though not born in Dundee, **William Topaz McGonagall** is looked upon as one of Dundee's great, if not overly-talented, literary figures. He later wrote a poem to commemorate the disaster, which has became almost as famous as the disaster itself:

Beautiful Railway Bridge of the
Silv'ry Tay!
Alas! I am very sorry to say
That ninety lives have been taken away
On the last Sabbath day of 1879,
Which will be remember'd for a very
long time.

It has been called, rather unfairly perhaps, "the worst poem ever written". Perhaps we should not judge it so harshly. McGonagall was a simple handloom weaver whose formal education stopped when he was seven years old, and he was trying to put into words the horror he felt at the tragedy.

He was born in Edinburgh in 1830, the son of Irish immigrants, and came to Dundee with his parents after having lived in Paisley and Glasgow. In 1877, he took to writing poetry, having felt "a strange kind of feeling stealing over me". He then wrote until he died in September 1902. His finest hour was the "knighthood" that was bestowed upon him, making him

Tay Rail Bridge

•

In 1999, The Verdant Works, in West Henderson's Wynd, was voted Europe's top industrial museum. Jute was once a staple industry in Dundee, employing over 40,000 people. Here, in a former jute mill, you are taken on a tour of the industry, from its beginnings in India to the end product in all its forms. You will see the processes involved in jute manufacture, you'll see the original machinery, and you'll see the living conditions of people both rich and poor who earned their living from the trade. There are interactive displays, film shows, and a guided tour.

•

151 MILLS OBSERVATORY

Dundee

The UK's only full time public observatory where you have the opportunity to view stars and planets through an impressive telescope.

 see page 495

"Sir William Topaz McGonagall, Knight of the White Elephant of Burmah". He used the title for the rest of his life, never once realising that it was a cruel joke.

The 160 feet tall **Old Steeple** of St Mary's Church, in the heart of the city, dates from the 15th century, and is reckoned to be one of the finest in the country. The rest of the building dates from the 18th and 19th centuries, and was once divided into four separate churches. Until the 1980s, when they finally amalgamated, there were still three churches within the building - the Steeple Church, Old St Paul's and St David's. The original medieval church had, it is said, the longest transepts of any church of its size in Europe.

Another reminder of Dundee's past is the **Wishart Arch** in the Cowgate. It is one of the city's old gateways, and from its top, George Wishart the religious reformer, is said to have preached to plague victims during the plague of 1544 (see also Montrose and St Andrews). Near the arch is the Wishart Church, where **Mary Slessor** used to worhip. She was born in Aberdeen in 1848, and moved to Dundee when she was 10. Inspired by David Livingstone, she went to Africa as a missionary, and died at Calabar in 1915.

St Paul's Cathedral in the High Street is the cathedral for the Episcopalian Diocese of Brechin. It was built between 1853 and 1855 to the designs of Sir George Gilbert Scott on the site of a medieval castle, and fragments of

the castle can still be seen within its grounds. In 1905 it became a cathedral. It contains the ornate tomb of Bishop Alexander Penrose Forbes, who was instrumental in having the cathedral built.

RSS Discovery, Captain Scott's ship, was built in Dundee and launched in 1901. It now forms the centrepiece of the five-star **Discovery Point**, at Discovery Quay. It was one of the last wooden three-masted ships to be built in Britain, and the first to be built solely for scientific research. You can explore the ship, "travel" to Antarctica in the Polarama Gallery and find out about one of the greatest stories of exploration and courage ever told.

At Victoria Dock you'll find **HM Frigate Unicorn**, the oldest British-built wooden frigate still afloat. It was built at Chatham in 1824 for the Royal Navy at a time when iron was beginning to replace wood in ship building, and carried 46 guns. The ship re-creates the conditions on board a wooden sailing ship during Nelson's time, with officers' quarters, cannons, and the cramped conditions within which the crew lived.

Sensation is Dundee's science centre. Located in the Greenmarket, it is a place where "science is brought to life" using specially designed interactive and hands-on exhibits. Here you can find out how a dog sees the world, how to use your senses to discover where you are, and why things taste good or bad. The latest exhibition is Roborealm, the only one of its kind in the world. It will give visitors a chance to interact with a team of robots. The **Mills Observatory** (see panel) in Balgay Park a mile west of the city centre and accessed from Glamis Road, also deals with matters scientific. It is Britain's only full time public observatory, and houses a ten inch Cooke refractor telescope. It also has a small planetarium and display area. It is named after a local businessman called John Mills, who, in the late 19th century, left a bequest to the city to build such an observatory. It was not built until 1935.

The **McManus Galleries** are housed within a Gothic-style building in Albert Square, and contain many 18th and 19th century Scottish paintings. Within it there is also a museum of more than local interest, with a particularly fine collection of artefacts from Ancient Egypt. The **Dundee Contemporary Arts Centre** in the Nethergate specialises in contemporary art and film, and has galleries, cinemas and workshops.

Dudhope Castle, at Dudhope Park in Dundee, dates originally from the 13th century, and was once the home of the Scrymgeour family, hereditary constables of Dundee. The present building dates from the late 16th century. In its time it has also been a woollen mill and a barracks. It now forms part of the University of Abertay and is not open to the public, though it can be viewed from the outside. And at the junction of Claypotts

Road and Arbroath Road is the wonderfully named **Claypotts Castle** (Historic Scotland), built between 1569 and 1588 by John Strachan. It was once owned by John Graham of Claverhouse, better known as "Bonnie Dundee". It can be viewed by prior appointment.

The ruins of **Mains Castle**, sometimes called Mains of Fintry, is in Caird Park, and was once owned by John Graham, a cousin of Viscount Dundee. It now houses a restaurant. To the east of the city is **Broughty Ferry**, once called the "richest square mile in Europe" because of the many fine mansions built there by the jute barons. Up until 1913, it was a separate burgh, with its own councillors and provost, but in that year it was absorbed into Dundee. The **Broughty Ferry Museum** is at Castle Green, and housed within a castle built by the Earl of Angus in 1496 as a defence against marauding English ships. It has displays on local history, and tells the story of Dundee's former whaling fleet, at one time Britain's largest. If you visit Broughty Ferry at New Year, you can see the annual **N'erday Dook** ("New Year's Day Dip") held on January 1st, when swimmers enter the waters of the Firth of Tay. It is organised by Ye Amphibious Ancients Bathing Association, one of the country's oldest swimming clubs, and is done for charity. It attracts about 100 - 150 bathers a year, and it is not unknown for the crowd of spectators, which can be over 2,000

On the Coupar Angus Road is Camperdown Country Park, Dundee's largest park. Its name celebrates the Battle of Camperdown, when the British defeated the Dutch fleet in 1797 at Camperdown off the Dutch coast. Commanding the British fleet was Admiral Adam Duncan, who bought the estate and called it Camperdown after he retired. It was his son who built Camperdown House (not open to the public). Within the park there is a wildlife centre, with a fine collection of Scottish and European wildlife, including brown bears, Scottish wildcats, wolves and bats. Templeton Woods, also within the park, is home to red squirrels, owls and roe deer. There is a woodland visitor centre which explains what can be seen. Next to Camperdown is Clatto Park, which has a 24 acre reservoir used for water sports.

strong, to be wrapped up in warm woollens, scarves and gloves as the swimmers enter the water dressed only in swimsuits. On some occasions, it has even been necessary to break up ice before entering the water (see also South Queensferry).

To the west of the city, on the north bank of the Tay, is the **Carse of Gowrie**, one of the most fertile areas of Scotland. The Dundee artist **James Macintosh Patrick**, who died in 1988, regularly painted scenes on the Carse. He is reckoned to be one of Scotland's finest 20th century landscape painters and etchers..

AROUND DUNDEE

MONIFIETH

6 miles E of Dundee on the A930

This little holiday resort sits at the entrance to the Firth of Tay, and has some good sandy beaches. Its golf courses were used in the qualifying rounds of the British Open. At one time it was an important Pictish settlement, and some Pictish stones were discovered at **St Rule's Church** that are now in The National Museum of Scotland in Edinburgh.

CARNOUSTIE

11 miles E of Dundee on the A930

Golf is king in Carnoustie. This small holiday resort on the North Sea coast hosted the British Open Championships in 1931 and 1999, and is a favourite destination for golfing holidays.

But it has other attractions. **Barry Mill** (National Trust for Scotland) is a 19th century working corn mill, though a mill has stood here since at least the middle of the 16th century. You can see the large water wheel turning, and also find out how corn is ground. There is an exhibition explaining the historical role of the mill, as well as a walkway along the mill lade. Three miles northwest of the town are the **Carlungie and Ardestie Souterrains** (Historic Scotland), underground earth houses dating from the 1st century AD.

North of the town are two country parks. **Monikie Country Park** was opened in 1981, and is centred on Monikie reservoir, built to supply clean water to the growing city of Dundee in 1845. **Crombie Country Park** is also centred on a reservoir dating from 1866, which was supplying Dundee with water until 1981. In 1993 it opened as a country park.

Carlungie Souterrain

BALGRAY

4 miles N of Dundee off the A90

Four miles north of the city centre, near Balgray, is the **Tealing Souterrain** (Historic Scotland), an underground dwelling dating from about AD 100. It was accidentally discovered in 1871, and consists of a curved passage about 78 feet long and seven feet wide with a stone floor. The **Tealing Dovecote** (Historic Scotland) dates from 1595 and was built by Sir David Maxwell of Tealing.

FOWLIS EASTER

6 miles W of Dundee on a minor road off the A923

This small village has one of the finest small churches in Scotland. The **Parish Church of St Marnan** dates from about 1453, and still has part of its rood screen, as well as medieval paintings dating to about 1541 and a sacrament house that is reckoned to be the finest in Scotland. Lord Gray built it on the site of an earlier church, which in turn was built in about 1242 by a member of the local Mortimer family as an offering to God so that her husband, who was fighting in the Crusades, might return safely. (see also Fowlis Wester).

Fowlis Castle, home of the Grays, dates from the early 16th century, and replaced an earlier structure. It is not open to the public.

GLAMIS

10 miles N of Dundee on the A94

Glamis Castle is famous as being the childhood home of the late Queen Mother and the birthplace, in 1930, of her daughter, the late Princess Margaret. The lands of Glamis (pronounced "Glams") were given to Sir John Lyon in 1372 by Robert II, the first Stewart king and grandson of Robert the Bruce, and still belong to the family, who are now the Earls of Strathmore and Kinghorne. In 1376 Sir John married Robert's daughter, Princess Joanna, and the castle has had royal connections ever since. The present castle was built in the 17th century to resemble a French château, though fragments of the earlier 14th century castle still survive in the tower.

Shakespeare's *Macbeth*, which he wrote in 1606, is set in Glamis, and Duncan's Hall, the oldest part of the castle, is said to have been built on the spot where Macbeth murdered Duncan. Shakespeare, like most playwrights, was more interested in drama than historical fact, and history tells us that Duncan most probably died in battle near Elgin. It may even be that Shakespeare visited Glamis as he and his troupe of actors were on their way to Aberdeen in 1599 to perform before James VI (see also Aberdeen).

Glamis has the reputation of being one of the most haunted castles in Scotland. There is a Grey Lady who haunts the chapel (said to be the aforementioned Janet), a Black Page, and a window which looks out from a room that does not appear to exist. Legend has it that in the room, which might be

Tragedy seems to stalk Glamis Castle. In 1537 Janet Douglas, the widow of the 6th Lord Glamis, was burnt as a witch in Edinburgh. The main instigator of the charges of witchcraft was the Scottish king, James V, a man who took an unhealthy interest in witches at the best of times. By the time of the charges, Janet had remarried, her second husband being Archibald Campbell. Both she and her husband were found guilty, and imprisoned in Edinburgh Castle. Though Archibald escaped Janet herself was burned on Castlehill . It was a totally trumped up charge, as Janet's grandfather had been Angus Douglas, 5th Earl of Angus. James hated the Douglases, and saw this as a way of dealing the family yet another blow. However, she was later declared innocent of all the charges, with the lands being restored to her son.

Angus Folk Museum, Glamis

153 THE TOLBOOTH

Forfar

A traditional pub and lively bistro selling great food, right in the heart of the historic market town of Forfar.

¶ see page 496

within the thickness of the walls of the castle, one of the Lords of Glamis and the Earl of Crawford played cards with the devil, and was sealed up because of it.

The castle is also noted for its gardens, and in springtime the mile-long driveway is lined with daffodils. In summer there are displays of rhododendrons and azaleas.

Within the village of Glamis, at Kirkwynd, is the **Angus Folk Museum** (National Trust for Scotland), housed in a row of six 18th century stone cottages. It contains one of the finest folk collections in Scotland, including a "Life on the Land" exhibition based in an old courtyard, and a restored 19th century hearse.

A few miles north of the village is Pictish **St Orland's Stone** (Historic Scotland), with, on one side, the carving of a cross and on the other a carving of men rowing a boat and a hunting scene.

FORFAR

13 miles N of Dundee on the A932

Once the county town of Angus, Forfar is now a small royal burgh and market town. It gives its name to one of Scotland's culinary delights - the **Forfar Bridie**. It has meat and vegetables within a pastry crust, and used to be popular with the farm workers of Angus, as it was a self-contained and easily portable meal.

The **Meffan Museum and Art Gallery** in West High Street gives you an insight into the town's history and industries. It was built in 1898 after a daughter of a former provost left a sum of money to the town. During the Dark Ages this part of Scotland was inhabited by the Picts, who, as far as we know, had no alphabet. However, they were expert carvers, and in the museum is a superb display of carved stones. You can also walk down an old cobbled street and peer into shops and workshops. A more unusual display is one about witchcraft in Angus.

Queen Margaret, wife of King Malcolm Canmore, had a castle and chapel on top of Castle Hill in the 11th century, though all traces of them are now gone. Her husband held a parliament in the castle in 1057. Robert the Bruce had the castle destroyed in the 14th century in case it fell into the hands of the English.

The **Forfar Market Cross** was

moved to the top of Castle Hill in 1785 when the new Town House was built. It was carved by Alexander Adam, who was associated with the great family of architects, in 1684. However, he got some of the coats-of-arms wrong, and eventually had to recarve them.

On the 572 feet high **Balmashanner Hill** (nicknamed the "Boammie") is a war memorial - perhaps one of the grandest and most unusual in the country. It consists of a square, castellated tower with one pepper pot turret on a corner at the top. It sits about a mile out of town

Five miles east of Forfar is **Balgavies Loch**, a Scottish Wildlife Trust reserve, where you can see great crested grebe, whooping swans, cormorant and other birds. Ospreys can also be seen from time to time. Keys to the hide are available from the ranger at the Montrose Basin Wildlife Centre. There is a hide which is open on the first Sunday of each month. **Forfar Loch Country Park**, to the west of the town, has viewing platforms where wildfowl can be observed feeding.

The ruins of **Restenneth Priory** (Historic Scotland) sit about a mile-and-a-half from the town, on the B9113. It once stood on an island in Restenneth Loch, but this was drained in the 18th century. It was founded by David I for Augustinian canons on the site of a much earlier church no doubt founded by the Picts, and its square tower, which is surmounted by a

later spire, has some of the earliest Norman - and possibly Saxon - work in Scotland. It was sacked by Edward I, but under the patronage of Robert the Bruce it soon regained its importance. Prince John, one of Bruce's sons, was buried here in 1327.

A few miles north of Forfar, near Tannadice, is the **Mountains Animal Sanctuary**, for rescued ponies, horses and donkeys. It was founded in 1982.

KIRRIEMUIR

15 miles N of Dundee on the A926

At 9 Brechin Road is **JM Barrie's Birthplace** (National Trust for Scotland). The creator of *Peter Pan* (first performed in 1904) was born here in 1860, the son of a handloom weaver, and the building's outside washhouse was his first theatre. The house next door has an exhibition about Barrie's life. He was a bright child, attending both Glasgow Academy and Dumfries Academy (see also Dumfries) before going on to Edinburgh University. He wrote many stories and novels, setting them in a small town called "Thrums", which is a thinly disguised Kirriemuir. So proud of Barrie are the people of Kirriemuir that has two statures of Peter Pan - one in the centre of the town and one in a garden near his birthplace.

The **Kirriemuir Aviation Museum,** at Bellie's Brae, has a private collection of World War II memorabilia. It was established in 1987, and largely confines itself to British aviation history.

154 LITTLETON OF AIRLIE COTTAGES

Kirriemuir

Two superior self-catering cottages on a farm amid the relaxing, rural scenery of Angus.

see page 495

155 VISOCCHI'S

Kirriemuir

Long-established ice cream makers; also a café serving wide choice of light meals and snacks.

see page 497

156 THRUMS HOTEL

Kirriemuir

Family-run and recently refurbished, offers fine dining and excellent en suite accommodation.

see page 498

In 1930, when he was given the freedom of the town, Barrie donated a Camera Obscura (National Trust for Scotland) to Kirriemuir, one of only three such cameras in the country. It is situated within the cricket pavilion on top of Kirriemuir Hill, and is open to the public. The town was the birthplace of one other famous person - Bon Scott, the late lead singer with the Australian group AC/DC, and an engraved stone set in the pavement at Cumberland Close commemorates the event. When he was six, Scott (real name Ronald Belford Scott) emigrated to Australia with his family. He was one of rock music's "bad boys".

Kirriemuir is the gateway to many of the beautiful Angus glens, and in the **Gateway to the Glens Museum** in the former town hall in the High Street you can find out about life in the glens and in Kirriemuir itself. The glens lie north of the town, and go deep into the Cairngorms (see also Brechin). They are extremely beautiful, and well worth a visit. The B955 takes you into **Glen Clova**, then, at its head, forms a loop, so you can travel along one side of the glen and return along the other for part of the way. The **Airlie Monument** on the 1,269 feet high Tulloch Hill was built in 1901 to commemorate David Ogilvy, 9th Earl of Airlie, who was killed a year earlier at the Battle of Diamond Hill in South Africa.

A minor road at the Clova Hotel takes you up onto lonely **Glen Doll** before it peters out. At Dykehead, further down the B955, you can turn off onto a minor road for **Glen Prosen** and follow it as it winds deep into the mountains. A cairn close to Dykehead commemorates the Antarctic explorers Robert Falcon Scott and Edward Adrian Wilson. Wilson was born in Cheltenham, the son of a doctor, but lived in Glen Prosen, and it was here that some of the Antarctic expedition was planned. He died along with Scott in Antarctica in March 1912.

Glen Isla is the southernmost of the Angus glens, and you can follow it for all of its length along the B951, which eventually takes you onto the A93 at Glenshee and up to Braemar if you wish. You will pass the **Lintrathen Loch**, which is noted for its bird life. **Reekie Linn Falls** lie to the west of the loch. They get their name from the smokey ("reekie") water spray the falls give off. A couple of miles further up the glen a minor road takes you to lonely **Backwater Reservoir** and its dam.

DUNNICHEN

13 miles NE of Dundee on minor road off the B9128

Close to the village was fought, in AD 685, the **Battle of Nechtansmere** between the Picts, under King Nechtan, and the Northumbrians. It was a turning point in early Scottish history, as it was decisive in establishing what was to become Scotland as an independent nation, and not part of an enlarged Northumbria and later England (see also Brechin).

Northumbria was aggressively trying to extend its boundaries, and had already taken the Lothians and Fife. It now wanted to conquer the land of the Picts, and its army, under the Northumbrian king Ecgfrith, moved further north. Necttan moved south, and took up a stance near the shores of a shallow loch, later called Nechtansmere. The Northumbrians were roundly beaten, and Ecgfrith himself and most of the royal court were killed. Nechtan's battle plan, according to Bede, was simple. He would send in half his troops to do battle, but hide the rest behind Dunnichen Hill. The Pictish troops, vastly outnumbered, pretended to flee, and the Northumbrians gave chase. However, they found themselves exactly where Nechtan wanted them - between the hill and an area of swamp beside the loch, where they were trapped. The rest of the Pictish troops came charging down the hill and easily wiped out the Northumbrian army. Ecgfrith and all the Northumbrian court were killed.

It was a battle that was every bit as important to Scotland as Bannockburn. If the Northumbrians had won, the Picts would have been absorbed into Ecgfrith's kingdom, which would have stretched from the Tees to the Moray Firth. It is to Scotland's shame that there were once plans to quarry on Dunnichen Hill - a plan that was eventually abandoned. At the crossroads in the village is a cairn which commemorates the battle, and a newer one was erected in 1998 close to the actual battlefield. Some people claim to have seen a ghostly re-enactment of the fighting take place in modern times. The "mere", or loch, which gave its name to the battle, was drained many years ago.

The picturesque village of **Letham**, which is close by, was founded in 1788 by George Dempster, the local landowner, as a settlement for farm workers who had been forced to leave the land because of farming reforms. It became a centre of weaving and spinning, though the introduction of power looms in nearby towns killed it off.

ARBROATH

15 miles NE of Dundee on the A92

The ancient town of Arbroath is special to all Scots. It was here, in 1320, that the nobles of Scotland met and signed the **Declaration of Arbroath**, which stated that the country was an independent kingdom, and not a province of England. It was sent to a sceptical Pope John XXII in Avingon (Bruce had previously been excommunicated), and in it, they claimed that they were not fighting for glory, riches or honour, but for freedom. They also, in no uncertain terms, claimed that they would remain loyal to their king, Robert the Bruce, only as long as he defended Scotland against the English. It was a momentous declaration to make in those days, when unswerving loyalty to a

Letham

A recently refurbished village inn that combines tradition with a modern feel, and which is proud of its food and drink.

🛏 ‖ see page 499

Arbroath

158 COLLISTON INN

Arbroath

A great wine bar and bistro on the outskirts of Arbroath that is not only stylish and welcoming, but represents great value for money.

see page 500

159 BUT 'N' BEN

Auchmithie

A great pub/restaurant, in a small fishing village, famous for its seafood, its well stocked bar and its great prices.

see page 501

sovereign was expected at all times. The Declaration also traced the dubious history of the Scots nation from the Scythians, who travelled via the "Pillar of Hercules" to Scotland, something that was firmly believed in the 14th century.

The Declaration was drawn up in **Arbroath Abbey** (Historic Scotland), with Bernard de Linton, the abbot of the abbey, being the writer. The ruins of the abbey still stand within the town, and sometimes a re-enactment of the signing is held there. A Visitor Centre tells the story of the abbey and the Declaration.

The abbey ruins date from the 12th century and later, and are of warm red sandstone. It was founded in 1176 by William the Lion (who was later buried there) for the Tironensian monks of Kelso, and dedicated to St Thomas of Canterbury. Portions of the great abbey church remain, including the south transept, with its great rose window. In 1951 the abbey was the temporary home of the Stone of Destiny after it was removed from Westminster Abbey by students with Scottish Nationalist sympathies.

In 1446 the **Battle of Arbroath** took place around the abbey. It had been the custom for the abbot to nominate a baillie to look after the peacekeeping and business side of Arbroath. He appointed Alexander Lindsay to the lucrative post, but later dismissed him for "lewd bahaviour", appointing John Ogilvie in his place. Lindsay took exception to this and arrived at the abbey with

an army of 1,000 men. The ensuing battle, fought in the streets of the town, killed over 600 people, with Lindsay's army emerging triumphant. However, it was a hollow victory, as Lindsay himself was killed.

The award-winning **Arbroath Museum**, at Ladyloan, is housed in the elegant signal tower for the Bellrock Lighthouse, and brings Arbroath's maritime and social history alive through a series of models, sounds and even smells. The **Arbroath Art Gallery** is within the public library on Hill Terrace. There are works by local artists, and two paintings by Pieter Brueghel the Younger.

Arbroath has had a harbour at the "Fit o' the Toon" (Foot of the Town) since at least the 14th century, and it supported a great fishing fleet. The town gave its name to that delicacy called the **Arbroath Smokie** (a smoked haddock) though the origins of the delicacy are to be found not in the town, but in **Auchmithie**, a fishing village four miles to the north. The story goes that long ago it was the practice to store fish in the lofts of the fishermen's cottages. One day, a cottage burned down, and the resultant smoked fish was found to be delicious. Not only that - it preserved them.

The **Seaton Cliffs Nature Trail** winds for one and a half miles along the red sandstone cliffs towards Carlinheugh Bay. There is plenty of birdlife to see, as well as fascinating rock formations. The town is also a holiday resort, and at West Link Parks is the 10¼ inch gauge **Kerr's Miniature Railway**, always a favourite with holidaymakers. It is open during the summer months, and is Scotland's oldest miniature railway, having been built in 1935. It runs for over 400 yards alongside the main Aberdeen to Edinburgh line.

Within the village of St Vigeans, on the outskirts of Arbroath, is the **Parish Church of St Vigeans**, which was built in the 12th century, but not consecrated until 1242. While being refurbished in the 19th century, 32 sculptured Pictish stones were discovered. They are now housed in the **St Vigeans Museum**, converted cottages close to the small knoll where the church stands. The most important stone is the Dristan Stone, dating from the 9th century.

St Fechan, or St Vigean, was an Irish saint who died in about AD 664. The village of Ecclefechan in Dumfriesshire is also named after him.

ABERLEMNO

18 miles NE of Dundee on a minor road off the B9134

Within the village are the Pictish **Aberlemno Sculptured Stones** (Historic Scotland). One is situated in the kirkyard of the parish church, and the others are within a stone enclosure near the roadside north of the church. The one in the kirkyard shows a fine cross on one side surrounded by intertwining serpents and water horses, and a typical Pictish hunting scene on the other. It dates from the 8th or 9th century. The other

two have crosses, angels, and battle or hunting scenes. Because of possible frost damage, the stones are boxed in between October and May.

BRECHIN

22 miles NE of Dundee off the A90

If the possession of a cathedral makes a town a city, then Brechin is indeed a city, even though it has a population of only 6,000. **Brechin Cathedral** dates from the 12th century, though most of what we see today is 13th century and later. It was the successor to a Celtic church which stood on the site, and which had been endowed by Kenneth II King of Scots between AD 971 and 995. It soon became the premier church for Angus, though by the 11th century Roman Catholic clergy had succeeded the Culdee priests.

In 1806 the nave, aisles and west front were remodelled, and between 1901 and 1902 were restored to their original design. Adjacent to the cathedral, and now forming part of its fabric, is an 11th century **Round Tower**, which rises to a height of 106 feet. These towers are common in Ireland, though this is the only one of two to have survived in Scotland (see also Abernethy). From the top a monk rang a bell at certain times

Aberlemno Sculptured Stones

To the north west of Brechin is Glen Lethnot, one of the beautiful Angus glens (see also Kirriemuir). Flowing through it is the West Water, and near the head of the glen is an old trail that takes you over the Clash of Wirren into Glen Esk. Illicit distillers used this as a route in days gone by, and hid their casks in the corries among the hills. For this reason it became known as the Whisky Trail.

160 MONTROSE BASIN WILDLIFE CENTRE

Montrose

View the wildlife of this enclosed tidal estuary through powered telescopes and see unique displays on the migrating birds that visit here.

 see page 501

during the day, calling the monks to prayer. It was also used as a place of refuge for the monks during troubled times.

In Maison Dieu Lane is the south wall of the chapel of the **Maison Dieu** almshouses (Historic Scotland) founded in 1267 by Lord William de Brechin. Here the poor and the sick of the town would have been looked after. It survived well after the Reformation.

Brechin Museum, on the ground floor of the former Town House in St Ninian's Square, has exhibits and displays about the cathedral, the ancient city crafts and local archaeology. **Brechin Castle** (not open to the public) was built largely in the 18th century, and is the seat of the Earls of Dalhousie. Within the grounds of the castle is the **Brechin Castle Centre**, which has a garden centre, walks and a model farm. There is also **Pictavia**, an exhibition about the enigmatic Picts, who occupied this part of Scotland for centuries. One of the displays explains the Battle of Nechansmere (see also Dunnichen). Their name means the "painted people", and they fought the Romans, the Vikings and the Angles. The various tribes eventually amalgamated, forming a powerful kingdom, which ultimately united with the kingdom of the Scots of Dalriada in AD 843 to form an embryonic Scotland.

At Menmuir, near the town, are the White and Brown **Caterthuns** (Historic Scotland), on which are the well-preserved remains of Iron Age forts. The hills also give good

views across the surrounding countryside.

The **Caledonian Railway** runs on Sundays during summer and on Saturdays also during the peak season, when passengers can travel between the Victorian Brechin Station on Park Road and the nearby Bridge of Dun. The railway has ten steam engines and 12 diesels, and is run by the Brechin Railway Preservation Society. The Brechin branch line, on which the trains run, was closed in 1952.

MONTROSE

27 miles NE of Dundee on the A92

Montrose is an ancient royal burgh which received its charter in the early 12th century. It sits on a small spit of land between the North Sea and a shallow tidal inlet called the Montrose Basin, which is a local nature reserve founded in 1981 famous for its bird life. The **Montrose Basin Wildlife Centre** is visited by thousands of bird watchers every year who come to see the many migrant birds.

At the old Montrose Air Station, where some of the Battle of Britain pilots trained, is the **Montrose Air Station Heritage Centre**. In 1912, the government planned 12 such air stations, to be operated by the Royal Flying Corps, later called the Royal Air Force. Montrose was the first, and became operational in 1913. Now it houses a small collection of aircraft, plus mementoes, documents and photographs related to flying. It also houses a ghost.

The **William Lamb Memorial**

Studio is in a close off Market Street, and is open to the public during the summer. It celebrates the life of a local artist who died in 1951. He was born in Mill Street in 1893, and became a monumental sculptor and stone mason. He later attended night school art classes at Montrose Academy and eventually Edinburgh College of Art. He was wounded twice in World War I (one of the wounds to his right hand), yet in 1932 was commissioned by the Duchess of York to make busts of her daughters, Princess Elizabeth and Princess Margaret. So impressed was she that she then commissioned a bust of herself.

Montrose was adopted as the title of the Graham family when it was ennobled, and the most famous member was James Graham, 5th Earl and 1st Marquis of Montrose. He was born in 1612, and succeeded to the earldom in 1625. At first he was a Covenanter, then changed sides. He was made Lieutenant-General of Scotland by the king, and unsuccessfully tried to invade the country with an army. He later went to the Highlands in disguise to raise a Royalist army. During a succession of skirmishes, he defeated Covenanting forces due to his brilliant leadership and almost reckless courage. Charles's defeat at Naseby, however, left him powerless, and his forces were eventually soundly beaten at Philiphaugh in 1645. Afterwards he fled to the Continent but returned in 1650 in support of Charles II. Charles, however, disowned him and he was hanged, still protesting that he was a good Covenanter and at the same time supporter of the king

Though not born in Montrose, George Wishart the religious reformer has close associations with the town. He attended the grammar school here in the 1520s, and went on to Aberdeen University. He later returned and taught at the grammar school, where he used the Greek translation of the Bible while teaching his pupils. For this he was accused of heresy, and he had to flee to England. In 1546 he was burnt at the stake in St Andrews on the orders of Cardinal Beaton (see also Dundee and St Andrews).

EDZELL

27 miles NE of Dundee on the B966

There has been a castle at Edzell since at least the 12th century, when one was built by the Abbot family. The present ruins of **Edzell Castle** (Historic Scotland) date from the early 16th century. It was a seat, first of the Abbots, and then of the Lindsays, and reckoned to be the finest castle in Angus. It clearly shows that life in a Scottish castle was not the cold, draughty experience that people imagine from seeing bare, ruined walls. They could be places of refinement and comfort, and at Edzell we have evidence of this.

The gardens were especially tasteful and elegant, and were laid out in 1604 by Sir David Lindsay, though he died in 1610 before they could be completed. The walled garden has been described as an

To the west of the town of Montrose, beyond the Basin, is the House of Dun (National Trust for Scotland). From 1375 until 1980 the estate was home to the Erskine family, with the present house being designed by William Adam in 1730 for David Erskine, High Court judge and 13th Laird of Dun, and contains good plasterwork, sumptuous furnishings and a collection of embroidery carried out by Lady Augusta Kennedy-Erskine, natural daughter of William IV by his mistress Dorothea Bland, also known as Mrs Jordan. There are also formal gardens and woodland walks.

"Italian Renaissance garden in
Scotland", and featured heraldic
imagery and an array of carved
panels representing deities, the
liberal arts and the cardinal virtues.

The castle was added to in
1553 when David Lindsay, 9th Earl
of Crawford and a high court
judge, built the west range. In 1562
Mary Stuart spent two nights here,
and held a meeting of her Privy
Council.

In 1715 the Jacobite Lindsays
sold the castle to James Maule, the
fourth Earl of Panmure, who was
also a Jacobite sympathiser, so that
they could raise a Jacobite regiment.
After the rebellion the castle and
lands were forfeited to the crown
and sold to an English company
called the York Building Company,
which went bankrupt in 1732. The
castle gradually became ruinous,
and in the 1930s the gardens were
restored to their former glory. The
summerhouse contains examples of
the carved panelling that was in the
castle in its heyday.

One of the delights of Edzell
village is the **Dalhousie Arch**,
erected in 1887 over a road into the
village as a memorial to 13th Earl
of Dalhousie and his wife, who
died within a few hours of each
other.

Up until 1995 American navy
had a base with an RAF airfield to
the east of the village. A monument
now marks the spot. Edzell is the
gateway to **Glen Esk**. It is the
longest and most northerly of the
glens, and you can drive the 19
miles to Invermark Lodge, close to
Loch Lee, where the road peters

out. Along the way you can stop at
the Retreat, where you will find the
Glen Esk Folk Museum, which
traces the life of the people of the
glen from about 1800 to the
present day. **Invermark Castle** is a
ruined tower house dating from the
16th century, and built by Sir David
Lindsey of Edzell. It was used by
the locals as a place of safety when
Highland marauders came to steal
cattle.

KINROSS

Once the main town in the tiny
county of Kinross, which measures
no more than 15 miles by nine, this
small burgh now sits quietly on the
shores of Loch Leven. The
opening of the M90 motorway has
put it within half an hour of
Edinburgh, and over the last 15
years it has expanded to become a
peaceful haven for commuters.

The town's **Tolbooth** dates
from the 17th century, and was
restored by Robert Adam in 1771.
On the **Mercat Cross** are the
"jougs", an iron collar placed round
the neck of wrongdoers. **Kinross
House** dates from the late 17th
century, and was built for Sir
William Bruce of Balkaskie, Charles
II's surveyor and master of works,
who was responsible for the fabric
of the Palace of Holyrood in
Edinburgh. It is an elegant
Palladian mansion with wonderful
formal gardens that are open to the
public from April to September.
Bruce himself never stayed in the
house, and the story goes that it
was intended as a home for the ill-

fated James VII, then Duke of York, in anticipation of the fact that he might not succeed to the throne, though this is unlikely.

Loch Leven is one of Scotland's most famous lochs, not because of its size (it covers 3,500 acres) or its spectacular beauty, but because of its wonderful trout fishing. Though this has gone into decline in recent years, the trout are still highly prized for their delicate pink flesh, caused by the small fresh water shellfish on which they feed.

The loch was formed at the end of the last Ice Age, about 10,000 years ago. As the ice retreated, some was left in a depression, and as it melted the depression filled up with water. On the south shore of the loch, close to the B9097, is the **Vane Farm Nature Reserve**, administered by the Royal Society for the Protection of Birds and part of the Loch Leven National Nature Reserve. It hosts a programme of events throughout the year, and was the first educational nature reserve in Europe.

The loch has seven islands. On the 35 acre **St Serf's Island** (the largest), a Celtic monastery was established by Brude, the last Pictish king, in the early 9th century. Later, the island was given to monks from St Andrews by David l, and they established a small Augustinian priory. All that remains are the scant walls of the chapel. One of the priors was Andrew of Wynton, author of the *Orygynale Cronykil* ("Original Chronicle"), which was a history of Scotland .

On another island are the ruins of **Lochleven Castle** (Historic Scotland). It was a Douglas stronghold, the surrounding lands and the loch having been gifted to the family by Robert III in 1390. From June 1567 until May 1568 Mary Stuart was held prisoner here, having been seized in Edinburgh for her supposed part in the murder of her husband Lord Darnley. She was 25 years old at the time, and married to Bothwell, who was also implicated in Darnley's murder. While kept prisoner, she was constantly being asked to abdicate and divorce Bothwell, but this she refused to do, as she was already pregnant by him. Shortly after she arrived on the island, she gave birth to stillborn twins, and eventually agreed to their terms.

But it was not her stay on the island that made the castle famous; rather it was the way she escaped. The castle was owned by the Dowager Lady Douglas, mother of

Lochleven Castle

There is an interesting story attached to Burleigh castle. In 1707 the heir to the castle fell in love with a servant girl, which so displeased his father that he sent him abroad. However, he declared his undying love for her, and swore that if she married someone else while he was away, he would kill him when he returned. After a year or so he returned, only to find that she had married a schoolmaster. True to his word, he shot him dead. He then fled, but was captured and sentenced to death. However, he escaped the gallows by changing places with his sister and donning her clothes. He later fought in the Jacobite army during the 1715 Uprising. For this, his castle and lands were taken from the family and given to the Irwins. It later passed to the Grahams.

Mary's half brother the Earl of Moray, who became regent when Mary abdicated. Both she and her other sons Sir William and George Douglas looked after Mary during her imprisonment. But George gradually fell under Mary's spell, and hatched various plans for her escape. All failed, and he was eventually banished from the island.

Someone else had also fallen under Mary's spell - 16-year-old Willie Douglas, who was thought to be the illegitimate son of Sir William, and who was kept as a page. Mary was being held in the third storey of the main tower, above the Great Hall where the Douglas family dined. One evening young Willie "accidentally" dropped a napkin over the castle keys, which his father had placed on the table while dining. On picking up the napkin, he picked up the keys as well.

As the meal progressed, Mary and one of her attendants crept out of her room and made for the main doorway, where Willie met them. He unlocked the door, and they both slipped out. He then locked the door behind him and threw the keys into the water before rowing the two women ashore. There they were met by George Douglas, Lord Seton and a troop of loyal soldiers, and taken to the safety of Niddrie Castle.

In those days, the loch was much bigger and deeper than it is now, and the water came right up to the doors of the castle. Between 1826 and 1836 it was partially drained, reducing its size by a quarter and dropping the water level by four and a half feet. Amazingly, the keys were recovered from the mud. Nowadays, trips to the island leave from the pier at Kinross.

The **Scottish Raptor Centre** at Turfhills has falconry courses and flying displays. It is the largest centre of its kind in Scotland, with about 80 birds. Close to Kinross at Balado is held Scotland's biggest outdoor rock festival, **T in the Park**. Every year in July it attracts over 69,000 music lovers. And every Sunday the **Kinross Market** is held, the largest indoor market in Scotland, featuring a flea market and car boot sale.

AROUND KINROSS

MILNATHORT

2 miles N of Kinross off the M90

Milnathort is a small, former wool-manufacturing town. To the east are the ruins of 15th century **Burleigh Castle** (Historic Scotland), built of warm red stone, which was a stronghold of the Balfour family. All that remains nowadays is a curtain wall and a four-storey tower, and is said to be haunted by the ghost of a woman called Grey Maggie.

The **Orwell Standing Stones** are just off the A911. Two huge stones, dating to about 2000 BC, stand on a slight rise. One of them fell down in 1972, and during restoration work cremated bones were discovered buried at its foot.

SCOTLANDWELL

5 miles E of Kinross, on the A911

Scotlandwell takes its name from the springs that bubble up to the surface in this part of the county, which is on the western slopes of the Lomond Hills. In the mid 13th century William Malvoisin, Bishop of St Andrews set up a hospice here, and his successor gave it to the "Red Friars", or "Trinitarians", a monastic order that had originally been founded to raise money for the release of captives in the Holy Land during the Crusades. They built a friary and exploited the springs, and established a **Holy Well**. Soon it became a place of pilgrimage, bringing huge revenue to the monks. Robert the Bruce came here to find a cure for his leprosy, and held a parliament. On the slopes above the village are the **Crooked Rigs**, remnants of a medieval runrig field system.

The local landowners, the Arnots of **Arnot Tower,** the ruins of which can still be seen set within ten acres of garden, gazed enviously at the wealth of the Trinitarians, and decided to "muscle in" on their "healing waters" venture. They placed younger sons of the family within the order as fifth columnists, and when enough of them were in place, they occupied the friary and ejected those friars who weren't Arnots. They established Archibald Arnot, the Laird of Arnot's second son, as minister (the name given to the head of the friary), and began creaming off the vast wealth. At the Reformation, the lands and income of the friary were given to them, and the takeover was complete.

The holy well still exists today. In 1858 the Laird of Arnot commissioned David Bryce to turn it into a memorial to his wife Henrietta, and this is what can be seen today. The friary has completely disappeared, though a small plaque in the graveyard marks the spot where it once stood.

At Portmoak near Scotlandwell there's the **Scottish Gliding Centre**, where the adventurous can try an "air experience flight".

CROOK OF DEVON

5 miles W of Kinross on the A977

This small village has twice won an award for being the "best kept village in Kinross". It seems quiet enough now, but in the 1660s it achieved notoriety as a centre of witchcraft. A coven of witches had been "discovered" in the area, and in 1662 three women were tried and sentenced to be strangled to death and their bodies burnt at a "place called Lamblaires". A few weeks later four women and one man were executed in the same manner, and not long after two women were tried, one of them escaping death because of her age. The other was burnt at the stake.

By this time the other members of the "coven" had fled from the area. But in July two further women were put on trial, one of whom was executed and the other, called Christian Grieve, acquitted. The acquittal was looked upon as an

At Kinnesswood, north of the village, is the Michael Bruce Museum. Bruce was known as the "Gentle poet of Loch Leven", and died in 1767 aged only 21. Keys for the museum are available from the local garage.

affront by the local people - especially the clergy - and she was retried and eventually executed.

There is no doubt that the trials were a travesty, and that many old scores were settled by naming people - especially old women - as witches. It was also not unknown in Scotland at that time for the accused, knowing their fate was sealed, to get their own back on the accusers by naming them as witches and warlocks as well. Thus Scotland seemed to be awash with devil worship, when in fact it was very rare.

Today Lamblaires is a small grassy knoll in a field adjoining the village. It looks peaceful enough, and nothing reminds you of the horrible stranglings and burnings that took place there.

PERTH

The "Fair City" of Perth sits on the Tay, and in medieval times was the meeting place of Scottish kings and parliaments. Though a large place by Scottish standards, having a population of about 43,000, its location away from the Central Belt ensured that it never succumbed to the intense industrialisation that many other towns experienced. But it did succumb to the ravages of modernisation, and many of the ancient buildings that played a part in Scotland's story have been swept away.

The city centre lies between two large open spaces, the **North Inch** and the **South Inch**, and is filled with elegant 18th and 19th century buildings. Up until the local government reorganisations of the mid '70s, it had a lord provost, and was truly a city. It even has **St Ninian's Cathedral**, which dates from the 19th century and was designed by William Butterfield. It is the cathedral for the diocese of St Andrews, Dunblane and Dunkeld, each of which, before the Reformation was a diocese in its own right. It was the first cathedral to be built in Britain since the Reformation, having been consecrated in 1850. It stands on the site of the Blackfriar's Monastery.

Perth has played a large part in the history of Scotland. James I chose it as his capital, and if he had not been murdered in the city in 1437, it might have been Scotland's capital to this day. The story of James's murder has been embellished over the years, but the facts are simple. He was an unpopular monarch, and when he was staying in the city's Dominican Friary (now gone), he was attacked by a group of nobles under the Earl of Atholl, who hoped to claim the crown. James tried to make his escape through a sewer which ran beneath his room, but was caught and stabbed to death. An embellishment to the story is that one of his Queen's ladies-in-waiting stuck her arm through the boltholes of the door as a bar to prevent the entry of the assassins. However, it is probably a later invention.

In the centre of the city is **St John's Kirk**, one of the finest medieval kirks in Scotland. From this church, the city took its earlier name of St Johnstoune, which is remembered in the name of the local football team. It was consecrated in 1243, though the earliest part of what you see nowadays, the choir, dates from the 15th century, with the tower being added in 1511. It has some Renaissance glass, and it was here, in May 1559, that John Knox first preached after his exile in Europe. It more or less launched the Reformation in Scotland.

After the Reformation of 1560, the building was divided into three churches, with three distinct congregations. It was not until the early 20th century that the church housed one congregation again. The architect for the scheme was Sir Robert Lorimer, and the furnishings in the nave are mostly his work.

The city was the scene, in February 1437, of the assassination of James I of Scotland. James had been captured by the English and brought up at the English court. When he returned to Scotland after a ransom had been paid, he found the country in a state of anarchy. He immediately set about restoring royal authority, his first act being the execution of the Duke of Albany and his accomplices, who had bled the country dry (see also Stirling and Doune).

However, many of the nobles objected to the charges he was introducing, and some of them hatched a plot to assassinate him. When James gave a reception at the Blackfriars Monastery in Perth

(now the site of St Ninian's Cathedral) the nobles turned up unannounced, and James hid himself in a secret room, or perhaps drain. beneath the monastery, with a passage through which he could make his escape.

However, the passage turned out to be blocked, and the king was trapped. Eventually the nobles, under Sir Robert Graham, found him and stabbed him to death. In the aftermath of the assassination, the nobles discovered that their deed had not made them as popular as they thought it would, and James's wife, Queen Joan, had them rounded up, tortured and executed for treason. The king himself was buried in Blackfriars.

The **Perth Museum and Art Gallery** is in George Street, and is one of the oldest in Britain. It houses material whose scope goes beyond the city and its immediate area, as well as a collection of fine paintings, sculpture, glass and silver. The **Fergusson Gallery** in Marshall Place is dedicated to the painter John Duncan Fergusson (1874-1961), who, along with Peploe, Cadell and Hunter formed a group called the Scottish Colourists, who were heavily influenced by the vibrant colours of contemporary French painters. The gallery, which opened in 1992, is housed in a former waterworks dating from 1832.

In 1928 Sir Walter Scott's novel *The Fair Maid of Perth* was published, the heroine of which was Catherine Glover, daughter of Simon Glover, who lived in Curfew

In Balhousie Castle in Hay Street near the North Inch you'll find the Black Watch Regimental Museum. Raised in 1725 from the ranks of clans generally hostile to the Jacobites, such as the Campbells, Frasers and Grants, its purpose was to patrol or "watch" the Highlands after the first Jacobite Uprising. (see also Aberfeldy). The regiment became the third battalion of the Royal Regiment of Scotland in 2006.

165 THE ROOST

Bridge of Earn

Outstanding coffee shop and restaurant close to junction 9 of the M90.

📖 *see page 506*

166 BAIGLIE INN & COUNTRY RESTAURANT

Aberargie, Perth

A picturesque country pub and former coaching inn south of Perth that is now a food lovers' paradise.

📖 *see page 507*

167 THE SCONE ARMS

Scone

Charming 200-year-old village pub with excellent restaurant, two bars and beer garden.

📖 *see page 508*

Row. It was set in the 14th century, and tells of how Catherine, a woman noted for her piety and beauty, was sought after by all the young men of the city. David Stewart, Duke of Rothesay and son of Robert III, also admired her, though his intentions were not honourable. He was thwarted by Hal Gow, who came upon the Duke and his men trying to enter Catherine's house in the dead of night.

The ensuing skirmish resulted in one of the Duke's retainers having his hand hacked off by Hal before they fled in disarray. Catherine slept through it all, though Hal wakened her father and showed him the severed hand. The story ends happily when Hal subsequently marries Catherine. The present **Fair Maid's House** in North Port (now used as a small arts centre) does not go back as far as the 14th century. However, it is over 300 years old, and incorporates some medieval walls, which may have belonged to the original house that stood on the site. In 1867 Bizet wrote his opera *The Fair Maid of Perth* based on Scott's book, and the story became even more popular.

Bell's Cherrybank Gardens is an 18-acre garden on the western edge of the city. It incorporates the National Heather Collection, which has over 900 varieties of heather. On Dundee Road is the **Branklyn Garden** (National Trust for Scotland), developed by John and Dorothy Renton. One of its more unusual plants is the rare blue

Himalayan poppy. **Kinnoull Hill**, to the east of Perth, rises to a height of 729 feet above the Tay, and forms part of the Kinnoull Hill Woodland Park. If you are reasonably fit, you can walk to the summit, and get some wonderful views across the Tay to Fife, over to Perth and beyond, and down over the Carse of Gowrie. There is a folly on top of the hill, built in the 18th century by the 9th Earl of Kinnoull in imitation of a Rhine castle.

AROUND PERTH

SCONE PALACE

2 miles N of Perth off the A93

Historically and culturally, Scone (pronounced "Scoon") is one of the most important places in Scotland. When Kenneth MacAlpin, king of Dalriada, also became king of the Picts in AD 843, he quit his capital at Dunadd and moved to Scone. He made the move to be nearer the centre of his new kingdom and to escape from the constant Norse raids on the western seaboard. This was the beginning of the kingdom of Scotland as we know it, though it would be another 170 years before the Lowland kingdoms of Strathclyde and the Lothians were absorbed.

Scone Abbey, (now gone) was built by Alexander I in 1114 for the Augustinians, and was totally destroyed after the Reformation. Outside of it, on the **Moot Hill** (which can still be seen) the Scottish kings were crowned sitting on the **Stone of Destiny** (see also

Dunadd and Edinburgh). It was here that Robert the Bruce was crowned king of Scotland in 1306, in defiance of Edward I of England. Traditionally, the Earl of Fife placed the crown on the monarch's head, but as he was being held in England, he could not perform the duty. Therefore his sister, Isobel MacDuff, Countess of Buchan, took his place, incurring the wrath of both Edward I and her own husband, who supported Edward's claim to the throne.

Scone Palace itself is the home of the Earls of Mansfield, and dates from the 18th century. It has collections of fine furniture, porcelain and needlework.

Scone Palace

STANLEY

6 miles N of Perth on the B9099

The picturesque village of Stanley sits on the River Tay, and is a former mill village. Sir Richard Arkwright had an interest in the mill here, the first of which was founded in 1786. Three large mills were built in the 1820s, powered by seven waterwheels. They were the most northerly mills in Britain. Four miles away are the ruins of 13th century **Kinclaven Castle**, once a favourite residence of Alexander II, who had built it. William Wallace ambushed a small force of English troops near here in 1297, and when they took refuge in the castle, Wallace besieged it.

BANKFOOT

7 miles N of Perth on A9

This small village sits just off the A9. The **Macbeth Experience** is within the Perthshire Visitor Centre, and is a multi-media show that explains all about one of Scotland's most famous kings. It debunks the Macbeth of Shakespeare's play and instead concentrates on the actual man and his achievements.

MEIKLEOUR

10 miles N of Perth on A984

The **Meikleour Hedge,** just outside the village on the A93, is the world's largest. It borders the road for over 600 yards, and is now 100 feet high. It is of pure beech, and was supposed to have been planted in 1745 by Jean Mercer and her husband Robert Murray Nairne, who was later killed at the Battle of Culloden. Jean immediately left the area, and the hedge was allowed to grow unattended for many years.

BLAIRGOWRIE

14 miles N of Perth on the A93

This trim town, along with its sister town of **Rattray**, became one burgh in 1928 by an Act of

A replica of the Stone of Destiny is to be found at the summit of Moot Hill in Scone Palace, along with a small chapel. The last king to be crowned at Scone was Charles II in 1651. This stone is also called Jacob's Pillow, and is supposed to have been the pillow on which the Biblical Jacob slept, though the present one, housed in Edinburgh, was almost certainly quarried in Perthshire. However, there are those who say that when Edward I seized the stone in 1296, he was given a worthless copy by the monks of the abbey.

305

The finest collection of Pictish stones in Scotland was found in and around Meigle, 16 miles NE of Perth on the B954, and they are now on display at Meigle Museum (Historic Scotland), in a converted schoolhouse. The largest stone, at eight feet tall, is known as Meigle 2, and shows a fine carved cross one side and mounted horsemen and mythical animals at the bottom. The central panel shows what appears to be Daniel surrounded by four lions, but some people have put another intepretation on it. They say it depicts the execution of Queen Guinevere. It seems that she was captured by Mordred, king of the Picts, and that when she was released, Arthur ordered her execution by being pulled apart by wild animals. The museum is open from April to September.

Parliament. It is noted as the centre of a raspberry and strawberry growing area. It sits on the Ericht, a tributary of the Tay, and the riverside is very attractive. Within the library in Leslie Street is the **Blairgowrie Genealogy Centre** where you can carry out research on the old families of the area.

The **Cateran Trail** is named after medieval brigands from beyond Braemar who used to descend on Perthshire to wreak havoc and steal cattle. It is a 64-mile long circular route centred on Blairgowrie, and uses existing footpaths and minor roads to take you on a tour of the area. It has been designed to take about five or six days to complete, with stops every 12 or 13 miles, and takes in parts of Angus as well as Perthshire.

Craighall Castle, the earliest parts of which date from the 16th century, are perched on a cliff above the Elricht. Sir Walter Scott visited it, and he used it as a model for Tullyveolan in his book *Waverley*. It now offers holiday accommodation.

The **Lays of Marlee**, south of the village, is a stone circle, with the B947 passing right through it.

COUPAR ANGUS
12 miles NE of Perth on the A94

Situated in Strathmore, Coupar Angus is a small town which was given its burgh charter in 1607. The scant remains of the gatehouse of **Coupar Angus Abbey**, founded by Malcolm IV for Cistercians from Melrose in the mid 12th century, stand in the kirkyard. At one time it

was the wealthiest Cistercian abbey in Scotland. The town's **Tolbooth** dates from 1702, and was used as a courthouse and prison. To the east of the town are the remains of a Roman camp.

ALYTH
19 miles NE of Perth on the B952

The ruins of St Moluag's Church, known as the **Alyth Arches**, lie within the old graveyard. and contain a fine sacristy. In Commercial Street is the **Alyth Folk Museum**. To the north east, on **Barry Hill**, are the remains of an Iron Age Fort. According to legend, Athur's Guinevere was imprisoned here for loving a Pictish prince.

ERROL
8 miles E of Perth on a minor road off the A90

Set in the Carse of Gowrie, a narrow stretch of fertile land bordering the northern shore of the Firth of Tay, Errol is a peaceful village with a large **Parish Church** of 1831 designed by James Gillespie Graham which is sometimes called the "Cathedral of the Carse". The village gives its name to an earldom, which means that there is an "Earl of Errol" (see Slains Castle). A leaflet is available which gives details of most of the old kirkyards and kirks in the Carse. In 1990s the **Errol Station Trust** opened the former railway station as a heritage centre.

ELCHO
3 miles SE of Perth on a minor road

Elcho Castle (Historic Scotland) was the ancient seat of the Earls of

Wemyss. The present castle was built in the mid 1500s by Sir John Wemyss, who died in 1572, on the site of an earlier fortification dating from the 13th century.

By about 1780, the castle had been abandoned, and it gradually became ruinous. It was re-roofed in 1830. It is open between April and September each year.

ABERNETHY

6 miles SE of Perth on the A913

The 75-feet high **Abernethy Round Tower** (Historic Scotland) is one of only two round towers in Scotland (see also Brechin). It dates from the end of the 11th century, and was used as a place of refuge for Celtic priests during times of trouble. At the foot of the tower is a carved Pictish stone.

FORTEVIOT

6 miles SW of Perth on the B935

This little village was at one time the capital of the Pictish kingdom, and was later the place chosen by Kenneth l as the capital of a united Scotland. In a field to the north of the River Earn stood the **Dupplin Cross**, erected, it is thought, in the 9th century by King Constantine I, who died in AD 877. It was taken to the National Museum of Scotland in 1998 for restoration, after which it was housed in St Serf's Church in Dunning.

The village itself was redeveloped in the mid 1920s by the first Lord Forteviot to resemble a garden city, a style which was popular in England at the time.

DUNNING

8 miles SW of Perth on the B934

This quiet village is mainly visited because of **St Serf's Parish Church**, with its fine early 13th century tower. The original church was probably built by Gilbert, Earl of Strathearn, in about 1200. It now houses the Dupplin Cross. A couple of miles outside the village, near the road, is a monument topped with a cross which marks the spot where, according to its inscription, **Maggie Wall**, a witch, was burned in 1657. It is the only memorial to a witch in Scotland, though no record has ever been found about the trial or execution of anyone called Maggie Wall. Maybe it was what nowadays would be called a "lynching". The whole thing - including who actually built the cairn - remains a mystery.

AUCHTERARDER

12 miles SW of Perth on the A824

Situated a couple of miles north of the Gleneagles Hotel, Auchterarder (nicknamed "The Lang Toun") is a small royal burgh with a long main street. It has been bypassed by the busy A9, and retains a quiet charm. At **Auchterarder Heritage**, within the local tourist office in the High Street, there are displays about local history. It was in Auchterarder Castle (now gone) in 1559 that Mary of Guise, Mary Stuart's mother, signed the Treaty of Perth acknowledging that Scotland was a Protestant country.

In 1072 Malcolm III met William the Conquerer in Abernethy and knelt in submission, acknowledging him as his overlord. This was an act which had repercussions down through the ages, as Edward I used it to justify his claim that Scottish kings owed allegiance to him. The Abernethy Museum, founded in the year 2000, explains the village's history, and is housed in an 18th century school building.

168 SMIDDY HAUGH HOTEL

Aberuthven

A friendly welcome awaits at the Smiddy Haugh Hotel with its superb food and comfortable rooms.

see page 509

The Tullibardine Distillery is built on the site of Scotland's first public brewery. At James IV's coronation in 1488 beer from the brewery was drunk. The visitors centre is open from May to September each year.

169 DRUMMOND CASTLE GARDENS

Muthill

Stunning formal gardens first laid out in the 17th century.

 see page 509

Another royal visitor to the castle was Edward l of England, who rested here in 1296 during his campaign to subdue Scotland.

About three miles west of the town, near the A823, is the cruciform **Tullibardine Chapel** (Historic Scotland), one of the few finished collegiate chapels in Scotland that have remained unaltered over the years. It was founded by Sir David Murray of Tullibardine, ancestor of the Dukes of Atholl, in 1446, and altered in 1500.

MUTHILL

15 miles SW of Perth on the A822

Within Muthill (pronounced "Mew-thill") are the ruins of the former **Muthill Parish Church** (Historic Scotland), which date mainly from the early 15th century, though the tower was probably built four centuries earlier. A Celtic monastery was founded here in about AD 700, and before the medieval church was built it was served by Culdee priests and monks. The **Muthill Village Museum** is housed in a cottage built about 1760. It is open on Wednesdays, Saturdays and Sundays from June to September each year from 12.30 pm until 3 pm.

Three miles east of Muthill, at Innerpeffray, is **Innerpeffray Library**, the oldest public library in Scotland. It was founded in 1680 by David Drummond, 3rd Lord Maddertie and brother-in-law of the Marquis of Montrose, and is housed in a building specially built for it in 1762 by Robert Hay Drummond, who at the time was

Archbishop of York. In 1968 the library ceased to be a lending library due to a fall in demand from local readers. It contains many rare books, such as a copy of the 16th century Treacle Bible, so called because the translation of Jeremiah chapter 8 verse 22 reads, "Is there not triacle (treacle) at Gilead". There is also a copy of the *Chronicles of England, Scotlande and Irelande* by Raphael Holinshed, which Shakespeare used as his historical source for the play *Macbeth*. Before moving to its present building it was housed in **Innerpeffray Chapel**, (Historic Scotland), built in 1508 and dedicated to St Mary. It still retains its pre-Reformation altar. The ruins of **Innerpeffray Castle** are nearby. It is a simple tower house dating from the 15th century which was heightened in 1610 for the 1st Lord Maddertie.

Drummond Castle Gardens, to the west of the village, are well worth visiting. They were first laid out in the 17th century by the second Lord Drummond, who served in the court of both James Vl and Charles l, improved and terraced in the 19th, and replanted in the middle of the 20th. In 1842, Queen Victoria visited, and planted some copper beech trees, which can still be seen. The castle itself is not open to the public.

To the east of the village are the sites of two Roman signal stations - the **Ardunie Signal Station** (Historic Scotland) and the **Muir O'Fauld Signal Station**. They were two of a series of such stations running between Ardoch and the Tay, and date to the 1st century AD.

BRACO

19 miles SW of Perth on the A822

Half a mile north of the village are the **Blackhall Camps**, two Roman marching camps which date to the 3rd century AD.

HUNTINGTOWER

2 miles W of Perth on the A85

Huntingtower (Historic Scotland) is a restored 15th century tower house once owned by the Ruthvens, Earls of Gowrie, and then the Murrays. Mary Stuart visited the castle twice, and in 1582 the famous "Raid of Ruthven" took place here, when the Earl of Gowrie and his friend the Earl of Mar tried to kidnap the young King James VI. Justice in those days was swift, as the perpetrators were first executed, and then tried for treason. The castle has no connection with the John Buchan spy yarn, also called Huntingtower, which was set in Ayrshire.

The castle has two towers, and there is a story about the daughter of an Earl of Gowrie who spent the night with her lover in one of the towers, then leapt the nine feet to the other tower, where her own bedroom was, when her mother nearly discovered her. The gap became known as *The Maiden's Leap*.

FOWLIS WESTER

12 miles W of Perth on a minor road off the A85

Fowlis Westers church sits on a spot where a place of worship has stood since at least the eighth century. The present one dates from the 13th century, though it is much restored, and is dedicated to an 8th century Irish saint, grandson of the King of Leinster, who preached in the area. The church has a leper's squint - a small window which allowed lepers to see the chancel area without coming into contact with the congregation. Two Pictish cross slabs from the 8th or 9th centuries are housed within the church - a ten feet high cross slab and a smaller one. The larger one shows two horsemen and some animals on one side and a man leading a cow and six men on the other. The smaller slab shows two men - possibly priests - seated on chairs. A replica of the larger one stands on the village green. Also in the church is a fragment of the McBean tartan, taken to the moon by American astronaut Alan Bean, who was the lunar module pilot on Apollo 12 during the second mission to the moon in November 1969, and the fourth man to walk on its surface.

CRIEFF

15 miles W of Perth on the A85

This inland holiday resort is the "capital" of that area of Scotland known as Strathearn, and the second largest town in Perthshire. It sits at the beginning of Glen Turret, within which are the picturesque **Falls Of Turret**. At the **Crieff Visitor Centre** on Muthill Road you can see paperweights, pottery and miniature

•

The first name of the small village of Fowlis Wester (pronounced "fowls") comes from the Gaelic "foghlais", meaning "stream" or burn. However, there is another, more intriguing derivation. It seems that long ago three French brothers settled in Scotland - one at Fowlis Wester, one at Fowlis Easter near Dundee and one at Fowlis in Ross-shire, and they each named their village after the French word for leaves, "feuilles". Above an archway in the Parish Church of St Bean in Fowlis Wester is a carving showing three leaves.

•

animal sculptures. The **Glenturret Distillery** at the Hosh, home of the famous "Grouse Experience", is Scotland's oldest, and tours (with a dram at the end) are available. The beech-lined **Lady Mary's Walk**, beside the River Earn, was gifted to the town in 1815 by Sir Patrick Murray of Ochtertyre in memory of his daughter Mary. **Macrosty Park** is said by some to be the finest municipal park in Scotland, and was named after a provost of the town who laid it out in 1902.

The **Baird Monument** stands on a hill to the west of the town, and was erected in memory of Sir David Baird (1757-1829) by his widow. Also to the west of the town is the ruined church of **Monzievaird**, where, in 1490, 120 members of Clan Murray (including women and children) took refuge to escape the Drummonds and Campbells, who had scores to settle with them. They were burned to death when the Drummonds and Campbells set fire to the building. The elder son of Lord Drummond and some of his followers were later executed for the crime.

MADDERTY

10 miles W of Perth off the A85

To the northeast of this village is the site of **Inchaffray Abbey**, of which nothing now remains apart from a low mound. The name means "island of the smooth waters", as at one time the mound was an island within a small loch.

Maurice, Abbot of Inchaffray was Robert the Bruce's chaplain, and the keeper of a holy relic called the Arm of St Fillan. At the Battle of Bannockburn he paraded it before the Scottish troops to bring good fortune (see also St Fillans, Tyndrum and Pittenweem). A later abbot, Laurence Oliphant, was killed at the Battle of Flodden in 1513.

COMRIE

21 miles W of Perth on the A85

This village is often called the "earthquake capital of Scotland" and the "shaky toun" as it sits right on the Highland Boundary Fault. James Melville, writing in his diary in July 1597, mentions an earth tremor, though the first fully recorded one was in 1788. A 72-feet high monument to him - the **Melville Monument** - stands on Dunmore Hill. In 1874 it was struck by lightning, and the man who climbed to its top to repair it swore he could see Edinburgh Castle.

In 1839 a major earthquake took place, causing the world's first seismometers to be set up in the village. The recently refurbished **Earthquake House**, built in 1874, now houses an array of instruments to measure the tremors. North of the village, in Glen Lednock, is the **De'ils Cauldron Waterfall**, and to the south of the village, off the B827, is the **Auchingarrich Wildlife Centre**, with animals, a wild bird hatchery, woodland walks and an adventure playground.

Every New Year in the village the **Flambeaux Ceremony** takes place, when tall "flambeaux", or torches soaked in paraffin are lit. They are laid against the wall of the old graveyard, and as the clock strikes midnight they are picked up and set alight. They are then paraded round the village accompanied by a pipe band and people in fancy costume.

Comrie was the "Best Large Village" in the 2001 Britain in Bloom contest.

ST FILLANS

26 miles W of Perth on the A85

St Fillans stands at the eastern end of Loch Earn, where the River Earn exits on its way to join the Firth of Tay, and is a gateway to the new Loch Lomond and Trossachs National Park. It is named after the Irish missionary St Fillan (see also Pittenweem, Tyndrum and Madderty). Two relics of the saint - his bell and his pastoral staff - are now housed within the National Museum of Scotland. On an island in Loch Earn stand the scant ruins of the 13th century **Loch Earn Castle**, which belonged to Clan MacNeish. From here they plundered the surrounding countryside before retreating to the safety of their castle, where they thought they were safe. The McNabs, whom they attacked in 1612, gained their revenge by carrying a boat over the mountains, unseen by the MacNeishes, launching it on the loch, and mounting a surprise attack. The MacNeish clan chief was killed, as was most of his followers. Since then, the McNab crest has featured the head of the chief of Clan McNeish.

At the top of **Dunfillan Hill** (600 feet) is a rock known as **St Fillan's Chair**. To the southwest, overlooking Loch Earn, is **Ben Vorlich** (3,224 feet). The ruins of **Dundurn Chapel**, which date from pre Reformation times, can be found to the east of the village, off the A85. It was the burial place of the Stewarts of Ardvorlich.

PITLOCHRY

This well-known Scottish town is one of the best touring bases in Scotland. It was a quiet Highland village until Victorian times, when Queen Victoria popularised the Highlands as a holiday destination, and many of the buildings in Pitlochry date from that time. It is said to be at the geographical heart of the country, and as such, it is as far from the sea as it is possible to be in Scotland. It was the 2003 winner as the "best small country town" in the Britain in Bloom contest.

Though not a large town, it relies heavily on tourism, and is full of hotels and guesthouses, and as it sits just off the A9, this makes it a good stopping off point for those travelling north or south. But it has its own attractions, not least of which is the marvellous scenery surrounding it. The B8019, the start of the famous **Road to the Isles** goes west towards beautiful **Loch Tummel**, whose waters have been harnessed for electricity. It passes the **Forestry Commission Visitor Centre**, which interprets

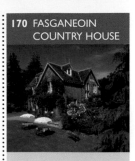

170 FASGANEOIN COUNTRY HOUSE

Pitlochry

A small, friendly country house with a great history and 40 years of offering the very best in hospitality.

see page 510

the wildlife of the area. From the **Queen's View** at the west end of the loch there is a magnificent view west towards Loch Tummel and beyond. Queen Victoria stopped at this point during her "incognita" Highland tour in 1866 and praised the scenery, though it is said that it was Mary Stuart who originally gave the place its name when she visited in 1564.

Loch Faskally is close to Pitlochry, and is a man-made loch over which the A9 passes It is a lovely stretch of water, and forms part of the Tummel hydroelectric scheme. At the **Pitlochry Visitor Centre**, near the dam, there is the famous **Salmon Ladder**, which allows salmon to enter the loch from the River Tummel below. There is a viewing gallery, which allows you to watch the salmon, and displays about how electricity is produced from flowing water. Beside the loch is a picnic area, with an archway called the **Clunie Arch**. It is the exact internal dimensions of the tunnel that brings the waters from Loch Tummel to the Clunie Power Station.

The **Edradour Distillery,** situated among the hills to the east of Pitlochry, is Scotland's smallest, and possibly its most picturesque distillery. It was established in 1837 and produces handcrafted malt using only local barley. Conducted tours, finished off with a tasting, are available. Bell's **Blair Atholl Distillery** is the oldest working distillery in Scotland, and is also in Pitlochry.

The **Pitlochry Festival Theatre** was founded in 1951, and presented its first plays in a tent. It continued like this until 1981, when a purpose-built theatre was opened at Port-na-Craig on the banks of the Tummel. It presents a varied programme of professional plays every summer, and is one of Scotland's most popular venues.

The A924 going east from Pitlochry takes you up into some marvellous scenery. It reaches a height of 1,260 feet before dropping down into Kirkmichael and then on to Bridge of Cally. On the way, at Enochdhu, you will pass **Kindrogan**, a Victorian country house where the Scottish Field Studies Association offer residential courses on Scotland's natural history. The house itself dates from the early 19th century, and was owned by the Keirs. The **Dunfallandy Standing Stone** lies south of the town near Dunfallandy House, and west of the A9. It dates from Pictish times, and has a curious legend attached to it. A nun called Triduana was being

Loch Tummel

forced into marriage with the son of a Scottish king, but escaped to a small chapel at Dunfallandy, where she erected the "praying stone" in gratitude.

There are many fine guided walks in the area, some organised by such bodies as National Trust for Scotland, the Scottish Wildlife Trust and the Forestry Commission. A small booklet about them is available.

AROUND PITLOCHRY

SPITTAL OF GLENSHEE

13 miles NE of Pitlochry on the A93

As the name suggests, a small medieval hospital, or "spittal", once stood close to this village, which lies in the heart of the Grampian Mountains at a height of 1,125 feet. It sits on the main road north from Perth to Braemar, and surrounding it is some marvellous scenery. The Glenshee skiing area (Britain's largest) lies six miles north of the village, and is dealt with in the North East Scotland section of this guidebook.

The **Four Poster Stone Circle** at Bad an Loin is unusual in that it only has four stones. Legend says it is the burial place of Diarmid, the great Ossianic folk hero, who was killed in a boar hunt. From it there are fine views of Glen Shee.

DUNKELD

11 miles S of Pitlochry off the A9

Though it has all the appearance of an attractive town, Dunkeld is in fact a small cathedral city. **Dunkeld Cathedral** sits on the banks of the Tay, and consists of a ruined nave and a restored chancel, which is now used as the parish church.

For a short period Dunkeld was the ecclesiastical capital of Scotland. Kenneth I, when he ascended the throne as the first king of Scots in AD 843, established his capital at Forteviot, and then Scone, near Perth, bringing relics of St Columba with him, no doubt because Iona was too vulnerable to Viking attack. He placed them in the church of a Celtic monastery set up at Dunkeld, which in AD 865 was the seat of the chief Scottish bishop.

The cathedral as we see it nowadays dates from many periods. The choir (the present parish church) was built mainly in the early 14th century, while the nave (now ruined) was built in the early 15th century. Within the church is the tomb of Alexander Stewart, son of Robert II and known as the Wolf of Badenoch, the man who sacked Elgin Cathedral in the 14th century after a disagreement with the Bishop of Moray (see also Elgin, Grantown-on-Spey and Fortrose). After the Reformation the cathedral fell into disrepair, and it was not until 1600 that the choir was re-roofed and used as the parish church.

In 1689 the town was the scene of the **Battle of Dunkeld**, when Jacobite forces were defeated by a force of Cameronians under **William Cleland**. This was an unusual battle, as the fighting and

The Devil's Elbow on the A93 lies about five miles north of Spitaal of Glenshee. A combination of steep inclines and double bends made it a notorious place for accidents in days gone by, though it has been much improved. The Cairnwell, at 3,058 feet high, is a Munro standing almost adjacent to the A93. The road reaches a height of 2,199 feet, making it the highest public road in Britain. During the winter months the road can be blocked by snow for weeks on end.

172 BALLINLUIG INN HOTEL

Ballinluig, Pitlochry
This former drover's inn now offers the best in food, drink and accommodation.

see page 511

At the Birnam Institute in Dunkeld is the Beatrix Potter Gardens, and within the Institute itself there is a small exhibition, which tells the story of the young Beatrix. She used to holiday at Dalguise House near Dunkeld as a child, and gained some of her inspiration from the surrounding countryside.

gunfire took place among the streets and buildings of the town, and not in open countryside. William Cleland was fatally wounded during the encounter, and now lies in the ruined nave of the cathedral.

Another, but not so famous, man lies in the nave of the cathedral. Curiously enough he lies beside William Cleland, and yet he was the grandson of the greatest Jacobite of them all, Charles Edward Stuart. The Prince's illegitimate daughter Charlotte had an affair with the Archbishop of Bordeaux, Ferdinand, Count of Rohan, the result being two daughters and a son - Charles Edward August Maximilien de Roehenstart, better known as **Count Roehenstart** (a name made up from "Rohan" and "Stuart"). On a trip to Scotland in 1854 he was killed in a carriage accident near Dunkeld when a wheel came off his coach. Though his mother and grandfather were both Catholics, Count Roehenstart was brought up a Protestant.

Most of the "little houses" in Dunkeld date from the early 18th century, as they were built to replace those that had been destroyed in the battle. Now the National Trust for Scotland looks after most of them. On the wall of one house in the square, the **Ell Shop,** is portrayed an old Scottish length of measurement called the "ell", which corresponds to 37 inches. Also in the square is the **Atholl Memorial Fountain,** erected in 1866 in memory of the 6th Duke of Atholl.

The **Loch of the Lowes** lies to the east of the city, and has a visitor centre. The star attraction of its 242 acres from late April to August is a pair of breeding ospreys. The **Hermitage** (National Trust for Scotland) is a riverside walk, along the banks of the River Braan, to the north west of the town, on the other side of the A9

This is the heartland of the "big tree country", and it was in Dunkeld, in 1738, that the first larches were planted in Scotland.

GRANDTULLY

7 miles SW of Pitlochry on the A827

Grandtully is pronounced "Grantly". **Grandtully Castle**, to the west of the village, dates from the 15th century, and was a Stewart stronghold. It was abandoned in the 19th century, but rebuilt in the 1920s. **St Mary's Church** (Historic Scotland) was built by Sir Alexander Stewart in 1533, and was remodelled in 1633 when a painted ceiling was added that shows heraldic motifs and coats-of-arms of families connected with the Stewarts.

ABERFELDY

8 miles SW of Pitlochry on the A827

In 1787 Robert Burns wrote a song called *The Birks of Aberfeldy*, and made famous this small town and its surrounding area. "Birks" are birch trees, and the ones in question can still be seen to the south of the village in an area known as **The Birks**. Some people claim, however, that Burns was actually writing about Abergeldie near Crathie in Aberdeenshire, though this is doubtful. The River Moness, a tributary of the Tay, falls through The Birks, and at its head are the **Falls of Moness**.

The village sits on the River Tay, and crossing it is **General Wade's Bridge**, built in 1733 (but not opened until 1735) by Major-General George Wade, Commander-in-Chief of North Britain from 1724 until 1740 ("Scotland" was not a name that was liked by the English establishment at the time). It is 400 feet in length, with a middle arch that spans 60 feet, and was part of a road network used to police the Highlands during the Jacobite unrest. It was formally opened in 1735, and cost £3,596, which in today's terms in close to £1m.

At about the same time, six independent regiments were raised to "watch" the Highlands for signs of this unrest. These six regiments later amalgamated to form the 43rd Highland Regiment of Foot under the Earl of Crawford, and it paraded for the first time at Aberfeldy in May 1740. The regiment later became the Black Watch, and the **Black Watch Memorial**, built in 1887, commemorates the event. The regiment now forms the third battalion of the Royal Regiment of Scotland.

Right on the A827 is **Dewar's World of Whisky**. Here you will find out about one of Scotland's most famous whisky firms, located in the distillery where Aberfeldy Single Malt is made. The **Aberfeldy Water Mill**, a combination of bookshop, art gallery and coffee shop, is housed in an old mill built in 1835.

A mile or so north west of the village, near Weem is **Castle Menzies**, home to Clan Menzies (pronounced Ming -iz in Scotland). The clan is not Scottish in origin, but Norman, with the name coming from Mesnieres near Rouen. James Menzies of Menzies, son-in-law of the then Earl of Atholl, built the castle in the 16th century. In 1665 the clan chief was created a baron of Nova Scotia. The last member of the main line died in 1918, and the clan was left without a chief. In 1957 the descendants of a cousin of the first baron were recognised as clan chiefs, and the present one is David Steuart Menzies of Menzies. During the Jacobite Uprising, most branches of the clan supported Charles Edward Stuart, while the main branch, based at Castle Menzies, tried to remain neutral, though the castle played host to Charles Edward Stuart for two nights as he retreated north in 1746.

173 WEEM HOTEL

Weem

An old coaching inn that combines traditional hospitality and modern standards of service.

see page 511

General Wades Bridge

Ben Lawers National Nature Reserve

174 COURTYARD RESTAURANT AND LOUNGE BAR

Kenmore

A restaurant and lounge bar where modern cuisine and stunning Perthshire scenery combine to give a great dining experience.

🍴 see page 512

175 FORTINGALL HOTEL

Fortingall

A stylish yet friendly hotel set in a historic village that offers the very best in Scottish hospitality.

🛏 see page 512

316

The castle is now owned by the Menzies Charitable Trust. Parts of it are open to the public, and it houses a Clan Menzies museum.

KENMORE

13 miles SW of Pitlochry on the A827

Kenmore sits at the eastern end of **Loch Tay**, and was founded in about 1540 by the Earls of Breadalbane. The loch is the source of the River Tay, one of the most picturesque in Scotland. It is 14-and-a-half miles long, less than a mile wide, and plunges to a maximum depth of over 500 feet. Overlooking it, on the northern shore, is **Ben Lawers** (3,984 feet), with the **Ben Lawers Mountain Visitor Centre** (National Trust for Scotland) on a minor road off the A827. There is a nature trail, and a booklet is available at the centre.

The Scottish Crannog Centre, run by the Scottish Trust for Underwater Archaeology, explains how people in the past lived in crannogs, which were dwelling houses situated in the shallow waters of a loch that

offered defence against attack. They were either built on artificial islands or raised on stilts above the water, and were in use from about 2500 BC right up until the 17th century. Off the north shore of the loch is **Eilean nan Bannoamh** ("Isle of the Holy Women") where once stood a small Celtic nunnery. Alexander I's wife Queen Sybille (illegitimate daughter of Henry l of England), died here in 1122, and Alexander founded an Augustinian priory in her memory. She was buried in Dunfermline Abbey.

The **Croftmoraig Stone Circle** lies to the west of the village, and was excavated in 1965. It is said to be the most complete example of this kind of stone circle in Scotland.

FORTINGALL

15 miles SW of Pitlochry on a minor road off the B846

—

This little village has a unique claim to fame. It is said to be the birthplace of **Pontius Pilate**, the governor of Judea at the time of Christ's execution. It is said that his father, a Roman officer, was sent to Scotland by Augustus Caesar to command a unit which kept the local Pictish clans in check. Whether Pontius was born of a union between his father and a local woman, or whether his father had brought a wife with him, is not recorded. There is no proof that the story is true, but there was certainly a Roman camp nearby. One further story says that Pilate's mother was a Menzies, but as that family is descended from someone who came over to England with the Norman Conquest in the 11th century, this cannot possibly be true.

Sir Donald Currie laid out Fortingall as a model village in the 19th century, and it has some picturesque thatched cottages that would not look out of place in a South of England village. In the kirkyard of the early 20th century parish church is the **Fortingall Yew**, said to be the oldest living thing in Europe. The tree looks rather the worse for wear nowadays, but as it may be as much as 3,000 years old (a plaque next to it says 5,000 years, but this is doubtful), perhaps this is not surprising.

The village sits at the entrance to **Glen Lyon**, at 25 miles long, Scotland's longest, and perhaps loveliest, glen. Tumbling through it is the River Lyon, which rises at Loch Lyon, part of a massive hydroelectric scheme. At Bridge of Balgie a minor road strikes south, rising into some wild scenery and passing **Meall Luaidhe** (2,535 feet) before dropping down towards the Ben Lawers Mountain Visitor Centre (see Kenmore) and the shores of Loch Tay. On the B846 four miles north of Fortingall at the foot of **Schiehallion** (3,546 feet) is the **Glengoulandie Deer Park**, with its herd of red deer,

Highland cattle, goats and rare breeds of sheep. Schiehallion translates as the "Fairy Hill of the Caledonians", and is owned by the John Muir Trust.

KINLOCH RANNOCH

17 miles W of Pitlochry on the B846

This small village, laid out in the 18th century by James Small, a government factor, sits at the eastern end of **Loch Rannoch**, which has roads on both the northern and southern sides.

The **Parish Church** is one of Telford's parliamentarian churches, and was built in 1829. Usually a parliamentarian church was nothing but a plain, T-shaped preaching box, but Kinloch Rannoch is more like a conventional church, with the Holy Table at the east end.

The ruins of the old church stand at **Lassintullich**, to the east of the village. They date from the 17th century, though a church has stood here since medieval times.

The B846 carries on westward past Kinloch Rannoch, and skirts the northern shores of Loch Rannoch. It eventually comes to an end at **Rannoch Station**. This station, on the Glasgow/Fort William line, is the loneliest in Britain, and stands at a height of over 1,000 feet. Beyond it is **Rannoch Moor**, said to be the most desolate spot in Scotland, and "Europe's last great wilderness". In winter, when snow covers it, it is treacherous, and no one should venture out onto it unless they're experienced. Even in summer, when it is hauntingly beautiful, it

In a field next to the village of Fortingall is the Carn na Marbh, or Cairn of the Dead which marks the mass grave of plague victims during the galar mhor, or great plague in the 14th century. It is said that one old woman, who was still sufficiently healthy, carried the bodies to the field on a horse-drawn sledge.

An obelisk in the centre of Kinloch Rannoch commemorates Dugald Buchanan, the local schoolmaster who died here of a fever in 1763. He wrote in Gaelic and Latin, and was one of the Highland's greatest religious poets. He was buried at Balquidder, where he was born. He had eight children, and they too died of a fever within a short time of Dugald's death.

176 TALLADH-A-
BHEITHE LODGE

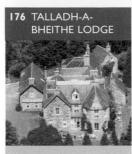

Loch Rannoch

An elegant guest house and
restaurant on the shores of
Loch Rannoch where you
are assured of a relaxing
time.

see page 513

should still be treated with respect.
It took 5,000 men to build the rail
line over this daunting moor, and it
rests on a "floating" bed of wood
and straw.

But the moor's landscape is not
a natural one. Even here, man has
made his mark. The whole of the
moor was once covered in the trees
of the old Caledonian Forest, but
man gradually cleared them to use
as fuel and for building. The whole
of the moor is littered with small
lochs and large boulders carried by
the glaciers that once covered this
area.

KILLIECRANKIE

3 miles N of Pitlochry off the A9

The rather unusual name comes
from the Gaelic *Coille Creitheannich*,
meaning "aspen wood". It was
here, in 1689, that the **Battle of
Killiecrankie** was fought. The Pass
of Killiecrankie is a narrow defile,
and as government troops (not
Englishmen but Scottish
Lowlanders) under General Mackay
passed gingerly through it, they
were attacked from above by
Jacobite forces under Bonnie
Dundee (see also Blair Atholl). The

government troops had the River
Garry behind them, so escape was
impossible, and it ended in a
victory for the Jacobites. Bonnie
Dundee himself was killed before
the battle could get underway
properly, however. The
Killiecrankie Visitors Centre
(National Trust for Scotland) has
displays explaining the battle.

A curious tale says that after
Dundee's body had been recovered,
he was discovered to have been
wearing a Templar cross beneath
his clothing (see also Blair Atholl).

At the north end of the pass is
a spot known as the **Soldier's
Leap**, high above the River Garry.
It is said that, after the battle, a
government trooper called Donald
McBean leapt across the 18-feet
wide gap to escape from some
Jacobites who were chasing him.

BLAIR ATHOLL

6 miles NW of Pitlochry off the A9

Blair Castle is one of the most
famous castles in Scotland. It sits
above the village, and with its
whitewashed walls looks more like
a great fortified mansion house
than a castle. It is the ancestral

Killiecrankie

home of the Murrays, Dukes of Atholl, and originally dates from 1269, though what you see nowadays is mainly from 18th and 19th century refurbishments. About 30 furnished rooms are open to the public, with fine furniture, paintings, china and armour on display. The Duke of Atholl is the only person in Britain who is allowed to have a private army, the **Atholl Highlanders**, and a small museum has displays of uniforms, weapons and musical instruments associated with the regiment. It was raised in 1778 by the 4th Duke of Atholl to fight the colonists in the American War of Independence. However, after a posting to Ireland they were disbanded. The regiment as we know it today dates from 1839. In 1844 Queen Victoria stayed at Blair Atholl and a year later presented the regiment with two sets of colours.

In a vault beneath the ruined **St Bride's Kirk**, in the castle grounds, lies the body of John Graham, 1st Viscount Dundee, known as "Bonnie Dundee", who was killed at the Battle of Killiecrankie in 1689 (see also Killiecrankie). At Bruar, four miles north of Blair Atholl, is the **Clan Donnachaidh Museum**. Though the name translates into English as Donnachie, it traces the history of the Clan Robertson, and shows their place in local and Scottish history. **The Falls of Bruar** are close by, and fall through a picturesque ravine with footbridges over them.

North East Scotland

The area normally referred to as North East Scotland is not, in fact, within northeast Scotland, which is further north and centred on the town of Wick. Instead, it is that vast area of the country jutting out into the North Sea and centred on the city of Aberdeen. It consists of the old counties of Aberdeenshire, Kincardineshire, Banffshire and Morayshire.

The area abounds in fine scenery of all kinds. High mountains, wooded glens, cityscapes, beaches, rich farmland, towering cliffs and moorland - it's got the lot. And yet it is relatively unknown to those outside Scotland, apart from the city of Aberdeen and along Royal Deeside. The beaches are quiet and clean, the country lanes are a joy to drive along, and there is history and heritage aplenty.

And always in the background are the Grampians, that mountain range which has its highest peaks here. Queen Victoria, when she bought Balmoral, popularised Deeside, a glen which goes deep into the heart of the mountains, and it has remained firmly on the tourist trail ever since. But as with many parts of Scotland, while the tourist traps swarm with people, other places, equally as interesting and picturesque, are bypassed.

To go off the beaten track in the North East is to be rewarded with some wonderful discoveries. Who, for instance, has explored the farmlands of Buchan, with their rich soil, which, even though they are above the Highland line, are firmly in the Lowlands, and have a Lowland dialect called "The Doric" that even other Scots have difficulty understanding at times? How many people stop in Kincardineshire, with its fishing villages and its literary associations? It was here that Robert Burns's father was born. It was here that local man Lewis Grassic Gibbon set his dark novels of country life - novels that owed nothing to the prevalent custom of writing novels with happy, rustic people living in harmony with the land. And who, except those in the know, visit Elgin, a charming small city with the ruins of what was one of the largest and grandest cathedrals in Scotland?

Nowhere else in Europe is there such a concentration of historic castles - around 1,000 at the last count. There is even a Castle Trail, with a leaflet that explains their history and how to get to them. And then there are the distilleries. The industry is centred mainly on Banffshire and Moray, where the streams are swift flowing and the water pure. It's amazing that two distilleries a mile or so apart can make whiskies that are so different in character. The Whisky Trail takes in most of them, and like the Castle Trail there is a leaflet to guide you as you explore it.

The inland villages are quiet and peaceful, and the market towns, such as Inverurie, Forres and Huntly, are packed with history and charm. The coastline is as dramatic as anywhere in Britain. Yet another trail, the Coastal Trail, takes you on a tour from St Cyrus in the south, northwards to Fraserburgh then westwards to Findhorn on the Moray Firth coast. The ruins of Dunnottar Castle are perched dramatically above the sea, while the Ythan Estuary (pronounced "eye-than") is a Site of Scientific Interest, rich in aquatic and bird life as well as having archaeological sites dating back to Neolithic times. Slains Castle, south of Peterhead, was one of the inspirations for Bram Stoker's *Dracula*, and the fishing port of Fraserburgh was, for a very short time, a university town.

For all its crowds (especially in late summer when the Queen is in residence at Balmoral), Deeside cannot be missed. This long glen follows the Dee up into the heart of the Grampians with Braemar, at its heart, being officially Britain's coldest place (though summer days can be balmy and long). But don't let the seeming remoteness put you off - the glen is green and wooded for most of its length. Ballater - Crathie - Aboyne - the names are familiar to us all through news programmes, and yet the reality of seeing them makes you realise why Queen Victoria, and subsequent monarchs, fell in love with Royal Deeside in the first place.

Aberdeen is Scotland's third largest city and Europe's oil capital. The name, which

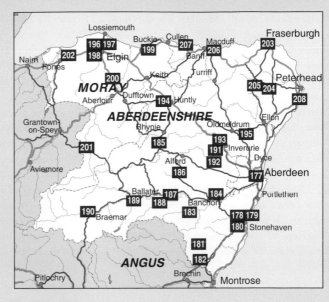

ACCOMMODATION

FOOD & DRINK

PLACES OF INTEREST

means "at the mouth of the Dee and the Don", sums up its location precisely, as the two rivers enter the North Sea here. The oil industry has brought money to the city, and it has also brought a cosmopolitan lifestyle that includes smart restaurants, boutiques, nightclubs and stylish pubs. But even here history is never far away. It was granted a royal charter by King William the Lion in 1175, and Old Aberdeen, which used to be a proud separate burgh, was granted its charter in 1489.

The other city in the region is Elgin, at one time one of the most important places in Scotland. It has lost some of that importance now, but has not lost any of its charm. It is still a busy place, and is the shopping and administrative centre for a large fertile area called the Laigh of Moray. Here too there are quiet country lanes and small villages to explore, while at Findhorn there is the Findhorn Foundation, where the emphasis is on spiritual living and alternative lifestyles. And south of the city is the only medieval abbey in Britain that still houses monks.

Farming is a vital industry in North East Scotland, and sometimes it seems that the area known as Buchan - to the north of Aberdeen - has more Aberdeen Angus cattle than people, and the perception is not far wrong. And the countryside in Banff and Moray is where the distilleries get their barley. Plus there is fishing, with Peterhead being the main port. In fact, it is now the largest white fish port in Britain.

ABERDEEN

The Brig o' Balgownie over the Don, near the cathedral, has a single, elegant, Gothic arch. Work started on it in about 1290, but it was not until the early 14th century that it was completed. It is said to have been built using money given by Robert the Bruce, and is reckoned to be the finest single arch structure in Scotland. Aberdeen's other old bridge, to the south of the city, is the seven-arch Bridge of Dee, built by Bishop Dunbar in the early 1500s. It once marked the southern boundary of the city. A battle was fought here in 1639 between Royalist troops and Covenanters.

With a population of about 220,000, Aberdeen is Scotland's third largest city. Its nickname is the "Granite City" because of the predominant building material - one which has created a stylish and attractive place that seems to glisten in the sun - or even the rain. It prides itself on being Scotland's most prosperous city, due to the oil fields that lie beneath the North Sea. For this reason it is also known as the "Oil Capital of Europe", and the docks and harbours, which were once full of fishing boats, now pulse with supply ships ferrying men and machines out to the oil rigs. It also has the ferry terminal for the Shetland ferry.

But Aberdeen has two more nicknames - "Scotland's Garden City" and the "Flower of Scotland". Both derive from the many gardens and colourful open spaces that can be visited. In fact, it boasts six city parks, seven local parks and 32 neighbourhood parks, plus many green spaces dotted round the place. It has won awards for its floral displays (including many "Britain in Bloom" awards), with **Johnston Gardens, Hazelhead Park, Union Terrace Gardens, Bon Accord Terrace Gardens, Westfield Park** and **Duthie Park** offering particularly fine examples. In Duthie Park is the magnificent 70 feet tall **James McGrigor Monument**, which commemorates a notable military surgeon who died in 1851. He is credited with having reformed the army's medical facilities. The monument once stood at Marishal College, of which McGrigor was once rector, but was moved in the

1890s. The eleven acre **Cruickshank Botanic Gardens** is partly owned by the University of Aberdeen, and though open to the public, is used for teaching and research purposes. In 2003 Aberdeen took silver in the "Nations in Bloom" competition, beaten only by Seattle, USA, and Quanzhou, China.

It is also a centre of learning, administration, shopping and business. But it has never been scarred by industry in the way that some Scottish central belt towns have. It has managed to remain above such things, and its quality of life is among the best in urban Britain.

And for all its bustle and modern office blocks, it is an ancient city, having been granted a charter as a royal burgh in 1175. Even then it was an important and busy port, trading with the Baltic States as well as the Netherlands and France. During the Wars of Independence it was sacked three times by the English, and finally razed to the ground by Edward III in 1337. One unexpected visitor to Aberdeen was William Shakespeare, who, with his troupe of actors, was sent by Elizabeth I to appear before the court of James VI in 1601 (see also Glamis).

There are two Aberdeens - the original one, and Old Aberdeen, which was at one time a separate burgh. Perversely Old Aberdeen was only granted its charter in 1489, and is a captivating area of old, elegant buildings and quiet cobbled streets.

The buildings you see throughout the city nowadays however, are mainly Georgian, Victorian and later, with some older buildings among them to add historical depth. The **Cathedral Church of St Machar** in Old Aberdeen was founded in about 1131, and is dedicated to a saint who was son of Fiachna, an Irish prince. He was also a companion of St Columba, and came over from Ireland with him to found the monastery on Iona. Legend states that Columba sent him to convert the Picts in the area, and he had a vision from God to build a church at a point where a river bends in the shape of a bishop's crosier just before it enters the sea. As the Don bends in this way, he established his church here in about AD 580. It's a fascinating tale, but probably untrue, as a bishop's crosier in those days was not curved, but straight.

St Machar's as we see it today dates from the 14th century and later. The choir has completely disappeared, and what you see now was the nave of the original cathedral with the ruins of the two transepts, which are in the care of Historic Scotland. In 1688 the central tower collapsed, leaving a rather truncated building with a beautiful west front with two towers. Perhaps its most famous bishop was **William Elphinstone**, Chancellor of Scotland and producer of the first book of liturgy in the country, the *Aberdeen Breviary*. Its heraldic ceiling, containing 48 coats-of-arms, is

The Church of St Nicholas stands in St Nicholas Street. The first mention of a church on the site is a Papal Bull dated 1157, though there may have been a previous building which was burned down during a great fire that swept through the city in 1153. At the Reformation it was divided into two churches, the East and the West. These were later united once more when the church was largely rebuilt in the 18th and 19th centuries. Of the original church only the transepts and the crypt survive. Its carillon of 48 bells is the largest of any church in Britain. There are six entrances to the kirkyard, the grandest being the granite colonnade in Union Street, designed in 1830 by John Smith, Aberdeen's city architect. Beneath what was the East Kirk is St Mary's Chapel, built by Lady Elizabeth Gordon. When she died in 1438 she was buried within it.

In King Street is St Andrews Episcopal Cathedral, dating originally from 1817, but greatly expanded in 1880. In 1914 it became the cathedral for the diocese. After the Jacobite Uprising, Episcopalians in the city (who generally supported Charles Edward Stuart) were forced to leave their churches, and a man called John Skinner held services in a chapel in his house. It was in this chapel, in 1784, that Samuel Seabury was consecrated bishop of America by Skinner, Bishop Kilgour of Aberdeen and Bishop Petrie of Moray. This flew in the face of government policy at the time, which saw no need for Anglican bishops for the colonies, but as it was a perfectly legal ceremony, they could do nothing about it. However, it eventually forced parliament to change the law so that bishops for the colonies could be consecrated. In 1884 a window was consecrated within the cathedral to commemorate the 100th anniversary of the event.

magnificent, and is the work of Bishop Gavin Dunbar, who succeeded Elphinstone in 1518. Curiously enough, one of the coats-of-arms is that of Henry Vlll of England. Dunbar also erected the two west towers.

At Bridge of Don is **Glover House,** the family home of Thomas Blake Glover, the Scotsman who, it is said, inspired Puccini's opera *Madame Butterfly*. Born in Fraserburgh in 1838, his family moved to Bridge of Don in 1851 when he was 13 years old. When he left school, he began working for a trading company, and got a taste for overseas travel.

When he first went to Japan at the age of 21, he was entering a feudal society that had been closed to the west for over 300 years. However, within one year he was selling Scottish-built warships and arms to Japanese rebels during the country's civil war. At the same time he sent young Japanese men to Britain to be educated.

He was called the "Scottish Samurai", and helped found the Mitsubishi shipyards, the first step Japan took to becoming a great manufacturing power. He also helped found the famous Kirin Brewery, and his picture still appears on Kirin labels to this day. He was later presented with the Order of the Rising Sun, Japan's greatest honour. He built himself a house at Nagasaki, and married a Japanese woman called Tsura, who invariably wore kimonos decorated with butterfly motifs. When Puccini came across a short story and

subsequent play based on this relationship, it sowed the seeds for Madame Butterfly.

The house was previously owned by the Mitsubishi Company, but was given to the Thomas Blake Glover Trust in 1997. It has been restored to the way it would have been in Victorian times.

St Mary's Roman Catholic Cathedral in Huntly Street, was opened in 1860, and had a spire added between 1876 and 1877. It was the first RC cathedral in Britain to be refurbished to take advantage of the reforms in liturgy of the Second Vatican Council.

Union Street, Aberdeen's main thoroughfare, is over a mile long, and thronged with shops. It was laid out in the early 1800s to celebrate the union of Britain and Ireland. At one end, in Castlegate, is the city's **Mercat Cross**, standing close to where Aberdeen's long-gone medieval castle stood. Built in 1686 by local stonemason John Montgomery, it has carvings of the ten Stuart monarchs, from James l to James Vll. Almost opposite is the city's Tolbooth, dating from the 17th century, and housing the **Tolbooth Prison Museum**.

Provost Skene's House, off St Nicholas Street, dates from about 1545, and is named after a former lord provost of the city, Sir George Skene, who bought it in 1669. It is a tall, solid building of turrets and chimneys, and has wonderful painted ceilings and period furniture, as well as displays on modern history. **Provost Ross's House** is in Shiprow, said to be

Aberdeen's oldest street still in use. The house was built in 1593, but is named after its most famous owner, John Ross, lord provost of Aberdeen in the 18th century. It now houses part of the **Aberdeen Maritime Museum**, with exhibits and displays on Aberdeen's maritime history, plus a re-created "helicopter ride" out to an offshore oilrig. In the former Skene Square School can be found the **Museum of Education Victorian Classroom**, which re-creates a typical classroom in the city in Victorian times.

Provost Skene's House

Aberdeen University was founded by Bishop Elphinstone in 1494 under a Papal Bull from Pope Alexander IV. **King's College** stands in Old Aberdeen, and its chapel, built in 1505, forms one side of a quadrangle in the middle of which is a 20th century monument to its founder. The chapel's crown steeple, built in honour of James VI, was blown down in a storm in 1633, and there were dark mutterings all over Aberdeen that witchcraft was involved. The following year work started on rebuilding it. The **King's College Conference and Visitor Centre** explains the college's history.

Marischal College, another university, was founded in 1593, 99 years after King's College, which meant that the city had two universities at a time when the whole of England had the same number. It was founded by George Keith, 5th Earl Marischal of Scotland, as a Protestant alternative

to the Catholic-leaning King's College. The present imposing granite building in Broad Street dates from the 19th century, and is the second largest granite building in the world. In 1860 the two universities united to form Aberdeen University. The **Marischal College Museum**, founded in 1786, houses a collection of classical and Egyptian objects, as well as local collections. Aberdeen University's **Zoology Museum**, in the university's Zoology Building at the corner of St Machar's Drive and Tillydrone Avenue, has the largest collection of zoological specimens in the north of Scotland. Some of its treasure include a mounted Bengal tiger, seized at Aberdeen Airport in 1996, twelve bird skins from North American birds, presented by the American natural history artist John James Audubon to William McGillivray, professor of Natural History at the university in the late 19th century, and a replica of a coelacanth.

The Aberdeen Art Gallery and Museum is at Schoolhill, near Robert Gordon's College. Apart from a fine collection of paintings and sculpture by such artists as Degas, Reynolds, and Epstein, it houses displays on Aberdeen's history, including finds made at various archaeological digs throughout the city. James Dun's House, dating from 1769, forms part of the museum.

177 GORDON
HIGHLANDERS
MUSEUM

Aberdeen

The heroic story of the 200-year history of the Gordon Highlanders, is illustrated with displays and re-creations.

 see page 513

On the north bank of the Dee, where it enters the North Sea, is an area called Footdee, or, as it is known by Aberdonians, "Fittie". This is where Aberdeen's original fishing community lived, in rows of cottages that have now been tastefully renovated and modernised.

The **Planetarium** at Aberdeen College in the Gallowgate Centre is a star dome, which shows the planets and stars as they "move" through the heavens. And the **Gordon Highlanders Museum** on Viewfield Road tells the story of what Sir Winston Churchill called "the finest regiment that ever was". In 1994 it was merged with the Queen's Own (Seaforth and Camerons) regiment, to become the Highlanders. In 2006 the Highlanders became the 1st battalion of the Royal Regiment of Scotland. There is an audiovisual theatre, gardens, a children's "handling area", a shop and a café. **Stratosphere,** in Justice Mill Lane, is a hands-on science centre where children can explore all aspects of science, and watch a science show that explains things like colour and bubbles. The **Doonies Rare Breeds Farm** near Nigg, to the south of the city, has a collection of rare breeds, and is a recognised breeding centre for endangered species.

At one time there were well over 100 quarries in the city mining granite. **Rubislaw Quarry**, near the Gordon Highlanders Museum, was one of the biggest. It was still being worked right up until 1971, when it was about 465 feet deep and 900 feet across. Now it has been filled with water to a depth of 180 feet and fenced off. However, it can still partially be seen from Queen's Road. During 230 years of quarrying, it is said to have produced over six million tonnes of granite, not just for Aberdeen, but for places like London, Russia and Japan.

At 164 King Street is the **Aberdeen and North East Scotland Family History Society**, which has a wide range of reference material for family and genealogical research. It was the first such facility in Scotland. At Blairs, on South Deeside Road, there was once a Catholic junior seminary, which closed in 1986. The **Blairs Museum** now holds the Scottish Catholic Heritage Collection, and is open to the public. There are objects connected with the Stuart line (including Mary Stuart and Charles Edward Stuart) on display, as well as a collection of rich vestments, church plate and paintings. Group tours and tailored tours can be arranged.

AROUND ABERDEEN

STONEHAVEN

16 miles S of Aberdeen on the A92

Stonehaven was once the county town of Kincardineshire. It is a fishing community, though the industry has gone into decline. Near the harbour stands the 18th century **Mercat Cross**, and the **Steeple**, from where James VII was proclaimed king in 1715 after landing at the town's harbour. The Tolbooth was built in the late 16th century, and is the town's oldest building. It stands on the north side of the harbour, and was formerly a storehouse belonging to the Earl Marischal of Scotland, who lived in nearby Dunnottar Castle. Now it is the **Tolbooth Museum**, with displays and exhibits about the town's history and its fishing fleet. It was officially opened in 1963 by the Queen Mother.

Each year at Hogmanay the traditional **Fireball Festival** is held in Stonehaven. It takes place in the "Auld Toon", with up to 60 men parading at midnight while swinging huge fireballs on the end of stout wires. The origins are rooted in paganism, with the light from the balls supposedly attracting the sun, ensuring its return after the dark days of winter. Today the whole ceremony lasts about half an hour, but in days gone by it could last for up to an hour or more.

Two miles south of the town is **Dunnottar Castle**. It is magnificently sited, as it stands on a promontory 160 feet above the sea and guarded on three sides by the North Sea and on the fourth by St Ninian's Den, a steep ravine. A fortification has stood here since at least Pictish times, if not before, though the present castle dates from the 13th century and later. It was the home of the Keiths, hereditary Earl Marischals of Scotland, who organised all the great ceremonial occasions in the country, such as coronations, state funerals and the like. The tenth and last Earl Marischal was stripped of his lands and possessions because of his support for the Jacobites in 1715.

The castle has seen some gruesome episodes in Scotland's history. In 1297 William Wallace torched it, burning to death every English soldier within its walls. In 1652 Cromwell's troops laid siege to it for eight months to capture Scotland's Crown Jewels. However, they were foiled by the wife of the minister of Kinneff Church, who smuggled them out (see also Inverbervie) under the very noses of the troops.

In 1685 167 Covenanters were imprisoned in an underground cellar. Those that tried to escape were killed, while most of those that remained succumbed to disease and starvation. Those that survived were taken to the colonies.

INVERBERVIE

25 miles S of Aberdeen on the A92

Though no bigger than a village, Inverbervie is in fact a royal burgh, having been granted its charter in 1341 by David II, who, along with Queen Joanna (daughter of Edward II of England), was shipwrecked off the coast as he returned from imprisonment in France, and was "kindly received" by the people of the village. John Coutts, whose son **Thomas Coutts** founded the famous bank, was born here in 1699. **Hallgreen Castle** (not open to the public) sits close to the sea, and has associations with the Dunnet family. The village's **Mercat Cross** dates from 1737.

At the south end of the Jubilee Bridge, built in 1935 for the jubilee of George V, is the **Hercules Linton Memorial**, which commemorates the man who designed the famous tea clipper *The Cutty Sark*, and was a partner in the Dumbarton yard that built her. He was born in the burgh in 1831, and

178 ST LEONARDS HOTEL

Stonehaven

A hotel that is special - it offers value for money, traditional hospitality and high standards of service.

see page 514

179 MOLLY'S

Stonehaven

A stylish and trendy café bar by day and a superb restaurant in the evenings - you can't go wrong if you pay a visit!

see page 514

180 THE SHIP INN

Stonehaven

A superb harbour side inn with comfortable, en suite accommodation, a cosy, welcoming bar, and great food.

see page 514

Three miles north, at Kinneff, is Kinneff Church, built in 1738. The previous church on the site, dedicated to St Anthony and built in about 1242, has a unique place in Scotland's history. In 1651 the Scottish Crown Jewels (known as the "Honours Three") were used at the coronation of Charles II at Scone, then taken to Dunnottar Castle (see Stonehaven) so that Parliamentarian troops could not find them. But when their whereabouts became known to Cromwell, and he laid siege to the castle, they were smuggled out by the wife of Kinneff's minister, and hidden within the church. There they lay for nine years, beneath the floor next to the pulpit. Every three months the minister and his wife dug them up, cleaned them and aired them before a fire. With the Restoration of Charles II in 1660, they were taken to Edinburgh Castle. There they lay, forgotten about, in a locked chest in the Crown Room. In 1817, at the instigation of Sir Walter Scott, they were rediscovered and eventually put on display. Though no longer used for worship, the church is still open to the public and under the care of the Kinneff Old Church Preservation Trust.

after leaving school worked in the Aberdeen shipyards. For a while he served as a councillor in the town, and is now buried in the local churchyard.

ARBUTHNOTT

23 miles S of Aberdeen on the B967

The village of Arbuthnott lies in what is called The Mearns. **Arbuthnott Collegiate Church**, is dedicated to St Ternan, a Pictish saint. The choir was consecrated in 1242, with the rest of the church being later. It was here that James Sibbald, priest of Arbuthnott, wrote the **Arburthnott Missal** in 1491. It laid out the form of service to be used at masses celebrated within the church, and in 1897 was purchased by Archibald Coats of the Paisley thread making firm, who presented it to Paisley Museum, where it can still be seen (see also Paisley). The **Arbuthnott Aisle** contains the tomb and effigy of Robert Arbuthnott.

The ashes of James Leslie Mitchell the writer, otherwise known as **Lewis Grassic Gibbon**, lie within the kirkyard, and there is a memorial to him. He was born in Auchterless in Aberdeenshire in 1901 and later moved to Arbuthnott, where he spent most of his childhood. He spent brief spells as a journalist in Aberdeen and Glasgow (where he was sacked for "fiddling his expenses") and, after some time in the army, married and settled with his wife Rebecca in Welwyn Garden City near London. Here he wrote dark brooding novels about Mearns farm

life, far removed from the couthy stories about simple, cheerful Scottish country folk that had been published before. He died in 1935, aged only 33, from peritonitis. **The Lewis Grassic Gibbon Centre**, next to the parish hall, traces the life and works of a man who became one of the most important British writers of the 20th century. It is open between March and October.

The area has other literary associations. Robert Burn's father was born here before setting up home in Ayrshire, and in the kirkyard of the church at **Glenbervie** four miles to the northwest is the grave of Burns's great grandfather, James Burnes (the "e" in the name was dropped after Burns's father moved to Ayrshire). He farmed at nearby Clochnahill. Also in the churchyard is the **Douglas Aisle**, formed from part of the chancel of the now gone medieval church.

Arbuthnott House, home to the Arbuthnott family, dates mainly from the 18th and 19th centuries, and is open to the public on certain days of the year. It was originally an Oliphant stronghold, but passed through marriage to Hugh of Swinton, who assumed the family name of Arbuthnott. The gardens are open all year round.

MARYCULTER

6 miles SW of Aberdeen off the B9077

The lands surrounding Maryculter were granted to the Knights Templar by William the Lion in the 12th century, and the order of monastic soldiers established a church and preceptory, dedicating it to St Mary. Pope Clement V suppressed the order in 1312, and at trials held at Holyrood Abbey in Edinburgh in 1319 the last Preceptor of the house at Maryculter was given as William de Middleton of the "tempill house of Culther". The lands formerly owned by the Knights Templar were then granted to the Knights of the Order of St John. On the opposite bank of the Dee a church had been established and dedicated to St Peter, and this parish became known as Peterculter. It now lies within the City of Aberdeen, while Maryculter is in Kincardineshire.

Four miles west of the village is **Drum Castle** (National Trust for Scotland), built in the late 13th century, probably by the wonderfully named Richard Cemantarius, king's master mason and provost of Aberdeen. In 1323 it was given to William de Irwyn by Robert the Bruce, and the Irvines lived in it right up until 1975. It was enlarged in 1619 by the creation of a grand Jacobean mansion.

The 28 acre **Storybook Glen** is in Maryculter, and is a children's park where over 100 fairy tale and nursery rhyme characters can be found.

FETTERCAIRN

27 miles SW of Aberdeen on the B974

On the edge of the fertile Howe of the Mearns, Fettercairn is an attractive village with, at its heart, the **Mercat Cross** of 1670. In 1861 Queen Victoria and Prince Albert visited the village, staying overnight, and the **Fettercairn Arch** commemorates the event. The B974 goes northwards from the village up over Cairn o' Mount (from where there are good views) until it reaches Banchory in Deeside. It is regularly closed in the winter due to snow.

Close to the road, about a mile north of the town, is **Fasque**, former home of William Gladstone, prime minister in the late 19th century. It was bought in 1829 by his father, Sir John Gladstone, son of a Leith corn merchant, from its original builder, who was bankrupted by the huge building costs. William so loved the place that he used to catch a train to Banchory, 15 miles away, and walk over the hills to visit it. It has a deer park, and is open for groups of more than 12 by prior arrangement.

Fettercairn Distillery, founded in 1824, sits to the northwest, and has guided tours (with a free dram at the end) and a visitor centre.

GARLOGIE

10 miles W of Aberdeen on the B9119

The **Garlogie Mill Power House Museum** has a rare beam engine - the only one to have survived intact

Mercat Cross, Fettercairn

181 CLATTERIN' BRIG RESTAURANT

Nr Fettercairn

A friendly establishment, on the Fettercairn to Banchory road, that serves some of the best food in the area and has wonderful views.

❙❙ *see page 515*

182 SAUCHIEBURN HOTEL

Luthermuir

A wonderful hotel, in a small village, that offers great, affordable accommodation and good food and drink.

⊢ ❙❙ *see page 516*

183 FEUGHSIDE INN

Strachan

A superior Scottish inn that makes the perfect base for exploring Deeside and its royal connections.

 see page 515

184 CRATHES CASTLE AND GARDENS

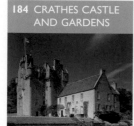

Banchory

A 16th century tower house, standing in beautiful grounds, that still retains some original features and holds interesting collections of furniture and portraits.

 see page 517

in its location - which used to power this wauk mill, which finished off woven cloth. The mill is open to the public, and there are displays about how it worked, its history and machinery.

The **Cullerlie Stone Circle**, close to the village just off the B9125, dates from the Bronze Age, and consists of eight stones placed in a 33-feet diameter circle. Later on, it was used as a cemetery to bury cremated remains. The shallow **Loch of Skene**, to the north of the village, is a special protection area and supports an important colony of Icelandic greylag geese and Whooper swans. Three miles to the west of the village, near Echt, is the **Barmekin of Echt**, an ancient fortified hill settlement. It consists of five concentric lines of defence enclosing an area 340 feet in diameter.

BANCHORY

17 miles W of Aberdeen on the A93

This little 19th century burgh stands at the point where the River Freugh enters the Dee, and is often called the "Gateway to Royal Deeside". It once stood on the Deeside railway line that closed in 1966, and there are now plans to reopen a section between the town and Crathes, three miles to the east. In Bridge Street is the **Banchory Museum**, which has collections featuring tartans, royal commemorative china and the natural history of the area. The Scottish musician and composer **James Scott Skinner**, "the

Strathspey King", was born at Arbeadie, just outside the town, in 1843, and a further display in the museum is dedicated to his life. Curiously, his father William also played the fiddle, though he lost three fingers on one hand - the one that depressed the stings - after an accident. James died in 1927 and now lies in Allenvale Cemetery in Aberdeen. There is a memorial plaque to him in Banchory's High Street.

Three miles east of the town is **Crathes Castle** (National Trust for Scotland - see panel). It dates from the 16th century, with some of the rooms retaining their original painted ceilings, which were only rediscovered in 1877. It was built by the Burnetts of Ley, who were granted the lands of Ley by Robert the Bruce in 1323. The ancient **Horn of Leys** hangs in the Great Hall. It is made of ivory and encrusted with jewels, and was presented to the Burnetts by Bruce at the time of the land grant. The family's coat-of-arms includes the horn. On the main stairway there is a "trip stair", which tripped up attackers who did not know it was there. Watch out also for the castle's ghost - the Green Lady, which is said to haunt the Green Lady's Room. The house remained with the family until 1951, when Sir James Burnett presented it to the National Trust for Scotland. Eight themed gardens have been laid out within the old walled garden, separated by yew hedges. There is also a shop and restaurant.

KINCARDINE O'NEILL

23 miles W of Aberdeen on the A93

This little village, with its Irish sounding name, claims to be the oldest village on Deeside. It is in fact a small burgh, which was granted its charter in 1511. It was here, in 1220, that the first bridge was constructed across the Dee beyond Aberdeen, so it became an important place. The ruins of the **Kirk of St Mary** date from the 13th century. It may have been the chapel for a hospital that stood here before the Reformation. It was in use up until 1862, when a new church was built. St Mary's was thatched up until 1733, when someone shot at a pigeon perching in its roof and it caught fire.

ALFORD

26 miles W of Aberdeen on the A944

Alford (pronounced "Afford" locally, with the accent on the first syllable) is a pleasant village within a fertile area known as the Howe of Alford. The **Grampian Transport Museum**, with its white arched entrance, has displays and working exhibits about transport in the Grampian area. You can even clamber aboard some of the exhibits. Each year the Eco-marathon takes place at the museum, where vehicles have to travel as far as possibly on a set amount of fuel. In 2001 a world record was set at Alford when a team called Fancy Carol NOK from Japan achieved the equivalent of 10,240 miles per gallon. The **Alford Valley Railway and Railroad**

Museum is a two-mile long two feet gauge passenger railway with steam and diesel locomotives that runs between the Transport Museum and the 99 acre **Haughton Country Park,** where there are woodland walks, a wildflower garden and a caravan park.

LUMPHANAN

24 miles W of Aberdeen on the A980

Lumphanan was founded when the Deeside railway was constructed, and was the highest point on the line. The **Peel Ring of Lumphanan** (Historic Scotland) is a huge 12th century motte and bailey where a castle built by the Durward family once stood. Edward 1 of England visited it in 1296, and it was still occupied in the late 18th century. After the Battle of Dunsinane, it is said that Macbeth was slain at Lumphanan three years after his defeat at the hands of Malcolm lll at the Battle of Dunsinane, near Perth, in 1054.

ABOYNE

27 miles W of Aberdeen off the A93

This small Royal Deeside town is famous for the **Aboyne Highland Games**, held in August each year. The village was laid out in 1676 around a huge village green, where the games are now held. It prospered with the coming of the railway in the 19th century, and is now a quiet settlement, popular with tourists. It is also the home of the **Aboyne and Deeside Festival**, held in July and August, which features music, drama and

Four miles south of Alford, on the A980, is one of Aberdeenshire's finest castles, Craigievar Castle (National Trust for Scotland). With its many turrets and small windows, it looks like something from a fairy tale. It was built by William Forbes, who bought the land in 1610 and completed the castle in 1626. It has a fine collection of 17th and 18th century furniture, as well as family portraits. William Forbes was also known as "Danzig Willie" (Danzig being the old name for the modern Polish port of Gdansk), and was a rich Aberdeen merchant who traded with the Baltic countries.

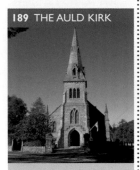
art. There is a lovely, but in places difficult, walk up **Glen Tanar**, two miles west of Aboyne. The **Braeloine Interpretive Centre**, has walks, a nature trail, a picnic site and guided tours by rangers.

Five miles north of the town, and two miles north east of Tarland is the **Culsh Earth House**, a souterrain, or underground chamber, which is over 2,000 years old. It is a long, doglegged tunnel, which was probably used not as a house, but as a store for foodstuffs. A torch is needed to explore it. The **Tomnaverie Stone Circle** (Historic Scotland) is a mile to the south west, and dates from about 1600 BC.

BALLATER

34 miles W of Aberdeen on the A93

Set among the spectacular scenery of Royal Deeside, Ballater is surrounded by wooded hills of birch and pine, and makes an excellent base for exploring an area of outstanding beauty. It is a comparatively modern settlement, and, like Aboyne, owes its growth to the coming of the railways in the 19th century. In fact, this was as far as the Deeside line came, as Prince Albert stopped a proposed extension to Braemar in case it spoiled the Balmoral estate. **The Old Royal Station** in Station Square has been restored, and shows what it would have looked like in Victorian times when the Royal Family used it. There is also a small exhibition called "Royalty and Railways". It was also used by many of the crowned heads of Europe as

they visited Victoria at Balmoral, including Nicholas ll, the last Czar of Russia. The **Muir of Dinnet Nature Reserve** lies between Ballatar and Aboyne, and covers 2,000 acres around Lochs Kinord and Davan.

There is plenty of good walking country around the village, and **Glen Muick**, to the south of Ballater, has a narrow road that takes you up towards Loch Muick (the road ends before the loch is reached, so you have to walk part of the way), in the shadow of **Lochnagar**, which, notwithstanding its name, is a mountain rising to a height of 3,786 feet. It gave its name to Prince Charles's book, The *Old Man of Lochnagar*. The drive is a particularly fine one, and takes you past **Birkhall** (not open to the public) which was bought by Edward VII before he became king. It was the Deeside home of the late Queen Mother.

BALMORAL

42 miles W of Aberdeen off the A93

The Queen's private home in Scotland was purchased by Prince Albert in 1852. Four years previously, Queen Victoria had visited and fallen in love with the area. Though the castle as you see it today only dates from that time, a castle has stood here for centuries. The first recorded reference we have is in 1484, when it was called "Bouchmorale". The 50,000 acre estate is closed when the Royal Family is in residence. The present castle is in Scots Baronial style, and built from local granite. Its foundation stone was laid in 1853, with the architect being William Smith, city architect for Aberdeen.

A quarter of a mile east of the castle is the small **Crathie Kirk**, where the Royal Family worships while at Balmoral. It dates from 1893, when Queen Victoria laid the foundation stone, and overlooks the remains of the original 14th century kirk. Many of the fittings and furnishings have been donated over the years by members of the Royal Family. **John Brown**, Queen Victoria's controversial ghillie who died in 1883, lies in the adjoining cemetery. The **Royal Lochnagar Distillery**, established in 1845, is near the kirk, and has a visitors centre. It was given a Royal Warrant by Queen Victoria in 1864.

A **Victorian Heritage Trail** has been laid out (with distinctive brown signs) which traces the footsteps of Queen Victoria, not just on Deeside, but throughout the area, and a leaflet is available from most tourism offices. While on the trail, visitors should look out for the coats of arms which signify that business and shops supply the royal family with goods "by royal appointment".

BRAEMAR

50 miles W of Aberdeen on the A93

This little village high in the Cairngorms is officially Britain's coldest place. Between 1941 and 1970 its average temperature was only 6.4 degrees Celsius. On two occasions, in 1895 and 1982, it experienced the lowest temperature

Deeside, near Balmoral

ever officially recorded in Britain - minus 27.2 degrees Celsius. And during the depths of winter, it can only achieve a maximum of three and a half hours of sunshine a day due to the surrounding mountains. However, it only manages 35 inches of rain a year - on a par with Glasgow. It sits at an altitude of 1,100 feet, and is famous for the **Braemar Gathering and Highland Games**, held every September, and visited by the Royal Family. In fact, the ruling monarch has the official title of the "Chieftain of the Braemar Gathering" There have been formal games at Braemar since 1832, though the history of the gathering goes back to the times of Malcolm Canmore in the 11th century.

Braemar Castle is the seat of

190 GORDON'S RESTAURANT AND B&B

Braemar

A tearoom/restaurant plus B&B that offers the best in accommodation and food.

see page 519

191 BURNETT ARMS HOTEL

Kemnay

A lovely small hotel in a rural village that has a friendly, bustling bar, good, well priced meals and en suite accommodation

🛏 ‖ see page 519

192 LAIRDS THROAT PUB & RESTAURANT

Kemnay

A newly established pub and restaurant that is ideally placed for anyone exploring all that Aberdeenshire has to offer.

‖ see page 520

193 BREASLANN GUEST HOUSE

Inverurie

A friendly guest house in a picturesque town with a good reputation for hospitality.

🛏 see page 521

the Farquharsons of Invercauld, and was built in 1628 by the Earl of Mar on the site of an older castle. It was used as a base by Hanovarian troops after the 1745 Rebellion, and they left some graffiti on window shutters. In the drawing room can be seen the world's largest Cairngorm (a semi-precious stone) weighing 52 pounds. And in the morning room display is a collection of Native American items from the Great Lakes area of Canada. They were sent to this country by two members of the family who went there seeking their fortunes.

The 72,598-acre **Mar Lodge Estate** (National Trust for Scotland) lies five miles west of Braemar on a minor road, and is part of the **Cairngorms National Park**, which came into being in September 2003 (see Grantown-on-Spey). The estate has some of the wildest landscapes in Britain, and has been described as the most important nature conservation area in Scotland, containing four out of its five highest mountains. In medieval times, when it was owned by the Earls of Mar, it was one of Scotland's most important hunting estates. It contains many of the features normally associated with Highland landscapes, and has a wealth of wildlife, plants, trees and archaeological sites. The estate is open daily, and the Lodge itself has special open days that are well advertised.

To the south of Braemar, on the A93, is one of Scotland's most popular winter sports areas,

Glenshee. The snowfields stretch over three valleys and four Munros, with about 25 miles of marked pistes as well as off-piste skiing. The village of Spittal of Glenshee is dealt with in the Perthshire, Angus and Kinross section of the book.

KINTORE

10 miles NW of Aberdeen off the A96

Kintore is a small picturesque royal burgh four miles south east of Inverurie. **Kintore Tolbooth** dates from 1747, when the Earl of Kintore was the provost, and **Kintore Parish Church** was built in 1819. Incorporated into the west staircase is a piece of the sacrament house of the 16th century Kinkell Church (see Inverurie) .

INVERURIE

15 miles NW of Aberdeen city centre off the A96

The royal burgh of Inverurie sits where the River Urie meets the Don, in an area known as "Garioch" (pronounced "Geery"). A legend tells of how a Roman soldier who came to this area exclaimed "urbi in rure!" (a city in the countryside) when he first saw the settlement. The town adopted the words as its motto, and it is on the coat of arms of the burgh. However, in reality the town's name has a more prosaic meaning - the "mouth of the Urie". It was founded in the 11th century by the Earl of Garioch, brother of Malcolm IV, king of Scotland.

Mary Stuart visited the town in 1562, and stayed in the royal castle which once stood where the mound known as the **Bass** is situated. The **Battle of Harlaw** was fought near the town in 1411, and a monument now marks the spot. A Lowland army under the Earl of Mar fought a Highland army under Donald, Lord of the Isles, and while the result was a draw, it stopped the Highlanders from moving into the Aberdeenshire lowlands and controlling them. It was one of the bloodiest battles ever fought on Scottish soil, which earned it the nickname of "Red Harlaw".

To the west of the town stood a Roman camp known as **Deer's Den Roman Camp**, or sometimes "Devona". The northern slopes of the 1,732 feet high Bennachie (known as "Aberdeenshire's Mount Fuji", because of its shape), to the west of the town, is one of the likely locations for the **Battle of Mons Graupius**, fought in AD 84, and no doubt the camp played a major part. It was fought between a confederation of Caledonian tribes and the army of Agricola, with no clear victor emerging. The **Bennachie Visitor Centre** has displays about the natural history of the area.

Two miles south of the town are the ruins of the 16th century **Kinkell Church** (Historic Scotland), which has a particularly fine sacrament house. The ornate grave slab of Gilbert de Greenlaw, who was killed at the Battle of Harelaw, can also be seen. **Castle Fraser** (National Trust for Scotland) lies six miles south west

of the town, near the village of Craigearn. Work was started on it in 1575 by Michael Fraser, the sixth laird, and it was finished in 1636. It has a traditional "Z" plan, and contains many Fraser portraits, fine carpets, linen and curtains.

The **Brandsbutt Symbol Stone**, in the midst of a housing estate, dates from Pictish times. It was reconstructed after being broken up for wall building material. To the west of the town is the **Easter Aquhorthies Stone Circle**, well signposted from the A96.

OLDMELDRUM

15 miles NW of Aberdeen on the A920

This small town of just over 2,000 people was created a burgh of barony in 1672, 12 years before **Oldmeldrum Parish Church** was built. The **Glen Garioch Distillery** was established in 1794, though it was subsequently closed in 1968, reopened, and again closed in 1995. It reopened again in 1997, and now has a visitor centre and shop.

The **Battle of Oldmeldrum** was fought in 1308 between an army headed by Robert the Bruce and the forces of John Comyn, Earl of Buchan. Bruce was victorious, paving the way for him to become King of Scotland.

DAVIOT

20 miles NW of Aberdeen off the A920

The Loanhead Stone Circle is possibly over 4,000 years old, and sits to the north of the village. It was excavated in 1934, and charcoal and pottery was recovered.

In 1805, the Aberdeenshire Canal was opened which linked Inverurie with Aberdeen. Designed by John Rennie, it was never a great success, and in 1845 it was sold to the Great North of Scotland Railway Company, who drained it, filled it in, and used part of its route to carry their railway line to Inverurie and eventually Inverness. Port Elphinstone, to the south east of the town, recalls the canal, and part of its channel can still be seen there. It was the only canal in Britain to be closed every winter because of ice and snow. Within the Carnegie Inverurie Museum in the Square is a small display dedicated to the canal, as well as displays on local history.

The old Scottish ballad The Bonny Lass o Fyvie, with its line "There was a troop o' Irish Dragoons cam' marchin' doon through Fyvie o", recalls a skirmish that took place near the village in 1644 between a troop of Irish Dragoons, commanded by the Marquis of Montrose, and a troop of Covenanters. Before the battle, a captain of the dragoons called "Ned" fell for the "pretty Peggy " of the song, but alas, she did not reciprocate. Ned didn't survive the battle, though the song suggests that he deliberately got himself killed because of a broken heart.

MONYMUSK

17 miles W of Aberdeen off the B993

Monymusk was once the site of an Augustinian priory, founded in 1170 by the Earl of Mar. The **Monymusk Reliquary**, in which was kept a bone of St Columba, was one of its treasures. It dates from the 8th century, and is a small wooden box covered in silver and bronze and decorated in semi-precious stones. It was paraded before Bruce's troops at the Battle of Bannockburn, and is now in the Museum of Scotland.

The **Parish Church of St Mary**, which formed part of the priory, dates from the early years of the 12th century. In 1929 it was restored to its original condition, and it is now one of the finest parish churches in Scotland. Inside it is the **Monymusk Stone**, on which is carved Pictish symbols.

Though the original village was of great antiquity, the present village dates only from the early 19th century, when it was entirely rebuilt for estate workers by a member of the Grant family.

OYNE

21 miles NW of Aberdeen on the B9002

Over 7,000 ancient sites have been identified in Aberdeenshire, from Pictish carvings to stone circles, and these form the basis for the **Archaeolink Prehistory Park,** which bridges the gap between ancient history and modern times by way of exhibits and hands-on displays, both indoor and out. It has some of the finest collections of ancient remains in Europe.

FYVIE

23 miles NW of Aberdeen city centre off the A947

The oldest part of **Fyvie Castle** (National Trust for Scotland) dates from the 13th century, and was once a royal stronghold. There are 17th century panelling and plaster ceilings, as well as a portrait collection that includes works by Raeburn, Romney and Gainsborough. One of the legends attached to the castle is that its five towers were built by the five great families in the northeast who owned it - the Gordons, the Leiths, the Meldrums, the Prestons and the Setons. Both Robert the Bruce and and his descendent Charles I stayed here.

The **Parish Church** dates from the 19th century, and has a fine laird's pew and wine glass pulpit. In Fyvie Old Manse in 1864 was born **Cosmo Gordon Lang**, who became Archbishop of York in 1908 and Archbishop of Canterbury in 1928.

Fyvie Castle

A small Benedictine priory once stood in the village, and the site is now marked by a cross. The village lies on the River Ythan, once famous for its fresh water pearls. It is said that a large pearl in the Scottish crown was taken from the Ythan near Fyvie.

HUNTLY

33 miles NW of Aberdeen on the A96

Huntly is an old burgh, which was granted its charter in 1488. It sits in an area called Strathbogie, and is famous for the ruins of **Huntly Castle** (Historic Scotland). It was originally called Strathbogie Castle, and was built by the Earl of Fife in the late 12th century. While in the area in the early 1300s, Robert the Bruce took ill, and spent some time in the castle, as the then Earl, David, was one of his supporters. However he changed sides and joined the English just before Bannockburn, and subsequently forfeited the lands of Strathbogie.

They were subsequently given to Sir Adam Gordon of Huntly, who lived in the Scottish Borders (see Gordon), and he moved north to claim them in 1376. In the 16th century the name of the castle was changed to Huntly, and in the early 1550s it was rebuilt by George, 4th Earl of Huntly.

During the Reformation, the Gordons of Huntly were one of the most important Catholic families in Scotland, and fought on the side of Mary Stuart. James VI, her son, had the castle demolished when the 6th Earl, George, was implicated in an uprising against

him. George fled to France, but returned, made his peace with James, and had the castle rebuilt. During the turbulent Covenanting times, the castle changed hands many times until it finally came into the hands of the Covenanters in the early 17th century.

From about the early 18th century the castle fell into decay. But even today you can see just how stately and comfortable the place must have been in its heyday. It entertained many famous people, including Mary of Guise, mother of Mary Stuart, and Perkin Warbeck, pretender to the English throne.

In the town square is a statue to the 4th Duke of Richmond, erected in 1863. He inherited the Gordon estates through his mother's side when the last Duke of Gordon died in 1836. Beneath it are the two **Standing Stones of Strathbogie**, or as they are known in Huntly, the "Stannin Steens o Strathbogie". At one time they formed part of a stone circle.

On the corner of the Square and Duke street is the birthplace of **James Legge**, who became a missionary in China and was later the first professor of Chinese at Oxford.

Six miles south of Huntly, on the B9002 near Kennethmont, is **Leith Hall** (National Trust for Scotland). It was the home of the Leith (later Leith-Hay) family from 1650 onwards, and contains many of their possessions. The family had a tradition of military service, and its most famous member,

194 GORDON ARMS HOTEL

Huntly

A hotel right in the heart of a historic town that offers great food and drink, as well as comfortable, affordable accommodation.

see page 521

The Brander Museum in the Square in Huntly has collections dealing with local history, arms and armour and the works of local author George MacDonald, who died in 1905. His most popular stories were of fantasy and fairies, with a strong religious message. He rejected the Calvinist view, still held by some people in the Church of Scotland at the time, that art was self-indulgent and iconoclastic. Instead he argued that God could be understood through art and imagination.

195 EAT ON THE GREEN

Udny Green, Ellon

Eat on the Green is a superb restaurant serving a good selection of contemporary and classic dishes, using the freshest of local produce.

❙ *see page 522*

Andrew Hay, fought for Charles Edward Stuart. The hall started as a typical Scottish tower house built in 1650 by James Leith which was added to in the 18th and 19th centuries. The surrounding gardens can also be visited.

Not far from here is **Rhynie**, known for its Celtic sites, Pictish stone circles, vitrified forts and castles. The village is situated on crossroads from which there is easy access to the distilleries, Deeside, Aberdeen and the coast. The local hill, **Tap O'Noth** is a favourite spot for hang-gliders. An Iron Age fort can be found at its summit.

ELLON

15 miles N of Aberdeen on the A920

Situated within an area known as the Formartine, Ellon is a small burgh or barony, which was granted its charter in 1707. It was one of the places burned down during what became known as the "Harrying of Buchan" in 1308 soon after Robert the Bruce defeated John Comyn, Earl of Buchan, at Oldmeldrum.

The town sits on the River Ythan, with a **Parish Church** that dates from 1777. It's hard to imagine nowadays that this little town, five miles from the coast, was once a port for a small steamer that took goods up and down the river. It is also one of the stops on the **Formartine Buchan Way**, based on disused railway tracks from Dyce, just outside of Aberdeen, to Fraserburgh. The **Moot Hill Monument** sits on Moot Hill, from where justice was dispensed by the Earls of Buchan in the 13th and early 14th centuries.

The ruined **Ellon Castle** (once known as Ardgirth Castle) once belonged to the Earls of Aberdeen, and was last lived in in the early 20th century. The **Deer Dykes** were built in the 19th century not only to keep deer from straying from the castle estate, but to provide work for the unemployed.

Five miles west of the town, on the A920, is the **Pitmedden Garden** (National Trust for Scotland). The centrepiece is the Great Garden, laid out by Sir Alexander Seton, 1st Baronet of Pitmedden, in 1675. In the 1950s the rest of the garden was re-created using elaborate floral designs. Four parterres were created, three of them being inspired by designs possibly used at the Palace of Holyrood in Edinburgh, and the fourth based on Sir Alexander's coat-of-arms. There is also a visitor centre and a Museum of Farming Life, which has a collection of old farming implements once used in this

Forbes Tomb, Ellon

largely farming area.

Near the gardens are the substantial ruins of **Tolquhon Castle**, built by William Forbes, 7th Lord of Tolquhon in the 1580s. In 1589 James VI visited the house, and both his and the Forbes' coats-of-arms were carved over the doorway. William Forbes and his wife Elizabeth are buried in an elaborately carved tomb in the south aisle of the parish church at Tarves. The church has since been demolished, but the **Forbes Tomb** survives to this day.

ELGIN

Situated in the fertile Laigh of Moray, Elgin is a charming city with the ruins of what was one of the finest cathedrals in Scotland. Before the local government reforms in the mid-70s, there were only six towns - or cities - in Scotland that were allowed to have lord provosts, and Elgin was one of them.

The city's layout is still essentially that of a medieval burgh, with a High Street that goes from where the royal castle once stood on **Lady Hill** to the cathedral. It widens in the middle into a market place called the **Plainstanes**, and close to it stands **St Giles Church**. It is in neoclassical style, and was built in 1828. It is believed that a church was originally built on this site in Pictish times, though the first recorded church was built in the 12th century. In 1390 this was burned down by the Wolf of Badenoch, and a new church was erected in its place. By 1801 the last

vestiges of this church - the chancel - was demolished in 1801. In the square at its east end is the **Muckle Cross**, a Victorian rebuilding of a cross erected during the reign of Charles l. On Lady Hill is a monument to the 5th Duke of Richmond, dating from 1839, with the statue being added 16 years later. The hill takes its name from the chapel of the former castle, dedicated to Our Lady. At the far east end of the High Street is another cross. It marks the spot where Alexander MacDonald of the Isles did penance for despoiling the cathedral. It also marks the western limit of the "sanctuary area" of the cathedral.

Just off the High Street is the **Thunderton Hotel**, housed in what was a grand medieval town house. It was once the royal residence of the town, and was where the monarch stayed when he visited. It was surrounded by orchards, gardens and a bowling green. In 1746 Charles Edward Stuart stayed here while on his way to Culloden.

Three 17th century arcaded merchants' houses are to be found in the High Street, one of which at one time housed the bank of William Duff, a member of the family which went on to become substantial landowners in the area and eventually Earls of Fife. The award-winning **Elgin Museum** is also in the High Street, and has many important collections, including natural history, archaeology and the social history of the area. Another museum

Haddo House (National Trust for Scotland), one of the grandest stately homes in Aberdeenshire, lies six miles northwest of Ellon. It was designed by William Adam for the 2nd Earl of Aberdeen in the early 1730s, and restored in the 1880s. It is noted for its Victorian interiors within an elegant Georgian shell, and features furniture, paintings and objets d'arts. It also has a terraced garden with rose beds and a fountain. In the grounds is Kelly Lake, one of the few natural (as opposed to man made) sheets of water called "lake" rather than "loch" in Scotland (see Lake of Menteith, Kirkcudbright and Stenton).

198 THUNDERTON HOUSE

Elgin

Popular town centre hostelry occupying historic building dating back to 1655.

❙❙ *see page 522*

•

Off Greyfriars Street in Elgin stands the restored Greyfriars Monastery, now reckoned to give the best idea of what a medieval Scottish friary looked like. It was built in 1479 at the behest of Bishop Innes for the Observantine Friars of the Franciscan order, and restored in the late-19th century.

•

worth visiting is the **Moray Motor Museum** in Bridge Street, with its collection of old cars and motorcycles.

Work was started on **Elgin Cathedral**, or to give it its proper name, the Cathedral of the Holy Trinity, in about 1224. It was one of Scotland's grandest churches, and could compare to the great cathedrals of Europe. There had been three cathedrals in the dioceses before this one, at Birnie, Spynie and Kinneder, but the locations had all been unsuitable. By the end of the 13th century, building work was complete, though in 1390 the Wolf of Badenoch and his men (see also Dunkeld, Grantown-on-Spey and Fortrose), set fire to it after a violent quarrel with the Bishop of Moray, who had ordered him to give up his mistress and return to his wife, Euphemia Ross.

The damage was extensive, and work on repairing it continued right up until the Reformation in 1560. After the Reformation, the cathedral became a quarry for the

people of the town. In 1807 a keeper of the ruins was appointed, and from then on what was left was cared for and preserved. The east gate to the cathedral precincts, known as the **Panns Port**, still stands.

To the northwest of the cathedral are the ruins of the so-called **Bishop's Palace**. It had nothing to do with the bishop, and was instead the manse of the cathedral's preceptor, who looked after the sacred music. It was one of about 20 such manses around the cathedral which housed the cathedral staff. And to the north east of the cathedral is the **Brewery Bridge**, built in 1798 and so called because a brewery stood close by until 1913. The three acre **Biblical Garden** is adjacent to the cathedral, in King Street, and is open each year from May to September. It has been planted with all 110 plants mentioned in the Bible.

At the west end of the high street is the imposing façade of Dr Gray's Hospital, the town's main infirmary. It was founded by Dr Alexander Gray, who amassed a fortune in India, and built between 1816 and 1819.

Johnston's Cashmere Visitor Centre is at Newmill. There are tours round the mill, and an exhibition and audiovisual that explains the making of the luxury material. There is also a shop where Johnston products can be bought, and a coffee shop.

The **Old Mills** is the last remaining meal mill on the River

Elgin Cathedral

340

Lossie. Its history goes back to the 13th century, when it was owned by Pluscarden Abbey. The **Glen Moray Distillery,** on Bruceland Road near the banks of ther River Lossie, has a visitors centre. It was established in 1831 as a brewery, but in 1897 turned instead to distilling.

North of the city are the impressive ruins of **Spynie Palace** (Historic Scotland), the home of the bishops of Moray. The palace sits on the shores of tiny Loch Spynie, and dates from the 14th century and later. David's Tower, the main part of the building, dates from the 16th century. Spynie Church, which stood nearby until 1736, was at one time the cathedral of the diocese. Now all that is left is a kirkyard, a mortuary building and a tall stone cross that marks where the eastern end of the church stood.. The church was founded by Bishop Bricius of Moray in the 12th century. In the kirkyard is the grave of **James Ramsay MacDonald**, Britain's first Labour prime minister (see also Lossiemouth).

AROUND ELGIN

DUFFUS

5 miles NW of Elgin on the B9012

The ruins of the **Church of St Peter** (Historic Scotland) stand near the village. Though mainly 18th century, it incorporates work that is much older. Opposite the porch is the medieval **Parish Cross**, showing that long ago people used the kirkyard as a site

for their weekly markets and fairs.

Close by are the ruins of **Duffus Castle**, founded in the 12th century by Freskin, Lord of Strabrock, who later took the title and name of Lord of Duffus and Freskin or Moravia. He is the ancestor of the great Moravia, (later Moray, or Murray), family, which has played such a prominent part in Scotland's history. The castle would originally have been a wooden tower surrounded by a wooden palisade which not only encompassed the castle on top of its motte, or hill, but a bailey as well, where a small settlement would have flourished. The castle as we see it today dates from the 14th century onwards, and still has the finest motte and bailey of any castle in the north of Scotland.

LOSSIEMOUTH

5 miles N of Elgin on the A941

This holiday resort sits at the mouth of the River Lossie, and was established as a small port for the city of Elgin in the 18th century after Elgin's original port at Spynie was cut off from the sea as the River Lossie silted up. There are fine sandy beaches, and the **Lossiemouth Fisheries and Community Museum**, in a former net mending loft at Pitgaveny Quay, traces the history of the town and its fishing industry. There is also a reconstruction of the study used by **James Ramsay Macdonald**, Britain's first Labour prime minister, who was born illegitimate in a small cottage in the town in 1866 (see also Elgin).

Gordonstoun School, attended by Prince Philip, Prince Charles, Prince Andrew and Prince Edward, is close to Duffus, and is housed in an 18th century mansion. It was founded by the German educationalist Dr Kurt Hahn in 1934. Another famous pupil was the late Roy Williamson of the Corries folk group, who wrote Scotland's unofficial national anthem, **Flower of Scotland.**

341

West of the village centre of Fochabers and overlooking the Spey is Baxter's Highland Village, home to one of the best-known food firms in Scotland. It all started in 1868, when George Baxter, who worked for the Duke of Gordon, opened a small grocery shop in Fochabers. This is one of the most fertile areas in Britain, famed for its fruit, vegetables and cattle, and soon George's wife was making jams and conserves in the back shop. Now the factory and associated shops, restaurants and kids' play areas are tourist attractions in their own right.

199 HIGHLANDER HOTEL

Buckie

Recently renovated hotel in small fishing village offering good home-made food and en suite accommodation.

see page 523

Kinneddar, to the south west of the town, is where one of the predecessors of the present Elgin Cathedral once stood.

FOCHABERS

8 miles E of Elgin on the A96

Fochabers dates from 1776, when the then Duke of Gordon decided that he didn't like the dilapidated huddle of thatched cottages that was old Fochabers within his parkland to the north of the present village. He therefore built a new village further south with a large spacious square, and the present day Fochabers was the result. The architect was John Baxter, an Edinburgh man who had already worked on Gordon Castle. Within the former Pringle Church in the High Street is the **Fochabers Folk Museum**, and in the square is the elegant, porticoed **Bellie Church**. Its rather quaint name comes from the Gaelic "beul-aith", meaning "the mouth of the ford".

The imposing **Milne's High School** - surely one of the grandest looking primary schools in Scotland - dates from 1844, and was built using money gifted by a native of the town who made his fortune in New Orleans.

BUCKIE

13 miles E of Elgin on the A990

Buckie is a major fishing port. In the **Buckie District Fishing Heritage Museum** in Cluny Place and the **Buckie Drifter** in Freuchny Road are displays that tell the story of the fishing industry on the Morayshire coast.

Four miles west of the town is the mouth of the River Spey. It is half a mile wide, though no great port sits here. The village of **Kingston** dates from 1784, and was founded by Ralph Dodworth and William Osbourne. They came from Kingston-upon-Hull in Yorkshire, and named their village after it. It was near here that Charles II arrived from Holland on 23rd June 1650 and signed the Solemn League and Covenant. His ship grounded in shallow water, and he had to be taken ashore "piggyback" style on the back of a villager who had a daughter called Maggie. He is said to have developed a crush on the young woman, and today's **Maggie Fair**, held each year in June in nearby Garmouth, celebrates the event. He granted Maggie her dearest wish, and it was to have a fair named after her.

On the opposite shore of the Spey is the **Tugnet Ice House**, the largest ice house in Scotland. When the Spey froze in winter, ice was cut from it and stored in the ice house. It kept salmon caught from the river in summer fresh until it could be shipped out. The **Moray Firth Wildlife Centre** is part of the Whale and Dolphin Conservation Society, and has displays and exhibitions on local wildlife.

The small fishing communities round about, such as **Findochty** (pronounced locally as "Finechtay") and **Portnockie** are very attractive, and well worth visiting. The **Bow Fiddle Rock** at Portnockie has been carved by the sea into the shape of an inverted "V" with one leg thicker than the other. Five miles southwest of the town are the ruins of **Deskford Church** (Historic Scotland), within the village of the same name. It is noted for its ornately carved sacrament house, and was founded by Alexander Ogilvie in 1551. **St Mary's Church**, which dates from 1543, sits in the small fishing village of **Cullen**, to the north of Deskford, and was formerly collegiate. Cullen, a former fishing village, gives its name to one of Scotland's best known dishes - Cullen skink, a fish soup enriched with potatoes, onion and cream. The word "skink" comes from the Gaelic word for "essence".

In the village of **Fordyce**, south east of Cullen, is the **Fordyce Joiner's Workshop and Visitor Centre** in West Church Street, dedicated to the skills and tools of carpentry in northeast Scotland. **Fordyce Castle**, which sits right on the village's main street, was built in 1592 by Sir Thomas Menzies of Durn, a provost of Aberdeen. It is an L-plan tower, and is not open to the public. The ruins of **St Talarican's Church** are close to the castle, and date from 1272.

CRAIGELLACHIE

12 miles S of Elgin off the A95

The **Craigellachie Bridge** dates from 1814, and is Scotland's oldest iron bridge. It was designed by Thomas Telford, and has one single graceful arch spanning the Spey. The village is on the 65-mile-long **Speyside Way**, a long distance footpath that runs from Ballindalloch, southwest of

Craigellachie, to the mouth of the Spey. It also sits at the heart of the **Malt Whisky Trail**, and most of the distilleries organise tours round the premises, with a tasting at the end. The **Speyside Cooperage**, on the Dufftown road, has a visitor centre where you can learn about the skills involved in making and repairing whisky casks.

Craigellachie Distillery, which dates from 1891, lies within the village, as does the **Macallan Distillery**, and four miles north is the **Glen Grant Distillery**. The **Glenfarclas Distillery** is seven miles southwest, near **Ballindalloch Castle.** The castle dates from the 16th century, and is the home of the McPherson-Grant family, who have lived there continuously since it was built. It is open to the public during the summer months. About four miles south of Ballindalloch is the **Glenlivet Distillery**, which again has organised tours. A couple of miles southwest is the village of Aberlour, where there is **Aberlour Distillery**, which has a visitor centre.

A mile outside Archiestown, west of Craigellachie on the B9102, is the **Ladycroft Agricultural Museum**, with horse drawn vehicles and a display of farming tools used in the area over the ages.

DUFFTOWN

16 miles S of Elgin on the A941

Dufftown is the world capital of malt whisky and was founded in 1817 by James Duff, the 4th Earl of Fife. Built to provide

200 SEAFIELD ARMS HOTEL

Rothes

A traditional hotel in a historic village that offers a warm Scottish welcome.

⊨ ‖ *see page 524*

One of the most dramatically situated castles in the area is Findlater Castle, which sits on a small promontory jutting into the sea. The ruins you see now date from the 15th century, and were built by the Ogilvie family, though a castle may have stood here since at least the 13th century. Care should be taken when approaching or exploring it. The name comes from the Norse "fyn", meaning "white" and "leitr" meaning "cliff", as the cliffs in this part of the country are studded with quartz.

employment after the Napoleonic wars, it is based around a number of distilleries, including the world famous **Glenfiddich Distillery**. The most prominent feature is the **Clock Tower**, originally built in 1839 as the town jail. The clock itself came from Banff, where it was known as the "Clock That Hanged MacPherson". McPherson of Kingussie, a notorious bandit who had the reputation for being the Scottish Robin Hood, had been

sentenced to death in 1700, but was later pardoned. While the pardon was on its way to Banff, Lord Braco, the local sheriff, put the clock forward to ensure that MacPherson would hang.

Mortlach Church, which is a Scottish Heritage site, was founded on the site of a much earlier church, thought to have stood here since the community began in AD 566 and to have been in regular use as a place of worship ever since. Although much of the church was reconstructed in the 19th century, parts of the original building still survive. It is said that Malcolm ll extended the church that stood there at the time in thanks for a victory over the Danes nearby in 1010. In the graveyard is an old Pictish cross, and inside the church is the **Elephant Stone**, again with Pictish associations. **Balvenie Castle** (Historic Scotland), lies a mile north, and was once home to the Comyns and later the Stewarts and the Douglases. In the 13th century it was visited by Edward I of England, and Mary Stuart spend two nights here in 1562.

The **Keith and Dufftown Railway** connects Dufftown to the market town of Keith, 11 miles away. It was reopened in 2000/2001 by a group of enthusiasts, and runs services between the two towns.

The 18-hole Dufftown Golf Club on the Tomintoul Road boasts the highest tee in the UK. It is 1,294 feet above sea level. Besides golf, the town caters for all types of outdoor activities including

Clock Tower, Dufftown

walking, fishing, shooting and cycling.

KEITH

15 miles SE of Elgin on the A96

Keith is divided into two communities, separated by the River Isla. The old Keith was founded in the 12th century on the west bank of the river as a market centre for the selling of cattle. The newer, and larger, Keith was laid out in 1755 by the Earl of Findlater on the east bank.

The town is home to the **Glenisla Distillery**, which is open to the public. The old **Packhorse Bridge** dates from 1609, though the town's oldest building is **Milton Tower**, dating from 1480. It was a stronghold of the Ogilvie family, whose most famous member was John Ogilvie. Raised a Protestant, he later converted to Roman Catholicism on the Continent and was sent back to Scotland to promote the faith, posing as a horse dealer and soldier called John Watson. He was eventually hanged in Glasgow in 1615, and was made a saint in 1976. There is a **Scottish Tartans Museum** in Keith's Institute Hall. The town is the eastern terminus of the Keith and Dufftown Railway (see Dufftown).

TOMINTOUL

27 miles S of Elgin on the A939

Tomintoul dates from 1775, when the 4th Duke of Gordon decided to lay out a new village in the aftermath of the Jacobite Uprising. It is situated at a height of 1,160 feet and is said to be the highest

village in the Highlands (but not in Scotland). The A939 southwest to Cockbridge is called "**The Lecht**", and is notorious for being blocked by snow in winter. The ski area of the same name lies six miles from Tomintoul. The small **Tomintoul Museum**, in the village square, has displays on local history and wildlife.

At Cockbridge is **Corgarff Castle** (Historic Scotland), a tower house set within a curious star-shaped walled enclosure. Though built by the Elphinstone family in about 1550, it was leased to the Forbes family. There was a long running feud between the Forbes and the Gordons, and in 1571 a troop of men led by Adam Gordon tried to take the castle in the name of Mary Queen of Scots. At the time the castle was occupied by women and children, including Margaret, the wife of John Forbes. She shot one of the Gordon troops in the leg, and an enraged Adam Gordon burned the castle down, killing the 24 people within it, including Margaret.

PLUSCARDEN

6 miles SW of Elgin on a minor road

Pluscarden Priory was founded in 1230 by Alexander II and settled firstly by Valliscaulian and then Benedictine monks. In the 19th century the Bute family acquired the ruined buildings, and in 1943 presented them to the monks of Prinknash in England, who took up residence in 1948. It is the only medieval abbey in Britain still used for its original purpose. At first it

201 THE GLENAVON HOTEL

Tomintoul

A friendly, family-run hotel in the heart of the Cairngorms that offers the best in food, drink and accommodation

🛏 🍴 *see page 524*

345

was a priory, but became an abbey in its own right in 1974. It is open to the public, and has a small gift shop.

FORRES

12 miles W of Elgin off the A96

This small royal burgh, which was granted its charter in the 13th century, was once one of the most important places in Scotland, and is mentioned in Shakespeare's Macbeth. It is also thought to be the "Varris" on Ptolemy's maps. The ground plan of the medieval settlement still forms the basis of the town today, though it is much more open and green than it was then, thanks to some large areas of parkland.

The 20-feet high **Sueno's Stone** (Historic Scotland) dates from the 9th or 10th century, and is the largest known Pictish stone in Scotland. One side shows a cross, while the other shows scenes of battle. One of the scenes might be the battle fought at Forres in AD 966 where the Scottish king, Dubh, was killed. It is now floodlit, and under glass to protect it from the weather. **The Falconer Museum** in Tolbooth Street was founded in 1871, and highlights the history and heritage of the town and its surroundings. It was founded using money from a bequest left by two brothers who left Forres for India. One was Alexander Falconer, a merchant in Calcutta, and the other was Hugh Falconer, a botanist and zoologist.

The cathedralesque **St Laurence Church** was built between 1904 and 1906 on the site of the town's former churches (with the original having been built in the 13th century), all dedicated to St Laurence. Though impressive from the outside, its inside is spectacular.

Dominating the town is the **Nelson Tower**, opened in 1812 in Grant Park to commemorate Nelson's victory at Trafalgar seven years before - the first such building to do so in Britain. If you're fit enough to climb its 96 steps, you'll get spectacular views over the surrounding countryside and the Moray Firth.

Brodie Castle

Brodie Castle (National Trust for Scotland) lies four miles west of the town. It is a 16th century tower house with later additons. In about 1160 Malcolm IV gave the surrounding lands to the Brodies, and it was their family home until the late 20th century. It contains major collections of paintings, furniture and ceramics, and sits in 175 acres of ground. Within the grounds is Rodney's Stone, with Pictish carvings.

A couple of miles northeast of Forres is **Kinloss**, with an RAF base and the scant remains of an old abbey. It was founded in about 1150 by David I, and colonised by Cistercian monks from Melrose. It is said that in 1150 David founded it in thanks after getting lost in a dense forest. Two doves led him to an open space where shepherds were looking after their sheep. They gave him food and shelter, and as he slept he had a dream in which he was told to found an abbey on the spot. Before the Reformation, it was one of the wealthiest and most powerful abbeys in Scotland.

On the coast north of Forres is perhaps Scotland's most unusual landscape, the **Culbin Sands**. In 1694 a storm blew great dunes of sand - some as high as 100 feet - over an area that had once been green and fertile, causing people to flee their homes. The drifts covered cottages, fields, even a mansion house and orchard, and eventually created eight square miles of what became known as "Scotland's Sahara". Occasionally, further

storms would uncover the foundations of old cottages, which were then covered back up again by succeeding storms. The sands continued to shift and expand until the 1920s, when trees were planted to stabilise the area. Now it is a nature reserve.

Dallas Dhu Distillery (Historic Scotland) sits to the south of Forres, and explains the making of whisky. It was built between 1898 and 1899 to produce a single malt for a firm of Glasgow blenders called Wright and Greig.

FRASERBURGH

Fraserburgh sits on the coastline just at that point where the Moray Firth becomes the North Sea. It is one of the main fishing ports in northeast Scotland, and the largest shellfish port in Europe. It was founded in the 16th century by Alexander Fraser, eighth laird of Philorth, who built the first harbour in 1546. Between 1570 and 1571 he also built **Fraserburgh Castle**. A powerful lantern was added in 1787, and it became a lighthouse, now known as **Kinnaird Lighthouse**, owned by Historic Scotland. It is a museum dedicated to Scotland's lighthouses.

The **Old Kirk** in Saltoun Square isn't as old as its name would suggest. It was built in 1803 to replace the original church built by Alexander between 1570 and 1571. Beside it is the **Fraser Burial Aisle**.

One of Alexander's grander schemes was the founding of a

202 STABLES INN

Kinloss
Friendly hostelry in former village school offering local brews and good home-cooked food.

see page 524

At Findhorn, on the Moray Firth coast, is the Findhorn Foundation, one of the most successful centres in Britain for exploring alternative lifestyles and spiritual living. It was founded by Dorothy Maclean and Peter and Eileen Caddy in 1962 in a caravan park. The Findhorn Heritage Centre and Museum has displays on the history and heritage of the place. The village of Findhorn itself was once a busy port, trading with the Low countries and Scandinavia. Now it is a sailing and wildlife centre.

Kinnaird Lighthouse

university in the town, and he even went so far as to obtain James VI's permission to do so. The Scots Parliament gave it a grant, and the Reverend Charles Ferme became its first principal. Unfortunately, the Reverend Ferme was later arrested for attending the 1605 General Assembly of the Church of Scotland in defiance of the king. The embryonic university subsequently collapsed, though one street in the town, College Bounds, still commemorates the scheme.

In Quarry Road is the **Fraserburgh Heritage Centre**, which has exhibits about the history of the town, including some haute couture dresses designed by the late fashion designer **Bill Gibb**, who hailed from Fraserburgh. The most unusual building in Fraserburgh is the **Wine Tower**, next to the lighthouse. It too was built by Alexander Fraser, possibly as a chapel. It has three floors, but no connecting stairways.

At Sandhaven, to the west of the town, is the **Sandhaven Meal Mill**, dating from the 19th century. Guided tours and models show how oatmeal used to be ground in

Scotland. At Memsie, three miles south of Fraserburgh on the B9032, is the **Memsie Burial Cairn**, dating from about 1500 BC. At one time three stood here, but only one remains.

AROUND FRASERBURGH

OLD DEER

12 miles S of Fraserburgh on the B9030

In a beautiful position on the banks of the River South Ugie are the ruins of **Deer Abbey** (Historic Scotland), founded in 1219 by William Comyn, Earl of Buchan, for the Cistercian order of monks, who colonised it from Kinloss. Little remains of the abbey church, but the walls of some of the other buildings are fairly well preserved. It is said that it was built on the site of a Celtic monastery founded by St Columba and his companion St Drostan in the 6th century. It was here, in the early 10th century, that the famous **Book of Deer**, which contains the four Gospels, was written. 11th century additions give the story of the founding of the Columba monastery.

MINTLAW

11 miles S of Fraserburgh on the A952

In the village you'll find the 230-acre **Aden Farming Museum**, which sits within a country park. It traces the history of farming in this rich area of Aberdeenshire through the "Weel Vrocht Grun" ("well worked ground") exhibit. Hareshowe Farm has been restored to what it would have been like in the 1950s.

MAUD

12 miles S of Fraserburgh on the B9029

Maud grew up around a junction in the railway line that once connected Aberdeen to Fraserburgh and Peterhead. In the **Maud Railway Museum**, housed in the village's former station, you can relive the days of the Great North of Scotland Railway through exhibits, photographs, artefacts and displays.

TURRIFF

20 miles SW of Fraserburgh on the A947

Set close to the River Deveron in the heart of the Buchan farmlands, Turriff is an ancient burgh that was given its charter in 1512 by James IV. The Knights Templar once owned land in the area, and a Templar chapel stood here. **Turriff Parish Church** was built in 1794, and there are some good carvings on its belfry and walls from the previous kirk that stood on the site. In 1693 a Covenanting army controlled Turiff, but in May of the same year a force led by the Marquis of Huntly put them to flight, an event which became known as the "Turiff Trot". The ruined **St Congan's Church** was founded on the site of a Pictish fort by Malcolm IV in the 12th century.

Hatton Castle sits in its own spectacular grounds. It is not open to the public, though it can be rented for holidays or sporting breaks. It was the home of **Sir Beauchamp Duff**, a World War 1

general who committed suicide in 1918 after the failure of a British offensive against the Turks in 1915 in what is now Iraq. Over 9,000 troops from the Indian Division were surrounded, and three failed attempts to relieve the men resulted in the death of nearly 23,000 troops, some of them in Turkish prisons. The leader of the force, General Charles Townsend, was exonerated at a subsequent enquiry in 1917, while Duff was censured.

Turriff was the scene of a famous incident concerning the **Turra Coo** ("Turriff Cow"), which received widespread publicity throughout Britain. New National Insurance Acts were passed by Lloyd George's government in 1911 and 1913 which required employers to pay 3d per week for each of their employees. The farmers of Aberdeenshire, in common with others all over Britain, did not want to pay, as they reckoned that farm workers had a healthy lifestyle, and would not need much medical treatment. Curiously enough, the farm workers themselves supported the farmers on this issue.

One Turriff farmer in particular, Robert Paterson of Lendrum, refused to comply with the new regulations, so one of his cows was taken to be sold at auction to pay off his arrears. However the auction, held in Turriff, turned into a fiasco, as the cow, which had the slogan "Lendrum to Leeks" painted on its body ("leeks" being a reference to Welshman Lloyd George), took

Delgatie Castle, close to Turriff, was founded in about 1050, though the castle as you see it today dates from the 16th century. It is the ancestral home of Clan Hay, and has been in the Hay family for just under 700 years. It belonged to the Earls of Buchan until after the battle of Bannockburn in 1314, when Robert the Bruce gave it to the Hays. In 1562 Mary Stuart stayed in the castle for three days after the Battle of Corrichie, which took place to the west of Aberdeen. The Queen's troops under Donald, Chief of Clan Cameron, easily defeated a force of men led by the 4th Earl of Huntly, who was found dead on the battlefield after the victory. It is thought he was smothered by his armour.

349

Pennan

Delgatie Castle, close to Turriff, was founded in about 1050, though the castle as you see it today dates from the 16th century. It is the ancestral home of Clan Hay, and has been in the Hay fame 4th Earl of Huntly, who was found dead on the battlefield after the victory. It is thought he was smothered by his armour.

---

fright and bolted through the streets of the town. Meanwhile, the auctioneer was pelted with raw eggs and bags of soot. Three days later the cow was taken to Aberdeen, where it was sold for £7.

It was a hollow victory for the authorities, which had spent nearly £12 in recovering the sum. And they were further annoyed to hear that Paterson's neighbours had clubbed together and bought the cow so that it could be returned to him. So, while the authorities were out of pocket over the whole affair, it had not cost Robert Paterson a penny. There are now plans to erect a statue of the "Turra Coo" to commemorate the event.

The town has two small museums - the **Auld Post Office Museum** in the High Street and the **Cottage Museum** in Castle Street. Seven miles south west of Turriff along the B9024 is the **Glendronach Distillery**, founded in 1826 and situated on the banks of the Dronach Burn. Tours are available, and there is a visitor centre and shop.

PENNAN

9 miles W of Fraserburgh on the B9031

Pennan is possibly the most spectacular of the little fishing villages on the northern coast of Aberdeenshire. It is strung out along the base of a high cliff, with many of the cottages having their gable ends to the sea for protection. It is a conservation village, and is famous as being the setting, in 1983, for the film *Local Hero*, though parts were shot on the west coast (see also Arisaig). The red telephone box, famously used in the film, was a prop. However, Pennan's real telephone box, about 15 yards away from where the prop stood, is still a favourite place for photographs.

BANFF

20 miles W of Fraserburgh on the A98

Banff was once the county town of Banffshire, and is a small fishing port close to the mouth of the River Deveron. It is an ancient royal burgh, having been granted its charter in 1163 by Malcolm IV. The **Banff Museum** in the High Street is one of Scotland's oldest, having been founded in 1828. It has a nationally important collection of Banff silver.

Duff House is a unique country house art gallery run by a unique partnership between Historic Scotland, the National Galleries of Scotland and Aberdeenshire Council, with a fine collection of paintings by such artists as Raeburn and El Greco, as well as tapestries and Chippendale furniture. It was designed by William Adam and built between 1735 and 1740 for William Duff of Braco, who later became Earl of Fife. After a bitter wrangle with Adam, William Duff abandoned it, and it was left to James, the 2nd Earl Fife, to complete the grand plan, including the grounds. Over the years it has had a chequered career, having been a hotel, a sanatorium, a prisoner-of-war camp and the scene of an attempted murder, when a Countess of Fife tried to do away with her husband.

The small town of **Macduff** sits on the opposite shores of the small bay where the Deveron enters the Moray Firth, and contains the **Banffshire Maritime and Heritage Museum**. The lands were bought by the 1st Earl of Fife in 1733, and in 1783 the 2nd Earl founded the town as a burgh of barony. The **Macduff Marine Aquarium** in the High Shore has a central tank open to the sky surrounded by viewing areas so that you get a good view of fish and marine mammals from all angles. The aquarium has a wave-making machine which adds to the experience of seeing underwater life in its true state.

Six miles west of Banff, on the A98, is the attractive little fishing port of **Portsoy**, which is well worth visiting if only to soak in the atmosphere. Though its burgh charter dates from 1550, it was Patrick Ogilvie, Lord Boyne, who realised its potential and developed it as a port to export marble from the nearby quarries. Louis XIV used Portsoy marble on his palace at Versailles.

CRIMOND

7 miles SW of Fraserburgh on the A90

The village's main claim to fame is fact that the music to which *The Lord's My Shepherd* is sung was named after the village. It was written by Jessie Seymour Irvine, born in 1836, whose father was minister at Dunnottar, Peterhead and latterly Crimond.

PETERHEAD

16 miles SE of Fraserburgh on the A90

Peterhead is the largest town (as opposed to city) in Aberdeenshire, and one of the chief fishing ports in the northeast. It was founded by George Keith, the 5th Earl Marischal of Scotland in 1587, and is Scotland's most easterly burgh. It is Europe's largest white fish port, and also benefits from being one of the ports that services the offshore gas industry. The **Arbuthnot Museum** in St Peter Street tells the story of the town and its industries, and has a large collection of Inuit artefacts. It was given to the town in 1850 by Adam Arbuthnot, a local man who had acquired a huge collection of antiquities.

In South Road, in purpose-built premises, is **Peterhead Maritime Heritage Museum**. This tells of

206 WATERFRONT HOTEL

Macduff

A friendly, family-run hotel that offers good food, great drink and weekend entertainment.

see page 526

207 THE STATION HOTEL

Portsoy

A delightful small hotel that offers keenly priced holiday breaks as well as comfortable accommodation and fine dining.

see page 527

208 ROCKSLEY INN

Boddam

A recently refurbished inn that offers great value-for-money accommodation

 see page 526

the town's connections with the sea over the years, from its fishing fleet (which went as far as the Arctic in search of fish) to its whaling fleet (in its day, the second largest in Britain) and finally to the modern offshore gas and oil industries. The shape of the building resembles a "scaffy", a kind of fishing boat once used in the area.

The village of Boddam, two and a half miles south of the town, is typical of the small fishing villages that dotted the North Sea coastline of Aberdeenshire. **Boddam Castle**, now in ruins, belonged to the Keith family. One of its most famous sons was Sir William Keith, who rose to be Governor of Pennsylvania and Delaware before losing everything and dying in penury in London in 1749.

A few miles south of the town, at Cruden Bay, are the ruins of **Slains Castle**, built by the 9th Earl of Errol in 1597 to replace an earlier castle. It has been rebuilt and refurbished several times since then, and the ruins you see now date from the early 19th century. Now there are plans to restore it yet again, this time as holiday flats. It has literary associations of an unusual kind. While staying at the nearby village of **Cruden Bay** in 1895, Bram Stoker began writing Dracula, and based the vampire's Transylvanian castle on Slains. In an early draft of the novel he even has the Count coming ashore at Slains rather than Whitby. If you want to explore the area round Slains, great care must be taken, as it sits close to a cliff top above the sea.

The Highlands

When people talk of Scottish scenery, they inevitably mean the scenery of the Highlands - mountains, dark, heather-clad glens and deep, brooding lochs. And though other areas can also claim their fair share of these features, this is the one that has them in abundance.

The Highlands area has no set boundaries, and some places described in earlier chapters, such as Aberdeen and Grampian, Argyllshire and parts of Perthshire, can lay claim to being in the Highlands as well. But the area described in this chapter has the same boundaries as the local government area, and can legitimately be called the true Highlands. It stretches from the northernmost coast of mainland Scotland down to Perthshire, and from the borders of Aberdeenshire and Moray to the rugged west coast, taking in one or two of the Inner Hebridean islands on the way.

It is mostly wild country, with fewer roads than other parts of Scotland. Some areas are totally inaccessible unless you go by foot over difficult terrain, and if you do decide to take to the hills or moors, remember that Highland weather can be unpredictable, even in summer. Take the correct clothing, and always tell someone about your intended route and your estimated times of arrival at various stages.

The capital of the Highlands is Inverness. It is a thriving city with an enviable quality of life, and its environs are reckoned to be one of the most rapidly growing areas in Britain, if not Europe. The recently announced plans for a large development (in essence a "new town") to the east of the city will se it grow even more.

Seen from the A9 as you head over the Kessock Bridge, Inverness has all the appearance of a large metropolis, with suburbs that sprawl along the Moray and Beauly Firths. But in fact its population is no more than 50,000, though this is growing daily. And some of the countryside surrounding it looks more like the Lowlands than the Highlands, with neat fields, villages and winding country road. However, if you head southwest along the A82 towards Loch Ness, or south along the A9, you'll soon find yourself in what is undoubtedly Highland scenery.

Within the Highlands you'll find Scotland's most famous features. Ben Nevis, Scotland's highest mountain, is here, as is Loch Morar, the country's deepest loch. Loch Ness, undoubtedly the most famous stretch of water in Europe, is a few miles from Inverness's city centre, and the last full battle on British soil was fought at Culloden. Here too is Glencoe, scene of the famous massacre, as well as John O' Groats, Aviemore, Monarch of the Glen Country, Skye, Fort William, Cape Wrath and Plockton, the setting for the books and TV series *Hamish Macbeth*.

The west coast is rugged, with sea lochs that penetrate deep into the mountains. Settlements are few and far between, and most of them are to be found right on the coast. Some visitors to the west coast of the Highlands are amazed at the sub-tropical plants that seem to thrive here. It's all down to the Gulf Stream, which warms the shores and keeps snow at bay.

The east coast, from Nairn to Inverness then north to John O' Groats, is gentler, with many more settlements. Dornoch, though small, has a medieval cathedral, so is more of a city than a town, and at Fortrose there are the remains of another cathedral. Strathpeffer was once a thriving spa town, with regular trains connecting it to Edinburgh and London.

And between the east and west coasts are the mountains, the lochs, the tumbling streams and the deep glens. The scenery can be austere and gaunt, but never anything less than beautiful.

No Gulf Stream here, and in some sheltered corners, snow lies well into May or even June. Glencoe/Nevis and Aviemore take advantage of this by being skiing centres, though of late snow has been in short supply.

In Caithness and Sutherland - Scotland's two northernmost counties - you will find the Flow Country, mile upon mile of low peaks, high moorland and small, shallow lochans. This is not the dramatic scenery of the West Highlands where mountain seems to pile on mountain, but

it has a ruggedness and grandeur of its own.

The Highlands takes the breath away at every turn. There are areas that are all mountains, lochs and glens, and there are areas that are as green and intensely cultivated as the Lowlands. There are lonely places, where another human being is likely to be miles away, and there are crowded holiday towns such as Fort William and crowded cities such as Inverness. All these qualities ensure that the Highlands is one of the most rewarding areas in Britain to visit.

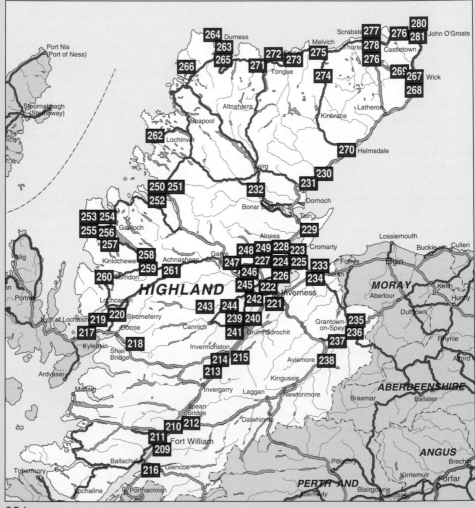

209 CORRIE DUFF

Fort William

A splendid guest house boasting six en suite rooms plus two self-catering cottages that have been fitted out to a very high standard.

🛏 see page 528

•

Fort William is where the Caledonian Canal begins (see also Inverness). It is not one uninterrupted canal, but a series of canals connecting Loch Lochy, Loch Oich and Loch Ness (see Drumnadrochit for details of Loch Ness). Work started on building it in 1803, and it was finally finished in 1822. However, it was found to be not deep enough for larger ships, so in 1847 work began on deepening it.

•

FORT WILLIAM

The small town of Fort William lies at the western end of Glen Mhor. or More, (meaning "Great Glen"), in an area known as Lochaber. Though it is small, in the summer months it gets crowded with visitors all seeking the solitude of the Highlands. It is the northern "terminus" of the 95-mile long West Highland Way, which snakes through Western Scotland from Milngavie on the outskirts of Glasgow.

The fort referred to in the town's name was built by General Monk in the 1650s, then rebuilt and renamed Maryburgh during the reign of William III to house a garrison of 600 troops to keep the Highland clans in order. Only parts of the wall of this fort survive, as the rest was dismantled in the 19th century to make way for the West Highland Railway.

It was from Fort William that thousands of Scots sailed for the New World during that time known as the Clearances. In the early 19th century, landowners could squeeze more profit from their estates if it had sheep on rather than people, so Highlanders were evicted from their cottages and small parcels of land. Some settled on the coast, and some emigrated.

It was the coming of the railway in 1866 that established Fort William as one of the Highland's main tourist centres, and it has remained so to this day. A few miles east of the town is **Ben Nevis**, at 4,406 feet, Britain's

highest mountain. The five-mile climb to the top, along a well-trodden path, is fairly easy if you're reasonably fit. It can also get crowded at times. The summit is reached by way of **Glen Nevis**, often called Scotland's most beautiful glen, though there are other contenders for the title. If you do decide to climb Ben Nevis, let people know, and dress appropriately. While it may be warm and sunny at sea level, the weather on the mountain's slopes can be changeable. The rewards of the climb are immense. The Cairngorms can be seen, as can the Cuillin range on Skye and the peaks of Argyllshire. On an exceptionally clear day even the coast of Northern Ireland can be glimpsed through binoculars. At the **Glen Nevis Visitors Centre** there are exhibits about local heritage and wildlife, and, importantly, information about the weather on the mountain.

Aonach Beag (4,058 feet) and **Aonach Mor** (3,999 feet) are Ben Nevis's little brothers, lying just over a mile to the east. In the winter this is a skiing area, but it is equally popular in the summer. Britain's only mountain gondola takes you half way up the range to a restaurant and bar, and there are several walks to enjoy when you reach them.

Within the town, in Cameron Square, is the **West Highland Museum**, with exhibits and displays about the area. The most famous exhibit is the 18th century "Secret Portrait of Prince Charles

Edward Stuart". It is a meaningless swirl of colours which, when reflected onto a polished cylinder, gives a likeness of the Prince. It was necessary, after the Jacobite Rebellion was suppressed, to keep secret any admiration you had for the Stuarts, and portraits of any of them were not allowed. Another secret ritual that the Jacobites had was to pass their wine, brandy or whisky glasses over a bowl of water before drinking it. This signified the "kings across the water". Within the museum there are also some pieces of eight brought up from the Spanish galleon which sank in Tobermory Bay (see also Tobermory). On the A830 at Corpach, northwest of the town, is the award-winning **Treasures of the Earth**, one of Europe's finest collections of crystals and gemstones. The **Underwater Centre**, on the banks of Loch Linnhe, is the world's leading diving instruction and training centre.

The impressive ruins of 13th century **Inverlochy Castle** (Historic Scotland) sit one-and-a-half miles north east of Fort William. It was originally built by the Comyn family in the 13th century on the site of an even earlier fort, though the ruins you see now date from much later. It was here that Montrose had an important victory over the Covenanting Campbells in 1645, when most of the Campbells who weren't killed during battle or who later surrendered were massacred.

Not far away, on the A82, is the 174-year-old **Ben Nevis Distillery and Whisky Centre**, which has conducted tours. One of its products is a blend of whiskies called The Dew of Ben Nevis.

Fort William is the northern terminus of the West Highland Way, a long distance footpath that starts at Milngavie just outside Glasgow. It is also the western terminus for the **Great Glen Way**, which opened in 2002. It is another long distance footpath that follows the Great Glen and Loch Ness, ending at Inverness, 73 miles away.

Neptune's Staircase at Banavie, near Fort William, was designed and built by Thomas Telford in the early 1800s, and takes the canal through a series of eight locks while raising it over 60 feet.

In the summer months, the **Jacobite Steam Train** travels the famous Fort William to Mallaig line. It passes along the northern shores of Loch Eil - a continuation of Loch Linnhe after it turns westwards - on a 45-mile journey that has some of the most beautiful scenery in Britain.

210 LEASONA

Torlundy

A modern, attractive villa, offering superb B&B accommodation in four comfortable, well-furnished rooms.

see page 529

211 THE BRIDGE CAFÉ

Lochybridge

A superb café just north of Fort William where you will find good food beautifully cooked - all at realistic prices.

see page 529

Inverlochy Castle

At Roy Bridge, to the east of Spean Bridge, was fought the Battle of Mulroy in 1688 between Clan MacDonald of Lochaber and the Macintoshes, with the MacDonalds being the victors. It was the last great inter-clan battle fought in the Highlands, and the last one on British soil where bows and arrows were used. A cairn marks the spot. The Parallel Roads in Glen Roy are a series of lines running parallel to each other on glen hillside. They mark the shorelines of a great loch that once filled the glen thousands of years ago, and which drained away when a great dam of ice at the beginning of the glen melted after the last Ice Age.

Spean Bridge sits eight miles northeast of Fort William. It was around here that commandos trained during World War II, and they are remembered by the **Commando Memorial**. It was designed by the sculptor Scott Sutherland, and depicts three commando soldiers. It was unveiled by the late Queen Mother (at that time consort of King George) in 1952 (see also Achnacarry). **The Spean Bridge Mill,** which is nearby, has demonstrations of tartan weaving as well as a clan tartan centre.

AROUND FORT WILLIAM

ACHNACARRY

9 miles NE of Fort William on a minor road off the B8005

Since 1665 **Achnacarry Castle** had been the home of Cameron of Locheil, known as "Gentle Locheil", one of Charles Edward Stuart's most ardent supporters. After 1745 it was burned down by Hanoverian troops. Locheil's family was banished from the country, but they were allowed to return in 1784, and built a new home a few years later. In 1942 the Cameron chief had to leave his home once again, when it was taken over by the British army as a training centre for commandos (see also Fort William).

A 17th century croft house close to where Achnacarry once stood now houses the **Clan Cameron Museum**, which has displays, charts and exhibits relating

to the history of the clan and to the commandos who trained here during the Second World War. A minor road takes you past the museum and along the lovely banks of **Loch Arkaig,** finally petering out near its western end. On its northern shore is the 180 acre **Allt Mhuic Nature Reserve**, which supports two populations of rare butterflies - the chequered skipper and the pearl bordered fritillary.

LAGGAN

19 miles NE of Fort William on the A82

Laggan sits between Loch Lochy and Loch Oich, two of the lochs that make up the Caledonian Canal. It was here, in July 1544, that the so-called **Battle of the Shirts** took place, fought between Clan Fraser and the combined forces of Clan Ranald and Cameron. It was fought on a hot summer's day, and the clansmen removed their plaids and fought in their shirts. However, this may be a mistranslation of the original Gaelic, which more probably translates as the "Battle of the Swampy Meadow". There were many casualties, including the chief of Clan Fraser and his son.

FORT AUGUSTUS

28 miles NE of Fort William on the A82

Fort Augustus Abbey, on the shores of Loch Ness, was founded for Benedictine monks. It was established in 1876 on the site of a fort (named after George II's son, the Duke of Cumberland) built on the orders of General Wade between 1729 and 1742 to keep Jacobite sympathisers in check.

However, this it failed to do, and was actually taken by the Jacobite army in 1745. The buildings were bought in 1867 by Lord Lovat, and he in turn leased them to the Benedictine monks in 1870. The abbey eventually closed in 1998, due to a decline in the number of monks. Many of the valuable books and manuscripts that were in the abbey library are now owned by the National Library of Scotland

The **Caledonian Canal Heritage Centre** is located in a converted lock keeper's cottage near the locks that lower the canal before it enters Loch Ness, and explains the history and uses of the canal.

The **Highland and Rare Breeds Croft** is on Auchterawe Road, and you can see Highland cattle, red deer and rare breeds of sheep. At the **Clansman Centre**, housed in an old school, there are presentations on ancient Highland life, and demonstrations about such things as putting on a belted plaid and handling a claymore.

KINLOCHLEVEN

10 miles SE of Fort William on the B863

This little town sits at the head of Loch Leven, and is on the West Highland Way. It was developed as an industrial village in the early 20th century when the North British Aluminium Company built the Blackwater reservoir and a hydro electric scheme to power an aluminium smelter which was the largest in the world at the time. Before that, it had been two small villages called Kinlochmore and

Killochbeag. The **Aluminium Story Visitor Centre** on Linnhe Road at the library tells the story of the smelting works right up until the year 2000. Outside the centre is a giant sundial designed by blacksmith Robert Hutcheson that takes its inspiration from the area's history and scenery.

The **Ice Factor** on Leven Road is Britain's premier indoor mountaineering centre, and features the world's largest indoor ice climbing wall as well as Britain's largest articulated rock climbing wall. Built within what was part of the old smelting works, there is also a children's activity zone, audiovisual lecture theatre, steam room, plunge pool and hot tub and a cafeteria and restaurant.

The **Atlas Brewery** opened in 2002, brewing a range of real ales. From Easter to September there are conducted tours round the premises at 5.30pm every day except Sunday. Special group tours can be arranged by prior notice at other times.

BALLACHULISH

10 miles S of Fort William on the A82

The area surrounding Ballachulish (pronounced Balla-hoolish" and meaning"settlement near the narrows") was once famous for its slate quarries. There are actually three villages - Ballachulish itself, and west of it of North Ballachulish, on the northern shore of Loch Leven, and South Ballachulish on the southern shore. The last two were once connected by a ferry which stopped running

213 THE SCOTS KITCHEN

Fort Augustus

A delightful restaurant right in the heart of Fort Augustus that sells coffees, teas, lunches and takeaway meals.

see page 530

214 INCHNACARDOCH LODGE HOTEL

Fort Augustus

A superb hotel overlooking Loch Ness, with well appointed rooms and serving a good range of Scottish dishes.

see page 530

215 DEER VIEW BED & BREAKFAST

Whitebridge

A superb, modern B&B, set in the heart of breathtaking Highland scenery, that offers the very best in Scottish hospitality.

see page 530

Ballachulish

A five star hotel and golf resort on the banks of Loch Linnhe that offers the last word in luxurious living.

see page 531

in 1975 when a bridge was built across the loch.

South Ballachulish straggles along the southern shore of Loch Leven. To the west of the village a cairn marks the spot where Jacobite sympathiser James Stewart, known as **James of the Glen**, was hanged for a crime he did not commit in 1752. He was found guilty, by a Campbell judge and jury, of the murder of **Colin Campbell**, known as the "Red Fox", a government agent. Robert Louis Stevenson used the incident in his book *Kidnapped*. Another cairn marks the site of the murder.

The **Lochaber Water Sports Centre** can be found at Laroch, on the southern shores of Loch Leven. It offers tuition in most water sports, including yachting and power boating.

To the east of Ballachulish, on the A82, is one of the most evocative place names in Scotland - **Glencoe**. It was here, in 1691, that the infamous Massacre of Glencoe took place. Because of bad weather, McIan of Clan MacDonald had failed to take the oath of allegiance to William III before the deadline, and a party of Campbell troops were sent to Glencoe to massacre his people. They pretended at first to come in peace, and were offered hospitality. But in the early hours of February 13th they set about systematically killing McIan's people - men, women and children - with few escaping. The massacre did not take place at one location, but in small clachans all over the glen. Thirty eight people were killed, while many more died of exposure after the clachan cottages were burnt down. A monument in the shape of a tall Celtic cross commemorates the event.

Glencoe, further east than the village, is a wild, beautiful place, though it does get crowded with hikers and climbers in summer months . On the north side is **Aonach Eagach**, a long ridge, and on the south side three peaks of Beinn Fhada, Gearr Aonach and Aonach Dhu, known as the **Three Sisters**. About 14,000 acres within Glencoe are now owned by the National Trust for Scotland, and it has set up the **Glencoe Visitor Centre**, which tells the story of the

Loch Leven, near Ballachulish

massacre. In Glencoe village itself is the **Glencoe and North Lorn Folk Museum**, which has exhibits about the history of the area and its people, including slate quarrying.

About nine miles east of Glencoe, on a minor road off the A82, is the Glencoe skiing area with a chair lift that is open in the summer months, and gives wonderful views over Glencoe and Rannoch Moor.

ARDNAMURCHAN

30 miles W of Fort William

The B8007 leaves the A861 at **Salen** (where a small inlet of Loch Sunart is usually crowded with yachts, making a picturesque panorama) and takes you westwards onto the Ardnamurchan Peninsula. It is single track all the way, so great care should be taken. It heads for Ardnamurchan Point and its lighthouse, the most westerly point of the British mainland, and in doing so passes some wonderful scenery.

At Kilchoan there are the ruins of **Mingary Castle**, originally built in the 13th century as a stronghold of Clan MacIan before passing to the Campbells. It was visited by James IV in 1493 on one of his expeditions to subdue the Western Isles. It was briefly used in the 2002 movie *Highlander: Endgame*. Kilchoan is Britain's most westerly mainland village, and up until 1900, when the B8007 was constructed, it was also Britain's most inaccessible, as it could only be reached by boat. Nowadays, in summer, a ferry connects it to Tobermory on Mull.

Glencoe

A few miles North of Salen, reached by a minor road off the A861 and on the edge of the area known as Moidart, are the ruins of **Castle Tioram** (pronounced "Chirrum"). The castle sits on a small tidal island and was originally built in the 14th century by Lady Anne MacRuari, whose son Ranald gave his name to Clan Ranald. It was burnt by the Jacobites in 1715 to prevent it being used by Hanovarian forces, and has been a ruin ever since.

At the head of Loch Moidart, and to the east of Castle Tioram, is a line of five beech trees. Originally there were seven, and were known as the **Seven Men of Moidart**. They commemorate the seven men who landed with Charles Edward Stuart and sailed with him up Loch Shiel, and were originally planted in the early 19th century (see Glenfinnan).

STRONTIAN

20 miles SW of Fort William on the A861

Strontian (pronounced "Stron - tee - an", and meaning "point of the

---

●

At Glenborrodale on the Ardnamurchan peninsula you can glimpse the late Victorian Glenborrodale Castle, built by C.D. Rudd of the De Beers Mining Company and owned from 1933 to 1949 by Lord Trent, otherwise known as Jesse Boot, founder of the chain of chemists. The red sandstone was quarried at Annan on the Solway Firth and brought to Ardnamurchan by boat. It is now a luxury hotel.

●

The narrow B849 from Lochaline (with passing places) follows the shores of the Sound of Mull as far as Drimnin, and makes a wonderful drive. A ferry connects Fishnish on Mull with Lochaline, and a small, private passenger ferry connects Drimnin with Tobermory and Laga Bay on Ardnamuchan during the summer.

fairies") sits in an area known as Sunart, which lies to the south of Loch Shiel. The village gave its name to the metal strontium, which was discovered in 1791 in the local lead mines by a chemist called Adair Crawford. A few years later Sir Humphrey Davie gave it its name.

In 1843, the then local landowners, the Riddell family, refused to allow the villagers to build a Free Presbyterian church, as they supported the established Church of Scotland, and believed that everyone should worship there. The villagers took matters into their own hands, and had a ship built on the Clyde, which they sailed up to Strontian and had anchored offshore. The Riddells were powerless to stop it, and it became known as the **Floating Church**.

To the north of the village are the **Ariundle Oakwoods**, a national nature reserve.

MORVERN
24 miles SW of Fort William

Morvern is that area of the mainland that sits immediately north of the island of Mull. The A884 leaves the A861 east of Strontian and travels down through it as far as Lochaline on the Sound of Mull, where there is the restored **Kinlochaline Castle.** It sits at the head of Loch Aline, and was once the ancestral home of Clan MacInnes. The clan takes a special pride in being one of the few clans in Scotland without a chief. The last one, and all his family, was butchered by John, Lord of the

Isles, in 1354 at **Ardtornish Castle**, the ruins of which can still be seen a few miles from Lochaline.

SALEN
27 miles W of Fort William on the A861

Salen (not to be confused with Salen on the Isle of Mull) sits on the shores of Loch Sunart, and is known as the gateway to Ardnamurchan. Three miles east (not accessible by road) is **Claish Moss**, a good example of a Scottish raised bog. Water is held in the peat, and the landscape is dotted with lochans. The peat has preserved seeds and pollen for thousands of years, so it is of interest to biologists researching the flora of the Western Highlands.

GLENFINNAN
13 miles W of Fort William on the A830

It was here, at the northern tip of **Loch Shiel**, Scotland's fourth longest freshwater loch, that Charles Edward Stuart raised his standard in 1745, watched by 1,200 Highland followers, after having been rowed a short distance up the loch from the house of MacDonald of Glenaladale on the western shores. The **Charles Edward Stuart Monument** (National Trust for Scotland) was erected in 1815 by Alexander MacDonald of Glenaladale to commemorate the event, and a small visitors centre nearby tells the story.

The **Glenfinnan Station Museum** lies on the Fort William - Mallaig line, and tells of the building of the line by Robert McAlpine (known as "Concrete

Bob") in the late 19th and early 20th centuries. The museum's restaurant and tearoom is a restored 1950s railway carriage. The **Glenfinnan Viaduct**, also on the Fort William - Mallaig line, is 416 yard long, with a graceful curve. It has 21 graceful arches, the tallest being 100 feet high. It was designed by Sir Robert MacAlpine, and built between 1897 and 1898. Though it has always been an important example of civil engineering, it became famous when it was featured in the *Harry Potter* movies.

ARISAIG

29 miles W of Fort William on the A830

The tiny village of Arisaig sits at the head of Loch nan Ceall. Southeast of the village is **Loch nan Uamh**, where, on 25 July 1745, Charles Edward Stuart first set foot on the Scottish mainland. After his campaign to restore the Stuart dynasty failed, he left for France from the same shore. A cairn now marks the spot. The **Land, Sea and Islands Centre** in a derelict smithy in the village has exhibits and displays about the history and wildlife of the area. Parts of the film *Local Hero* were filmed here (see also Pennan).

MALLAIG

31 miles NW of Fort William on the A830

Mallaig, Britain's most westerly mainland port, is a busy fishing port and the terminal of a ferry connecting the mainland to Armadale on Skye. It is also the end of the "Road to the Isles" and

the western terminus for the Jacobite Steam Train (see Fort William). The **Mallaig Heritage Centre** on Station Road has displays and exhibits that tell the story of the districts of Morar, Knoydart and Arisaig. The **Mallaig Marine World Aquarium and Fishing Exhibition** sits beside the harbour, and tells the story of Mallaig's fishing industry and the marine life found in the waters off Western Scotland. Most of the live exhibits were caught by local fishermen.

KYLE OF LOCHALSH

40 miles NW of Fort William on the A87

Kyle of Lochalsh was once the mainland terminus of a ferry that made a short crossing across Loch Alsh to Skye. Now the graceful **Skye Bridge** has superseded it (for Skye see the Inner Hebrides chapter). Three miles east of the village on the A87 is the **Lochalsh Woodland Garden** at Lochalsh House, with sheltered walks beside the shores of Loch Alsh, as well as mature woodlands and a variety of shrubs, such as rhododendrons, bamboo, ferns, fuchsias and hydrangeas. There is a small visitors centre at the square in Balmacara, just off the A87. The Woodland Garden is within the 5,616 acre Lochalsh Estate, which takes in most of the Lochalsh Peninsula. Also centred on Kyle of Lochalsh is **Seaprobe Atlantis**, a glass-bottomed boat that takes you out into the Marine Special Area of Conservation and shows you the rich diversity of marine life in the

•

Southeast of Mallaig is water of another sort - Loch Morar, which is Britain's deepest fresh water loch, and the world's 17th deepest. Its western end is only just under half a mile from the sea, though it is much deeper than any of the sea lochs in the area. It plunges to a depth of 1,077 feet, and if you were to stand the Eiffel Tower on the bottom, its top would still be 90 feet below the surface. A minor road near Morar village, south of Mallaig, takes you to its shores. Like Loch Ness, it has a monster, nicknamed Morag, which, judging by people who have claimed to have seen it, looks remarkably like Nessie.

•

217 THE GATEWAY RESTAURANT

Kyle of Lochalsh

A licensed restaurant, in the shadow of the Skye Bridge, that is noted for its great, reasonably priced food.

║ **see page 532**

363

Eilean Donan Castle

218 OFF THE BEATEN TRACK - IN KINTAIL

Kintail

A cosy self-catering cottage, cradled in the mountains, ideal for the perfect get away.

⊨ see page 532

219 THE HAVEN HOTEL

Plockton

A quite superb hotel with first class facilities sitting in a part of Scotland that epitomises Highland scenery and grandeur.

⊨ ‖ see page 533

220 CROFT SELF CATERING

Strome Ferry

A self-catering cottage with three bedrooms that represents outstanding value-for-money holiday accommodation.

⊨ see page 532

waters surrounding Scotland. You can also see the wreck of the HMS Port Napier, built in 1940 and converted to a minelayer. She sank in 60 feet of water in November of the same year.

Six miles east of the village is one of the most photographed castles in Scotland, **Eilean Donan Castle**, which sits on a small island connected to the mainland by a bridge. It's name ("Donan's Island") comes from the legend that St Donan lived on the island as a hermit. He was killed during a Viking raid on the island of Eigg in AD 617. Parts of the castle date back to 1220, when it was built by Alexander II and given to an ancestor of the Mackenzies who fought beside him at the Battle of Largs. Most of it, however, dates from a rebuilt carried out between 1912 and 1932 by Lieutenant Colonel John MacRae Gilstrap. It is now the ancestral home of Clan MacRae, and has a small clan museum. It has also featured in many films, most notably *The World is Not Enough* and *Highlander*.

If you continue eastwards

along the A87 you will eventually arrive at **Shiel Bridge**, at the head of Loch Duich. To the southeast is Glen Shiel, where five peaks, called the **Five Sisters of Kintail** (National Trust for Scotland) overlook the picturesque glen. Close by is the site of the **Battle of Glen Shiel**, fought in 1719 between a Hanovarian Army and a force of Jacobites (which included 300 Spaniards). It was the last battle fought on British soil between British and foreign soldiers, and it had no clear victor, though the Hanovarians claimed victory. There is a **Countryside Centre** (National Trust for Scotland) at Morvich Farm, off the A87, and it makes a good starting point for walking on some of the surrounding hills and mountains.

Northeast of Kyle of Lochalsh is the conservation village of **Plockton**, with its palm trees and idyllic location. This was the Lochdubh of *Hamish Macbeth* fame, as it was here that the TV series was filmed. It sits on Loch Carron, and on the opposite bank, opposite Strome Ferry and a few miles inland off a minor road, are the ruins of **Strome Castle** (National Trust for Scotland). It was built in the 15th century, and was a stronghold of the MacDonalds, Lords of the Isles. On **Craig Highland Farm**, near the village, you can view rare breeds, as well as feed the farmyard animals.

Kyle of Lochalsh is the western terminus for the famous Dingwall - Kyle of Lochalsh railway line (see Dingwall).

INVERNESS

Inverness is the capital of the Highlands. It is said to be the most rapidly expanding city in Britain, if not Europe, and though it only has a population of about 50,000, its hinterland supports a further 20,000. Plans for a major new development to the east of the city could boost this figure even further. But for all its modest size at present, it still has all the feel and bustle of a much larger place, and its shopping - especially in the pedestrianised High Street, where the Eastgate Shopping Centre is located - is superb.

The city sits at the northeast end of the Great Glen, at a point where the River Ness enters the Moray Firth. It was once the capital of the Northern Picts, and it was to Inverness that St Columba came in the 6th century to confront King Brude MacMaelcon and convert him and his kingdom to Christianity. The doors of Brude's fort were firmly closed, but Columba marked them with the sign of the cross and they miraculously flew open.

No one knows where this stronghold stood, though people have suggested **Craig Phadraig**, a hill that overlooks the town, and on which there are the remains of a Pictish fort, and others have suggested **Torvean**.

The present **Inverness Castle** dates from 1835, and houses the local courthouse. Castles have stood on the site since at least the 12th century. However, Macbeth's castle, where Shakespeare set the murder of Duncan, was to the east of the present building, and closer to the River Ness, at a spot where people have claimed to have seen the ghost of Duncan in full kingly attire. General Wade enlarged Inverness Castle after the uprising of 1715, and its garrison surrendered to Charles Edward Stuart when he occupied the town in 1745. Wade then ordered the castle to be blown up. Close to the present castle is a statue of Flora MacDonald, who helped Charles Edward Stuart evade capture. Parts of the castle are open to the public during the summer.

Across from the castle is the **Tolbooth Steeple**, dating from the late 18th century. It was once part of a complex of buildings that contained a courthouse and jail. **Inverness Museum and Art Gallery**, on Castle Wynd, is closed until further notice. Inverness Library has a dedicated genealogy room, where people can learn about the people living in Inverness through the ages, and possibly come upon their own ancestors.

The oldest secular building in the city is **Abertarff House** in Church Street (National Trust for Scotland), which dates from 1593. It was built as a town house for the Frasers of Lovat, and is now the local headquarters for the National Trust for Scotland. **Dunbar's Hospital** is also on Church Street, and dates from 1668. It was founded by Provost Alexander Dunbar as a hospital for the poor. It has now been divided into flats.

221 LOCH NESS HOUSE HOTEL

Inverness

A top city hotel and restaurant to the west of the city centre that is also handy for exploring the Cairngorms, Loch Ness and the Western Highlands.

🛏 ❙ see page 534

Near the castle, in Bridge Street, is the Town House, which was completed in 1882. It was in the council chamber here, in 1921, that the only cabinet meeting ever held outside London took place when Lloyd George, the Prime Minister, wanted to discuss the worsening Ireland situation.

The stately **Balnain House** (National Trust for Scotland), on Huntly Street on the opposite bank of the River Ness, was built in 1726 for an Inverness merchant, and for a time was a music heritage centre. Also on the opposite bank is **Inverness Cathedral,** dedicated to St Andrew, a gem of a building designed by Alexander Ross and consecrated in 1874. It was supposed to have had two large spires, but these were never built. The Eden Court Theatre, next to the cathedral, incorporates parts of the old Bishop's Palace.

The Old High Church in Church Street is Inverness's parish church, and was built in 1770, though parts of the tower may date from medieval times. After the battle of Culloden, the church was used as a jail for Jacobite soldiers, some of whom were executed in the kirkyard. It is said to be built on a site where St Columba once preached. The **Old Gaelic Church** was originally built in 1649, though the present building dates from a rebuilding of 1792.

Inverness is one of the few Scottish towns to have retained its traditional market, and the indoor **Victorian Market** in the Academy Street building dates from 1890, when it was rebuilt after a disastrous fire.

The magnificent **Kessock Bridge**, opened in 1982, carries the A9 over the narrows between the Moray and Beauly Firths and connects Inverness to the Black Isle. At North Kessock is the **Dolphins and Seals of the**

Moray Firth Visitor and Research Centre. The Moray Firth is famous for its bottlenose dolphins, and boats leave from many small ports so that you can observe them. This visitor centre gives you one of the best opportunities in Europe to learn about the creatures, and to listen to them through underwater microphones.

A few miles west of the town at Kirkhill is the **Highland Wineries**, based around Moniack Castle, an old Fraser stronghold dating from 1580. There are country wines, liqueurs, preserves and sauces.

AROUND INVERNESS

CROMARTY

16 miles NE of Inverness on the A832

This picturesque small royal burgh, which received its charter in the 13th century, sits on a small headland near the mouth of the Cromarty Firth. It is probably the best-preserved 18th century town in Scotland, and was where many Highlanders embarked for Canada during the clearances of the early 19th century.

It was the birthplace, in 1802, of Hugh Miller, writer and the father of geology. **Hugh Miller's Cottage** (National Trust for Scotland), where he was born, is open to the public. It has a collection of fossils and rock specimens, as well as some of his personal possessions such as his geological hammer and microscope. **The Old Orchard** surrounds

Cromarty's oldest still inhabited house, the Old Manse. It's wall was built in 1770, though the present garden dates only from 1997.

The **Cromarty Courthouse Museum**, as its name suggests, is housed within the old courthouse. There is a reconstruction of an 18th century trial in the courtroom itself, plus you can see the old cells, children's costumes, a video presentation giving 800 years of Cromarty history and an audio tape tour of the old part of the town.

The Cromarty Firth has always been a safe anchorage for British ships. On 30th December 1915 *H.M.S. Natal* mysteriously blew up here, with the loss of 421 lives. Many of those killed lie in the kirkyard of the **Gaelic Chapel**, which is now ruined. Cromarty has always been a Lowland-Scots speaking town, and the chapel was built for Gaelic incomers in the 18th century.

Ross and Cromarty was one of the counties of Scotland lost in the local government reforms of 1975. Originally it was two counties, each with its own Lord Lieutenant, though Cromarty, for historical reasons, was fragmented into enclaves within the whole width of Ross-shire, which spread from the Atlantic to the North Sea coastlines. The two were amalgamated in 1889.

FORTROSE

8 miles NE of Inverness on the A832

Fortrose Cathedral (Historic Scotland) was founded by David I as the mother church of the diocese of Ross. Building began in the 1200s, though the scant remains you see nowadays date from the 14th century. One of the three fine canopied tombs is of Euphemia Ross, wife of the thoroughly bad Alexander Stewart, son of Robert I and nicknamed the "Wolf of Badenoch" (see also Dunkeld, Grantown-on-Spey and Elgin). She was the daughter of the Uilleam, Mormaer of Ross (a mormaer being a high steward), and on the death of her husband in 1394 she became Prioress of Elcho Priory in Perthshire and died four years later. The other two are of bishops, possibly Robert Cairncross and John Fraser.

Nearby **Chanonry Point** is one of the best places to observe the Moray Firth dolphins. Here, where the Firth is at its narrowest, you can sometimes see up to 40 of these graceful creatures glide through the waters or put on a fine display of jumping and diving. It was at Chanonry Point that Kenneth Mackenzie, better known as the **Brahan Seer**, was executed in 1660 (see also Strathpeffer). He was born on Lewis, and had, from an early age, the gift of second sight. It is said he predicted the Caledonian Canal, the Battle of Culloden and North Sea oil. Like so many famous predictions, however, they are cloaked in such language that they could mean anything. When he was asked by Isabella, the 3rd Countess of Seaforth why her husband, also called Kenneth Mackenzie, was late returning home from Paris, he said that he was with a lady. She was so enraged that she

224 THE ANDERSON

Fortrose

Truly outstanding restaurant with rooms, with extensive menu changing daily; huge choice of beers and over 250 whiskies.

🍴 🛏 *see page 535*

225 EILEAN DUBH RESTAURANT

Fortrose

Recently established restaurant specialising in dishes based on produce from the Black Isle area.

🍴 *see page 535*

226 CROFTERS CAFÉ BAR

Rosemarkie

Café Bar in seaside village offering tasty home-made dishes based on fresh local produce.

🍴 *see page 536*

227 CULBOKIE INN

Culbokie

A village hostelry that attracts people from all over to sample its fine food and its outstanding range of drinks.

🍴 see page 536

228 THE SHIP INN

Invergordon

Comfortable B&B accommodation in former Temperance Hotel.

🛏 see page 537

229 FEARN HOTEL

Hill of Fearn

Recently refurbished hotel in scenic countryside offering excellent food and comfortable en suite accommodation.

🛏 🍴 see page 537

had Kenneth tried for witchcraft and executed by being immersed in a barrel of tar which was then set alight. A cairn marks the spot.

In nearby **Rosemarkie** is the **Groam House Museum,** with exhibits and displays that explain the culture of the Picts, those mysterious people who inhabited this part of Scotland in the Dark Ages. The cathedral for the diocese of Ross was established here before moving to Fortrose, the site now being occupied by the parish church of 1819.

TAIN

23 miles N of Inverness on the A9

In medieval times, Tain was a great Christian centre, drawing pilgrims from all over Europe to the shrine of St Duthus within **St Duthus Collegiate Church**. Now an exhibition and visitors centre called **Tain Through Time** explains about St Duthus (sometimes called Duthac) himself, the pilgrimage, and the people who made it. The museum, which is part of the centre, also has displays about Clan Ross. A church near the mouth of the river and now in ruins was built, it is said, on the site of St Duthac's birthplace. He was born about 1000, and died in Armagh, Ireland, in 1065. His body was subsequently brought back to Tain and buried in the old church. He is said to have accomplished many miracles during his lifetime. One story, if a somewhat flimsy one, tells of him being sent to the blacksmith as a boy for hot coals. The smith, obviously a bad

tempered man, scooped up some red hot coals in a shovel and threw them at Duthac. He calmly collected them in the folds of his coat and took them back to his master. On another occasion Duthac was attending a feast when a guest became ill. A kite swooped down and stole the sick man's food and ring. Duthac immediately prayed for the return of the ring and the food, and the kite miraculously reappeared and dropped all the items. Duthac allowed it to keep the food, but returned the ring to its owner.

Tain Tolbooth was built in 1707 by Alexander Stronach, a local mason, replacing an earlier building. Half a mile north of the town is the **Glenmorangie Distillery**, which has guided tours and a museum, with a tasting at the end of the tour.

Edderton lies north west of the town, and is famous for **Edderton Old Church**, built in 1743 and largely unaltered since then. When it was built, it had a thatched roof which was replaced by slate a few years later. At its east end is a burial mausoleum for the Baillie family made from what was probably the chancel of the church's medieval predecessor.

DORNOCH

30 miles N of Inverness on the A949

Dornoch Cathedral dates originally from the early 13th century. However, the church as we see it today is largely a rebuilding of the early 19th century, though there are some old features still to be seen, mostly in the chancel and crossing. Sixteen Earls of Sutherland are said to be buried within it. **Dornoch Castle** sits opposite the cathedral, and was built in the 15th century with later additions. It is now a hotel. The **Historylinks Museum**, behind the hotel, tells the story of Dornoch from its beginnings up to the present day. It features a mock up of the workshop of local golf professional Donald Ross's workshop before he went on to design over 500 American golf courses. The Historylinks Trail takes you on a tour of the town, highlighting 16 sites of special interest.

Dornoch was the scene, in 1727 (though the stone says 1722), of Scotland's last execution for witchcraft, when an old woman called Janet Horne was burned for, among other things, supposedly turning her daughter into a pony and then getting Satan to shoe her. There is little doubt that Janet had Alzheimer's Disease, and that her daughter had a deformity of the hands and feet that were wholly natural. The sheriff, a Captain David Ross, was later reprimanded for his handling of the trial. Nine years after Janet's death, the trying and execution of witches in Scotland was outlawed. The **Witch's Stone**, within a garden in Littletown, marks the spot where Janet was executed.

GOLSPIE

40 miles NE of Inverness on the A9

A steep hill path takes you to the summit of the 1,300 feet high **Ben Bhraggie**, on which there is a statute by Chantry of the first Duke of Sutherland, who died in 1833. Locally, it is known as the "Mannie", and was erected in 1834 by "a mourning and grateful tenantry to a judicious, kind and liberal landlord". The words ring hollow, however, as the Duke, owner of the biggest private estate in Europe at the time, was one of the instigators of the hated Clearances of the early 19th century, and there have been continued calls to have the statue removed, and in some cases blown up. Others have argued that the statue should stay as a reminder of those terrible times.

North of Golspie, on the road to Brora, is **Carn Liath** ("the Grey Cairn"), which is over 2,000 years old. It overlooks the sea, and is all that is left of a once mighty broch. The walls are still 12 feet high in places. In the other direction, on the road to Dornoch, is the **Loch Fleet Nature Reserve**, covering 2,834 acres. It consists of a large tidal basin, sand dunes and wooded areas, and here you can see seals, sea birds and wildfowl.

BRORA

45 miles NE of Inverness on the A9

Brora is a picturesque coastal village at the mouth of the River Brora. The **Brora Heritage Centre** on Coal Pit Road has a hands-on guide to the history and wildlife of the area. At one time it was the location of the Highland's only coal mine, with the coal being

230 SUTHERLAND ARMS HOTEL

Golspie

Former hunting lodge, now a family-run hotel, offering quality cuisine and superior accommodation.

⊨ ∥ see page 538

Dunrobin Castle, the seat of the Dukes of Sutherland, is the most northerly of Scotland's stately homes and one of the largest in the Highlands. Though the core is 14th century, it resembles a huge French château, thanks to a remodelling in 1840 by Sir Charles Barry, designer of the Houses of Parliament. Some of the castle's 189 rooms are open to the public, and there is a museum in the summerhouse.

231 SUTHERLAND INN

Brora

Completely refurbished in early 2007, with excellent restaurant and top quality en suite accommodation.

⊨ ‖ *see page 537*

232 INVERSHIN HOTEL

Invershin

Scenically sited hotel offering en suite B&B or self-catering accommodation; regular music sessions.

⊨ ‖ *see page 539*

shipped out from the local harbour until the railways took over. The mine finally closed in 1974. The **Clynelish Distillery** has a visitors centre and shop.

LAIRG

40 miles N of Inverness on the A836

Lairg is an old village that sits at the southeast end of **Loch Shin**, which, since the 1950s, has been harnessed for hydroelectricity. The loch, which is famous for its fishing, is over 18 miles long by no more than a mile wide at its widest, with the A838 following its northern shoreline for part of the way. Due to the hydro electric scheme, it is 30 feet deeper than it used to be.

The village became important because it sits at a point where various Highland roads meet. Five miles south are the picturesque **Falls of Shin**, which has a visitor centre and a Harrods shop - the only one in Scotland. The falls are famous for the wild salmon that leap their way up to their spawning grounds from about April to October each year. **Ord Hill**, west

of the town, has a countryside centre and an archaeological trail, which takes you round a landscape rich in ancient sites, and a forest walk. **Ferrycroft Countryside Centre** explains land use in this part of Sutherland since the end of the last Ice Age.

FORT GEORGE

10 miles NE of Inverness on the B9006

Fort George (Historic Scotland) was designed by the Major General William Skinner, the King's Military Engineer for North Britain (the name given to Scotland after the Jacobite Uprising). It's purpose was to man the Highlands after the Jacobite Uprising, and ensure that nothing like that ever took place again. He originally wanted to build it at Inverness, but the councillors of the town objected, saying it would take away part of the harbour. The fort was named after George II, and sits on a headland near Ardersier that guards the inner waters of the Moray Firth. Work started on building it in 1748, and it was subsequently manned by government troops. It covers 42 acres, has walls a mile long, and the whole thing cost over £1bn to build at today's prices. It has been called the finest 18th century fortification in Europe, and has survived almost intact from that time. The **Queen's Own Highlanders Museum** is within the fort. The regiment was an amalgamation of the Seaforth Highlanders and the queen's Own Cameron Highlanders. Now it is the 4th Battalion of the Royal Regiment of Scotland.

Fort George

NAIRN

16 miles NE of Inverness on the A96

Nairn is a small, picturesque holiday and golfing resort on the Moray Firth. Local people there will tell you that the name is a shortened version of "nae rain" ("no rain"), and indeed this area is one of the driest in Britain. It has a fine, clean beach and a large caravan park. The River Nairn, which flows through the town, supposedly marks the boundary between the English speaking areas to the east and the Gaelic speaking areas to the west. A great royal castle stood here, built by William the Lion in 1179, but it is long gone. The **Nairn Museum** in Viewfield House in King Street has collections on local history, archaeology and wildlife.

At Auldearn (now bypassed), two miles east of the town, is the **Boath Doocot** (National Trust for Scotland), which sits within what was a small castle built in the late 12th century by William the Lion. The **Battle of Auldearn** was fought here in 1645 between 1500 Royalist troops of the Marquis of Montrose and a 4,000-strong Covenanting army under Sir John Hurry. The Covenanters, even though they outnumbered the Royalist troops, were routed, and some of the dead were buried in the kirkyard of **Auldearn Parish Church**, built in 1757.

Eight miles south of the town, at Ferness, is the **Ardclach Bell Tower** (Historic Scotland), dating from 1655. It sits above the parish church.

CAWDOR

12 miles NE of Inverness on the B9090

Cawdor Castle was made famous by Shakespeare in his play *Macbeth*, though the core of the present castle was built in the 14th century by the then Thane of Cawdor, who was sheriff and hereditary constable of the royal castle at Nairn. He built the core - essentially the central tower - round a thorn tree which can still be seen today. The story goes that the thane loaded a donkey with gold, and let it wander round the district. He vowed to built the castle where it finally rested. This it did beside a thorn tree, which was incorporated into the building. However, the present tree has been identified, not as a thorn, but as a holly. Recent carbon dating suggests it was planted in about 1372.

The connections between Shakespeare's Macbeth and Cawder Castle, especially the witches' prediction that Macbeth would become Thane of Cawder, attract a lot of attention. However, as Cawder Castle was not built until the 14th century, on a site where a castle had never stood before, and Macbeth lived in the 11th century, then there is no connection whatsoever. With its fairy tale looks and its turrets, however, Cawder is said to be one of the most romantic castles in Scotland.

CULLODEN

5 miles E of Inverness on the B9006

The Battle of Culloden was fought on a cold day in April 1746 when

Site of the Battle of Culloden

235 CULDEARN HOUSE

Grantown-on-Spey

Superb country house hotel, set in a Victorian villa with original features, offering luxury en suite accommodation and fine dining.

see *page 542*

can fail to be moved.

You can still see the stones that mark the graves of various clans, and there is a huge memorial cairn at the centre of the battlefield. **Leanach Cottage**, which survived the battle, has been restored, and the **Culloden Visitors Centre** (National Trust for Scotland) has displays and exhibits which explain the battle. The **Cumberland Stone** is where the 25-year-old Duke of Cumberland, third son of George II and commander of the Royalist troops, watched the battle. He earned the nickname "Butcher Cumberland" for his unspeakable acts of cruelty after the battle.

Not far from the battlefield are the **Clava Cairns** (Historic Scotland), a fascinating group of three burial cairns of the early Bronze Age, with the small burial chambers being aligned southwest/ northeast. On top of the chambers huge quantities of stones and boulders were heaped, Two of the cairns have passages which connect to the chambers, suggesting that the dead were visited at certain times of the year for various rituals to be carried out.

sleet and snow was falling heavily - an unusual occurrance for April in this part of Scotland. It was the last major battle to take place on British soil, and was a turning point in Scotland's - and Britain's - history. The hopes of the Jacobites to return a Stuart king to the British throne were dashed on that cold day, and the clan system was smashed forever.

The battlefield is on Drumossie Moor, which, in the 18th century, was a lonely, wild place. Now most of it has been drained and cultivated, though the battlefield site itself has been returned to the way it was in the 18th century. There is still a sadness about the place, and it was once said that no birds ever sang here. That is not quite true, but no one who visits

TOMATIN

13 miles SE of Inverness off the A9

Tomatin sits on the River Findhorn, just off the A9. The **Tomatin Distillery**, north of the village, is one of the highest in Scotland, and was founded in 1897. Now owned by a Japanese company, it has 23 stills, and draws its water from the Alt-na-Frithe burn. It has tours, a visitor centre and tastings.

NETHY BRIDGE

24 miles SE of Inverness on the B970

Dell Wood National Nature Reserve is in Abernethy Forest. It is famous for its rare bog woodland, which has largely disappeared from the area because of drainage and agricultural improvements.

GRANTOWN-ON-SPEY

26 miles SE of Inverness off the A939

This beautiful and elegant tourist centre is situated in the heart of Strathspey (never, ever the "Spey Valley"), and sits at a height of 700 feet above sea level. It was built by James Grant of Grantcastle from 1765 onwards, and laid out in a grid plan. The **Inverallan Parish Church** in Mossie Road was completed in 1856, and commemorates the 7th and 8th Earls of Seaforth. **Granton Museum**, in Burnfield Avenue, tells the story of the town since its beginnings

The 15,000-acre **Revack Country Estate** is to the south of the town, on the B970 to Nethy Bridge. It has gardens, woodland trails and an adventure playground. Revack Lodge was built as a shooting lodge in 1860.

Six miles northwest of the town are the ruins of **Lochindorb Castle**, built on an island in Lochindorb ("Loch of Trouble"), on bleak Dava Moor. It originally dates from the 13th century, and was built by the Comyns. It was the home of the infamous Alexander Stewart, son of Robert II, nicknamed the Wolf of Badenoch.

CARRBRIDGE

21 miles SE of Inverness on the A938

The arch of the original packhorse bridge across the River Dulnain still stands, and dates from 1717, when it was built by Brigadier-General Sir Alexander Grant of Grant. It also carried funeral processions to Duthil Church, and for this reason was given the nickname of the "Coffin Bridge".

South of the village is the **Landmark Forest Heritage Park**. It is carved out of woodland, and has such attractions as a Red Squirrel Trail, Microworld (where you can explore the world of tiny insects) and the Tree Top Trail, where you take a walk through the high branches of the trees. The Timber Tower gives amazing views over the surrounding countryside. At Dulnain Bridge, six miles east of the village on the A95 is the four star **Speyside Heather Centre**, with over 300 species of a plant that has become synonymous with Scotland.

AVIEMORE

24 miles SE of Inverness off the A9

Once a quiet Inverness-shire village, Aviemore has now expanded into one of the main winter sports centres in the Highlands. The skiing area and chair lifts lie about seven miles east of the village, high in the Cairngorms. This is also the starting point of **Cairngorm Mountain Railway**, which carries passengers all year round to the Ptarmigan Station, within 400 feet of the summit of the 4,084 feet

---

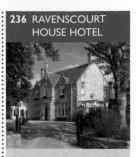

236 RAVENSCOURT HOUSE HOTEL

Grantown-on-Spey

Superior accommodation and first class dining in former Manse, in a charming small town.

see page 543

237 TIGH-NA-SGIATH COUNTRY HOUSE HOTEL

Dulnain Bridge

A superb country house hotel, within its own grounds, that offers the very best in Scottish hospitality.

see page 544

238 PINE BANK CHALETS

Aviemore

Self catering accommodation in beautiful Strathspey, one of Scotland's most scenic areas.

see page 545

The Rothiemurchus Highland Estate is a magnificent area with spectacular views, deep forests and woodland trails. You can try hill walking and mountain biking, and there are guided walks and safari tours in Land Rovers. The estate contains some of the last remnants of the great, natural Caledonian Pine Forest, which once covered all of the Highlands. Parts of Monarch of the Glen are filmed here (see also Kingussie). Details of all the activities are available from the Visitor Centre on the B970 south east of the village of Aviemore.

high Cairngorm itself. On the road to the skiing area is the **Cairngorm Reindeer Centre**, where Britain's only permanent herd of reindeer can be seen. The **Craigellachie Nature Reserve** (not to be confused with Craigellachie in Banffshire) is on the hill of the same name to the west of the village, and has mature birch woodland. There are trails through the trees, and sometimes peregrine falcons can be seen.

Aviemore is one of the termini of the **Strathspey Steam Railway,** which runs to **Boat of Garten**, five miles away. It was once part of the Aviemore to Forres line, which was closed in the early 1960s.

KINGUSSIE

28 miles S of Inverness off the A9

Kingussie (pronounced "King - yoosy" which means "the head of the pine forest") sits in Strathspey, with good views of the Cairngorms to the east, while to the west lie the **Monadhliath Mountains**, rising to over 3,000 feet. The main settlement in the area was not always at Kingussie, and it wasn't until 1799, thanks to the Duke of Gordon, that work began on the present village. In Duke Street sits the **Highland Folk Museum**, which gives an insight into the history and lifestyle of the ordinary people of the Highlands over 400 years. There is a reconstruction of a Black House (a Highland cottage) and a smoke house.

At **Newtonmore**, four miles south of the village, is another, similar museum called the **Newtonmore Highland Folk Museum**, where there is a reconstruction of an 18th century Highland township. Also in the village is the **Clan MacPherson House and Museum**, which, as its name implies, recounts the history of the MacPhersons. The whole museum covers 79 acres.

The ruins of **Ruthven Barracks** (Historic Scotland) lie to the west of Kingussie, on the other side of the A9. They were built in 1719 on the site of a castle dating from the 14th century and once owned by Alexander Stewart, the "Wolf of Badenoch" to house government troops when Jacobite sympathies were strong in the area. After the Jacobite defeat at Culloden, over 3,000 Jacobite troops mustered here to continue the fight. However, Charles Edward Stuart saw that further fighting was useless, and sent a message saying that each man should return home. Before they did, they burnt the place down. Four miles north of Kingussie is the **Highland Wildlife**, which has an array of Scottish wildlife, plus some animals that used to roam the Highlands but have now died out.

A few miles south west of Kingussie, along the A86, is **Loch Laggan**, where the BBC series *Monarch of the Glen* was filmed. The Ardverikie Estate, with its large house, played the part of Glenbogle (see also Aviemore). *Mrs Brown,* starring Judy Dench and Billy Connolly, was partly filmed here, as was *The Missionary* with Michael Palin and Maggie Smith.

The house itself was built in 1870. Queen Victoria visited the estate in 1847, staying for a month. She considered buying it before settling on Balmoral.

DRUMNADROCHIT

16 miles SW of Inverness on the A82

Drumnadrochit sits on the shores of **Loch Ness**, at Drumnadrochit Bay. With its village green, it is a quaint place, though it can get overcrowded in the summer due tourists flocking here to catch a glimpse of the Loch Ness Monster, nicknamed "Nessie". Whether a monster actually exists or not has never been proved, but that has never deterred the crowds. The loch measures just less than 23 miles long by a mile wide at its widest, and being over 700 feet deep at its deepest, contains more water than all the other lochs and lakes in Britain combined. In fact, the vertical cliffs that descend to the loch continue right down for several hundred feet below the waterline. The first mention we have of a monster - though in this case it was in the River Ness and not in the loch - occurs in Adamnan's *Life of St Columba*, written in the 7th century. In the year AD 565 St Columba was heading up the Great Glen towards Inverness, when he encountered a monster attacking a man in the River Ness at the point where it enters the loch. He drove it back by prayer, and the man's companions fell on their knees and were converted to Christianity.

Nowadays the monster is a bit more timid. Most sightings have been made at **Urquhart Castle** (Historic Scotland), about a mile from Drumnadrochit, and curiously enough, this is where the loch is at its deepest at 754 feet. The castle is one of the largest in Scotland, and sits on a promontory that juts out into the water. A fortification has stood here for centuries, but the present ruins date from the 16th

Loch Ness

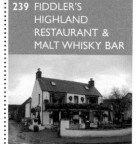

239 FIDDLER'S HIGHLAND RESTAURANT & MALT WHISKY BAR

Drumnadrochit

Superior food, superior drink and superior accommodation right on the banks of Loch Ness.

🍴 🛏 see page 545

240 GLEN ROWAN GUEST HOUSE

Drumnadrochit

A superb guest house standing in its own grounds that offers not only great accommodation, but the personal, friendly touch.

🛏 see page 546

241 BENLEVA HOTEL

Drumnadrochit

A superb hotel that is renowned for its real ales, its value for money tariffs and its comfortable guest rooms.

🛏 🍴 see page 546

242 THE OLD NORTH INN

Inchmore

Excellent food, real ale and comfortable en suite accommodation in long-established village inn.

¶ ⊨ see page 547

243 CULLIGRAN COTTAGES

Glen Strathfarrar

Superb self-catering accommodation, consisting of a traditional cottage and four chalets, within an area of outstanding beauty.

⊨ see page 547

244 CNOC HOTEL

Struy

Outstanding Highland country house hotel with award winning restaurant, nestling in picturesque Strathglass.

⊨ see page 548

century, when the Grants occupied it. Urquhart Castle has nothing to do with Clan Urquhart, whose homeland was on the Black Isle, north of Inverness, though there may have been early links. In 1689 a government force held out against a Jacobite army which was trying to capture it, but when the government troops moved out they blew the place up, rendering it useless to both sides. A visitor centre contains a model of the castle showing what it was like in its heyday.

Two exhibitions vie for attention in the village, the **Loch Ness 2000 Exhibition Centre** within the grounds of a hotel and the **Original Loch Ness Monster Exhibition.** They each have displays about the Loch Ness Monster, and in reality there is little to choose between them.

BEAULY

7 miles W of Inverness on the A862

Within this picturesque village are the ruins of **Beauly Priory** (Historic Scotland), founded by the Bisset family in 1230 for monks of the Valliscaulian order. What can be seen nowadays, however, dates from between the 14th and 16th centuries, when the Frasers of Lovat were the dominant family. The north transept, which is more or less complete, is the burial place of the MacKenzies of Kintail.

It is said that the village got its name when Mary Stuart stayed in the priory in 1564 on her way to Dingwall and declared it to be a "beau lieu", or beautiful place. However, it was called Beauly long before she arrived by the original monks, and the name may indeed come from the Latin for "beautiful place".

The **Beauly Centre**, next to the priory, has displays about the history of the area. There is also a reconstructed village store, a weaving centre and a Clan Fraser exhibition.

To the southwest is **Strathglass**, one of the most beautiful glens in the area. It was here, in the early 19th century, that the Sobieski Stuarts lived in some style, claiming to be the legitimate grandsons of Charles Edward Stuart. Their claims were believed by many people, notably the Earl of Moray, Lord Lovat and the Earl of Dumfries. There is no doubt, however, that they were charlatans.

Close to Beauly, at Kirkhill, is the **Wardlaw Mausoleum**, built on to the east end of Kirkhill Parish Church. It is one of the burial places of Clan Fraser, and was built in 1634. In 1998 it was restored by Historic Scotland. A couple of miles outh of Kirkhill is Moniack Castle, home to the famous **Moniack Winery**, which makes wines, liqueurs and preservatives. There are nine country wines, ranging from silver birch wine to sparkling perry. You can see the wine making process, and have a tasting in the visitors centre.

STRUY BRIDGE

19 miles W of Inverness on the A831

Struy is the gateway to the beautiful Glen Strathfarrar, which is reached by a private road branching off the

A831. In this beautiful glen you will find the **Glen Strathfarrar National Nature Reserve,** which, if you manage to overcome the access problems (there is a locked gate restricting vehicle access), is well worth visiting. The pinewood here is a remnant of the old Caledonian Forest, which once covered the whole of the Highlands. Aspen, alder, rowan, birch, sessile oak and willow can all be found among the pine trees. There are also many flower species to be discovered, as well as birds such as Scottish crossbill, the crested tit and the coal tit.

On a small island at the centre of **Loch a' Mhuillidh** are the remains of a cottage where Lord Lovat hid after the Jacobites were defeated at Culloden.

Permits to traverse the private road are available at certain times from a cottage next to the gate. Cars are only allowed access in summer, and there is no access on Tuesdays throughout the year.

STRATHPEFFER

14 miles NW of Inverness on the A834

At one time, this small village was one of the most famous spa resorts in Britain, and trains used to leave London regularly carrying people who wanted to "take its waters". For this reason, it is full of hotels, B&Bs and genteel guesthouses. So fashionable was it that the local paper used to publish a weekly list of the crowned heads and aristocratic families who were "in town".

The spa days are over now,

though the **Pump Room** has been refurbished and re-creates the halcyon days of the village when the cream of society flocked here. You can even sample the curative waters yourself. The adjacent Victorian gardens, where Victorian society used to promenade and play croquet, have also been restored.

Within the disused railway station is the **Highland Museum of Childhood**, with photographs, toys, games and videos. The Angela Kellie Doll Collection is particularly fine. On the eastern outskirts of the village is the **Eagle Stone**, with Pictish symbols. Scotland's own Nostradamus, the Brahan Seer (Kenneth Mackenzie, born in the early 17th century) predicted that if the stone fell over three times, the waters of the Cromarty Firth, five miles to the east, would rise so that ships could drop anchor near where the stone stood. The stone has fallen over twice so far, and as some of the Seer's other predictions have come true, it is now embedded in concrete to be on the safe side.

Three miles west of the village, off the A835, are the **Rogie Falls** on the Blackwater, reached by a footpath from a car park on the main road. A fish ladder has been built to assist salmon to swim upriver. There are also woodland walks in the surrounding area.

DINGWALL

11 miles NW of Inverness on the A862

Dingwall's name derives from the Norse "thing vollr", meaning "the place of the parliament", which

249 BALCONIE INN

Evanton

A traditional Scottish inn offering five comfortable rooms, a good range of drinks and value for money bar snacks.

see page 550

250 THE TEA STORE

Ullapool

A friendly eating place that offers delicious, high quality food and outstanding service at down to earth prices.

see page 550

251 THE SHEILING GUEST HOUSE

Ullapool

A welcoming, comfortable guest house offering six en suite rooms and the chance to fish in local lochs free of charge.

see page 551

shows that even in ancient times it was an important settlement. It is a royal burgh, and received its charter from Alexander II in 1227. Its castle was the birthplace of Macbeth in 1010. The castle is long gone, though the **Castle Doocot** on Castle Street was built from stones from the castle.

Another famous son is **Sir Hector MacDonald**, a crofter's son who was born in 1853 and joined the army as a private, rising through the ranks to become a major general and national hero. He was known as "Fighting Mac", and eventually commanded the British Army in Ceylon. In 1903, on his was back to Ceylon after a trip to London, he committed suicide in Paris after unproved accusations of homosexuality from those who objected to his lowly birth. After his death, his accusers were stunned to discover that he had a secret wife and child. A monument to him, known as the **Mitchell Tower**, stands on a hill to the south of the town on Mitchell Hill.

A curious story grew up about MacDonald after he had committed suicide. Some claimed that he faked his death and assumed the identity of a German officer called Field-Marshal August von Mackensen, who, conveniently enough, was dying of cancer at the same time.

Eagle Stone, Strathpeffer

Von Mackensen fought against the British in the First World War and died in 1945, in his 96th year.

Within the old Tolbooth of 1730 is the award-winning **Dingwall Museum**, where the town's history is explained by way of displays and exhibits. Dingwall is the eastern terminus for the famous Dingwall - Kyle of Lochalsh railway line, which runs through some of the most beautiful scenery in Scotland as it crosses the country. The **Dingwall Canal** (now closed) is Britain's most northerly canal, and was designed by Thomas Telford in 1817, though by 1890 it had closed. It is just over a mile in length. At the end of the canal is the **Ferry Point,** which has a picnic area.

ULLAPOOL

This fishing port and ferry terminal on Loch Broom was founded by the British Fisheries Society in 1788 and laid out in a grid plan to designs by Thomas Telford. By 1792 much of the work on the port buildings and some houses was completed, settlers having been given a plot of land, free stone to build a home, and land for a garden. Over the years the fortunes of the village fluctuated as the fishing industry prospered or went into recession, though it has always managed to survive.

Now the town is a tourist resort, and a centre for hill walking, sightseeing, wildlife study and fishing. It is also the mainland terminus for the Stornoway ferry, and can be a busy place during the summer months. The award-winning **Ullapool Museum and Visitor Centre** is housed in a former church designed by Thomas Telford - one of the so-called "parliamentary churches". In 1773, before the town was established, the very first settlers bound for Nova Scotia left Loch Broom in the *Hector*, and there is a scale model of the ship within the museum.

One of the hidden jewels of the West Highlands are the **Leckmelm Gardens**, three miles south of the town just off the A835. They were planted in about 1870, but by 1985 had become overgrown. In that year work began in re-establishing them and revealing the beauty that had been lost for so long. The area

surrounding Ullapool is famous for its golden beaches, the best ones being at **Achnahaird**, **Gruinard Bay** and **Achmelvich**.

Isle Martin, northeast of the town, is run by a trust, and here you can see a variety of birds. It is said that the island got its name from a St Martin, a follower of Columba, who lived and died here in the 6th century. In the old burial ground an upright stone is said to mark his grave.

AROUND ULLAPOOL

GAIRLOCH

22 miles SW of Ullapool on the A832

This little village, on the shores of Loch Gairloch, has one of the loveliest settings in Scotland. The **Gairloch Heritage Museum,** housed in old farm buildings, has an "illicit" still, village shop, lighthouse interior and other displays that explain how life was lived in northwest Scotland in the past.

Five miles northeast, on the banks of Loch Ewe are the famous **Inverewe Gardens** (National Trust for Scotland). They have plant collections from all over the world, which thrive in these northern latitudes due to the Gulf Stream. The gardens were founded by Sir Osgood Mackenzie, third son of the Laird of Gareloch. He had bought the Inverewe and Kernsary estate in 1862 and there built Inverewe House and surrounded it with gardens. The most amazing thing about Inverewe is that it is further north than some parts of

252 THE SEAFORTH

Ullapool

Multi award-winning seafood restaurant with two bars and outstanding takeaway; major centre for live music gigs.

see page 552

253 MILLCROFT HOTEL

Gairloch

A quality hotel that boasts five en suite rooms plus superior self-catering accommodation within the same building.

see page 551

254 BLUEPRINT CAFÉ AND RESTAURANT

Gairloch

A café by day and a restaurant by night - this is the place for coffees, teas, snacks and fabulous full dinners!

see page 553

255 STEADING RESTAURANT

Gairloch

A small, highly-rated restaurant in the quiet coastal village of Gairloch that combines quality and service with down-to-earth prices.

see page 553

Inverewe Gardens, Gairloch

Greenland, yet still manages to grow some exotic species.

Sixteen miles south east of Gairloch, and beyond beautiful Loch Maree, is the quiet village of **Kinlochewe**. It is in the heart of what is recognised to be some of the finest mountain scenery in Scotland. The **Beinn Eighe Nature Reserve**, Britain's first, has a visitor centre and nature reserve. It sits just west of Kinlochewe, along the A832.

Also west of Kinlochewe along the A832 is **Loch Maree**, a beautiful stretch of water. One of the islands - Isle of Maree - has a curious legend attached to it. It seems that at one time this whole area was ruled by a Norse prince who had an uncontrollable temper. He also fell in love far too easily, and in his usual manner fell for a girl, and he had a wooden tower built for her on the Isle of Maree. He lived happily with his bride on the island, and gave up his former life of sailing and marauding.

However, the lure of his former life was too strong, and he took command of a long sea voyage with his former colleagues. But his wife was worried, so he told her that on his return a black flag would be raised on the boat taking him across to the island should it be transporting his corpse, and a white one should he be alive.

Similarly a white flag would be raised on Isle Maree should she still be alive, or a black one should she have died while he was away.

Eventually the wife saw a boat flying a white flag crossing to the island. But still she was worried, and wondered if the prince had been faithful to her while away. So she raised a black flag and placed herself on a deathbed surrounded by mourners. The prince saw the flag and when he got to the island and saw his wife's body plunged a dagger into his breast. On seeing what she had done, the wife withdrew the dagger and plunged it into her own breast. The pair were buried side by side on the island, and carved stones still mark the site of the graves.

TORRIDON

28 miles SW of Ullapool on the A895

Torridon sits at the head of Upper Loch Torridon, and at the beginning of Glen Torridon. The Torridon Estate is owned by the National Trust for Scotland, and the **Countryside Centre** explains about what can be seen on the estate and the surrounding area.

LOCHINVER

17 miles N of Ullapool on the A837

This small fishing port sits on Loch Inver, at the end of the A837. A few miles east is Loch Assynt, on whose shores you will find the ruins of **Ardvreck Castle**, built in the 16th century by the MacLeods of Assynt. It was here, in 1650, that Montrose was kept prisoner before being taken to Edinburgh

for execution. The **Assynt Visitor Centre** in Lochinver's Main Street has small displays and exhibits about local history. The centre is the main base for the ranger service, which organises guided walks in the area.

Four miles south east of the village is what has been called "the most beautiful mountain in Scotland" - **Suilven**. At a mere 2,389 feet, it is not even a Munro, nor is it the highest in the area. Seen from Lochinver, it appears to be a solitary mountain that rises sheer on all sides. It's name comes from the Norse, and means the "Mountain Pillar". However, it is the western end of a high ridge, and makes for some superb walking and climbing country.

At Achiltibuie, 10 miles south of Lochinver, and reached by a narrow road, is the **Hydroponicum**, a "garden" where plants grow without soil. It calls itself the "garden of the future" and kits are available so that you too can start growing plants without soil. It was set up in the mid-1980s to show that some of the problems found in this part of Scotland -- poor soil, a short growing season and high winds - could be overcome. It now provides high quality produce (from lettuces to bananas) for homes and businesses in the area. It also now features renewable sources of energy and green technologies.

Offshore at Achiltibuie are the **Summer Isles**. The largest, Tanera Mor, issues Summer Isles postage stamps by permission of the Post

---

260 RIVENDELL GUEST HOUSE & RESTAURANT

Shieldaig

A popular guest house and restaurant that combines great food and accommodation with outstanding prices and service.

⊨ ∥ see page 555

261 LEDGOWAN LODGE HOTEL

Achansheen

A quite superb three-star hotel, within a former hunting lodge, that offers true Highland hospitality at affordable prices.

⊨ ∥ see page 556

262 MOUNTVIEW

Lochinver   *Muir-làn*

Quality self-catering accommodation. in log cabins and and stone cottage in a stunning location on the waterside of Loch Inver Bay.

⊨ see page 556

Smoo Cave, Durness

Office for sending letters to Achiltibuie,, where they are forwarded by the regular mail service to places on the mainland.

DURNESS

50 miles N of Ullapool on the A838

Durness, in Sutherland, is one of the most northerly villages in Scotland, and sits close to **Cape Wrath** - one of only two "capes" in Great Britain, the other being Cape Cornwall. To reach the cape, you have to cross the Kyle of Durness (a narrow sea loch) from Durness itself on a small ferry and walk or take a minibus to the cape, ten miles away.

The peculiarly named **Smoo Cave** is in the cliffs a mile-and-a-half west of the village. It consists of three chambers, and goes underneath the coast road. The name may come from the Old Norse smjugga, meaning "rock". A walkway with railings takes you down to the cave, which has had

lights fitted. There are also many clean, golden beaches in the area, most of them uncrowded. The best ones are **Balnakeil**, **Ceann na Beinne**, **Sango Beag** and **Sango Mor**.

The village has associations with John Lennon of the *Beatles*, who used to spend holidays here with his family when he was young. The **John Lennon Memorial Garden** commemorates his stays, and there is a small display of Lennon letters in the village hall to his cousin Stanley Parkes, who donated them at the opening of the garden in 2002..

WICK

Wick has been an ancient royal burgh since 1589, and in the mid 19th century was the leading herring port in Europe. Situated on the North Sea Coast, it was, until 1975, the administrative capital of Caithness, Scotland's most northerly mainland county. The name comes from the Old Norse word *vik* meaning "bay", and this whole area owes more to Norse culture than it does to the culture of the Gaels. **Parliament Square** near the Market place recalls the fact that James V held a parliament at Wick as he made a royal progress through Scotland in 1540.

The award-winning **Wick Heritage Centre** in Bank Row has exhibits and displays about life in Wick and Caithness. In Huddart Street in Pulteneytown on the south bank of the River Wick is the **Pulteney Distillery**, which makes the world-famous "Old Pulteney" single malt whisky. It has a visitor centre and shop, and there is a tour of the distillery plus tastings.

The **Old Parish Kirk**, dedicated to St Fergus, dates from 1830, though a church has stood here since medieval times. In the kirkyard is the **Sinclair Aisle**, burial place of the old Earls of Caithness.

An old story featuring George Sinclair, the 4th Earl, explains just how bloodthirsty times were in the 16th century. He was suspected of murdering the Earl and Countess of Sutherland so that he could marry off his daughter to their heir, and thus claim the Sutherland lands. However, in 1576, the heir left the country, and Sinclair's plans were thwarted. In revenge, he ordered his son John to lay waste to the Sutherland lands, but when he refused Sinclair had him thrown into a dungeon.

With the help of his jailer, John hatched a plot to escape. John's brother William found out about this and told his father, who executed the jailer. When William went down to the dungeon to goad his brother, John killed him with his chains. For this, his father punished him by denying him food for five days, then feeding him salt beef without giving him anything to drink. John died in agony, his tongue swollen through lack of water. His father had him buried in the Sinclair Aisle, and years later, just before he too died, full of remorse for what he had done, he asked that his heart be buried beside his son.

One mile south of the town, on a cliff top, are the ruins of the **Castle of Old Wick** (Historic Scotland), built by Harald Maddadson, Earl of Caithness, in the 12th century. It was later held by Sir Reginald de Cheyne, and then the Sinclairs, Oliphants, Campbells and Dunbars. Care should be taken when exploring the ruins. The castle name - Old Wick, does not mean what it seems. The "old" comes from the Gaelic *allt*, meaning a stream or river. Therefore the correct name of the castle is the "Castle of the River of Wick"

On a hill to the south of Wick Bay is a memorial to the engineer **James Bremner**, who was born in Caithness and who died in Wick in 1856. He designed and built many of the harbours in Caithness, and collaborated with Brunel, and salvaged the SS Great Britain when it ran aground off Ireland.

266 KINLOCHBERVIE HOTEL

Kinlochbervie

Harbourside hotel with exceptional cuisine (seafood a speciality) and quality en suite accommodation.

see page 559

267 QUEEN'S HOTEL

Wick

Former church manse offering the very best in food, drink and accommodation in a relaxed and friendly atmosphere.

see page 558

268 MEIKLEJOHN'S TEA ROOMS

Wick

Excellent traditional tea room serving delicious home-baked meals, cakes, pastries and slices.

see page 560

269 BILBSTER MAINS

Wick

Four-star self-catering accommodation in 2 delightful stone-built cottages in tranquil location.

see page 560

270 LA MIRAGE

Helmsdale

Once a favourite of Barbara Cartland, a unique restaurant offering extensive menu of outstanding food.

see page 561

271 BEN LOYAL HOTEL

Tongue

Superb family-run hotel in magnificent location with AA Rosette restaurant and quality en suite accommodation.

see page 563

272 BORGIE LODGE HOTEL

Skerray

Outstanding family-run country house hotel in quiet, secluded glen; fine cuisine and en suite rooms.

see page 562

North of Wick, the two castles of **Girnigoe** and **Sinclair** stand above Sinclair Bay. They were strongholds of the Earls of Caithness. Girnigoe is the older of the two, dating from the end of the 15th century, and it was in its dungeons that George Sinclair had his son incarcerated. Sinclair Castle dates from about 1606.

On the northern edge of the town is **Wick Airport**, Scotland's most northerly mainland commercial airport. For all its size, Wick received plenty of attention from German bombers during World War ll. Wick was attacked six times, and over 222 bombs fell in the county of Caithness. The first bombs fell in July 1940, before the London Blitz and during that time known as the "Phoney War".

AROUND WICK
LATHERON
15 miles S of Wick on the A9

Latheron, unlike other villages in the area, has a name derived from Gaelic "làthair roin", meaning "resort of seals". Within the old church, which dates from 1735, is the **Clan Gunn Heritage Centre**. It traces the history of the clan from its Norse origins right through to the present day. At Dunbeath, three miles south of Latheron, is the thatched, whitewashed **Laidhay Croft Museum**, which explains the layout of a typical Highland croft house, with living quarters, byre and stable all under the one roof. And in an old schoolhouse at Dunbeath is the

Dunbeath Heritage Centre, managed by the Dunbeath Preservation Trust. It has displays, photographs and documents about the village.

Neil Gunn, one of Scotland's finest writers (author of *The Silver Darlings*), who was born in Dunbeath in 1891 and died in 1973, attended the very school in which the Heritage Centre is located.

HELMSDALE
30 miles SW of Wick on the A9

The name Helmsdale comes from the Norse *Hjalmundal*, meaning "dale of the helmet". A great battle is supposed to have been fought here between two Norse chiefs, Swein and Olvir. Swein was victorious, and Olvir fled and was never heard from again.

Within this little fishing port is **Timespan**, a visitor centre that tells the story of Helmsdale and its surrounding communities. There are exhibits about the Clearances, Picts, Norse raids, witches, a riverside garden and so much more.

Helmsdale Castle once stood in Couper Park, but the last vestiges of it were demolished in the 1970s due to the unstable state of the ruins. In 1567 a famous tragedy - said to inspired Shakespeare to write Hamlet - was enacted here. Isobel Sinclair had hopes that her son would claim the earldom of Sutherland. She therefore invited the then earl and countess and their son and heir to dinner one evening where she poured them poisoned wine. The earl and countess died, but the heir survived. Unfortunately, Isobel's own son drank the wine and died also. Isobel later committed suicide.

The **Strath of Kildonan**, through which flows the River Helmsdale, was the scene of a famous gold rush in 1868. A local man called Robert Gilchrist, who had been a prospector in Australia, began searching for gold in the river. He eventually found some, and once his secret was out, the Duke of Sutherland began parcelling off small plots of land to speculators. At its height, over 500 men were prospecting in the area, and a shantytown soon sprung up. But in 1870, when sportsmen complained that the prospectors were interfering with their fishing and hunting, the Duke put a stop to it all, and the gold rush was over. There is still gold there today, and it is a favourite spot for amateur gold panners.

TONGUE

50 miles W of Wick off the A838

Tongue is a small village situated near the shallow Kyle of Tongue, a sea loch. It's name means exactly what it says, as it comes from the Norse *tunga*, meaning a tongue, in this case a tongue of land. In 1972 a causeway was built across the kyle to take the A838 westwards towards Loch Eriboll and Durness. On a promontory to the west of the village are the ruins of the small **Castle Varrich** ("Caisteal Bharraigh in Gaelic), which once belonged to Clan Mackay.

The 16th century **House of**

Tongue, overlooking the Kyle of Tongue, was also a Mackay stronghold. It was destroyed in the 17th century, with the Mackays building a new house sometime in the 18th century. The gardens are open to the public.

In 1746 a ship - the *Hazard* - carrying gold coinage for Charles Edward Stuart's Jacobite army tried to take shelter in the Kyle of Tongue to escape *HMS Sheerness*, a government frigate. The crew took the coinage ashore for safekeeping, but were followed and captured by some Mackay clansmen, who were supporters of the government. The crewmen threw the coins into Loch Haken, but most were later recovered.

Nine miles northeast of the village, within the old St Columba's Church at Bettyhill, is the **Strathnaver Museum**, with exhibits about local history, most notably the Clearances and Clan Mackay. Strathnaver was probably the most notorious area in the Highlands for the eviction of tenants so that they could be replaced with the more profitable sheep. The whole area abounds with prehistoric archaeological sites, and within the kirkyard of the museum is a burial stone dating to the 8th or 9th century. The **Strathnaver Trail** to the east of the village takes you round 16 sites, which date from 5000 BC to the 20th century.

ALTNAHARRA

51 miles W of Wick on the A836

Sitting close to the western tip of

273 FARR BAY INN

Bettyhill

Charming inn in former Manse built in 1819; excellent cuisine and quality en suite accommodation.

see page 564

274 STATION COTTAGE

Forsinard

Welcoming B&B close to remote railway station in outstanding location.

see page 563

275 HALLADALE INN

Melvich

Fine inn, good restaurant, chalet accommodation and caravan park, all close to superb beach.

see page 565

276 COMMERCIAL HOTEL

Halkirk

Family-run village hotel offering excellent cuisine, occasional live entertainment, and comfortable en suite accommodation.

see page 566

Dunnet Bay, Thurso

277 THE STATION HOTEL

Thurso

Friendly, family-run hotel with all modern amenities and excellent restaurant; self-catering apartments also available.

see page 566

278 THE PARK HOTEL

Thurso

Long-established family owned and run hotel with fine restaurant, quality accommodation and conference facilities.

see page 567

386

Loch Naver, Altnaharra is a small village famous as a centre for game fishing. Loch Naver is the source of the River Naver, one of the best salmon rivers in Sutherland, which flows northwards through Strathnaver to the sea.

Nine miles from Altnahara. on a narrow, unclassified road from Altnaharra to **Strath More** and **Loch Hope** are the remains of the **Dun Dornaigil Broch**. Some of its walls rise to 22 feet, and over the entrance is a strange triangular lintel. A few miles beyond the broch is **Ben Hope**, at 3,041 feet Scotland's most northerly Munro.

The B873 strikes east from Altnaharra along Strathnaver, following the loch and then the river until it joins the B871, which joins the A836 south of Bettyhill. It is a superb run, with magnificent scenery.

THURSO

19 miles NW of Wick on the A9

Thurso is a former fishing port on Caithness's northern coast, and is the most northerly town on mainland Britain. It was once a Norse settlement, with its name meaning "river of the god Thor". The substantial ruins of **St Peter's Church** sit in the old part of the town, and date from the 16th century, though a church has stood here since at least the 13th century. It was once the private chapel of the Bishop of Caithness, whose summer retreat was **Scrabster Castle**, of which only scant ruins survive. In 1654 a witch called Graycoat was held in the church's tower. The story goes that a man was having difficulty getting his whisky to ferment properly, and blamed a stray cat that had dipped its paw in it. He attacked the cat and cut off its paw, which fell into the whisky. When he drained the barrel, he found, not a paw, but a human hand. Graycoat was then seen nursing a bandaged hand, and people quickly put two and two together, getting five. She was summoned before the kirk elders and convicted of being a witch.

Six miles west of Thurso are the ruins of St Mary's Church, in the village of Crosskirk. They date from the 12th century, making the church one of the oldest in Caithness. To reach the ruins, you have to walk through open countryside.

At the mouth of the river are the ruins of the mock-Gothic

Thurso Castle, built in 1878 by Sir Tollemarche Sinclair on the site of a much older castle. At Holborn Head is the 90 feet high **Clett Rock**, a huge natural pillar, or stack, situated just offshore. It is a nesting place for many birds.

Eight miles west of the town, on the A836, is Dounreay, where Scotland's first operational nuclear reactor was built. The **Dounreay Visitor Centre** explains about nuclear power and the history of the site. It is open from Easter to October each year.

JOHN O'GROATS

13 miles N of Wick on the A99

John O' Groats is 873 miles by road from Land's End in Cornwall, and 290 miles from Kirkmaiden in Wigtownshire, Scotland's most southerly parish. It is supposed to be named after a Dutchman called Jan de Groot, who, to settle an argument about precedence within his family, built an eight sided house with eight doors which gave onto an eight-sided table. This house has now gone, though a mound marks its site. The **Last House in Scotland Museum** contains displays and artefacts about the area.

To the west is **Dunnet Head**, the most northerly point on the British mainland. Between the two is the **Castle of Mey**, the late Queen Mother's Scottish home and the most northerly castle on the British mainland. It is an ancient castle of the Earls of Caithness, and was built in the 16th century by the 4th Earl. When Queen Elizabeth first saw it in the early 1950s it was a ruin. She subsequently bought it, changed its name from Barrogill Castle to Castle of Mey and rebuilt it. The castle and its fine gardens are now open to the public.

Mary-Ann's Cottage at Westside shows how successive generations of one crofting family lived and worked over the last 150 years. It is named after its last owner, Mary-Ann Calder. It had originally been built by her grandfather in 1850, and the croft lands had been worked first by her parents then by herself and her husband James, who left their former home in Westkirk to do so. In 1990, when she was 93 years old, she left the cottage and entered a nursing home in Wick, where she died.

The **Northlands Viking Centre** in the Old School House at Auckengill, Keiss, five miles south of the village, tells the story of the Vikings and Norsemen in the area, as well as recounting the life of John Nicolson, a local artist and mason. Ten minutes away are the remains of the **Nybster Broch**, built about 200 BC to AD 200.

279 CASTLE ARMS HOTEL

Mey

Former 19th century coaching inn opposite entrance to the Castle of Mey and noted for its fine dining.

🍴 🛏 *see page 568*

280 SEAVIEW HOTEL

John O'Groats

Popular family-run establishment with panoramic views, good home-cooked food, and en suite accommodation.

🛏 🍴 *see page 568*

281 THE SCHOOLHOUSE RESTAURANT

John O'Groats

Restaurant in former Victorian schoolhouse offering superb home-cooking based on local produce.

🍴 *see page 569*

The Western Isles

The Western Isles resembles a huge kite with a long tail streaming out behind it. The body of the kite is the island of Lewis and Harris, and the tail consists mainly of the smaller islands of North Uist, Benbecula, South Uist and Barra. The whole length between Barra in the south and the Butt of Lewis in the north is about 130 miles, and they are separated from the mainland by a stretch of water called the Minch.

These islands are the last bastion of true Gaeldom in Scotland, and in some places English, though spoken and understood perfectly, is still a second language. Some are also bastions of Free Presbyterianism, where the Sabbath is strictly observed, and work or leisure activities of any kind on a Sunday is frowned upon. Visitors should, of course, respect these Sabbath customs. Unfortunately, they have given the islanders the reputation of being dour and strict, frowning on anything that smacks of pleasure. Nothing could be further from the truth. They are fun loving, friendly and always helpful.

WESTERN ISLES

(Map with numbered locations: 289 Port Nis (Port of Ness); 290, 288; 282 283 Steornabhagh (Stornoway); 284 285; 286 287; 291 292 Tairbeart (Tarbert); 293; 295 Loch nam Madadh (Lochmaddy); 294; 296; 297; 298 299 Loch Baghasdail (Lochboisdale); 300 Bagh a Chaisteil (Castlebay). Mainland locations: Uig, Dunvegan, Portree, Ardvasar, Mallaig.)

ACCOMMODATION

FOOD & DRINK

PLACES OF INTEREST

The Western Isles are full of such contradictions. They may be where Gaelic culture is cherished and preserved, but there are more Norse influences here than Celtic, and many of the place names (especially in the north) have Norse origins. Up until the Treaty of Perth in 1266 the Western Isles were ruled by Norway, but in that year Magnus IV surrendered all of his Scottish possessions, with the exception of Orkney and Shetland, to Alexander III of Scotland.

Plus many of the inhabitants of the islands are not Presbyterian, but Roman Catholic. South Uist and Barra especially never embraced the Reformation of 1560, or if they did only superficially, and kept the old ways up until the present day.

The weather in the Western Isles, especially in winter, can be harsh, though there are occasions where it can be astonishingly mild and sunny. Snow is rare because of the Gulf Stream, but there are between 45 and 50 inches of rain a year, and the winds blowing in from the Atlantic are invariably strong. The compensations, however, are enormous. The long summer evenings can be still and warm, and at midnight in the north of Lewis it is still possible to read a newspaper out of doors.

And the wildlife is astounding. Deer and otters abound, and the machair (the meadows bordering the sandy beaches) brim with flowers in summer. The seas are home to dolphins, basking sharks, whales and seals. In fact, some people claim that the waters surrounding the Western Isles are the most populated in Britain.

The main island is divided into two parts, Lewis and Harris, an ancient arrangement going back as far as the 13th century. Though joined geographically, they are usually considered to be two separate entities, and indeed the differences between them are marked. A natural boundary of mountains and high moorland runs between Loch Resort on the west and Loch Seaforth on the east, explaining the differences.

Lewis is the northern, and larger part, and up until the mid 1970s was within the county of Ross and Cromarty. Harris (and the smaller islands to the south) came under Inverness-shire. Now they all form one administrative area, with the capital being at Stornoway.

The underlying rock of Lewis is gneiss, one of the oldest in the world. It is largely impermeable, so does not absorb water. For this reason the interior of the island is a large, empty peat moorland dotted with shallow lochs (called "lochans"), while most of the settlements are on the coast. Harris is more mountainous, and has peaks reaching 2,500 feet. It is also an area where the underlying rocks break through to the surface like bones, giving an essentially bleak but never less than attractive landscape. It in turn is divided into two parts, North and South Harris, with the narrow isthmus between West Loch Tarbert and East Loch Tarbert being the boundary.

Of the main southern islands, Berneray, North Uist, Benbecula, South Uist and Eriskay are joined by causeways. North Uist connects to Harris by a ferry between An t-Obbe and Berneray, and Barra has a ferry connection with Eriskay. Each island in the chain has its own flavour, and all are noted for their quality of light, especially in summer.

The Western Isles sit on the farthest edge of Europe, with North America being the next stop. But for all their seeming isolation, they have a long history. The standing stones at Callanish - the second largest stone circle in Britain - are over 4,000 years old, and were built for pagan ritual and to record the passing of the seasons so that crops could be sown and harvested. And there are individual standing stones, duns, brochs and old forts dotted all over the landscape. The local people are proud of their history, and have established small, village-based museums everywhere.

During the Dark Ages the Western Isles were at the crossroads of trade. To the south were the Lowlands of Scotland, as well as

England, Wales, Ireland and the Isle of Man. To the east, beyond Scotland, were the Norse and Baltic countries. This made for a mixture of cultural influences that enriched the islands - influences that can still be seen today.

Norse invasions began in earnest in the 8th century, and by about AD 850 Norsemen ruled all of the Outer Hebrides. In 1266 the islands came into Scottish hands through the Treaty of Perth. However, this did not stop the Lords of the Isles from acting almost independently of the crown. For this reason there was much friction between them and the Scottish kings, though the kings gradually imposed their authority. The islands eventually accepted this and became fully integrated into Scotland. Some historians claim, however, that the Norse language did not fully die out until the late 16th century.

Various attempts have been made over the years to encourage industry, most notably when Lord Leverhulme bought both Lewis and Harris in 1918 and tried to promote fishing. Today all the islands rely on fishing, crofting and tourism, with the weaving of Harris Tweed being an important industry on Lewis and Harris. Weaving is a cottage industry, with the weavers working at home or in sheds at the back of the house. Some will welcome you into their weaving rooms and explain the processes involved in turning wool into fine cloth.

Ferries for Stornoway leave from Ullapool, and there is also a ferry connection between Oban, South Uist and Barra, as well as one from Uig on Skye to Lochmaddy and Tarbert.

STORNOWAY

With a population of about 6,000, Stornoway (from the Old Norse stjorna, meaning "anchor bay") is the only town of any size in the Western Isles. It is the administrative, educational and shopping centre, and is a surprisingly cosmopolitan place.

It was founded in the middle ages round an old MacLeod castle, built by the MacNicols and later taken by Leod, son of Olaf the Black, a Viking. The town has a fine natural harbour and an airport. On Lewis Street is **The Parish Church of St Columba**, dating from 1794, and in **St Peter's Episcopal Church** (1839) is David Livingstone's Bible and an old font from a chapel on the Flannan Isles, about 33 miles west of Lewis in the Atlantic. Its bell, which was made in 1631, was once the town bell that summoned townspeople to important meetings. The **Free Church** in Kenneth Street once had the distinction of being the best attended church in all of Britain, with the Sunday evening congregation regularly exceeding 1,500.

Lews Castle was built in the 1840s and 50s by James Matheson, a businessman who earned a fortune in the Far East trading in tea and opium. In 1843 he bought Lewis, and began a series of improvements in what was then an isolated and inward looking island. He built new roads, improved housing and brought running water and gas to the town. The castle has recently deteriorated, though there are now plans to refurbish it.

One of his pet projects was a plant to extract oil from the peat that blanketed the island, and in 1861 the Lewis Chemical Works began production. But problems beset the plant, and it actually blew up, putting the citizens of Stornoway into a state of fear and alarm. The venture finally folded in 1874.

The **Museum nan Eilean** was opened in 1984 by the then local authority, and is located in Francis Street. It has artefacts and exhibits highlighting the history and archaeology of both the island of Lewis and Stornoway itself, and makes a good starting point if you want to explore the area. The **An Lanntair Arts Centre** sits across from the ferry terminal, and has contemporary and traditional exhibitions, as well as varied programmes of music and drama highlighting the Gaelic culture.

One of Stornoway's most famous sons was the 18th century explorer and fur trader Sir Alexander Mackenzie, who gave his name to the Mackenzie River in Canada. In Francis Street, on the site of his house, is **Martins Memorial Church**, built in 1885. Over 1,150 men of Lewis died in the two world wars, and the **Stornoway War Memorial** must be the most imposing in Britain. It stands on the 300-feet high Cnoc nan Uan, and itself rises to a height of 85 feet.

It was off Stornoway, on New Year's Day 1919, that the **Iolaire** struck rocks off the coast near Stornoway. The ship was bringing Lewis and Harris men back from fighting in the First World War, and over 284 were drowned and only 79 rescued. In a storm the ship struck rocks known as the Beasts of Holm only two hours into the new year, when it should have been heading for the entrance to Stornoway Harbour. It is a tragedy still remembered today in the Western Isles, even though few other people have even heard of it. A memorial overlooking the rocks commemorates the event.

The Western Isles are synonymous with Harris tweed, and at the **Loom Centre** on Bayhead you can find out about its history and about how it is woven. To attain the "orb" symbol of genuine Harris tweed, the cloth needs to be woven from "virgin wool produced in Scotland", then spun, dyed and hand woven in the Outer Hebrides.

West of Stornoway, on the Eye Peninsula, are the ruins of **St Columba's Church**, built in the 14th century on the site of a small monastic cell founded by St Catan in the 6th century. It is said that 19 MacLeod chiefs are buried here.

AROUND STORNOWAY

CALLANISH

16 miles W of Stornoway on the A858

Dating back at least 4,000 years, the **Callanish Stone Circle** (Historic Scotland) is second only to Stonehenge in importance in Britain. It is more than just a circle of upright stones. Four great arms

284 ROYAL HOTEL

Stornoway

Close to the marina, this historic hotel offers excellent cuisine and superb en-suite rooms.

🛏 ❙ see page 571

285 DIGBY CHICK

Stornoway

Outstanding cuisine in this distinguished restaurant with seafood dishes particularly popular.

❙ see page 572

286 THE CALEDONIAN HOTEL

Stornoway

Close to the quayside with an outstanding restaurant, bar food, regular entertainment and en suite rooms.

🛏 ❙ see page 573

287 THE COFFEE POT

Stornoway

Long-established tearoom/ coffee shop, close to the harbour, serving fresh wholesome food to order.

❙ see page 574

288 TIGH MEALROS

Garynahine
Superb dining at this well-established rural restaurant with seafood as the speciality.

❙❙ see page 574

made up of monoliths radiate from it to the north, south east and west, with the northern arm (which veers slightly to the east) having a double row of stones as if enclosing an approach way. And in the middle of the circle is the tallest stone of them all, measuring over 15 feet in height.

It is a mysterious place, and has attracted many stories and myths over the years. One story tells of a race of giants who met to discuss how to defeat the new religion of Christianity that was spreading throughout the islands. This so incensed St Kieran, a Celtic monk and missionary, that he turned them all to stone. Another says that the stones were brought to Lewis by a great priest king who employed "black men" to erect them. The men who died building the circle were buried within it.

Plus there are the more modern, and unfortunately predictable, theories that the stones were erected by mysterious beings from outer space as a means of guiding their spacecraft, though why people with such technology

should need a guidance system made of stones seems equally as mysterious.

A visitors centre next to the stones tries to uncover the truth behind them, which may have something to do with primitive ritual and predicting the seasons for agricultural purposes.

People visit Callanish for the stone circle alone, not knowing that there are two further circles close by, known as **Callanish ll** and **Callanish lll**. Though not as spectacular as the main one, they nevertheless should be visited as well. Callanish ll once had nine uprights, but only five survive. Callanish lll consists of twelve uprights which may have formed part of a double circle.

Two miles to the southeast is the **Garynahine Stone Circle**, sometimes known as Callanish lV. It consists of five stones.

CARLOWAY

17 miles W of Stornoway on the A858

The 2,000-year-old **Dun Carloway Broch,** overlooking Loch Roag, is one of the best preserved brochs in Scotland. It is over 47 feet in diameter, and its walls are 22 feet high in places. Some of the galleries and internal stairways are still intact. The Doune Broch Centre has displays explaining what life must have been like within fortifications such as this.

Though probably not complete, the broch was still in use in the 11th century, when the Morrisons used it as a fortification in their feuds with the Macauleys.

Dun Carloway Broch

One-and-a-quarter miles north of Carloway is the **Gearrannan Blackhouse Village**. It faces the Atlantic, and is a huddle of traditional cottages dating from the 19th century. They were lived in up until 1974, and restored by the Garenin Trust between 1989 and 2001.

SHADER

16 miles NW of Stornoway on the A857

The **Steinacleit Stone Circle and Standing Stones** sit on a low hill near Loch an Duin, and date from between 2000 and 3000 BC. The stones are in the shape of an oval rather than a circle, and archaeologists are unsure whether it is indeed a stone circle, a burial cairn or the remains of a settlement of some kind.

SHAWBOST

16 miles W of Stornoway on the A858

Housed within the community centre, the **Sgoil Shiaboist Museum** (Shawbost School Museum) has artefacts and objects collected by school pupils 30 years ago as part of a project that illustrates the way people used to live in Lewis. Near it is the thatched **Shawbost Norse Mill and Kiln**, a restored water mill of the type used in Lewis up until the mid-20th century.

The **Shawbost Stone Circle**, near the shores of the small Loch Raoinavat, only has two stones left standing. They are difficult to find, and good walking gear is recommended if you want to search them out.

BARVAS

13 miles NW of Stornoway on the A858

At one time, most of the population of Lewis lived in small cottages known as blackhouses. On the west coast of the island, at Arnol, is the **Arnol Blackhouse** (Historic Scotland), which shows what life was like in one of them. People and animals lived under the one roof, separated by thin walls, with the roof usually being of thatch and turf. They had tiny windows because of the seasonal gales and rain and the fact that glass was very expensive. The thick, dry stone walls (with a central core of clay and earth) kept the cottage cool in summer and warm in winter.

The Arnol house has been furnished in typical fashion, and it has a clay floor. There is no fireplace, the fire being placed centrally, with no chimney. The houses got their name in the mid-19th century to distinguish them from the more modern white houses, which had mortar binding the stones.

There is also an interpretation centre in a nearby cottage, which has a model of a typical blackhouse showing how they were made. The term "blackhouse" is of comparatively recent date, and doesn't refer to thr darkness of the interiors or the dark stone used in their building. The name was introduced to differentiate them from more modern cottages that were being built in Victorian times, which were usually painted or

289 GALSON FARM

South Galson

Ideal for animal lovers, working croft offering 4-star guesthouse and adjoining bunkhouse accommodation.

see page 575

290 5 HACKLETE

Great Bernera

A truly Hidden Place on island off the west coast of Lewis offering comfortable self-catering accommodation.

see page 575

291 ISLE OF HARRIS INN

Tarbert

Outstanding cuisine with strong emphasis on island produce, especially salmon and lamb.

see page 576

292 HARRIS HOTEL

Tarbert

Established family-owned hotel with friendly attentive service, superb food and a relaxing atmosphere..

see page 577

---

harled in white. They became known as "whitehouses".

During archaeological excavations at Barvas, a 200-year-old Iron Age cemetery was uncovered. One of the finds was a beautiful iron and copper alloy bracelet, the first of its kind to be found anywhere in Scotland.

BALLANTRUSHAL

15 miles NW of Stornoway on the A857

The **Clach an Trushal** (Historic Scotland), at 18 feet high, is the tallest standing stone in Scotland, and is said to mark the site of an ancient battle, though this is unlikely. In the 19th century several feet of peat were cut away from around its base, revealing the true height.

PORT NIS

25 miles NW of Stornoway on the A857

This is the most northerly of the Lewis villages, and sits at the end of the A857 close to the Butt of Lewis (in Gaelic *Rudha Rhobhainis*), the island's most northerly point. **St Moluag's Church** lies close to Port Nis, and dates from medieval times (the exact date is unknown). It was restored in the early 20th century.

One legend says that it was founded by a Norse prince who had converted to Christianity. However, he could find no wood for the roof, so prayed that wood might be provided. His prayers were answered when he was told to go to a local bay, where he would find a roof. This he did, and saw a roof of the exact proportions floating in the

sea. Another story says that, at one time, a pilgrimage to the church would cure mental illnesses.

GREAT BERNERA

18 miles W of Stornoway off the B8059

The small island of Great Bernera measures only six miles long by three miles wide at it's widest. It is connected to the mainland by the **Great Bernera Bridge**, opened in 1953 and the first bridge in the country made from pre-stressed concrete girders. The **Community Centre and Museum** has displays about the island, and also sells tea, coffee and cakes. On the lovely beach at **Bostadh** an Iron Age village has been excavated, and a reconstruction of an Iron Age house built. A cairn commemorates those men who took part in the **Bernera Riot** of 1874, when crofters stood up for their right of tenure. Three of them eventually stood trial, though a later Act of Parliament gave them the rights they were fighting for.

The **Great Bernera Lobster Pond** was built in the 1860s, and is the largest of its kind in the Western Isles. Fisherman used them to keep the lobsters they had gathered before having them transported to the mainland when prices were high.

TARBERT

33 miles S of Stornoway on the A859

The small village of Tarbert has a ferry connection with Uig on Skye. This is the starting point of South Harris, and an isthmus no more that half a mile wide separates East

Loch Tarbert, which is an arm of the Minch, from West Loch Tarbert, which is an arm of the Atlantic. In fact, *Tairbeart* in Gaelic means "isthmus" or "place of portage", where boats were dragged across land from one stretch of water to another.

Amhuinnsuidhe Castle, with its beautiful hillside gardens, was built in 1868 by the Earl of Dunsmore, who owned Harris. It was the Earl's wife who introduced the weaving of Harris tweed to the island. The castle was subsequently owned by the Bulmer family, which founded the cider firm. It was here that J.M. Barrie wrote his play *Mary Rose*. It is now used as an upmarket conference centre.

SCALPAY

33 miles S of Stornoway on a minor road

The tiny island of Scalpay, measuring three miles by two, lies off Harris's east coast. It is connected to the mainland by the £7m **Scalpay Bridge**, the biggest civil engineering project ever undertaken in the Western Isles. It was opened in 1998 by Tony Blair, the first serving prime minister ever to visit the Western Isles. The visit is also remembered because of the biting criticism he received from one of the island's more militant inhabitants - *culiciodes impunctatus*, more commonly known as the midge. However, the first official crossing was made in December 1997, when the island's oldest inhabitant, 103-years-old Kirsty Morrison, was taken across it in a vintage car.

RODEL

48 miles S of Stornoway on the A859

Rodel sits near the southern tip of Harris, and is famous for **St Clement's Church**, burial place of the MacLeods. It was built in 1500 by Alasdair Crotach ("hunchback") McLeod, who lived in the church's tower from 1540 to his death in 1547. He is still within the church, in a magnificent tomb that shows carvings of his home at Dunvegan on Skye. By 1784 the church was ruinous, but in that year Alexander MacLeod of Berneray, a captain with the East India Company, restored it.

OTHER WESTERN ISLES

NORTH UIST

59 miles SW of Stornoway

Like most of the Western Isles, North Uist is low lying, with more water than land making up its total area of 74,884 acres. **Loch Scadavay** is the biggest of the lochs, and though it only has an area of eight square miles, it has a shoreline measuring 51 miles in length. The island was given by James IV to the MacDonalds of Sleat in 1495, who sold it in 1855, having cleared many of the tenants to make way for sheep. The highest point on the island, at 1,127 feet, is **Eaval**, near the southeast corner. The island has a ferry service to An t-Obbe in Harris from Berneray, and one to Skye from **Lochmaddy**,

293 BORVEMOR COTTAGES

Scarista

Four unique self-catering cottages, one of them thatched, sited on the scenic western seaboard of the Isle of Harris.

🛏 *see page 578*

294 LANGASS LODGE

Locheport

Former hunting lodge now a family run small hotel ideal for outdoor enthusiasts.

🛏 ‖ *see page 579*

295 RUSHLEE HOUSE

Lochmaddy

Outstanding B&B establishment with a 4-star rating set beside a peaceful freshwater loch.

🛏 *see page 580*

296 NUNTON
STEADINGS

Isle of Benbecula

Two tea rooms, a gift, crafts and produce shop, and two exhibitions all on one site.

 see page 581

•

On Balashaval Hill, a few miles north of Lochmaddy, are three standing stones in a row, known as Na Fir Bhreige, or The Three False Men. Legend says they mark the burial places of spies who were buried alive. According to another legend, they are three men from Skye who were turned to stone after deserting their wives.

•

the island's capital, and where most of the hotels and B&Bs are to be found. **Taigh Chearsabhagh**, a museum and arts centre is housed in an old inn dating from the early 18th century. Near the village is **Barpa Langais** a Neolithic burial cairn with its burial chamber almost complete. Half a mile south east of it is the **Pubull Phinn Stone Circle**.

Teampull na Trionaid ("Trinity Temple"), on the southwest shore, was once the greatest place of learning in the Western Isles. Indeed some people claim that it was Scotland's first university, with scholars and students making their way here from all over the country, one being Duns Scotus (see also Duns).

It was founded in the early 13th century by one Beathag, a prioress from the priory on Iona and daughter of Somerled, Lord of the Isles. By the end of the 15th century, however, its influence began to wane, and during the Reformation it was attacked. Valuable books, manuscripts and works of art were tossed into the sea, and so much of the island's heritage was lost. The other building on the site is **Teampull MacBhiocair**, (MacVicar's Temple), where the teachers were buried.

It was in this area, in 1601, that the **Battle of Carinish** took place, the last battle on British soil not to have involved firearms. A troop of MacLeods from Harris was raiding the island, and took shelter in the Trinity Temple buildings when attacked by the MacDonalds. The

MacDonalds ignored the status of the temple, and slaughtered every MacLeod clansman except two, who escaped.

On the island's west coast, off the A865, is the **Balranald Nature Reserve**, where you can see waders and seabirds on various habitats.

BENBECULA

80 miles SW of Stornoway

Benbecula is Beinn bheag a' bh-faodhla in Gaelic, meaning "mountain of the fords". It is sandwiched between North and South Uist, with a landscape that is low and flat and dotted with shallow lochans, though **Rueval**, its highest peak, soars to all of 403 feet. The island marks the boundary between the Protestant islands to the north and the Roman Catholic islands to the south. There is no ferry terminal on the island, as it is connected to South Uist and North Uist by causeways.

The main settlement is **Balivanich**, or Baile na Mhanaich, meaning "Monk's Town". It sits on the west coast, and beside it is a small airstrip. The scant ruins of **Teampall Chaluim Cille**, founded by St Torranan, lie close to the village.

To the south of the village, on the B892, are the ruins of **Nunton Chapel**, supposed to have been a nunnery built in the 14th century. It was Lady Clanranald from nearby Nunton House (built from the stones of Nunton Chapel) who gave Charles Edward Stuart his disguise as a serving girl when he escaped from Benbecula to Skye in 1746.

Borve Castle

Borve Castle, about three miles south of Balivanich, was owned by Ranald, son of John of Islay, in the 14th century. The ruins show a typical tower house of the period. Within the school at **Lionacleit**, three miles south of Balivanich, is a small museum. **Benbecula Airport** near Balivanich was formerly an RAF station. It now has flights to Barra, Glasgow, Inverness and Stornoway.

SOUTH UIST

87 miles SW of Stornoway

Running down the east side of South Uist is a range of low mountains, with **Beinn Mhor** being the highest at 2,034 feet. The west side of the island is gentler, with fine white sandy beaches facing the Atlantic. **Lochboisdale**, in the southeast corner, is the largest village on the island, and has a ferry connection to Mallaig, Oban and Castlebay on Barra.

The island is one of the few places in Scotland never to have fully embraced the Reformation, and is predominantly Roman Catholic. To the northwest of the island, at Rueval, is the famous statute of **Our Lady of the Isles**, overlooking Loch Bee. It was erected in 1957 and sculpted by Hew Lorimer of Edinburgh. It stands 30 feet high. At the **Loch Druidibeag Nature Reserve**, which is close by, many birds such as greylag geese and mute swans, can be observed.

It was in South Uist, near **Milton** on Loch Kildonan, that Flora MacDonald was born in 1722. Her house is now completely ruinous, though the foundations can still be seen. She was no simple Gaelic lass, but the daughter of a prosperous landowning farmer who died when she was young. Her mother then married Hugh MacDonald, a member of the great

297 ORASAY INN

Lochcarnan

Friendly small hotel with exceptionally fine cuisine and very comfortable en suite rooms.

see page 582

298 LOCHBOISDALE HOTEL

Lochboisdale

Long-established hotel close to the ferry terminal offering excellent cuisine and great views.

see page 583

299 ARD NA MARA

Kilphedar

3-star quality en suite B&B in immaculate modern house.

see page 581

300 ISLE OF BARRA HOTEL

Tangasdale Beach

Overlooking a beautiful bay, the hotel offers excellent cuisine and en suite rooms.

see page 584

MacDonald of Sleat family. She was brought up in Skye and went to school in Sleat and Edinburgh.

Kildonan Museum, north of Lochboisdale on the A865, has displays and exhibits on local history, as well as a tearoom and shop. The basis of the museum is a collection of artefacts gathered by the island priest, Father John Morrison, in the 1950s and 60s. Further north along the A865 are the ruins of **Ormiclate Castle**, built between 1701 and 1708 as a sumptuous residence for the chief of Clanranald. Alas, the chief's stay there was short lived, as it burnt down in 1715 after a rowdy Jacobite party.

South Uist was once home to a **Missile Testing Range** which was built between 1957 and 1958. Here the Corporal missile, Britain (and indeed America's) first nuclear guided missile, was tested. It is still in use today.

Off the south coast of South Uist is the small island of **Eriskay** (from the Norse for "Eric's Island"), which is joined to South Uist by a causeway opened in 2002 and costing £9.8m. It is noted for one of the most beautiful of Gaelic songs, the *Eriskay Love Lilt*. It was here, on 23 July 1745, that Charles Edward Stuart first set foot on Scottish soil when he stepped off a French ship to reclaim the British throne for the Stuarts. The beach where he landed is now called Prince's Beach, and legend says that his first action was to plant the sea convolvulus which now thrives here.

It was in February 1941 that another event took place which was to make Eriskay famous. **The SS. Politician** was heading towards the United States from Liverpool with a cargo of 260,000 bottles of whisky when it was wrecked off Calvey Island in the Sound of Eriskay. Legend has it that as soon as the seamen were removed from the ship to safety, work began on "rescuing" the cargo. Eventually Customs and Excise men appeared on the island, but by this time the bottles had been spirited away into peat bogs and other hide-holes. Only 19 people were charged with illegal possession, as the people of the island, who considered the people who took the whisky heroes of sorts, kept their mouths shut.

Sir Compton Mackenzie used the incident as the basis for his novel *Whisky Galore*, made into a film in 1948. The wreckage can still sometimes be seen at exceptionally low tide. In the late 1980s an attempt was made to get at the rest of the cargo, but this proved unsuccessful. However, the story of the ship won't go away - now there is a single malt named *SS Politician* in honour of the men who liberated and eventually enjoyed the cargo.

The highest point on the island is **Ben Scrien**, at 609 feet. It is an easy climb, and gives magnificent views. The island's native pony, the grey and black Eriskay pony, was at one time used to carry seaweed and peat on panniers slung across their back. In the 1950s they nearly died out, but now are on the increase

Kisimul Castle, Barra

again. They are the last surviving examples of the once common Hebridean ponies, which were popular all over the islands.

BARRA

105 miles S of Stornoway

Barra ("Barr's Island") is the southernmost of the Western Isles, separated from South Uist by the Sound of Barra. To the south is a string of tiny islands, including Sanday, Rosinish, Mingulay and Berneray.

On an island in the bay itself is **Kisimul Castle** (Historic Scotland), the largest fortification in the Western Isles. Its name means "the place of taxes", and it was the home of the Macneils of Barra,

chiefs of Clan Macneill, who were granted the island in the 15th century, first by the Lord of the Isles and then by James VI. Others say, however, that the Macneils have been associated with the island since at least the 11th century.

The castle was originally built in about 1030, though the present building dates from the 15th century. The island on which it is built has its own fresh water wells, and this, coupled with its position, makes it almost impregnable. A story is told of how the castle was once being besieged by the Vikings, who wanted to starve it into submission. However, they soon gave up when they saw the castle guards hang bloody sides of beef from the ramparts. It was, of course, a ruse. What had been hung from the ramparts were cow hides used to make leather, smeared with dog's blood.

In 1838 the island was sold to Gordon of Cluny, who proceeded to remove the islanders from the land and ship them off to the New World. In 1937 the island was bought back by the 45th Chief of Clan Macneil, an American called Robert Lister Macneil. The 15th century castle had been burnt down in the late 1700s, and he set about restoring it. His son Ian, the present clan chief, continued the work of restoring the castle and handed it over to Historic Scotland in the year 2000. The castle is open to the public, and a small ferry takes you across to it.

The old chiefs of Clan Macneil had the reputation of being haughty and proud. A story is told of a Macneil chief at the time of Noah, who was invited aboard the Ark to escape the flood. He is supposed to have arrogantly replied, "Macneil already has a boat." Another story is told of later times. After Macneil had dinner, one of his servants would go up to the ramparts of Kisimul Castle and announce to the world: "as the Macneil has dined, the other kings and princes of the world may now dine also."

The **Dualchas Heritage and Cultural Centre** at Castlebay has changing displays and exhibitions about life on the island through the ages, as well as a café. The ruined **Cille-bharraidh** (Church of St Barr) is located at the north end of the island, and was the burial place of the Macneils. Also buried here is **Sir Compton Mackenzie**, who wrote *Whisky Galore* (see also Eriskay). The island is predominantly Catholic, and at Heaval, a mile north east of Castlebay, is a marble statue of the Madonna and Child called **Our Lady of the Sea**.

Orkney & Shetland

In 1469 James III married Margaret, the young daughter of Christian I of Denmark and Norway. Her father pledged Orkney and Shetland to the Scottish crown until such time as the dowry was settled in full. As he was crippled with debts, the dowry was never paid, and in 1472, the islands became part of Scotland, creating the kingdom of Scotland as we know it today.

The Norse influences are still strong. Gaelic was never spoken here, and the place names (and many family names) all have Norse derivations. Both sets of islands are nearer Oslo than they are London, and there have even been occasional calls for the islands to be independent of Scotland.

	ACCOMMODATION	
301	East Bank House, Kirkwall	p 403, 584
302	West End Hotel, Kirkwall	p 403, 585
303	Albert Hotel, Kirkwall	p 404, 585
304	Lynnfield Hotel, St Ola	p 404, 586
305	Sands Hotel, Burray	p 405, 585
306	The Galley Inn & Shore Restaurant, St Margaret's Hope	p 405, 587
307	Thira, Stromness	p 406, 587
308	The Ferry Inn, Stromness	p 406, 588
309	Ramsquoy Farm, Stenness	p 406, 588
310	The Orkney Croft, Stromness	p 407, 589
311	Leisburn Cottages, Burness	p 408, 589
313	Self Catering Shetland, Lerwick	p 411, 590
315	Glen Orchy House, Lerwick	p 411, 591
316	Orca Country Inn, Hoswick	p 412, 592
318	Busta House Hotel, Busta	p 414, 593
319	Midfield Croft Self-catering Cottages, Midfield Bardister	p 415, 593
320	Norwind Guest House, Mid Yell	p 415, 594

	FOOD & DRINK	
302	West End Hotel, Kirkwall	p 403, 585
303	Albert Hotel, Kirkwall	p 404, 585
304	Lynnfield Hotel, St Ola	p 404, 586
305	Sands Hotel, Burray	p 405, 585
306	The Galley Inn & Shore Restaurant, St Margaret's Hope	p 405, 587
308	The Ferry Inn, Stromness	p 406, 588
312	Havly Centre Café, Lerwick	p 410, 590
316	Orca Country Inn, Hoswick	p 412, 592
317	Mid Brae Inn, Brae	p 414, 592

	PLACES OF INTEREST	
314	The Shetland Fudge Company, Lerwick	p 411, 591

401

The Brough Ness on South Ronaldsay in Orkney is no more than eight miles from the Scottish mainland. The Shetlands sit much further out to sea, and Muckle Flugga, off the north coast of Unst in the Shetlands and the most northerly point in Great Britain, is 170 miles from the mainland. Few people realise the distances involved, as maps of the British Isles invariably put the Orkneys and Shetlands in a convenient box off Scotland's north east coast. However, fast ferries and air services put the islands within easy reach of the mainland.

In the past they were at a major trade crossroads, and gained an importance that far outweighed their size. They were on the main routes from Scandinavia to Scotland, England, Wales, Ireland and the Isle of Man. Vikings used them as a staging post as they struck west towards Iceland and the New World, and some eventually settled. They are rich in historical sites and remains (far too many to mention them all in this book), which show a continued occupation for thousands of years. Indeed, there are about 120 confirmed broch sites in the Shetland Islands alone. And because the landscape has never been intensely farmed or cultivated, many of these sites have remained relatively undisturbed.

The main difference between the two archipelagos can be summed up in the old saying that an Orcadian (an inhabitant of Orkney) is a crofter with a fishing boat, whereas a Shetlander is a fisherman with a croft. Orkney is therefore the more fertile of the two, though this is relative, as the landscape is nothing like the Scottish mainland farming areas, and trees are the exception rather than the rule. People sometimes ask why Vikings found this bleak landscape attractive enough to settle in. The answer is that the islands, for all their bleakness, offered land that was more fertile than the land they left behind in Norway.

One thing has brought prosperity to the islands, however, and that is North Sea oil. It has transformed their economies, but at the same time has remained remarkably unobtrusive, apart from places like Sullom Voe in Shetland, the largest oil terminal and port in Europe.

Up until local government reorganisation in 1975, Orkney and Shetland were separate counties (Shetland being known as "Zetland"). Now they comprise two "council areas", and each has its own local government set up.

The Orkney archipelago consists of about 70 islands, only 19 of which are inhabited. The largest island is Mainland, where the islands' capital, Kirkwall, is located. It is a small city as well as a royal burgh, as it has its own medieval cathedral, the most northerly in Britain and the most complete in Scotland. Most of the islands are connected by ferry, and the best way to explore the smaller ones is on foot rather than by car. Some of the sites, such as Skara Brae, are world famous and must not be missed.

Shetland has about 100 islands, with less than 20 being inhabited. Its largest island is again called Mainland, and it is here that Lerwick is situated. It is the island's capital, and the most northerly town in Britain. Every year in January the ancient "Up Helly Aa" festival is held, where a Viking ship is paraded through the streets of the town before being ceremonially burnt. Its origins go back to pagan times, when, in the depths of winter, people feared that the warmth of summer might not return. To attract it, they lit fires. - a case of like attracting like.

KIRKWALL

The capital of Orkney has a population of about 4,800, and was granted its charter as a royal burgh in 1486. It sits almost in the centre of Mainland, and divides the island into East Mainland and West Mainland. It is a lively, busy place of old stone buildings and streets paved in flagstones, with a shopping centre that serves all of the islands. The old name for the town was *Kirkjuvagr*, meaning the "church inlet", that church not being the cathedral, but the Church of St Olaf. All that is left of the early medieval building is a doorway in St Olaf's Wynd.

St Magnus Cathedral was founded in 1137 by Saint Magnus's nephew Rognvald Kolsson, though for his own reasons. In those days, Orkney was a Norwegian earldom which was shared between two earls. Already having one half of the earldom, he wanted to impress people so that he could claim the other half. He eventually succeeded, and was canonised.

The cathedral as you see it today dates from between the 12th and 16th centuries. The story goes that Magnus was the son of Erlend, one of the two earls who ruled Orkney at the time. The King of Norway deposed the earls, and appointed his own son Sigurd as Overlord. The King and his son then set out on a raiding party for Wales, taking Magnus with them. However, Magnus refused to take part in the usual rape and pillage, deciding instead to sing psalms. The Norwegian king was displeased, and young Magnus had to flee.

After the king's death, he returned to Orkney, and in 1117 arranged to meet with Haakon, the new ruler of the islands, to claim his inheritance. However, Haakon had him murdered by an axe blow to the skull. Magnus was buried at first in a small church on Birsay, but 20 years later his remains were taken to St Olaf's Church and finally to the newly consecrated cathedral. Some people regarded this story as more of a legend than historical fact, but in 1919, during some restoration work, a casket containing human bones was found embedded high up in one of the cathedral's pillars. The skull had been split open with an axe. In the 18th century the remains of St Rognval were also discovered embedded in a pillar.

The ruined **Bishop's Palace** (Historic Scotland) dates mainly

301 EAST BANK HOUSE

Kirkwall

En suite B&B or self-catering accommodation in charming 1824 house; conference facilities available.

see page 584

302 WEST END HOTEL

Kirkwall

A well-run and popular hotel which has character, comfortable accommodation and all the other things that will ensure an enjoyable stay.

see page 585

The Square, Kirkwall

303 ALBERT HOTEL

Kirkwall

A hotel in the heart of Kirkwall that offers stylish accommodation and great food and drink.

  see page 585

304 LYNNFIELD HOTEL

Kirkwall

A three star hotel which is being refurbished and upgraded, and which offers superb accommodation and fine food, all at affordable prices.

  see page 586

from the 12th century, when it was built for Bishop William the Old. The Round Tower (called the "Moosie Too" by locals), however, was built by Bishop Reid between 1541 and 1548. It was within the palace, in 1263, that King Haakon IV of Norway died, having just been defeated at the Battle of Largs (see also Largs). He was buried in Kirkwall Cathedral, but his body was later taken back to Bergen in Norway.

The notorious Patrick Stewart, 2nd Earl of Orkney (by this time Orkney had become a Scottish earldom) and grandson of James V, built the adjacent **Earl's Palace** (Historic Scotland) between 1600 and 1607. The Stewart earls were hated in the islands because they exploited their positions and bled the islands dry. Patrick himself was arrested by James VI and executed for treason in 1615.

Within Tankerness House, built in 1574, is the **Orkney Museum**, which contains artefacts and exhibits about the island. The wooden box that contained St Magnus's bones, discovered within a pillar in the cathedral, is one of the exhibits. Tankerness House originally belonged to the then cathedral, and was the home of Gilbert Foultie, the last archdeacon. It later became the property of the Baikie family, one of the islands' principle landowners. The Baikie Drawing room within the museum shows what a typical late 18th and early 19th century drawing room would have looked like. Tankerness House itself was owned by the

Cathedral, and for a short while was used as the residence of the Protestant archdeacon. Later it passed to the Baikie family, one of the island's main land owners.

The **Orkney Wireless Museum** is at Kiln Corner on Junction Road, and has examples of wartime and domestic wireless sets used on the islands. It was founded by local man Jim MacDonald, who had a lifetime's fascination with wireless and radio sets, and amassed a huge collection. He died in 1988.

On a building in Castle Street is a plaque commemorating **Kirkwall Castle**, which was dismantled in 1615 and finally demolished in 1865. It had been built in the 14th century by Henry Sinclair, first Earl of Orkney. He had been given the title by Haakon of Norway in 1379, long before the islands became part of Scotland. His descendent William, the third earl, built Rosslyn Chapel in Midlothian, and his name has been linked to a pre-Columbus transatlantic crossing, the holy grail and the Knights Templar (see also Rosslyn).

Every year on Christmas Eve and Hogmanay, the young men of Kirkwall take part in the traditional **Kirkwall Ba' Game** ("Ball Game"), played between two teams known as the "Uppies" (who come from the Laverock area of the town) and the "Doonies" (who come from the burgh area). It is played through the streets of the town, and shops and businesses usually board up their windows and barricade their doors, as there is no quarter given or taken. The ball is specially made from cork and leather on the islands.

AROUND KIRKWALL

LAMB HOLM

7 miles S of Kirkwall on the A961

After the sinking of the Royal Oak by a U boat in 1939 a string of islands to the south of Mainland were joined by causeways, the whole thing being called the **Churchill Barriers**, which would prevent submarines from slipping through again. On the 99-acre Lamb Holm, one of the islands, is the ornate **Italian Chapel**. It was built by Italian prisoners-of-war captured in North Africa in 1942 who were working on the causeways. The work is remarkable considering its basis is two Nissen huts and various pieces of cast-off metal and wood. In 1960 some of the ex-POWs were invited to return to the island to restore it. Mass is still said here every day during the summer months, and it is one of the most visited places on Orkney.

SOUTH RONALDSAY

10 miles S of Kirkwall

This small island is connected to Mainland by the Churchill Barriers (see Lamb Holm). Brough Ness is its most southerly point, and is only eight miles from John o' Groats. The island is mainly visited for the Isbister Cairn, more commonly known as **Tomb of the Eagles**. It is a chambered burial cairn. It is about 5,000 years old, and when

opened revealed the bones of about 342 people, plus the skeleton of an eagle. Lined round the walls were skulls, with a small pile of bones beside each one..

MINE HOWE

5 miles SE of Kirkwall on the A960

This deep, subterranean structure within a large mound was examined by the TV programme *Time Team*, but its real purpose still remains a mystery. It was originally uncovered in 1946 and reburied again to preserve it. It consists of a chamber accessed by a stone lined tunnel with steps, and the latest thinking is that it dates from the Iron Age and has a religious significance.

Five miles west of Mine Howe, at Mull Head, is **The Gloup**, a curious cave whose roof has collapsed at its end.

MAES HOWE

8 miles W of Kirkwall off the A965

Maes Howe (Historic Scotland), on Mainland, is Britain's largest chambered cairn, and was excavated in 1861. In 1910 it was taken into state care, at which time the mound was "rounded off" to give it the appearance we see today. When archaeologists reached the main chamber, they discovered that the Vikings had beaten them to it, as there was Norse graffiti on the walls. The name "Maes Howe" comes from the Old Norse and means "great mound". It is a great, grassy hill, 36 feet high and 300 feet in circumference, and was built about 2,700 BC. A long, narrow

305 SANDS HOTEL

Burray
A recently refurbished four-star hotel with comfortable, high quality rooms and a reputation for fine food.

see page 585

306 THE GALLEY INN & SHORE RESTAURANT

St Margaret's Hope
A delightful inn and restaurant overlooking the quay.

see page 587

405

307 THIRA

Innertown

Purpose-built, non-smoking guesthouse enjoying superb sea views, just 2 miles from picturesque seaport of Stromness.

see page 587

308 THE FERRY INN

Stromness

A lively and welcoming harbour-side inn that is close to the ferry terminal, and has value for money accommodation, good drink and great food.

see page 588

309 RAMSQUOY FARM

Stenness

A warm, friendly B&B that has been welcoming people from all over the world for the last 30 years.

see page 588

passage leads into a central chamber with smaller side chambers, which are roofed and floored with massive slabs. At the winter solstice, the setting sun shines directly down the main passage.

Also looked after by Historic Scotland are the four **Stenness Standing Stones**, the largest such stones in Orkney. Originally, it is thought, there were 12, and they formed a circle 104 feet in diameter, and date from about the same time as Maes Howe. The tallest stone is 16 feet tall. Not far away is an even taller stone, the **Watch Stone**, which is 18-and-a-half feet tall. To the north of the Stenness Stones, and near the shore of Harray Loch, is the **Barnhouse Settlement**, a neolithic village discovered in 1984. Agricultural activity over the years has destroyed much of it, though it is reckoned there were 15 dwellings on the site.

The **Ring of Brodgar**, also dating from about 2700 BC, still has 27 of its original 60 stones, surrounded by a ditch. They are smaller than the Stenness Stones, and stand on a strip of land between two small lochs. Legend says that long ago a group of giants came to this spot during the night, and that one of their number began playing the fiddle. The giants began to dance in a circle, and so carried away were they that they never noticed the sun starting to rise. When the light struck them, they were turned to stone. A short distance east is a single stone known as the **Comet Stone**, and a

mile or so northwest is the **Ring of Bookan**, a circular mound surrounded by a massive ditch. And close to it is another Neolithic site - the **Bookan Cairn**. It was excavated in 1861, and human remains were found. This whole area is part of the Orkney World Heritage Site, designated in 1999.

ORPHIR
9 miles W of Kirkwall off the A964

During early Norse rule, Orphir was one of the main Orcadian settlements. **Orphir Church** was built in the 11th or 12th century and dedicated to St Nicholas. Some say that King Haakon, the man who murdered St Magnus, founded it, possibly as an act of penance after a pilgrimage to Jerusalem. It was a circular church about 18 feet in diameter, with a small apse at its eastern end, and was the only such medieval church in Scotland. Nothing now remains apart from the apse and some of the east wall. The **Orkneyinga Saga Centre** is close by, which interprets the old Orkney Saga, from which much of Orkney's early history is taken.

STROMNESS
15 miles W of Kirkwall on the A965

This little burgh, huddling beneath Binkie's Brae, a ridge behind the town, faces Orkney's second largest island, Hoy. Though it looks old and quaint, it only received its burgh charter in 1817, and was founded in the 17th century. The **Stromness Museum** in Alfred Street has displays on **Scapa Flow**,

Stromness

whaling, lighthouses and the Hudson's Bay Company (which had a base here, and employed many Orcadians). Scapa Flow, between Hoy and Mainland, is one of the best natural harbours in the world. After World War I the German fleet was brought to Scapa Flow while a decision was made about its future. However, the German officers decided the fleet's future themselves - they scuttled the ships, and most still lie at the bottom of the sea, a constant attraction for divers (see also Hoy).

HOY

17 miles W of Kirkwall

Hoy is Orkney's second largest island, and sits off the west coast of Mainland. The **Old Man of Hoy** is Great Britain's tallest and most famous sea stack. Made of sandstone, it is over 445 feet high, and sits off the island's north west coast, a constant challenge to climbers. The first successful climb was in 1966, and TV cameras were there to record it.

Betty Corrigall's Grave marks the burial site of a young Orcadian woman who lived in the 18th century, though she is more remembered for a series of bizarre events that took place 200 years later. Her lover deserted her when he found out she was pregnant, and she tried to take her own life. She threw herself into the sea, but was rescued. Then she was more successful - she hanged herself. As she had committed suicide, she was not allowed to be buried on consecrated ground, so was buried in an unmarked grave on moorland, between two parishes, as was the custom then. In 1933 some men who were cutting peat came across her coffin. Eventually it was opened, revealing the body of a young, long-haired woman which had been well preserved by the peaty soil. By her side was a noose. She was reinterred at the same spot, and forgotten about. However, during the Second World War her grave was once again discovered, this time by a troop of soldiers, who returned again and again to exhume the body and gaze at it. This caused the body to decompose.

Officers soon put a stop to this bizarre ritual, and moved the grave,

310 THE ORKNEY CROFT

Hoy

Wonderful self-catering accommodation on the quiet yet breathtakingly beautiful island of Hoy.

see page 589

407

Firth

Two self-catering cottages that offer peace and tranquillity and yet are equipped with modern conveniences that will make your stay enjoyable and comfortable.

see page 589

placing a concrete slab over it. In 1976 her grave finally got a memorial stone - albeit one made of fibreglass. So ended the curious saga of Betty Corrigall.

At the southwest end of the island at Longhope is a **Martello Tower**, erected between 1813 and 1815 to protect the island from the French. The **Lyness Interpretation Centre** has displays about the role the Orkneys played during both World Wars, especially Scapa Flow (see also Stromness). There is also an outdoor collection of armaments.

The **Dwarfie Stone** is unique in the United Kingdom - a burial chamber dating from at least 3000 BC cut into a great block of sandstone. Some people claim, however, that it was not a tomb, but an ancient dwelling. The most amazing thing about it is that it was hollowed out using nothing but horn tools, antlers and pieces of stone.

CLICK MILL

13 miles NW of Kirkwall on the B9057

Click Mill (Historic Scotland), east of Dounby, with its turf covered roof, is the islands' last surviving example of a horizontal watermill, and got its name from the clicking sound it made when turning. They were once common throughout Scandinavia.

At Harray, a couple of miles south of the mill, is the **Corrigall Farm Museum**, housed in a 19th century farmhouse. Exhibits include a working barn with grain kiln and a loom.

SKARA BRAE

17 miles NW of Kirkwall on the B9056

In 1850, at the Bay of Skaill, a storm uncovered the remains of a village which was at least 5,000 years old - older even than the Pyramids. It is the oldest known prehistoric village in Europe, and the remains are now looked after by Historic Scotland. They show that the people who built it from stone were sophisticated and ingenious, and that the houses were comfortable and well appointed, with beds, dressers and cupboards made of stone, as wood was hard to come by. Archaeological evidence tells us that it was built by Neolithic people who farmed, hunted and fished. When it was built, it stood some distance from the sea, but due to erosion over the years the sea is now on its doorstep.

Close by is **Skaill House**, the finest mansion in Orkney, surrounded by lawned gardens. The main part of the house was originally built in 1620 for George Graham, Bishop of Orkney, though it has been extended over the years. It houses a fine collection of furniture, including Bishop Graham's bed, on which are carved the words GEO. *GRAHAM ME FIERI FECIT* ("George Graham caused me to be made").

When the Skaill was being built, 15 skeletons were uncovered to the south of the South Wing. In the 1930s skeletons were also uncovered under the house itself. It is now thought that the house was built on the site of a Christian Pictish cemetery. It is no wonder that Skaill is said to be haunted.

BROUGH OF BIRSAY

21 miles NW of Kirkwall off the A966

This little island, which is connected to the mainland at low tide by a narrow causeway, has the remains of a Norse settlement and the early medieval **St Peter's Church** (once the cathedral of the diocese of Orkney), built on the foundations of a chapel that may date back to the 7th or 8th centuries. After he was killed, St Magnus was possibly buried here until such time as his body could be taken to the newly built St Magnus Cathedral in Kirkwall. Within the churchyard is a Pictish stone, though it is a copy of the original one that stood here. When visiting the island, the times of tides must be taken into account. The tourism office at Kirkwall can advise.

The area on Mainland opposite the island is also called Birsay, and here you can see the ruins of **Earl Stewart's Palace**. It was built between 1569 and 1579 for Robert, Earl of Orkney, a cruel, unpopular man and father of Patrick, who was even more cruel and unpopular. He was an illegitimate son of James V, and took full advantage of his royal connections to amass himself a huge fortune at the islanders' expense. The **Kirbuster Farm Museum**, also on Mainland, has examples of farm implements used on Orkney over the years, and a Victorian garden.

ROUSAY

14 miles N of Kirkwall

This island is sometimes known as the "Egypt of the North", as it brims with archaeological sites, most with delightful names. The 5,000 year old **Taversoe Tuick Chambered Cairn** has two chambers, one above the other. The **Blackhammer Cairn,** the **Knowe of Yarso Cairn** and the **Midhowe Cairn** can also be seen. **The Broch of Midhowe** has walls that still stand 13 feet high.

On **Egilsay**, a small island to the east, are the superb ruins of the 12th century **St Magnus's Church**, with its round tower. It was on Egilsay in 1115 that Magnus was killed. A cairn marks the spot of the martyrdom.

WESTRAY

27 miles N of Kirkwall

The substantial ruins of **Noltland Castle** lie to the north of the island. It was built by Gilbert Balfour, who was Sheriff of Orkney and Master of the Household to Mary Stuart. At Pierowall, the island's main settlement, are the ruins of **St Mary's Church**, dating from the 17th century with medieval fragments. and at Tuquoy are the ruins of the **Cross Kirk** with the remains of a Norse settlement. Near Inga Ness are the remains of the **Knowe O' Burristae Broch**, which has been partly destroyed by sea erosion,

To the east of Westray is the smaller island of **Papa Westray**. It

At Marwick Head is a squat, crenellated tower - the Kitchener Memorial. It was erected in memory of Kitchener of Khartoum, who was killed when HMS Hampshire, on which he was travelling to Russia to discuss the progress of the war with Tzar Nicholas, struck a German mine near here in June 1916. Only 12 people survived the sinking of the ship. The monument was paid for by the people of Orkney.

312 HAVLY CENTRE CAFÉ

Lerwick

A stylish yet comfortable Christian café that is open to everyone for delicious coffees, teas, home baking and light lunches.

❙❚ see page 590

is connected to Westray by air, the flight (which lasts two minutes) being the shortest scheduled air flight in the world. The ruins of **St Tredwell's Chapel** are medieval, and beside them are the remains of an early monastery, with the remains of beehive cells clearly visible. As late as the 18th century, St Tredwell's was a place of pilgrimage.

SANDAY

20 miles NE of Kirkwall

The 7¼ inch gauge **Sanday Light Railway** is Britain's most northerly passenger carrying line. Two steam engines and two petrol driven engines ply the route, which includes Britain's most northerly level crossing.

The island has many cairns, standing stones, and other archaeological sites, including the **Quoyness Chambered Cairn**, the **Styes of Brough** and the **Viking Boat Burial**.

LERWICK

The name "Lerwick" comes from the Norse for "muddy bay", and up until the 17th century that's all it was - a muddy bay surrounded by a handful of crude dwellings. It is capital of Shetland and was granted its burgh charter in 1818. It was originally developed by the Dutch in the early 17th century to service their herring fleet, and from there gradually grew into a small town. It is the most northerly town in Britain, and, with a population of about 7,000, sits on the island of Mainland. It is so far north that during June you could read a newspaper at midnight out of doors without any artificial light.

Every year, on the last Tuesday in January, the festival of **Up Helly Aa** is held. After being hauled through the streets of the town accompanied by men carrying torches and dressed as Vikings, a Viking longboat is set on fire. Though an enjoyable and spectacular sight, it is a ritual which dates back to pagan times, when darkest days of winter were feared. It was thought that the light from celebrations of this kind attracted the light of the sun, which would then gradually return, lengthening the days. The introduction of a Viking ship, however, was a Victorian idea. Before that tar barrels were used.

Lace Knitting, Lerwick

410

Like Orkney, all the islands are rich in ancient remains. There are also many small interpretation centres and museums - too many for all of them to be mentioned in this book.

The number of days in the year when the temperatures rise above 75 degrees are few in Shetland, but there are compensations, not least of which is the quality of light and the almost 24 hours of daylight at the height of summer. And there is less rain here than in Fort William or even North Devon.

Fort Charlotte, named after George III's wife, was built in the 1780s on the site of 17th century fortifications to protect the town from the Dutch, whom, the British government felt, had too much power in the area due to its large herring fleet, which was based here. **Shetland Museum** has been relocated to Hay's Dock, and will not be reopening until some time in 2007. It gives an insight into the history of the islands and its people, and has some marvellous displays on archaeology. There is also an excellent photograph archive and occasional art exhibitions.

The wonderfully named **Böd of Gremista** is located to the north of the town, and was the birthplace in 1792 of **Arthur Anderson**, co-founder of the P&O line. He joined the Royal Navy, and subsequently fought in the Napoleonic wars. In 1833 he co-founded the Peninsular Steam Navigation Company, which, in 1937, became the Peninsular and Oriental Steam Navigation Company. The building has been restored as a small museum and interpretation centre highlighting the island's maritime history. It is a typical Shetland "böd", (farmhouse or warehouse), of the 18th century.

AROUND LERWICK

BRESSAY

1 mile E of Lerwick

The island of Bressay sits opposite Lerwick, and shelters its harbour. Due to the frequency of the ferries, it is a favourite place for Lerwick commuters to live, and has a population of over 400. **Bressay Heritage Centre** illustrates through displays and exhibits what life was like on the island in former times. As it sits close to the ferry terminal, any visit to the island should start here. The tiny island of **Noss**, off its west coast, is a nature reserve, one of the oldest on the Shetlands. Boat trips to the island are available. Bressay has some fine walks, notably on its east coast. Its highest point is **Ward Hill**, at 742 feet.

The ruined **St Mary's Chapel** is at Cullingsbrough Voe, on the island's east coast. It may date back to Viking times, and is the only cruciform church on the Shetland Islands.

MOUSA

13 miles S of Lerwick

There are about 70 confirmed broch (round, fortified tower) sites in Shetland, and the best preserved

313 SELF CATERING SHETLAND

Lerwick

A range of self catering properties within and on the outskirts of Lerwick that are comfortable and represent amazing value for money.

⊨ see page 590

314 THE SHETLAND FUDGE COMPANY

Lerwick

Family-run business producing hand-made fudge, truffles and chocolates.

🏛 see page 591

315 GLEN ORCHY HOUSE

Lerwick

A superior guest house that offers high standards of service and amazing value for money in Lerwick, Shetland's capital.

⊨ see page 591

316 ORCA COUNTRY INN

Sandwick

A superb country inn on Shetland that offers comfortable accommodation, great food and a range of drinks.

❚ ⊨ *see page 592*

on this tiny uninhabited island off the east coast of Mainland. The **Broch of Mousa** (Historic Scotland) was built sometime during the Iron Age from local stone, and is over 40 feet high and 49 feet in diameter. It has lost its uppermost courses, but is still in a remarkable state of preservation, and shows the typical layout of these curious buildings, which are found nowhere else but in Scotland. The double walls slope inwards as they get higher, and embedded in them are staircases (which you can use to climb to the top) and defensive galleries. Like other brochs, no mortar was used in its construction. A small ferry takes you to the island from Sandsayre Pier at Sandwick.

BODDAM

20 miles S of Lerwick on the A970

The **Crofthouse Museum** comprises a thatched house, steading and water mill, and illustrates what life was like in a 19th century Shetland Island croft. Furnished in home-made furniture of the type used on the Shetland Islands, it would have housed an extended family of children, parents and grandparents, Within a croft, the men would have earned their living from the sea while the women worked the land. People visiting should be aware that there are low roof beams and an uneven floor.

JARLSHOF

25 miles S of Lerwick on the A970

Lying close to Sumburgh Airport on Mainland, Jarlshof is one of the most important historical sites in Europe, and has been continuously occupied from the Bronze Age right up until the 17th century. There are Bronze Age huts, Iron Age earth houses, brochs, wheelhouses from the Dark Ages, Norse longhouses and medieval dwellings. It is managed by Historic Scotland, and there is a small museum and interpretation centre. It was exposed in the 19th century when high winds and waves blew the sand away from the ancient walls. The site got its name from Sir Walter Scott's book *The Pirate*. He named a house in this part of Shetland "Jarlshof", and the name stuck.

At **Old Scatness**, close to Jarlshof, is an archaeological site centred on a number of ancient brochs, wheelhouses and medieval dwellings. There is a living history area with demonstrations that reproduce ancient technologies using authentic materials. It was discovered in 1975 when a road was cut through what was thought to be a natural mound. Old walls were discovered, and work began on excavating the site in 1995 by archaeologists from Bradford University.

The **Ness of Burgi**, a small promontory jutting out into the sea, lies to the west of Jarlshof, and has an Iron Age fort within a circular ditch.

FAIR ISLE

46 miles S of Lerwick

The most southerly of the Shetland Islands lies almost half way between Shetland and Orkney. It is owned by the National Trust for Scotland, and is one of the remotest inhabited islands in the country, with a population of about 65. It was originally called Fridarey, meaning "island of peace", by Norse settlers. In 1588 one of the Spanish Armada vessels, the *El Gran Grifon*, was shipwrecked here. About 200 men managed to struggle ashore, and they were looked after by the islanders as best they could. However, the sailors, hungry and exhausted, began killing off the islanders' animals for food, and they were eventually shipped off to Shetland from where they were sent home. Over 50 Spaniards died of hunger while on the island. In 1948 a Spanish delegation dedicated a cross on the island to those Spaniards who had died, and the wreck was excavated in 1970 by archaeologists from St Andrews University.

The island was once owned by George Waterston, who was the Scottish Director of the Royal Society for the Protection of Birds, and who founded a bird observatory in 1948. **The George Waterston Memorial Centre and Museum** at Utra has displays about the history and wildlife of the island. **The Fair Isle Lodge and Bird** Observatory was built in 1970, and is open from April to October. Visitors can book accommodation and spend time observing the wide variety of birdlife on and around the island. The **Feely Dyke**, a turf wall separating common land from

Fair Isle

modern crofting land, may date from prehistoric times.

Fair Isle knitting is famous the world over, and it is a craft that is still carried out to this day, using traditional patterns.

SCALLOWAY

6 miles W of Lerwick on the A970

Though only six miles from Lerwick, this small village sits on the Atlantic coast while its larger neighbour sits on the coast of the North Sea. Its name comes from the Norse "Scola Voe", which means the "Huts by the Bay".

Up until 1708 it was Shetland's capital, but as Lerwick expanded so the centre of power shifted eastwards. **Scalloway Castle** dates from around 1600, and was built by Patrick Stewart, who was executed 15 years later in Edinburgh for treason (see also Kirkwall).

During World War II the village was a secret Norwegian base, and from here Norwegians used to be ferried across to their country in fishing boats (nicknamed

413

317 MID BRAE INN

Brae

An old inn on Shetland that not only offers a range of drinks, but also great food that is cooked on the premises.

see page 592

318 BUSTA HOUSE HOTEL

Busta, Brae

A superb country house hotel with 22 comfortable en-suite rooms and fine food served in the restaurant.

see page 593

"Shetland buses") to mount sabotage operations and bring back resistance fighters who were on the run from German troops. The **Shetland Bus Memorial** commemorates these men, and the small **Scalloway Museum** in Main Street tells their story, as well as the story of Scalloway itself.

TINGWALL

6 miles NW of Lerwick on the A970

Law Ting Holm near Tingwall was where the ancient Shetland Islands parliament, or Althing, used to meet. It sits on a small promontory (which in Norse times was an island) jutting out into the Loch of Tingwall.

Just off the A970 is the **Murder Stone**, a prehistoric standing stone. It got its name from a local legend, which states that murderers were made to run between Law Ting Holm and the stone pursued by relatives of the murdered person. If the murderer made it to the stone unscathed, he was not executed, if he did not, his pursuers killed him. The **Tingwall Agricultural Museum,** within an 18th century grain store, has a collection of old crofting tools.

TANGWICK

33 miles NW of Lerwick on the B9078

The **Tangwick Haa Museum**, based in Tangwick Haa at Northmavine, has displays and artefacts about the local history of the northern part of Mainland. The haa ("hall") itself dates from the 17th century, and was built by the Cheyne family, the local

landowners. It was restored by the Shetland Amenity Trust and opened as a museum in 1988. One of the characters of Northmavine was John Williamson, known as "Johnnie Notions". Though uneducated, he devised an inoculation for smallpox long before anyone else, and it seemed to work. He inoculated over 1000 people, and not one of them died of smallpox, even when it was raging through the islands..

WHALSAY

18 miles NE of Lerwick

This small island, no more than six miles long by two miles wide, is connected to Mainland by a ferry from Dury Voe. There are superb coastal walks and many ancient remains. The 393-feet high **Ward of Clett** is its highest point, and from here a good view of the east coast of Mainland can be enjoyed. The granite **Symbister House**, in the island's ferry port, is the finest Georgian house in Shetland. It was built by the Bruce family, who nearly bankrupted themselves in doing so, something that did not trouble the people of the island, as the family had oppressed them for years. It now forms part of the local school. The grounds are said to be haunted by the ghost of a sailor. The island is home to Britain's most northerly golf course and to the **Symbister Pier House Museum**, which tells the story of the island's links with the merchants of the Hanseatic League, The pier house was one of two Hanseatic warehouses on the island where the

German merchants stored their merchandise. After the 1707 Union of Parliaments, new import duties forrced the German merchants to leave. The road beside the Pier House is still called the Bremen Strasse.

FETLAR

40 miles NE of Lerwick

The island of Fetlar, the fourth largest of the Shetland Islands, is seven miles long by five miles wide at its widest, and sits off the east coast of Yell, to which it is connected by ferry. The soil here, compared to other islands, is fertile, so the Vikings named it the "rich land", from which the name Fetlar comes. **The Fetlar Interpretive Centre** at Beach of Houbie has displays on the island's history, wildlife and folklore, as well as genealogical archives. There is also an archive of over 3,000 photographs.

In the middle of the island are three mysterious stone circles known as **Fiddler's Crus**, which almost touch each other. Close by is the **Haltadans**, another stone circle, where 38 stones enclose two stones at its centre. The story goes that the two inner stones are a fiddler and his wife who were dancing with 38 trolls in the middle of the night. As the sun rose in the morning, its light turned them all to stone. Another site is the wonderfully named **Stone of the Ripples**, a standing stone over six feet high. The name has nothing to do with ripples, but comes from the coastline where it is located, called

De Ripels. The island supports over 300 varieties of plants, and is a bird sanctuary which has the highest density of breeding waders in Britain.

YELL

30 miles N of Lerwick

The second largest island in Shetland is about 20 miles long by seven miles wide at its widest, and is connected to Mainland by a 15 minute ferry crossing. Though its population is close to 1,000, it still has lonely moorland and a varied coast that lend themselves to hill walking and bird watching.

The whitewashed **Old Haa of Burravoe** ("Old Hall of Burravoe"), at the island's south east corner, is the oldest complete building on the island, and dates from 1637. It now houses a small museum and interpretation centre, and has a digital recording studio. A tapestry commemorates the crashing of a Catalina aircraft in 1941 close to Burravoe, with only three out of the crew of ten surviving. The **Lumbister RSPB Reserve** sits between Whale Firth (said to be the smallest "firth" in Scotland) and the A968, the island's main road. It is a large tract or moorland with many lochans, bogs and ruined crofting cottages. Here you can see the red-throated diver, eider, dunlin, great and Arctic skua, wheatear, curlew, merlin and snipe.

UNST

46 miles N of Lerwick

Unst is the most northerly of the Shetland Isles, and off

319 MIDFIELD CROFT SELF-CATERING COTTAGES

Ollaberry

Two well appointed self-catering cottages that offer the opportunity for quiet, relaxed holidays on a coastal location.

⊨ see page 593

320 NORWIND GUEST HOUSE

Mid Yell

One of the best bed and breakfast establishments on the Shetlands - one that makes the ideal base from which to explore all that they have to offer

⊨ see page 594

Hermaness, where there is a nature reserve and visitor centre, is **Muckle Flugga**, with its Out Stack, or "Oosta", which is the most northerly point in the United Kingdom. At the southeast corner of the island are the gaunt ruins of **Muness Castle**, the most northerly castle in Britain. The castle dates from 1598, and was built by Lawrence Bruce of Cultmalindie, a relative of the wayward Stewart dynasty that ruled the islands, and a man every bit as cruel and despotic as they were. He was appointed sheriff of Shetland, and when Patrick Stewart succeeded his father Robert as the Earl of Orkney, Lawrence felt so threatened that he built the castle as a place of safety. In 1608 Patrick came to Unst with 36 men to destroy it, but retreated before he had a chance to do so. In about 1627 a party of French raiders attacked and burnt the castle, and it was never rebuilt.

At **Haroldswick**, in the north of the island, is **Harold's Grave,** an ancient burial cairn that is supposed to mark the grave of Harold the Fair of Norway. **Burra Firth**, on the northern coast, is one of Britain's tiniest firths, and certainly its most northerly. In fact, everything here is Britain's "most northerly" something or other. The Post Office is Britain's most northerly post office, the village's Methodist church is the counrty's most northerly church, and **Wick of Shaw** is the most northerly dwelling house. The church with its white walls and red roof, has a simple layout based on a traditional Norwegian church, and was built between 1990 and 1993.

Accommodation, Food & Drink
and Places to Visit

The establishments featured in this section includes hotels, inns, guest houses, bed & breakfasts, restaurants, cafés, tea and coffee shops, tourist attractions and places to visit. Each establishment has an entry number which can be used to identify its location at the beginning of the relevant county chapter. This section is ordered by county and the page number in the column to the right indicates the first establishment in each county.

In addition full details of all these establishments and many others can be found on the Travel Publishing website - **www.travelpublishing.co.uk**. This website has a comprehensive database ocovering the whole of Britain and Ireland.

Coldingham Sands,
Berwickshire TD14 5PH

☎ 018907 71450

e-mail: info@dunlaverock.com

🌐 www.dunlaverock.com

Dunlaverock is an elegant Edwardian country house in a superb location commanding spectacular views and with direct access from its garden to the beach and seashore. The house is surrounded by an extensive peaceful garden where guests can enjoy a game of croquet or just relax.

Scenic walks and trails along the cliff tops or fishing trips from St. Abbs or on Coldingham Loch provide local leisure facilities, along with the numerous fine golf courses within a thirty-mile drive.

With its spacious proportions and period features Dunlaverock is a superb place to stay, long or short, in Berwickshire. The lounge, dining room and the two main bedrooms with their large picture windows have a magnificent view of the coastal panorama. All the rooms – there are 6 in all – are tastefully decorated in traditional but varied style so that each has its own character and style. There is one ground floor room that is wheelchair accessible with walk-in shower and rails.

Included in the room rate is a sumptuous full Scottish Breakfast. All the food is freshly cooked using local ingredients where possible. There is a wide selection of cereals, yoghurts and fresh grapefruits together with a range of fruit juices followed by a full hearty Scottish Breakfast of bacon, sausage, black pudding, mushrooms, tomatoes, hash browns and eggs. The eggs are all free range and may be fried, poached, boiled or scrambled. Alternatively a full continental breakfast is available with a wide range of cold meats. Eyemouth Kippers are available as a fish alternative at breakfast and vegetarians will feel at ease with the options available. An evening meal is also available if desired, where again the emphasis is on using local produce, particularly sea foods whenever possible. Dunlaverock House has a

licence for residents and a wide range of beverages is available. The Wine List whilst not extensive

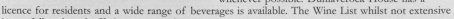

is carefully selected offering a comprehensive range of wines at eminently reasonable prices. After dinner guests are able to partake of coffee and drinks in front of the real log fire. Owners Bill and Jane Foulis are also happy to cater for small functions and the house also has a licence for civil marriages.

Special mid-week and weekend breaks for two or more nights stay are available. Credit cards are accepted and there's ample parking.

Incidentally, if you prefer self-catering, the Foulis's also have a house and flat in nearby Coldingham village.

3 CHIRNSIDE INN ¶

Chirnside, Duns, Berwickshire TD11 3XH
☎ 01890 818034
e-mail: david@thechirnsideinn
🌐 www.chirnsideinn.co.uk

A traditional Scottish welcome awaits guests at the **Chirnside Inn**, a delightful old coaching inn dating back to the 1820s. It stands just outside the pretty Borders village of Chirnside, on the Coldstream road.

Now under new ownership, the hotel has recently been completely refurbished and upgraded, but essentially it's still a cosy wayside inn – albeit with an added touch of class. With its roaring log fire and a vast selection of malt whiskeys, real ales and real people, this is a place to savour. The inn serves bar lunches and suppers all year round. The food is locally produced and freshly cooked in the kitchens by the helpful and friendly staff under the eye of the new head chef. He does his best to ensure that wherever possible, the ingredients are locally produced and grown. All meals are cooked freshly on the premises. There's a very popular bar lunch menu and the bar suppers are renowned for their fresh, local ingredients. The staff take pride in offering good, home-cooked food at reasonable prices. Many of the regulars prefer to eat in the bar with its roaring fire, cosy atmosphere and local chit-chat. It's also a smoke-free zone following recent legislation which means all licensed premises in Scotland are now non-smoking throughout. In the traditional restaurant which, like the rest of the hotel has been totally refurbished, menu offers a mix of the traditional and contemporary with both Haggis, neeps & tatties and Smoked venison with rocket salad among the starters. Main courses range from a hearty 8oz sirloin steak with pepper sauce and home-made hand-cut chips through a delicious fresh Eyemouth haddock & chips, to Mediterranean vegetables with lime and coconut couscous. To accompany your meal, the inn offers a selection of fine wines and the bar stocks over 30 single malt whiskeys along with various real ales, including guest ales which change throughout the year. The inn also has an outdoor area for al fresco eating and drinking – this area is sheltered from the elements and heated during the colder months.

If you are planning to stay in this lovely part of the country, the Chirnside Inn has five stylish bedrooms, 2 of which have 4-poster beds. Three of the rooms have new en suite facilities and all of them have been individually designed with the guests' total comfort in mind.

4   HOME ARMS HOTEL

High Street, Eyemouth TD14 5EY
☎ 018907 50220
e-mail: homearmshotel@btconnect.com

As you enter Eyemouth's one-way High Street the first building you will see is the **Home Arms Hotel,** a large brick pile that was named after former Prime Minister Lord Home. Built in the early 1900s, the hotel enjoys a fine position overlooking the sea. Bruce Gillie took over here in the summer of 2006 and is gradually re-decorating and upgrading the guest bedrooms. There are 6 of them, all en suite, as well as a dormitory that can sleep up to 15 people. There's a very spacious, well-stocked bar and from Easter 2007 sensibly priced, honest-to-goodness pub food will be on sale here.

1 CEDAR CAFÉ

Grantshouse, Berwickshire TD11 3RP
☎ 01361 850371
e-mail: thmsangl23@aol.com

Conveniently located beside a layby on the A1, a quarter of a mile south of Grantshouse, the **Cedar Café** offers wholesome and appetising food in pleasant surroundings. It's owned and run by Angela and Keith Brown, with Keith doing the cooking. The regular menu is supplemented by daily specials – Aberdeen

Angus Steak Pie, perhaps, Mince 'n' Tatties, or Scottish Pork & Leek Sausages. The café is licensed and open from

8am to 8pm, Sunday to Friday, and from 8am to 5pm on Saturday. Credit cards are accepted and there's ample parking. Keith and Angela also have a self-catering flat to let in nearby Reston.

5 THE SHIP HOTEL

The Harbour, Eyemouth, Berwickshire TD14 5HT
☎ 018907 50224
e-mail: theroyaloak40@btinternet.com
⊕ www.theroyaloakhawkeridge.co.uk

Set right beside Eyemouth's picturesque harbour, **The Ship Hotel** is a traditional whitewashed hostelry with oodles of olde worlde charm. It was extensively refurbished in early 2007

but care was taken to maintain its many period features. Naturally, with fresh fish being landed just a

few yards away, seafood takes pride of place on the menu with Eyemouth Haddock and the superb Special Fisherman's Pie as specialities. But there are plenty of other choices, including vegetarian dishes. If you are planning to stay in this delightful little town, The Ship has 6 comfortable guest rooms, 3 of them with en suite facilities.

6 THIRLESTANE CASTLE

Lauder, Berwickshire TD2 6RU
☎ 01578 722430 Fax: 01578 722761
e-mail: enquiries@thirlestanecastle.co.uk
⊕ www.thirlestanecastle.co.uk

Thirlestane, one of the oldest and finest castles in Scotland is set in lovely Border hills at Lauder, 28 miles south of Edinburgh and 68 miles north of Newcastle, on the A68. Built originally as a defensive fort in the 13th century it was re-built in the 16th century as the home of the Maitlands. As the seat of the Earls and Duke of Lauderdale it was enlarged and embellished over the centuries but it still remains home to the Maitland family. The Duke's ghost is said to haunt the castle.

See the Panelled Room and the Library with their defensive walls up to 13' thick. Absorb the atmosphere of the Billiard Room with its fascinating salmon fly screen. Climb the ancient turnpike stair to the Duke's Suite, including the incomparable 17th century plasterwork ceilings. Relish the

splendour of the Green Drawing Room and the Ante Drawing Room with their exquisite ceilings and joinery. Meet the Maitlands through the portrait collection in the State Dining Room and discover some of their fascinating treasures. Sink into nostalgia as you enter the Family Nurseries with their unique collection of historic toys. Some are in replica form for children to use and dipping into the dressing up chest can create some memorable moments on a family holiday. Discover the old Kitchens and Laundries, and explore the Border Country Life exhibitions showing domestic, sporting and agricultural life over the centuries.

7 THE KINGS ARMS HOTEL

High Street, Melrose,
Roxburghshire TD6 9PB

☎ 01896 822143 Fax: 01896 823812

e-mail: enquiries@kingsarmshotel.co.uk

⊕ www.kingsarmsmelrose.co.uk

The three-star **Kings Arms Hotel** is one of the Scottish Borders' best loved inns. It sits right in the heart of Melrose, a delightfully picturesque town that boasts the ruins one of the finest abbeys in the country. This former coaching inn is over 300 years old, and has now been lovingly restored to offer modern standards of service while still retaining period features that make it a place full of character and charm.

The hotel is ideally placed for a host of activities, from golf to fishing and from bird-watching to hiking and horse riding. Most can be arranged by the hotel on your behalf. In fact, it was in the hotel that the Melrose rugby Club once met and founded that branch of rugby called Rugby Sevens, which is now played all over the world.

It is a family run hotel, owned and managed by Linda and Malcolm McDonald, who are maintaining the long history of keeping to the highest standards. The atmosphere is friendly, welcoming and fun, with value for money being the key watchwords. The seven comfortable bedrooms on offer are all fully en suite, and are decorated and furnished to an extremely high standard, with a traditional Scottish feel to the décor. You're sure of a good night's sleep here! The courtyard cottage is the perfect place for a self-catering break. It sleeps up to four in double and twin rooms, and has a kitchen and sitting room.

If you enjoy good food, you've made the right choice if you dine here! The cuisine is traditional Scottish with over 30 main courses available, all cooked to perfection, using only fresh local produce wherever possible, such as beef, game, fish and locally grown vegetables. The select wine list carries many fine vintages, and there's sure to be a wine that will match your meal to perfection. Lunches are served from noon until 2pm, and dinners are served between 6.30pm (5.30pm on Sunday) and 9.00pm on weekdays and 9.30pm on Saturdays. All are served either in the cosy, comfortable bar or in the no-smoking family restaurant.

The Kings Arms Hotel is also the perfect place to have that quiet, relaxing drink; and indeed, it recently won a "Perfect Pub Award" from Greene King. There is a fine range of wines, spirits,

liqueurs and soft drinks on offer, and the hotel has been recognised by the Campaign for Real Ale for its beers. You have the choice of a public bar - which is popular with locals - or an elegant cocktail bar.

The staff are friendly and knowledgeable, and are determined that you are going to enjoy your stay at the Kings arms Hotel. Packed lunches and flasks can be made up by prior arrangement. Holiday packages and special offers can be arranged round particular themes such as shopping breaks, with Edinburgh, Glasgow, Newcastle and Carlisle are within easy driving distance. Well behaved pets are welcome by prior arrangement, and there is a private car park.

8 WAGGON INN

10 Coalmarket, Kelso TD5 7AH
☎ 01573 224568
e-mail: waggoninn@virgin.net
🌐 www.thewaggoninn.com

The Waggon stands at the top of this charming historic border town. A treat awaits within, with excellent fresh food offerings, pleasant service and great value for money. Operated by Joe Wright (a Chef, himself) and his happy team, a warm welcome is extended as you enter this 'fresh, airy and 'friendly' environment. The varied menu provides a wealth of dishes to cater for all. Cosmopolitan creations from fresh local produce are delivered beyond expectations, home- cut chips make such a difference. The Inn has an added bonus of a Toddlers Playroom and the 'Kiddies Menu' provides the same 'fresh' quality (under two's eat free). Pub quiz Tuesday Evening and an excellent Carvery on Sunday!!!

11 CLINT HOUSE COUNTRY LODGE

Clint Hill, St Boswell's,
by Melrose TD6 0DZ
☎ 01835 822027 Fax: 01835 822656
e-mail: clintlodge@aol.com
🌐 www.clintlodge.co.uk

Dating back to 1869, **Clint House Country Lodge** is a splendid former sporting lodge which enjoys outstanding views over the magnificent Borders countryside. It's the home of Bill and Heather Walker who have been welcoming bed & breakfast guests here since 1996.

The house has 5 beautifully furnished guest bedrooms, 4 of them en suite, 1 with a private bathroom. If you prefer self-catering, just across the yard is a well-appointed cottage that sleeps up to six people. Heather and Bill also offer a superb 3-course evening meal which is highly recommended. Credit cards are accepted.

10 DRYBURGH ABBEY HOTEL

Dryburgh, St Boswells, Melrose,
Roxburghshire TD6 0RQ
☎ 01835 822261 Fax: 01835 823945
e-mail: enquiries@dryburgh.co.uk
🌐 www.dryburgh.co.uk

From the outside, the **Dryburgh Abbey Hotel** looks like an old country house, tucked into the Borders countryside, close to the ruins of Dryburgh Abbey itself. But from the inside it is one of the country's leading hotels, with all the modern comforts and conveniences that people look for nowadays. It has elegant, well-equipped bedrooms that are fully en suite, two beautiful lounges where guests can relax over a welcoming drink, and a luxurious indoor swimming pool. The abundance and quality of local fresh produce is reflected in the hotel's menu, which changes daily. Choose the tranquil setting of the Tweed Restaurant overlooking the river, or the bistro-style Courtyard Bar. Either way, you'll enjoy a tradition of service and hospitality championed by the Gross family, who have been providing high standards of service for over 100 years. The ambience is unstuffy and informal, while still retaining the country house hotel feel, and there are many opportunities for country pursuits in the surrounding area. The hotel can arrange shooting for individuals or groups, and it offers a free booking service with the local agent covering 14 beats. Within a short distance there are also 14 superb and challenging golf courses, and there are fine walks to be had in the surrounding countryside.

Dryburgh Abbey is only a short stroll from the hotel and the historic town of Melrose, with its wonderful abbey ruins, is a couple of miles away. The Dryburgh Abbey hotel is a wonderful base from which to explore the beautiful Scottish Borders or the ideal location for a business conference, or a celebration such as a party or wedding!

9 THE PLOUGH HOTEL

Main Street, Town Yetholm,
Kelso TD5 8RF
☎ 01573 475215
e-mail: dianecuthbert@yahoo.com
🌐 www.ploughhotelyetholm.co.uk

Standing in the historic centre of Town Yetholm, **The Plough Hotel**, in common with many of the village cottages, is officially listed and protected as a building of architectural importance. The main building dates back to the late 1700s – early 1800s. It was remodelled and extended in the late 19th to early 20th century. However, history suggests there is every likelihood of an earlier inn on this site long before the 18th century. One documentary source (circa 1860) describes the Plough as "a nice respectable country Inn and the first house of entertainment in Town Yetholm, where there is good accommodation for travellers and suitable stabling for horses". No more stabling, of course, but there is car parking for guests in front of the hotel building, off the road side.

The Plough's location makes it the natural centre of social life in the village and features like the real log fire, real ale and home cooking all add to its appeal. Owners Diane and Andrew Hay take great pride in the food served at the Plough and do most of the

cooking themselves. Set daily, each menu is prepared using local produce and seasonal vegetables. At least one vegetarian dish is included in each course and they will try to accommodate any special dietary requirement – just let your server know when you arrive. Half portions are available for children or those with smaller appetites, and food can be puréed for babies.

The five bedrooms at The Plough have all recently been upgraded to a high standard under Andrew and Diane's personal supervision. They are clean, sumptuously decorated and all have spacious en suite facilities, TV and hospitality tray. All told, a relaxing environment in which to unwind before enjoying a meal in the restaurant or a snack at the bar. Children are welcome at the Plough, and pets can sometimes be accommodated with tariff.

The Plough stands within one mile of the Scottish-English border and is a natural destination for many families exploring the B roads south of Kelso. The area is popular with walkers since it is on the 80-mile St Cuthbert's Way, which links Melrose and Lindisfare (Holy Island), and is also at the northern end of the 250-mile Pennine Way, from Edale in Derbyshire to Kirk Yetholm. In 1999 Yetholm also became the terminus of an ambitious European footpath, the E2, which will extend in due course across mainland Europe.

12   THE PLACE

73 High Street, Selkirk,
Selkirkshire TD7 4BZ
☎ 01750 23303

The Place is one of the best pubs in the small, picturesque market town of Selkirk. The atmosphere is warm and friendly, the food is great and the drink is marvellous. Here you'll get one of the best pints of Belhaven in the country! A selection of freshly ground coffees from a local supplier are also served. The food is all cooked on the premises from good, fresh local produce with steak pie being a firm favourite with locals and visitors alike. The

prices are keen and the clientele ranges from 19 to 90. In fact, there is a popular senior citizens' menu that contains many mouth watering dishes that are sure to please! So if you're in Selkirk, The Place is the place for you!

14   THE NIGHTJAR

1 Abbey Close, Jedburgh,
RoxburghshireTD8 6BG
☎ 01835 862552

For those who like fine dining and good wine, **The Nightjar** in Jedburgh is the place

to eat. This intimate bistro has an excellent reputation, and is a favourite with locals and tourists alike. It serves innovative dishes using carefully sourced ingredients. This, together with the relaxed, friendly

atmosphere, ensures that you will linger long over a memorable meal.

13   THE GLEN CAFÉ AND BISTRO

St Mary's Loch, Selkirk,
Selkirkshire TD7 5LH
☎ 01750 42241
e-mail: enquiry@glencafe.co.uk
🌐 www.glencafe.co.uk

The Glen Café & Bistro is situated in the heart of the Southern Uplands in the Scottish Borders, beside the beautiful St Mary's Loch and offers outstanding views across Loch of the Lowes. This is an area which is rich in beauty and has a depth of history ready to be explored.

This is the place to relax over wonderful food and drink while looking out over one of the best views in Scotland. Home cooking and baking is a speciality. A range of Fair Trade coffee & tea is served along with snacks, light lunches and meals which are individually prepared to order all day.

Take the time to let your friends and family know where you are by using the free internet access or keep up to date with current events with the daily newspapers.

Before you go spend some time browsing through

the range of local crafts, gifts and cards.

It is open through the year with a variety of musical functions at regular intervals. Musical themes are varied, following the tradition of excellent local talent, many of international renown, with the accompanying food using the best of fresh local produce. More details can be found of the café website.

15 JEDFOREST DEER AND FARM PARK

Camptown, Jedburgh TD8 6PL
☎ 01835 840364 Fax: 01835 840266
e-mail: mervinslaw@ecosse.net
[◉] http//www.aboutscottand.co.uk/
jedforest/

The Jedforest Deer and Farm Park is located just off the main A68 Edinburgh to Newcastle road some 5 miles south of Jedburgh. There are magnificent herds of deer and you can find out more about farming today. You can see how they look after the animals and protect the countryside and watch the farm in action on our special demonstration days. In addition explore the farm animals of yesteryear within the large conservation collection of rare breeds of sheep, pigs, cattle, chickens, ducks and others.

There is a coffee shop, barbecue area, picnic area as well as both indoor and outdoor adventure areas. Rangers offer walks through the lovely Scottish Borders' countryside and allow you to discover more about the environment, nature and wildlife.

16 BAILEY MILL ACCOMMODATION, TREKKING & RACE BREAK CENTRE

Bailey Mill, Newcastleton,
Roxburghshire TD9 0TR
☎ 016977 48617
e-mail: pam@baileymill.fsnet.co.uk
[◉] www.ridingholidays.uk

Set in a part of the Borders that has hardly changed since the days of the Border reivers, the **Bailey Mill Accommodation and Trekking Centre** offers not only superb B&B or self catering accommodation, but also a range of equestrian activities that will let you explore this wonderful area. It can organise riding holidays tailor-made for your own abilities, and you can either hire one of their horses or ponies, or bring your own - the equestrian accommodation is superb. There is a licensed bar where you can enjoy a drink and a meal and there is also a wealth of other attractions in the area to enjoy.

19 THE GEORGE HOTEL

Walkerburn, Peeblesshire EH43 6AF
☎ 01896 870336
e-mail: georgehotelscotb@aol.com

With its stepped gables and half-moon feature window, **The George Hotel** in the village of Walkerburn looks the very model of a traditional Borders hostelry. Inside there's a bar full of character and a cosy restaurant serving a menu with lots of old favourites such as home-made Steak & Ale Pie, Gammon Steak & Pineapple, and a Roast of the Day. For vegetarians there are dishes such as the Raj Vegetable Curry and a vegetable lasagne. If you plan to stay in this scenic part of the country, The George has 7 comfortable en suite rooms and 1 with private bathroom.

39 Eastgate, Peebles EH45 8AD
☎ 01721 725100
e-mail: mail@halcyonrestaurant.com
🌐 www.halcyonrestaurant.com

The name of the **Halcyon** restaurant in the heart of Peebles was inspired by the many beautiful legends connected with the European kingfisher, which the Greeks called Halcyon. An old belief was that the seven days preceding the shortest day of the year were used by these birds to build their nests which, it was thought, floated on water; and the seven days following were devoted to hatching the eggs. During this period 'The Halcyon Days' the ancients believed the sea was always calm. Hence 'Halcyon' to describe calm peaceful days.

At the Halcyon Restaurant, chef/patron Ally McGrath offers cutting edge food and wine set within a beautiful restaurant interior, with paintings from Scottish artists alongside specially commissioned bronze castings from Beltane Studios of Peebles. This atmospheric restaurant with its brilliant white linen tablecloths, sparkling glass and gleaming utensils, is the perfect location for lunches, dinners and private or company events.

The food ion offer s made from only the very finest produce available. Ally prides himself on using local suppliers wherever

possible and he also thinks it is very important to only use fresh fruit and vegetables when they are in season in the UK whenever this is possible. The fruit and vegetables are also organic – again whenever possible. The menus change regularly but, typically, you might find Braised hare shoulder with choucroute amongst the starters; poached haddock fillet with gnocchi and puree, or braised beef shin with mash and roast root vegetables as main courses. And don't miss out on desserts such as the caramelised pineapple with lemon grass cream, or the warm chocolate brownie with fennel ice cream. Vegetarians are well catered for but if you have any special dietary requirements just let Ally know beforehand. The Halcyon is open Tuesday to Saturday for lunch from 12 noon until 2pm; and for dinner from 6pm to 9pm. Credit cards are accepted.

18 THE CROWN HOTEL

High Street, Peebles, Borders EH45 8SW
☎ 01721 720239
e-mail: info@hotel-scottish-borders.co.uk

Located in the heart of the picturesque town of Peebles, **The Crown Hotel** dates back to the early 1600s and for many years has been owned and run by the Cassidy family, now in the 3rd generation of the family to preside over the inn.

The hotel has a friendly atmosphere and its main goal is to offer a homely and welcoming stay. The hotel has a well-stocked bar which is open all day and serves excellent cuisine in the restaurant, eyemouth haddock being a speciality, which is open from 12 noon until 9pm. There's a pleasant patio beer garden and the hotel also offers a large function room for weddings or large celebrations.

The Crown has 5 guest bedrooms, all of them en suite with tea and coffee making facilities – advance booking is recommended for all accommodation. If you are looking for a fishing, golfing, biking or shooting holiday The Crown is ideal. There are two 18-hole golf courses and one 9-hole course within a 15-minute drive, shooting is available locally, and the hotel also sell fishing permits on site. Credit cards and children welcome.

Traquair Road, Innerleithen,
Peeblesshire EH44 6PD
☎ 01896 830229 Fax: 01896 830260
e-mail: info@traquairarmshotel.co.uk
⊕ www.traquairarmshotel.co.uk

For many, the words "Scottish Borders" conjures up magical images of rolling heather-clad hills, woodland horizons and meandering rivers. In the heart of this exceptional countryside lies the **Traquair Arms Hotel.** Nestling on the edge of the picturesque town of Innerleithen, 6 miles south of Peebles and less than an hour from Edinburgh, it is the perfect hub for relaxation and adventure.

Popular with guests and locals alike for its warm welcome, the Traquair Arms offers great food, inviting surroundings and comfortable accommodation. The whole hotel has recently been completely refurbished but all the old charm and character remains. And the cuisine too remains as outstanding as ever. With the best of fresh Scottish produce on the doorstep and an imaginative chef in the kitchen, diners at the Traquair are offered a hearty and varied menu. Some of the most popular dishes include Caramelised Duck, and Seared King Scallops to start, with roast rack of lamb, **Halibut Fillet** or **Chilli & Lime Chicken** as tasty main dishes. Vegetarians are well served with offerings such as the wild mushroom and goat's cheese lasagne.

Food is also available in the two bars, each serving fresh, home-cooked bar meals and an extensive range of beers, wines and spirits. In good weather, you can also enjoy your refreshments in the spacious beer garden. If it's chilly, settle down in front of the cosy log fire or in front of the TV in Traqs Bar to watch all major sports events. Incidentally, the Traquair Arms is one of only two establishments where you can sample the delicious Traquair Bear ale, brewed a stone's throw away at historic Traquair House – the oldest continuously inhabited house in Scotland.

For accommodation, the hotel offers a choice of 16 newly refurbished en suite rooms, each finished in simple, unfussy and soothing shades. All rooms have remote control TV and hospitality tray. Dogs are also welcome.

Innerleithen itself is an excellent centre for golf, fishing and walking – the town being a stop-off on the coast-to-coast Southern Upland Way route. It also boasts some of the world's best mountain biking, including the Red Bull Trail. These internationally renowned cross-country and downhill trails are just five minutes from the hotel. The town also enjoys a busy events calendar with many musical, cultural and sporting events taking place throughout the year.

21 LAST POST

38 Academy Street, Dumfries,
Dumfries & Galloway DG1 1BZ
☎ 01387 249045 Mobile: 07718407290
e-mail: sharonsloan@btconnect.com
🌐 www.lastpost.co.uk

Situated at the corner of Academy Street and
Loreburn Street, close to the centre of the centre
of the historic town of Dumfries, the **Last Post** is
one of the best and friendliest inns in the whole of
the area. Since they established the place over five
years ago, Sharon and Robert have created a must-
visit pub that offers the very best in good drink and accommodation. Robert used to work for the
Post Office, so the 'Last Post' seemed the ideal name for the
establishment! It is open all day and every day, and has a cosy bar
area with a well-stocked bar selling beers, wines, spirits and soft
drinks should you be driving, so call in here for a relaxing and
quiet drink after exploring the town, or better still book one of
their immaculate rooms and either use it as a base from which to
explore Dumfries and Galloway or as an overnight stop.

There are four fully en suite rooms on offer plus a suite, and
all are tastefully decorated and
furnished to a very high

standard. The rooms can be either twins or doubles, and the
'studio' style suite can be used either for bed and breakfast or
self-catering. A full Scottish breakfast, or something lighter if
required, is included in the tariff. There is ample parking, and an
excellent beer garden for those warm, sunny summer days.
From 8 pm on each second Saturday there is karaoke. So, when
in Dumfries, make your first stop the Last Post. You won't be
disappointed!

22 MARCHILLS RESTAURANT

Moffat Road, Dumfries,
Dumfries & Galloway DG1 1NY
☎ 01387 268728

Housed in a refurbished barn in the lovely old
town of Dumfries, the **Marchills Restaurant** is
one of the best eating establishments in the town.
It is owned and run by Sue and Kevin Jelley, who
opened it 18 months ago to great acclaim, and who are
determined to build on the reputation it has already earned in
that time.

The exterior is of red Locharbriggs sandstone - a material
that lends so much character to the town of Dumfries. The
interior is on two floors, with a brasserie on the ground floor
that provides dining for all tastes and appetites from 11am to
11pm seven days a week. This is the place to have a three
course meal, a delicious snack or a cup of excellent coffee and
one of the daily made cakes or pastries. Upstairs is a

sophisticated restaurant in
modern style offering the best in à la carte dining. Like the
brasserie, it is open all day, though bookings are recommended.
The menu encompasses tastes from all around the globe, with
only the finest and freshest of local produce being used
wherever possible. Everything - including the bread, desserts
and the ice cream - is made on the premises!

The reception area has a small shop where condiments,
sauces and the bread can be bought. So, if you're staying in
Dumfries or just passing through, why not treat yourself by
visiting the Marchills Restaurant?

23 THE LINEN ROOM

53 St Michael Street, Dumfries DG1 2QB
☎ 01387 255689
e-mail: enquiries@linenroom.com
⊕ www.linenroom.com

The only fine dining restaurant in Dumfries, **The Linen Room** was opened in November 2004 with the declared aim of becoming not only the finest place to eat in the region but to establish itself as one of the leading restaurants in Scotland. An ambitious target but one that chef/patron Russell Robertson has triumphantly achieved. Food reviewers have heaped praises on "the intelligent selection of local and seasonal ingredients", and "the air of unshakeable excellence with each and every aspect of the business fully under control in a way that delivers natural and unobtrusive perfection".

The main theme to the food is that is based on using as much local produce as possible and preparing it on the premises freshly every day. "In our opinion" says Russell, "the secret to creating a dining experience like the one at The Linen Room is purely down to the quality of produce you source. When the ingredients are so good, you only have to complement them as they serve themselves". The fish and shellfish have been landed at Kirkcudbright; Mr Ballard of

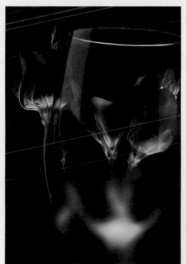

Castle Douglas provides the Texel lamb bred there, and Mr Little, also of Castle Douglas, supplies the local pork. "Mr Byrne's venison and game birds, and the nationally known Buccleuch beef are just some examples of what the region has to offer not only the rest of the country, but the world". And the culmination of little things like the home-made bread baked daily, the hand-made pasta and petit fours, and the extensive wine list ensure that your evening at The Linen Room is a truly memorable experience.

A typical menu might offer Diver-caught sea scallop with parsley two ways and yoghurt among the starters; Magret duck, sleek parsnip, apple and calvados as a main course, and wild strawberry, basil mutiny with szechuan pepper as dessert. No wonder the restaurant has won so many awards, amongst them two rosettes from the AA for 2006/2007 and the Scottish New Restaurant of the Year,

2005. The restaurant also features in the Good Food Guide and is a member of the Scottish Beef Club. As another reviewer reported in his review of The Linen Room "To be honest, everything was sublime. How refreshing it is to see people with real talent coming back to our town and providing that – dare I say it – "Missing Ingredient".

24 BARNSOUL FARM

Shawhead, Dumfries,
Dumfries & Galloway DG2 9SQ
☎ 01387 730249
e-mail: barnsouldg@aol.com
🌐 www.barnsoul.co.uk

Just off the A75 Dumfries to Stranraer road you will find **Barnsoul Farm**, a superb caravan and camping park that has everything for the tourist. Passing through, or looking for a base from which to explore beautiful Dumfries and Galloway, the place has everything.

It has 50 pitches for tents and caravans, as well as chalets and Wigwam mountain bothies/bunk houses. There is electricity and water throughout, plus a modern, comfortable shower unit with mirror, seat, basin etc, which is open 24 hours a day. There is also a kitchen with gas cooker, fridge, microwave, laundry facilities and constant hot water day and night.

The compact, comfortable and cosy mountain bothies have been described as 'camping without a tent'.

Constructed from timber, they have bunks for four to six people. They are heated, and come with basic furniture, cushions, mattresses, pillows, kettle, toaster and fridge. Each one has an exterior patio with bench table and stone barbecue. People using the bothies still have full use of the site kitchen and its appliances.

Barnsoul has nearly 300 acres of paddocks, woodland, and ponds, and is famous for its wildlife.

25 MORLICH HOUSE

Ballplay Road, Moffat,
Dumfries & Galloway DG10 9JU
☎ 01683 220589
e-mail: meg.Maxwell@virgin.net
🌐 www.morlichhouse.com

Moffat sits just off the M74 motorway linking England with Glasgow and the Highlands, and is the perfect stopping off place as you travel north or south. Only half a mile from the town's centre is the substantial, four star **Morlich House**, a superb B&B that offers three en suite rooms that are comfortable, spacious and well-appointed. It stands within half an acre of grounds and has superb views of the town and surrounding hills. Older children are very welcome at this no smoking establishment, and there is plenty of parking.

26 THE OLD STABLES

Main Street, Beattock,
Dumfries & Galloway DG10 9QX
☎ 01683 300134

Just a short drive from junction 15 on the M74 is the village of Beattock, where you will find **The Old Stables**, an inn with a fine reputation for its drink, food and accommodation. After a complete refurbishment, it reopened in December 2005 and is now a favourite with both visitors and locals alike. Food is available at lunchtimes and in the evening, and the one guest bedroom is fully en suite. This makes the ideal stopping off place as you travel along the M74.

27 BUSH OF EWES

**Ewes, Langholm,
Dumfries & Galloway DG13 0HN
☎ 01387 381241
e-mail: jandsfisher@aol.com**

Sitting in a quiet, rural spot in the Ewes Valley, the quaintly named **Bush of Ewes** is a picturesque stone-built farmhouse offering superb yet affordable B&B accommodation to people touring Dumfries and Galloway or the Scottish Borders. The farm itself extends to 2,000 acres of land, and supports Blackface sheep (Scotland's native breed) and Aberdeen Angus and Limousin suckler cows. It is owned and run by Jane and Stuart Fisher, who have farmed here for over eleven years, and who bring a wealth of knowledge not only to farming, but to providing genuine Scottish hospitality.

Guests are free to explore the farm and its surrounding countryside or, if they feel so inclined, they can just relax in the farmhouse's lounge and let the world go by! It sits close to the town of Langholm ('the Muckle Toon'), as well as Dumfries, Carlisle and Hawick, so makes the ideal base from which to explore the area.

There are three rooms on offer, all fully en suite and all immaculately decorated and furnished, with tea/coffee making facilities and central heating. As you

would expect on a working farm, the breakfasts are hearty and filling, with only the freshest of local produce being used. Of course, lighter options are available if required, and packed lunches can be prepared by prior arrangement. There is plenty of secure parking space, plus a garden where you can sit and enjoy the fresh air, the feeling of calm and the scenery. The prices are all inclusive.

A self-catering cottage is also available. At one time a traditional shepherd's cottage, it has now been refurbished to an extremely high standard. It sits just half a mile from the farmhouse, and is available all year round. It

sleeps four in absolute comfort in a double and a twin room, and well-behaved children and pets are more than welcome. It can be hired weekly, though short breaks are also available.

If you're looking for a holiday that is totally relaxing and far away from the bustle of modern life, then the Bush of Ewes - both the farmhouse B&B and the self-catering cottage - are for you. And if you're just passing through, then why not stop for the night at the farmhouse and experience genuine Scottish hospitality at its very best?

28 ARDBEG COTTAGE

19 Castle Street, Lochmaben,
Dumfriesshire DG11 1NY
☎ 01387 811855
STB grade; 3 star B&B

Ardbeg Cottage is a small B&B near the centre of Lochmaben, a friendly village just 4 miles west of the M74 at Lockerbie. It enjoys much repeat business. There are two letting bedrooms, one twin and one double, and a shared lounge/diner all on the ground floor, and one step up from the footpath, and one down to the paved garden at the back.

All beds have posturepaedic mattresses, or equivalent, for comfort. Each bedroom has TV, tea/coffee facility, hair dryer, washbasin, alarm clock, towelling dressing gown and slippers, power sockets, and an ensuite shower, shower caps and toilet. There is soap, face cloth and quality towelling for each guest.

The twin room has a low entry shower with folding seat and handrail, lever controls are fitted to the shower and washbasin taps. A toilet seat raiser and frame are available, if required. It is approved for guests with mobility problems. The double room has a 6 foot wide superking bed, which can be made up as two standard single beds if preferred.

Substantial breakfasts are available between 7.30am and 9am. Three course evening meals are available, given prior notice, and are served at 6.30pm. Rates on request. No smoking, no pets.

29 SAVINGS BANK MUSEUM

Ruthwell, Dumfries DG1 4NN
☎ 01387 870640
e-mail: info@savingsbankmuseum.co.uk
⊕ www.savingsbankmuseum.co.uk

Dr Henry Duncan was an accomplished artist and some of his work is displayed in the museum, but he is best remembered as the man who identified the first fossil footprints in Britain. Minister of the Ruthwell parish church for 50 years, he opened the world's first commercial savings bank in 1810. The museum

also houses a large collection of early home savings boxes, coins and bank notes from many parts of the world. Open 10am-1pm and 2pm-5pm, Tuesday to Saturday 1st October to Easter and every day Easter to 30th September. Admission free.

30 CARRUTHERSTOWN HOTEL

Carrutherstown,
Dumfries and Galloway DG1 4LD
☎ 01387 840268
Mobile: 07933 485883

Carrutherstown is a small hamlet just off the A75 eight miles east of Dumfries, and can be easily seen from the main road. The **Carrutherstown Hotel** is an attractive, whitewashed building that makes the ideal B&B stopping place as you travel east or west,

and is also the perfect base from which to explore beautiful Dumfriesshire, with all it has to offer. You can also stop here for lunch at weekends and evening meals throughout the week.

The hotel is owned by Angela and David Howe, and since they took over in June 2006 they have spent much time, thought and money refurbishing it so that it is now one of the best establishments in the area. The bar area is warm and cosy, and carries a great selection of beers, wines, spirits and soft drinks if you're driving. It has six fully en suite rooms on offer - four twin and two family - and they are furnished and decorated to a high

standard, offering maximum comfort at affordable prices.

Good food is served between 12 noon and 9pm on Saturday and Sunday, and between 6pm and 9pm on weekdays. You can choose from a printed menu or a specials board that takes advantage of local produce in season. The hotel has a good relationship with Buccleuch Foods, and the signature dish here is a juicy Buccleuch steak with all the trimmings.

So if you're looking for a place to stop while on the A75, choose the Carrutherstown hotel!

31 THE CRIFFEL INN

2 The Square, New Abbey,
Dumfries & Galloway DG2 8BX
☎ 01387 850305
e-mail: enquiries@criffelinn.com
⊕ www.criffelinn.com

Set in a picturesque village overlooked by Criffel Hill, the **Criffel Inn** is the premier guest house for mountain bikers in Scotland. The country is famous for its mountain biking facilities, and Dumfries and Galloway is at the heart of the sport. The inn boasts five fully en suite guest rooms, and each one

has a TV and tea/coffee making facilities. Of course, if you're a walker, angler or sail enthusiast, you'll find the inn is just as handy for your particular activity as well. Plus it makes the ideal base from which to explore the area by car.

It is the brainchild of Clive Forth, extreme-endurance.com Rider/Skills Tutor & Rider Guide, and is housed in an old coaching inn dating from the 18th century. It has a restaurant plus a cosy bar and snug, and is the 'local' for the village. It's

interior is inviting and warm, and here you can relax over a drink or two and chat to the local people.

The restaurant serves excellent, home-cooked food, all made from fresh, local produce wherever possible to give you that authentic and honest Dumfries and Galloway taste. You can choose from a menu or a daily special board.

There are many excellent mountain biking trails in the area, varying in length, from Mabie Forest just 3 miles away to Glentress/Innerleithen 69 miles away.

32 THE GORDON HOUSE HOTEL

116 High Street, Kirkcudbright,
Dumfries & Galloway DG6 4JQ
☎ 01557 330670
e-mail: mail@gordon-house-hotel.co.uk
🌐 www.gordon-house-hotel.co.uk

Kirkcudbright is famous for its artists and writers, such as A.E Hornel and Dorothy L. Sayers. It is also famous for one of the best hotels in Dumfries and Galloway- **The Gordon House Hotel**, right on the town's High Street. It dates from 1455, and the owners, Helen and Robin Murray, are proud of its fine reputation, both among locals and tourists, for its accommodation, its fine food and its drink.

It offers eight spacious, well furnished rooms to discerning guests making this the ideal base from which to explore Dumfries and Galloway, one of Scotland's most scenic and historic areas. The food here is excellent, and you can eat in the Pegasus Restaurant or comfortable lounge bar, with its open fire and welcoming atmosphere. Everything is home-cooked from fresh local produce wherever possible, and the meals represent amazing value for money.

The establishment is the 'local' for many of this captivating town's residents, and in its friendly public bar you can enjoy a relaxing drink while joining in the conversations. There is a fine selection of beers, wines and spirits, including a large selection of malt whiskies.

Dumfries and Galloway is one of Scotland's hidden gems - an area that is rich in scenery, history and heritage. While you're there, stay at the Godron House Hotel - you won't be disappointed!

34 KENMURE ARMS HOTEL

High Street, New Galloway,
Dumfries and Galloway DG7 3RL
☎ 01644 420240

Once an old coaching inn dating to 1741, the Kenmure Arms Hotel is now one of the best hotels in the area, offering the modern concepts of value for money, high standards of service and a warm, friendly welcome.

The food is outstanding, as is the fine selection of drinks in the bar. Plus there are nine comfortable, beautifully furnished guest rooms, seven of which are fully en suite. People who visit the Kenmure come back again and again, and if you visit, you will too!

33 THE CASTLE RESTAURANT ¶

Castle Street, Kirkcudbright,
Dumfries & Galloway DG6 4JA
☎ 01557 330569
e-mail: info@thecastlerestaurant.net
⊕ www.thecastlerestaurant.net

The Castle Restaurant, within an elegant Regency building on Kirkcudbright's Castle Street, is a superb establishment that is appreciated far beyond the town, as it attracts patrons from all over. It is owned and managed by the husband and wife team of Fiona and Paul Wilkinson, a Yorkshire couple who so fell in love with Dumfries and Galloway that they moved here to live and work.

This is the perfect place to have a lunch, a light snack or dinner while exploring an area that is filled with history, heritage and things to do. The exterior, with its small-paned window and 'olde worlde' feel, seems to invite you in. Once inside you will be entranced with the décor, which is smart yet welcoming and warm yet spacious. The crisp linen on the tables, the polished wood, the gleaming cutlery and the tartan carpeting show that this is a place where you can eat with confidence.

Paul is the chef and he uses imagination and flair when preparing his many dishes. All the produce used in the kitchen is local and in season wherever possible, so you know you are getting the very best at value for money prices. The lunch menu includes such things as prawn salad, steak and onion baguettes, soup of the day with warm bread and a selection of ice creams and home made desserts.

The dinner menu contains such starters as salmon mousse with oatcakes and rocket salad, local roast smoked salmon with lemon and honey, roast duck breast with sesame seed and balsamic dressing . The main dishes are sure to set your mouth watering as well. What about fillet of beef with a wild mushroom duxcelle? Or sea bass with a roast pepper and spinach sauce? Then there's monkfish with basil and olives and a pepper dressing, bacon wrapped breast of chicken filled with roasted vegetables and parmesan roulade with roast vegetables. All are beautifully cooked and presented, and each one represents amazing value for money.

Across from the restaurant are the romantic ruins of MacLellan's Castle, once home to Sir Thomas MacLellan of Bombie, provost of Kirkcudbright, local landowner and a friend of the king. Plus the town is famous as being Scotland's 'artists' town', and was once home to AE Hornel the famous painter. Dorothy L. Sayers was a frequent visitor, and for a short while Lawrence of Arabia lived here as well. It's a fascinating place, and when you are visiting, The Castle Restaurant is the place to eat!

35   DOUGLAS ARMS HOTEL

206 King Street, Castle Douglas,
Dumfries & Galloway DG7 1DB
☎ 01556 502231
e-mail: enquiries@douglasarmshotel.com
⊕ www.douglasarmshotel.com

Owned and managed since February 2006 by Marie and Robert McLaren, the **Douglas Arms Hotel** is situated right in the heart of Castle Douglas, Scotland's 'food town'. It is a picturesque, whitewashed building dating from 1779, and was once a coaching inn on the route between

Dumfries and Stranraer. They both have plenty of experience in the trade and are now building on the hotel's already solid reputation as a place for comfortable accommodation, good food and great drink.

It boasts many original features and has 23 fully en suite guest rooms, each one individually decorated and furnished to a very high standard. Every room is equipped with colour TV, radio, trouser press, tea and coffee making facilities, direct dial telephones and internet access, as well as complimentary toiletries. In addition, an upgrade ensures there are slippers and bathrobes. There is even a honeymoon suite with a luxurious four poster bed. This makes the hotel one of the finest bases from which to explore beautiful Dumfries and Galloway, surely one of the grandest and most scenic areas in Scotland, every bit as good as the Highlands.

The hotel is renowned for its fine dining, and has two dedicated restaurants - the Wallace and the Cameron. The Wallace has a play area for kids so that parents can eat in peace, while the Cameron offers the finest of à la carte dining, featuring fresh, local produce in season, in a relaxed intimate atmosphere. Or why not enjoy an informal snack or bar meal in the St Andrew's Lounge Bar?

The bar has an excellent range of drinks on offer, including some exceptionally fine malts for you to savour. There is also real ale from Castle Douglas' own brewery - the Sulwith Brewery.

There are a range of rooms available for functions large and small, with wedding receptions and formal celebrations being a speciality. Parking is available in the hotel courtyard to the rear, which is locked at night to provide a secure area.

This area of Dumfries and Galloway has many things to see and do. It is especially rich in history and heritage with many old castles, ruined abbeys, small villages and meandering country lanes. You can also take part in bird-watching, angling, walking, fishing, sailing, mountain biking and a whole host of activities that make the Douglas Arms Hotel the perfect base for a great holiday!

36 THE MAD HATTER

53 King Street, Castle Douglas,
Dumfries & Galloway DG7 1AC
☎ 01556 502712

Castle Douglas is Scotland's food town, with many small outlets selling fresh, local produce. In the main street you will find **The Mad Hatter**, the place to visit for a delightful lunch or snack made from this produce. It will shortly be opening in the evening, so you'll be able to have dinner here as well!

It is owned and run by Sue and David Lewis, who have been here for two years. David is the cook, and Sue looks after the 'front of house', offering you a warm welcome. It has an attractive frontage on the town's main street, and it is cosy and narrow, while still giving a feeling of spaciousness. Soon it will be split into a daytime café and an evening restaurant with a totally different décor, but each with the same high standards of cuisine, attention to detail and excellent value for money.

All the food is prepared on the premises and represents good, honest Scottish fayre, some with a Continental hint to make it that little bit different. Try the filled paninis, the baked potatoes or the all day breakfast! This is a café/restaurant with a difference - it places great emphasis on the quality of the ingredients and the way they are prepared and cooked. Plus Sue and David are determined to keep prices as low as possible so that you get a great eating experience at prices you can afford!

38 CLONYARD HOUSE HOTEL

Colvend, Near Dalbeattie,
Dumfries & Galloway DG5 4QW
☎ 01556 630372
e-mail: info.clonyard@virgin.net
⊕ www.clonyardhotel.co.uk

The **Clonyard House Hotel** sits in a secluded position on the beautiful Solway coast, within seven acres of mature gardens and woodland, between Rockcliffe and Kippford. It boasts 15 fully en suite rooms (12 on the ground floor) that are individually furnished and

decorated (some with antiques), each one having a colour TV, direct-dial telephone and tea/coffee making facilities. One room has been specially adapted for those with limited mobility.

The hotel is renowned for its cuisine, and you can either eat à la carte in the spacious restaurant or have a delicious bar meal in the bar area. Food is served between 12 noon and 2pm and 5.30pm and 9pm. The produce is sourced locally wherever possible, making it fresh and full of flavour. The bar serves a wide range of drinks and is a favourite with both locals and visitors alike.

It is open Monday to Friday from 11am to 11pm, and midnight on Friday and Saturday.

The Clonyard is a family-run establishment that always offers great value for money, and has been in the ownership of the Thompson family for over 30 years. There is ample, floodlit parking and a safe play area for children. Dogs are welcome, but must not enter the restaurant area. All major credit cards with the exception of Diners are accepted. The hotel is ideally based for golf, sailing, walking, bird watching, mountain biking and angling.

37 THE SHIP INN

**High Street, Dalbeattie,
Dumfries and Galloway DG5 4DS
☎ 01556 610419**

The Ship Inn is one of the best inns in the small, attractive town of Dalbeattie, in southwest Scotland. It is the ideal place to stop for a quiet drink and a chat to the locals as you explore Dumfries and Galloway - an area that has often been called 'Scotland's hidden gem'. There is a full verandah along the front of the inn - just right for those long summer evenings!

39 BURNSIDE HOUSE

**23 Main Street, Auchencairn,
Dumfries & Galloway DG7 1QU
☎ 01556 640283
e-mail: burnsidehousebb@yahoo.co.uk**

For the very best in B&B accommodation in Dumfries and Galloway, you can't better **Burnside House**, in the quiet little village of Auchencairn, once a centre for smuggling. It offers two extremely comfortable rooms to discerning guests, one with a single and a double bed and one with a double bed and two singles, making it ideal for families. Each one has a TV, DVD player and tea/coffee making facilities. The breakfasts here are hearty and filling, with lighter options if required. Special diets are catered for by prior arrangement.

40 GEORGE METRO HOTEL

**49 George Street, Stranraer,
Dumfries and Galloway DG9 7RJ
☎ 01776 702487
e-mail: mail@georgemetrohotel.co.uk
🌐 www.georgemetrohotel.co.uk**

Situated in the centre of Stranraer, the superb **George Metro Hotel** is a new concept - it gives customers what they want at prices they can afford without compromising quality or high standards of service. There are fourteen luxury rooms on offer, with every room being, in effect, a suite of bedroom, bathroom and lounge.

The hotel also houses a fine, independent restaurant, and you have the choice of eating there or in one of the many other restaurants within Stranraer itself.

41 TORWOOD COUNTRYSIDE

**nr Glenluce, Newton Stewart,
Dumfries and Galloway DG8 0PB
☎ 01581 300469
e-mail: torwoodglenluce@aol.com
🌐 www.torwoodhotel-and-logcabins.com**

Set in 30 acres of beautiful countryside, **Torwood Countryside** will soon be one of Scotland's premier luxury leisure developments. 40 luxurious plots for log cabins are on offer here, all at keen prices, to people who want a superb holiday home-away-from-home. Already people are buying, and if you're quick, you too can take advantage of a development that offers everything. The cabins, in seven configurations, are imported from Finland, and are available as freehold, leasehold or holiday let. This is an opportunity you can't afford to miss!

43 CORSEWALL LIGHTHOUSE HOTEL

Nr Kirkcolm, Stranraer,
Dumfries and Galloway DG9 0QG
☎ 01776 853220
🌐 www.lighthousehotel.co.uk

A hotel within old lighthouse buildings? Correct! That's what makes the four-star **Corsewall Lighthouse Hotel** unique. Everyone who visits this famous place, whether to sample its award winning food or to take advantage of its luxury accommodation, are captivated and entranced by it. And they are amazed to see that the light still beams out across the waters, guiding ships and ferries into the safety of Loch Ryan.

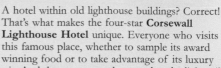

It sits within 20 acres of grounds right at the northern point of the Mull of Galloway, that hammer-shaped peninsula sticking out from Scotland's southwest coast, and has truly stunning views out over the North Channel towards Northern Ireland, Ailsa Craig and Kintyre. You can also watch the Stranraer Ferry ply backwards and forwards between Stranraer and Northern Ireland.

The hotel prides itself on being a friendly, welcoming place, where you can relax completely away from the stresses of modern life. It has six en suite rooms on offer, and by the year 2007 it will also have five cottage suites. Each one is luxuriously appointed and individually named, decorated and furnished. The

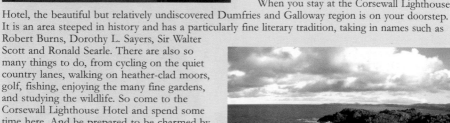

spectacular Lighthouse Suite, only 30 seconds from the main building, has two bedrooms, as well as a sea-facing conservatory with superb views and all the other usual offices. The North Channel Suite is particularly suited to business hospitality and meetings, and the Galloway Room is disabled friendly.

The food here is outstanding. The hotel has won a coveted AA Red Rosette, and is recommended by Taste of Scotland. Imaginative use is made of fresh, locally sourced produce, and the menus could include such dishes as supreme of wood pigeon, roasted field mushrooms, premier Scotch beef fillet, roast loin of pork or sea bass fillet.

When you stay at the Corsewall Lighthouse Hotel, the beautiful but relatively undiscovered Dumfries and Galloway region is on your doorstep. It is an area steeped in history and has a particularly fine literary tradition, taking in names such as Robert Burns, Dorothy L. Sayers, Sir Walter Scott and Ronald Searle. There are also so many things to do, from cycling on the quiet country lanes, walking on heather-clad moors, golf, fishing, enjoying the many fine gardens, and studying the wildlife. So come to the Corsewall Lighthouse Hotel and spend some time here. And be prepared to be charmed by the informal ambience and exceedingly high standards!

42 HOUSE O' HILL HOTEL

Bargrennan, nr Newton Stewart,
Dumfries and Galloway DG8 6RN
☎ 01671 840243
e-mail: r_davey@bt.connection.com
🌐 www.houseohill.co.uk

Bargrennan is an unspoilt village set in the heart of the Galloway countryside and it is here you will find the **House o' Hill Hotel,** a superb, cosy inn that offers good food, great drink and two en suite guest rooms for discerning travellers.

There is also a self-catering cottage nextdoor to the inn that is ideal for those wanting a break away from the bustle of modern life. The village sits close to The Merrick, southern Scotland's highest hill, and all around is superb walking country, as well as facilities for golf, fishing, sailing, bird watching, cycling, and so on.

44 COUNTY HOTEL

Stoneykirk, nr Stranraer,
Dumfries and Galloway DG9 9DH
☎ 01776 830431
🌐 www.thecountyhotelstoneykirk.co

The **County Hotel** sits in Stoneykirk, a delightful village a few miles south of Stranraer. It is a free house and offers great food and drink and superb accommodation, which consists of eight en suite rooms and one with private facilities. It is a firm favourite with locals and visitors alike, and anyone visiting this corner of Scotland should make their way to Stoneykirk and the County Hotel!

45 LOGAN FISH POND

Port Logan, Stranraer
☎ 01776 860300
🌐 www.loganfishpond.co.uk

The first time visitor to **Logan Fish Pond** is often amazed and surprised by what they see. Not until they enter through the original Fish Keepers Cottage and have their first glimpse of the pond below do they have any idea of what this unique and historic attraction holds.

In 1788 Andrew McDouall Laird of Logan decided to create a Fish Larder for storing live sea fish by adapting a natural rock formation in the form of a blow hole, formed during the last ice-age. The work took 12 years and was finished in 1800. Many visitors return year after year and indeed some have been doing so for fifty or sixty years, feeding the fish today as they remember doing so as children.

In the springtime, the area around the Pond is a carpet of daffodils, primroses and bluebells and later in the year these are replaced with an abundance of wild flowers, including thrift and sea campion.

On the rocks next to the Fish Pond is a restored Victorian Bathing Hut which adjoins a Bathing Pool. Recent additions to the original pond include Touch Pools, Cave Aquarium and Gift Shop. Open 1st February to 30th September 10am to 5pm and 1st October to early November 10am to 4pm. Some disabled access.

46 THE WELLTREES INN

9 Welltrees Street, Maybole,
Ayrshire KA19 7AW
☎ 01655 883317
Mobile: 07747 895863
e-mail: gwelltreeinn@hotmail.co.uk

The **Welltrees Inn** is situated just off the main A77 in the charming old town of Maybole, at one time the capital of that ancient division of Ayrshire called Carrick. With its whitewashed walls, small-paned windows and dark red shutters, it is a picturesque hostelry, dating from the early part of the 19th century.

Since Bill Torbett took it over more than three years ago, it has become one of the most popular inns in the town, and is the 'local' for many of its inhabitants. The interior is equally as appealing with bare stone walls, comfortable furniture and warm, friendly atmosphere. It is open seven days a week and food is served every day up until 9pm. This is the place to enjoy a relaxing drink in the evening or at lunchtime while chatting to the friendly locals, or enjoying one of the superb meals for which the establishment is justly famous. The bar is adorned with old photographs and prints of the town, and has a wide range of beers, ales, lager, wines, spirits and soft drinks. The lounge has that 'olde worlde' feel about it, with its

comfortable seating and a collection of old jugs adorning its walls and beams. Some of the whisky is bottled especially for the Welltrees, and it boasts a good range of single malts. Every month it features one malt in particular as the 'Malt of the Month'.

The food at the Welltrees Inn is superb and people travel from near and far to sample its outstanding dishes. Dining takes place in the conservatory, which has views out over the town to the Galloway hills and is the perfect place for a dinner or romantic meal. The menu contains many fine dishes, and only fresh local produce is used in the kitchen wherever possible.

Children are very welcome at the Welltrees Inn and, in the summer months, there is nothing finer than sitting in the well appointed beer garden and enjoying a drink while the kids take full advantage of the play area. This area, known as the 'hidden gem' even boasts an aviary, and perhaps you'd like to take your children there to admire the many birds in the collection. The garden is floodlit in the evening, and there is no finer place for enjoying a bottle of wine, sourced from Maybole's own famous wine merchants. So why not make The Welltrees Inn your first stop when you come to Carrick, the most beautiful part of Ayrshire?

47 MAYBOLE CASTLE

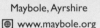

Maybole, Ayrshire

🌐 www.maybole.org

Maybole Castle is the oldest inhabited house in the town having been built about the middle of the sixteenth century (believed to be around 1560). It was the town house of the Earls of Cassillis who spent most of the winter months in Maybole, and was the largest and finest of the twenty-eight lairds' houses written about by Abercrummie in 1696. It was built in the style of a typical Scottish castle, with square tower and round turrets, and strong enough to protect its occupants from unfriendly neighbours, of whom there were many at that time. The main hall was above vaulted cellars which still remain and above the hall were the sleeping apartments. The retainers' quarters were on the other side of a gateway which gave entrance into the castle yard, built round the well, locally known as "The Pump".

The tower is capped by a lovely little oriel window with heads carved round it which local people wrongly believe represent the heads of Johnnie Faa and his gypsies. The corbels to the roof of the little room at the top of the tower (known as the Countess's Room) are carved with male and female heads and symbols of fertility. The walls are extremely thick (in some places about seven feet) and it must have been a safe retreat in troublesome times when the Earls lived in it, with their own men around them in the small township clustered on the hillside below it.

It was from Maybole Castle that the Earl of Cassillis and his men sallied forth to the fight at Ladycross in December 1601, when young Bargany was killed in the bitter feud between the Cassillis and Bargany families. Locally there is an old tale of the Countess of Cassillis being imprisoned at the top of the tower, after she had allegedly eloped with Johnnie Faa, King of the Gypsies, but while the story is a delightful one, facts disprove it.

As years passed the Earls spent less of their time in Maybole, and gradually the old Castle fell into disrepair and was practically abandoned except for a few old retainers who lived in outbuildings. In 1805 the Earl of Cassillis agreed with the town council that the part sited where the Post Office now stands could be demolished to allow a road to be formed from the foot of the High Street to Duncanland Toll at the bottom of Redbrae. When the old buildings were removed the Earl decided to repair the Castle and in 1812 reroofed it and built some additions. The gardens and park had walls erected round them and from 1812 the Castle has remained as it is now, apart from repairs to the roof following a fire in 1919.

The Historical Society has been very active in promoting Maybole Castle since May-Tag (founded by the Community Council in 1986 as a training company to promote local unemployment) moved out and has said, "The Castle goes from strength to strength and we have a very good relationship with the factor and through him the Estate and Trustee. We are putting together proposals and plans for opening the castle regularly to the public; improving and expanding the display material in the castle; and the future of the castle as a heritage centre".

48 BUCHANAN'S VILLAGE SHOP

72 Main Street, Ballantrae,
Ayrshire KA66 0NB
☎ 01465 831500

When travelling north or south along the beautiful Ayrshire coast, you must stop at **Buchanan's Village Shop** in Ballantrae. If you are touring, or are enjoying a caravanning or self-catering holiday in South Ayrshire, this is the place to stock up on all your essentials. It is so much more than a typical village shop and, after a major refurbishment, was reopened in October 2006. It not only carries all the usual convenience items expected of a shop of this quality, such as newspapers and tinned goods, but a wide range of produce that is sourced locally. Vegetables, cuts of meat, fish and dairy products are stocked, and where possible all come from local farmers, fishermen and growers. In addition you can also purchase superb locally made ice cream, as well as pies and cold meats. It also stocks a wide range of craft and gift items, many of which again are made locally.

This is a village shop as it used to be, with friendly service and realistic prices. It is also licensed, so you can stock up on beers, wines and spirits .Why not call in on your way past for excellent coffees, teas and snacks? It has a small eating area that serves traditional farmhouse baking such as pies, cakes and desserts, and filling bowls of home made soup. You can choose from a printed menu, and takeaways are available. Children are most welcome at this friendly shop, so why not call in? You won't be disappointed!

49 KINGS ARMS HOTEL

Ballantrae, Ayrshire KA26 0NB
☎ 01465 831202
⊕ www.kingsarmsballantrae.com

Situated within the delightful old fishing village of Ballantrae on the Ayrshire coast, the **Kings Arms Hotel** is part of the village's history. It is over 250 years old and in all that time has been offering superb hospitality to locals and visitors alike. It boasts six attractive and comfortable guest rooms, many with en suite facilities, as well as great food and drink (including a superb range of malt whiskies).

50 WILDINGS HOTEL & RESTAURANT

Harbour Road, Maidens KA26 9NR
☎ 01655 331401
e-mail: bookings@wildingsrestaurant.co.uk
⊕ www.wildingsrestaurant.co.uk

Situated in the former fishing village of Maidens, on the A719 between Ayr and Stranraer, **Wildings Hotel and Restaurant** is the place to stay and eat in this part of Ayrshire. It has ten luxury, en suite rooms on

offer plus a suite with two bedrooms, lounge and bathroom. The food served in the restaurant is famed throughout the area - so much so that you are well advised to book in summer and at weekends throughout the year. Children are most welcome, and all credit cards are accepted with the exception of American Express and Diners.

51 THE TOWN HOTEL ⊨ ⫘

9/11 Barns Street, Ayr, Ayrshire KA7 1XB
☎ 01292 267595

Ayr is an old, historic, royal burgh and seaside resort on the Firth of Clyde. Situated close to the centre of the burgh is **The Town Hotel**, housed in an elegant Georgian town house dating back 200 years. It has been owned and managed personally for the last nine years by Lin and Arthur Warwick who have created an establishment that is one of the finest and friendliest in Ayrshire. The cosy yet spacious bar and lounge offers a wide range of beers, wines, spirits and, should you be driving, soft drinks. The most popular ales among the regulars are McEwan's 60 shilling and Tennent's Lager. Why not drop in and chat to the locals while enjoying a drink or two? Or you could sample one of The Town Hotel's excellent bar meals, which are served daily from 12 noon to 3pm. The cuisine is traditional Scottish, with only the finest and freshest of local Ayrshire produce being used wherever possible.

The hotel boasts 18 superbly furnished en suite guest rooms in a mixture of sizes from double to single. Nine rooms are on the ground floor, which makes them ideal for the disabled. The B&B tariff includes a hearty cooked Scottish breakfast or something lighter if required. Ayrshire is full of history, and The Town Hotel makes the ideal base from which to explore. Stately Culzean Castle, perched on a cliff top above the Firth of Clyde, is close by, as is Alloway, birthplace of Robert Burns and the golf courses at Troon and Turnberry. Lin and Arthur will be happy to arrange a round of golf for you, and provide transport to and from their local course.

52 FOUTERS ⫘

2a Academy Street, Ayr,
Ayrshire KA7 1HS
☎ 01292 261391
e-mail: chef@fouters.co.uk
⊕ www.fouters.co.uk

Fouters is undoubtedly one of the finest restaurants in Scotland, and is famed throughout the country for its commitment to fine cuisine. It is to be found in the 18th century basement of a former bank, and has been serving superb food since 1973. People travel miles to dine here, and for good reason. The cuisine is Scottish with French influences, and the chef, who has 30 year's experience, believes in letting the flavours of the food speak for themselves. Booking is advisable at all times, and all major credit cards are taken.

53 COZY NOOK CAFÉ AND RESTAURANT ⫘

88 Main Street, Ayr, Ayrshire KA8 8EF
☎ 01292 292935 Fax: 01292 292935
e-mail: cosynookcafe@btconnect.com

The **Cozy Nook Café and Restaurant** serves some of the best food in the attractive holiday resort of Ayr. It is clean, spacious and bright, and uses "Fair Trade" produce wherever possible. Here you will find "good food cooked fresh", with an interesting menu selection, including vegetarian and gluten free choices. When you're in Ayr, make this your first stop. You won't be disappointed!

54 THE CAFÉ PRESTWICK

10/12 The Cross, Prestwick,
Ayrshire KA9 1AJ
☎ 01292 470597

You just can't beat **The Prestwick Café** for good food at reasonable prices. It is open seven days a week for wonderful, home-cooked dishes that are almost always prepared from fresh local produce. This is food at its very best, and there is everything on the menu from all day breakfasts to pasta, chicken supreme,

filled rolls, steak pie and baked potatoes. The café opens from 8am to 5pm (8pm on Thursday and Friday). So for the very best in teas, coffees, snacks and full meals, head for The Prestwick Café!

55 THE POSTAGE STAMP

66 Portland Street, Troon,
Ayrshire KA10 6QU
☎ 01292 314471

Named after the eighth hole on the world famous Royal Troon Golf Course, the **Postage Stamp** is a superb little pub, close to the town centre and on the road to the ferry terminal, that is justly renowned for its hospitality and warm welcome. The premises date from the 1880s and are a very popular 'watering hole' for the people of the town and for visiting golfers.

In fact, the walls are adorned with golfing memorabilia. Pamela Wilcock took over in April 2006 and is now 'mine host'. She is determined to build on the pub's solid reputation and create a friendly, welcoming place where you can have a relaxing drink or a superb meal. The bar sells a wide range of popular drinks and good, honest pub food is served from 12

noon until 6pm seven days a week. You can choose from a printed menu or a specials board. On Wednesday, which always features Thai food, you choose from the menu only. Children are very welcome if eating, and payment is by cash or cheque only. On the second Sunday of each month there is an 'open mike' night from 7.30pm, and on Tuesday evenings there is a quiz night, to which everyone is invited. The patio to the rear is a favourite place to eat or drink during the summer months.

56 POOSIE NANSIE'S INN

21 Loudoun Street, Mauchline,
Ayrshire KA5 5BA
☎ 01290 550316
e-mail: marion.young5@btinternet.com

The small, attractive village of Mauchline is forever associated with Scotland's national poet, Robert Burns. In fact, part of Burns's poem *The Jolly Beggars* was written in **Poosie Nansie's Inn**, which was one of the poet's favourite watering holes. It is still going strong to this day, and offers fine food and drink to people who seek out one of the most historic inns in Scotland. The building dates from 1700, and one of the rooms has been turned into a shrine to the poet, with the actual chair he used while composing the poem on display.

The inn is open from 11am to 12 midnight on Monday. Tuesday and Wednesday, 11am to 1am on Thursday, Friday and Saturday and 11am to 12.20am on Sunday. The bar is cosy and attractive, with many period features to admire, and sells a wide range of beers, wine, spirits and soft drinks. Food is served from 12 noon to 3pm from Monday to Thursday, and on Friday, Saturday and Sunday from 12 noon to 9pm. During the winter months, no food is served on Tuesday and Wednesday, and the times for Saturday and Sunday are 12 noon to 8pm.

Fresh local produce is used wherever possible in the kitchen, and three course special dinners are available every day. You choose from a printed menu, and are well advised to book on Saturday and Sunday. Children are most welcome, and payment is by cash or cheque only. There is occasional live entertainment and karaoke every Thursday evening.

57 THE MERCAT HOTEL

40 The Square, Cumnock,
Ayrshire KA18 1BL
☎ 01290 424618

The **Mercat Hotel** is a picturesque old inn dating from the early 1800s. It sits right in the heart of the old town of Cumnock, opposite the parish church and is handy as a place for a quiet drink or an overnight stop as you head north or south along the A76, which now bypasses the town. Mine hosts in this free house are Sadie and Ian, who have been here a year and are determined to improve the premises even further. Soon, for instance, they will be introducing good, home cooked food through the day and in the evenings.

At present B&B is offered to discerning guests all year round. The rooms are homely, comfortable and newly decorated. All are upstairs and there is a mix of various sizes to suit everyone. The well-stocked bar has drinks to

suit most tastes including beers, wines, spirits and, should you be driving, soft drinks. The atmosphere within the bar is friendly and inviting, as this is one of the town's favourite 'locals', with good use being made of polished wood and comfortable seating. There is also plenty of off-road parking. The bar areas are disabled friendly, though people should phone beforehand about the guest rooms, which are upstairs.

58 COACH HOUSE INN

1 Furnace Road, Muirkirk,
Ayrshire KA18 3RE
☎ 01290 661257

Since taking over in July 2006, Audrey and Frank Bone have made the **Coach House Inn** one of the best establishments of its kind in Ayrshire. It sits in the old mining village of Muirkirk, on the A70 between Ayr and the M74 motorway

It was once the stables for a coaching inn that stood just across the road, and dates from the late 18th century. It is an impressive, well-proportioned building, and its interior has been modernised to a very high standard, though some period features have been retained. The bar is especially attractive with its low beams, dark polished wood and well-stocked bar. There is no finer place to stop and enjoy a quiet relaxing drink as you listen to the 'patter' of the regulars. The inn is open every day, all day, and has a great selection of ales, lagers, spirits, wines and soft drinks

Good food is served in the newly refurbished restaurant, which is spacious and inviting. It has been furnished and decorated to an exceptional standard, and is a popular eating place for people living in the area. The cuisine is traditional Scottish, with all the produce used in the kitchen being sourced locally wherever possible, ensuring freshness and full flavour. This ensures that you have a dining experience that you will long remember. The lunch menu contains such favourites as home made steak pie, scampi, home made lasagne and chicken with white sauce, while the evening menu includes breast of duck on a bed of farmhouse cabbage and mushroom sauce, tornados Rossini served on an Italian crouton and pate, and cajun chicken with a creamy sauce and wild rice. A kid's menu is also available and contains such tried and tested favourites as burger and chips and fish fingers and chips. No food is served on Tuesday or Wednesday, and you are advised to book a table at weekends.

The Coach House Inn boasts two upstairs guest rooms which, by 2007, should be fully en suite. They are comfortable, clean and well furnished, and represent amazing value for money. The tariff includes a full Scottish breakfast or a lighter option if you prefer. Children are very welcome, and all major credit cards are taken in payment, as well as cheques. Friday night is karaoke night, so come along and listen to the music! There are no problems for the disabled downstairs, but you should phone about the accommodation.

Craigie, By Kilmarnock, Ayrshire KA1 5LY
☎ 01563 860286
🌐 www.craigieinn.com

The **Craigie Inn** is well off the beaten track, and sits in the small village of Craigie, set among the low, green hills south of Kilmarnock. You can reach it by leaving the A77 at Bogend Toll and heading east along the B730 before taking the third minor road north. The village consists of a few old cottages and an ancient church, but it is well worth seeking out for the inn alone, as it is one of the best-known hostelries in Ayrshire, and has a fine reputation. People come from miles around to seek out its friendly atmosphere, its real ales and its superb food.

The interior is as inviting as the outside of the whitewashed building, with a cosy, quaint atmosphere, carpeted floors, comfortable seating and warm, polished wood. The inn is open at lunchtime and in the evenings from Monday to Saturday, and all day Sunday. It's the kind of place where people come to relax over a drink, or sit down to a meal that they will long remember. In fact, the inn is justly proud of its food, which is served seven days a week. There is a downstairs dining area and an upstairs restaurant, which can also be used for private functions. The produce used in the

kitchen is sourced locally wherever possible, ensuring freshness and full flavour. This is fresh food, not fast food, and everything is cooked beautifully to order. You can choose from a printed menu or a specials board that takes advantage of produce that is in season.

Dishes on the menu might include traditional haggis, neeps and tatties with Drambuie sauce, breast of chicken stuffed with brie, wild mushroom and courgette Stroganoff, juicy steaks with all the trimmings, Scottish salmon stuffed with prawns and ginger farce, and beef olives with spring onion mash. The specials board

usually features fish caught in the Firth of Clyde or game sourced from the local Ayrshire countryside. Booking is advised at weekends.

The bar carries a fine selection of beers, wine, spirits and soft drinks, and also features two rotating real ales. Occasional Scottish banquets are held (ring for details), and once a month there is a folk night. For excellent local accommodation, why not stay at the Craigie Inn's sister establishment, the Fenwick Hotel to the north of Kilmarnock?

61 DALGARVEN MILL

Dalgarven, Kilwinning KA13 6PL
☎ 01294 552448
⊕ www.dalgarvenmill.org.uk

There has been a mill on the site since the 14th century, set up by the monks of Kilwinning Abbey. The present mill was erected in 1640 and rebuilt in 1880 after being damaged by fire. The Garnock waters power a 6 metre diameter breast shot wheel that drives the French millstones through cast iron gearing. Traditional methods of producing flour can be traced and the wheel turns when possible.

The 3 storey grain store has been converted to house an extensive collection of Ayrshire farming and domestic memorabilia and there is an exhibition drawn from a collection of over 6000 costumes and accessories ranging from 1775 to 1980. The top floor is a re-creation of the mill owners house as it would have been in the 1880s. There are delightful walks by the river, a coffee shop in a farmhouse kitchen setting and an antique shop to complete your visit.

59 MINISHANT INN

28 Main Road, Minishant,
Ayrshire KA19 8EU
☎ 01292 442483

Situated south of Ayr on the A77, the **Minishant Inn** is a traditional village pub that offers the very best in Scottish food and drink.

62 THE TALL SHIP AT GLASGOW HARBOUR

100 Stobcross Road, Glasgow G3 8QQ
☎ 0141 222 2513
e-mail: info@thetallship.com
⊕ www.thetallship.com

Sail through 100 years of maritime history at the Tall Ship at Glasgow Harbour. Follow the remarkable restoration of the Glenlee from an abandoned hulk in Seville harbour to her fully rigged splendour today and learn about the living conditions aboard a deep sea trading ship.

Explore the cargo hold where you will see what goods she carried, the deck house where the crew lived, the poop deck and the galley. Also in the harbour is the Pier 17 restaurant, a gift shop and various exhibitions and events. Phone for details.

63 GREYSTONELEA LODGE

Greystonelea, Gartocharn, Loch Lomond,
Dunbartonshire G83 8SD
☎ 01389 830419
e-mail: gerard.wood2@btinternet.com

Greystonelea Lodge is not just a charming self-catering cottage but also an eco-friendly showhouse for renewable energy. Built in the autumn of 2005, the house occupies a superb location, set in more than 120 acres of woodland and open countryside in a small village close to Loch Lomond and within the Loch Lomond and Trossachs National Park. So good are its facilities it has been awarded 4 stars from Visit Scotland.

Everything in the cottage is eco-friendly and of the very best quality. Solar panels heat the water and power the lighting, and there is a beautiful remote-control operated modern wood-burner in the lounge which is capable of heating the whole building with an A-rated oil-fired central heating system as back-up. Light switches can be adjusted

from low to high levels and the fully fitted kitchen is equipped with many labour-saving, state of the art devices. Greystonelea is also disabled friendly. The shower on the ground floor is also invalid-capable with grab handles and an emergency cord. Other amenities include an en suite master bedroom with a balcony commanding wonderful panoramic views. Children are very welcome – there is an outdoor play area for them, and a high chair is available if required.

64 ANCHORAGE TEAROOM & GUEST HOUSE

Balloch Road, Balloch, Nr Dumbarton,
Dunbartonshire G83 8SS
☎ 01389 753336 Fax: 01389 729606
e-mail: anchorage-gh@balloch.co.uk
⊕ www.anchorage-guesthouse-balloch.co.uk

The village of Balloch lies close to the southern shores of Loch Lomond, and it is here that you will find the **Anchorage Tearoom and Guest House**. As the name implies, it offers both great food and exceptional accommodation to travellers, and is one of the most popular establishments of its kind in the area. The tearoom serves light snacks and breakfasts, teas, coffees and cold drinks, and is open each year from May to September. It seats 20 in comfort, with a further 30 out of doors in the summer months.

The guest house is a picturesque cottage dating from 1886, and has five fully en suite rooms (all on the ground floor) on offer, plus toilet and shower facilities for the disabled. The rooms (one family, one twin and two doubles) are all comfortable and spacious, and the establishment gets many repeat visitors due to the high standards of service and outstanding value for money. The B&B tariff includes a full Scottish breakfast, with lighter options if required. All credit

cards with the exception of American Express and Diners are accepted, and children are more than welcome.

There is plenty of parking space, and the cottage can be used either as a stopping off place as you travel north or south, or as a base to explore the Loch Lomond and Trossachs National Park and the countryside surrounding Loch Lomond, surely Scotland's loveliest loch.

65 THE WISHING WELL

63 Montgomery Street, Eaglesham,
Renfrewshire G76 0AU
☎ 01355 302774

Eaglesham is one of the most picturesque villages in Scotland and sits on the B764, between East Kilbride and the M77 motorway. Here you will find **The Wishing Well**, a small tearoom and restaurant that sells superb food and snacks. It is perfectly positioned opposite the village green (which has the delightful

name of 'The Orry') and is open during the day for breakfasts, lunches, teas, coffees and, on Thursday, Friday and Saturday, evening meals. It is a famous establishment, and people travel from all over to sample its cuisine and cosy interior.

68 COFFEE SPOT

152A & B High street, Biggar,
Lanarkshire ML12 6DH
☎ 01899 221902

The **Coffee Spot** in Biggar offers a warm welcome to one and all. Come and enjoy delicious home baking. Freshly baked scones are a speciality, along with a range of home made soup and savoury and sweet pies freshly made daily. Open 7 days, sit in or take away.

Looking for:
- *Places to Visit?*
- *Places to Stay?*
- *Places to Eat & Drink?*
- *Places to Shop?*

www.travelpublishing.co.uk

66 DUNSYRE MAINS

Dunsyre, Carnwath,
Lanarkshire ML11 8NQ
☎ 01899 810251

Dunsyre Mains is a 400 acre beef and sheep farm that can be found off either the A721 via Newbigging or A702 via Dolphinton, among some of the best walking country in Scotland The farmhouse itself dates to the 1700s, and offers three spacious yet cosy guest rooms to discerning tourists. They are rated three-star, and all of them are furnished and decorated to an extremely high standard. The owners, Margaret and Lance Armstrong, have lived here for 39 years, and for 30 of them having been offering superior bed and breakfast. So good is the place that people keep coming back again and again to experience the warm welcome and the great Scottish hospitality. One room can be used as a family room, while the other two have a double and a single bed within them. One of the rooms is on the ground floor.

This is a superb area for outdoor activities, from walking to fishing, and from golf to mountain biking. The landscape is rugged, and there are many places of historic interest to visit plus, of course, the town of Lanark, where William Wallace began his campaign for Scottish freedom.

The farmhouse breakfasts here are hearty and filling, and will set you up for a full day of travelling or exploring. Evening meals are available by prior arrangement, and payment is by cash or cheque. So good is the hospitality here that once you visit, you are sure to return!

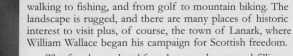

515 Carlisle Road, Lesmahagow,
Lanarkshire ML11 0JU
☎ 01555 892293

Lesmahagow is an old, historic village lying off the M74 motorway - one of the main routes north for tourists visiting Scotland - connecting Glasgow and Carlisle. It dates back many centuries, and was founded by monks who established Lesmahagow Priory in the mid 12th century. The foundations of this Tironensian monastery can still be seen in the village, next to the parish church. On the former main road (now the B7078) on the south side of the village, you will find **The Star Inn**, which offers great food and drink to travellers.

It is the ideal stopping off point as you head north or south along the M74. You can't miss it - leave the motorway at Junction 11 (the Happendon Services turn off) and head north. Or exit at Junction 10 and head south. Since April 2006 it has been owned and run by the Rossi family, and already it is gaining a fine reputation among locals and visitors alike. It was once a truck stop, and is still occasionally used by truckers, who certainly recognise a place that offers great hospitality at affordable prices!

It is open all day, every day except Tuesday, when it opens at 5.30 pm. The bar area is cosy and inviting, with carpeted floors, a well-stocked bar, luxury sofas and polished wood, and is the ideal place to relax for an hour or so. The bar sells a great range of beers, lagers, cider, wine, spirits, liqueurs and, if you're driving - soft drinks. You can also meet and chat with the locals, who appreciate the ambience of the place and its value-for-money prices.

Scottish cuisine is served here, as well as a selection of Italian dishes. Good, fresh local produce is used in the dishes wherever possible, ensuring a meal that is beautifully

cooked on the premises and full of flavour. You can choose from a printed menu or a daily specials board, which takes advantage of produce that is in season. Starters include such favourites as Japanese breaded king prawns as well as mozzarella sticks. Main courses include beef stir fry, a choice of six juicy steaks and a further choice of six fish dishes.

Children are most welcome, and all major credit cards are accepted. The Star Inn is a must-visit place when you're travelling along the m74. Be sure to call in for a drink or meal!

69 FARMHOUSE KITCHEN

Carmichael Visitor Centre,
Carmichael Estate,
South Lanarkshire ML12 6PG
☎ 01899 309111

Whether visiting the Carmichael Visitor Centre or just looking for a place to enjoy a meal as you travel along the A72, you should head for the **Farmhouse Kitchen**, where you will find delicious food at affordable prices. Operated by Marjory Smith, the Farmhouse Kitchen uses fresh meat and eggs from the Carmichael Estate. Whether it's a hot meal you want, or just a coffee with home baking, the Farmhouse Kitchen is the place for you!

70 MUSEUM OF SCOTLAND

Chambers Street, Edinburgh EH1 1JF
☎ 0131 247 4422
🌐 www.nms.ac.uk

The Museum of Scotland tells the remarkable story of a remarkable country. From the geological dawn of time to modern day life in Scotland, you'll discover the roots of a nation - a land steeped in fascinating cultures and terrible wars, passionate religion and scientific invention. A land of creative struggle - and occasionally of glorious failure. In a unique and purpose - built museum are gathered together the treasured inheritance and cultural icons which tell Scotland's many stories. The people, the land, the events that have shaped the way they live now.

If you weren't aware of the extraordinary history and impressive achievements of this small country, then it's time to find out. Because after more than 3,000 million years of Scotland's story, there is the perfect place in which to celebrate it - the Museum of Scotland. The exhibits include the earliest known fossil reptile found in Bathgate, dating back to 338 million years BC, artifacts from around 8,000 BC when the first settlers arrived and a tiny shrine thought to date from AD750.

The museum shop sells a wide variety of souvenirs and a cafe and restaurant ensure that all appetites are catered for. Guides are available and there is a rooftop garden with spectacular views. Open Monday to Saturday 10am-5pm and Sunday 12 noon-5pm. Disabled access.

71 THE ROYAL YACHT BRITANNIA

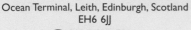

Ocean Terminal, Leith, Edinburgh, Scotland
EH6 6JJ
☎ 0131 555 5566
e-mail: enquiries@tryb.co.uk
🌐 www.royalyachtbritannia.co.uk

For over forty years **The Royal Yacht** *Britannia* served the Royal Family, travelling over one million miles to become the most famous ship in the world. Travelling to every corner of the globe, in a career spanning 968 royal and official visits, she played a leading role in some of the defining moments of recent history. To Her Majesty The Queen and the Royal Family, *Britannia* proved to be the perfect royal residence for glittering State Visits, official receptions, honeymoons and relaxing family holidays. Since her decomissioning *Britannia* has now made Edinburgh's historic Port of Leith her final home and is open to the public throughout the year. Now owned by The Royal Yacht *Britannia* Trust, a non profit making charity, any proceeds go towards *Britannia's* maintenance.

Your tour of *Britannia* starts in the Visitor Centre on the second floor of Ocean Terminal. Here you can learn about *Britannia's* fascinating history through exhibits and photographs before you collect your complimentary audio handset and step on board *Britannia,* a privilege previously reserved for guests of Her Majesty The Queen and the Royal Family. Starting at the Bridge and finishing at the gleaming Engine Room, come and discover the reality behind life and work on board this Royal Yacht. Viewing five decks, using the lift or stairs for easy access, you will tour *Britannia* at your own pace and enjoy highlights that include the State Dining Room, the Drawing Room, the Sun Lounge, the Wardroom and the Chief Petty Officers' Mess. *Britannia* is furnished with artefacts from The Royal Collection, which are on loan from Her Majesty The Queen.

72 SAM'S

High Street, Dalkeith,
Midlothian EH22 1AZ
☎ 0131 663 2515
e-mail: cat.m2@btopenworld.com

Located at the top end of Dalkeith's busy High Street, **Sam's** is a great place for a quiet relaxing drink or a bar lunch of fresh, simple food at sensible prices. The building dates back to the early 1800s and retains many original period features. Owner Catherine McGregor presides over the open plan bar/lounge which is tastefully and

comfortably furnished. From this area, a door leads out to the ever-popular beer garden and smokers' area. Sam's hosts regular music sessions and there's a pub quiz every Wednesday evening. Credit cards are accepted and Sam's has its own car park.

73 VICTORIA INN

35 The Braes, Auchendinny
Midlothian EH26 0QU
☎ 01968 673088
e-mail:
victoriainn@auchendinny.wanadoo.co.uk

The **Victoria Inn** sits in a small village among the lovely Midlothian countryside. With its traditional interior, both visitors and locals alike enjoy the freshly prepared dishes, served in the restaurant. Regular live music.

74 THE COUNTY HOTEL

15-17 High Street, North Berwick,
East Lothian EH39 4HH
☎ 01620 892989
e-mail: ianianstee@aol.com

The County Hotel is a handsome Victorian
building with a black and cream frontage that
adds distinction to North Berwick's High
Street. The inside is absolutely immaculate
and although owners Ian and Irene Steele
only moved
here in early
2007 they
are both
very
experienced
in running
pubs. The
hotel has 7
guest
bedrooms,

all attractively furnished and decorated, and
all with en suite facilities. Good food is also
available in the newly reopened restaurant.
The hotel has a pleasant beer garden to the
rear and its own car park.

75 12 QUALITY STREET

12 Quality Street, North Berwick,
East Lothian EH39 4HP
☎ 01620 892529 Fax: 01620 897113
e-mail: bookings@no12qualitystreet.co.uk
 www.no12qualitystreet.co.uk

12 Quality Street is only minutes from the
beach,
the golf
links
and the
harbour
of this
popular
holiday
resort.
This
boutique
hotel,

housed within an 18th century building, has
recently been renovated, so that the eleven en
suite rooms reflect the highest standards of
hospitality available. The ground floor bistro
is fully licensed, and uses only the finest local
produce in its cuisine.

76 NETHER ABBEY HOTEL

20 Dirleton Avenue, North Berwick,
East Lothian EH39 4BQ
☎ 01620 892802 Fax: 01620 895290
e-mail: bookings@netherabbey.co.uk
 www.netherabbey.co.uk

The **Nether Abbey Hotel** is one of the most
popular hotels in North Berwick, and people
come back again and again to sample its great
hospitality and friendly atmosphere. It has 13
rooms, all en suite. The restaurant uses only
fresh local produce wherever possible, and in
the bar you can enjoy not only a relaxing drink,
but a selection of tapas that is sure to please.
The hotel has disabled facilities.

77 THE WESTGATE GALLERY

39/41 Westgate, North Berwick,
East Lothian EH39 4AG
☎ 01620 894976 Fax: 01620 890452
e-mail: info@westgate-gallery.co.uk

If you're looking for home and gift ideas, you
can't afford to miss **The Westgate Gallery**
in North Berwick It sits at the west end of
the high street, and has a wide range of
artwork, ceramics, glass, homeware and gifts
for everyone. Pay it a visit, even if you're not
buying. It
has a
licensed
café
serving
teas and
coffees,
home
baking
and light
lunches -
just right

for when you want a break from exploring
this fascinating seaside town!

78 FENTON TOWER

Kingston, North Berwick,
East Lothian EH39 5JH
☎ 01620 89 0089
e-mail: manager@fentontower.com

Set in rolling countryside just 20 miles east of Edinburgh, Fenton Tower provides a unique and unforgettable experience. It was built in the late 1500's and its first notable visitor was James VI (later James I of England) in 1591 as he fled from the Earl of Bothwell, the third husband of Mary, Queen of Scots. More the 400 years later Ian Simpson and John Macaskill decided to restore the Tower and convert it into a comfortable modern residence for the 21st Century. The restoration was completed in 2002 and the Tower now provides luxurious accommodation for up to 12 guests. Here they can relax in unparalleled comfort, sample gourmet foods and sip fine wines from the Tower cellar.

Using an exclusive team of architects, engineers and designers, the Tower's original features have been meticulously restored. Gentle pastels reflect the abundance of natural light from the exceptionally large windows. Elegant antique furniture has been sourced from across Europe, and the heating, lighting and plumbing all use the very latest technology while maintaining the castle's luxurious ambience.

Enter through the fortified front door and you will find yourself in the vaulted dining room. It is designed to serve anything from two to twenty four guests with ease. Guests can discuss their preferences with the staff to ensure they receive the kind of dishes they wish. Service is discreet, professional and individual.

Wander up to the first floor and you will find the great hall with its impressive beamed ceiling, roaring log fire, and private library. The Tower's four main bedrooms are all individually styled with their own luxurious en-suite bathrooms. At the very top of the Tower sits the Garret Suite, complete with double en-suite bedroom and private sitting room. You can also venture out onto the battlements and take in the spectacular views of the East Lothian countryside.

79 MUSEUM OF FLIGHT 🏛

**East Fortune Airfield,
East Lothian EH39 5LF
☎ 01620 897240
⊕ nms.ac.uk/flight**

The Museum of Flight is based at East Fortune Airfield, a Scheduled Ancient Monument and one of the most famous sites in world aviation history. It tells the history of East Fortune (established in 1915 as a fighter base to protect Scotland from Zeppelin attacks) and of the Scottish built airship R34 which left East Fortune and flew to Long Island, New York, becoming the first return Transatlantic flight. The Museum collection is housed in the original hangars and restoration work can be seen in progress. A large selection of models, toys and books is on sale in the shop and the Parachute Cafe serves light refreshments.

80 BLACK BULL 🍴 🛏

**High Street, Dunbar EH42 1JH
☎ 01365 863026**

Dating back to the late 1700s, the **Black Bull** is one of Dunbar's oldest hostelries and is very popular with local people. It's a compact place with just one room on the ground floor and two guest bedrooms upstairs with a private bathroom. The bar has a large screen TV and juke box, and once a month a karaoke session is held here

on Sunday afternoon. The bar also hosts a folk music evening, also once a month on Wednesday. There's no food served – this is very much a place for drink and congenial company.

82 THE CREEL 🍴

**25 Lamer Street, Dunbar EH42 1HG
☎ 01368 863279
⊕ www.creelrestaurant.co.uk**

Although Logan Thorburn only took over **The Creel** in late summer 2006, word has spread incredibly quickly about the quality of the cuisine on offer here. Logan's experience with seafood king Rick Stein and Michelin starred chef John Campbell no doubt helped. Located close to the harbour in a sturdy, stone-built house, The Creel has a stylish modern décor and offers a menu that ranges from traditional

crispy local fish and chips, or Aberdeen Angus Rib Steak to less familiar dishes such as the Broschetta of Chicken and Brie. The Creel is open for lunch and dinner, Thurs to Mon (closed Tues and Wed). Credit cards are accepted; ample parking.

83 THE VOLUNTEER ARMS 🍴

**17 Victoria street, Dunbar,
East Lothian EH42 1HP
☎ 01368 862278
e-mail: doniw@btinternet,com**

The 250-year-old **Victoria Arms** sits near the harbour of this pretty holiday town. As well as being a traditional Scottish pub with cask ales, it also boasts a bistro-style restaurant, which serves range of seafood dishes and quality pub food.

81 THE ROSSBOROUGH HOTEL

Queen's Road, Dunbar EH42 1LG
☎ 01368 862356
e-mail: info@therossborough.com
🌐 www.therossborough.com

Only 2 minutes walk from the historic town centre of Dunbar, **The Rossborough Hotel** was built in 1902 as a luxury hotel. Many of the original Edwardian features are still intact and recent refurbishment has restored this fine old hotel to its former state of grace. The Rossborough is family-owned and run by Ann and Robin Rossborough who continue to upgrade the hotel's amenities.

There are two separate eating places within the hotel. Ritchie's Restaurant serves grill and à la carte menus, Tuesday to Saturday. The chef (formerly at The Ivy in London) uses only the very best of local produce to create a varied menu that offers Belhaven Smoked Salmon or Farmhouse Venison amongst the starters; pan-fried fillet of sea bass or Chump of Lamb as main courses; and a selection of Scottish Cheeses and Oatcakes as an alternative to dessert. In addition to evening meals, Ritchie's will also serve High Teas to groups by arrangement.

In the friendly Stones Bar & Bistro bar

meals are available every day. The extensive choice ranges from sandwiches and toasted paninis through salads and soups to substantial chicken and steak dishes.

The Rossborough also has two function rooms. The Carlisle can seat 100 for wedding parties, or 200 theatre style for conferences. The Lewis is ideally suitable for public meetings seating 40, boardroom style meetings for 20, and family gatherings or small wedding parties for up to 30 guests. Should you be interested, just contact Ann who has a BA (Hons) in Hospitality Management and a Diploma in Industrial Studies. She also has more than 30 years experience in hotels and has worked in Conference and Banqueting at Belfast Castle, the city's premier conference and wedding venue.

If you are planning to stay in Dunbar, accommodation at The Rossborough comprises 19 stylish and very comfortable bedrooms, all en suite and equipped with colour TV, telephone, hair-dryer and hospitality tray.

Dunbar is an ideal resort for a sporting or activity holiday. There are many walks, clifftop trails, geology and nature trails, plus a great variety of castles, museums and historic buildings to visit. The Rossborough is just a 5-minute drive from 2 golf courses, one of championship level and close to a further 18 East Lothian courses. A 30-minute road or rail journey will bring you to Edinburgh and its many metropolitan attractions.

84 LIVINGSTON'S RESTAURANT

52 High Street, Linlithgow,
West Lothian EH49 7AE
☎ 01306 846565
e-mail: conatct@livingstons-
restaurant.co.uk
⊕ www.livingstones-restaurant.co.uk

For 13 years, the husband and wife team of
Christine and Ronald Livingston have owned
and run **Livingston's Restaurant**, right in
the heart of the historic burgh of Linlithgow.
During that time they have earned an
enviable reputation for the quality of the
cuisine they offer,
described as
"Scottish food with a
French flavour". All
the produce used is
fresh and local
wherever possible,
and people come
from far and wide to
sample the food, the
ambience and the
friendly welcome.

86 INVERKEITHING MUSEUM

The Friary, Queen Street, Inverkeithing, Fife
KY11 1LS
☎ 01383 313594

Inverkeithing Museum is housed in the
upper floor of a wonderful 14th century
Friary guest house, standing amidst well
tended gardens. The gallery is only small but
has a lovely collection of local photographs,
paintings and artefacts, illustrating the history
of the area. Admiral Greig, Inverkeithing's
most famous son
- the "Father of
the Russian
Navy", is
featured. Open
Thursday, Friday,
Saturday and
Sunday 11am to
12.30 pm and
1pm to 4pm.
Admission is free
but access is by
stairs only and so
is not suitable for
the disabled.

85 THE CLIPPIE'S FAYRE

2/8 Main street, Kelty, Fife KY4 0AA
☎ 01383 839544

People come from near and far to sample the
good home cooking of **The Clippies Fayre**.
The surroundings are light and airy, with a
large conservatory overlooking the bowling
green. The wide ranging menu includes
traditional Scottish fare, exotic fresh fish
dishes and pasta. Vegetarians are also catered
for. Disabled access.

87 THE SHIP TAVERN BAR & RESTAURANT

Bruce Street, Kinghorn, Fife KY3 9TJ
☎ 01592 890655

Kinghorn is a picturesque village in an area
rich in local history. At the recently
refurbished **Ship Tavern Bar and
Restaurant** you can enjoy a drink or have a
meal in the well appointed restaurant which
overlooks the attractive beer garden. Food is
cooked to order using fresh local produce.

88 MILTON HOUSE

13 Aberdour Road, Burntisland,
Fife KY3 0HA
☎ 01592 873507
e-mail: wendygarrod73@msn.com

Milton House is a popular, busy little inn
that is cosy and compact, and makes the ideal
stopping off place for a drink or snack while
exploring the area. It is a picturesque place,
with hanging baskets and whitewashed walls,
and the
interior is
equally as
appealing.
There is a
full range
of local
ales such
as Calders
and
Belhaven,
plus

wines, spirits (including malts!) and soft
drinks for those who are driving. On the last
Saturday of the month there is always a live
music night.

89 THE NEW INN

21 St Mary's Street, St Andrews,
Fife KY16 8AZ
☎ 01334 472105

Sitting close to the picturesque harbour in St Andrews, **The New Inn** is the place for a quiet drink or a meal and attracts tourists and locals alike. Inside the place is comfortable and inviting with a rustic feel, and a range of traditional dishes are on offer. To the rear is a beer garden.

90 MARINE HOTEL

54 Nethergate, Crail, Fife KY10 3TZ
☎ 01333 450207
e-mail: marinerosebery@tsicali.co.uk

The three star **Marine Hotel** has ten en suite rooms, and sits in a beautiful and quaint part of Fife, right on the magnificent coastline.

91 THE SMUGGLER'S INN

High Street East, Anstruther
Fife KY10 3DQ
☎ 01333 310506 Fax: 01333 312706
e-mail: ian.Lawson@smugglersinn.org
🌐 www.sunriseinns.com/smugglersinn

The **Smuggler's Inn** in Anstruther boasts six fully en suite rooms that are both comfortable and spacious. It is a quaint, whitewashed building, with a lounge/restaurant that boasts bare stone walls and an open fire. Here you will traditional Scottish fare, prepared on the premises.

The bar is warm and welcoming. The inn makes the perfect base from which to explore a beautiful area of Fife.

92 SCOTTISH FISHERIES MUSEUM

St. Ayles, Harbourhead, Anstruther,
Fife KY10 3AB

☎ 01333 310628

e-mail: enquiries@scotfishmuseum.org
🌐 www.scotfishmuseum.org

Fishing has always been important to the small villages that fringe the East Neuk of Fife and in the **Scottish Fisheries Museum** you can learn all about the industry, not just in Fife, but throughout Scotland. It is a truly fascinating place, and is housed in buildings dating from the 16th to the 19th centuries. There are displays on many facets of the industry, and a trip round makes a great day out for children and adults alike. It begins by examining a replica dug-out canoe dating from AD500, created in the museum workshop to illustrate that fishing in Scotland goes back to ancient times. After it was made in 1991, it was tested in Anstruther Harbour, and performed beautifully!

There are many galleries, each one highlighting a facet of the industry. There is an area on whaling, for example, plus a gallery called 'The Herring Market', with a net-loft where nets were repaired, a fish merchant's office, and lively herring lassies gutting and packing the catch. There are also, of course, fishing boats, and you can see and touch the craft that took hardy fishermen out into the seas round Britain in days gone by. One of the most fascinating galleries is the one dedicated to Zulu fishing boats. How did they get their name? What key role did they play in the industry? There is also a tearoom, a room which you can book to enjoy your packed lunch, and a shop, where you can pick up well-crafted souvenirs to remind you of your trip to one of the most interesting and enjoyable museums in Scotland. It is wheelchair friendly, and special themed visits can also be arranged. It makes a memorable day out.

93 THE VILLAGE INN

Cupar Road, Pitlessie, Fife KY15 7SU
☎ 01337 830595
e-mail: the villageinn@hotmail.co.uk
⊕ www.thevillageinnpitlessie.co.uk

The Village Inn is an old coaching inn that dates from the 17th century, and is popular with both locals and tourists alike. Situated between Edinburgh and St Andrews, it makes the perfect break when travelling north. The inn serves traditional Scottish fare - lunches, evening meals and a high tea every Sunday between 4.30 and 6.30pm - in the spacious restaurant, and its bar is both cosy and inviting.

94 HILLPARK HOUSE

96 Main Street, Leuchars, St Andrews
Fife KY16 0HF
☎ 01334 839280 Fax: 01334 839051
e-mail: enquiries@hillparkhouse.com
⊕ www.hillparkhouse.com

Built in 1906 as a family home, Hillpark House now offers splendid accommodation in five comfortable and spacious rooms, three of which are fully en suite. It sits five miles from St Andrews in open countryside, and is a dog-friendly  establishment that offers the very best in Scottish hospitality. The breakfasts - ranging from full Scottish to vegetarian, can be served in an airy conservatory.

95 THE ROYAL OAK HOTEL

7 Bedford Place, Alloa,
Clackmannanshire FK10 1LJ
☎ 01259 722423 Fax: 01259 215523
e-mail:
ahilton@theroyaloakhotel.freeserve.co.uk
⊕ www.theroyaloakhotel.alloa.co.uk

The Royal Oak Hotel is situated in the conservation area of Alloa, and dates originally from the 19th century. It is now an extremely comfortable family owned hotel that boasts eleven fully en suite rooms, a popular restaurant and a function suite. It appeals to both holidaymakers and locals, who flock to sample the hotel's high teas. The food is superb, as are the beers, wines and  spirits served in the cosy Oak Pub and beer garden. This is the ideal base from which to explore the region. Dogs are allowed in the rooms by arrangement.

96 FORMULE 1 HOTEL

Beancross Farm, Polmont,
Falkirk FK2 0XS
☎ 01324 719966 Fax: 01324 720926
e-mail: E5829@accor-hotels.com
⊕ www.formule1-hotels.com

Situated right in the heart of the Scottish Lowlands, the dog-friendly Formule 1 Hotel at Falkirk is the ideal stopping off point when heading north into the Highlands. It also makes an ideal base from which to explore all the Scottish Lowlands, from Edinburgh to Glasgow and from Stirling to the Scottish  Borders and Ayrshire. It has 75 rooms with shared facilities, which are clean, comfortable and affordable. Continental breakfasts are available at a cost of £2.50.

101 RED LION HOTEL

Balkerach Street, Doune,
Perthshire FK16 6DF
☎ 01786 842066
e-mail: info@redlion-doune.com
🌐 www.redlion-doune.com

The **Red Lion Hotel** in Doune combines all the traditional values of Scottish hospitality with the modern concepts of high standards, efficient, friendly service and outstanding value for money. The 200 year old building stands on the town's main street, almost next to the old Merkat Cross, and is a delightfully picturesque place, with its whitewashed walls and dormer windows.

The place speaks of traditional comfort and a warm, friendly welcome, should you be using the inn as a B&B base from which to explore the area. It has four extremely comfortable rooms, two of which are fully en suite. Each one has its own individual feel, but they all come with TV and tea/coffee making facilities. Hair driers and irons are available on request, as are extra beds or cots.

Food is served in the stunning Stewart Room restaurant, which is smart and stylish while still having a traditional Scottish feel to it. All the dishes are made on the premises from fresh local produce wherever possible, and combine imagination with flare. The menu is changed four times a year to

reflect the produce in season, and there is ample choice for all the family. Private parties of up to 35 can be accommodated in the Quaich. The Stewart Room takes up to 20, so this is the ideal place for a small wedding reception or party.

With its own external entrance, the hotel's bunkhouse is ideal for walkers, cyclists or large parties, and sleep up to ten in absolute comfort. It has all mod cons - shower, loos, kettle, microwave and fridge. Backpacks and cycles can be stored away safely, and packed lunches can be prepared.

The Red Lion Hotel is also one of the village's most popular locals, with people

meeting and chatting over a relaxing drink in the friendly bar. A wide range of good ales, beers, wine, spirits and soft drinks is served. So you can meet and chat here to your heart's content, knowing that you are in convivial company.

For functions such as large meetings, seminars or wedding receptions, the Quaich Room is the ideal place to hold it. It opens out onto a sun trap patio area that is just right for those summer months!

Doune is one of Scotland's most historic villages, and Doune Castle was where many scenes from *Monty Python and the Holy Grail* were filmed. So visit the village and stay in the Red Lion Hotel!

97 CASTLE CROFT

Ballingeich Road, Stirling FK8 1TN
☎ 01786 474933
e-mail: castlecroft@supanet.com
🌐 www.castlecroft-uk.com

Nestling below the ramparts of the castle, **Castle Croft** is one of the best B&B establishments in the historic city of Stirling. There are six extremely comfortable en suite rooms, a pleasant garden and private parking. A full Scottish breakfast is included.

98 THE ALLANWATER CAFÉ

15 Henderson Street, Bridge of Allan, Stirlingshire FK9 4HN
☎ 01786 833060

With seating for 80, the **Allanwater Café** is bright and spacious, being decorated in the "ice cream parlour" style. It is popular with visitors and locals alike and offers a menu which includes many freshly made Scottish dishes, as well as a large selection of ice-creams and ice-cream sundaes.

99 CHIMES HOUSE

Cathedral Square, Kirk Street, Dunblane, Perthshire FK15 0AL
☎ 01786 822481
e-mail: moira@bedandbreakfast-scotland.co.uk
🌐 www.bedandbreakfast-scotland.co.uk

With two twin rooms and one double room (all en suite), **Chimes House** is one of the best and most comfortable B&Bs in Dunblane, and sits overlooking the medieval cathedral.

100 THE COACH HOUSE

Main Street, Aberfoyle, Stirlingshire FK8 3UG
☎ 01877 382822

For good accommodation, food and drink, you can't beat the **Coach House** in Aberfoyle, a small town known as the "gateway to the Trossachs". A good diverse menu is served in the traditional bar or in the conservatory dining room. Three rooms are available for B&B and there is a patio beer garden.

103 DALGAIR HOUSE HOTEL

113-115 Main Street, Callander FK17 8BQ
☎ 01877 330283
🌐 www.dalgair-house-hotel.co.uk

Callander is often called 'the gateway to the Highlands' and it is here, in this small, picturesque town, that you find one of the best hotels in this area of Perthshire - **Dalgair House Hotel**. It sits right on Main Street, and has eight en suite rooms that are supremely comfortable. Each one boasts bath and shower, colour TV, direct dial telephone, tea/coffee making facilities, hair drier and trouser press. Some even have four posters!

The Trossachs Restaurant sells superb food to residents and visitors, with the kitchens using only the finest and freshest of local produce wherever possible. Its speciality is Scotch beef, lamb, fish and game, and every dish is

prepared by the resident chef with imagination and flair. The Back Bar is a welcoming hostelry that is popular with both visitors and locals alike, and has a wide selection of drinks, including malt whiskies. You can eat here as well, either a tasty bar meal or a choice from the à la carte menu, served from early to late. There is live music every Friday and Saturday night, and karaoke every Saturday evening.

102 THE WAVERLEY HOTEL

Main Street, Callander FK17 8BD
☎ 01877 330245
🌐 www.thewaverley.co.uk

With its striking pillared frontage of white stone and ornamental glass, **The Waverley Hotel** is one of the most distinctive buildings in the attractive little town which will be familiar to viewers of the 1970s BBC-TV series *Dr Finlay's Casebook*. More than 100 years old, the building was taken over in September 2006 by Charlotte Halladay and Martin Graham who have carried out a comprehensive refurbishment. Both of them grew up in Callander and studied Hospitality Management in Glasgow. They then worked for a few years gaining experience with different hotel companies before deciding they wanted to run somewhere of their own.

A very traditional Scottish theme is featured in The Waverley's bar and restaurant with various claymores, swords and targes hanging on the walls and the floor covered with the old favourite tartan carpet. The restaurant offers an appetising menu based on locally sourced food and includes some of Scotland's favourite and classic meals. The bar was winner of the CAMRA Forth Valley Pub of the Year 2006 and stocks a fabulous selection of

regular and guest ales that are constantly changing. They are sourced from breweries throughout Britain, including local micro-breweries. At the end of August/early September the bar hosts the Annual Beer Festival when there are 12 cask ales on at one time – 20 different types of beers for you to sample – as well as real cider. Also available is a balanced selection of Scottish Malt Whiskeys, local and continental lagers and a few speciality beers. From April through October the bar hosts live music at weekends with various types of bands and music. And you can test your knowledge at the monthly quiz nights.

Accommodation at The Waverley comprises 10 fully en suite newly renovated rooms – 5 doubles, 2 family rooms, 2 singles and 1 suite. Each room is equipped with flat screen television providing Sky TV, hospitality tray and bathroom amenities. The tariff includes a full breakfast. The hotel's other facilities include a TV lounge showing all major sporting events; a function room to the rear of the building which can seat approximately 60 theatre style, or 50 persons dining; and, new for 2007, a heated smoker's area also at the rear of the hotel.

Callander itself is a popular tourist town – the Gateway to the Highlands and to the National Park. A wide range of activities is available including golf, fishing, shooting, walking, hiking, horse-riding, cycling and watersports.

104 MYTRLE INN

Stirling Road, Callander FK17 8LE
☎ 01877 330919
e-mail: myrtleinn@btconnect.com

When in Callander, the delightful, white-washed **Myrtle Inn** must be visited. This traditional roadside inn is an ideal place for a quiet drink or a superbly cooked meal as you explore an area that is stunningly beautiful. There are two menus - lunch and evening - with food being served in a restaurant  area as well as in the bar. The favourite dishes here are roast lamb, using local lamb, and Wallace Chicken - chicken stuffed with haggis and served with Wallace Liqueur. Disabled access is no problem.

HIDDEN PLACES GUIDES

Explore Britain and Ireland with *Hidden Places* guides - a fascinating series of national and local travel guides.

Packed with easy to read information on hundreds of places of interest as well as places to stay, eat and drink.

Available from both high street and internet booksellers

For more information on the full range of *Hidden Places* guides and other titles published by Travel Publishing visit our website on

www.travelpublishing.co.uk or ask for our leaflet by phoning **0118-981-7777** or emailing **info@travelpublishing.co.uk**

105 THE BYRE INN

Brig o' Turk
☎ 01877 376292
🌐 www.incallander.co.uk/byreinn.htm

The **Byre Inn** is set within the small village of Brig o' Turk within the Loch Lomond and Trossachs National Park. This is truly one of the outstanding inns in the area, between Lochs Venachar and Achray. The small, picturesque, whitewashed building is everything you think a Scottish inn should be, and once you step over the threshold you won't be disappointed. It has even won a 'Which Pub Guide Award' for 2005.

It's 30-seat restaurant is open for coffees, lunches, snacks, suppers and dinners, and features local produce such as trout, beef, lamb and game. People staying at the Dalgair House Hotel in Callander can also eat here, as well as enjoying the hospitality in the traditional bar area with its log fire and low beams. On summer days, you can sit outside on a decked area and enjoy the local scenery.

The Byre Inn, as well as the Dalgair House Hotel, is the perfect place for a small, romantic wedding reception, with the church, which overlooks Loch Achray, being close by. The Byre Inn also offers a lovely, small self-catering cottage, 'An Tuiric', for quiet, get-away-from-it-all holidays. At the end of 2007 the inn also hopes to offer comfortable guest rooms.

Lochay Road, Killin, Perthshire FK21 8TN
☎ 01567 820349
e-mail: coachhousehotel@btinternet.com
🖳 www.hotelkillin.co.uk

For comfortable accommodation, superb food and great drink in the Killin area there is no finer place than **The Coach House Hotel**. It is housed in a substantial, elegant building of local stone that dates to 1872, and is well known among those who appreciate high standards of service at affordable prices. It is a family-run establishment, with an informal, welcoming atmosphere that you will be sure to appreciate. It sits in one of the most picturesque villages in Scotland, and only seven miles from the geographical heart of the country. All around are high mountains with stunning views across the River Lochay towards Loch Tay.

Breakfasts and dinners are served in the spacious, pleasant restaurant. The breakfasts are always hearty and filling, though lighter options are always available as well. There is also an extensive dinner menu, and everything is cooked to perfection by a resident chef, who insists on only the finest and freshest of local produce being used wherever possible. A good selection of wines are kept in the hotel's cellars, so there will always be a bottle that will complement your meal perfectly.

Why not enjoy a relaxing drink in the resident's lounge or the lounge bar? Coffee and tea is always available, as is a wide range of beers, wines, spirits and soft drinks. The lounge bar in particular is a friendly, cosy place, converted from the House's former stables It is full of atmosphere, and has exposed stone walls and original beamed ceilings. As well as eating in the dining room, you can also eat here, with tasty home-cooked bar meals being served. It is a popular place with local people, and at least once a week from May until September there is live music in the evening, played by local folk, blues and Scottish ceilidhs bands. It makes for a wonderful night, and you are sure to be entertained by it!

The hotel's accommodation is superb. It has five guest rooms, three of which are fully en suite, and on the top floor there is dormitory accommodation taking up to nine people, at very competitive rates. This is particularly suitable for walking or fishing parties. The hotel makes the ideal base for exploring the area - one in which there is so much to do and see. Wind surfing, sailing, water skiing, bowling, fishing, golf, horse riding, clay pigeon shooting, walking, climbing and cross country skiing facilities are all close at hand.

107 SUIE LODGE HOTEL

Glen Dochart, Crianlarich,
Perthshire FK20 8QT
☎ 01567 820417
e-mail: suielodge@btinternet.com
🖰 www.suielodge.co.uk

Situated in an area of outstanding natural beauty which is steeped in Scottish history and heritage, the two star **Suie Lodge Hotel** is an 18th Century former hunting lodge within the Breadalbane estate and sits in its own attractive 5 acres of ground.

The hotels name, 'suie', translated from Gaelic literally means 'seat' as it is situated in the vicinity of the 'seat of learning' founded by St Fillan in the 8th Century. Located across the road from the hotel is an old McNab burial ground, containing a stone with a Latin Cross that may date back to the great man himself!

It is located mid-way between Crianlarich, 8 miles to the east and Killin, 7 miles to the west, on the A85 route north to Oban and Fort William. Whether you head north or south it is the ideal Bed & Breakfast stopping off point. It also makes an ideal base from which to explore the surrounding area. Within one and a half hours drive are Stirling Castle and the Wallace monument, Doune Castle, Callander and the Rob Roy Museum, Loch Lomond, Fort William and Ben Nevis, not forgetting the picturesque harbour town of Oban.

The hotel is family run providing outstanding value for money accommodation, food and drink in a friendly and informal atmosphere. The Suie Lodge has nine guest rooms, seven of which are en-suite. The rooms are all furnished and decorated to a high standard and all have colour television, shaver points, tea and coffee making facilities and hair dryers.

As you plan your days ahead, relax and enjoy a drink in the bar, where a welcoming roaring fire will warm you on a cold winters evening. The bar carries a fine range of beers, lager, wine, liqueurs and spirits, including a superb collection of single malts for you to try.

Why not enjoy a good home-cooked meal served in the bar or in the spacious and inviting dining room. To ensure maximum flavour and freshness locally sourced produce is used wherever

possible making a memorable and enjoyable eating experience.

The hotel is justly famous amongst ramblers, walkers, stalkers and fishermen for its facilities which include deep freezers and driers.

Children are welcome and dogs are welcome by prior arrangement. The hotel offers ample parking space and all major credit cards are accepted.

108 VAILA GUEST HOUSE

277 Argyll Street, Dunoon,
Argyll PA23 7QY
☎ 01369 707540
e-mail: vailaindunoon@tiscali.com

The **Vaila Guest House is a** quite superb establishment that stands just a short walk from Dunoon town centre. It offers wonderful, value for money accommodation, and has three comfortable guest rooms, one of which is completely en suite with the other two sharing a bathroom. It is the ideal place to stay while having a family holiday in the lovely old town of Dunoon on the Firth of Clyde.

110 HUNTERS QUAY HOLIDAY VILLAGE

Hunters Quay, Dunoon Argyll PA23 8HP
☎ 01369 707772
e-mail: david@hqhv.co.uk
🌐 www.argyll.co.uk

The family-run **Hunters Quay Holiday Village** is undoubtedly one of the finest establishments of its kind in Scotland, and offers all the facilities for a superb, fun holiday among some of the best scenery in Scotland. It has been awarded five coveted stars for its holiday park and three stars for its self-catering accommodation, and offers panoramic view across the Holy Loch. Accommodation is within two and three bedroom lodges, or a wide range of caravans, and all are superbly equipped for a holiday that will be truly memorable. The holiday village boasts the Dolphin Leisure Centre, one of the finest in the whole of Argyll. It has a 25-metre indoor swimming pool, a 25-metre indoor fun pool for kids, a state of the art gym, facilities for badminton, table tennis, snooker and mountain bike hire. And if that wasn't enough, there is a licensed bar and lounge area, plus superb entertainment for all the family.

Hunters Quay Holiday Village is the perfect place for a fun-packed family holiday. It is set among some superb scenery, and yet is only a short drive from Glasgow and the main road south and north. You can even get discount tickets (if requested with 14 days notice) from the village's reservation office for the ferry crossing from Gourock to Hunters Quay! All around is superb Scottish countryside that is just crying out to be explored, and the bustling, friendly town of Dunoon is close by for all your needs.

109 ABBOT'S BRAE HOTEL

West Bay, Dunoon, Argyll PA23 7QJ
☎ 01369 705021
e-mail: info@abbotsbrae.co.uk
🌐 www.abbotsbrae.co.uk

High above Dunoon, in two acres of grounds, you will find the quite superb four star **Abbot's Brae Hotel**. Originally built in 1843 as a holiday retreat for a wealthy Glasgow glass merchant, it is now a small, family-run establishment that offers luxurious guest rooms, a warm welcome and a friendly, unfussy ambience. Many of the building's original features have been retained, both inside and out, and it manages to combine an air of elegance with informality and a relaxed atmosphere that could almost be a home-from-home.

It is owned and run by the husband and wife team of Christine and Colin Macpherson, who are determined to build on the hotel's already envious reputation as one of the premier establishments in Argyll. It boasts eight fully en suite rooms, each one luxuriously furnished and decorated. One room is on the ground floor, three on the first floor and four on the top floor - and the higher you go, the more stunning the views out over the Firth of Clyde. All are extremely spacious, and come in a variety of sizes to suit most needs. They are individually named after places within the Cowal Peninsula, and have photographs and prints connected with the history of it's namesake.

Dining at the Abbot's Brae is an experience not to be missed. The cuisine is traditional Scottish, with possibly the hint of foreign influences now and then. Only the finest and freshest of local produce is used wherever possible, guaranteeing maximum flavour. The menu contains such dishes as local wild venison pate, bacon and lentil soup, juicy steaks with all the trimmings, steamed fillet of Loch Fyne salmon, slow cooked lamb shank and a host of other marvellous dishes that are sure to please. Plus there is a fine selection of wines to complement your meal exactly.

The Abbot's Brae Hotel sits close to the ferry terminal connecting Dunoon to Gourock and the Scottish motorway system, and Glasgow is only 30 miles away as the crow flies. Plus there is all that the Cowal Peninsula - one of Argyll's loveliest areas - has to offer. Historic sites - old towns such as Inveraray - marvellous coastal scenery - they're all here and waiting for you, as are golf courses, fishing rivers and great walking country. You just can't afford not to stay at the Abbot's Brae Hotel!

471

111 ENMORE HOTEL

111 Marine Parade, Kirn, Dunoon,
Argyll PA23 8HH
☎ 01369 702230
e-mail: enmorehotel@btinternet.com
🌐 www.enmorehotel.co.uk

The absolutely stunning four-star **Enmore Hotel** sits above the shores of the Cowal Peninsula, next to the holiday resort of Dunoon, known as the 'jewel of the Clyde'. It was built in 1785 as a holiday retreat for a Glasgow businessman, and has mature gardens to the front and rear. It has been lovingly restored over the years to create a magnificent hotel where luxury comes as standard and high levels of service are the norm. It boasts ten fully en suite rooms of varying sizes (but with no single rooms), each one individually furnished and decorated to an extremely high standard and with wonderful views out over sea, garden or mountain. Some rooms have four-poster or canopied beds, with the en suite facilities including double Jacuzzis or spa baths. The Enmore is a special place - small enough to ensure personal attention from the highly trained staff and yet of a size to ensure the very best in good food and drink. Personal towelling robes and carefully chosen books in the rooms, and fresh flowers everywhere in the public areas, illustrate the lengths that the owners, Wendy and Robert Thomson,

go to ensure that guests are constantly surprised and delighted.

Dinner is served each evening between 7 pm and 9 pm, though guests can stay on a B&B basis if required. Food is important here, and the chefs have put together a menu that takes advantage of fresh, locally sourced produce wherever possible. Starters include crispy whitebait, avocado and smoked salmon, and artichoke in a cream sauce. For a main course, you can chooses from such dishes as medallions of venison fillet in a blueberry sauce, roast breast of duck with an orange and ginger sauce, or juicy fillet or sirloin steaks. The restaurant is open to non-residents, though you

are well advised to book in advance.

One room has been created on the ground floor which is ideal for those unable to climb stairs. All credit cards with the exception of Diners and Amex are accepted, and children and dogs are welcome. The hotel holds a civil marriage license, so this is the ideal place for a romantic wedding and reception. It also makes an ideal base from which to explore Argyll. So for a relaxed break where you are sure to be pampered, come to the Enmore Hotel on the Cowal Peninsula!

113 SEAFIELD HOTEL

Kilkerran Road, Campbeltown,
Argyll PA28 6JL
☎ 01586 554385
e-mail: info@seafieldhotel.co.uk
🌐 www.seafieldhotel.co.uk

Overlooking the sea at Campbeltown is one of the best hotels in the whole of Argyll - the **Seafield Hotel**. It has been owned by Mr and Mrs Archer since August 2006 who, since then, have built on its reputation for fine food, great drink, and accommodation. It is set in a historic old building that dates from 1836, and was built for the owners of the Springbank Distillery, which is still in existence.

The Seafield is a family-run establishment that combines great service and outstanding value for money. It has six fully en suite rooms with showers, four doubles and two twins, and all are on the ground floor. They are located in the garden court annex, and are richly and comfortably furnished, ensuring a peaceful sleep. This is the perfect place to use as a base when exploring the area, or if you are exploring Argyll by car you can use it as B&B accommodation. The tariff always includes a hearty and filling Scottish breakfast (or lighter option if required) - just right to set you up for the day. If you book a stay, you will receive a ten per cent discount on green fees from the famous Machrihanish Golf Club, which is situated a few miles away on the west coast of the Mull of Kintyre.

The restaurant is open to residents and non-residents alike. Mrs Archer does the cooking, and

makes sure that only the finest and freshest of local produce is used wherever possible. You can choose from a menu or from a specials board that takes advantage of produce in season. Children's menus are also available, and vegetarians are catered for. Plus there is a fine range of wines to choose from, so you are sure to get something that complements your meal perfectly. There is also a good range of single malts representing most whisky-producing areas of Scotland.

To the back of the hotel is a patio and beer garden area where you can relax in the evening

over a glass of ale or a single malt. Or, if you wish, you can sit in the cosy yet spacious lounge bar and reception area. In the colder months, an open log fire proves a centrepiece and is the ideal spot to enjoy a pre-dinner drink.

Mr & Mrs Archer have refurbished the hotel rooms in order to attain a third star. The hotel sits overlooking Campbeltown Loch with views to Davaar Island and Arran, and is only a few minutes walk from the centre of town. Stay here and you won't be disappointed!

112 BENMORE BOTANIC GARDEN

Dunoon, Argyll PA23 8QU
☎ 01369 706261
e-mail: benmore@rbge.org.uk
🌐 www.rbge.org.uk

A member of the National Botanic Gardens of Scotland, Benmore Botanic Garden is famous for its collection of trees and shrubs. Set amid dramatic scenery, the west coast climate provides ideal growing conditions for some of the finest Himalayan rhododendrons. Guided walks are available to discover the secrets of this sensational garden, including the historic formal garden with Puck's Hut and established conifers. There is something of interest all year round and autumn provides a beautiful array of colours. There is a cafe for refreshments and a shop to buy gifts and plants, whilst various exhibitions and events take place in the Courtyard Gallery. Phone for details.

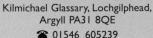

114 EMPIRE TRAVEL LODGE

Union Street, Lochgilphead,
Argyll PA31 8JS
☎ 01546 602381
e-mail: enquiries@empirelodge.co.uk
🌐 www.wmpirelodge.co.uk

The three-star **Empire Travel Lodge** sits in the centre of the historic town of Lochgilphead. Formerly the town's cinema, it now offers wonderful accommodation in nine fully en suite guest rooms. All the rooms are well-equipped and are mainly twin, double and family. All are on the ground floor, and  one has been specially equipped for the disabled. The place is very popular with tourists, and people come back again and again so sample the superb hospitality!

116 DUNADD COTTAGES

Kilmichael Glassary, Lochgilphead,
Argyll PA31 8QE
☎ 01546 605239
e-mail: listerdunadd@aol.com
🌐 www.dunaddcottages.co.uk

Dunadd Hill was the capital of the kingdom of Dalriada, and it was from here, in AD843, that King Kenneth MacAlpine, its king, set off to Scone in Perthshire to become the first king of a united Scotland. For over ten years, Margaret and Tim Lister have been providing wonderful self-catering accommodation in the three-star **Dunadd Cottages** that lies at the foot of the hill. They have been converted from old farm buildings, and offer the kind of facilities that make for a truly memorable holiday. They are named after kinsmen of *Fergus mor mac Eric*, who founded Dalriada in the 5th century. One cottage, *Comgall*, sleeps up to four, while the other, *Gabran*, sleeps up to three, and many people return again and again because of the historic location, the stunning scenery and the comfort and spaciousness that the cottages offer. They are open all  year round, and special short breaks are available in the winter months. *Comgall* is all on one level, and is suitable for the disabled.

Children and well-behaved pets are very welcome. Tariffs are weekly, and electricity and linen are included in the prices. Cots and high chairs can be provided. Each cottage has a TV and video, CD & DVD player, microwave, cooker, dishwasher and patio with barbecue. There is ample parking, plus a large shared garden where children can play in safety. These cottages represent amazing value for money, so are very popular. Book now and you'll be delighted with your choice of holiday accommodation!

115 ARGYLL TRAIL RIDING & CASTLE RIDING CENTRE

Brenfield Farm, Ardrishaig,
Argyll PA30 8ER
☎ 01546 603274
Fax: 01546 603225
e-mail: activities@brenfield.co.uk
🌐 www.brenfield.co.uk

Argyll Trail Riding and Castle Riding Centre were established by expert horsewoman Tove Gray-Stephens 25 years ago, and has grown to become one of the most renowned trail and riding centres in Britain. Being in Argyll, it offers truly memorable holidays amid some of the most wonderful scenery in Britain.

Come and join Tove and her son David for a ride in the hills above Brenfield on well-trained and reliable horses. Beginner or advanced, you will be entranced at how much more of the wonderful Argyll scenery you can see from horseback. Discover the splendour of the West Highlands of Scotland! Ride over Bens and through glens, ford rivers and burns and even ride out along the shore to the sea. Everything from an hour's ride to a full day pub ride, family holidays, weekend breaks and corporate events are available. Training and tuition in all things equestrian including the up and coming sport of Le Trec. You could try your hand at clay pigeon shooting also with expert tuition for the complete beginner or the expert.

For those who are more experienced riders there are three exciting and challenging trails available. The week-long *Wild Boar Trail* takes you through spectacular Dalriada, birthplace of the Scottish nation. You will explore historic sites and old castles, gallop across beaches, swim with the horses and climb mountains. The *Rob Roy Trail*, which again lasts one week, follows in the footsteps of Rob Roy McGregor and takes you from Inveraray Castle to the foothills of Ben Nevis, passing through historic Glencoe on the way. The *Loch and Forest Trail* lasting six days follows ancient drove roads as you discover hidden Argyll. In the evenings good food in comfortable inns and hotels is provided along the way.

The centre is fully licensed and approved by all leading equestrian organisations, the staff are friendly, helpful and knowledgable.

Argyll Trail Riding and Castle Riding Centre is on the coast just south of Lochgilphead, only two hours drive from Glasgow.

117 KILMARTIN HOTEL

Kilmartin, Near Lochgilphead,
Argyll PA31 8RQ
☎ 01545 510250
e-mail: kilmartinhotel@aol.com
🌐 www.kilmartin-hotel.com

The village of Kilmartin sits in what is possibly the most historic part of Scotland, surrounded by old burial cairns, stone circles, castles and standing stones. At the centre of the village is the **Kilmartin Hotel**, famous for its accommodation, warm welcome, well-stocked bar and great food.

There are six spacious bedrooms, four of which are fully en suite. Each one has tea/coffee making facilities and colour TV. This makes the hotel the ideal base from which to explore Argyll, possibly the most beautiful and historic area of Scotland. You can also eat here, either in the restaurant or in the cosy lounge, though you are advised to book beforehand. The hotel offers what it calls 'wholesome fayre',

with all dishes being realistically priced without compromising quality. The cuisine is traditional Scottish, with a great emphasis on locally caught seafood. There is a great selection of wines, so you are sure to find one that will suit your taste.

Plus the bar offers two real ales and a range of single malts, as well as a selection of beers, wines, spirits and, if you're driving, soft drinks. Why not relax and enjoy a quiet drink as you head north or south, or use the hotel as an overnight B&B? It is comfortable, welcoming, friendly, and represents great value for money.

118 THE CRAFTY KITCHEN

Ardfern, By Lochgilphead,
Argyll PA31 8QN
☎ 01852 500305
🌐 www.craftykitchen.co.uk

Ardfern is an extremely attractive small village in beautiful surroundings nestling on the shores of Loch Craignish, a sea loch popular with yachtsmen. **The Crafty Kitchen** is in the centre of the village, and is housed in what was, up until 14 years ago, a general store. Three years ago it was taken over by Taryn Blair, who has lived in the village for over nine years. Now it is a justly famous establishment selling good food at realistic prices.

It is open each year from the beginning of April until the end of October from Tuesday to Sunday each week, and on Saturday and Sunday only in November and December. Taryn is determined to offer imaginative meals at wonderful prices, and uses only the finest and freshest of local produce wherever possible in all the dishes created by her. Argyll has a number of producers providing a range of foods from beef, lamb, fish and shellfish to organic vegetables and fruits. In this way, the local economy thrives, and you are assured of

food that is full of flavour and beautifully home-cooked on the premises.

The ambience of the place is relaxed and friendly, with an interior that makes good use of pine furniture and timber flooring. In the summer months you can even eat out of doors. You can choose from printed menus or from a daily specials board that takes advantage of whatever local produce is in season. The dishes are cooked with imagination and flair, but always with due regard to the fresh flavour of the produce itself. The dinner menu contains such dishes as Islay scallops with either lemon, butter and parsley or cream, horseradish and chives,

cured meat platter, which has smoked local fish and various cured meats, home-made salmon fishcakes, and beef burgers using meat form a local farm. There is also a menu for snacks and light lunches and one for puddings.

The Crafty Kitchen is aptly named, as it also sells a great range of craft and toy items, some of them made locally. Here you can browse for a gift or souvenir without obligation.

This is a great place to eat while in this beautiful part of Argyll, and you can't go far wrong if you stop off and sample the great food on offer!

119 ANCHOR HOTEL

Harbour Street, Tarbert, Argyll PA29 6UB
☎ 01880 820577

Sitting right on the harbour side in the old fishing village of Tarbert on the Mull of Kintyre you will find one of the best hotels in the area - the **Anchor Hotel**. It is a warm, friendly place with plenty of character, and has a great reputation for its high standards of service, its food and its outstanding value for money.

The building itself has, in the past, been a church and a cinema before finally becoming a hotel called 'The Bruce' in the 1970s. Since November 2006 it has been under new management, with the owners formerly having worked together in a well-known Edinburgh hotel for over seven and a half years, and great things are planned for it, making it even better. It boasts 13 guest rooms, all of them en suite and all being furnished and decorated to an extremely high standard. Most are doubles and twins, though there is a family room, with none of them being on the ground floor. Six of the rooms have great views out over the quaint harbour, where picturesque fishing boats and yachts bob in the water.

The hotel is more of a dining pub with rooms, plus a bar that is cosy and inviting. In the summer months, you can sit outside and enjoy a pint of beer of a single malt while watching fishing boats unload their catch - some of which will no doubt be featuring in the hotel's menu that same evening. In fact, the Anchor Hotel is famous for its seafood, and appears in the famous 'Seafood Trail', which features elite establishments on Argyll's coast that place great emphasis on seafood (http://www.theseafoodtrail.com/members.php). The mussels are renowned, as are the scallops served in their own shells with maybe some garlic butter or Crabbie's Green Ginger. The hotel's seafood platter has become a legend, and is full of plump langoustines, lobster, razor fish and crab.

But the hotel is also renowned for its other dishes and most of the produce, such as Islay beef and Ifferdale lamb from just down the road in Saddell, is sourced locally to ensure maximum flavour and freshness. Plus soups and sandwiches are available throughout the day. Children are very welcome in the dining area at the Anchor Hotel, and both the bar and the restaurant are disabled friendly. However, you are advised to telephone about the accommodation, and during the summer months you should book in advance if you are eating.

120 FURNACE INN

Furnace, Inverary PA32 8XN
☎ 01499 500200
e-mail: thebeerjedi@aol.com
🌐 www.thefurnaceinn.co.uk

Small though it, the village of Furnace on the shore of Loch Fyne still has a post office/ village shop and a thriving traditional hostelry, the **Furnace Inn**. Built in the late 1700s with stone from the local quarry, the inn has a great atmosphere. The bar and restaurant are cosy and inviting, with an open log fire and walls covered with old pictures

of the village, the quarry and famous local shinty team. The Furnace has a fantastic reputation for good home-made food – and plenty of it! Other attractions here include a pool table, live music or a pub quiz most Saturday nights, and a beer garden.

122 BEN ARTHUR'S BOTHY

Main Street, Arrochar, Argyll G83 7AF
☎ 01301 702347
e-mail: benarthur01@aol.com

For the best in good drink and food in Arrochar, head for **Ben Arthur's Bothy** in the Main Street, close to the shores of Loch Long. It is open seven days a week, and uses only local produce wherever possible in its dishes. You can choose from a printed menu or a daily specials board, with everything being home-cooked to perfection. Fish - juicy steaks - chicken - vegetarian dishes - they are all here at very reasonable prices. Make this your first stop when in Arrochar!

123 THE UPPER CRUST

88A West Clyde Street, Helensburgh
Dunbartonshire G84 8BB
☎ 01436 678035
🌐 www.theuppercrustrestaurant.info

Many people have visited and recommended **The Upper Crust**, one of the Clyde coast's best restaurants. It sits on the seafront in the holiday resort of Helensburgh, west of Glasgow, and offers exceptional Scottish cuisine prepared from fresh local produce wherever possible. People come from far and near to sample the cooking, and many of the local B&Bs send their guests here for a meal. So highly thought of is it that you are advised to book at all times.

It is open at lunchtimes and in the evening from 6.30 pm during the summer months, and evenings only, with the exception of Wednesday, outside the holiday season. The interior is a delight, with a charm that can only be described as 'olde worlde'. It was formerly a bake house, and the old ovens can still be seen. It seats 26 in absolute comfort, and can accommodate a further 20 in the beautiful walled garden when the weather is warm.

Eating here is an experience not to be missed. Game and fish dishes are a speciality, with everything home cooked to order. This is not the place for fast food! You can choose from the daily menu or a specials board, although, with such attractive dishes, choosing might be difficult! The restaurant accepts all credit cards with the exception of Diners and American Express, and children are most welcome.

121 THE SHORE HOUSE INN ⁐

Lochgoilhead, Argyll PA24 8AD
☎ 01301 703340 Fax: 01301 703322
e-mail: theshorehouseinn@bt.connect.com
🖳 www.theshorehouse.net

The **Shore House Inn** in Lochgoilhead is an exceptional establishment that is famous for its good food, its great views and its elegant guest rooms. The village sits at the head of Loch Goil, approximately 90 minutes by car from Glasgow or Oban, and about 45 minutes from Dunoon. All around it is the stunning scenery of the Loch Lomond and Trossachs National Park, which adds to its attractiveness as a place to stay, eat or enjoy a quiet drink. It also sits at the head of the Cowal Peninsula, one of Argyll's most picturesque and historic areas.

The house itself is close to the waterfront, and is a former manse dating from 1847. Owners Gillian and Mark Curtis, soon after they took over in July 2004, closed the hotel for six months while it was completely refurbished. It opened to the public in June 2005 with the rooms opening in April 2006. It now offers all the modern conveniences you would expect from a VisitScotland 3-star rated hotel, while still retaining many original features which add to the elegance and charm of the place.

The hotel has four fully en suite rooms,

three doubles and a twin, all located upstairs. Each one is individually furnished and decorated, and combines great comfort with spaciousness. Two face the loch, and have wonderful views out over the water.

The bar is a welcoming, cosy place where you can enjoy a relaxing drink. Choose from a range of real ales (including the local Fyne Ale), plus beers, lager, spirits (including single malts), wine and soft drinks. It is the favourite haunt of musicians, and on a Thursday evening, during the 'pizza and pint' special offer, you can usually hear them play. If you are a musician yourself, bring your instrument along and join in!

The Lochside Restaurant serves some of the best food in the area, with all the produce used in the kitchen being sourced locally wherever possible. Prime Scottish steaks and succulent seafood are the specialities here, cooked with imagination and flair. Or try the pizzas cooked in an authentic wood-fired oven. There is a daytime menu that features home baking, open sandwiches, soup and salad, as well as children's options. The evening menu features many fine dishes such as breast of chicken stuffed with haggis, Shore House beef and vegetable curry, and Scottish venison steaks with orange and port sauce.

It is disabled friendly on the ground floor, and has ramped access to the dining and drinking areas.

124 THE HILL HOUSE

Upper Colquhoun Street,
Helensburgh G84 9AJ
☎ 01436 673900 Fax: 01436 674685
🌐 www.nts.org.uk

The finest of Charles Rennie Mackintosh's domestic creations, **The Hill House** sits high above the Clyde, commanding fine views over the river estuary. Walter Blackie, director of the well known Glasgow publishers, commissioned not only the house and garden but much of the furniture and all the interior fittings and decorative schemes. Mackintosh's wife, Margaret MacDonald, contributed fabric designs and a unique gesso overmantel. The overall effect is daring, but restrained in its elegance: the result, timeless rooms, as modern today as they must have been in 1904 when the Blackie family moved in.

An information room interprets the special relationship between architect and patron and provides a historical context for Inspirations, a dazzling exhibition in the upper east wing and the gardens. It brings together exceptional pieces of domestic design by great living designers, all of whom, in some way, pay homage to Mackintosh's elegance and invention, Inspiring comparisons may,be drawn between the work of Mackintosh, now recognised as one of the geniuses of the early 20th century, and pieces that themselves have become 21 st century icons.

The gardens have been restored to their former glory, and reflect features common to Mackintosh's architectural designs, They also contain a kinetic sculpture given to the house by the artist George Rickey.

125 THE BARRIEMORE

Corran Esplanade, Oban,
Argyll PA34 5AQ
☎ 01631 566356
e-mail: reception@barriemore-hotel.co.uk
🌐 www.barriemore-hotel.co.uk

"At the end of the day.... location matters."
And nowhere is this more evident than at **The Barriemore**, one of Oban's finest small guest houses. It sits right on the Corran Esplanade, with wonderful vistas out over the bay to the islands of Kerrera, Mull and Lismore. It has an historical background as it was built in 1895 by John Stuart McCaig, who also built McCaig's Folly in the town.

The four-star hotel boasts eleven fully en suite rooms (doubles, twins and one triple) which have alarms, colour TVs, (many having DVD or video facilities) and hospitality trays. Each one is individually and opulently furnished, and from five of them the whole panorama of Oban Bay can be seen. The residents' lounge is comfortable and tastefully decorated, with a large open fire and plenty of books and magazines. This leads into the warm, cosy bar, which is for residents only. Here you can enjoy a wide range of beers, wines or single malts after a hard day exploring all that Argyll has to offer. The spacious dining room overlooks the bay, and is where full Scottish breakfasts (including locally produced kippers and smoked haddock) are served. Overnight tariffs include breakfast, and all credit cards with the exception of American Express and Diners are accepted. Oban itself has a wide range of attractions, including many fine restaurants, so there is always something to do.

128 SOROBA HOUSE HOTEL

Soroba Road, Oban, Argyll PA34 4SB
☎ 01631 562628
e-mail: dochieblack@aol.com
🌐 www.sorobahousehotel.co.uk

The **Soroba House Hotel** sits only five minutes from the centre of the lovely small town of Oban, on Scotland's west coast. It is housed in an 18th century building that has retained many of its period features. In 2006 the hotel came under the personal management of Duncan and Donald Black, and since they bought it they have preserved and enhanced the unique ambience of the place.

It is set in lovely surroundings and gardens, and you could be mistaken for thinking that you were in the heart of the beautiful Scottish countryside rather than on the outskirts of the "Gateway to the Isles".

The hotel has four rooms/apartments, two of which are self-catering. All are spacious and decorated and furnished to an extremely high standard. The hotel also boasts two bars that sell

a great range of drinks, from single malts to beer and ales, wines, spirits, liqueurs and soft drinks. Delicious food is served in the dining area and the produce used in the kitchen is all sourced locally wherever possible, and is as fresh as can be. The cuisine is Scottish with subtle overseas hints.

This is a hotel that places great emphasis on service and value for money. The ambience is friendly and unfussy, and you are always sure of a warm welcome. It can also cater for weddings, anniversaries, birthdays and small conferences.

126 CORRIEMAR GUEST HOUSE

6 Corran Esplanade, Oban.
Argyll PA34 5AO
☎ 012931 562476 Fax: 01931 564339
e-mail: info@corriemarhouse.co.uk
🌐 www.corriemarhouse.co.uk

Corriemar Guest House has an outstanding position right on the seafront at Oban. The delightful four star Victorian building boasts 14 fully en suite rooms (one a suite consisting of sitting room, bedroom and en suite toilet). The décor is exceptional, using many materials and motifs from around the world, and this ensures a comfortable stay in an establishment that is friendly and welcoming. Breakfasts, lunches and dinners are served, with the kitchen using fresh local produce wherever possible.

127 GLENARA

Rockfield Road, Oban, Argyll PA34 5DQ
☎ 01631 563172
🌐 www.glenara.co.uk

Glenara is one of the most delightful and friendly B&Bs in Oban. Owned by Jenny and Bernard Childs, it has recently been completely refurbished, and offers three fully en suite rooms (two doubles and a triple) to discerning guests. This is a friendly, welcoming place that people return to again and again because of the high standards of service

and amazing value for money. The Scottish breakfasts are hearty and filling, and will set you up for the rest of the day!

129 OYSTER INN & FERRYMAN'S OF CONNEL

Connel Bridge, Near Oban,
Argyll PA37 1PJ
☎ 01631 710666
e-mail: stay@oysterinn.co.uk
⊕ www.oysterinn.co.uk

The Oyster Inn and Ferryman's of Connel sits four miles north of Oban in the village of Connel, where there was once a ferry across the mouth of Loch Etive. This is a splendid hostelry and traditional ferryman's pub dating from when you had to cross the loch by ferry. The Oyster Inn is an informal hotel boasting 11 four-star, en suite rooms and five three-star bunkhouses, each sleeping two. The rooms have TVs, CD and DVD players and radios.

The inn is famed for its food, and is open all day during the summer months, though you are well advised to book in advance. The speciality here is locally caught seafood, which is prepared by the resident chef, who uses flair and imagination in the dishes.

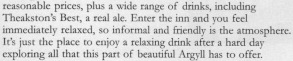

The Ferryman's is a traditional 18th century Scottish inn serving good food all day at

reasonable prices, plus a wide range of drinks, including Theakston's Best, a real ale. Enter the inn and you feel immediately relaxed, so informal and friendly is the atmosphere. It's just the place to enjoy a relaxing drink after a hard day exploring all that this part of beautiful Argyll has to offer.

Both establishments are owned and personally managed by Beth and Malcolm MacAuley, who are determined to build on the great reputation the places have enjoyed over the years. Visit and you're sure to agree!

130 APPIN HOLIDAY HOMES

Appin, Argyll PA38 4BQ
☎ 01631 730287
e-mail: info@appinholidayhomes.co.uk
⊕ www.appinholidayhomes.co.uk

Discover the west coast with ease from **Appin Holiday Homes**. With lochs, castles, glens, great hill, forest and island walks all on your doorstep, you won't have to spend all day in the car. Your home-from-home has tennis, sea life centre, horse riding, gardens, restaurant, country inn,

bike hire, village shop, craft shop and pottery all within 5 miles. With caravans on the shoreline, lodges on the edge of the woodland and houses around the restored railway station, Appin Holiday Homes is your natural holiday choice.

131 THE PIERHOUSE HOTEL & SEAFOOD RESTAURANT

Port Appin, Argyll PA38 4DE
☎ 01631 730302
e-mail: reservations@pierhousehotel.co.uk
🌐 www.pierhousehotel.co.uk

The Pierhouse Hotel & Seafood Restaurant is situated in one of the most beautiful and historic areas in Argyll - on the spectacular coastline of Loch Linnhe with 10 private moorings for guests. The hotel offers 12 ensuite bedrooms, including two superior four poster Loch View rooms and three family rooms, that are comfortable and tastefully furnished. Perhaps it is the magnificent views, stunning location and warm, friendly atmosphere that ensures people return again and again. The Pierhouse is just a few yards from the Port Appin ferry crossing to Lismore and as its name suggests, is renowned for its restaurant that specialises in delicious, fresh local seafood. The restaurant, which seats 60 people and boasts spectacular panoramic views, has

won a reputation for quality that has spread well beyond Argyll. It uses only the finest and freshest of produce (caught locally wherever possible). Lobsters, scallops, salmon, prawns and langoustine are all caught in Loch Linnhe and Loch Etive, while the mussels and oysters are gathered just offshore from Lismore. Venison and beef are sourced locally from neighbouring estates. The restaurant has an excellent cellar and an exciting winelist that is the perfect accompaniment to the excellent A La Carte Menu. Candlelit tables, crisp white linen and breathtaking views ensure an unforgettable culinary experience, whilst the choice of Bar Menu and Childrens Menu offers an alternative dining choice. The Pierhouse Hotel & Seafood Restaurant is out of the ordinary - a special place to hold like a secret.

Recommended by AA, Harden's UK Restaurant Guide, Peter Irvine's 'Scotland The Best', and Awarded AA Seafish Pub of the Year 2007.

132 AIRDENY CHALETS

Glen Lonan, Taynuilt, Argyll PA35 1HY
☎ 01866 822648
e-mail: jenifer@ardenychalets.co.uk
🌐 www.airdenychalets.co.uk

For the perfect hideaway among some of the finest scenery in Scotland, you can't beat the three and four star self-catering **Airdeny Chalets,** a mile from the village of Taynuilt. The seven timber chalets have two or three bedrooms, and come complete with everything you need for a holiday that is as hectic or relaxing as you want. The chalets are within a small development covering 3.5 acres, and look up towards the magnificent Ben Cruachan.

The living area in each chalet is open plan, with armchairs and a sofa which, in the two-bedroom version, converts into two single beds. Plus there is a television, DVD player and CD player. The kitchen is well-equipped and linen for the bedrooms is supplied. Towels, cots and high chairs can be hired by prior arrangement. For the cooler months, there is heating in the chalets and double glazing. Electricity is extra and payable at the end of your stay. There are laundry facilities on site and, for a small charge, dogs are welcome.

This part of Scotland brims with history and heritage, and there is a wide choice of activities in the area from golf, fishing and walking, to bird watching and sailing. The area is also renowned for its gardens and there so many lovely ones to visit. Oban and Fort William are within easy reach by car, and the ferry at Oban can take you across to Mull or the other islands of the Inner Hebrides.

133 CRUACHAN VISITOR CENTRE

Dalmally, Argyll PA33 1AN
☎ 01866 822618 Fax: 01866 822509
e-mail: visit.cruachan@scottishpower.com
🌐 www.scottishpower.com/cruachan/

Hidden deep within the mountain of Ben Cruachan on the shores of Loch Awe is Cruachan Power Station. Here, a short distance from Oban, you can discover one of the hidden wonders of the Highlands. A power station buried one kilometre below ground. At its centre lies a massive cavern, high enough to house the Tower of London! Here enormous turbines convert the power of water into electricity, available to you in your home at the flick of a switch. Take an unforgettable journey into Ben Cruachan and find out how power is generated. Experienced guides will lead you along a tunnel cut from solid rock. A coach will transport you into a different world, a place so warm that sub-tropical plants grow.

Find the nerve centre of the station and understand how the power of water from Loch Awe is harnessed to provide a rapid response to sharp rises in demand for electricity such as at mealtimes. A generator can go from standstill to an output of 100,000 kilowatts in two minutes to provide as much electricity as necessary.

Back on the surface, the visitor centre has many things to see and do. The Exhibition includes touch screens and demonstrates the way in which power will continue to be generated in the future. To finish off, there is a lochside cafeteria and gift shop. Open all year 9am-5pm.

135 RAERA FARM

Kilninver. By Oban, Argyll PA34 4UT
☎ 01852 316271
e-mail: inglis@talktalk.net

South of Oban, off the A816, is Kilninver, where you'll find a lovely self-catering accommodation at **Raera Farm**. The four units - a flat, a cottage a chalet and part of the 18th c farmhouse - are set within some of the best countryside in Argyll, and offer comfort, modern amenities and outstanding value for

money. So good is the accommodation that people come back again and again, drawn by its peace and tranquillity and its handy central location for exploring the area. The units are open all year except for the chalet, which is closed in winter.

136 CUILFAIL HOTEL

Kilmelford, Argyll PA34 4XA
☎ 01852 200274 Fax: 01852 200264
e-mail: info@cuilfail.co.uk
🌐 www.cuilfail.co.uk

The **Cuilfail Hotel** is different. For a start, it is an authentically traditional Highland inn that offers good, old fashioned Highland hospitality to people passing through or holidaying in this beautiful

part of Argyll on the west coast. Here you can enjoy good food, good drink and an unstuffy ambience that speaks of friendliness, relaxation and great value for money. There is so much to see and do in this part of Scotland, and if you visit the Cuilfail Hotel should be your first port of call.

134 BLARGHOUR FARM COTTAGES

Blarghour Farm, Lochaweside, By Dalmally,
Argyll PA33 1BW
☎ 01866 833246
e-mail: blarghour@btconnect.com
🌐 www.self-catering-argyll.co.uk

The four-star **Blarghour Farm Cottages** are truly outstanding self-catering cottages in Argyll. This is holiday accommodation at its very best, and yet at amazingly reasonable prices. They sit on a working hill farm on the shores of beautiful Loch Awe, and offer a holiday experience in a part of Scotland that is truly spectacular and filled with history. There are four cottages on offer, one of which has wheelchair access, so is ideal for the disabled. Each one is beautifully appointed, with a fully equipped kitchen, superb furnishings and great views out over Loch Awe. *Barr-Beithe Upper* is the largest of the cottages, and sleeps six people in three bedrooms - a double (with king-sized bed), a twin (with beds that zip together to form a double) and a further twin. The cottage is all on the one level. It also boasts a spacious conservatory with glorious views.

Barr-Beithe Lower sleeps five, and has three bedrooms - a double, a twin (with beds that can zip together to form a double) and a further single. All rooms are on the same level, and there

is a wheelchair ramp at the entrance. *The Stable* sleeps four in two twin bedrooms, each with beds that can zip together to form doubles. One of the features of this cottage is a handsome spiral staircase. *The Barn* is the smallest of the cottages, and sleeps two in one bedroom with twin beds that can covert to a double.

Each cottage is double-glazed, and boasts a cosy yet spacious lounge where you can relax and enjoy the great views. The kitchens all boast a cooker, microwave, fridge/freezer, iron and ironing board, washer, and a host of other labour saving devices. Each cottage has a well-appointed bathroom, and in addition *Barr-Beithe Upper* and *Barr-Beithe Lower also* have shower rooms. Each cottage has a colour TV, telephone, double-glazing, gas fires and plenty of car parking space. The cottages are open all year round, and short winter breaks are available between November and the end of March.

The countryside surrounding the Blarghour Holiday Cottages is rugged and spectacular, yet they are only an hour's drive from all that the bustling town of Oban has to offer with its restaurants, pubs and supermarkets and Inveraray with its famous castle and jail only 35 minutes away.

486

138 LUNGA ESTATE

Craobh Haven, Nr Lochgilphead,
Argyll PA31 8QR
☎ 01852 500237 Fax: 01631 572248
e-mail: colin@lunga.com
ⓦ www.lunga.com

The **Lunga Estate** covers 4,000 acres and offers the perfect facilities for a holiday that can be as relaxing or as activity-filled as you desire. It stands on the Craignish Peninsula on the western seaboard of Argyll, which is one of the loveliest areas in western Scotland, with history and heritage aplenty to explore.

Within the estate you will find superb self-catering and serviced accommodation that offers everything for a holiday that will be truly memorable. Lunga House was originally a fine old tower house but is now a castellated and turreted building, set romantically among woodland, and having fine views out to the Firth of Lorne and the Sound of Jura. It has four self-contained flats (two of which sleep up to ten people) and two serviced rooms.

Adjacent to the house are two studio rooms and a self-catering cottage that sleeps up to five people, and north of Lunga are a further two self-catering cottages that sleep six. Within the picturesque village of Ardfern is a

further self-catering cottage, *The Old Schoolhouse*, which sleeps up to ten. All the properties are equipped to an exceptional standard to make a stay as comfortable and carefree as possible. Cots, dinners and other amenities can be supplied by prior arrangement and at a small extra charge. Dinners for large parties of about 30 are sometimes held in the dining room of the house - an experience not to be missed!

Craignish Peninsula is a beautiful area that repays a careful exploration. There are old castles, wells, Viking burial sites, romantic ruined church sites with the graves of clan chiefs and crusader knights, and the village of Ardfern, which contains one of the most picturesque inns in Argyll. Plus there is a wide range of activities. There are riding stables just north of the estate, a boat club at Ardfern, yachting marinas, fishing on the estate's six lochs and superb walking and climbing. In addition, there are golf courses at Oban and Lochgilphead, not forgetting the championship course an hour away at Machrihanish. Or why not cross over to the island of Colonsay, play a round there, and return in the evening?

Lunga is a traditional estate that offers superb hospitality, and a holiday here will be long remembered. The laird, Colin Lindsay-Macdougall, is anxious to offer you a warm Scottish welcome to his Highland estate!

137 CRAOBH HARBOUR COTTAGES

Colonsay Cottage, Craobh Haven,
By Lochgilphead, Argyll PA31 8UA
☎ 01852 500648
🌐 www.holidaycottageshighlands.co.uk

Set in the small, modern village of Craobh Haven ('Tree Haven'), the **Craobh Harbour Cottages** feature six purpose-built self-catering units that offer everything the modern holiday maker needs for a restful holiday among the stunning scenery of the West Highlands. There are two kinds, sleeping either  four or six, and they come with well-equipped kitchens, an open plan lounge area and spacious, comfortable bedrooms. You can't afford to miss these stunning cottages!

139 TOROSAY CASTLE & GARDENS

Craignure, Isle of Mull PA65 6AY
☎ 01680 812421 Fax: 01680 812470
e-mail: info@torosay.com
🌐 www.torosay.com

Torosay Castle, completed in 1858 in the Scottish Baronial style by the eminent architect David Bryce, is a fine example of his work, and one of the few still used as a family home while open to the public. Bryce's clever architecture results in a combination of elegance and informality, grandeur and homliness. A combination of formal terraces and dramatic scenery makes Torosay a spectacular setting,  which, together with a mild climate results in superb specimens of rare, unusual and beautiful plants. There is also a tearoom, a shop and free parking. Open Easter to October 10.30am-5pm. Gardens open all year.

141 TIGH HOLM COTTAGES

Sculamus Moss, Breakish, Isle of Skye,
Inverness-shire IV42 8QB
☎ 01471 822848
e-mail: info@tigh-holm-cottages.com
🌐 www.tigh-holm-cottages.com

Tigh Holm Cottages are situated at the junction of the A850 and the A851 on the Isle of Skye, only half a mile from Broadford. Two cottages and one house are available as self-catering accommodation for discerning tourists, and each one is extremely cosy yet spacious. So good are they that they have been given a three-star rating from VisitScotland. They sit close to the shore and are ideal for walkers, wildlife enthusiasts, climbers, photographers and lovers of Scottish scenery.

Each cottage has a modern lounge/dining room on the ground floor, along with a well-equipped kitchen and utility room. Upstairs has a twin, a double room and a bathroom, meaning that they sleep up to four in absolute comfort. The house is more substantial and sleeps up to eight people.

Each has been furnished and decorated to a superior standard  to give you a holiday to remember. There is full central heating, a video recorder, DVD player, TV, radio/CD player and a pack containing information on what to do and where to go in the area. A starter grocery pack is also made available containing fresh bread, milk and anything else you need by arrangement. Further groceries are available from Broadford.

Short, out of season breaks are available with a minimum stay of three days. There is plenty of off road parking, and children and pets are most welcome.

140 THE MACKINNON COUNTRY HOUSE HOTEL

Kyleakin, Isle of Skye,
Inverness-shire IV41 8PQ
☎ 01599 534180
e-mail: info@mackinnonhotel.co.uk
🌐 www.mackinnonhotel.co.uk

Standing in its own beautiful four-acre gardens, the three-star **The MacKinnon Country House Hotel** represents all that is great about traditional Scottish hospitality. It is owned and run by the Smith-Tongs family, whose one aim is to make their guests feel relaxed and perfectly at home in one of the best

hotels on the Isle of Skye. It sits just over the Skye Bridge, and makes a superb B&B stopping off place or a base from which to explore the area. The building itself dates back to 1912, when it was built as a private residence, and today's hotel retains many of the original features, giving it a charm and warmth.

The hotel is open all year round, and has sixteen fully en suite guest rooms, nine of which are in the main building with a further seven in the delightfully secluded Lodge nearby. All the rooms are individually furnished and decorated to an exceptional standard, and all have

central heating, direct dial phone, colour TV, hair drier and tea/coffee making facilities.

One guest once described the Bein Na Caillich as 'one of the loveliest restaurants I have ever eaten in', and this is praise richly deserved. It has wonderful views out over the gardens to the mountains beyond, and this is complemented by the superb cuisine. Local produce from the Isle of Skye is used by the talented Head Chef, and if you have a favourite dish he will do his best to cook it for you. An excellent wine list is available, and you are sure to find something that

will complement your meal admirably. The restaurant is open every evening from 7 pm until very late.

If you just wish to relax in friendly, informal surroundings, then this is the hotel for you. If, however, you want to have a more active time, then there is just so much to see and do in the area, from sightseeing to golf, fishing to walking, and from sailing to mountain biking!

142 HEBRIDEAN HOTEL, BAR AND RESTAURANT

14 Harrapool, Broadford,
Isle of Skye IV49 9QA
☎ 01471 822486
e-mail: enquiries@hebrideanhotel.co.uk
🌐 www.hebrideanhotel.co.uk

The **Hebridean Hotel, Bar and Restaurant** is famed throughout the Isle of Skye for its comfortable accommodation, good food and great drink. It sits in Harrapool, east of Broadford, and offers superb rooms to discerning tourists who recognise high standards of service and great value for money. The building itself is imposing and modern, and of its eleven rooms, three are fully en suite. There are four doubles, two en suite twins, four singles and an en suite family room that sleeps three. All are decorated and furnished to a very high standard.

The licensed restaurant sells delicious, home-cooked food from noon until 9 pm in summer and from noon to 2.30 pm and 6 pm to 9 pm at other times. All the produce is sourced in Scotland, and you can choose from a printed menu or a specials board that takes advantage of produce in season. The well stocked bar offers a wide range of drinks, including, during the summer months, real ale. There is also a wide selection of single malts, plus beers, wines, spirits and soft drinks. Children are very welcome if eating.

There is plenty of off road car parking, and all credit cards with the exception of American Express and Diners are accepted. Though the bar and restaurant areas pose no problems for the disabled, guests should ring about the accommodation.

143 BEINN NA CAILLICH CAFÉ

Ford Road, Broadford, Isle of Skye,
Inverness-shire IV49 9AB
☎ 01471 822616
e-mail: skye-gifts@fsmail.net

The **Beinn Na Caillich Café** is more than just a café. It is a superb licensed restaurant selling some of the best food in the Broadford area. It is open seven days a week, and the impressive menu includes such dishes as venison pie, grilled fresh salmon and cheesy nut roast. Lighter options include salads, jacket potatoes, baguettes, burgers and toasted paninis. Plus there are always other dishes on the daily specials board. This is the place to eat when you're in Broadford!

144 CAFÉ ARRIBA

Quay Brae, Portree, Isle of Skye,
Inverness-shire IV51 9DB
☎ 01478 611830

Café Arriba is a lively bistro/café located in the heart of Portree. Traditional on the outside and modern, funky and smart on the inside, it is more than just a café - it is a great eating place where good food and value for money go hand in hand.

By day you can relax and enjoy great teas and coffees, as well as light snacks and lunches. In the evening, from 6pm onwards during summer, the ambience changes and it becomes an intimate yet spacious restaurant, serving some of the best food on the island. The cuisine is always imaginative, with the produce being local wherever possible, and though there is a strong vegetarian influence to many of the dishes, the food is sure to appeal to everyone.

There is always an informal feel to the place, and the service is efficient while still remaining friendly. You can choose from a menu

or a specials board, which has been known to change two or three times a day as popular dishes run out and are replaced by something else! The place is open six days a week from 7 am to 10 pm in the summer and 8 am to 5 or 6 pm in the winter.

Once you've eaten in the café, why not visit Vanilla Skye, a colourful shop opposite that sells its own hand made chocolates plus carefully chosen produce from elsewhere. Do you have a sweet tooth? Then this is the place for you!

145 URQUHART CALEDONIAN HOTEL

Wentworth Street, Portree, Isle of Skye,
Inverness-shire IV51 9ET
☎ 01478 612641
e-mail: celedonianhotel@quista.net
⊕ www.urquhartcaledonianhotel.co.uk

The **Urquhart Caledonian Hotel**, right in the heart of Portree, has recently been refurbished to a high standard to give some of the best tourist and business accommodation on the Isle of Skye. It is a friendly, family-run establishment that puts informality and a warm welcome first, without compromising high standards of service or outstanding value for money.

There are eight rooms on offer, each one extremely comfortable and furnished and decorated to a high standard. They are fully en suite, as you would expect, and have a colour TV, tea/coffee making facilities, a hair drier, radio alarm clock and a telephone. The Caley Bar is a favourite haunt of local people, and it is the ideal place to meet people, relax and have a quiet drink. Sit by the open fire and enjoy one of the many blended whiskies and single

malts, or have a game of darts, pool or one of the board games.

And when it's eating time, enjoy one of the no-frills meals that are cooked on the premises. There is an extensive menu, and most of the dishes are prepared from fresh local produce. The bar is a child friendly area up until about 9 pm, so the whole family can eat here.

Skye is a wonderful place for sightseeing and outdoor activities such as walking and fishing, so ironing and laundry facilities are always available.

146 GLENVIEW HOTEL

Culnacnoc, Staffin, Isle of Skye,
Inverness-shire IV51 9JH
☎ 01470 562248
e-mail: enquiries@glenviewskye.co.uk
🌐 www.glenviewskye.co.uk

The **Glenview Hotel** sits on the Trotternish Peninsula, twelve miles north of Portree, on the stunningly beautiful island of Skye. This pet-friendly hotel is owned and run by Doreen and Ian, and offers five superb guest rooms, four of which are fully en suite while the other has private facilities. There is a good mix of room sizes - two doubles with four-poster, a double and two double/twins. Each one is extremely comfortable, with a high standard of furnishings and decoration ensuring that you have a relaxing and enjoyable time.

You can book on a B&B or dinner, B&B basis. The full Scottish breakfasts (or lighter options if required) will really set you up for the day. Dinner is served each evening in the spacious dining room from 6.30 pm, with Doreen doing all the cooking. In fact, she is an expert cook, and people have raved about the many fine dishes she prepares from fresh, local produce wherever possible. Comments about her food have included '...the food alone is worth the 1200km drive', and 'hosts

and food exemplary'. She even opens the place to non-residents in the evening, as her reputation has spread throughout the area. Non-residents however, need to book beforehand. The dining room seats up to ten in absolute comfort, so get your booking in quickly!

The house was built in 1903 for a local merchant, and it has retained a lot of its Edwardian charm. It has lovely views out over the Old Man of Storr, and there is nothing finer than sitting in the garden in the evening and drinking in the peace and quiet while admiring the scenery. When the weather is a wee bit colder, there is a cosy yet spacious guest lounge, with log burner, TV, video and DVD player. Here you can read or watch TV while enjoying a relaxing drink.

The whole area is rich in history and heritage, with many castles, ruined churches and deserted crofting communities. Plus there are so many things to do. Golf is available at Portree, the Trotternish Peninsula seems to have been made for walking, and there is plenty of river and loch fishing. Charter boats can be hired for sea fishing excursions into the Minch, and on the coastline you can see seals, dolphins, sea birds and sometimes whales.

147 LODGE HOTEL

Edinbane, Isle of Skye,
Inverness-shire IV51 9PW

☎ 01470 582217 / 0700 Skyelodge

e-mail: skyelodge@AOL.com

🌐 www.the-lodge-at-edinbane.co.uk
www.isleofskyehotel.com

The **Lodge Hotel** at Edinbane on Skye is a famous old coaching inn and hunting lodge that dates right back to 1543. It is a picturesque place, built of old stone, and is situated just off the A850 between Portree and Dunvegan. Here you will find traditional Highland hospitality coupled with modern amenities and high standards of service.

It has six spacious and comfortable guest rooms that have that genuine 'country feel' to them - two doubles, two twins, a triple and a single. Four are en suite, and each one is furnished and decorated to an exacting standard, with colour TVs and tea/coffee making facilities. There will also soon be a room specially adapted for the disabled. Snuggle down in a four-poster here and you'll get a great night's sleep!

The restaurant serves delicious food, as the owners of this family-run hostelry are passionate about their fine cuisine. It uses the finest and freshest local produce, and it open to residents and non-residents alike. Venison, locally caught fish, Scotch beef and lamb all feature on the menu. After your meal why not enjoy a glass or two of single malt in the hotel bar as a nightcap? It offers a wide range of welcoming drinks, and is both cosy and welcoming. Usually it is open between 12 noon and 1 am. And single malts are not the only spirits to be found here! The hotel boasts several ghosts, who are said to haunt the downstairs areas. But fear not - they seem to be friendly and harmless!

149 MORAR

Ardvasar, Sleat, Isle of Skye,
Highlands IV45 8RU

☎ 01471 844378 / 07775 668223

e-mail: info@accommodation-on-skye.co.uk

🌐 www.accommodation-on-skye.co.uk

Morar is a large, luxurious and comfortable B&B less than a mile from the Mallaig to Armadale ferry terminal, in the village of Ardvasar on the Sleat Peninsula, known as the 'Garden of Skye'. It is a modern building on a working croft which has a quiet charm, and overlooks the sea. If you arrive on foot via the

Armadale ferry, you can arrange for the owners of the B&B to pick you up at the terminal and take you to the house.

It has three guest rooms - two large, double rooms (one suitable for a family) and a smaller twin room. Each one is well equipped and comfortable, and comes with tea/coffee making facilities, television, video and hair drier. Pre recorded videos are freely available. From the south facing terrace and the dining room, you get splendid views out over the mountains of the mainland and the sea, and dolphins and whales can often be seen. Guests can walk in

the extensive grounds or go down to the shore at the foot of the garden, where otters are sometimes seen. Morar has its own heated indoor swimming pool. Breakfast options include free range eggs, home-made bread and preserves, and local produce such as fish and bacon. Lighter options, including vegetarian, are also available.

The B&B is the perfect place to spend a day or two, or even a week, as it makes the ideal base from which to explore Skye and Lochalsh. Come along and see for yourself!

Knock Bay, Sleat, Isle of Skye,
Inverness-shire IV44 8RE

☎ 01471 833231 / 0845 055 1117

e-mail: info@skyehotel.co.uk

🌐 www.skyehotel.co.uk

Toravaig House is a truly outstanding small hotel that fully merits its four star rating. It sits on the Sleat Peninsula, on the beautiful Isle of Skye, and speaks of luxury and elegance while still retaining an informal and friendly atmosphere. Owned and managed by Ann Gracie and her partner Kenneth

Gunn since December 2003, it exemplifies all that is good about traditional Scottish hospitality. In fact, it won the 'Scottish Island Hotel of the Year' award from Hotel Review Scotland in 2005, and Conde Nast Johansen's 'Most Excellent Service UK' award for 2006. The hotel has nine individually designed rooms that reflect the high standards that have been set. They are all en suite, and come with Sky satellite TV, CD player, telephone modem and hospitality products. Each one is cosy yet spacious, and is luxuriously decorated and furnished, ensuring that guests feel relaxed and get a great night's sleep!

The dining room is elegant but unfussy, and here you can enjoy a dining experience that you will long remember. The chef insists on only the finest and freshest of produce for his imaginative dishes. Seafood - prime Scotch beef and lamb - venison - poultry - crisp local vegetables - they are

all sourced locally to ensure maximum flavour and freshness. The small but select wine list contains many fine wines, and you are sure to find something that is just perfect. There is a splendid range of sweets and the meal can be rounded off by a coffee and a glass of cognac or single malt whisky.

Why not relax afterwards in the splendid drawing room, with its baby grand? Or, during the summer months, take a stroll around the landscaped gardens and admire the view out over the sea to Knoydart on the mainland?

The hotel is also the ideal venue for business meetings, conferences and seminars up to a maximum of 20 people, far away from the distractions of the big city. The hotel can arrange all the facilities you will need, plus a range of free time and team-building activities such as clay pigeon shooting, golf, archery and so on.

150 THE SHED ¶

Armadale Pier, Armadale, Sleat,
Isle of Skye, Inverness-shire IV45 8RS
☎ 01471 844222

For good food while on the Isle of Skye, you just can't beat **The Shed**, situated at the pier in Armadale. This small restaurant is famous for the quality of its many dishes, the most popular being its fresh herb salads, which are available in the summer months. It also serves delicious seafood such as locally caught scallops and crab. Vegetarian options are also available. Pay it a visit - you won't be disappointed!

151 MILLS OBSERVATORY 🏛

Glamis Road, Balgay Park,
Dundee DD2 2UB
☎ 01382 435967 Fax: 01382 435962
e-mail:
mills.observatory@dundeecity.gov.uk
⊞ www.dundeecity.gov.uk

Mills Observatory, housed in a classically styled sandstone building, is the UK's only full time public observatory. Here you can see the stars and planets for yourself through an impressive Victorian telescope and look at safe projected images of the sun. The planetarium has an artificial night sky giving you the chance to view constellations and planets. More can be learnt through the changing displays, audio and visual presentations and an interactive computer. The shop offers a range of gifts and educational items. Admission to the observatory is free.

152 THE OLD MANOR ⊨

Panbride, Carnoustie, Angus DD7 6JP
☎ 01241 854804 Fax: 01241 855327
e-mail: stay@oldmanorcanoustie.com
⊞ www.oldmanorcarnoustie.com

As soon as you enter **The Old Manor**, you find yourself back in the days when comfort and elegance were the order of the day. This superb four star establishment has five rooms on offer, each one named after a Scottish castle, and each one comfortable and cosy, with tea and coffee making facilities. The public rooms are spacious and elegant, with wide-screen digital TV in the lounge and a roaring log fire in the colder months. There is also a self-catering cottage

available which sleeps five to six people. This makes an ideal base from which to explore Dundee and the surrounding countryside.

154 LITTLETON OF AIRLIE COTTAGES ⊨

Littleton of Airlie, Kirriemuir,
Angus DD8 5NS
☎ 01575 530422
e-mail: yvonne_mallet@hotmail.com
⊞ www.littletonofairlie.com

For superior self-catering accommodation in a rural setting in Angus, you can't beat the 19th century **Littleton of Airlie Cottages**, on a farm west of Kirriemuir. There are two cottages on offer - both of them sleep two, with cottage number one having a double bed and

cottage number two having zip-link beds. Both cottages are beautifully appointed, and come equipped for a relaxing holiday in the tranquil countryside of Angus.

153 THE TOLBOOTH

West High Street, Forfar, Angus DD8 1BE
☎ 01307 464350

The Tolbooth is a lively pub and restaurant in the centre of the historic old market town of Forfar in Angus. It dates from the 18th century in parts, and is housed in a picturesque old whitewashed building on a prominent corner site. The pub is a cosy, welcoming place, full of polished wood and comfortable furniture where you can enjoy a quiet drink as you watch Premier League football (a speciality in the pub!) on TV.

The bar carries a wide range of drinks including ales, beers, wines, cider, spirits, liqueurs and soft drinks should you be driving. It is a favourite place for locals and visitors alike, and you will be assured of a friendly, Scottish welcome from Jacqui Garven, who is the manager.

The Tolbooth also serves great food. There is seating for 30 to 40 people in the downstairs restaurant, plus there is a smart, trendy bistro upstairs. Only the finest and freshest of local produce is used, wherever possible, in the many dishes on offer, and every one is home-cooked to perfection on the premises. You can choose from the main menu or from a daily specials board, which takes advantage of local seasonal produce.

There is a separate menu for the upstairs bistro, which is a popular place for local people to eat. The cusine is traditional Scottish, with Italian influences. Dishes on the menus for both upstairs and downstairs include tomato and basil soup with focaccia bread, turkey with all the trimmings at Christmas time, juicy Aberdeen Angus steaks with all the trimmings, popcorn and blue cheese salad, wild duck in a morello cherry sauce and Highland game pie. Jacqui is determined to give her customers an eating experience they will long remember for all the right reasons, and you will be amazed at the value-for-money prices. There are no disabled access problems downstairs, though people should phone about access to the upstairs bistro.

Jacqui looks forward to welcoming you to her pub and restaurant. It's the place to go after a hard day exploring all that the lovely county of Angus has to offer. Pay it a visit and experience it for yourself!

155 VISOCCHI'S

37 High Street, Kirriemuir,
Angus DD8 4EG
☎ 01575 572115

During the three quarters of a century since it was established, **Visocchi's** has become something of a legend in the Kirriemuir area. It is still owned and run by the Visocchi family – Michael and Elena – and it still produces the famous ice cream that is made fresh each day in their factory from the finest ingredients using their remarkable 77 year old recipe.

Although best known for its ice cream, Visocchi's is also a café serving a good choice of snacks, light meals, filled baguettes, toasties, omelettes, burgers, mini pizzas and baked potatoes and Costa coffee. Naturally, ice cream also features prominently on the menu with a wide choice that includes Banana Split, Banana Royale, Knickerbocker Glory, sundaes and – apologies to the calorie police – mouthwatering confections such as "Brown Derby": a hot muffin topped with ice cream, chocolate sauce and whipped cream.

Visocchi's also has a thriving retail counter where you can buy ice creams to take out or purchase some of the confectionery and snacks on sale.

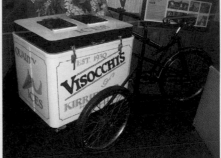

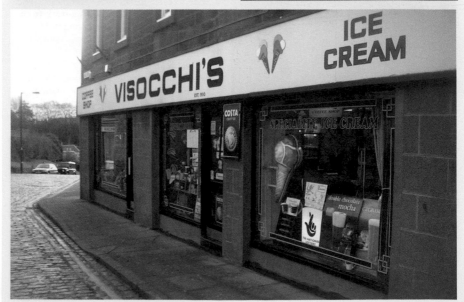

156 THRUMS HOTEL

Bank Street, Kirriemuir, Angus DD8 4BE
☎ 01575 572758
e-mail: enquiries@thrumshotel.co.uk
🌐 www.thrumshotel.co.uk

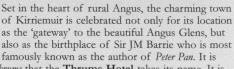

Set in the heart of rural Angus, the charming town of Kirriemuir is celebrated not only for its location as the 'gateway' to the beautiful Angus Glens, but also as the birthplace of Sir JM Barrie who is most famously known as the author of *Peter Pan*. It is from another of Barrie's works, *A Window in Thrums* that the **Thrums Hotel** takes its name. It is situated in the heart of the town and offers quality accommodation and a welcoming, friendly atmosphere within charming surroundings.

The hotel is fully licensed and the lounge, with its traditional interior and pleasant atmosphere, provides an enjoyable environment in which to unwind. The bar stocks an extensive range of drinks including a wide selection of some of Scotland's finest malt whiskeys. If you prefer, meals can be enjoyed here in the lounge rather than the dining room. Children are welcome in the lounge area providing they are accompanied by a supervising adult.

Dining at the hotel is a real pleasure. The chefs create an excellent, varied menu that is renowned for its quality and ranges from light snacks to traditional wholesome fare. Many of

the most popular dishes contain local produce, amongst them fresh Scottish Salmon, marvellous local game and excellent seafood fresh from the East Coast. The dining room is fully licensed and there's an extensive selection of wine to cater for all tastes and meals. The dining room is open seven days a week from midday through until 8pm each night. High teas are served from 4.30pm to 7.30pm daily, and breakfast is from 7am to 9.30am daily.

Along with the rest of the hotel, the guest bedrooms have recently undergone a major refurbishment and are now of the highest standard you would expect. There's a choice of single, twin, double or family rooms to cater for all requirements. Each room has full en suite facilities and is equipped with colour TV and hospitality tray.

A statue of JM Barrie's most enduring creation, Peter Pan, stands in the market place in Kirriemuir. There's also an imaginative exhibition about Barrie's life and work which is housed in his birthplace. And, on Kirriemuir Hill, the camera obscura he donated to the town can be visited. It gives a unique 360 degree panoramic view of the surrounding countryside and is one of only three remaining in Scotland today.

157 LETHAM HOTEL

The Square, Letham, by Forfar, Angus
☎ 01307 818218
e-mail: lethamhotel@hotmail.co.uk

With five fully en suite rooms on offer in various sizes, the **Letham Hotel** must surely make the best base from which to explore historic Angus and even beyond. Each one is comfortable and spacious, and comes well furnished and decorated. There is also a colour TV and tea and coffee making facilities.

The hotel itself sits in the centre of the village, in the main square, and is a picturesque, whitewashed building dating from the early 19th century with a distinct 'olde worlde' charm about it. The interior has recently had a major £200,000 refurbishment, which has created a warm, friendly establishment that is modern without losing many of the period features that make it such a welcoming place. So you are assured of the highest standards of service here, coupled with realistic prices.

The hotel is famous throughout the area for the high standards of its cuisine. The dishes are all individually cooked to order, so there is no 'fast food' here! Only the finest and freshest

of local produce is used in the kitchen wherever possible, which means that guests experience a meal that is full of flavour. Everything is home-cooked on the premises, and there is almost nothing that is 'boil in the bag' or defrosted before serving here! Why not enjoy an evening meal after a hard day exploring Angus and beyond? Every day there is a specials board that takes advantage of local produce in season, and there is also a printed menu.

If you stay on a B&B basis, you will discover that the breakfasts, also cooked from local produce, are hearty and filling, will serving times being arranged beforehand to suit you. The hotel is also the village's 'local', and the bar is a cosy, friendly place with a modern feel to it, where you can chat to the local people over a relaxing drink. There is a superb range of drinks behind the bar - ales, beers, cider, lager, wines, spirits, liqueurs and soft drinks are all available, and all at competitive prices. There is an adjoining games room where yo can place pool or darts. The downstairs areas are disabled friendly, though you should phone about the rooms, which are upstairs. The toilet contains a baby-changing room. There is ample parking, and all credit and debit cards are accepted.

Collistion, Arbroath, Angus DD11 3RP
☎ 01241 890232
e-mail: colliston@btconnect.com
🌐 www.thecollistoninn.co.uk

On the busy A933, on the outskirts of Arbroath, you will find the substantial, family-run **Colliston Inn**, housed in a former manse dating from 1850. It is a picturesque, well-proportioned building with plenty of parking space and a relaxing feel to it. It is owned and personally managed by Winnie and Grant Scott who have, in the four years they have been here, created a warm, friendly establishment that is appreciated by locals and tourists alike.

It boasts a bistro-style wine bar, a restaurant and a huge function room, and soon the inn will be extended to accommodate guest rooms where people can stay for short breaks or overnight B&B stays. The restaurant is a large, old fashioned room, beautifully lit in the evenings and naturally lit at lunchtimes. The twelve tables have crisp linen and sparkling cutlery which, along with fresh flowers, gives an elegance that adds to the dining experience. Winnie and Grant's sons are the chefs here, and they make as much use as possible of locally sourced produce, from beef, lamb and

vegetables to fish, game and poultry. The cuisine is traditional Scottish with a modern twist. A lunch menu, for instance, might contain such dishes as pan fried lamb's liver with onions and mash, salmon fish cakes with parsley sauce, home made steak and ale pie and pan fried rib-eye steak. Snacks such as soup and sandwiches are also available, and just as much attention is given to these as to the more formal dishes.

The wine bar is special. It boasts a selection of wines specially chosen for the Colliston, including the famous Boland cellar in South Africa, and the curiously named Tiddy Widdy well from South Australia. The bar is also stocked with a great range of beers, spirits, liqueurs, lagers, cider and soft drinks for those who are driving.

The Collinstin Inn is also the perfect place to host a wedding reception, party or other function. The Broust function suite can easily hold up to 110 people, and has its own bar, entrance and dance floor. It is made of timbers from the infamous Britannic cruise ship of the early 1900s. The walls are adorned with prints of the ship.

Arbroath is a town steeped in history, and is famous as the place where, in its now-ruined abbey, the Declaration of Arbroath was signed. If you are visiting, you must come along to the Colliston Inn and experience some of the best hospitality in Scotland!

159 BUT 'N' BEN

**Auchmithie, Nr Arbroath,
Angus DD1 5SQ
☎ 01241 877223**

Three miles north of Arbroath you will find the **But 'n' Ben**, a great eating place in the small village of Auchmithie. It is a pub/restaurant that serves great food and drink to discerning guests, and is housed in a row of old cottages, some of which date back to the 13th century. Pride of place goes to seafood here, including the famous Arbroath Smokie, which was invented in the village. The welcome here is warm, and the prices represent great value for money!

HIDDEN PLACES GUIDES

Explore Britain and Ireland with *Hidden Places* guides - a fascinating series of national and local travel guides.

Packed with easy to read information on hundreds of places of interest as well as places to stay, eat and drink.

Available from both high street and internet booksellers

For more information on the full range of *Hidden Places* guides and other titles published by Travel Publishing visit our website on

www.travelpublishing.co.uk
or ask for our leaflet by phoning
0118-981-7777 or emailing
info@travelpublishing.co.uk

160 MONTROSE BASIN WILDLIFE CENTRE

**Rossie Braes, Montrose, Angus DD10 9TJ
☎ 01674 676336 Fax: 01674 678773**

Montrose Basin is the 750 hectare enclosed estuary of the South Esk river. Virtually untouched by industrial development and pollution, the Basin provides a rich feeding ground for thousands of resident and migrant birds. The daily tidal cycle and passing seasons, each with its own characteristic pattern of birds - winter and summer visitors and passage migrants - ensure something new and different every month of the year. From here you might see eider ducks, pink footed and greylag geese, otters and much more.

Magnificent views of the wildlife can be seen through high powered telescopes and binoculars, whilst television cameras bring the wildlife right into the centre! Unique displays show how a tidal basin works and the routes taken by the migrating birds. There are lots of buttons to press, boxes to open, touch tables and microscopes - ideal for children - and there is a fully equipped

classromm for children to enjoy a range of educational activities. A nearby hide provides a closer view of the wildlife and the shop is stocked with a range of unusual and exciting gifts. Open 15th March to 15th November, daily 10.30am-5pm and 16th November to 14th March, Friday, Saturday and Sunday 10.30am-4pm.

161 GREEN HOTEL

2 The Muirs., Kinross,
Kinross-shire KY13 8AS
☎ 01577 863467 Fax: 01577 863180
e-mail: jm@green-hotel.com
🌐 www.green-hotel.com

Kinross is a small town with a character and history all of its own.. And in it you will find the **Green Hotel**, an intimate, private establishment that retains all the traditional values of Scottish hospitality while also offering up to the minute standards of service and value for money. It started

life in the 18th century as a coaching inn for people travelling from Edinburgh to the Highlands, and even then its reputation was second to none.

The hotel is family-owned and family-run, and has a relaxed and inviting ambience. Kinross is in just the right location to act as a base for exploring a wide area of Scotland, from the delights of Edinburgh and Glasgow to the East Neuk of Fife, the Trossachs, the Burns Country, Perthshire, Angus and the Borders. There are also two golf courses on hand, with special rates for hotel

guests, fishing on Loch Leven, plenty of good walking country, and a superb ice facility for one of Scotland's national sports - curling. Guests can also enjoy the hotel's own leisure facilities which include a heated swimming pool, sauna, solarium, fitness centre and tennis and squash courts.

There are 46 rooms in the hotel, and all are all fully en suite. They are also spacious, comfortable and furnished and decorated to an extremely high standard. Four of the rooms are family rooms, and two have four posters. In addition, each room has satellite TV, radio, direct dial telephone, coffee and tea making facilities, a hair drier, trouser press and 24-hour service. Many of the rooms face out over the hotel garden or the quiet courtyard and fountain.

Food is important at the Green Hotel. The recently refurbished Basil's is the hotel restaurant, and here you will find dishes that marry imagination with good, fresh, local produce. The elegant setting makes a meal here doubly enjoyable and of course there is a great selection of wines available to accompany your meal.

If you require a quiet, relaxing drink then the courtyard's cocktail bar is the place for you. Or you could have coffee here after dinner. It is relaxing, unfussy and informal.

Scotland has always had a fine reputation for its hospitality, and the green Hotel continues this tradition. Pay it a visit - you won't be disappointed!

Kinross, Perth & Kinross KY13 8AU
☎ 01577 862270
e-mail: themuirsinn@fsmail.net

Located on the outskirts of Kinross, just off the M90, **The Muirs Inn** is a picturesque listed building dating back to the 1800s. It was originally a small farmhouse where the blacksmith of the area lived and serviced travellers' horses, carts and carriages. At that time the house was just a small, single level cottage of croft type design – this is now the Mash Tun public bar. Next to the cottage was a byre which now houses the Wee Still Lounge. Later, the original building was extended by the addition of another floor above for accommodation along with a single storey extension for use as stables. These in turn became a garage and today the Maltings and Cellar Food Parlour Rooms occupy the space. Around 1900 the property became a small hotel where the owners initially served drink and refreshments through the living room window to mounted horse riders outside. The owners lived on the premises – and this is the case today.

The Mash Tun Bar still features the original – and much admired – custom-built gantry constructed by a local craftsman around 1909. Also still in place are the much coveted and now scarce original hand-etched ornamental glass porch windows and bar mirrors. The Wee Still Lounge features its own "wee still" which was used in the now defunct Stronachie Distillery in nearby Milnathort. Later it was used by a local chemist for the distillation of water before being acquired by the Muirs' innkeeper of the day.

The extensive menu offers a wide choice of traditional Scottish dishes and pub favourites. Amongst the starters there's a Bothy Broth – the inn's own home-made traditional kitchen soup, and Smokehouse Scotia – a hot smoked fish which is an established favourite. As a main course, choose between a selection of grills, succulent home oven roasted joints and country classics such as the Muirs Steakhouse Pie or the Chicken Cleish – tender breast of chicken marinated in white wine and mushroom cream sauce. Many of the dishes are available in petite and pensioner's portions at reduced prices. To accompany your meal there's a choice of wines, real ales, spirits and Scottish fruit wines, all at very reasonable prices.

The Muirs Inn also offers comfortable accommodation in 5 guest bedrooms. Four of them have en suite facilities; the fifth is a family room with its own private bathroom.

164 CAFFÉ CANTO

62-64 George Street, Perth PH1 5JL
☎ 01738 451938
e-mail: enquiries@caffecanto.fsnet.co.uk

Caffé Canto is a smart café/bistro that sits right in the heart of the Fair City of Perth. Owned and personally managed by Theresa and Keith Smaill, it is a stylish yet friendly establishment that is open seven days a week offering the very best in Scottish food and drink. If you are exploring the city of Perth, this is the place at which to stop off at lunchtime or in the evening for a snack, light lunch, dinner or even just a refreshing cup of the best coffee in town. The clientele includes not only local people and tourists from the UK, but visitors from such European countries as France, Belgium, Holland and Germany.

All the produce used in the kitchen is locally sourced wherever possible, making for a memorable eating experience. During the day you can choose from a full house breakfast (served until noon), bacon and sausage butties, baked potatoes, panninis, sandwiches, salads and soups. Plus there

is a daily specials board. The evening menu includes pasta, stir fries, risottos, steak baguettes and other tempting dishes that are all beautifully cooked and which all taste delicious. There is also a wine list that is sure to contain something you will like. You could even try the evening special - a starter or side, main course, and a glass of the House wine, all for a modest £11.25!

163 CHERRYBANK INN

210 Glasgow Road, Perth,
Perthshire PH2 0NA
☎ 01738 624349
e-mail: kenscot.findla@btconnect.com
⊕ www.cherrybankinn.co.uk

Since 1761, when it was first opened, the **Cherrybank Inn** has been providing great accommodation, food and drink to weary travellers. It started life as a drover's and coaching inn, and even then was reckoned to be one of the best inns in the whole of Perthshire. It is now justly famous, and sits just off the A9 on the south side of the city. It overlooks the Glasgow Road, and its

entrance can be found by driving north towards the city centre then taking first right and then left. The establishment has recently been completely refurbished to a high standard without losing any of its ambience. It is a picturesque place, both inside and out, and has a feeling of great history about it, while still maintaining the high standards that guests have come to expect nowadays. It is also a friendly, informal place that will offer you a warm Scottish welcome if you visit. The inn has seven extremely comfortable guest rooms - a double and six twins - each one fully en suite and each one furnished and decorated to a high standard, with pine predominating. One room has even been specially designed for wheelchair users. A colour TV and tea/coffee making facilities come as standard. and tariffs include a Continental breakfast pack..

The bar/lounge is a friendly, informal place, with comfortable furnishings, polished wood and soft carpeting. The bar has a wide selection of drinks, including ales, lager, cider, spirits (including a range of single malts), wines, liqueurs and soft drinks if you are driving. You can sit here enjoying a quiet drink and admire the view from the window. Or why not have one of the inn's wonderful bar lunches? The produce used in the kitchen is sourced locally wherever possible, with very little use being made of frozen or 'boil in the bag' ingredients, ensuring freshness and flavour. The cooking is simple, direct, and always delicious, and represents amazing value for

money. A menu could include such things as juicy steaks with all the trimmings, lamb chops , smoked salmon, vegetable stir fry and the famous Cherrybank mixed grill. You can also order various salads, burgers, filled baguettes and baked potatoes.

The inn stands a few yards from Craigie Hill Golf Club, so is ideal for golfing breaks. Tee bookings can be made by the inn. Or you could use it as a base from which to explore Perthshire and the city of Perth itself. It is also ideal as a B&B stop while driving north or south. There is plenty of car parking, and all credit cards are accepted.

165 THE ROOST

Forgandenny Road, Kintillo,
Bridge of Earn PH2 9AZ
☎ 01738 812111
e-mail: ispoon2006@hotmail.co.uk

Close to junction 9 of the M90 you will find a wonderful coffee shop and restaurant called **The Roost** which has been established since December 1999. Here, in a quaint redstone building which was once a farm outhouse, you will find some of the best food in the area, along with a fine range of teas and coffees.

It is owned and run by Sheila and Ian Wotherspoon who extend a very warm and friendly welcome when you stop off for a while in the area. You will be pleasantly surprised by the relaxed and unique atmosphere here that instantly captures you. Enjoy a full breakfast, tea coffee and a home-baked scone or cakes, all of which are produced on the premises by Sheila. Local produce is used wherever possible and all the meats have been bred within a 15-mile radius.

The Roost also offers a very large lunch menu served from 12 noon until 3pm; dinners are served from 7pm, Wednesday to Saturday. Booking is strongly recommended for dinner – bring your own wine or beer if you wish. Most major credit cards are accepted and there's ample parking space.

166 BAIGLIE INN & COUNTRY RESTAURANT ¶

Aberargie, Nr Bridge of Earn,
Perthshire PH2 9NF
☎ 01738 850332
e-mail: steve.whiting@baiglieinn.co.uk
⊕ www.baiglieinn.co.uk

The small village of Aberargie sits south of the 'Fair City' of Perth, on the B9112 just west of the A 912 and the M90 (leave at Junction 9). It is here, on the edge of Glenfarg, that you will find one of the best country inns in Scotland - the **Baiglie Inn & Country Restaurant**, set in some lovely countryside. It was once a coaching inn, and dates from at least the early 19th century. The exterior is everything a country inn should be - whitewashed and picturesque, and the interior is cosy and appealing, with exposed stone walls, open fires and timber beams within its two contrasting dining areas and spacious lounge/bar.

People come here from all over for the wonderful food. The new owner, Steve Whiting, has many year's experience in the hospitality trade and, since he arrived, he has created a place that is noted for the warmth of its welcome and its reasonable prices. The cuisine is traditional and contemporary, with a few foreign influences, and all the dishes are put together with imagination and flair, while still letting the flavours of the ingredients

speak for themselves. All the produce used in the kitchen is sourced locally, from the thick juicy steaks to the fresh fish and seafood delivered daily from the East Coast. Favourites are Thai salmon fishcakes, Scottish steaks, fresh penne pasta and steak pie. If it is a light snack you are after, or just a cup of tea or coffee, you are more than welcome. Every Sunday there is a traditional roast on offer.

Food is served seven days a week. From Monday to Saturday the times are 12 noon to 2.30pm and 5.30pm to 9pm and on Sunday from 12 noon until 8.30pm. So popular is the Baiglie that you are well advised to book a table in advance.

The bar has a wide range of drinks on offer,

including a selection of wines to accompany your meal, and it now also features real ales. The inn looks across to the Ochil Hills to the west and, in the summer months, you can sit on the café style decking as you eat or drink and take in the glorious views.

Since Steve Whiting took charge, the inn has gained a fine reputation for its high standards of service, its warm Scottish welcome and its attention to detail. It is a food lover's paradise, and as the menu says, 'Sorry - no chicken nuggets here…' Children are most welcome, and there is a special menu dedicated to them.

167 THE SCONE ARMS

Perth Road, Scone, Perth PH2 6LR
☎ 01738 551341 Fax: 01738 551393
e-mail: gordon@thesconearms.co.uk
🌐 www.thesconearms.co.uk

The Scone Arms looks really inviting with its whitewashed walls, latticed windows and hanging baskets. This charming old building dates back to 1807 when it served as the Toll Booth, the large window facing the crossroads being the Toll window. The building is L-shaped with the 70-cover restaurant facing Cross Street and linking to the low-beamed Lounge Bar through to the "wee and top bars" on Perth Street. The public bars have many original features with wood-panelled walls and ceiling, and original gas lamps. The walls are dotted with photographs and memorabilia of past team successes and local "worthies".

The spacious and light restaurant serves fresh, locally sourced food cooked to the highest standards by Head Chef Neil O'Rourke. Traditional Scottish fare merges with the more exotic to provide a menu and specials board at affordable prices. The restaurant caters for both intimate dining and for functions of up to 70 which can use the separate bar and dance floor. The bars offer a

diverse range of drinks from real ales to traditional malt whiskeys and fine wines. A pool and darts area is provided and to the rear of the inn there is a recently constructed Beer Garden and a good sized private car park.

The owners of the Scone Arms, brothers Alistair and Gordon Cook, promote local talent in the form of bands and musicians performing a variety of different genres of music on a monthly basis. The inn also acts as host to, and supports, several local teams and clubs, amongst them the Quiz Team, the Whiskey Tasters, and the football and darts teams. Indeed, the inn is essentially a community facility which has served the village for 200 years. All sections of the community use the

Scone Arms as a meeting place or as a venue for their various activities.

Scone itself is a historic village, home to Scotland's Stone of Destiny for nearly 500 years. Scone Palace, gardens and maze are within a mile of the inn, as is the famous Perth Racecourse and its adjacent caravan and camping site. Lying on a main arterial route North, the pub and restaurant are a popular stopping off point for travellers en route to the ski slopes and mountains or simply taking in the sights of Perthshire and Angus. The attractive city of Perth with its excellent shops and the River Tay are only 2 miles distant.

168 SMIDDY HAUGH HOTEL

Main Road, Aberuthven,
Perthshire PH3 1HE
☎ 01764 662013 Fax:01764 664433
e-mail: enquiries@smiddyhaughhotel.co.uk
⊕ www.smiddyhaughhotel.co.uk

With seven spacious and comfortable rooms,
three of which are en suite, the **Smiddy
Haugh Hotel** is one of the most popular
hotels in Perthshire - a favourite with golfers,
tourists, anglers and businessmen. It is also
poplar
with
locals,
who
appreciate
the
warmth
and
welcome
of the
friendly

bar, and the superb food served in the dining
room. It's the ideal base for visitors to an area
where there is just so much to see and do.

169 DRUMMOND CASTLE GARDENS

Muthill, Crieff, Perthshire PH5 2AA
☎ 01764 681433 Fax: 01764 681642
e-mail:
thegardens@drummondcastle.sol.co.uk
⊕ www.drummondcastlegardens.co.uk

Described as one of the finest formal
gardens in Europe, **Drummond Castle
Gardens** were first laid out in the early 17th
century by John Drummond, the 2nd Earl of
Perth and include a John Mylne sundial
erected in 1630. The gardens were renewed
in the 1950's by
Phyllis Astor,
preserving features
such as the ancient
yew hedges and the
copper beech trees
planted by Queen
Victoria to
commemorate her
visit in 1842. Open
Easter weekend and
then May to October
1pm-6pm. Castle not
open to the public.

171 PORT-NA-CRAIG INN & RESTAURANT

Port-na-Craig, Pitlochry,
Pethshire PH16 5ND
☎ 01796 472777
e-mail: info@portnacraig.com
⊕ www.portnacraig.com

The **Port-na-Craig Inn & Restaurant** has been
around since at least 1650, and has been serving
fine food and drink to the many people who have
passed through
its doors ever
since. The
present inn was built in the 1840s on the site of the former inn
buildings, and sits right on the banks of the River Tummell,
only a short distance from the Pitlochry Festival Theatre, the
hydroelectric dam and the famous salmon ladder.

Since March 2006 it has been under new management, and
the intention is to make it one of the best inns and eating
houses, in the whole area. Already the new owners are well on
their way to achieving their ambition, and eating here is an
experience that should not be missed. The produce is always
fresh and sourced locally wherever possible, with the dishes
being imaginatively cooked and presented. The ambience is
warm and welcoming, and the overall feeling is of a relaxed inn
and restaurant that puts the needs
and comfort of the customer
first.

Pitlochry is an attractive
tourist town that has always had the reputation of being at the centre
of Scotland, and is the ideal stopping off place when travelling north
or south.

509

170 FASGANEOIN COUNTRY HOUSE

Perth Road, Pitlochry,
Perthshire PH16 5DJ
☎ 01796 472387 Fax: 01796 474285
e-mail: Sabrina@fasganeoin.freeserve.co.uk
⊕ www.fasganeoincountryhouse.co.uk

The **Fasganeoin Country House** stands in one acre of ground overlooking lovely Glen Tummel in Pitlochry and surrounded by low Highland hills. It has a real "home-from-home" atmosphere, and people return to it again and again for its relaxed atmosphere, its warm, friendly welcome and its amazing value for money. The owner, Mrs Turk, is determined to keep up the high standards she has set since opening the Country House Hotel, meaning that Fasganeoin has three coveted stars from VisitScotland. In fact, the year 2007 is the 40th anniversary of Mrs Turk, her son Norbert and daughter Sabrina and her family running this small gem, something of which they are all justifiably proud.

The rooms are either fully en suite, or have private bathrooms, and each one is immaculately furnished and decorated, meaning that your stay here is comfortable and fuss free - just the place to recharge your batteries! Not only that - Sabrina and her brother speak perfect German, and they have an extensive knowledge of the area round Pitlochry, so can recommend places to go and things to see. Fasganeoin is the nearest country house to the Pitlochry Festival Theatre.

Food, as you would expect, is important in Fasganeoin. A full Scottish breakfast is served every morning - just right to set you up for a day exploring the area or taking part in one of the many activities available. For those who are visiting the theatre (or indeed, not!) tasty suppers are available to residents and non residents alike, although booking is necessary. All the produce used in the kitchen is fresh and local wherever possible.

The house itself has some history attached to it. It is a picturesque stone villa built in Victorian times, and was once the home of the architect Thomas Renny, whose great friend was a famous Japanese poet called Suseki Natsume. Renny was also a timber merchant who dealt with Japan and Russia, and had a fleet of ships on the Clyde. It has, over the years, been tastefully renovated to make it an oasis of calm and friendliness.

There is also so much to do in and around Pitlochry,. Apart from the theatre, there is golf, great fishing on the Tummel, the Tay and Loch Faskally, bird watching, climbing, walking, tennis and so much more. The surrounding countryside is full of heritage and history and from here you can have great days out in Inverness, Perth, the Trossachs and Aviemore.

Sabrina invites you to stay at Fasganeoin, and help her celebrate 40 great years of welcoming guests who return again and again to this small, friendly establishment. She is looking forward to continuing welcoming people. Make sure you are one of them!

172 BALLINLUIG INN HOTEL

Ballinluig, Pitlochry, Perthshire PH9 0LG
☎ 01796 482247 Fax: 01796 482506
e-mail: denisenixon@btinternet.com
⊕ www.ballinluiginn.co.uk

Set just a short distance from the A9, the **Ballinluig Inn Hotel** is an old drover's inn that offers the very best in accommodation, food and drink. It boasts six spacious and comfortable rooms, and is the ideal stopping off point when travelling north or south. It is also the perfect base from which to explore Scotland's heartland, where there is history galore, and ample opportunities for a wide range of outdoor pursuits.

HIDDEN PLACES GUIDES

Explore Britain and Ireland with *Hidden Places* guides - a fascinating series of national and local travel guides.

Packed with easy to read information on hundreds of places of interest as well as places to stay, eat and drink.

Available from both high street and internet booksellers

For more information on the full range of *Hidden Places* guides and other titles published by Travel Publishing visit our website on

www.travelpublishing.co.uk or ask for our leaflet by phoning **0118-981-7777** or emailing **info@travelpublishing.co.uk**

173 WEEM HOTEL

Weem, By Aberfeldy,
Perthshire PH15 2LD

☎ 01887 820381

e-mail: enquiries@weemhotel.com
⊕ www.weemhotel.com

The family owned and run **Weem Hotel** sits at the foot of Weem Rock near the historic town of Aberfeldy, and is a former coaching inn, dating originally from 1527. It was used by General Wade as barracks for his troops while building the nearby bridge across the Tay. Comfort and value for money are the watchwords here, and it has an intimate yet relaxed atmosphere that combines tradition with modern standards of service. The spacious rooms are simply but tastefully furnished, and all are fully en suite. They all have beautiful views either of the open countryside or of the Weem Rock and courtyard garden. Each one has colour TV, clock radio, hair dryer and tea and coffee making facilities. The hotel has Wi-Fi Broadband Internet Access available.

The hotel's menu changes every six weeks, with the cuisine combining imagination and flair with the best of fresh Scottish produce. The wine list contains many fine wines, all competitively priced, and a range of real ales.

The Weem Hotel is the ideal base from which to explore beautiful Perthshire or indulge in golf, fishing, clay pigeon shooting, bird watching, mountain biking and so much more!

174 COURTYARD RESTAURANT AND LOUNGE BAR

Kenmore, Perthshire PH15 2HN
☎ 01887 830763
e-mail: info@thecourtyard-restaurant.co.uk
🌐 www.thecourtyard-restaurant.co.uk

Situated in beautiful Kenmore on Loch Tay, the **Courtyard Restaurant and Lounge Bar** is a brasserie and bar that offers an upbeat and sophisticated eating experience at surprisingly low prices. Its cuisine is modern, though sometimes with a hint of the traditional, and uses fresh, local produce wherever possible. This, combined with imagination and flair, gives you an eating experience that will long be remembered.

Special diets are also catered for, and between 12 noon and 5pm there is a snack menu that includes such things as light bites and what the restaurant calls "hungry nibbles". The Courtyard Restaurant and Lounge Bar has, of course, an extensive cellar of choice wines to accompany your meal, all carefully chosen to match the style of cuisine found here. Plus there is a great selection of single malts. The place can also be

booked for corporate events, parties and weddings, and the attentive staff will make sure your function is a resounding success!

The restaurant is fortunate enough to be at the heart of some beautiful Perthshire scenery, and in the warmer months you can dine indoors or out, taking in the peace and tranquillity of a place where hustle and bustle are strangers. So make your way to Kenmore and sample the fantastic cuisine of the Courtyard Restaurant and Lounge Bar!

175 FORTINGALL HOTEL

Fortingall, Aberdeldy, Perthshire PH15 2NQ
☎ 01887 830367
e-mail: hotel@fortingallhotel.com
🌐 www.fortingallhotel.com

Whether it's a base from which to explore wonderful Perthshire, or a B&B when passing through, the **Fortingall Hotel** is the hotel for you! It sits in a beautiful conservation village of thatched cottages at the foot of Glen Lyon, and boasts ten en suite rooms that are both stylish and comfortable. Each one has been individually refurbished to reflect the history and heritage of the area, making use of estate tweeds.

The whole atmosphere is a mix of informality and contemporary décor, guaranteeing you a relaxed time among some of the finest scenery in Scotland. Fishing - walking - golf - country pursuits - exploring - sailing - all these activities, and a whole lot more, are on the doorstep. The staff are friendly, attentive and knowledgeable about what's on offer, and the attention to detail makes this hotel extra special.

Of course, the hotel offers fine dining. The produce is all locally sourced and as fresh as possible, which means that Tay salmon, Fortingall lamb and Glen Lyon venison feature in many of the dishes on offer. The cuisine combines imagination and tradition, ensuring a dining experience to be remembered. There is a good wine list and the bar has a fine selection of malt whiskies, beers, cognacs and soft drinks.

The Fortingall Hotel offers all that is best in Scottish hospitality, and the staff look forward to welcoming you.

176 TALLADH-A-BHEITHE LODGE

Loch Rannoch, North Lochside Road,
Near Pitlochry PH17 2QW
☎ 01882 633203 Fax: 01882 633203
e-mail: info@tab-lodge.co.uk
🌐 www.tab-lodge.co.uk

The imposing **Talladh-a-Bheithe Lodge**, on the banks of Loch Rannoch, west of Pitlochry, started life as a hunting lodge of Clan Menzies, one of the large local estates. Now it is a licensed guest house and restaurant offering the best in accommodation and food. It has fifteen comfortable and spacious rooms, single, twin/double and family rooms, each one decorated and furnished to an extremely high standard so that you enjoy the very best when you holiday in this part of Scotland. The

lodge sits in seven acres of parkland, ensuring a relaxing, peaceful time, and all public rooms in the lodge have Adam fireplaces, adding a touch of elegance to the surroundings. There are also 3 self catering cottages available close to the lodge.

The food marks this place out as somewhere special. The produce used in its many delicious dishes is always as fresh as can be, and sourced locally wherever possible. The breakfasts are always filling because the good, clean air will give you a hearty appetite! You can also order lunches, high teas and evening meals which are out of this world, and are becoming popular with non-residents.

The Talladh-a-Bheithe Lodge is ideal for a relaxing break, where you can recharge your batteries among some of the most magnificent scenery in Scotland.

177 GORDON HIGHLANDERS MUSEUM

St Lukes, Viewfield Road,
Aberdeen AB15 7XH
☎ 01224 311200
e-mail: museum@gordonhighlanders.com
🌐 www.gordonhighlanders.com

The story of The Gordon Highlanders spans 200 years of world history and is packed with tales of courage and tenacity on the field of battle. At the museum you can re-live the compelling and dramatic story of one of the British Army's most famous regiments, through the lives of its outstanding personalities and of the killed soldiers of the North East of Scotland who filled its ranks.

The spectacular exhibition includes a unique collection of the finest of the regiments treasures, including a remarkable display of Victoria Crosses; strikingly detailed life size and scale reproductions of some of the Regiment's finest moments in battle; state of the art touch screens to let you explore the deeds and values that made the Regiment great and stunning film presentations which convey the story of the 'Gordons'.

A stroll in the delightful museum gardens can be rounded off with light refreshments in The Duchess Jean Tea Room. A range of souvenirs are available at The Gordon Gift Shop. Open April to October, Tuesday to Saturday 10.30am-4.30pm and Sunday 12.30pm-4.30pm; November, February and March Thursday to Saturday 10am-4pm.

178 ST LEONARDS HOTEL

2 Bath Street, Stonehaven,
Kincardineshire AB39 2DH
☎ 01569 762044 Fax: 01569 766222
e-mail: info@stleonardshotel.com
⊕ www.stleonardshotel.com

As soon as you step over the threshold of the **St Leonards Hotel** in Stonehaven you know you are somewhere special. It is owned by Wilma and Allan Bruce, who have recently refurbished it to an extremely high standard so that you can have the very best in service and good, old fashioned Scottish hospitality. The hotel boasts nine comfortable en suite rooms, all furnished and decorated to the highest standards, with telephone, dial-up Internet points (with broadband pending), television and tea/coffee making facilities.

The cuisine, as you would expect, is outstanding, with all the produce locally sourced and as fresh as possible. This is a gastronomic experience to be savoured, within an informal friendly atmosphere that adds to the ambience. You can eat in the 70-seat Orangery Restaurant, with its stunning views of Stonehaven Bay, or in the Robert Burns Restaurant, which seats 30 and is ideal for a business lunch or an evening celebration.

The welcoming and cosy William Wallace lounge bar, with its oak panelling and old pictures of

famous battles, is an ideal place to enjoy a relaxing drink after a hard day's sightseeing.

So if you find yourself in or near Stonehaven, make for the St Leonards Hotel and enjoy the warm welcome and high standards of service!

179 MOLLY'S

The Promenade, Stonehaven,
Kincardineshire AB39 2RD
☎ 01569 762378

Molly's sits right in the heart of Stonehaven. By day it is a trendy café/bar offering great coffee, snacks and lunches and in the evenings it offers superb gourmet cooking. This is the perfect place to stop for a refreshing break while exploring the town, or to celebrate a special occasion such as a birthday or anniversary in the evening. The produce is sourced locally wherever possible, ensuring full flavour and freshness. Pay it a visit - you won't be disappointed!

180 THE SHIP INN

Shorehead, Stonehaven,
Kincardineshire AB39 2JY
☎ 01569 762617
e-mail: enquiries@shipinnstonehaven.com
⊕ www.shipinnstonehaven.com

Dating from 1777, **The Ship Inn** is the oldest pub in Stonehaven. It boasts six en

suite guest rooms that are both comfortable and affordable, all but one having a view out over the harbour. The cosy lounge/bar is popular with locals, and here you can relax over a drink or two after a hard day's sightseeing. The food is exceptional, and outstanding value for money.

181 CLATTERIN' BRIG RESTAURANT

Nr Fettercairn,
Kincardineshire AB30 1HB
☎ 01561 340297

The purpose-built **Clatterin' Brig Restaurant** sits in a picturesque spot above the Clatterin' Brig, north of Fettercairn on the B974. It is not a place you can afford to miss if you want good, wholesome food and friendly service at realistic prices. Plus the views are outstanding! It is licensed, and opens every day with the exception of Monday.

HIDDEN PLACES GUIDES

Explore Britain and Ireland with *Hidden Places* guides - a fascinating series of national and local travel guides.

Packed with easy to read information on hundreds of places of interest as well as places to stay, eat and drink.

Available from both high street and internet booksellers

For more information on the full range of *Hidden Places* guides and other titles published by Travel Publishing visit our website on

www.travelpublishing.co.uk or ask for our leaflet by phoning **0118-981-7777** or emailing **info@travelpublishing.co.uk**

183 FEUGHSIDE INN

South Deeside Road, Strachan,
Aberdeenshire AB31 6NS
☎ 01330 850225

Sitting no more than five miles from Banchory in Royal Deeside, the **Feughside Inn** is a superior hotel close to the River Feugh, and boasts ten rooms, four of which are fully en suite. Each one is well furnished and from most of the rooms there are great views over the surrounding countryside, especially the 1,932 feet high Clachnaben. The inn is the perfect base from which to explore one of the most scenic and historic areas of Scotland. It is also the ideal place to stay if you want to indulge in some of the many activities in the area, such as fishing, shooting, pony trekking, motor biking, hill walking, bird watching (there are ospreys in the district), and so on.

The restaurant and carvery serve some of the finest food in Deeside. Only the freshest of local produce is used wherever possible, guaranteeing you a gastronomic experience you will long remember for all the right reasons. The wine list is comprehensive, and there is sure to be something to suit your taste. The cuisine is Scottish/European, specialising in game, fish, local beef and locally grown vegetables. Special dietary requirements can be accommodated by prior arrangement.

The Feughside Inn prides itself on its Scottish high teas, which are available by arrangement. Afternoon teas are served during the season, and the bar serves a great range of drinks - real ales, beer, malt whisky, spirits, wine, liqueurs and soft drinks.

182 SAUCHIEBURN HOTEL

Luthermuir, By Laurencekirk, Kincardineshire
☎ 01674 840587

South of Laurencekirk, and just off the A90, is the small village of Luthermuir, where you will find the **Sauchieburn Hotel**, a superior establishment that offers everything that is good about Scottish hospitality. The building itself is over 200 years old, and brims with historic detail. However, it has been totally upgraded and refurbished to offer all the modern conveniences travellers and tourists expect nowadays without losing any of its character.

The hotel is open to non-residents, and boasts two fully en suite rooms to discerning guests, that are both comfortable and spacious. They have been furnished and decorated to an exceptionally high standard, and provide the perfect base from which to explore Kincardineshire and Aberdeenshire, from Royal Deeside and the lush farmlands of The Mearns to the cosmopolitan city of Aberdeen itself and the attractions of Stonehaven. Or you could simply use the hotel as an overnight B&B stop. The tariff includes a superb full Scottish breakfast, with lighter options available if required.

The bar is cosy and inviting, and has a wide range of drinks on offer - beer, ales, wine, lager, cider, spirits (including single malts), liqueurs and soft drinks. Why not relax here after a hard day exploring the area, and plan your next days' trip? The food is outstanding and the kitchen features only the finest and freshest of local produce in its many imaginative dishes. Great prime Scottish steak with all the trimmings is one of the specialities, also fresh fish from the local coast. Everything is home-cooked on the premises, and you can choose from an ever-changing menu or a specials board that takes advantage of produce that is in season. The attractive restaurant seats 40 in absolute comfort, and with its crisp linen and panelled walls, it is a pleasure to eat here.

In addition to the two rooms, the Sauchieburn Hotel also offers a self-catering cottage, *The Stables*, which is impeccable throughout. It comes with all the things you'll ever need for an enjoyable holiday, even if the weather isn't kind to you! Prices are amazingly reasonable considering the high standards of comfort being offered. Everything is on the one level, so it is disabled friendly. There is plenty of car parking for both the hotel and the self-catering cottage, and all major credit cards are accepted.

There is no doubt that the Sauchieburn Hotel offers some of the finest accommodation in Aberdeenshire, and people keep coming back again and again to sample it. If you visit, you're sure to come back as well!

516

184 CRATHES CASTLE AND GARDENS

Banchory, Aberdeenshire AB31 5QJ
☎ 0870 118 1951
Ranger service: 01330 844810
e-mail: crathes@nts.org.uk
🌐 www.nts.org.uk

King Robert the Bruce granted the lands of Leys to the Burnett family in 1323: the ancient Horn of Leys, which can be seen today in the Great Hall, marks his gift. The castle, built in the second half of the 16th century, is a superb example of a tower house of the period. Some of the rooms retain their original painted ceilings and collections of family portraits and furniture.

A visit is enhanced by the walled garden, which

incorporates herbaceous borders and many unusual plants, providing a wonderful display at all times of the year. The great yew hedges, fascinating examples of the art of topiary, date from as early as 1702. Explore the estate on the seven

waymarked trails (including one suitable for wheelchairs) that lead through the mixed woodlands, along the Coy Bum and past the millpond. In the Visitor Centre a new exhibition, *A Walk on the Wild Side*, explores the wildlife on the Crathes Estate.

185 LUMSDEN ARMS HOTEL

Main street, Lumsden,
Aberdeenshire AB54 4JN
☎ 01464 861712
e-mail: lumsdenarmshotel@aol.com
🌐 www.lumsdenarmshotel.co.uk

With five spacious and comfortable rooms - two doubles, a family and three singles - the **Lumsden Arms Hotel** is the perfect base from which to explore an area that is rich in history and heritage. This is a family run hotel, warm and friendly, where

people can relax. All rooms have TVs and tea/coffee making facilities, and the family room has a wash hand basin. Enjoy a quiet drink, or have a meal in the dining room.. All the produce is locally sourced wherever possible, meaning that you get a superb eating experience.

187 THE CANDLESTICK MAKER

Charleston Road, Aboyne,
Aberdeenshire AB34 5EJ
☎ 01339 886060
e-mail: enquiries@thecandlestick-maker.com
🌐 www.thecandlestick-maker.com

The Candlestick Maker is one of the finest restaurants in the whole of Royal Deeside. Contemporary in style, it serves superb food, and is the ideal place for a lunch or dinner when exploring the area. It proudly supports local produce, which it uses wherever possible in its kitchens. The service is outstanding, and the prices always realistic. Visit The Candlestick Maker and you're sure to agree!

186 CROSSROADS HOTEL

Nr Lumphanan, By Banchory,
Aberdeenshire AB31 4RU
☎ 01339 883275
e-mail: Deeside crossroads@yahoo.co.uk
⊕ www.deesidecrossroads.com

The **Crossroads Hotel** was built during the early 1800s as a coaching inn and still retains all the warmth and character of a place that had long offered the highest standards of hospitality. The views from the hotel are breathtaking, and its position makes it an ideal base from which to explore Royal Deeside and much further afield - Aberdeen itself, the small city of Elgin, the Speyside Whisky Trail, the Castle Trail and the villages and towns of the Moray Firth.

It has seven bright, spacious en suite bedrooms on offer, each one offering all the amenities you would expect of a good hotel - telephone, tea/coffee making facilities and colour television. You can choose from double, single, twin or family rooms.

The restaurant is a popular place with both locals and tourists alike, and the kitchens use only the finest and freshest of local produce in season wherever possible.

During your stay, why not enjoy the wonderful cuisine by booking a table for dinner? You can also relax in the stylish lounge bar with its range of spirits (including, of course, single malts), beers, wines, liqueurs and soft drinks. Or you can meet the local people in the friendly public bar, where the atmosphere is informal, and there is a pool table.

So, if you're looking for a holiday base, or you're just passing through, make for the Crossroads Hotel!

188 STRACHAN COTTAGE

9 Strachan Cottages, Tarland, Aboyne,
Aberdeenshire AB34 5PG
☎ 01339 881401

In the charming village of Tarland, four miles northwest of Aboyne, you will find **Strachan Cottage**, a stone-built cottage that offers the very best in self-catering accommodation. It sleeps six in three bedrooms, and has a spacious and comfortable lounge, a well-equipped kitchen and a bathroom. It is the ideal place

for people who want a quiet holiday close to Royal Deeside, or for the more energetic, such as anglers, golfers or ramblers. It is owned and run by Evelyn Smith, who keeps it spotlessly clean so that guests have a memorable holiday.

189 THE AULD KIRK

31 Braemar Road, Ballater,
Aberdeenshire AB35 5RQ
☎ 01339 755762
⊕ www.theauldkirk.com

Set in the heart of Royal Deeside, **The Auld Kirk** is a superb small hotel housed in a former Victorian "kirk" - or church - the oldest such building in Ballater. It has recently been refurbished to an extremely high standard, and boasts six en suite rooms, each individually furnished and decorated, making them stylish and comfortable. The interior blends contemporary styling with the many period features that have been retained, such as high, timbered ceilings and leaded windows, creating an atmosphere of informal elegance.

Food is the focus of attention at The Auld Kirk, and dining is a real pleasure in the restaurant, where all the produce used in the kitchen is fresh and locally sourced.

This small hotel is the ideal base from which to explore an area where history, heritage and sport combine to give the holiday of a lifetime. Being situated within the Cairngorms National Park, golf, shooting, angling, walking and a host of other outdoor activities are on the doorstep. Whilst set in the beauty of the Grampian Highlands, near to the royal residence of Balmoral, the Auld Kirk is less than an hours drive from the bustling city of Aberdeen.

The Auld Kirk offers Highland hospitality at its very best. The service is efficient, courteous and friendly, and the food - naturally enough - is out of this world!

190 GORDON'S RESTAURANT AND B&B

20, Mar Road, Braemar,
Aberdeenshire AB35 5YL
☎ 013397 41247/41906
e-mail: moira.ebruce@btinternet.com
⊕ www.gordonsbraemar.com

The award winning **Gordon's Restaurant and B&B** sits right in the heart of Royal Deeside, and is the ideal place to stay and eat while exploring this historical part of Scotland. The restaurant is a traditional Scottish tearoom during the day, and a restaurant in the evening that offers beautifully cooked Scottish fayre. The B&B has three comfortable rooms with Sky TV, and a spacious residents' lounge with Internet access. Make it your base when exploring Royal Deeside!

191 BURNETT ARMS HOTEL

Bridge Road, Kemnay,
Aberdeenshire AB51 5QS
☎ 01467 642208

The **Burnett Arms Hotel** is owned and managed by Steve Morrice, who has created a hotel that is full of character and offers outstanding value for money. It dates from 1877, and offers six comfortable en-suite guest rooms. The bar lounge is a firm favourite with locals - always a good sign - and sells a great range of drinks. Relax and enjoy the ambience as you sample a single malt among the friendly regulars! Good, straightforward food is served, and you can choose from the daily specials board which includes chicken, curry and gammon steaks. All the produce is sourced locally wherever possible and is all home-cooked on the premises.

17 Station Road, Kemnay,
Aberdeenshire AB51 5RB
☎ 01467 643617

The wonderfully named **Lairds Throat Pub and Restaurant** sits in the small Aberdeenshire village of Kemnay, on the B993 between Deeside and Donside. It is a new venture, and has already attracted much attention and approval from people who appreciate good food and fine drink. It is housed in a very picturesque stone building that dates from the mid 18th century, and offers all that is best in good, old-fashioned Scottish hospitality.

There is a fine range of drinks on offer, and already the place has become extremely popular with the locals as a place to meet, have a drink and relax. The bar serves ales, beers, lager, cider, wines, spirits (including single malts), liqueurs and a range of soft drinks for people who are driving. The interior has been furnished and decorated to an extremely high standard, and is all dark, polished wood, comfortable furniture, carpets and walls hung with old prints. The ambience is cosy and warm, while still retaining an air of spaciousness and great service.

The place is gaining an enviable reputation throughout the area for its fine food. The airy and comfortable lounge/restaurant area is where the eating takes place. The cuisine is mainly Scottish, and everything is home-cooked on the premises from only the finest and freshest of local produce wherever possible. Try the Aberdeen Angus steaks, for instance, with all the trimmings. Choose from a printed menu or a daily specials board that takes advantage of local produce in season. Or why not go for 'mince and tatties ' - a great Scottish favourite that consists of 'tatties' (potatoes) with mince and diced vegetables in a rich sauce. Another Scottish favourite served here is 'stovies' - usually layers of tender beef with sliced potato and seasoning. It is absolutely delicious! Plus, of course, there are the old favourites like cottage pie and succulent burgers.

There is also a function room, the ideal place for small wedding receptions, birthday parties and so on. All major credit cards are accepted, and there is plenty of parking space nearby. The pub also hosts occasional live music nights.

Kemnay is ideally placed to take advantage of everything that Aberdeenshire has to offer, from the sophisticated city of Aberdeen itself to the rich farmlands of Buchan and, of course, Royal Deeside. Why not call in when you're in the area for a quiet drink or a superb meal?

193 BREASLANN GUEST HOUSE

Old Chapel Road, Inverurie,
Aberdeenshire AB51 4QN
☎ 01467 621608 Fax: 01467 622224
e-mail: breaslann@btconnect.com

Breaslann Guest House offers modern, comfortable accommodation in a quiet residential area of Inverurie. All five rooms are all fully en suite and a spacious guest lounge is available to relax in throughout the day.

There is also ample off-street private parking. Be assured of a warm welcome and an excellent breakfast. Many of the guests return again and again and are very happy to recommend Breaslann Guest House.

196 RESTAURANT 55

55 High Street, Elgin, Moray IV30 1EE
☎ 01343 551273 Fax: 01343 500228
e-mail: dave@restaurant55.co.uk
www.restaurant55.co.uk

Chef/patron Dave Buchanan only took over recently at **Restaurant 55** but he has already made it *the* place to eat in Elgin. Formerly chef at the town's Mansion House, Dave has created enticing bills of fare with different menus for lunch and dinner. There's a strong emphasis on fresh, local Scottish produce with a traditional Scotch Broth soup with shredded Lamb Flank amongst the

starters and Scotch Sirloin Steak as a main dish. But the menu also offers fish and poultry dishes along with vegetarian options such as organic mushroom ravioli with basil infused cream. A comprehensive wine list offers plenty of choices.

194 GORDON ARMS HOTEL

The Square, Huntly,
Aberdeenshire AB54 8AF
☎ 01466 792288 Fax: 01466 794556
www.gordonarms.demon.co.uk

Situated in the heart of the small market town of Huntly, the **Gordon Arms Hotel** is a favourite with tourists and locals alike. It has fourteen comfortable, fully en suite rooms, each one decorated and furnished to a high standard, and each one boasting TV, telephone, alarm clock, hair drier and tea and coffee making facilities.

This is the ideal place to use as a base when exploring Aberdeenshire and beyond, as Huntly itself has excellent communications, both by road and rail, with Aberdeen, Inverness, The Aberdeenshire Castle trail, the Speyside Whisky Trail and the many picturesque fishing villages on the Moray Firth coast. In addition, there are excellent local facilities for hill walking, fishing, sailing, golf and exploring historic sites.

Cheers is within a separate building, and is a friendly bar

where you can play pool, listen to music on the juke box or take part in karaoke at weekends. The lounge bar is quieter, and also serves a wide range of drinks. As you would expect, there is a good selection of single malts. Here you can also enjoy a bar lunch or supper, with a separate children's menu being available. Or if you prefer a more formal dining experience, you can eat in the dining room, which seats up to 60 in absolute comfort. All the food is freshly prepared on the premises from good, fresh produce.

The hotel also caters for parties of up to 200, so it is the ideal place for a wedding, seminar or conference.

521

195 EAT ON THE GREEN

Udny Green, Ellon,
Aberdeenshire AB41 7RS

☎ 01651 842337   Fax: 01651 843362

e-mail: enquiries@eatonthegreen.co.uk

🌐 www.eatonthegreen.co.uk

Eat on the Green brings a new dining experience to the picturesque village of

Udny Green, tucked away in the green Aberdeenshire countryside between Oldmeldrum and Ellon. Owned and managed by Craig Wilson, it has earned a fine reputation for its imaginative range of contemporary and classic dishes using only the finest and freshest of specially selected local produce. Craig is an award-winning chef who brings a wealth of experience to the superb food served in the restaurant, and you will be

looked after 'front of house' by the restaurant staff who ensure that your dining experience takes place in a relaxed and informal atmosphere while still retaining the hallmarks of a great restaurant – high standards of service coupled with value-for-money prices.

Eat on the Green seats up to 70 in absolute comfort, while the adjoining lounge offers light snacks and fresh coffee in a warm and inviting ambience. A sample lunch or dinner menu might include Parsnip, Honey & Ginger Soup, Thai-style Smoked Haddock Fishcakes, Seared Fillets of Salmon with Lime Hollandaise and Wok-Fried Greens or Chargrilled Sirloin of local Aberdeen Angus with Roasted Shallots and Homemade Chunky Chips. Desserts might include: Caramelised Lemon Tart, Banana and Cinnamon Pavlova, or Iced Terrine of White & Dark Chocolate.

Eat on the Green is closed on Monday and Tuesday.

197 MORAYDALE GUEST HOUSE

276 High Street, Elgin,
Morayshire IV30 1AG
☎ 01343 546381
e-mail: moraydale@btinternet.com
🌐 www.moraydaleguesthouse.com

Conveniently located on Elgin's High Street, **Moraydale Guest House** is an imposing stone-built Victorian villa dating back to 1881. Beautifully furnished and decorated throughout, Moraydale is the home of Wilma Roger who offers a warm welcome to her bed & breakfast guests. There are 7 guest bedrooms, all of them with brand new en suite facilities complete

with a proper sized shower. At breakfast time you'll find plenty of choice but most guests opt for the full breakfast which one of them described as "more of a feast than just breakfast!" All major credit cards are accepted and there's ample off road parking.

198 THUNDERTON HOUSE

Thunderton Place, Elgin,
Morayshire IV30 1BG
☎ 01343 554921
e-mail: kareenmchardy@fsmail.net
🌐 www.thundertonhouse.co.uk

Dating back to 1655, **Thunderton House** is most impressive, a lofty stone building resembling a castle – Bonnie Prince Charlie stayed here before the fateful Battle of Culloden. Today it's a friendly and popular hostelry run since 1996 by Kareen McHardy. The inn has a spacious bar with an open fire, serving breakfast, lunch and dinner. Steak Pie is the speciality of the house and the fully stocked bar offers a wide selection of beverages including Cask Marque approved ales. There's a large screen TV showing Sky Sports, and a Quiz on Sunday evenings.

199 HIGHLANDER HOTEL

**75 West Church Street, Buckie,
Banffshire AB56 1BQ
☎ 01542 834008**

Located in the small fishing village of Buckie, the **Highlander Hotel** is a sturdy stone building dating from the 1880s which became a hotel in the 1940s and was extensively refurbished in the winter of 2007/7. Highly popular with local people, the hotel has a public bar, lounge bar and a separate small dining room. Bar snacks and meals, including daily specials, are served throughout the day, and in the evening there's another menu which features some more exotic dishes. Everything on offer is based on fresh, local produce and a speciality of the kitchen is delicious fresh haddock served in a special beer batter. In good weather, refreshments can be savoured in the pleasant beer garden with a covered area at the rear, where there is also a car park for residents. Children are welcome throughout the hotel.

Accommodation at the Highlander comprises 6 comfortable guest bedrooms, all stylishly furnished and well-equipped. Five of them have recently modernised en suite facilities; the 6th has its own modern private bathroom. The hotel has good access for wheelchairs and disabled toilets; all major credit cards are accepted.

200 SEAFIELD ARMS HOTEL

73 New Street, Rothes, Moray AB38 7BJ
☎ 01340 831587
⊕ www.seafieldarmshotel.co.uk

The **Seafield Arms Hotel** is popular with
both tourists and locals alike. It has five
rooms on offer, and has recently been given a
complete refurbishment by its new owners.
Built of local sand stone, it lies on the
northern
edge of
the quiet
village of
Rothes, in
the middle
of the
whisky
trail and a
stones
throw

away from the famous Glen Grant Distillery.
There is a good selection of malts, and the
food is all prepared on the premises from
good, local produce. It's sister establishment,
the **Rocksley Inn** near Peterhead, has the
same high reputation.

202 STABLES INN

Findhorn Road, Kinloss, Moray IV36 3TS
☎ 01309 690218
e-mail: sandys132@hotmail.com

The **Stables Inn** is an unusual pub in that it
was originally the village school and later used
for stabling. It's now a friendly hostelry run
by Sandy and Gill Sutherland who took over
here in 2002. Sandy is a former Royal Marine
and a local man who looks after the bar; Gill
is in charge of the kitchen, serving up a good
choice of home-cooked food at sensible
prices. The pub has an elegant lounge/diner
with two large leather couches set in front of
an open fire and there's also a public bar with
pool and darts.

201 THE GLENAVON HOTEL

The Square, Tomintoul,
Banffshire AB37 9ET
☎ 018076 580218   Fax: 01807 580733
e-mail: enquiries@glenavon-hotel.co.uk
⊕ www.glenavon-hotel.co.uk

The **Glenavon Hotel** is set in the square of
picturesque Tomintoul, the highest village in the
Scottish Highlands. It is a family run establishment
with a reputation for its warm, friendly welcome
coupled with the highest standards and keen prices.
There is a choice of standard or en suite rooms,
each one spacious and comfortable. Sky TV comes as standard, as do
tea and coffee making facilities. Extra fold-down beds can be supplied
on request. You can relax in the hotel's lounge bar over a pint of real
ale, or a dram of the finest malt whisky - the hotel is only a few miles
from the famous Speyside Whisky Trail. The bar itself is warm and
cosy, and here you can meet and chat to the local people while
enjoying a drink and a meal. The food is prepared from only the
finest, freshest local produce wherever possible, and you are sure to
find something on the menu to suit your palate. There's local cuisine,

international and vegetarian, as well as
a children's menu.

The key words in the Glenavon
are "relaxation" and "informality" and
while the standards remain high, this
is the kind of place where guests can relax and unwind . The staff
are friendly, approachable and always on hand to attend to your
wishes. The hotel caters for coach groups, motorists, cyclists and
bikers, and well behaved pets are always welcome.

203 BECCA'S & THE COFFEE SHOP

**High Street, Fraserburgh,
Aberdeenshire AB43 9ET
☎ 01346 512900**

Becca's and **The Coffee Shop** are two delightful café/restaurants right in the heart of Fraserburgh. Of the two Becca's is the newer, and offers great Scottish cuisine at tempting prices. Everything is cooked on the premises from produce which is sourced locally wherever possible, and there is even a kid's play area! The Coffee Shop sells value for money snacks such as paninis and so on. Come along and see for yourself how good they are!

205 JJ'S CAFÉ

**Deer Road, Maud,
Aberdeenshire AB42 5LY
☎ 01771 613444**

JJ's Café sits in the small village of Maud, deep in the delightful Aberdeenshire countryside. It is well worth seeking out for its great food and affordable prices. It offers homemade cakes, scones and preserves, as well as delicious teas and coffees. Or why not ask for the fish and chips, which are renowned in the area? Other dishes include all-day breakfasts, homemade soups, toasties and baked potatoes. There is even a takeaway service!

204 ADEN ARMS HOTEL

**19 Abbey Street, Old Deer, Mintlaw,
Aberdeenshire AB42 5JA
☎ 01771 622573
e-mail: info@adenarmshotel.com
⊕ www.adenarmshotel.com**

With six fully en suite rooms, from single to family, the **Aden Arms Hotel** is one of the best small hotels in Aberdeenshire. It is situated within the small village of Old Deer, famous for the ruins of an old abbey, and is a favourite for locals and tourists alike. This whole area, known as Buchan, is rich in history and heritage, with the old fishing port of Peterhead being ten miles to the east, Aden Country Park close by, and the many castles of Aberdeenshire on the doorstep.

This family-run hotel also offers great food. Everything is freshly prepared from only the finest and freshest of local produce, and served in the small but spacious dining room. The service is friendly and attentive, and the staff are knowledgeable about the many attractions that can be visited and experienced in the area. Why not enjoy a quiet drink in the lounge bar? There is a wide range of whiskies (including many single malts), beers, wines and soft drinks, and here you can relax after a hard day's sightseeing. The hotel has been completely refurbished by the new owners, Elaine and Ian Grubb, and they are proud of the comfortable rooms, the attention to detail and the informal, relaxed atmosphere that they have created.

This is the perfect base from which to explore Aberdeenshire, and it makes a great overnight B&B for those touring Scotland. So pay the Aden Arms Hotel a visit - you will not be disappointed!

206 WATERFRONT HOTEL

25 Union Road, Macduff,
Aberdeenshire AB44 1UD
☎ 01261831661 Fax: 01261 831662
e-mail: info@waterfrontmacduff.co.uk
⊕ www.waterfrontmacduff.co.uk

'The Waterfront Hotel at Macduff is something special. Tucked away on the outskirts of this picturesque fishing village, it offers comfortable accommodation, fine dining and tremendous value for money. Whether you're passing through and are looking for B&B accommodation, or looking for a base from which to explore a historic and scenic area, then it's the place for you.

It boasts 15 fully en suite bedrooms, from single to twin and from double to family. Each one has a colour TV, telephone and tea/coffee making facilities, and each one is beautifully furnished and decorated. The staff are attentive, knowledgeable and friendly, and will make your stay in the hotel one you will long remember.

Dining at the Waterfront Hotel is an experience that cannot be missed. Whether it's an evening dinner, a lunch, a snack or afternoon tea, the food is all freshly prepared from only the finest and freshest of local ingredients. Plus the hotel can cater for meetings, conferences, weddings and family occasions. Every Sunday there is a carvery between 12 noon and 3 pm.

This part of Scotland has much to offer the tourist, from the Speyside Whisky Trail to castles, old fishing villages, sports such as fishing, walking, sailing and golf, and museums. Why not relax over a drink or two in the hotel's friendly bar? There is a full range of beers, wines, spirits and soft drinks, including a good selection of single malts. And at weekends there is always entertainment that will set your toes tapping!

208 ROCKSLEY INN

Stirling Village, Boddam, nr Peterhead,
Aberdeenshire AB42 3AP
☎ 01779 472594

The family run **Rocksley Inn** has comfortable rooms, excellent service and offers real value for money. Only a short distance from Cruden Bay and Peterhead, it is an ideal overnight stop or base for a holiday in this historic part of Aberdeenshire. In the new modern bar and lounge snacks and home cooked food can be enjoyed in an informal and friendly atmosphere.

There is also a beer garden at the rear. It's sister establishment, the **Seafield Arms Hotel**, is in Rothes in Moray, and should not be missed.

HIDDEN PLACES GUIDES

Explore Britain and Ireland with *Hidden Places* guides - a fascinating series of national and local travel guides.

Packed with easy to read information on hundreds of places of interest as well as places to stay, eat and drink.

Available from both high street and internet booksellers

For more information on the full range of *Hidden Places* guides and other titles published by Travel Publishing visit our website on

www.travelpublishing.co.uk or ask for our leaflet by phoning **0118-981-7777** or emailing **info@travelpublishing.co.uk**

207 THE STATION HOTEL

Seafield Street, Portsoy,
Aberdeenshire AB45 2QT
☎ 01261 842327
e-mail:
enquiries@stationhotelportsoy.co.uk
⊕ www.stationhotelportsoy.co.uk

Portsoy is a town on the Moray Firth which is steeped in history. It claims to have the oldest natural harbour in Europe, and was granted its town charter by Mary Queen of Scots. Nowadays people seek it out because of **The Station Hotel**, one of the finest small hotels in the area. It is owned and run by the husband and wife team of

Susan and Ewan Cameron, who take a quiet pride in the high standards of service, the warm welcome and the relaxing atmosphere of the place.

It boasts eleven fully en suite rooms that are comfortable and immaculately clean. Each one is furnished and decorated to a very high standard, and comes with TV and tea/coffee making facilities. You are assured of a good night's sleep here!

Food is important in The Station Hotel. The restaurant is spacious and elegant, and is open to non-residents. In fact, it is one of the favourite eating places in the town for local people! This is because Susan and Ewan want

people to enjoy the full dining experience, and in this they have succeeded admirably.

There is an extensive a la carte menu that contains many fine dishes created by the hotel's head chef. He insists on only the finest and freshest of local produce wherever possible, and combines imagination and flair without compromising the natural flavours. Being on the Moray Firth coast, locally caught seafood is something of a speciality, with the fish and shellfish coming from a merchant just a mile down the road. And being in Aberdeenshire, famous for its Aberdeen Angus cattle, the hotel can guarantee that the beef and steak, which come from the local award-winning butcher, are of the finest quality. The hotel is also famous for its high teas, a Scottish institution. The cake stand is always full of tasty, locally baked scones and cakes which are sure to delight those with a sweet tooth. Plus the teas and coffees are freshly brewed every time!

Close to the hotel are many fine golf courses, and it offers a range of golf breaks, from three nights bed and breakfast and three rounds of golf at different courses, to what it called a 'lazy golf break', where the hotel will arrange to pick you up from your home, transport you to Portsoy, arrange the golf, then take you home again. All are keenly priced, and are proving very popular.

So come to Portsoy and stay at The Station Hotel. It makes the ideal base for an activity holiday or for sightseeing in an area full of history and heritage!

209 CORRIE DUFF

Glen Nevis, Fort William.
Inverness-shire PH33 6ST
☎ 01397 701412
e-mail: gill@corrieduff.co.uk
🌐 www.corrieduff.co.uk

For outstanding guest house and self-catering accommodation close to Fort William, you simply can't beat **Corrie Duff**, owned and managed by the husband and wife team of Gill and Keith Williams. It has been given a coveted three star rating by VisitScotland, and is situated in Glen Nevis, only a ten minute stroll from the centre of Fort William and close to the slopes of Ben Nevis, Britain's highest mountain. Here you will find Scottish hospitality at its very best. Gill and Keith took over the place in 2006, and since then their reputation has certainly spread!

They offer six beautifully furnished and decorated rooms to discerning guests all year round. The entrance to the guest house is ramped, and one of the rooms - a twin - has an especially wide entrance door, disabled facilities and a walk in shower, making it particularly suitable for people in wheelchairs. Another room is a bunkroom which sleeps two, and this is very popular with youngsters! The tariff includes a full Scottish breakfast, and these are always filling and hearty. They feature locally sourced produce wherever possible, and will set you up for a hard day's sight seeing in one of the most beautiful areas of Scotland. In addition, Corrie Duff offers two stunning self-catering cottages. These were built two years ago, and feature everything that the modern holiday-maker expects nowadays. Each sleeps up to six in absolute comfort, and come with fully equipped kitchen and plenty of parking space. The cottages are also three-star, which means that you are getting the very best. They are on offer all year round, and short breaks are available (ring for details).

Gill and Keith are determined to offer the holidaymaker something special while still keeping prices as low as possible. The place is friendly and informal, and both children and well behaved pets are more than welcome. They also know the area, and can offer good advice on what to see and do.

One of the obvious things to do is climb Ben Nevis - it's a great day out for people who are reasonably fit and healthy. Plus there are the restaurants and pubs of Fort William, attractions such as the West Highland Museum, the Treasures of the Earth Exhibition, the Underwater Centre and, of course, trips on the famous Caledonian Canal.

Gill and Keith are anxious to welcome you to their guest house and self-catering accommodation. If you come along, you're assured of a great Highland welcome!

210 LEASONA

Torlundy, Fort William,
Inverness-shire PH33 6SN
☎ 01397 704661
e-mail: leasona@hotmail.com
🌐 www.leasona.co.uk

Leasona is an attractive, modern villa only two and a half miles north of Fort William that offers outstanding B&B accommodation to discerning tourists. It is a cheery, informal place that has four lovely rooms, two of which are en suite.

It has a three-star rating, and the tariff includes a full Scottish breakfast that is filling and cooked to perfection. There are wonderful views of Ben Nevis from the front of the building, which adds to its attractiveness as a place to stay.

212 MEHALAH RIVERSIDE HOUSE

Spean Bridge, Inverness-shire PH34 4EU
☎ 01397 712893
e-mail: mehalahrh@btinternet.com
🌐 www.mehalah.co.uk

Mehalah Riverside House is a superb 4 star bed and breakfast establishment, privately situated in its own grounds overlooking the river Spean. Warm and inviting, tastefully decorated throughout, with two en suite rooms. It is an ideal base for touring and exploring the wonderful countryside. A very warm welcome, peace, tranquility, good food and wonderful views make happy memories to take home with you when you stay here.

211 THE BRIDGE CAFÉ

Lochybridge, Fort William,
Inverness-shire PH33 7NU
☎ 01397 700532
e-mail: bridgecafe@btinternet.com

North of Fort William, close to the junction where the A82 meets the A830, you will find **The Bridge Café**, a licensed eating establishment that combines great food with outstanding value for money. Formerly part of the Ben Nevis Distillery, it became a café six years ago, and was taken over in June 2006 by new owners, who have already added to its already enviable reputation.

It is open seven days a week in the summer months, and closed on Sunday in winter. The opening times are 9 am to 10 pm in summer and 9 am to 4.30 pm in winter. It seats up to 50 in absolute comfort, and you can choose from a printed menu or a daily specials board. It sits close to the Great Glen Way, and walkers - as well as tourists, cyclists, motor-cyclists and passers by - are more than welcome. The homemade soup - usually there are nine varieties! - is very popular, as is the all-day breakfast, steak and ale pie, fish and chips and pizzas. Vegetarian options are always available.

The produce used in the kitchen is sourced locally wherever possible, and takeaways are always available during opening hours. Children are more than welcome, and payment is by cash or cheque only. So if you're feeling hungry in Fort William, head for the Bridge Café, where you will find great food at amazing prices.

529

213 THE SCOTS KITCHEN

Main Street, Fort Augustus,
Inverness-shire PH32 4DD
☎ 01320 366361
e-mail: johnshonsheila@hotmail.com

The **Scots Kitchen** is a delightful licensed restaurant right in the heart of Fort Augustus, opposite the tourism information centre. It is owned and run by the mother/son team of Sheila and Hamish Johnson, who are proud of the high standards they have set. Why not stop for a refreshing

coffee, a lunch, or a takeaway meal? It uses only the finest and freshest of local produce wherever possible. And while you're eating - take a look at Sheila's wonderful collection of tea pots!

214 INCHNACARDOCH LODGE HOTEL

Fort Augustus, Inverness-shire PH32 4BL
☎ 01456 4590900
e-mail: lochness97@aol.com
🌐 www.inchnacardoch.com

With fabulous views out over Loch Ness and the surrounding hills, the **Inchnacardoch Lodge Hotel** has 16 fully en suite rooms, most with antiques and fine furniture. The cuisine is Scottish with international influences, and the dishes combine fair and imagination, ensuring that people come back again and

again. The bar is the place to meet the locals and relax over a drink after a hard day exploring the area!

215 DEER VIEW BED & BREAKFAST

Lower Knockchoilum, Whitebridge,
Inverness IV2 6UR
☎ 01456 486276/486647
e-mail: deerviewbnb@hotmail.co.uk
🌐 www.deerviewbedandbreakfast.co.uk

There are some bed and breakfast establishments that stick in the mind for all the right reasons. The **Deer View Bed & Breakfast**, three miles from Foyers on the south side of Loch Ness, is one such establishment. It is a modern bungalow, built in 2003, that offers the best of Scottish hospitality and value-for-money prices. All around are breathtaking views, and the wildlife of the Highlands can be observed, sometimes just yards from the front door.

Julie and Ian Mitchell, who own Deer View, offer all visitors a warm Highland welcome. They offer three rooms - two doubles and a family room, all comfortable and well appointed, and all with TV and video. There is one large bathroom with bath and shower and one small shower room. In addition there is a private sitting/dining room plus another

dining room. For those days when the Highland weather might not be at its best, there is a summer house that

contains a pool table and dartboard. For a small charge, Internet access is available. The breakfasts are hearty and filling, and served at a time to suit you. Packed lunches and evening meals are available by prior arrangement.

Deer View is the ideal base from which to explore the area. Loch Ness is close by, as is Fort Augustus and Inverness.

Ballachulish, Argyll PH49 4JX
☎ 01855 811266 (main house)
01855 811695 (house and golf)
Fax: 01855 811498
e-mail: mcloughlins@btconnect.com
🌐 www.ballachulishhouse.com

There is no doubt that **Ballachulish House and Golf Course** is one of the best and most famous establishments of its kind in Scotland. It has five coveted stars from VisitScotland, five diamonds from the AA, and a restaurant that has been awarded two rosettes for its superb food. It's no wonder that it prides itself on being world class and a 'truly unique experience'.

The house is set in its own grounds on the shores of Loch Linnhe, and was built in 1640. It became the HQ for Captain Campbell, who led the troops that massacred the MacDonalds in Glencoe, so it is steeped in history. It now boasts eight luxurious en suite rooms, each one individually furnished in the Georgian style. Though there is elegance and good taste aplenty, the hotel still has that unstuffy, welcoming atmosphere that leads to complete relaxation, and older children are more than welcome. It is open all year round, and you can stay on a B&B or dinner, B&B basis. You are also welcome to visit if you just wish a superb

lunch or dinner.

The food, of course, is outstanding, with a Michelen award-winning menu. The cuisine is Scottish, with French influences. Local produce is always used in the kitchens, where the chefs create dishes that show imagination and flair, while still remaining simple and true to the original flavours. The five course table d'hôte menu contains such dishes as a tartlet of peat-smoked fish with wild mushrooms crusted with Mull-cheddar rarebit, rosette of prime Highland beef glazed with Arran mustard and herd crumble, rack of Skye lamb with spinach and wild mushroom face, and cranachan set in a cage of spun sugar with fresh Highland raspberries.

This is dining at its finest, and is an ideal way to celebrate a special occasion such as birthday or anniversary. The golf course itself was opened in 2001, and is open to non-members. It is a par 68/65 course of 5038 yards, and presents a unique challenge to golfers at all levels. The clubhouse has a bar and grill, and you can enjoy simpler, but no less beautifully cooked, fare, such as soup, baked jacket potatoes, Angus steak burgers with chips, and home baking. These facilities are open to non-members.

The establishment holds a civil marriage license, so you can tie the knot in one of the most luxurious and unique locations in Scotland. So f you're in Argyll, don't miss Ballachulish House and Golf Course!

217 THE GATEWAY RESTAURANT

Station Road, Kyle of Lochalsh,
Inverness-shire IV40 8AB
☎ 01599 530258
e-mail: oorrestaurant@aol.com
🌐 www.thegatewayrestaurant
@daisybroadband.co.uk

Kyle of Lochalsh, on the mainland opposite the Isle of Skye, is where you will find **The Gateway Restaurant**, one of the best eating places in the area. It serves wonderful food at reasonable prices and is open seven days a week during the summer months from 8.30 am until 10 pm. During the winter, it is closed on Sunday, Monday and Tuesday, reopening on Wednesday at 5 pm.

The interior seats 80 in absolute comfort and is smart and modern, with plenty of space, pine furniture, large windows and delightful prints on the wall. It is a popular eating place for tourists and locals alike due to the high standards the owners, Catriona and Andrew Morrison, have set. The food is outstanding, and features local, fresh produce wherever possible. This being Scotland's western coast, locally caught seafood is a speciality. Try the pan-seared Lochalsh scallops, for

instance! Or why not go for the tower of haggis, neeps (mashed swede) and champit tatties (mashed potato)? Absolutely delicious! There is also a unique children's menu, where the dishes were all suggested by local children. It includes such dishes as macaroni cheese with chips or potatoes, buffet platter (carrot, cheese, cucumber, fruit, roast meat of the day and bread and butter) and a bowl of soup and half a sandwich.

The premises, which are upstairs, are licensed, and they are available for private hire for birthdays, anniversaries and so on.

218 OFF THE BEATEN TRACK - IN KINTAIL

The Old House, Innisachro, Kintail,
Kyle of Lochalsh,
South West Ross-shire IV40 8HQ
☎ 01599 511385
e-mail: offbeatkintail@freeuk.com
🌐 www.offbeatkintail.freeuk.com

Off the Beaten Track in Kintail. The Old House is a cosy, homely self-catering cottage in one of the most beautiful parts of Western Scotland. Tucked up the glen at the foot of the Five Sisters of Kintail, it offers modern comforts with original character. It has one double

bedroom, one family room, dining kitchen, sitting room with open fire and bathroom. It is the place to really get away from it all and enjoy a holiday walking, bird watching or exploring the area with its mountains, islands and lochs, castles and brochs.

220 CROFT SELF CATERING

167 Portachullin, Strome Ferry,
Ross-shire IV53 8UW
☎ 01599 577267 Fax: 01599 577267

Situated on the edge of Loch Carron, with excellent sea views, **Croft Self Catering** is a superb modern cottage that offers the very best in comfortable, affordable holiday accommodation. It has been furnished and decorated to an extremely high standard, which is reflected in its VisitScotland four star grading. It has three bedrooms, a double, twin and single, and is let on a weekly basis. Children and a single pet are very welcome.

219 THE HAVEN HOTEL

Plockton, Ross-shire IV52 8TW
☎ 01599 544223
e-mail:
reception@havenhotelplockton.co.uk
🌐 www.havenhotelplockton.co.uk

Imagine a small Scottish village on the edge of a sea loch, washed by the warm waters of the Gulf Stream. Imagine warm, friendly people and picturesque cottages, framed by high, purple hills. Then imagine Plockton, one of Scotland's loveliest villages, made famous in the *Hamish Macbeth* series, but unspoilt by the fame it brought. It is indeed a lovely place, and in this setting you will find a hotel that epitomises everything that is good about Highland hospitality - **The Haven Hotel**. This

family-run establishment is renowned for the warmth of its welcome, its high standards of service and reasonable prices. It was once the home of a merchant, and has been refurbished to a very high standard without losing any of the period features that give it its great character. There are thirteen guest rooms on offer, all but one being fully en suite. They are all comfortable and welcoming, with high standards of furnishings and decoration. Each has a TV, tea/coffee making facilities, telephone, hair drier and trouser press. The public areas and rooms are equally as welcoming, and the staff is friendly and knowledgeable without being intrusive. Take time out from your hectic sight seeing

schedule, and sit before a roaring log fire as you read your paper and enjoy a coffee or something stronger!

Mutley's Bar is a cosy, friendly place that is popular with the locals - always a good sign. Teas, coffees, home baking, light luncheons and bar meals are served throughout the day, with cooked bistro meals available in the evenings. The bar has a great range of drinks, from draft ales to wines, soft drinks and single malts.

You can also eat in the more formal Symphony's Restaurant. It represents the very best in Scottish cuisine, and raids Scotland's larder of fine produce for its inspiration. Wild salmon - venison - prime Scottish beef - hill lamb - fresh

vegetables and fruit - it uses them all with imagination and flare. The care, understanding and skill of the chefs are the other ingredients, ensuring that you get a unique dining experience that will long be remembered for all the right reasons. There is also an extensive wine list to complement the menu.

The countryside surrounding Plockton is undoubtedly the essence of the Highland experience, even though you will - surprisingly - find palm trees growing in the village! And The Haven Hotel is the essence of Scottish hospitality and friendliness. Pay it a visit and you're sure to agree.

221 LOCH NESS HOUSE HOTEL

Glenurquhart Road, Inverness,
Inverness-shire IV3 8JL
☎ 01463 231248 Fax: 01463 239327
🌐 www.lochnesshotel.co.uk

Situated on the outskirts of the beautiful city
of Inverness, the **Loch Ness House Hotel**
is a comfortable, family-run establishment
that offers 22 en suite bedrooms. It has the
Copper Kettle Bar, which also sells bar meals
and is the hotel's "pub", plus the Stag and
Haggis Restaurant selling superb food
prepared from fresh, local produce. The Loch
Ness

House
Hotel is
one of the
best hotels
in the city,
and is
handy for
Loch Ness,
the Black
Isle and all
the glories
of the
Highlands.

223 CROMARTY ARMS INN

Church Street, Cromarty IV11 8XA
☎ 01381 600230

One of the oldest buildings in this delightful
little town, the **Cromarty Arms Inn** is a
charming old hostelry offering good food,
real ale and comfortable accommodation.
Owned and run by Helen and Kenneth
MacFarlane, the inn starts the day by serving
breakfast,
followed by
meals
throughout
the day
from noon
until 10pm.
Locally
caught
prawns and
crab dishes
are particularly popular. At least one real ale is
always available. On Saturday evenings there's
live music from 9pm. The inn also offers
accommodation with 2 doubles and a family
room available. Children are welcome and
dogs are also taken.

222 ANCHOR AND CHAIN HOTEL

Coulmore Bay, near Charlestown,
Ross-shire IV1 3XB
☎ 01463 731313
e-mail: macnachten@aol.com
🌐 www.anchorandchainhotel.co.uk

Occupying a position of outstanding beauty and
tranquillity, the **Anchor and Chain Hotel** makes
the most of its superb location looking out towards
Beauly and the Muir of Ord. Its Waterside
Restaurant also looks out across the Bay where,
depending on the season, diners can watch
dolphins playing, ospreys fishing or seals basking. When the
weather is favourable, you can also sit out at tables on the
spacious lawn which also enjoys the same grand views.

The fully licensed restaurant is open throughout the day
for light lunches and an evening menu based on local food –
delicious fish from Mallaig, venison from Tarradale and
Aberdeen Angus or Black Isle beef, for example. The dining
room and all 10 of
the bedrooms are all
on the ground floor
and have only
recently been built.
All the rooms are en suite with TV, and have been superbly
furnished and decorated in varying styles by owners Maura
and Peter MacNaughton who have been in the hospitality
business for some 40 years, five of them at Coulmore Bay.
The front bedrooms command wonderful views over the
Bay. Children are welcome and all major credit cards are
accepted.

224 THE ANDERSON

Union Street, Fortrose IV10 8TD
☎ 01381 620236
e-mail: info@theanderson.co.uk
⊕ www.theanderson.co.uk

A truly outstanding restaurant with rooms, **The Anderson** is a striking Victorian building with many flamboyant architectural features. But it's the superb food that brings diners here from far and wide. Formerly known as The Station Hotel and then the Royal Hotel, The Anderson now takes its name from the owners, Jim and Anne Anderson. Both had many years experience in the hospitality business before taking over here in 2003.

Anne is the Chef and her regular "everyday" menu includes her famous Black Isle Burger served with bacon and a thick slice of haggis. But each day, Anne offers an extensive and exciting choice of daily specials that might include a Lebanese Falafel Salad or Wild Grouse Pâté amongst the starters; Acapulco Red Snapper, Saltimbocca di Vitello or Rabbit, Feta and Chorizo as main courses. To accompany your meal there's a huge choice of beers and ales – and a mind-boggling selection of more than 250 different varieties of single and malt whiskeys to savour. The restaurant is open every evening and from noon until 2pm on Saturday and Sunday. The Anderson also has 9 superb guest bedrooms available, all with en suite facilities and with lots of character.

225 EILEAN DUBH RESTAURANT

18 High Street, Fortrose IV10 8SX
☎ 01381 620690

Graham and Anne Law created the **Eilean Dubh Restaurant** in December 2006 after 3 years running the village pub.

Eilean Dubh means "Black Isle" in Gaelic and they designed their menu to reflect the local produce of this area. "We also run a small farm" they say, "where we produce our own lamb and grow many of our vegetables. The rest we source from local farmers, fishermen or growers". So, the dishes on offer include pan-fried steak of Black Isle venison, baked fillet of Moray Firth salmon and "Chicken Highlander" – breast of chicken stuffed with haggis. All very tasty indeed!

226 CROFTERS CAFÉ BAR ❢

I Marine Terrace, Rosemarkie, Fortrose,
Ross-shire IV10 8UL
☎ 01381 620844

The village of Rosemarkie occupies a fine position on the Black Isle looking out across the Moray Firth. It is fortunate in having a delightful eating place in the form of the **Crofters Café Bar**. The extensive menu is home-made and based on fresh local produce, offering tasty dishes such as Highland Steak & Ale Pie or Venison Casserole, fish dishes (locally caught salmon, for example) and vegetarian options.

To accompany your meal, there's a wide choice of draught and bottled beers, including a locally brewed real ale and organic bottled beers from the

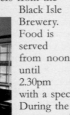

Black Isle Brewery. Food is served from noon until 2.30pm with a special evening menu available from 5.30pm. During the summer months, booking ahead is recommended. The well-stocked bar is open from 11am until 11pm, all year round. Children are welcome; all major credit cards except Diners are accepted, and there's ample parking.

227 CULBOKIE INN ❢

Culbokie, Ross-shire IV7 8JH
☎ 01349 877280
e-mail: info@culbokieinn.com
⊕ www.culbokieinn.co.uk

Sitting a few miles north of Inverness on the picturesque Black Isle, Culbokie is a pleasant country village where you will find The **Culbokie Inn**, one of the best hostelries in the area. It is an idyllic spot, with lovely views out over the Cromarty Firth to the shoreline beyond.

It is owned and managed by Angus Murray, who places great emphasis on food. People come from far and near to eat here, and you are well advised to book a table if you wish to dine from Thursday to Sunday. Angus is a chef, and he ensures that all the produce is sourced locally wherever possible, so that it fresh and flavoursome. The menu contains some outstanding dishes, from traditional Scottish to stir fries, lasagne and vegetarian dishes. You can also choose from a daily specials board which takes advantage of local produce in season. The wine list offers a fine selection, so

there is sure to be one to complement your meal.

The cosy, inviting bar serves a wide range of drinks, including two real ales (Deuchars IPA and a rotating ale in the summer months). There is also a range of beers, wines, spirits (including single malt), liqueurs and soft drinks if you're driving.

There is occasional live entertainment (ring for details), plenty of parking, a beer garden and, unusually, a pétanque court. Children are very welcome, and all major credit and debit cards are accepted.

228 THE SHIP INN

33 Shore Road, Invergordon IV18 0ER
☎ 01349 852427

Situated in the heart of Invergordon, **The Ship Inn** dates back more than 200 years and served for a long time as a Temperance Hotel. It is now the home of Allan and Sue who have been welcoming bed & breakfast guests here since 2003. It's a very popular establishment with a large part of its custom being repeat visitors. Guests are welcome all year round except at Christmas and the New Year.

There are 7 comfortable guest bedrooms – 2 singles, 3 twins, 1 double and a room with 3 single beds. Allan and Sue are very hospitable hosts and you'll find that the hearty breakfast served between 8.30am and 9.30am will truly set you up for the day. Children are welcome. Cash or cheques are accepted. The Ship Inn is located about 5 minutes off the main A9 road.

229 FEARN HOTEL

Hill of Fearn, Tain, Ross-shire IV20 1TJ
☎ 01862 832234 Fax: 01862 850342
e-mail: fearnhotel@yahoo.co.uk

Set in scenic countryside, the **Fearn Hotel** was bought in 2006 by experienced owners Paul and Heather Hart who carried out an extensive refurbishment to the highest standards and re-opened in October 2006. Paul is an accomplished chef and his extensive menu offers a tasty selection of dishes based on fresh local produce. Such is his reputation it is essential to book during the summer months. Children are welcome and have their own menu. If you are planning to stay in this attractive corner of Easter Ross, the hotel has 6 comfortable guest bedrooms, 3 double/twins and 3 singles, all with en suite facilities.

231 THE SUTHERLAND INN

Fountain Square, Brora KW9 6NX
☎ 01408 621209 Fax: 01408 622442
e-mail: sutherlandinn@aol.com
 www.sutherlandinn.co.uk

Conveniently located on the A9 in Brora with the River Brora flowing past at the rear of the building, **The Sutherland Inn** is a family-run establishment owned and run by Leon and Kerry Sims. Leon is the chef and offers a varied and enticing menu whose ingredients are 90% locally sourced. Friday night is Steak Night but with exotic choices, not the standard fare. There's an outstanding wine list, reasonably priced, and a huge choice of malt whisky. The whole hotel has just been completely refurbished and now offers 7 top quality guest bedrooms, all en suite.

537

230 SUTHERLAND ARMS HOTEL

Old Bank Road, Golspie,
Sutherland KW10 6RS
☎ 01408 633234
e-mail: sutherlandarms@aol.com
🌐 www.sutherlandarmshotel.com

Conveniently located alongside the north-east coastal road, the A9, in the village of Golspie, the **Sutherland Arms Hotel** is an impressive building that started life in 1808 as a hunting and shooting lodge. The Dorward family arrived here at the beginning of 2007 – Sue Dorward, her daughter Heather and son Rob. Sue used to be a PA/Conference Organiser at Guy's Hospital in London but loves to cook. Heather has many years experience in management at some well-known London hotels so she looks after the practical details while Rob is an enthusiast in the 'bar' department.

The hotel has a full on licence and stocks a good range of well-kept draught keg ales. The bar is open throughout the day. At lunchtime (noon until 2pm) Sue's menu offers a wide choice of main meals, light bites, sandwiches and "spuds" (oven-baked potatoes), as well as a selection of "Wee Kiddies Meals". On Sundays, the choice also includes 3 different roasts. Dinner is available in 'The 1808 Restaurant' from 6pm to 8.30pm and among the locally sourced dishes are Lamb Shank in a red wine sauce; smoked salmon or Atlantic prawn cocktail as starters; poached salmon, breaded haddock or scampi, and steaks. For vegetarians there's a homemade vegetable goulash or a wild mushroom risotto. Amongst the desserts, don't miss the delicious homemade sherry trifle. During the summer months it is advisable to book ahead for both lunch and dinner.

If you are staying at the hotel, there are 14 rooms of various sizes, but all spacious and all with en suite facilities. Children are welcome and all major credit cards apart from American Express and Diners are accepted.

232 THE INVERSHIN HOTEL

Invershin, Sutherland IV27 4ET
☎ 01549 421202 Fax: 01549 421268
🌐 www.invershin.com

Located in the midst of one of the most picturesque areas of the Scottish Highlands the **Invershin Hotel** is beautifully sited overlooking the waters of the Kyle of Sutherland. Also close by are the well-known Falls of Shin where, from May to November you can watch wild Atlantic salmon leaping upstream through the rushing waters.

Graham and Barry Lonsdale have recently refurbished the hotel and on a Bed & Breakfast basis they offer 8 comfortably appointed en-suite guest bedrooms all with TV and tea/coffee making facilities. For those who prefer self-catering, they also have 2 fully equipped Chalets sleeping upto 4 people and 3 self-catering twin bed units sleeping 2 people. For a nominal charge limited camping and overnight parking for caravans and camper vans is available.

Using the best fresh Scottish produce the extensive restaurant menu offers traditional dishes to tempt every palette and you can compliment your meal with a drink from the fully licensed, well stocked bar. The bar has had a long history of live music and session nights are a regular feature. Guests are encouraged to bring their instruments and join in.

Many pursuits from angling, shooting, walking, golfing, horse riding, cycling, bird watching or botany can be arranged for guests through local organisations or in-house facilities, angling permits for Salmon and Sea trout fishing in the Kyle and for wild brown trout in local lochs may also be purchased from the hotel.

A packed lunch for all outdoor ventures will be provided if required.

The many interesting and historic places in this area makes the Invershin Hotel an ideal base from which to explore the Highlands.

For further information and tariffs please visit:
www.invershin.com

233 WESTERLEA HOTEL

Inverness Road, Nairn IV12 4SD
☎ 01667 452136
e-mail: info@westerleahotel.co.uk
🌐 www.westerleahotel.co.uk

Situated directly on the A96 the **Westerlea Hotel** is a delightful Victorian building dating back to 1867, its walls of old stone now partly clad with ivy. It stands in its own grounds with a pleasant beer garden and a large parking area to the front. Inside, the beautiful original tiles are still in place in the entrance and around the fireplaces but the hotel has also been updated with all modern amenities. The bar is in traditional Scottish style and offers bar lunches 7 days a week with a roast dinner on Sundays with all the trimmings.

Owner Andrew McLauchlan spent several years with major Scottish hospitality companies and then 6 years self-employed as a publican before arriving here. His hotel has 5 guest bedrooms, all attractively furnished and decorated, and all with en suite facilities. The hotel is very conveniently located close to Nairn town centre and the Castle and Whiskey Trails. Golfers will be delighted to

find no fewer than 36 eighteen-hole courses within a one-hour drive! Westerlea is also close to the sea and a mere 6 miles from Inverness airport.

2 Academy street, Nairn,
Nairnshire IV12 4RJ
☎ 01667 453551
e-mail: aurorahotelnairn@aol.com
🌐 www.aurorahotelnairn.com

Nairn is one of Scotland's best holiday and golfing resorts, and nestles on the shores of the Moray Firth. It is one of the sunniest and driest places in Britain, and locals will assure you its name derives from "no rain"! At the west end of the town is the **Aurora Hotel and Italian Restaurant**, a superior establishment that combines the very best of accommodation with the very best of food.

Its ten rooms are all en suite, and are tastefully and comfortably furnished to make your stay as relaxing as possible. All have colour TV and central heating, and there is plenty of car parking. Overseas visitors will feel really at home, as the owners speak several languages, including Italian, Spanish and Portuguese, and are always keen to learn new ones!

While staying in the hotel, why not dine in the hotel's own restaurant? It is renowned throughout the area for the quality of its traditional Italian dishes, which uses only the finest and freshest of local produce wherever possible. You can dine in the elegant dining room or the spacious conservatory, and be assured of a meal to be remembered. You can even relax over a quiet drink beforehand in the hotel's well-stocked bar.

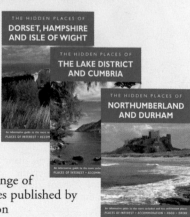

235 CULDEARN HOUSE

Woodlands Terrace, Grantown-on-Spey
Morayshire PH26 3JU
☎ 01479 872106 Fax: 01479 873641
e-mail: enquiries@culdearn.com
🌐 www.culdearn.com

Culdearn House is a fine granite Victorian villa dating from 1860 which has beautiful corniced ceilings, wood panelling and original marble fireplaces. It is owned and personally managed by William and Sonia Marshall, who have recently refurbished it making it one of the best small hotels in Speyside. Situated on the edge of Grantown-on-Spey, yet still within walking distance of the town, the house sits in its own grounds surrounded by mature trees.

With just seven bedrooms, all en suite, the house is more of a country house than a hotel, offering luxury accommodation, comfort and excellent hospitality. There is no smoking in the house.

Culdearn is renowned for its fine dining, excellent wines and selection of malt whiskies, some rare cask strengths. Accolades for the food include an AA red rosette, RAC Fine Dining Award, 3 medallions Taste of Scotland and the hotel is also a member of the Scotch Beef Club. The menu changes daily and offers a selection of

locally produced food using the finest ingredients, including Morayshire lamb, Highland Beef and some of the freshest and finest fish from the West Coast of Scotland, all prepared and cooked to perfection by Feona, the chef. Special diets can be catered for.

The Hotel has also won numerous awards including 'Scotland's Hotel of Year' and 'The Best Small Hotel in Speyside'.

Situated within the heart of Speyside, and in the National Park, Culdearn House is the perfect base for the many attractions in the area as well as being on the whisky and castle trails. Be it fishing

on the Spey, playing golf at some of the most spectacular courses in Scotland, walking in the Cairngorms Mountains or visiting the many bird sanctuaries in the area (including the Osprey at nearby Boat of Garten), or just for sheer relaxation, this is the ideal place to stay.

Open from March to December, the Hotel offers dinner, bed and breakfast either on a daily or weekly basis. Once you have stayed at this excellent country hotel you will certainly wish to return again and again.

236 RAVENSCOURT HOUSE HOTEL

Seafield Avenue, Grantown-on-Spey,
Morayshire PH26 3JG
☎ 01479 872286 Fax: 05601 162846
e-mail: info@ravenscourthouse.co.uk
🌐 www.ravenscourthouse.co.uk

Dating from around 1905, **Ravenscourt House Hotel** was originally built as a Church of Scotland manse. An impressive stone-built house, it stands in a quiet location just a 2-minute stroll from the centre of Grantown-on-Spey, a charming small town with a distinct village ambience, set amidst breathtaking countryside on the northern edge of the Cairngorms National Park.

Now an outstanding country house hotel, Ravenscourt is owned and run by Andrew, Sheena and Mark Williamson who extend a warm Scottish welcome to their guests. Since they took over in December 2006 they have raised the hotel's standards even higher and more than justify their 4-star rating from VisitScotland but the atmosphere still remains informal and relaxed. Arriving guests are offered tea or coffee when they check in, again when they return to the hotel after day trips, and also on a complimentary basis to residents guests after meals.

Arriving visitors enter through the vestibule into the reception hall where an enticing collection of whiskies is displayed behind the desk – the hotel can offer you a choice of 45 malts. The hotel has 7 luxurious en suite guest bedrooms with a choice of

double, twin or family rooms. There is also 1 twin room with a private bathroom. One double is on the ground floor for easier access. All the bedrooms are immaculately maintained, with period furnishings, and are provided with extras such as shortbread and other biscuits, along with complimentary *Ocean* toiletries. There's also a TV, radio/alarm, hair dryer and lots of local information. Like all hotels in Scotland, Ravenscourt House is completely non-smoking.

Downstairs again and into the inviting residents' lounge with its upholstered sofas and armchairs, rich drapes, and interesting pictures and curios. Across the Hall is the fine dining restaurant where the menu makes the maximum use of seasonal local produce to create modern Scottish dishes. You can dine either à la carte or select the 2 or 3 course dinners, all at very reasonable prices for such quality cuisine. An alternative to the restaurant is The Chop House, a delightful conservatory bistro looking out to the gardens.

237 TIGH-NA-SGIATH COUNTRY HOUSE HOTEL

Dulnain Bridge, Grantown-on-Spey,
Inverness-shire PH26 3PA
☎ 01479 851345
e-mail: iain@tigh-na-sgiath.co.uk
🌐 www.tigh-na-sgiath.co.uk

The **Tigh-na-Sgiath Country House Hotel** is centred on a magnificent former country house, and set in two-and-a-half acres of mature grounds. It sits in Strathspey, a couple of miles east of Grantown, and is the ideal base for exploring the beautiful Scottish Highlands, from Loch Ness to Aviemore, and from Royal Deeside and the whisky distilleries of Banffshire, to the cosmopolitan delights of Aberdeen.

It's name in Gaelic means "house on the edge", and it was built in 1902 for the founders of a shipping line. Many of the period features have been retained, giving the hotel a traditional feel while still offering all that is best in modern Scottish hospitality. It is said one of the previous owners loved the house so much that her benign ghost still haunts it - with her footsteps being heard as she climbs the stairs from the cellar!

Imagine entering a hotel as wonderful and welcoming as this one and being greeted by a richly panelled stairwell that speaks of fine Scottish craftsmanship. Imagine being greeted by attentive staff who are keen to make your stay as comfortable and enjoyable as possible. Imagine entering your room and being greeted by fine furnishings and decoration, and windows that give stunning views out over a landscape that encompasses fields and woodland with, in the distance, a rim of hills that adds a touch of romance.

Most of the rooms are fully en suite, as you would imagine, with each one being individually designed to express its own individuality. All have colour TVs, individually controlled heating, hair dryers and tea/coffee making facilities. The owners, Elaine and Iain MacDonald, look on the hotel not just as a business, but as their home, and to them attention to detail is everything.

The food in the Tigh-na-Sgiath is superb. The spacious dining room has elegant touches, fresh flowers and crystal. You can sit sipping fine wine from the hotel's cellars while you watch the sunset through the trees. The kitchens use only the finest, freshest produce in season wherever possible for their dishes, which marries the best of Scottish cooking with authentic French influences to give the diner a gastronomic experience that is long remembered. And the breakfasts are equally as satisfying! From the full Scottish to something lighter, they will set you up for a day's sightseeing or something a bit more energetic.

For all its period features, its attention to detail and its attentive staff, the hotel is still a home from home - a friendly place where you can completely relax and unwind among some of the most beautiful scenery in Scotland.

Why not make it your base as you explore the surrounding area? Or making it a stopping off point as you head north or south? It is just ten miles from the A9, and you'll be assured of a warm, Scots welcome!

238 PINE BANK CHALETS

Dalfaber road, Aviemore,
Inverness-shire PH22 1PX
☎ 01479 810000
e-mail: pinebankchallets@btopenworld.com
🌐 www.pinebankchalets.co.uk

Set in Strathspey, one of the most picturesque parts of the Highlands, the four star **Pine Bank Chalets** offer the very best in self catering accommodation. They provide the ideal base from which to explore an area that is rich in history, heritage and wildlife, and is yet only a few minutes from the A9 - the main route north to Inverness from the Scottish Lowlands. Here you can ski in the winter months, sail, walk, climb, fish and study nature.

There are thirteen chalets and log cabins in all, with one to three bedrooms and sleeping from one to six people. Situated right on the banks of the River Spey and a short walk from the centre of Aviemore, each one is extremely comfortable and welcoming. They come with a fully equipped kitchen, satellite TV, video and stereo.

In addition, the east wing of the charming Craigellachie House has two self-contained apartments available. The house has great character, and is set among Scots pines, with a cobblestone driveway, ample car parking and superb mountain views.

Pine Bank Chalets are the last word in comfortable yet affordable accommodation. There's just so much to do for all the family! Come and see for yourself. You won't be disappointed.

239 FIDDLER'S HIGHLAND RESTAURANT & MALT WHISKY BAR

The Village Green, Drumnadrochit,
Inverness-shire IV63 6TX
☎ 01456 450678
e-mail: info@fiddledrum.co.uk
🌐 www.fiddledrum.co.uk

Drumnadrochit sits right on the banks of Loch Ness, and it is in this village that you will find **Fiddler's**, an establishment that calls itself 'so much more than a restaurant'. It's an apt description for it also features a bar, a coffee shop and some of the best B&B accommodation in the area.

The restaurant serves delicious food, with much of the produce it uses being sourced locally. It seats 50, with more seating in the outdoor patio area in the summer months. It is open at lunchtime and in the evenings, and you choose from a menu which also includes daily specials. The resident chef produces some marvellous dishes that combine imagination with flair. So popular is Fiddler's that you are well advised to book at all times. The premises are licensed, with the bar

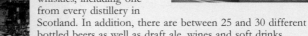

holding over 200 different whiskies, including one from every distillery in Scotland. In addition, there are between 25 and 30 different bottled beers as well as draft ale, wines and soft drinks.

The accommodation consists of six guest rooms, three in the inn itself and three in a villa situated opposite. Two are fully en suite, and they represent extremely comfortable accommodation at reasonable prices. Fiddler's also has a coffee shop and bakery, for sit-in or take-away food, open daily.

240 GLEN ROWAN GUEST HOUSE

West Lewiston. Drumnadrochit,
Inverness-shire IV63 6UW
☎ 01456 450235
e-mail: info@glenrowan.co.uk
🌐 www.glenrowan.co.uk

The four-star **Glenrowan Guest House** sits less than a mile from the picturesque Highland village of Drumnadrochit, on the shores of Loch Ness. It is owned by Vanessa and Alastair Ferguson, who offer comfortable, fully en suite guest rooms to discerning visitors. They are all tastefully furnished and decorated to a high standard, and as the guest house is in a peaceful location, you are assured of a good night's sleep! Each one comes complete with colour TV, tea/coffee making facilities, bedside lamps, radio alarm, heated towel rails and individual heating control.

Vanessa and Alastair pride themselves on offering the 'personal touch' and this friendly establishment has often been described by delighted guests as a 'home from home'. One person even called it 'the best guest house in Scotland'! There

are a number of lounges and a smart dining room where delicious home-cooked fare is served at individual tables. The full Scottish breakfasts are hearty and filling, just right to set you up as you search the waters of Loch Ness for Nessie, or explore the ruins of Urquhart Castle.

Surrounding the house are neat, well-tended gardens, which ensure privacy. There is plenty of parking, and the rooms at the back overlook the River Coiltie and the hills beyond. It is regretted that only guide or assist dogs are allowed.

241 BENLEVA HOTEL

Drumnadrochit,
Inverness-shire IV63 6UH
☎ 01456 450080
e-mail: enquiry@benleva.co.uk
🌐 www.benleva.co.uk

The **Benleva Hotel** sits in an acre of private grounds just a half a mile from Drumnadrochit. It is a picturesque and very historic building, being a former manse dating back over 300 years. Its tree-lined driveway even has a 400-year old hanging tree! The hotel is a friendly, welcoming establishment, famous for its good food, its comfortable accommodation and its ales

It has six en suite rooms that are comfortable, well furnished and decorated to an extremely high standard, including one that is a family room and one that boasts a four-poster. The ambience of the place is very welcoming and friendly, and if you stay here you are sure to return!

The hotel's two bars are famous for their wide selection of single malts and real ales. In fact, it was voted the CAMRA Highlands and Islands Pub of the Year in 2005 for the second time in three years. Fine food is available all day, with the produce used in the kitchens being sourced locally whenever possible, ensuring freshness and full flavour. Salmon - venison - lamb - beef - all appear on the menu in many imaginative dishes that are sure to appeal to your taste buds.

There is a small beer garden to the rear which is a sun trap in the summer months, and dogs and children are most welcome. You can use the hotel as an overnight B&B stop, or as a base to explore a wide area that takes in Loch Ness, Inverness, Fort William, the Moray Firth and the West Highlands.

546

242 THE OLD NORTH INN ¶ ⊨

Inchmore, Kirkhill, Inverness IV5 7PX
☎ 01463 831296
e-mail: oldnorthinn@btconnect.com
⊕ www.oldnorthinn.com

Whether you're looking for a quiet drink, a nice meal or a comfortable overnight stay, you can be assured of the finest Highland hospitality at **The Old North Inn.** You'll find it on the Inverness to Beauly road (A862), about 7 miles from Inverness, in the small village of Inchmore. Since 2004 the inn has been owned and run by Graham Cross who is dedicated to providing the very best in accommodation, food, drink and hospitality.

Food is taken seriously here with an extensive menu based on top quality Scottish produce – do try the locally produced haggis from Dingwall. Food is served from breakfast through to 8.30pm (9pm on Friday and Saturday). Children are welcome and have their own low fat, salt free

menu. Real ale lovers will be pleased to know that the inn offers one from the Isle of Skye

brewery. If you are planning to stay in the area, the inn has 10 comfortable bedrooms, all en suite with tea and coffee making facilities, telephone and TV. The tariff includes a full Scottish breakfast – "At The Old North Inn", says Graham, "we don't believe in buffet breakfasts – our breakfasts are prepared and cooked freshly to your requirements".

243 CULLIGRAN COTTAGES ⊨

Glen Strathfarrar, Struy, Nr Beauly,
Inverness-shire IV4 7JX
☎ 01463 761285
e-mail: info@culligrancottages.co.uk
⊕ www.culligrancottages.co.uk

The **Culligran Cottages** are situated in one of the most beautiful areas of Scotland - Strathfarrar, to the west of Inverness. All around is striking scenery, historical places to visit and plenty of opportunities for activities such as fishing, golf, walking, climbing, sailing or indeed just relaxing away from the bustle of every day life.

One of the cottages would make the idea base from which to explore the area. Owned and managed by Juliet and Frank Spencer-Nairn, they consist of a traditional stone-built cottage and four Norwegian-style chalets on the banks of the beautiful River Farrar, and within a naturally wooded area in the Culligran estate. The cottage sleeps up to seven people, and has three bedrooms, a spacious sitting room, a large, well-equipped kitchen, bathroom and a shower room.

The chalets have an open plan living room with kitchen/dining area, a bathroom and either two or three bedrooms. A sofa bed in the living room means they can sleep up to five in a two-bedroom chalet and seven in a three bedroom-chalet. All are comfortable and extremely well appointed, with double glazing, electric heaters, cookers and fridge. Frank offers Land Rover tours of Culligran Deer Farm, and a daily permit allows you to fish the River Farrar. Culligran Cottages are open from mid-March to mid-November each year.

244 CNOC HOTEL

Struy, by Beauly, Inverness-shire IV4 7JU
☎ 01463 761264 Fax: 01463 761207
e-mail: cnochotel@ta;l21.com
🌐 www.thecnochotel.co.uk

Standing in its own gloriously scenic grounds, the **Cnoc Hotel** is an outstanding Highland country house hotel which maintains the very best traditions of Scottish hospitality. It nestles in the picturesque countryside of Strathglass, at the foot of Glen Strathfarrar and was converted from four cottages which were once part of the Erchless Castle Estate, ancestral home of Clan Chisholm.

Since arriving here in 2001 owner Joanne Dixon has made the Cnoc Hotel a by-word for high standards, quality accommodation and excellent cuisine thanks to the award-winning Chef, Morag Fraser. Morag's menus offer an enticing selection of appetising dishes based on fresh, local produce wherever possible with venison and game as specialities. There's also an excellent choice of seafood dishes and around half a dozen vegetarian options. Fine wines and a wonderful range of single malt whiskeys are always available. The accommodation here sustains the same high standards evident throughout the hotel. The 7 guest bedrooms are all en suite, beautifully decorated and furnished, and equipped with colour TV, hospitality tray, radio alarm and hair dryer. Two of the rooms are family rooms and sleep at least 4 people with a cot available if required. Well-behaved dogs are welcome at a small supplementary charge.

245 ORD HOUSE

Muir of Ord,
Ross and Cromarty IV6 7UH
☎ 01463 870492
e-mail: admin@ord-house.co.uk
🌐 www.ord-house.co.uk

Ord House is a 17th century country house hotel set among some of the most beautiful scenery in Scotland. Still with many of its orginal features, it boasts twelve luxurious en suite rooms, one with a four poster bed, and is set in 40 lush acres of park, woodland and gardens. The food is a speciality, and only fresh, local produce (some from the hotel's own gardens) is used in the kitchens. This is the place to enjoy a relaxing, care free holiday where you can fish, golf, shoot, walk or generally laze around recharging your batteries! WI-FI Internet available.

246 THE COTTAGE BAR & RESTAURANT

Hood Street, Maryburgh,
Ross-shire IV7 8EB
☎ 01349 861230

Standing within its own grounds in the village of Maryburgh, **The Cottage Bar & Restaurant** is a charming family-run eating place offering an enticing menu of home-made dishes based on fresh local produce. The business is owned and run by the Payne family – Di, Kevin and their daughter, Traci. Di and a full-time chef produce the appetising fare which includes a notable deep fried Haggis with a whisky and onion cream sauce amongst the starters, vegetarian options and a selection of children's meals. The restaurant is open every day from noon until 2pm, and from 5pm to 8.30pm; and all day at weekends.

247 CRAIGVAR

The Square, Strathpeffer,
Ross-shire IV14 9DL
☎ 01997 421622
Mobile: 07732 837150
e-mail: craigvar@talk21.com
⊕ www.craigvar.com

There is no doubt that **Craigvar** is one of the Highland's most outstanding B&Bs. Under the personal management of its owner, Margaret Scott, it has become famous for its high standards of service, its truly outstanding accommodation and the warmth of its welcome.

The building itself is a substantial, well-proportioned Georgian villa built in 1839 that overlooks the square of this former spa village. It boasts three fully en suite rooms (the Blue Room, the Peach Room and the Beige Room) that are stylish, comfortable and extremely well appointed, and no expense has been spared to create an atmosphere in each one that speaks of traditional Scottish hospitality.

The breakfasts here are legendary, and are served in the elegant breakfast room overlooking the front garden. There is always an extensive menu which uses only the finest and freshest of local produce. The room even boasts a baby grand! The lounge is equally as elegant, and offers an informal atmosphere where you can relax as you read, write your postcards, plan the next day's outings or consult the extensive local history archive. Tea and coffee are always available on request.

The village sits north of Inverness, and yet is only 40 minutes from the delights of Ullapool and the Western Highlands, so makes the perfect base from which to explore the area.

248 THE STOREHOUSE

Foulis Ferry, Evanton,
Ross-shire IV16 9UX
☎ 01349 830038   Fax: 01349 830563
e-mail: storehouse@btconnect.com

The Storehouse run by Quintin and Michelle, stands alongside the A9 at Foulis Ferry near Evanton and from the rear of the premises there are grand views across the Cromarty Firth to the Black Isle. The Storehouse is both a restaurant/tea-room and a farm shop selling a huge range of quality produce along with local crafts, gifts and souvenirs. The restaurant, which has recently been refurbished, serves an enticing selection of home-cooked dishes, the majority of which are based on locally sourced produce. The home-baked cakes are particularly delicious. On Sundays a roast with all the trimmings is added to the menu and if the weather is favourable you can enjoy your refreshments outside where you

have a good chance of seeing a dolphin in the Firth.

Both farm shop and restaurant are open from 9am to 6pm, Monday to Saturday, and from 10am to 5pm on Sunday. Both have good access for wheelchairs and there is a disabled toilet. Incidentally, don't be misled by the name 'Foulis Ferry' – there used to be a ferry across to Resolis on the Black Isle but the last one left more than 100 years ago.

249 BALCONIE INN

10 Balconie Street, Evanton,
Ross-shire IV16 9UN
☎ 01349 830409
e-mail: balconieinn@hotmail.com

Set just off the A9 thirteen miles north of Inverness, Evanton is a small village standing almost on the shores of the Cromarty Firth. On its main street you will find the **Balconie Inn**, a superb small hotel that offers good food, comfortable accommodation and great drink. It makes a great stopping off point when travelling north or south for quality B&B accommodation, or even a central base for exploring the area.

There are five rooms on offer, two of which are fully en suite. Each one is comfortable and cosy while still having an air of spaciousness about them. The tariff includes a hearty Scottish breakfast, or something lighter if required.

The bar is open seven days a week for the sale of a wide range of beers, wines, spirits and soft drinks. Monday, Tuesday, Wednesday and Saturday it opens from 11am, Thursday and Friday

from 1pm and on Sunday from 12.30pm. Bar snacks are available, with the speciality of the House being delicious homemade pizzas. The front area of the premises is undergoing a complete refurbishment, with soft seating such as sofas and chairs, creating a plush, stylish area where you can relax.

On Sunday evenings from 8 pm there is always a 'jamming session' where local musicians turn up with their instruments to play traditional Scottish music - always an enjoyable occasion. There is plenty of off-road parking, plus a patio area with heater.

250 THE TEA STORE

27 Argyll Street, Ullapool.
Ross-shire IV26 2UB
☎ 01854 612995
e-mail: louise@theteastore.co.uk
🌐 www.theteastore.co.uk

The Tea Store is one of Ullapool's best eating places, and sits opposite the tourist information centre on Argyll Street. It is a place where quality meets outstanding value-for-money, which is why it is popular with both tourists and locals alike.

It sells quality food, and is renowned for being top of the range as far as high standards of service, a warm friendly welcome and imaginative cooking is concerned. It has been owned and managed by Louise Boyd for the last three years, and she is determined to maintain its popularity by offering only the very best. So much so that in 2005 she was runner up in the Prince's Scottish Youth Business Trust's Regional Business Award.

The food really is outstanding. Most of the produce used in the kitchen is sourced from local butchers, fishmongers, game shops and vegetable and fruit salesmen, ensuring the maximum flavour and freshness. Everything, as you would expect, is home-cooked on the premises. Breakfasts are particularly popular, with Lorne sausage (a square, skinless sausage cut into slices which is a Scottish delicacy) and haggis featuring. Or you could try the truly scrumptious venison burgers with red currant jelly.

Payment is by cash or cheque only, with the establishment seating 26 indoors and, during the summer months, 16 outside. It is open 8.30 am - 5 pm Monday to Saturday in winter and the same hours for seven days in the summer.

251 THE SHEILING GUEST HOUSE

Garve Road, Ullapool,
Ross-shire IV26 2SX
☎ 01845 612947
e-mail: mail@thesheilingullapool.co.uk
🌐 www.thesheilingullapool.co.uk

With a superb lochside location, **The Sheiling Guest House** has unbeatable views out over Loch Broom and the mountains opposite. It is owned and managed by experienced hoteliers Lesley and Iain MacDonald, and offers outstanding accommodation to those people who appreciate comfort, informality, high standards of service and great value for money. It sits in an acre of grounds with the loch to the rear, and offers six comfortable, cosy yet spacious, rooms. Each one is fully en suite and comes with a hospitality tray. There is a TV lounge and a split-level breakfast room where full Scottish breakfasts are served every morning. All the produce is sourced locally, and represents the best of Scottish fare.

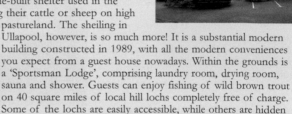

A sheiling was formerly a stone-built shelter used in the summer months by people tending their cattle or sheep on high

pastureland. The sheiling in Ullapool, however, is so much more! It is a substantial modern building constructed in 1989, with all the modern conveniences you expect from a guest house nowadays. Within the grounds is a 'Sportsman Lodge', comprising laundry room, drying room, sauna and shower. Guests can enjoy fishing of wild brown trout on 40 square miles of local hill lochs completely free of charge. Some of the lochs are easily accessible, while others are hidden away. All, however, offer a great day's sport to the experienced angler and the beginner.

253 MILLCROFT HOTEL

Gairloch, Ross-shire IV21 2BT
☎ 01445 712376
e-mail: reservations@millcroft-hotel.co.uk
🌐 www.millcroft-hotel.co.uk

Overlooking Loch Gairloch with magnificent views of the Torridon Mountains and the Isle of Skye, the **Millcroft Hotel** sits in one of the most magnificent parts of Western Scotland. It has five rooms that are well furnished and fully en suite, offering ideal holiday and business accommodation to discerning guests. Each has a colour TV, tea/coffee making facilities, central heating and hairdryers, ensuring a comfortable and relaxing stay. In addition, there are delightful self-catering apartments in the same building that are just right for holiday makers who want to explore the area at their leisure. One, two and three bedroom suites are on offer, all at the keenest prices. Each has a lounge, fully equipped kitchen and bathroom. All towels and bed linen are supplied.

This is a friendly, informal, family run hotel, where the welcome is warm and the service smart and efficient. There is always a member of staff on hand to help or advise with information of what to see and do in the area. The Red Room restaurant offers a varied menu, with most of the produce being sourced locally. The cuisine reflects the chef's experience in the Mediterranean, South East Asia and the West Indies combined with the best of traditional British cooking. Why not enjoy a quiet drink in the Fish Box Bar or the Stag's Head Lounge Bar? Both carry a good range of beers, wines, spirits and local malts, and are cheerful, friendly places that are popular with tourists and locals alike.

Quay Street, Ullapool,
Ross-shire IV26 2UE
☎ 01854 612122   Fax: 01854 613133
e-mail: drink@theseaforth.com
🌐 www.theseaforth.com

The Seaforth stands at the heart of Ullapool – both physically as well as culturally. It occupies a superb position with a patio overlooking the pier where the local boats land their catch and the ferry departs for Lewis. Customers have the opportunity of sampling award-winning food and music whilst savouring views over the pier and Loch Broom.

The Seaforth has been showered with awards over the years. In 2006 it won the Seafood Pub of the Year, and also the Pub of the Year for the whole of the UK. It has also been a finalist 4 times in the Music Pub of the Year for Scotland awards. The bar offers all year round entertainment and has hosted some of the finest performers playing, ranging from local bands to national and international chart acts. It has also hosted nights broadcast on BBC radio. Acts such as Shed Seven, Ash and Mull Historical Society have played here to audiences in the hundreds. Other evenings have involved a few individuals sitting around the fireplace enjoying a pint and chat. Throughout the summer months The Seaforth's owners,

Harry and Brigitte MacRae, try to put on live music most evenings.

The bistro is upstairs and offers a full range of refreshment, from snacks to full meals and has some of the finest local produce available, including its famous seafood dishes that match the finest restaurants of the world. The Seaforth was given a "Best Pint" award from Tennent for achieving "the highest level of quality". Also on offer is a range of McEwans, bottled lagers, guest bitters (some locally brewed), continental beers, a wide selection of wines and spirits -= and more than 70 malts! The restaurant is open 7 days a week from 9am to 10pm (9pm in winter).

Alongside The Seaforth is "The Chippy" which recently won BBC Radio 4's Best UK Takeaway award in 2004 as recognition of the high standards it maintains and the pride and their staff take in their service and products. Not only do they serve the finest fish and chips, they also offer the likes of langoustines, lobster and oysters.

The Seaforth is very much the social centre of the village. In the summer, there's a market in its car park every Saturday providing the opportunity of picking up some local produce and bargains.

254 BLUEPRINT LICENSED CAFÉ AND RESTAURANT ❙❙

Strath Square, Gairloch,
Ross-shire IV21 2BZ
☎ 01445 712397
e-mail: info@blueprintgairloch.com
🌐 www.blueprintgairloch.com

For excellent coffee and tea and really fabulous food, there is no better place that the **Blueprint Licensed Café and Restaurant** in the picturesque village of Gairloch.

By day it's a café, and in the evening it's a superb restaurant! From pizzas and pasta to

sandwiches and salads, and from soup to full dinners, you just cannot beat its marvellous choice and amazing prices. The interior is modern and comfortable, and there are facilities and a toilet for the disabled.

256 HARBOUR LIGHTS CAFÉ ❙❙

Pier Road, Gairloch, Ross-shire IV21 2BQ
☎ 01445 712137   Fax: 01445 712514

For good, simple, honest food at realistic prices, you can't beat the **Harbour Lights Café** in Gairloch. Everything is delicious and filling, from its all day breakfasts, hot meals with chips, home baking and nourishing soups. It sources its produce locally where possible, and uses only Fair Trade tea, coffee and chocolate. Delighted customers come back again and again, and admire the great food and the view out over Gairloch's working harbour!

255 STEADING RESTAURANT ❙❙

The Museum, Gairloch,
Ross-shire IV21 2BP
☎ 01445 712449 Mobile: 07775834425
e-mail: donaldcrerar@hotmail.com

Set in a picturesque granite building that forms part of the same complex as a small museum, the **Steading Restaurant** must surely be one of the finest eating places in Wester Ross. It is open six days a week from 10 am to 4 pm and from 6 pm until 9 pm, it uses only fine, fresh, local produce wherever possible in its kitchens to produce some wonderful dishes that combine imagination and flair.

Seafood, as you would expect in a coastal village, predominates, though steak, poultry, lamb and pork also feature on the menu. Try the filled fillet of salmon, the roast leg of scotch lamb, the juicy steaks, the smoked haddock mornay or the deep fried whole scampi tails - all are delicious!

You are well advised to book a table at all times in the summer and in the evenings in winter. The kitchen sources all its produce locally where possible, so that you get a dining experience you will long remember for all the right reasons. The restaurant is fully licensed, and children are most welcome. There is plenty of off road parking, and the establishment is disabled friendly. All credit and debit cards with the exception of American Express and Diners are accepted.

The Steading Restaurant is special, as it combines good food and high standards of service with great value-for-money. Pay a visit - you're sure to agree!

257 OLD INN ¶ ⊨

Flowerdale Glen, Gairloch,
Wester Ross IV21 2BD

☎ 01445 712006

e-mail: enquiries@theoldinn.net

🖳 www.theoldinn.net

The picturesque, three-star **Old Inn** dates from 1780, and is one of the best former coaching inns in the Western Highlands. It is an extremely popular place with both tourists and locals alike, and boasts up to seven real ales in its cosy bar and lounge during the summer months, including *Blind Piper of Gairloch*, a blend of ales sold exclusively in the inn. In 2003 it was the AA Pub of the Year for Scotland and Northern Ireland, and Seafood Pub of the Year for Scotland in 2006.

It also sells great food all day at reasonable prices, and as you would imagine seafood is its speciality. Try the fish and chips, for instance, tasting like fish and chips used to taste. Or how about its dishes based on Highland game? The kitchen uses local produce wherever possible, so the place has a reputation for its cuisine.

The inn also offers accommodation. There are 17 supremely comfortable en suite guest rooms on offer, each one

individually furnished and decorated. They come with TV, direct dial phones, tea/coffee making facilities and wireless broadband access. Family rooms are available, and one has been converted to suit the disabled.

The inn sits close to the quayside, and has superb views out over Loch Gairloch, making this the natural choice for a base from which to explore the area. So make your way to the Old Inn and experience the very best in Scottish hospitality!

258 HILL HAVEN B&B AND WEST HIGHLAND HAWKING ⊨ 🏛

Hill Haven, Kinlochewe, Achnasheen,
Ross-shire IV22 2PA

☎ 01445 760204

e-mail: (B&B): hillhaven@kinlochewe.info
e-mail (hawking): whh@kinlochewe.info
🖳 (B&B): www.kinlochewe.info
(hawking) www.westhighlandhawking.com

Hill Haven offers some of the best accommodation in Wester Ross, and fully deserves its three-star rating from Visit Scotland. It is a modern bungalow situated in its own grounds with the majestic Torridon mountains as a spectacular backdrop. There are three en suite guest

rooms, two doubles and a twin. Each one is cosy and comfortable - just right for an overnight stay or using as a base for exploring the area. The tariff includes a hearty breakfast, and each guest is presented with a courtesy tray on arrival. There is plenty of parking, and easy access to the A832.

Owners Lilah and David Ford also run **West Highland Hawking**, a small company that let's you experience the thrill of falconry. You don't need to be a falconer to appreciate the beauty and power of these birds, and anyone over the age of 12 (12-16 years must be accompanied by an adult) can participate. Why not combine a B&B stay at Hill Haven with a day spent among wonderful Scottish scenery with beautiful birds of prey? A day normally runs from 10 am to 4 pm, with prices being remarkably reasonable. Falconry has sometimes been called the 'sport of kings' and here is your chance, while holidaying in Scotland, to experience the exhilaration your self! Booking for the falconry must be made in advance.

259 KINLOCHEWE MOUNTAIN CHALETS

Kinlochewe, By Achnasheen,
Ross-shire IV22 2PA
☎ 01445 760334
Mobile: 07730 200037
e-mail: gregplus@btconnect.com
🌐 www.mountainchalets.co.uk

On the A832, 50 miles west of Inverness, you will find the Kinlochewe Mountain Chalets, which offer delightful self-catering accommodation in Wester Ross, an area of outstanding Highland scenery and just a short walk from the famous Loch Maree. There are four chalets on offer, set in three acres of land, on the

doorstep of the famous Beinn Eighe National Nature Reserve and within easy walking distance of shops, pub, garage and other amenities.

Each have beautiful views, and make the ideal base for people who appreciate the great outdoors, such as climbers, walkers, nature lovers, photographers or mountain bikers. Not only that, there are stunning coastal vistas, sandy beaches and golf courses just a short drive away.

The timber chalets have all the modern amenities you would expect nowadays, and sleep four in absolute comfort. They each have a microwave, fridge-freezer, hair dryer, colour television,

VCR, radio/CD, games and electric panel heaters. One of the chalets has a double and twin-bedded room with shower, while the three others have two twin-bedded rooms with both bath and shower.

A welcome pack including eggs, bread, milk, butter, jam, sugar, tea and coffee awaits your arrival, and well-behaved pets are always welcome for a small extra fee. Electricity is included in the tariff, and all duvets, pillows, blankets, bed linen and towels are provided.

260 RIVENDELL GUEST HOUSE & RESTAURANT

Shieldaig, Ross-shire IV54 8XN
☎ 01520 755250
e-mail: shieldaig50@aol.com
🌐 www.therivendell.co.uk

Shieldaig is to be found off the A896 on Scotland's spectacular west coast. Here you will find the **Rivendell Guest House and Restaurant**, a family-run establishment owned and run by the husband and wife team of Marilyn and Tom Taylor.

For over 27 years it has been providing great B&B accommodation to people who appreciate high standards of service and reasonable prices, with people coming back again and again.

There are ten comfortable guest rooms in the establishment, most of them with full en suite. But it's not only the accommodation that attracts people - it's the food as well. All of the family cook, and the kitchen uses the finest and freshest of local produce wherever possible. As you would expect, seafood is a speciality here, with locally caught crabs, prawns and other shellfish predominating. There is a

smokehouse in the village, and the restaurant makes good use of its produce as well. The premises hope to be licensed by May 2007 but until then you are welcome to bring your own, and you are advised to book at all times.

Rivendell is open all year round, and children are very welcome. All credit cards except American Express and Diners are accepted. It is a popular eating place for locals, which is an excellent recommendation. Pay a visit and you will be recommending it as well!

261 LEDGOWAN LODGE HOTEL

Ledgowan, Achansheen,
Ross-shire IV22 2EJ
☎ 01445 720252 Fax: 01445 720240
e-mail: info@ledgowanlodge.co.uk
🌐 www.ledgowanlodge.co.uk

The three-star **Ledgowan Lodge Hotel** calls itself a 'haven of Highland hospitality', and this is no idle boast. It is a quite superb establishment that always offers realistic prices without compromising on quality accommodation, food and drink . It is situated within its

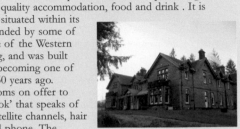

own grounds, which extend to 13 acres, surrounded by some of the best, most magnificent scenery in the whole of the Western Highlands. The building is elegant and imposing, and was built over 100 years ago as a shooting lodge before becoming one of the best country house hotels in the area over 50 years ago.

There are twelve spacious, fully en suite rooms on offer to discerning guests, each one with that 'period look' that speaks of great comfort and amenity, with TV that has satellite channels, hair drier, tea/coffee making facilities and direct dial phone. The award-winning Gowan Restaurant

serves great food. The breakfasts are always hearty and filling, and the extensive a la carte evening menu concentrates on locally sourced produce wherever possible, offering you a dining experience that is not to be missed. There is also the Bran Room for that intimate dinner or business lunch. The Strathban Bar is the place for a quiet drink. It is extremely popular with the locals, which is always a good sign. It has a wide range of drinks, including blended and single malts, and serves delicious bar meals and suppers.

262 MOUNTVIEW

70 Baddidarrach, Lochinver,
Sutherland IV27 4LP
☎ 01571 844648
e-mail: stay@mountview-lochinver.co.uk
🌐 www.mountview-lochinver.co.uk

Even by Highland standards the scenery around Lochinver is quite breathtaking with what has been called "the most beautiful mountain in Scotland", Suilven, rising sheer-sided on the horizon. At the heart of this glorious terrain is Loch Inver on whose shore stand 2 log cabins and a traditional cosy stone-built croft house, collectively known as **Mountview.** All 3 of these delightful properties are available to rent as self-catering accommodation.

The 2 log cabins – Muir-làn (Gaelic for *High Tide*) and Saorsa (*Freedom*) – sleep 4 and 2 people respectively and have an exclusive parking area within a private enclosure. Croft House sleeps 4 with parking available at the rear of the house. All the properties have full double glazing and are comprehensively equipped with colour TV, video/DVD and music centre; washing machine, dishwasher, microwave and coffee machine. Continental quilts and other linen are all provided, and

Saorsa

electricity, towels and linen are included in the rental. Children are welcome, pets are permitted by arrangement, and out of season 3 night stays are available. Facilities in the little fishing port of Lochinver include several excellent restaurants, the famous Highland Stoneware Pottery, a wide variety of shops including craft shops. A recent addition to the village's amenities is the brand new Leisure Centre.

263 SANGO SANDS OASIS

Sangomore, Durness,
Sutherland IV27 4PZ
☎ 01971 511222/511726
Fax: 01971 511205
e-mail: keith.durness@btinternet.com

Sango Sands Oasis was established by Francis Keith some 30 years ago and is now owned and run by Francis, James and Carol Keith. The site extends to almost 10 acres of well-drained and level ground, and overlooks the beautiful Blue Flag beach of Sango Bay. The caravan park is open all year round and can accommodate up to 90 tourers. Facilities on site include showers, laundry, chemical toilet disposal and a campers' kitchen. Booking is not normally necessary except to secure one of the 40 electric hook-ups. The Keiths also have 2 residential caravans sleeping 4 or 6 persons and fully equipped with all facilities including shower.

There's no need to cook your own meals when you're staying at the Sango Sands – the licensed restaurant, which is open from March to mid-October – serves a good choice of home-made dishes based on local produce

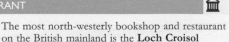

including locally caught fresh fish and grilled beef steaks. Children's portions are available on request and there's a well-balanced wine list. The lounge bar can accommodate up to 80 people and enjoys wonderful views over the bay. There's also a family room with pool table and darts. Debit cards are accepted; credit cards are not.

264 LOCH CROISPOL BOOKSHOP & RESTAURANT

2 Balnakeil Craft Village, Durness,
Sutherland IV27 4PT
☎ 01971 511777
e-mail: lochcroispol@btopenworld.com
⊕ www.scottish-books.net

The most north-westerly bookshop and restaurant on the British mainland is the **Loch Croisol Bookshop & Restaurant.** Early in 2007 the business moved into larger premises in the Craft Village so you will find an even more amazing range of titles, ranging through fiction, poetry, music biography, Scottish history, politics and culture, religion, children's books, natural history and the environment, humour, food and drink, and a whole lot more. The light and airy bookshop is owned and managed by Kevin Crowe and Simon Long who invite you to visit and browse to your heart's content. Book tokens can be bought or exchanged, and titles not in stock can be ordered quickly and simply. Kevin also offers a search facility for

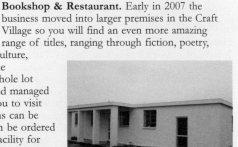

out-of-print books and books can be purchased online at

the website. The shop also hosts regular events such as book signings and poetry readings.

The restaurant side of the business has also expanded, creating 40 places in all. The menu offers a wide range of lunches, dinners, snacks and high teas; children are welcome and private parties can also be catered for. Another attraction being developed here is a sculpture garden displaying work by local artists..

265 GLENALADALE

99A Laid, Loch Eriboll,
Sutherland IV27 4UN
☎ 01971 511329
e-mail: Donald@gas2go.fsnet.co.uk
🌐 www.donnieandkate@glenaladale.org

Glenaladale stands on the single-track road, the A838, that winds its way around lovely Loch Eriboll. A smart modern bungalow, Glenaladale was built in 2005 by Katie and Donnie MacDougall, specifically to provide top quality bed & breakfast accommodation in a superb location. Guests enjoy true Highland hospitality and comfort along with magnificent views of the loch to the front and the mountain Meall Nacra to the rear. The 3 letting rooms are all on the ground floor, en suite with shower and toilet, and equipped with TV, hospitality tray and some thoughtful little extras. The bungalow is centrally heated throughout.

Guests have the use of a spacious, comfortable lounge with spectacular views over Loch Eriboll to Ben Hope, the most northwesterly Monro in Scotland. At breakfast, served in the dedicated guests' dining room, there's a choice of either a full Scottish breakfast or the Continental variety. Laid itself was created in 1832 to house people cleared from Eriboll, on the far side of the loch, to make way for sheep. It is an ideal base for exploring the solitude of the highlands, to watch the varied wildlife and birds, or enjoy a spot of fishing or golf.

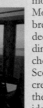

267 THE QUEEN'S HOTEL

16 Francis Street, Wick,
Caithness KW1 5PZ
☎ 01955 602992 Fax: 01955 606176
e-mail: petersutherland@btconnect.com

Located just a short walk from the centre of Wick, **The Queen's Hotel** is a stately stone building that was originally a church manse. Today this handsome old house offers visitors the very best in food, drink and accommodation in a relaxed and friendly atmosphere. The hotel is owned and run by a welcoming local couple, Peter and Sharon Sutherland, who took over here in 2005. Peter is an accomplished chef who offers a varied selection of dishes all based on fish, meat and vegetables that are sourced locally. During the summer months food is available every lunchtime from noon until 2pm, and every evening from 5pm. In winter, food is served every evening and on Friday and Saturday lunchtimes. It is highly advisable to book for Saturday evenings to avoid disappointment.

The hotel has 10 guest bedrooms, 8 of which have en suite facilities – the other two will also be upgraded by Spring 2007. The rooms are spacious and comfortable; 2 of them are family sized so children are very welcome. The hotel has a pleasant beer garden and good wheelchair access to the ground floor bar and restaurant. All major credit cards except American Express and Diners are accepted.

Kinlochbervie, by Lairg,
Sutherland IV27 4RP
☎ 01971 521275 Fax: 01971 521438
e-mail: klbhotel@btconnect.com
🌐 www.kinlochberviehotel.com

Enjoying views over the busy fishing harbour to one side and the North Atlantic to the other, **The Kinlochbervie Hotel** is a warm and welcoming place to stay with the very highest standards of food, drink and accommodation being maintained. Enez and Margaret Colan arrived here in 2005 and made it their mission to "provide a warm and friendly service and environment where all our customers feel that they have resided in comfort and enjoyed all our amenities". They take a special pride in the standard of the cuisine they offer, a priority that has resulted in a Taste of Scotland award. The fish and seafood they serve is so fresh you can watch the fishermen unload it at the nearby harbour. Just try the Kinlochbervie Haddock or the scampi made from fresh, locally caught monk fish. The hill lamb and venison has an unrivalled flavour and succulence only to be found in this part of Scotland. Vegetarians are also well-catered for with dishes such as Wild Mushroom Tart or Goat's Cheese and Cherry Tomato En Croute. To complement your meal, there's an excellent selection of fine wines from the expertly managed wine cellar. Evening meals are served from 6pm, with last orders at 8.30pm. An

alternative to the restaurant is the Garbet Bistro which offers a more informal atmosphere in which to enjoy an excellent selection of lunches and snacks.

The hotel has 14 comfortable guest bedrooms, all with an en suite bathroom, colour television and tea/coffee-making facilities. The rooms are warm and spacious, and some enjoy spectacular views. Children are welcome and guests can stay on either a bed & breakfast, or dinner, bed & breakfast basis. All major credit cards are accepted apart from Diners.

Kinlochbervie is a scattered coastal

settlement approximately 90 miles northwest of Inverness. The nearest village is Lairg, around 45 miles to the southwest. The coast here is dotted with countless sandy beaches and rocky coves, with particularly fine beaches at Oldshoremore, Polin and Sheigra. The area also provides great bird watching, fishing, hill walking and climbing, and there are several good golf courses in the area. And don't leave the area without paying a visit to the craft village at Balnakiel.

268 MEIKLEJOHN'S TEA ROOMS

1-2 Francis Street, Thurso,
Wick KW1 5PZ
☎ 01955 604379

As you enter **Meiklejohn's Tea Rooms** you breathe in that delicious smell of home baking – this is a real, traditional tea room of the very best kind. It occupies an impressive stone building in the centre of the town and is owned and run by Shelly Baines and her business partner Mandy who took over here in September 2006 after wide experience in the hospitality business. Naturally, the tempting selection of cakes, pastries and slices takes pride of place but the menu also offers a good choice of other meals, with all the meat and seafood for them sourced locally. The regular menu is supplemented by the specials listed on the board.

Children are very welcome – a high chair is available – the service is friendly and efficient, and there's good wheelchair access. The tea rooms are open Monday to Saturday from 8am to 5pm in summer, 9am to 4pm in winter. During the high season, it is also sometimes open on Sundays. Cash and cheques only are accepted. Perhaps the most authentic recommendation for Meiklejohn's is that it is extremely popular with local people.

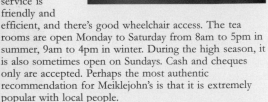

269 BILBSTER MAINS

Wick, Caithness KW1 4TA
☎ 01955 621226
e-mail: bilbster@farming.co.uk
🌐 www.caithness-cottages.co.uk

Bilbster Mains is a 1300-acre working farm straddling the delightful Wick River in a fertile little valley just east of the famous wild brown trout water Loch Watten. Jane and Donald Miller have been here for 38 years and for 16 of those have been offering self-catering accommodation in 2 delightful stone cottages – North Bilbster Cottage and Gardener's Cottage. Both have a 4-star rating from the STB and can sleep up to 4 guests and are comprehensively equipped with everything you will need, including a fully fitted kitchen with microwave and dishwasher, colour TV and video, and oil-fired central heating with a peat/log-burning stove. Children are welcome and kennels are available.

The cottages provide a tranquil and comfortable base from which to explore this scenic county or to participate in the many activities on offer. The area is an angler's paradise – Caithness alone has more than 100 lochs and Sutherland has nearer 1000! The cost of day and week permits for loch fishing are extremely reasonable and boats can be hired for you through outlets on some of the larger lochs. The area is also popular with shooters. A day's rough shooting at Bilbster could be a red-letter day in anyone's game book.

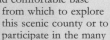

7 Dunrobin Street, Helmsdale,
Sutherland KW8 6JA
☎ 01431 821615
e-mail: sales@lamirage.org
⊕ www.lamirage.org

La Mirage Restaurant in Helmsdale on the north coast of Scotland is as famous for its hospitality and decor as it is for the food, and the food is very good indeed. Created by Nancy Sinclair and run with her son Don, the restaurant has a national and international reputation. Nancy retired a few years ago but the same wonderful atmosphere, good food and now wine can still be enjoyed under the new ownership of Pam and Mike Wakefield. Nancy still visits as often as possible and Don, a chef for more than 30 years, still manages the premises.

The interior is stunning and an experience in its own right. The predominant colour is pink, believed to have been chosen to match the pink limo that Barbara Cartland used to arrive in from her Scottish home nearby. The restaurant was regularly visited by Ms Cartland in her lifetime and the walls display not just pictures of her and Nancy, but of the many other celebrities who have visited. They include Victoria Wood who produced one of the numerous programmes that have been done on Nancy and La Mirage, Paul Young, TV's Mr

Fisherman, and Sally Whittaker of Coronation Street.

They came to enjoy the extensive menu on offer, a menu that varies according to the time of the year. Fresh seafood from langoustines to haddock, cod, plaice, monkfish and lobster are regularly on the menu when in season. Starters include prawn cocktail, deep fried camembert, a range of soups, garlic bread and deep fried mushrooms. Amongst the main courses are a range of salads, haddock, cod, plaice, langoustines, monk fish, T-bone steaks, chicken Kiev, gammon steaks, all day breakfasts and much more, including a vegetarian choice. And for dessert, the

marvellous meringues are not to be missed.

The restaurant also offers a range of snacks which include: baked potatoes and sandwiches with a variety of fillings, bacon, sausage and egg rolls, soup of the day and a variety of cakes and fresh baking.

A fine selection of wines and beers, including Orkney Island Beer, are also available in addition to the usual range of soft drinks

The restaurant can cater for 50 people and for those pressed for time the Take Away is very well known and used.

272 BORGIE LODGE HOTEL

Skerray, Tongue, Sutherland KW14 7TH
☎ 01641 521332 Fax: 01641 521889
e-mail: info@borgielodgehotel.co.uk
🌐 www.borgielodgehotel.co.uk

Set within the Countess of Sutherland's estate and about half a mile off the coastal A836, **Borgie Lodge Hotel** is an outstanding country house lying in a quiet, secluded Highland glen on the banks of the beautiful River Borgie. The family-run hotel is furnished "traditionally" with magnificent stags' antlers, Clan Sutherland tartan carpets and sporting prints. Crackling log fires add to the country house atmosphere.

A perfect and idyllic Highland retreat, Borgie is a haven for nature lovers, fishers, walkers, beach-goers or for simple relaxation. If it is an active sporting holiday you seek, the hotel has access to salmon fishing on several excellent rivers, and boats for wild brown trout on 20 hill lochs. It also has shooting and stalking on the 12,600-acre Tongue Estate. Keen surfers will be pleased to know that the hotel is located in one of the top surfing areas. For less demanding pleasure, there are delightful sheltered walks in Borgie Forest and Borgie Glen; splendid golf facilities at Reay and Durness; a local pony trekking centre; a wide and diverse

range of hill walks; and two miles of pure golden sand on Torrisdale Beach. Add craft shops, museums, and a leisure pool locally – there is much to see and enjoy with Borgie Lodge Hotel as your base.

After the day's activities, guests gather in the Lounge and chat over a pre-dinner dram while perusing the daily changing menu. The restaurant cuisine features fresh vegetables from the kitchen garden combined with succulent Caithness beef and lamb, Sutherland venison and a variety of seafoods and fresh fish from the clear blue waters of the North Sea. Salmon and wild brown trout are frequently on the menu – caught by hotel guests! The fine food is complemented by an

excellent selection of wines. An alternative to the Lounge is the friendly atmosphere of the Crofters Bar where guests may get acquainted with the local folk to hear a few stories, learn about the area, places to visit and to fish, and enjoy a game of darts, dominoes or pool.

Later, retire to one of the 8 eminently comfortable guest bedrooms, 7 of which are en suite – the 8th has its own private bathroom. One of the rooms is on the ground floor. Well-behaved pets and their owners are welcome.

271 BEN LOYAL HOTEL 🛏 🍴

Tongue, Sutherland IV27 4XE
☎ 01847 611216 Fax: 01847 611212
e-mail: benloyalhotel@btinternet.com
🌐 www.benloyal.co.uk

Centrally located within the village of Tongue, the **Ben Loyal Hotel** enjoys outstanding views out over the unspoiled Sutherland landscape. Many of the rooms command outstanding views out over the Kyle of

Tongue, Ben Loyal, Ben Hope and the ruin of Castle Varrich, which sits on the hill line opposite the hotel.

The restaurant, the An Garbh, has picture windows which frame similarly wonderful views. The restaurant is very well known for its outstanding cuisine, using predominately local produce; beef and lamb from Caithness and Sutherland, fresh fish from Scrabster, venison from local estates, oysters, crabs and lobsters from the Kyle of Tongue and prawns from nearby Loch Eriboll. Do book ahead, but if

you are unlucky, don't despair – the full menu is available in the Bistro Bar from the day the hotel opens on 1st March until it closes at the end of the season. The Ben Loyal has 11 centrally heated en suite bedrooms, each one tastefully decorated, and some containing original artwork by local artists. All have colour television, direct dial telephone, hairdryer and hospitality tray.

274 STATION COTTAGE 🛏

Forsinard, Sutherland KW13 6YT
☎ 01641 571262
e-mail: email@colinmair.f9.co.uk
🌐 www.scotlandindex.net

Situated alongside what is perhaps the most remote (and still functioning) railway station in Scotland, **Station Cottage** is the home of Susan and Colin Mair who have been welcoming bed & breakfast guests since 2000. Arriving guests receive a lovely warm welcome and an excellent cup of tea or coffee. Along with its outstanding location, the Cottage is highly recommended for its hospitality, facilities – and super breakfasts!
The house is beautifully decorated and furnished throughout, and all rooms have central

heating and TV. Evening meals are available by arrangement. Note for bird lovers: there's an RSPB Centre just the other side of the railway track.

273 FARR BAY INN

Bettyhill, by Thurso,
Sutherland KW14 7SZ
☎ 01641 521230
e-mail: farr.bay.inn@btopenworld.com
⊕ www.farrbayinn.co.uk

The delightful **Farr Bay Inn** started life in
1819 as the Manse attached to the adjacent
Church of Scotland church. A listed building,
it was converted to an inn in 1983 and since
May 2003 has been owned and run by Penny
and Rosemary who immediately make their
guests feel at home.

A major attraction here is the excellent
food on offer every day from 12.30pm to 8pm
during the summer months and at weekends;
from 4pm to 8pm at all other times. Choose from the standard menu or, after 5pm, from the daily
specials. Both Penny and Rosemary cook, using locally sourced produce. Their specialities include
homemade steak and ale pie and fresh fish dishes. The dining area seats 16 people but you can also
dine in the bar area – it's advisable for larger parties to book ahead. Children are welcome both in
the dining room and the lounge bar.

The bar stocks a good selection of
draught keg ales and hosts occasional live
music sessions. There's also a Bingo session
from 9pm on alternate Saturdays.

The inn has 4 guest bedrooms, all en suite
and provided with colour TV, DVD player and
hospitality tray. A limited selection of DVDs is
available – others can be hired from the local
store. Bathrobes, hair-dryer and extra pillows
are available on request. Pets are welcome to
stay in your room. Most guests will be pleased
to discover that mobile phones don't work
here – if you need to make a call, ask to use
the inn's landline. Alternatively, there are pay
phones opposite the village post office.

Incidentally, the whole of the Farr Bay Inn is non-smoking – all bedrooms are fitted with
sensitive smoke detectors which will set off the
main fire alarm.

Guests will find plenty to see and do in the
area. The beautiful Farr Beach is just a 5-
minute walk from the inn; loch or river fishing,
sea angling and boat trips can all be arranged.
There is pony trekking locally, and Farr Bay is
renowned for its surfing. The Strathnaver
Museum is next door in the former church and
the Tourist Information Office and Craft Shop
is right in front of the inn. Tongue is half an
hour away and has spectacular views of Ben
Loyal and Castle Varrich. Also well worth the
trip of about 1½ hours is the Castle of Mey,
the Caithness residence of the late Queen
Mother.

275 HALLADALE INN

Melvich, Sutherland KW14 7YJ
☎ 01641 531282
Mobile: 07796 133789
e-mail: mazfling@tinyworld.co.uk
⊕ www.halladaleinn.co.uk

The Halladale Inn is not just a welcoming hostelry but also offers a restaurant with a varied menu, self-catering accommodation and a camping park. It is situated in the small coastal village of Melvich, 17 miles west of Thurso on the A836 North Coast Road. Owners Ian and Marilyn Fling have recently completed a complete refurbishment of the inn to a very high standard indeed. There's a real fire in the bar lounge and the spacious restaurant is bright and cheery with its colourful tablecloths and serviettes. Chef Billy MacDonald offers a good choice of dishes based on local produce and the regular menu is supplemented by daily specials – look out for treats such as local brown trout. Food is available every day from 11am to 8pm; children are welcome and all major credit cards are accepted apart from American Express and Diners.

Just 100 metres from the inn, the Chalet Park has 4 self-catering chalets each of which sleeps up to 4 people and comprises 1 double bed and 2 single beds. Each chalet is comprehensively equipped, including bed

linen, although guests are asked to bring their own towels. Electricity is funded by a £1 slot meter; children and dogs are welcome. The Chalet Park has private parking within a fenced garden and there are outside drying facilities in the garden area. Guests have the option of using the laundry service situated in the Halladale Inn Caravan Site – a small charge is applicable.

The caravan park, which has been awarded a 4-star rating by the Scottish Tourist Board, comprises 14 pitches, six caravans or motor homes with optional electric hook-up and 8 tent pitches. The site is located next to the inn, which is open during normal licensing hours with extended times for Friday evenings (until 1am) and Saturday evenings (12 midnight).

Melvich itself is perfect for the quiet "get away holiday". A superb sandy beach is just a 10-minute walk away and is a favourite venue for surfing. If you are a keen fisherman then try the local lochs (permits can be arranged); birdwatchers can visit the Forsinard RSPB Bird Sanctuary, while for golfers there is Reay Golf Course just 5 miles away – apparently this course is "interesting"! Melvich is an ideal base for touring the North Coast of Scotland with the Orkney Islands just a short ferry ride away.

276 COMMERCIAL HOTEL

Bridge Street, Halkirk,
Caithness KW12 6XY
☎ 01847 831223
e-mail: halkirkcomm@tiscali.co.uk

Built as an inn in the 1860s, the **Commercial Hotel** in Halkirk is a handsome stone building with lots of character both inside and out. It is owned and run by James and Kate Campbell, a friendly and welcoming couple, with Kate having over 25 years experience in the hospitality business.

They arrived here in the summer of 2005 and have quickly established a glowing reputation for the quality of the food on offer and the varied but traditional, ever popular Scottish breakfast. Fish dishes and steaks are particularly popular and if you give them 24 hours notice you can enjoy their renowned Seafood Platter, a real work of culinary art. The dishes are made using 100% local produce, expertly prepared and attractively presented. You

should definitely book ahead if you wish to dine here on a Saturday evening.

Food is served every lunchtime (noon until 2pm) and evening (5pm to 8.30pm), Wednesday to Sunday. To accompany your meal there's a wide choice of beverages that includes draught keg ales, wines and some 8 or 10 malt whiskeys, plus a further 6 blends. The hotel hosts occasional live entertainment in the traditional lounge bar. The accommodation comprises 5 guest bedrooms, all en suite.

277 THE STATION HOTEL

54 Princes Street, Thurso,
Caithness KW14 7DH
☎ 01847 892003   Fax: 01847 891820
e-mail: station@northhotels.co.uk
🌐 www.northhotels.co.uk

Built in the 1860s to provide accommodation for the nearby railway station, **The Station Hotel** is a stone built building that has seen many guests passing through its door. The hotel provides a fine combination of a warm and friendly atmosphere in comfortable surroundings.

Fine cuisine is a priority here with a menu that offers the very best of Scottish fish and seafood, beef, lamb and game in season, traditionally cooked and served in order to preserve the natural flavours. In addition to the à la carte menu served in the restaurant, the lounge bar offers a blackboard menu with daily specials and vegetarian dishes. The bar boasts a good selection of beers and lagers, some

excellent malt and grain whiskies, and a personally selected choice of wines by the glass. The 38 guest bedrooms are

all beautifully appointed, en suite and equipped with remote control tele-video, digital television, hospitality tray, direct dial telephone and trouser press. Adjacent to the hotel, 11 self-catering apartments for 4 people each are also available.

278 THE PARK HOTEL

Thurso, Caithness KW14 8RE
☎ 01847 893251 Fax: 01847 804044
e-mail: reception@parkhotelthurso.co.uk
🌐 www.parkhotelthurso.co.uk

One of the North of Scotland's Premier Hotels, **The Park Hotel** stands on the A9 just a 5-minute walk from the centre of Thurso. It has been owned and run by members of the same family since 1963, and is currently run by the brother and sisters team of David, Karen and Sandra. They believe they have achieved the right balance of facilities and service to accommodate the demands of business travellers and tourists alike. In the relaxed atmosphere of the conservatory style 'Oldfields' restaurant, diners can enjoy an extensive choice of appetising fare with steaks and seafood as the specialities of the house. Lunch (noon until 2pm), dinner (5pm to 9pm) are all served here, bar suppers are also available. At weekends it is highly advisable to book ahead for the restaurant.

The newly refurbished lounge bar is a popular venue for rounding off a meal

with any of the extensive choice of liqueurs and malt whiskys. Or, if you prefer, there's always the public bar for a drink and a game of pool. Both bars are open until 11pm.

The accommodation at The Park reflects the same high standards maintained throughout the hotel. There are 21 en suite rooms, 10 of them on the ground floor and 2 of them are family rooms. Each room is well-equipped with TV, telephone, hospitality tray, hairdryer, iron and ironing board. Children are welcome, as are disabled guests – one room has been adapted for wheelchairs. Business travellers are well provided for with the Orange Room, which provides the solution for most conference and training situations.

The Park is an ideal base for touring the beautiful north coast of Scotland, including Caithness with its panoramic views, wonderfully open skies and dramatic seascapes. Birdwatchers will appreciate the range of special breeding species as well as the very visible migration of wildfowl during the autumn. Caithness also has its fair share of historical heritage – the Neolithic stone burial mounds at Camster and the Loch of Yarrows are older than the pyramids. But you will also find up-to-date amenities nearby for swimming, golf and much more.

279 CASTLE ARMS HOTEL

Mey, Caithness KW14 8XH
☎ 01847 851992   Fax: 01847 851244
e-mail: castlearms.mey@btinternet.com
🌐 www.castlearms.co.uk

Standing just across the road from the entrance to the Castle of Mey, the late Queen Mother's beloved Caithness home, the **Castle Arms Hotel** is a former 19th century coaching inn just bursting with charm and character. This is a good place to eat since the butcher who supplies the meat and the fishmonger who provides the fish both eat here – not a bad recommendation. The menu offers an excellent choice of dishes based on local produce, including vegetarian options. You can dine in the main restaurant which offers an a la carte menu; in the lounge dining room or in the bar where daily specials may well include freshly caught Orkney scallops.

The hotel has a full licence and stocks a good choice of draught keg ales. If you are

planning to stay in this fascinating corner of the county, the Castle Arms has 8 excellent en suite guest rooms, all spacious, well-decorated and with stylish furnishings. Three of the rooms are within the main building; the other 5 are situated around the rear courtyard. One room has been specially adapted for the disabled. Conveniently, the hotel also houses the village shop.

280 SEAVIEW HOTEL

John O' Groats, Caithness KW1 4YR
☎ 01955 611220
Mobile: 07733 472395
e-mail: seaviewhotel@barbox.net
🌐 www.johnogroats-seaviewhotel.co.uk

Only a couple of minutes from the Orkney and Gills Bay ferries, the **Seaview Hotel** is a small, popular family-run establishment which extends a warm welcome "at the end of the road" to everyone – including children and pets. The hotel boasts panoramic views of the Pentland Firth and Orkney Isles and you're sure to see some of the great flotilla of shipping that passes through daily. For owner Andrew Mowat good food is a priority so you can relax in the comfort of the restaurant, enjoying excellent food while watching the wonderful sight of a sunset over the Island of Stroma or even the Northern Lights.

Everything on the menu is home-cooked using local produce wherever possible and there's a personally selected range of

wines to accompany your meal. Food is also served in the attractively furnished public/lounge bar where you can also sample the vast range of more than 100 malt whiskeys, including local malts. Accommodation at the Seaview comprises 10 bedrooms, most of them en suite, and equipped with colour TV and hospitality tray. The hotel is open all year round, apart from Christmas Day and New Year's Day; has ample off road parking; a secure lock-up for bicycles and, best of all, friendly staff.

281 THE SCHOOLHOUSE RESTAURANT ⅂⅂

John O'Groats, Wick, Caithness KW1 4YS
☎ 01955 611714
e-mail: enquiries@dinecaithness.co.uk
🌐 www.dinecaithness.co.uk

As the name suggests, **The Schoolhouse Restaurant** occupies a former school, built in 1875 and closed as a school in 1974. It remained unoccupied for 2 years, then served other uses before the mother and son team of Ursula and David Shaw purchased the building in 2002. They have created a restaurant whose reputation for outstanding cuisine extends far beyond the Highlands. Locals drool over Ursula's home baking, visitors get inebriated on the sherry trifle, and even local licensees who provide food in their own inns dine here.

The menu is based on fresh local produce and changes every day. Typically you will find a homemade soup and baked trout amongst the starters; homemade fish pie, roast locally-raised beef, or Honeyed Lamb in Ginger as main

courses, and some glorious desserts such as Plum and Almond Tart. Everything of course is homemade, and that includes the breads. The Schoolhouse is definitely not a place for anyone trying to lose weight but it certainly is the place for anyone who appreciates lovingly prepared and wonderfully appetising food. The restaurant is open from 12.30pm until 2.30pm, and from 6.30pm to 8.30pm. Children are welcome, there's good wheelchair access, and all major credit cards except American Express and Diners are accepted.

283 STAG TEA ROOMS/THORLEE GUEST HOUSE ⅂⅂ 🛏

3 Cromwell Street, Stornoway,
Isle of Lewis HS1 2DB
☎ 01851 706300

Located side by side in the heart of Stornoway, the Stag Tea Rooms and Thorlee Guest House are both owned by Coinneach MacMillan. The tea rooms are very popular with local people and no wonder – everything is home-cooked and based on top quality fresh local produce.

Open Monday to Saturday, the tea room has a regular menu and a choice of specials that changes each week. Guests staying at Thorlee Guest House come here for a hearty breakfast that is included in the B&B rate. There are 16 guest bedrooms of varying sizes, all of which will become en suite during 2007.

HIDDEN PLACES GUIDES

Explore Britain and Ireland with *Hidden Places* guides - a fascinating series of national and local travel guides.

Packed with easy to read information on hundreds of places of interest as well as places to stay, eat and drink.

Available from both high street and internet booksellers

For more information on the full range of *Hidden Places* guides and other titles published by Travel Publishing visit our website on

www.travelpublishing.co.uk
or ask for our leaflet by phoning
0118-981-7777 or emailing
info@travelpublishing.co.uk

61 Bayhead Street, Stornoway,
Isle of Lewis HS1 2DZ
☎ 01851 702268/0845 644 8639
e-mail: hebgh@sol.co.uk
🌐 www.hebrideanguesthouse.co.uk

The Hebridean Guest House occupies a prime position in the heart of Stornoway overlooking the Castle Grounds and Golf Course. The ferry terminal is just 5 minutes away and the house is also within easy reach of Stornoway Airport. For guests with their own transport, the Hebridean has parking right outside. Built at the turn of the last century, the guest house has been developed into a modern, comfortable residence which has earned it a fine reputation – and a 3 star rating from the Scottish Tourism Board. Being situated so close to Stornoway town centre, the Hebridean provides ideal accommodation for not only tourists to the island, but also for those visiting the island on business.

The Hebridean has two living rooms where guests may socialise, as well as a spacious restaurant where a hearty breakfast is served, usually between 7.30am and 8.45pm, but owner Linda Johnson is flexible about the times.

The accommodation consists of 12 rooms over 2 floors, with single bedded,

twin bedded, and double bedded rooms, all with en suite bathroom facilities, independent heating and television, as well as tea and coffee making facilities.

The Hebridean is open all year round except over the Christmas and New Year period. Children are welcome and all major credit cards apart from American Express and Diners are accepted.

Stornoway is the principal town on the Isle of Lewis and is the main point for access to the island with a ferry service operated by Caledonian Macbrayne from Stornoway

harbour going to and from Ullapool on mainland Scotland. There are also air services operated by various operators travelling to and from Glasgow, Edinburgh and Inverness 7 days a week.

The Outer Hebrides, of which Lewis is part, boasts some of the most rugged and beautiful scenery in the world and also offers great freshwater and sea fishing, golf and of course sightseeing. Linda would be only to happy to help you organise any of these pursuits during your stay at the Hebridean – she can even organize day trips out to the island of St Kilda.

284 ROYAL HOTEL

Cromwell Street, Stornoway,
Isle of Lewis HS1 2DG

☎ 01851 702109 Fax: 01851 702142

e-mail: royal@calahotels.com

⊕ www.royalstornoway.co.uk

Stornoway's most historic hotel is just across the road from the marina, where you can relax, enjoy the hotel's cosy character and watch the world go by. Many of the locally owned hotel's period features have been retained in the front facing bedrooms, which overlook the marina and Lews Castle Grounds. It's said that Lord Leverhulme used to sit at the oriel window on the first floor, viewing the castle he bought in 1918.

Rear facing rooms are in more contemporary style and are a little quieter than those facing the street at the front - though this small town is rarely noisy! The 24 en-suite bedrooms, all renovated early in 2007, are well equipped with hospitality trays, colour TV, direct dial telephone and wireless broadband access.

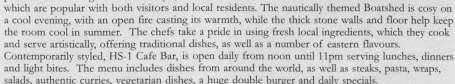

What matters so much more than bricks and mortar, though, is the warmth of the traditional Hebridean welcome you'll receive. The Royal is the first hotel on the island to receive the Hospitality Assured award, which measures 49 individual requirements.

There are two restaurants and a pleasant hotel lounge bar at the Royal, which are popular with both visitors and local residents. The nautically themed Boatshed is cosy on a cool evening, with an open fire casting its warmth, while the thick stone walls and floor help keep the room cool in summer. The chefs take a pride in using fresh local ingredients, which they cook and serve artistically, offering traditional dishes, as well as a number of eastern flavours. Contemporarily styled, HS-1 Cafe Bar, is open daily from noon until 11pm serving lunches, dinners and light bites. The menu includes dishes from around the world, as well as steaks, pasta, wraps, salads, authentic curries, vegetarian dishes, a huge double burger and daily specials.

Around 200 metres from the town centre, the hotel is convenient for a gentle stroll around the harbour or beside the River Creed, as it tumbles through a gorge-like valley in Lews Castle Grounds. Stornoway's 18 hole golf course is around five minutes walk and cycle hire is available at the bike shop, directly behind the hotel. Children are welcome throughout the hotel, with cots, high chairs and baby changing facilities all available.

285 DIGBY CHICK RESTAURANT

28 Point Street, Stornoway,
Isle of Lewis HS1 2XP
☎ 01851 700026

The Digby Chick Restaurant in the heart of Stornoway derives its unusual name from a dried herring dish called a Digby Chick. Apparently, the original Digby Chick was a whole herring, ungutted, that was heavily salted and then cold smoked for 2 to 3 weeks until it was hard. This delicacy was apparently popular in the past with sailors at a little fishing port called Digby in Nova Scotia.

You won't find Digby Chick on the menu at James and Marianne MacKenzie's distinguished restaurant. But amongst many other appetising dishes you will find local fish specials such as Sautéed scollops of monkfish with smoked bacon, wild mushrooms and pesto vinaigrette, or pan-fried scallops with a garlic, basil and red pepper cream. (Digby scallops, co-incidentally, provide the Nova Scotian town with its main claim to fame).

The restaurant has 3 different menus. For the set lunch (11.30am to 2pm) there's a choice of fish, pork, poultry and

vegetarian dishes, as well as a good selection of interesting panini sandwiches – how about Grilled goat's cheese with baby leaf spinach and peanut butter. From 5.30pm to 6.30pm, the restaurant offers an Early Menu with Loch Leurbost mussels among the starters and grilled local skate wing as one of the main courses. The à la carte dinner menu is served from 7pm to 8.45pm and features Breast of pigeon with caramelised leeks, sweet potato rosti and a wild garlic gravy amongst the starters; Roast loin of Lewis venison with smoked streaky bacon, Portobello mushroom, red onion marmalade and game jus as one of the main courses; and for dessert, how about Pear tarte tatin with brandy chocolate sauce and mascarpone ice cream?

The outstanding cuisine of the Digby Chick has made the restaurant understandably very popular so it is advisable to book at all times. Children are welcome – a small children's menu is available – and there's good wheelchair access throughout. The restaurant seats up to 58 diners and is licensed for those dining. There's also a separate function room that can cater for 22 and is available for private parties, meetings and so on. Dining vouchers can be bought as gifts. The restaurant is closed on Sundays; all major credit cards except American Express and Diners are accepted.

286 THE CALEDONIAN HOTEL

South Beach Street, Stornoway,
Isle of Lewis HS1 2XY
☎ 01851 702411 Fax: 01851 706210

Located just across the road from the quayside and enjoying spectacular views of the harbour, **The Caledonian Hotel** was built in 1968 after two previous hotels on the site had been destroyed by fires. It's now owned by Allan and Manna, who purchased it in December 2006. Allan, who has been a chef for 27 years, had previously worked at the hotel before buying it. Naturally, good food is a priority for him and the hotel restaurant enjoys a high reputation for quality cuisine. Allan's imaginative dinner menu offers his own classic Chicken Liver, Bacon, Garlic & Red Wine Parfait as one of the starters; Haddock fillet and fresh crab roulade on a crisp bed of leeks amongst the main courses; and a delicious roasted coffee tiramisu on a mandarin orange fruit coulis as one of the desserts. The restaurant is open from 5pm to 9pm, Tuesday to Saturday and such is its popularity it is advisable to make a booking. Food is also available in the bar areas from noon until

2pm, and from 5pm to 9pm every day including Sunday when it is available all day – very unusual in Stornoway where most places close on the Lord's Day. The extensive menu ranges from old favourites such as Steak & Kidney Pudding or Fish & Chips, through "hot'n'spicy" Tortilla Wraps or Mexi Burgers, to light bites of filled baguettes and burgers. If you are still hungry, return for a High Tea, served from 5pm to 6.30pm, Tuesday to Saturday. Dishes on offer include homemade lasagne served straight from the oven, and "Pigs in a Pond" – sausage and mash inside a Yorkshire pudding served with onion gravy. All food served at the Caledonian has been sourced locally wherever possible.

The hotel has a full on licence and its

popular draught keg beers are Tennant's lager and Tennant's 70sh. On Friday evenings, starting around 9.30pm, a local duo entertains customers with a programme of all types of music, and on Saturday evenings there are occasional live entertainment performances.

Accommodation at the Caledonian comprises 10 comfortable guest bedrooms of varying sizes, all with en suite facilities, telephone, TV, trouser press, hairdryer and hospitality tray. Rooms are available all year round. Children are welcome; all major credit cards except American Express and Diners are accepted.

287 THE COFFEE POT ¶

5 Kenneth Street, Stornoway,
Isle of Lewis HS1 2DP
☎ 01851 703270

Located close to the harbour, **The Coffee Pot** is surely the most popular tearoom/coffee shop in Stornoway. The business had its origins just after World War I when the present owners' grandfather opened premises in the town. They have been at the current location since 1972. The business is now owned and run by Peter and Marie Scaramuccia, together with their daughter, also Marie. They offer a wide choice of dishes and teatime treats, all of which are listed on boards near the counter. Their breakfasts are particularly popular and all dishes are cooked to order. As much as possible of the food is sourced locally and is always wonderfully fresh.

The good humour of the Scaramuccia family – they are always smiling, it seems – no doubt contributes greatly to the success of the enterprise. No wonder the Coffee Pot is highly popular with local people – the very best recommendation. Opening hours are from 7.30am until 7pm; cash and cheques only are accepted. There's good wheelchair access to the dining tables but the toilets are difficult.

288 TIGH MEALROS ¶

Garynahine, Isle of Lewis HS2 9DS
☎ 01851 621333
e-mail: mealros@hotmail.com

Opened in 1989, Tigh Mealros is now well established as one of the premier dining places in Lewis. Set amongst the druidical stone circles of Callanish, Tigh Mealros' menu features seafood as its speciality together with steaks, poultry and pork dishes also vegetarian dishes on request. It

is a family-run establishment with proprietor Ceit Crawford and son Iain preparing a menu that is freshly cooked to order. Booking is advisable in high season due to demand. Outside, customers are treated to a striking three meter high Stone Fish and a sculptured garden featuring a Moongate.
Open Mon – Sat evenings from 7pm.

289 GALSON FARM

38 South Galson, Isle of Lewis HS2 0SH
☎ 01851 850492
e-mail: galsonfarm@yahoo.com
🌐 www.galsonfarm.co.uk

Animal lovers looking for a congenial bed & breakfast establishment will be in their element at **Galson Farm.** Amongst the stock on this 40-acre working croft are native cattle, sheep, a Clydesdale horse and two donkeys. Owners of the farm, Hazel and David Roberts, have been welcoming guests to their 4-star rated accommodation since 2002. You can stay on either a bed & breakfast, or dinner, bed & breakfast basis – the latter is strongly recommended as Hazel is an accomplished cook. She creates a different menu each evening, basing many of her dishes on home-grown produce. For the rest, she tries to source the ingredients from produce grown on the island. The farmhouse is licensed so you can treat yourself to a drink with your meal.

The accommodation at

Galson Farm comprises 4 luxury, modern en suite bedrooms, (2 twins; 1 double and 1 kingsize double), all of them attractively furnished and decorated. Guests also have the use of elegant residents' lounges and the house enjoys some stunning views along the coast. For those travelling on a budget, Galson Farm also offers an adjoining 4-star self-contained Bunk House with 6 bunks.

290 5 HACKLETE

Great Bernera, Isle of Lewis HS2 9ND
☎ 01851 612269

5 Hacklete truly is a Hidden Place, tucked away on the island of Great Bernera off the west coast of Lewis. The island is connected to the mainland by a bridge and makes a wonderful centre for exploring the whole of Lewis and Harris. 5 Hacklete is a modern but picturesque cottage sitting on the shores of West Loch Roag at the southern end of the island.

The cottage has a large, wild garden and enjoys broad views of the sea and surrounding lochs. Available on a self-catering basis, the cottage has 3 attractively furnished and decorated bedrooms, providing comfortable accommodation for up to 5 people. There's a sitting room with colour TV, a well-appointed kitchen with cooker, fridge and washing machine, and guests have use of the large garden. The croft has a

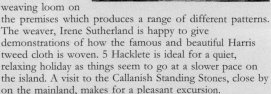

professional Harris tweed weaving loom on

the premises which produces a range of different patterns. The weaver, Irene Sutherland is happy to give demonstrations of how the famous and beautiful Harris tweed cloth is woven. 5 Hacklete is ideal for a quiet, relaxing holiday as things seem to go at a slower pace on the island. A visit to the Callanish Standing Stones, close by on the mainland, makes for a pleasant excursion.

291 ISLE OF HARRIS INN ¶¶

Scott Road, Tarbert,
Isle of Harris HS3 3DL
☎ 01859 502566 Fax: 01859 502354
e-mail: isleofharrisinn@btconnect.com
🌐 www.isle-of-harris-inn.com

Regarded by many as offering the best dining on the island, the **Isle of Harris Inn** is owned and run by Bill Scott who has been a chef since 1976. He started as manager/chef here in 1996 and became its owner in 2002. The inn was originally built in 1978 as a bar, part of the nearby Harris Hotel.

From Easter until the end of October, the inn is open from 11.30am to 9.30pm; out of season, the hours are from 11.30am until 2pm, and then from 4.45pm to 9pm. There are separate menus for the daytime and the evening. The daytime menu offers an extensive selection of popular bar meals (fish & chips; lasagne), burgers, omelettes, pizzas, wraps and baguettes. The evening menu also offers steakhouse grills and specials such as the highly popular fresh Harris or Uist Salmon or prime Lewis lamb. Wherever possible Bill tries to use local island produce. The specials change daily but

you might well find amongst the offerings The Haggis, "Great Chieftain o' the Puddin Race – haggis wi' bashed Neeps an champit Tatties, Rick wi' Whisky an Onions an Cream"! Haggis also features in the Fillet of Chicken filled with Haggis with whisky and peppercorn cream. The homemade soups are also particularly popular. To accompany your meal, there's an interesting selection of mostly New World wines available in full, one-third and quarter-size bottles and at very reasonable prices. If you prefer the "water of life", the inn stocks a good selection of Hebridean and Orkney malt whiskys including a 16-year-old Lagavulin.

The restaurant hosts occasional live entertainment and in summer hot buffets and barbecues are held outside – there is patio seating at the front.

Much of the restaurant's food can also be purchased to take away. Children are welcome in the restaurant; there's good wheelchair access, and all major credit cards are accepted apart from American Express and Diners.

Scott Road, Tarbert,
Isle of Harris HS3 3DL
☎ 01859 502154 Fax: 01859 502281
e-mail: harrishotel@btopenworld.com
🌐 www.harrishotel.com

For more than a hundred years the Cameron/ Morrison family have owned and run the **Harris Hotel** in Tarbert, just 500 yards from the ferry terminal. Today it is in the capable hands of the brother and sister team of Sarah and Andrew Morrison who continue to maintain the hotel's glowing reputation for friendly service, fine dining and comfortable accommodation. The impressive, very Scottish looking hotel was built around 1865 and one of its most distinguished visitors was the author of *Peter Pan*, JM Barrie, who visited Harris in the 1920s where he was inspired in his writing of *Mary Rose*. His initials, etched by himself, can still be seen in the dining room window.

Here you can also enjoy fine Scottish cuisine

featuring the best of local fresh produce – seafood, lamb and venison – after which you might like to sample one or more of the 100-plus whiskys in the cosy residents' bar. Food is served all day until 9pm during the season; morning coffee, bar meals at lunch time, afternoon tea and dinner in the evening. The hotel has 24 guest bedrooms, most of them recently refurbished, and many enjoy loch views, while the comfortable spacious lounges front onto a large, mature garden.

293 BORVEMOR COTTAGES

9 Scaristavore, Isle of Harris,
Outer Hebrides HS3 3HX
☎ 01859 550222
e-mail: borvemor@zetnet.co.uk
🌐 www.borvemor.zetnet.co.uk

Borvemor Cottages offer 4 unique self-catering properties, all on the southwestern seaboard of the Isle of Harris. Borvemor Blackhouse, or *Tigh Dubh* as it is called in Gaelic, was built in 1993 and is the first traditional "Blackhouse" to be built for over a century. Using the age-old materials of stone, wood and thatch, the classic shape of the dry-stone island house took shape in just 32 days and was completed within three months.

There are concessions to modern day requirements so Borvemor Blackhouse *does* have running water, electricity and excellent plumbing! The traditional features include a delightful Dover Stove complete with oven and a cosy box bed in a curtained recess off the living room with a box bed above which can be used for extra members of the family. The comfortable bedroom has a king size bed and antique furniture.

You might prefer either Stable Cottage or Byre Cottage, two comfortable self-contained semi-detached cottages created from a superbly converted steading. Stable Cottage has three bedrooms: one double room and two twin

rooms with bunk beds. The living room is spacious with comfortable seating and an open plan dining area at the other end. The modern fitted kitchen includes an electric cooker, a microwave and a washing machine/dryer.

The other half of the steading houses the Byre Cottage which sleeps six and has two bedrooms, one of which is a double / family room and the other has a bunk bed and a single bed. The modern fitted kitchen/living room is in an adjoining wing to the bedrooms, linked by a corridor opening on to a sunny conservatory.

The fourth property available through Borvemor Cottages is the two-storey Vallay House which was recently built up from the walls of the late 18th century Borvemor House. It is now fully modernised and provides self-catering accommodation for 5 or 6 people. Vallay House is at the corner of a dry stone walled garden and the sitting area at the back faces south and is very sheltered. Sun yourself! Access to the machair land and glorious Atlantic beach is a few minutes walk away on the west coast of Harris. Highland Cattle and Blackface Sheep are on the 30-acre working croft surrounding Vallay House and there is a trout loch just a quarter of an hour's hill walk away. There is also an excellent 9-hole links golf course just one mile away.

294 LANGASS LODGE

Locheport, Isle of North Uist,
The Western Isles HS6 5HA
☎ 01876 580285 Fax: 01876 580385
e-mail: langasslodge@btconnect.com
🌐 www.langasslodge.co.uk

Standing in splendid isolation in its own extensive grounds, **Langass Lodge** is a small hotel set beside a sea loch and enjoying spectacular views. It was originally built as a sporting lodge for the Duke of Hamilton but is now a popular retreat for all outdoor enthusiasts whether they are bird watchers, anglers or walkers. It is owned and run by Niall and Amanda Leveson Gower and another husband and wife team, John and Anne Buchanan, are in charge of cooking and hospitality. The fine cuisine served in the Lodge's restaurant is a major attraction here. North Uist in particular, and the Western Isles in general, are rich in game, fish and shellfish. At Langass Lodge the kitchen team prides itself on using as much of these as possible. Any shellfish they do not gather themselves or catch with their own boat and pots, they buy directly from local fishermen. They personally dive for their own scallops and endeavour to buy the freshest turbot, halibut, monkfish, cod and sole landed

on the island. Sea trout and brown trout appearing on the menu indicates that they have been caught either by a guest or by the ever keen staff. Most of the vegetables and fruit used in the kitchen is grown in the hotel's own poly-tunnel which enables them to continue well into the winter months. The Lodge's restaurant is open for lunch from 12.30pm until 2.30pm; and from 7pm to 9.30pm. Bar meals are also available from 6.30pm to 9pm.

Accommodation at the Lodge comprises 12 rooms (6 doubles; 4 twins; 1 single and 1 family room). All of them have been recently refurbished and have full en suite facilities. Children and dogs are welcome, and one of the ground floor rooms has been adapted for the disabled.

From the bedroom windows there are stunning views over Langass sea loch to Ben Eaval and the Minch beyond. In the foreground stands a stone circle around which a garden is being created and you will also see the wild deer that have made Langass Hill their home. Golden eagles and ravens are often seen over the Lodge and the sea loch is considered one of the best spots to sight an otter.

Langass Lodge is open all year except for February; all major credit cards except American Express and Diners are accepted.

295 RUSHLEE HOUSE

Lochmaddy, North Uist HS6 5AE
☎ 01876 500274
e-mail: rushleehouse@hebrides.net

Set beside a freshwater loch in a peaceful location less than a mile from the Lochmaddy ferry terminal, **Rushlee House** is an ideal base for exploring the Uists and surrounding islands with all their native wildlife. Built in 2004 for owners Linda and Sandy MacLeod this outstanding bed & breakfast establishment has been awarded a 4-star rating by Visit Scotland. Rushlee House stands in ¾ acre grounds leading down to Loch an Rubh Iar. Guests have the use of a comfortable lounge in which there are tea/coffee-making facilities and, if you are lucky with the weather, spectacular sunsets can be viewed from this room.

There are 3 double rooms, all with private en suite shower rooms, and all tastefully furnished and fully equipped with TV/video, radio, hair dryer and hospitality tray. The rooms are all on one level so there are no steps to negotiate and there are thermostatic controls in each bedroom. A full Scottish cooked or cold buffet style breakfast is included in the tariff and is usually served from 7.45am to 8.30am, but can be earlier if you need to catch a ferry. Other amenities include drying facilities for cyclists and walkers, ample parking and storage for cyclists. Rushlee House is open all year round; cash or cheques only are accepted.

North Uist island offers a truly amazing variety of outdoor pursuits as well as an abundance of wildlife – wild red deer, seals and otters as well as many inland and coastal birds. There's a bird sanctuary at nearby Balranald and anglers are spoilt for choice with so many lochs to explore.

296 NUNTON STEADINGS

Isle of Benbecula,
Outer Hebrides HS7 5LU
☎ 01870 603774 Fax: 01870 603452
e-mail: admin@nuntonsteadings.com
🌐 www.nuntonsteadings.com

At **Nunton Steadings** you will find not just one tea room but two, as well as a gift and farm shop, a small museum and more. This little complex is housed in buildings dating back to the 1700s and is leased and run by the Ladyman family, Mairi and Phil and their daughters, Maureen and Mairead.

Their tea rooms offer a good choice of tasty treats such as freshly baked scones or homebaking, along with light meals, fresh filled sandwiches, toasties, bagels, croissants, ciabatta, daily specials and a children's selection. One of your waiters is Edward Taylor who is also an artist and has some of his work on display here.

In between the tea rooms is a gift and produce shop selling local crafts along with Hebridean lamb and mutton and other locally produced

items such as home-made lemon curd. Outside, in a former stable, the Ladymans are creating an exhibition on the life of Mairi's grandfather, a well-known local figure known as Red Tie who used to farm here when Mairi was a young girl. Another stable contains an exhibition by the RSPB, while yet another is being converted into a cosy snug where customers can enjoy a wee dram.

299 ARD NA MARA

Kilphedar, South Uist HS8 5TB
☎ 01878 700452

Located in peaceful rural surroundings, **Ard Na Mara** is an immaculate bed & breakfast establishment. Built in 1979, the house boasts a 3-star rating from the Scottish Tourism Board. It's the home of Rosemary and Derek who offer between 4 and 6 rooms, depending on the number of guests. One upstairs room is a suite, with bedroom and adjoining lounge. Three of the other rooms have en

suite facilities. A full Scottish breakfast is included in the tariff and packed lunches are available. If required, your hosts will collect guests from the ferry terminal.

297 ORASAY INN

Lochcarnan, Isle of South Uist HS8 5PD
☎ 01870 610298 Fax: 01870 610267
e-mail: orasayinn@btinternet.com
🌐 www.orasayinn.co.uk

Owned and personally managed by Isobel and Alan Graham, the **Orasay Inn** is one of the best and friendliest small hotels on the beautiful island of South Uist. It is a modern building that blends beautifully into the surrounding landscape and offers the very best in Scottish hospitality. Isobel and Alan are committed to maintaining high standards at surprisingly keen prices which means that the hotel is also one of the most popular.

There are 9 rooms available, all fully en suite and all equipped with colour TV, telephone, hair dryer, central heating and hospitality tray. The beds are extremely comfortable and the furnishings and decoration are of the highest standard possible. Deluxe rooms have sofas and patio doors to a decked area where guests can relax on those long, lazy evenings for which the Western Isles are justly famous.

However, it's the food that makes the Orasay Inn so special. Isobel is a "Natural Cooking of Scotland" trainer and was even

one of the team picked to prepare the gala dinner for the grand opening of Scotland's new parliament in 1999. Her cooking philosophy is to always use fresh, local produce and to keep the dishes simple while still displaying imagination and flair. In this she has succeeded admirably and the inn now has a reputation extending far beyond the Western Isles for its fine cuisine. A quote from the *Sunday Times* travel section reads: "Finally, don't forget to eat some seafood. The scallops in particular are enormous and one of the best ways to enjoy them is as part of a seafood platter at the Orasay Inn on South Uist. Clean, functional and home to one of the best chefs in the Islands." Isobel's menu includes dishes based on locally caught seafood, dishes such as seared Isle of Uist scallops, baked fillet of Orasay halibut, and a gratin of seafood that includes local prawns, cockles, mussels and crab. The menu also offers chicken wrapped haggis, Hebridean venison, local lamb chops, duck and prime Scotch beef. Meals are served in the spacious dining room which commands superb views of sea and mountain. There is also a daily changing specials board where you might find such delightful surprises as deep-fried squid or red Thai curry. Co-chef Uilleam is also a qualified baker and produces wonderful fresh bread, scones and a selection of desserts.

298 LOCHBOISDALE HOTEL

Lochboisdale, South Uist,
Outer Hebrides HS8 5TH
☎ 01878 700332   Fax: 01878 700324
e-mail: karen@lochboisdale.com
🌐 www.lochboisdalehotel.co.uk

Overlooking the harbour at Lochboisdale and close to the ferry terminal, the **Lochboisdale Hotel** enjoys splendid views across the Minch to the islands of Canna and Rhum. Historically a sporting hotel, Lochboisdale has a unique fishing atmosphere enjoyed by anglers and tourists alike. The hotel is full of character and still houses the original records dating back to 1882 when the first visitors came to stay and fish on the famous lochs of South Uist. Owners of the hotel, Karen and Calum MacAuley, still maintain an association with South Uist Estates and fishing can be arranged through them for brown trout, sea trout or salmon.

The hotel is well-known for its excellent cuisine. The regular menu features the best of fresh local produce and the specials board is compiled daily after the owners have seen what the fishing boats have landed that morning. Food is served from noon until 2.30pm, and from 5.30pm until 9pm. The dining room, lounge bar and residents' lounge all enjoy beautiful sea and mountain

views. So, soak up the Gaelic atmosphere and enjoy the impromptu live music sessions in the lounge bar. The hotel has a full on licence and stocks a good range of beers, including one real ale from the island brewery, along with a wide choice of whiskeys.

The hotel has 15 guest bedrooms – 5 doubles, 5 twin rooms including a family room that can sleep 5 people, and 5 singles. All the rooms are en suite and individually designed. Travel cots are available on request, free of charge. Well-behaved dogs are welcome for a small charge.

In addition to fishing, South Uist offers a variety of activities. The island is a bird watcher's paradise with golden eagles living on the hills, black and red-throated divers on the moorland and hill lochs, and hen harriers, merlin and short-eared owls are common sights. The hotel is just 3 miles from the famous Tom Morris golf course in Askernish which is being restored to its former glory. From the harbour you can take the ferry to the Isle of Barra and there's also a small ferry to the Isle of Eriskay.

300 ISLE OF BARRA HOTEL

Tangasdale Beach, Isle of Barra HS9 5XW
☎ 01871 810383   Fax: 01871 810385
e-mail: isleofbarrahotel@btconnect.com

Beautifully located overlooking a glorious white, sandy bay washed by the Atlantic Ocean, the **Isle of Barra Hotel** is a family-run establishment owned and run by John and Elizabeth Johnston who previously ran the Caledonian Hotel in Stornoway. They arrived here in November 2006 and carried out major refurbishment of the 1973 building. Settle down in the spacious lounge and enjoy a drink as you look out over Halaman Bay with Ben Tangaval rising in the distance. In the dining room, which also commands stunning view, choose from the excellent selection of dishes based wherever possible on fresh local produce. Food is also available in the lounge and public bar, and there's a separate menu for children. Lunch is served from noon until 2pm; dinner from 5pm – booking is advisable in the summer months. After dinner, you can stroll out onto the patio with a coffee or single malt and admire the spectacular sunsets.

The hotel has 40 guest bedrooms, all with full en suite facilities and all equipped with colour TV and hospitality tray. Most enjoy those wonderful views across the bay. Children and small dogs are welcome. Barra is easily reached either by air from Glasgow (landing on the beach), or by ferry from Oban or Eriskay.

301 EAST BANK HOUSE

East Road, Kirkwall, Orkney KW15 1LX
☎ 01856 870179

East Bank House is located less than 5 minutes walk from the centre of Kirkwall town and its amenities, and makes an ideal base for exploring the Orkney Islands. Standing in its own grounds and dating back to 1824, the house was completely refurbished in 2005. It now provides comfortable en suite accommodation with 7 double/twin rooms; 3 family and 3 single rooms – all of them with en suite facilities. The ground floor consists of a large, fully fitted kitchen for the use of guests in the evening, a dining room and adjacent conservatory.

Guests are served a generous breakfast based on the very best of Orkney produce. Vegetarian or special diets can be catered for on request and everything is served in a friendly, informal atmosphere. Laundry and drying facilities are available, and a service wash can be undertaken on request. Children under 10 years old stay free, and dogs are also welcome.

East Bank House also offers self-catering options, as well as group and long stay reductions by negotiation. Accommodating up to 26 guests, with adjacent conference facilities, East Bank House is eminently suitable for small to medium-sized groups.

302 WEST END HOTEL

Main Street, Kirkwall, Orkney KW15 1BU
☎ 01856 872368 Fax: 01865 876181
e-mail: west.end@orkney.com
🌐 www.westendhotel.org.uk

You'll get a warm welcome at the **West End Hotel**, one of the best privately-run hotels in Orkney. It is renowned for its character, its friendliness and its down to earth prices, and you will surely return again and again if you stay here. Its restaurant sells excellent food, with the produce being sourced on the island wherever possible. The lounge bar is cosy and  welcoming, and serves a wide range of beers, wines and spirits to suit every taste. You can also sit in the West End's garden and enjoy the long, summer evenings.

303 ALBERT HOTEL

Mounthoolie Lane, Kirkwall,
Orkney KW15 1JK
☎ 01856 876000 Fax: 01856 875397
e-mail: enquiries@alberthotel.co.uk
🌐 www.alberthotel.co.uk

In the centre of Kirkwall, and close to all amenities, including ferries to the smaller islands, you will find the **Albert Hotel**, an establishment offering stylish accommodation and a relaxed, friendly atmosphere. The luxury rooms come with digital TV, internet connection, iron and board, tea/coffee making facilities and room service. Eat beautifully cooked  local produce in the restaurant or enjoy local ales and whiskies in the cosy Bothy bar. A favourite with locals and tourists alike, you too will be impressed with everything it has to offer!

305 SANDS HOTEL

Burray, Orkney KW17 2SS
☎ 01856 731298
e-mail: info@thesandshotel.co.uk
🌐 www.thesandshotel.co.uk

Originally built as a fish store in 1860, the four-star **Sands Hotel** has recently been refurbished and upgraded to an extremely high standard, making it one of the best hotels in the Orkneys. It overlooks Burray Harbour, Watersound Bay and South Ronaldsay, and is just four minutes away from the ferry terminal at St Margaret's Hope.

Owned and run by Evelyn and John Gunn, this is a friendly, informal establishment that offers six rooms to discerning tourists. Four are double and two are twin, and all are fully en suite, with telephone, tea and coffee making facilities and colour TV. Computer access is also available on request.

There is a cosy, welcoming bar serving a wide range of drinks, such as beer, spirits, wine and soft drinks, and the Watersound Restaurant, which has  a nautical theme about it, serves great food. The restaurant is a popular eating place for local people - always a good recommendation! - and serves fresh, flavoursome food that is, wherever possible, sourced locally. Orkney salmon - scallops - crab - lobster - beef - all feature in the menu.

The is a conservatory/garden room where you can relax over a drink and watch the activity at the harbour front, or enjoy a cup of tea or coffee as you look back on a day spent exploring these magical islands!

304 LYNNFIELD HOTEL

Holm Road, St Ola, Kirkwall,
Orkney KW15 1SU
☎ 01856 872505 Fax: 01856 870038
e-mail: office@lynnfield.co.uk
🌐 www.lynnfieldhotel.com

Within a building that dates back to at least 1880, the three-star **Lynnfield Hotel** is one of the most picturesque hostelries on Orkney. It's whitewashed walls, painted quoins and generous proportions speak of an inviting, welcoming place that places great emphasis on tradition mixed with modern concepts such as high standards of service and outstanding value for money.

The hotel was recently bought by Lorna Reid and Malcolm Stout, who owned the four-star Cleaton House Hotel on Westray, and now the whole place is being refurbished throughout, and by the year 2007 it will undoubtedly be one of the finest hotels in the whole of Orkney. It has always had a reputation among professional people and businessmen as a place that offers superb accommodation and high standards of cuisine at affordable prices, but now it is being discovered by tourists as well. It is ideally placed for touring, on the outskirts of Kirkwall, right next to the Highland Park Distillery, and you can make this the base while you explore the wonderful Orkney Islands, which are so rich in history and heritage.

There are 9 rooms in the hotel including 1 suite, 2 with four-posters and 1 ground floor, with facilities for the disabled. Each one is individually furnished and all are fully en suite. Each room has a colour TV and tea/coffee making facilities, and the furnishings and decorations are of an extremely high standard. The residents' room was totally refurbished in March 2006, and is now welcoming and cosy with fine wood panelling, comfortable furniture and, in the winter months, a roaring coal fire. This gives some idea of the standards that Lorna and Malcolm are setting themselves, and augers well for the upgrading and refurbishment of the rest of the hotel.

The view from the restaurant out over the bay can be distracting, but no doubt your attention will be drawn back to the food by its excellence. The kitchens use only fresh, local produce, and this is reflected in the menu, which can change according to what is available. Dishes could include Scapa Flow prawn salad with Marie Rose and coriander, juicy fillet steaks with steak mushroom and black pudding, topped with red onion chilli jam, vegetable stir fry and fillet of John Dory on a roasted hazelnut and orange salad.

There is plenty of parking space, and the hotel also has wireless facilities (YIFI).

306 THE GALLEY INN & SHORE RESTAURANT

Front Road, St Margaret's Hope,
Orkney KW17 2SL
☎ 01856 831526
e-mail: thegalleyinn@hotmail.com
🌐 www.galleyinn.co.uk

You should never visit the Orkneys without visiting **The Galley Inn and Shore Restaurant** in the picturesque village of St Margaret's Hope. Its patio overlooks the quayside, and is the perfect place to relax over a quiet drink as you take in the slower pace of life on these lovely islands. The Galley Inn has a relaxed, informal atmosphere, and serves a wide range of beers (including locally brewed bottled beers), wines, spirits and soft drinks, being a popular place for visitors and locals to mingle and chat. Hanging on the walls are works by local artists, and all are for sale. The B&B accommodation has recently been completely refurbished to an extremely high standard, and consists of three spacious rooms, a twin and two doubles, all fully en suite and all having remote control TV, hospitality tray, hairdryer and toiletries. They offer comfortable accommodation and great value for money.

The Shore Restaurant is open seven days a week and serves home cooked meals that are prepared from fresh, local produce such as Orkney beef and lamb, vegetables and fish. Everything from a simple bar meal to a lunch or dinner is available, and there's sure to be a wine in the small but comprehensive wine list that complements each dish perfectly. The Galley Inn and Shore Restaurant are non-smoking for your comfort and convenience, and the service is quick, efficient and friendly.

307 THIRA

Innertown, Stromness,
Orkney Islands KW16 3JP
☎ 01856 851181
e-mail: info@thiraorkney.co.uk
🌐 www.thiraorkney.co.uk

A warm welcome and a restful stay are assured at **Thira**, a purpose-built, non-smoking guesthouse just 2 miles from the picturesque 18th century seaport of Stromness in the peaceful parish of Innertown. Here you can enjoy unrivalled panoramic views of Hoy, Scapa Flow and the Scottish Munroes to the south.

Enjoying a 4-star rating from Visit Scotland, this warm, modern house offers comfortable en suite accommodation in 4 guest bedrooms – 1 double, 1 twin and 2 singles. Each room is equipped with colour TV tea and coffee-making facilities and generous

storage space. Home cooking is a speciality at Thira and you're

unlikely to forget the full and generous breakfast served in a dining room looking out to the hills of Hoy. As one visiting couple said of Thira: "it's hard to find…but harder to leave!" As well as being close to Stromness, the house is just 7 miles from famous sites such as the Ring of Brodgar, Skara Brae and Maes Howe.

308 THE FERRY INN

10 John Street, Stromness,
Orkney KW16 3AD
☎ 01856 850280
e-mail: adrian@ferryinn.com
🌐 www.ferryinn.com

Right on the seafront at Stromness you'll find **The Ferry Inn**, one of the best establishments of its kind on Orkney. It offers good food, good drink and first class accommodation. Its central location and its position right next to the ferry terminal makes it the ideal base from which to explore the islands, which makes it popular not only with locals, but tourists as well. It is particularly popular with diving groups as many of the dive-boats are berthed within 200 metres of the inn.

The Ferry Inn has 11 rooms on offer, seven of which are en suite. They are well furnished and decorated, and are extremely comfortable, representing astonishing value for money. The breakfasts are always hearty and filling, and are served in the restaurant. Also served in the restaurant are lunchtime snacks and

meals, and in the evening there is a full à la carte menu. Freshly caught seafood and quality Orkney beef form the basis of the menus.

The lively bar has a great selection of drinks, and is a friendly, welcoming place, popular with locals. It has been nominated many times for Scotland's 'best pub' awards. Here you can relax over a drink, or listen to the traditional musicians who perform midweek during the summer months. They live up an already lively place - one where you are sure to make new friends!

309 RAMSQUOY FARM

Stenness, Stromness, Orkney KW16 3EZ
☎ 01856 850316
e-mail: info@ramsquoy.com
🌐 www.ramsquoy.com

For superb B&B accommodation on Orkney, you must head for **Ramsquoy Farm,** overlooking the island of Hoy and Scapa Flow. Owners Mona and Jim Swannie have welcomed people to their 100-acre farm from all over the world in the last 30 years, and are determined to build on their fine reputation for warmth, friendliness and good, old-fashioned value for money. There are two rooms available - a double and a twin, both fully en suite and both extremely comfortable, with delightful furnishings and decoration. Children under five years stay for free, while there is a reduced rate for children over five. Well-behaved pets are also welcome by prior arrangement.

People return again and again to this establishment, so early booking is certainly recommended! And there is a discount for people who stay for seven days or more. There is a spacious lounge and dining room for guests, which has lovely views, and features a TV and tea/coffee

making facilities. This is the place to unwind over a cup of tea or coffee after a hard day exploring all that Orkney has to offer, be it history, walking, observing wildlife or one of the many sports that can be indulged in. A full Scottish breakfast is served each morning, with lighter options if required, and packed lunches and evening meals are available for an extra charge. Ramsquoy farm is a special place. Why not visit it when you're in Orkney, and find out for yourself?

310 THE ORKNEY CROFT

90 Dundas Street, Stromness,
Orkney KW16 3DA
☎ 01856 851116
e-mail: fioneil@fioneil.force9.co.uk
⊕ www.orkneycroft.co.uk

For self-catering accommodation for families, walkers, cyclists, anglers etc, you can't beat **The Orkney Croft**. The accommodation is on the beautiful and quiet island of Hoy, and consists of two units, each having two bedrooms and sleeping up to six people in absolute comfort. One building is an old barn that has been sympathetically converted to superior accommodation, and the other is more modern. Both were extensively renovated in 1999, and represent amazing value for money. Part of a complex of traditional stone buildings on a former farm, they received an award from the Orkney Heritage Society, named in honour of Laura Grimond, widow of the late Joe Grimond, MP. This was because of their attention to detail, and the use of traditional materials in building and restoring them.

This is self catering accommodation at its best, on an island that is renowned for its quietness and heritage - a place where you can recharge your batteries away from the turmoil of modern life. West Linksness cottage has a double room, a twin room and an

extra sofa bed. A further zed-bed can be supplied on request. Nether Linksness also has two bedrooms - a double and one with bunk beds (a double on the bottom and a single above, as well as a sofa bed. Both cottages have well-appointed kitchens, bathrooms and heating.

311 LEISBURN COTTAGES

Burness, Firth, Orkney KW17 2ET
☎ 01856 761442
e-mail: ann@the-stevensons.co.uk
⊕ www.orkneyselfcatering.co.uk

The four-star **Leisburn Cottages** are well placed to explore Mainland, Orkney's main island, or simply to enjoy the peace and tranquillity of a place where time seems to have stood still. The two cottages are situated on the edge of a stream, just before it enters the sea, via a tidal lagoon - a superbly romantic spot that speaks of the thousands of years of history you can explore on Orkney - history that has left its mark everywhere.

Each of the two semi-detached cottages sleeps four, and has two bedrooms, a bathroom with bath and shower, open plan kitchen/lounge with colour TV, microwave, oven, hob, fridge/freezer, washer/dryer and dishwasher. So you can see that, even though they offer peace and quiet, they still have all modern conveniences to make your stay here as comfortable and enjoyable as possible.

These no smoking cottages have all linen

supplied, and a cot or high chair can be provided. Electricity is by a 50p meter, and there is plenty of car parking. Why not sit in the garden and, during the summer months, marvel that you can still read a newspaper late at night. Or go for long walks and wonder at the many standing stones, burial cairns and other ancient monuments that seem to litter the landscape, showing that people have lived here for thousands of years.

312 HAVLY CENTRE CAFÉ

9 Charlotte Street, Lerwick,
Shetlands ZE1 0JL
☎ 01595 692100
e-mail: ravetvik@lineone.net

Owned and run by Astrid and Reidar Vetvik, The **Havly Centre Café** in Lerwick is a little piece of Norway in Shetland! Here, in a café that combines contemporary styling, comfort and outstanding value for money, you can relax over the best coffee in town with Norwegian waffles, home baked cakes, bread and rolls, all baked on the premises. The café also offers delicious light lunches such as home-made pizzas, beef burgers, soup, bacon rolls and so on.

This is a family-friendly, Christian establishment with a baby-changing room and a kid's corner with toys. It also provides a welcome break for business people to enjoy a cup of coffee away from the stresses of business life for a short while. Visitors from all over the world have eaten here, and once discovered, you are sure to come back again and again.

It is open from Monday to Saturday and offers a warm welcome to everyone.

The café is only a short walk away from many of Lerwick's attractions. Close by is the town hall, and next to it is a beautiful flower park with a children's play area. The Isleburgh Community Centre, with its summer exhibitions, is only five minutes away, and right at the back of the Havly Centre is the historic Fort Charlotte.

313 SELF CATERING SHETLAND

Inches, Bells Road, Lerwick,
Shetland ZE1 0QB
☎ 01595 692793
e-mail: info@selfcateringshetland.com
🌐 www.selfcateringshetland.com
(Online booking & 'up to the minute' availability calander)

Self Catering Shetland offers superior self-catering properties in Shetland's picturesque capital, Lerwick. The Decca sits on the outskirts of the town, yet only five minutes from all the amenities of the town centre. It was once Shetland's Navigational Signal Station, and has now been converted into apartments of various sizes, the largest sleeping six. It has ample car parking and is set in a spacious garden, with each apartment being given the Shetland dialect name for local birds, and each one individually decorated and furnished.

Corbie is a 19th century ground floor flat in the heart of Lerwick, and is full of period character. It is the perfect base from which to explore the islands, and has car parking to the front of the property and in the car park opposite. It boasts a

large family bedroom with a double and single bed and a second double bedroom. There is an open fire in the living room, a fully equipped kitchen, a dining area, a shared garden and a decked area.

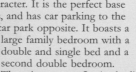

Bed linen, towels and dish towels are supplied in all the properties, and each one has Internet connection facilities. Most credit cards are accepted, but it is regretted that pets are not allowed. There are also laundry facilities in all of the properties.

314 THE SHETLAND FUDGE COMPANY

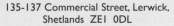

135-137 Commercial Street, Lerwick,
Shetlands ZE1 0DL
☎ 01595 741220
e-mail: sara.fox@shetlandfudge.com
⊕ www.shetlandfudge.com

The Shetland Fudge Company is a small family business famous for its traditional Scottish butter tablet, as well as its fudge, truffles and continental chocolates. It is the only company in Scotland that does this, with everything being hand-made in the shop in the centre of Lerwick, Shetland's capital, from only the finest local ingredients wherever possible.

The company manufactures in small batches, ensuring high quality every time, and you can call in at the shop to buy its products or order via its website. No preservatives of any kind are used, so you know you are getting the very best every time. The company sends to all over the world, and it is gaining a great name for itself! It also sells a rare, new delicacy - puffin poo! But don't be put off - people don't climb down steep cliffs and raid puffins' nests for it - it is made from the finest white

Belgian chocolate, and is becoming a firm favourite with people everywhere! Then there are the 'Shetland Hampers', which burst with goodies for the festive period. These too are very popular.

Why not call in if you are holidaying on the wonderful islands of Shetland? Or order via their website or by post? The products are usually dispatched within seven days of receiving the order, and the prices are very reasonable! So go on - indulge your sweet tooth and call in or place an order today!

315 GLEN ORCHY HOUSE

20 Knab Road, Lerwick,
Shetland ZE1 0AX
☎ 01595 692031
e-mail: glenorchy.house@virgin.net
⊕ www.guesthouselerwick.com

The superb facilities on offer at **Glen Orchy House** make it the perfect place to stay while holidaying in the lovely Shetland Islands. It was built in 1904 as a convent known as the "House of Charity", and then became the rectory for St Magnus Church. Now it is a guest house offering two family rooms, four double rooms, eleven twins and seven singles, all fully en suite and all furnished and decorated to a very high standard. One of the rooms is on the ground floor and is suitable for the disabled. The building has been sympathetically renovated and extended, while at the same time incorporating every modern convenience. It also boasts modern concepts such as high standards of service and outstanding value for money. All letting rooms in the new wing have underfloor central heating, air conditioning and satellite TV.

On the ground floor is an 'honesty bar' where guests can enjoy a quiet drink after a hard day's sightseeing, and there are also a selection of board games and books, some of them with a Shetland theme. Breakfast is served between 7.30 am and 8.30 am Monday - Saturday and 8.30 am and 9.30 am on Sunday unless otherwise requested. Authentic Thai cuisine is available 6.30pm to 9.30pm daily.

Pets and well behaved children are most welcome.

316 ORCA COUNTRY INN ‖ ⊢

Hoswick, Sandwick, Shetland ZE2 9HL
☎ 01950 431226
e-mail: lee@orcacountryinn.co.uk
⊕ www.orcacountryinn.co.uk

For superb hospitality on the Shetland Islands, head for the **Orca Country Inn** at Sandwick, fifteen miles south of Lerwick. It is owned and managed by renowned photographer Lee Mott, and boasts six beautifully decorated and furnished rooms, each one spacious yet cosy and comfortable. Five of the rooms are fully en suite, while the sixth has a private bathroom.

This splendid inn was built in 1880, and is a substantial whitewashed building that was converted to an inn/hotel in 1976. It offers real Scottish hospitality among some of the most spectacular scenery in the Shetlands.

The interior is delightful and appealing, and has a bar/restaurant where good, home-cooked food is available,

as well as a wide range of beers, wines, spirits and soft drinks. The kitchen uses locally sourced produce wherever possible, ensuring maximum flavour and freshness in its many dishes. Nature is on the doorstep of this splendid inn, and some of the best bird watching on the islands is available from the Observatory Restaurant. In the seas off the Shetlands killer whales can often be seen.

317 MID BRAE INN ‖

Brae, Shetland ZE2 9GJ
☎ 01806 522634
e-mail: andreamanson304@aol

Within the centre of the delightful village of Brae you will find the **Mid Brae Inn**, which dates back over 300 years. It seats 70 people in absolute comfort, and is open to all who appreciate good food and great drink.

The building, with its old stone, its slate roof and whitewashed walls, retains many of its original features, and the interior is just as impressive. Old beams, warm wood, stone walls and low lighting welcome you into an inn that is cosy, warm and inviting. But the establishment also places great emphasis on modern concepts, such as very high standards of service, a warm welcome to local and tourist alike and great value for money.

There are two bars, one restaurant/bar and a public bar, as well as a beer garden. Here you can relax in comfort and consider the selection of fine drinks on offer, from beers, lagers and cider to wines, spirits, liqueurs and soft drinks should you be driving. Plus the food is outstanding, and indeed the establishment is noted for its cuisine. All the produce used in the kitchen is sourced locally wherever possible to ensure freshness and maximum flavour, and it is all home cooked! Starters include such dishes as soup of the day, prawn cocktail, hot 'n' spicy chicken wings, mini vegetable spring rolls and garlic bread with melted cheese.

Main dishes range from juicy steaks with all the trimmings to steak and ale pie, roast gammon with peach sauce and chicken tikka marsala. Plus of course, this being the Shetland Islands, there are many and varied fish dishes to choose from.

318 BUSTA HOUSE HOTEL

Busta, Brae, Shetland ZE2 9QN
☎ 01806 522506 Fax: 01806 522588
e-mail: reservations@bustahouse.com
⊕ www.bustahouse.com

With 22 fully en suite rooms, the **Busta House Hotel** is one of the leading hotels on Shetland. The building is a historic place, dating back hundreds of years, with a 16th century Long Room (built during the reign of Elizabeth I of England), where the present Queen, Elizabeth II, had tea in 1961, and the non-smoking Gifford library, which dates from 1710.

But for all its age, the hotel is firmly in the 21st century where high standards of service, great cuisine, comfort and value of money are concerned. All the rooms are named after Shetland islands, and all have direct-dial telephone, modem port, tea/coffee making facilities, television and hair dryer. They are well furnished and decorated, and have a comfortable, welcoming feel to them. Regrettably, none are on the ground floor, and lifts or elevators were not invented in the 16th, 17th or 18th centuries!

Food is important at the Busta House Hotel. The Pitcairn Restaurant serves only the finest dishes, all

prepared from fresh local produce wherever possible, and bar meals are also available. The menu has been put together with imagination and flair, and this, along with a fine wine and malt whisky list, means that you will have a dinner to remember. You can relax in the lounge or bar area and Busta House has something which is a rarity on Shetland - a garden, where you can relax or stroll on a summer's evening. The hotel makes a perfect base and the staff are knowledgeable about what to do and see. There's even a ghost in the hotel - but don't worry! It's a warm, friendly one, and it will leave you alone to enjoy your stay!

319 MIDFIELD CROFT SELF-CATERING COTTAGES

Midfield Bardister, Ollaberry
Shetlands ZE2 9RU
☎ 01806 544277
e-mail: midfield-croft@freeuk.com
⊕ www.midfieldcroft@freeuk.com

Set on the B9079 in Ollaberry Northmavine are the three and four star **Midfield Croft Self-Catering Cottages,** located on a working, but quiet, croft close to the sea. This rural, northerly part of Shetland is ideal for hill and coastal walking with spectacular views. It's many lochs are superb for fishing and it is a popular destination for birdwatchers, as well as being home to a large number of otters. Askalong is a modern bungalow comprising of an open plan kitchen, dining room and lounge area. It has two double bedrooms with one ensuite, a single bedroom and a main bathroom. Midfield is a traditional crafting cottage. It has a cosy lounge/dining room with a wood burning stove, kitchen and bathroom on the ground floor. Upstairs there is a

double, twin and single bedroom. Both cottages are decorated to a very high standard and have spectacular views over Gluss Voe and of the north end of the island of Yell.

They both have their own laundry facilities, payphone and lovely paved patio gardens. There is plenty of parking to the front. A cot and highchair are available on request. There is a small charge for electricity. It is regretted that credit and debit cards are not accepted.

320 NORWIND GUEST HOUSE

Hillend, Mid Yell, Shetland ZE2 9BJ
☎ 01957 702312
e-mail: norwind@btinternet.com

Norwind Guest House is one of the finest bed and breakfast establishments on the Shetland islands. It is owned and run by Isobel Robertson who extends a warm welcome to all of her guests.

The building itself is a modern bungalow built of wood, with a tiled roof, sheltered garden and a balcony overlooking the sea. The interior is carpeted throughout, ensuring warmth, cosiness and a friendly, home-from-home atmosphere.

Isobel has three spacious, comfortable rooms that are fully en suite, each one being furnished and decorated to an extremely high standard. Being close to the sea, the B&B makes the ideal base for a quiet, restful holiday that takes in bird watching, fishing, walking or just lazing around away from the bustle of modern life.

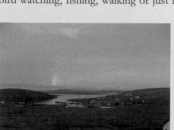

The home cooked breakfasts are hearty and filling and Isobel uses locally sourced produce wherever possible. Lighter options are, of course, available if required. Evening meals are available by prior arrangement.

The Shetlands are full of magic and discovery, with history and heritage all around. Norwind Guest House is an excellent base from which to visit all of the islands and so is the perfect place to stay to experience it all!

Tourist Information Centres

ABERFELDY

The Square, Perth & Kinross, Aberfeldy PH15 2DD
Tel: 01887 820276
Fax: 01887 829495
e-mail: aberfeldytic@perthshire.co.uk
website: www.perthshire.co.uk/

ABINGTON

Welcome Break Service Area, Junction 13 M74, Crawford,
Strathclyde ML12 6RG
Tel: 01864 502436
Fax: 01864 502765
website: www.southlanarkshire.gov.uk/

ALFORD

Railway Museum, Old Station Yard, Main Street, Alford,
Aberdeenshire AB33 8DF
Tel: 019755 62052

ANSTRUTHER

Scottish Fisheries Museum, Harbourhead, Anstruther,
Fife KY10 3AB
Tel: 01333 311073
e-mail: anstruther@visitfife.com

ARBROATH

Market Place, Arbroath, Angus and Dundee DD11 1HR
Tel: 01241 872 609
e-mail: enquiries@angusanddundee.co.uk
website: www.angusanddundee.co.uk

ARDGARTAN

Forestry Car Park, Glen Croe, Ardgartan, by Arrochar,
Dunbartonshire G83 7AR
Tel: 08707 200 606
Fax: 08707 200 606
e-mail: info@ardgartan.visitscotland.com
website: www.visitscottishheartlands.org/

AUCHTERARDER

90 High Street, Auchterarder ,
Perth & Kinross PH3 1BJ
Tel: 01764 663450
Fax: 01764 664235
e-mail: auchterardertic@perthshire.co.uk
website: www.perthshire.co.uk/

AVIEMORE

Grampian Road, Aviemore, Inverness-shire PH22 1PP
Tel: 0845 22 55 121
e-mail: info@visitscotland.com
website: www.visithighlands.com

AYR

22 Sandgate, Ayr, Ayrshire and Arran KA7 1BW
Tel: 01292 288 688
Fax: 01292 288 686
website: www.ayrshire-arran.com

BALLACHULISH

Ballachulish, Argyll and Bute PH49 4JB
Tel: 01855 811 866
Fax: 01855 811 866
e-mail: info@glencoetourism.co.uk
website: www.glencoetourism.co.uk/

BALLATER

Old Royal Station, Station Square, Ballater,
Aberdeenshire AB25 5RB
Tel: 013397 55306

BALLOCH

Balloch Road, Balloch, Dunbartonshire G83 8LQ
Tel: 08707 200 607
Fax: 01389 751704
e-mail: info@balloch.visitscotland.com
website: www.visitscottishheartlands.org/

BANCHORY

Bridge Street, Banchory, Aberdeenshire AB31 5SX
Tel: 01330 822000

BANFF

Collie Lodge, Banff, Aberdeenshire AB45 1AU
Tel: 01261 812419

BETTYHILL

Clachan Bettyhill, by Thurso, Sutherland KW14 7SS
Tel: 01845 22 55 121
e-mail: info@visitscotland.com
website: www.visithighlands.com

BIGGAR

155 High Street, Biggar, South Lanarkshire ML12 6DL
Tel: 01899 221066
Fax: 01899 221066
website: www.seeglasgow.com

BLAIRGOWRIE

26 Wellmeadow, Blairgowrie, Perth & Kinross PH10 6AS
Tel: 01250 872960
Fax: 01250 873701
e-mail: blairgowrietic@perthshire.co.uk
website: www.perthshire.co.uk/

TOURIST INFORMATION CENTRES

BO'NESS

Car Park, Seafield Place, Bo'ness, Lothian EH51 0AJ
Tel: 08707 200 608
Fax: 08707 200 608
e-mail: info@boness.visitscotland.com
website: www.visitscottishheartlands.org/

BOWMORE

The Square, Bowmore, Isle of Islay PA43 7JP
Tel: 08707 200 617
Fax: 01496 810 363
e-mail: info@islayvisitscotland.com
website: www.visitscottishheartlands.com

BRAEMAR

The Mews, Mar Road, Braemar,
Aberdeenshire AB35 5YP
Tel: 013397 41600

BRECHIN

Brechin Castle Centre, Haughmuir, Brechin,
Angus and Dundee DD9 6RL
Tel: 01356 623 050
e-mail: enquiries@angusanddundee.co.uk
website: www.angusanddundee.co.uk

BROADFORD

The Car Park, Broadford, Isle of Skye IV49 9AB
Tel: 01845 22 55 121
e-mail: info@visitscotland.com
website: www.visithighlands.com

BRODICK

The Pier, Isle of Arran, Brodick,
Ayrshire and Arran KA27 8AU
Tel: 01770 302140
Fax: 01770 302 395
website: www.ayrshire-arran.com

CAMPBELTOWN

MacKinnon House, The Pier, Campbeltown,
Kintyre PA28 6EF
Tel: 08707 200 609
Fax: 01586 553291
e-mail: info@campbeltown.visitscotland.com
website: www.visitscottishheartlands.org/

CARNOUSTIE

1b High Street, Carnoustie,
Angus and Dundee DD7 6AN
Tel: 01241 852 258
e-mail: enquiries@angusanddundee.co.uk
website: www.angusanddundee.co.uk

CASTLE DOUGLAS

Market Hill, Castle Douglas,
Dumfries and Galloway DG7 1AE
Tel: 01556 502611
e-mail: castledouglas@dgtb.visitscotland.com
website: www.visitdumfriesandgalloway.co.uk

CASTLEBAY

Main Street, Castlebay, Isle of Barra HS9 5DX
Tel: 01871 810336
Fax: 01871 810336
e-mail: castlebay@visithebrides.com
website: www.visithebrides.com

CRAIGNURE

The Pier, Craignure, Isle of Mull PA65 6AY
Tel: 08707 200 610
Fax: 01680 812497
e-mail: info@mull.visitscotland.com
website: www.visitscottishheartlands.org/

CRAIL

Crail Museum & Heritage Centre, 62-64 Marketgate, Crail,
Fife KY10 3TL
Tel: 01333 450869
e-mail: crail@visitfife.com

CRATHIE

The Car Park, Ballater, Crathie,
Aberdeenshire AB55 4AD
Tel: 01339 742 414

CRIEFF

Town Hall, High Street, Crieff,
Perth & Kinross PH7 3HU
Tel: 01764 652578
Fax: 01764 655422
e-mail: criefftic@perthshire.co.uk
website: www.perthshire.co.uk/

DAVIOT WOOD

Picnic Area (A9), Daviot Wood, by Inverness IV1 2ER
Tel: 01845 22 55 121
e-mail: info@visitscotland.com
website: www.visithighlands.com

DORNOCH

The Coffee Shop, The Square, Dornoch,
Sutherland IV25 3SD
Tel: 01845 22 55 121
e-mail: info@visitscotland.com
website: www.visithighlands.com

DRUMNADROCHIT

The Car Park, Drumnadrochit, Inverness-shire IV63 6T
Tel: 0845 22 55 121
e-mail: info@visitscotland.com
website: www.visithighlands.com

DRYMEN

Drymen Library, The Square, Drymen,
Dunbartonshire G63 0BD
Tel: 08707 200 611
Fax: 01369 660 751
e-mail: info@drymen.visitscotland.com
website: www.visitscottishheartlands.org/

DUFFTOWN

Dufftown, Moray, Grampian
Tel: 01340 820501

DUMBARTON

7 Alexandra Parade, A82 Northbound, Milton,
Dunbartonshire G82 2TZ
Tel: 08707 200 629
Fax: 01369 70685
e-mail: info@dunoon.visitscotland.com
website: www.visitscottishheartlands.org/

DUMFRIES

64 Whitesands, Dumfries,
Dumfries and Galloway DG1 2RS
Tel: 01387 253862
Fax: 01378 245555
e-mail: info@dgtb.visitscotland.com
website: www.visitdumfriesandgalloway.co.uk

DUNBAR

143a High Street, Dunbar, Lothian EH42 1ES
Tel: 0845 22 55 121
e-mail: info@visitscotland.com

DUNBLANE

Stirling Road, Dunblane, Stirlingshire FK15 9EP
Tel: 08707 200 613
Fax: 08707 200 613
e-mail: info@dunblane.visitscotland.com
website: www.visitscottishheartlands.org/

DUNDEE

21 Castle Street, Dundee, Angus and Dundee DD1 3AA
Tel: 01382 527 527
e-mail: enquiries@angusanddundee.co.uk
website: www.angusanddundee.co.uk

DUNFERMLINE

1 High Street, Dunfermline, Fife KY12 7DL
Tel: 01383 720 999
e-mail: dunfermline@visitfife.com

DUNKELD

The Cross, Dunkeld, Perth & Kinross PH8 0AN
Tel: 01350 727688
Fax: 01350 727688
e-mail: dunkeldtic@perthshire.co.uk
website: www.perthshire.co.uk/

DUNNET HEAD

Brough, Caithness KW14 8YE
Tel: 01847 851991
e-mail: briansparks@dunnethead.com
website: www.dunnethead.com/

DUNOON

7 Alexandra Parade, Dunoon, Argyll and Bute PA23 8AB
Tel: 08707 200 629
Fax: 01369 706 085
e-mail: info@dunoon.visitscotland.com
website: www.visitscottishheartlands.com

DUNVEGAN

2 Lochside, Dunvegan, Isle of Skye IV55 8WB
Tel: 01845 22 55 121
e-mail: info@visitscotland.com
website: www.visithighlands.com

DURNESS

Durine, Durness, by Lairg, Sutherland IV27 4PN
Tel: 01845 22 55 121
Fax: 01506 832 222
e-mail: info@visitscotland.com
website: www.visithighlands.com

ELGIN

17 High Street, Elgin, Moray IV30 1EG
Tel: 01343 542 666
e-mail: Elgin@visitscotland.com

EYEMOUTH

Auld Kirk, Market Place, Eyemouth,
Scottish Borders TD14 5HE
Tel: 0870 6080404
Fax: 01750 21886
e-mail: bordersinfo@visitscotland.com
website: www.scot-borders.co.uk

FALKIRK

2-4 Glebe Street, Falkirk, Stirlingshire FK1 1HX
Tel: 08707 200 614
Fax: 01324 638440
e-mail: info@falkirk.visitscotland.com
website: www.visitscottishheartlands.org/

FORFAR

East High Street, Forfar, Angus and Dundee DD8 2EG
Tel: 01307 467876
e-mail: enquiries@angusanddundee.co.uk
website: www.angusanddundee.co.uk

FORRES

116 High Street, Forres, Moray IV36 0NP
Tel: 01309 673 783
e-mail: Forres@visitscotland.com

FORT AUGUSTUS

Car Park, Fort Augustus, Inverness-shire PH32 4DD
Tel: 01845 22 55 121
e-mail: info@visitscotland.com
website: www.visithighlands.com

FORT WILLIAM

Cameron Centre, Cameron Square, Fort William,
Inverness-shire PH33 6AJ
Tel: 01845 22 55 121
e-mail: info@visitscotland.com
website: www.visithighlands.com

FORTH BRIDGES

c/o Queensferry Lodge Hotel, St Margaret's Head,
North Queensferry, Fife KY11 1HP
Tel: 01383 417759
e-mail: forthbridges@visitfife.com

FRASERBURGH

3 Saltoun Square, Fraserburgh, Aberdeenshire AB43 9DA
Tel: 01346 518315

GAIRLOCH

Achtercairn, Gairloch, Ross-shire IV22 2DN
Tel: 01845 22 55 121
e-mail: info@visitscotland.com
website: www.visithighlands.com

GATEHOUSE OF FLEET

Car Park, Gatehouse of Fleet,
Dumfries and Galloway DG7 5EA
Tel: 01557 814212
e-mail: gatehouseoffleettic@visitscotland.com
website: www.visitdumfriesandgalloway.co.uk

GLASGOW

11 George Square, Glasgow, Strathclyde G2 1DY
Tel: 0141 204 4400
Fax: 0141 221 3524
e-mail: enquiries@seeglasgow.com
website: www.seeglasgow.com

GRANTOWN ON SPEY

54 High Street, Grantown on Spey,
Inverness-shire PH26 3EH
Tel: 01845 22 55 121
e-mail: info@visitscotland.com
website: www.visithighlands.com

GRETNA GREEN

Unit 10, Gretna Gateway Outlet Village, Glasgow Road,
Gretna, Dumfries and Galloway DG16 5GG
Tel: 01461 337834
e-mail: gretna@dgtb.visitscotland.com
website: www.visitdumfriesandgalloway.co.uk

HAMILTON

Road Chef Services, M74 Northbound, Hamilton,
South Lanarkshire ML3 6JW
Tel: 01698 285590
Fax: 01698 891494
e-mail: hamilton@seeglasgow.com
website: www.seeglasgow.com

HARESTANES

Ancrum, Harestanes, Jedburgh,
Scottish Borders TD8 6UQ
Tel: 0870 6080404
Fax: 01750 21886
e-mail: bordersinfo@visitscotland.com
website: www.scot-borders.co.uk

HAWICK

Drumlanrig's Tower Knowe, Hawick,
Scottish Borders TD9 9EN
Tel: 0870 6080404
Fax: 01750 21886
e-mail: bordersinfo@visitscotland.com
website: www.scot-borders.co.uk

HELENSBURGH

Clock Tower, The Pier, Helensburgh,
Dunbartonshire G84 7NY
Tel: 08707 200 615
Fax: 01436 672 642
e-mail: info@helensburgh.visitscotland.com
website: www.visitscottishheartlands.org/

HUNTLY

9a The Square, Huntly, Aberdeenshire AB54 8BR
Tel: 01466 792255

INVERARAY

Front Street, Inveraray, Argyll and Bute PA32 8UY
Tel: 08707 200 616
Fax: 01499 302 269
e-mail: info@inveraray.visitscotland.com
website: www.visitscottishheartlands.org/

INVERNESS

Castle Wynd, Inverness, Inverness-shire IV2 3BJ
Tel: 01845 22 55 121
e-mail: info@visitscotland.com
website: www.visithighlands.com

INVERURIE

Book Store, 18a High Street, Inverurie,
Aberdeenshire AB51 3XQ
Tel: 01467 625800

ISLAY

The Square, Main Street, Bowmore,
Isle of Islay PA43 7JP
Tel: 08707 200 617
Fax: 01496 810363
e-mail: info@islay.visitscotland.com
website: www.visitscottishheartlands.org/

JEDBURGH

Murray's Green, Jedburgh, Scottish Borders TD8 6BE
Tel: 0870 6080404
Fax: 01750 21886
e-mail: bordersinfo@visitscotland.com
website: www.scot-borders.co.uk

JOHN O'GROATS

County Road, John O'Groats, Caithness KW1 4YR
Tel: 01845 22 55 121
e-mail: info@visitscotland.com
website: www.visithighlands.com

KELSO

Town House, The Square, Kelso,
Scottish Borders TD5 7HF
Tel: 0870 6080404
e-mail: bordersinfo@visitscotland.com
website: www.scot-borders.co.uk

KILCHOAN

Kilchoan Community Centre, Pier Road, Kilchoan,
Acharacle, Argyll and Bute PH36 4LJ
Tel: 01845 22 55 121
e-mail: info@visitscotland.com
website: www.visithighlands.com

KINGUSSIE

Highland Folk Museum, Kingussie,
Inverness-shire PH21 1JG
Tel: 0845 22 55 121
e-mail: info@visitscotland.com
website: www.visithighlands.com

KIRKCALDY

The Merchant's House, 339 High Street, Kirkcaldy,
Fife KY1 1JL
Tel: 01592 267775
e-mail: kirkcaldy@visitfife.com

KIRKCUDBRIGHT

Harbour Square, Kirkcudbright,
Dumfries and Galloway DG6 4HY
Tel: 01557 330494
Fax: 01557 332416
e-mail: kirkcudbright@dgtb.visitscotland.com
website: www.visitdumfriesandgalloway.co.uk

KIRRIEMUIR

Cumberland Close, Kirriemuir,
Angus and Dundee DD8 4EF
Tel: 01575 574097
e-mail: enquiries@angusanddundee.co.uk
website: www.angusanddundee.co.uk

KYLE OF LOCHALSH

Car Park, Kyle of Lochalsh, Ross-shire IV40 8AQ
Tel: 01845 22 55 121
e-mail: info@visitscotland.com
website: www.visithighlands.com

LAIRG

Ferrycroft Countryside Centre, Lairg,
Sutherland IV27 4AZ
Tel: 01845 22 55 121
e-mail: info@visitscotland.com
website: www.visithighlands.com

LANARK

Horsemarket, Ladyacre Road, Lanark,
South Lanarkshire ML11 7LQ
Tel: 01555 661661
Fax: 01555 666143
e-mail: lanark@seeglasgow.com
website: www.seeglasgow.com

LARGS

Railway Station, Main Street, Largs, Ayrshire and Arran
Tel: 01475 673 765
website: www.ayrshire-arran.com

LERWICK

Market Cross, Lerwick, Shetland ZE1 0LU
Tel: 08701 999 440
Fax: 01595 695 807
e-mail: info@visitshetland.com
website: www.visitshetland.com

LINLITHGOW

Burgh Hall, The Cross, Linlithgow, Lothian EH49 8RE
Tel: 0845 22 55 121
e-mail: info@visitscotland.com
website: www.edinburgh.org

LOCHBOISDALE

Pier Road, Lochboisdale, Isle of South Uist HS8 5TH
Tel: 01878 700286
Fax: 01878 700286
e-mail: lochboisdale@visithebrides.com
website: www.visithebrides.com

LOCHCARRON

Main Street, Lochcarron, Ross-shire IV54 4LX
Tel: 01520 722357
Fax: 01520 722324

LOCHGILPHEAD

Lochnell Street, Lochgilphead, Argyll and Bute PA30 8JN
Tel: 08707 200 618
Fax: 01546 606 254
e-mail: info@lochgilphead.visitscotland.com
website: www.visitscottishheartlands.org/

LOCHMADDY

Pier Road, Lochmaddy, Isle of North Uist HS6 5AA
Tel: 01876 500 321
Fax: 01876 500 321
e-mail: lochmaddy@visithebrides.com
website: www.visithebrides.com

MALLAIG

The Pier, Mallaig, Inverness-shire PH41 4SQ
Tel: 01845 22 55 121
e-mail: info@visitscotland.com
website: www.visithighlands.com

MELROSE

Abbey House, Abbey Street, Melrose,
Scottish Borders TD6 9LG
Tel: 0870 6080404
Fax: 01750 21886
e-mail: bordersinfo@visitscotland.com
website: www.scot-borders.co.uk

MOFFAT

Churchgate, Moffat, Dumfries and Galloway DG10 9EG
Tel: 01683 220620
e-mail: moffat@dgtb.visitscotland.com
website: www.visitdumfriesandgalloway.co.uk

MONTROSE

Bridge Street, Montrose, Angus and Dundee DD10 8AB
Tel: 01674 672 000
e-mail: enquiries@angusanddundee.co.uk
website: www.angusanddundee.co.uk

NAIRN

The Library, 68 High Street, Nairn,
Inverness-shire IV12 4AU
Tel: 01845 22 55 121
e-mail: info@visitscotland.com
website: www.visithighlands.com

NEWTON STEWART

Dashwood Square, Newton Stewart, Dumfries and
Galloway DG8 6EQ
Tel: 01671 402431
e-mail: newtonstewart@dgtb.visitscotland.com
website: www.visitdumfriesandgalloway.co.uk

NEWTONGRANGE

Scottish Mining Museum, Newtongrange,
Lothian EH26 8HB
Tel: 0845 22 55 121
e-mail: info@visitscotland.com
website: www.edinburgh.org

NORTH BERWICK

Quality Street, North Berwick, Lothian EH39 4HJ
Tel: 0845 22 55 121
e-mail: info@visitscotland.com
website: www.edinburgh.org

NORTH KESSOCK

Picnic Site, North Kessock, Ross-shire IV1 1XB
Tel: 01845 22 55 121
e-mail: info@visitscotland.com
website: www.visithighlands.com

OBAN

Church Building, Argyll Square, Oban,
Argyll and Bute PA34 4AN
Tel: 08707 200 630
Fax: 01631 564273
e-mail: info@oban.visitscotland.com
website: www.visitscottishheartlands.org/

OLD CRAIGHALL

Old Craighall Service Area (A1), Musselburgh,
Lothian EH21 8RE
Tel: 0845 22 55 121
e-mail: info@visitscotland.com
website: www.edinburgh.org

PEEBLES

High Street, Peebles, Scottish Borders EH45 8AG
Tel: 0870 6080404
Fax: 01750 21886
e-mail: bordersinfo@visitscotland.com
website: www.scot-borders.co.uk

PERTH

Lower City Mills, West Mill Street, Perth,
Perth & Kinross PH1 5PQ
Tel: 01738 450600
Fax: 01738 444863
e-mail: perthtic@perthshire.co.uk
website: www.perthshire.co.uk/

PERTH (INVERALMOND)

Caithness Glass, Inveralmond, Perth,
Perth & Kinross PH1 3TZ
Tel: 01738 638481

PITLOCHRY

22 Atholl Road, Pitlochry, Perth & Kinross PH16 5BX
Tel: 01796 472215/472751
Fax: 01796 474046
e-mail: pitlochrytic@perthshire.co.uk
website: www.perthshire.co.uk/

PORTREE

Bayfield House, Bayfield Road, Portree,
Isle of Skye IV51 9EL
Tel: 01845 22 55 121
e-mail: info@visitscotland.com
website: www.visithighlands.com

SELKIRK

Halliwells House, Selkirk, Scottish Borders TD7 4BL
Tel: 0870 6080404
Fax: 01750 21886
e-mail: bordersinfo@visitscotland.com
website: www.scot-borders.co.uk

SPEAN BRIDGE

The Kingdom of Scotland, Spean Bridge, by Fort William,
Inverness-shire PH34 4EP
Tel: 01845 22 55 121
e-mail: info@visitscotland.com
website: www.visithighlands.com

ST ANDREWS

70 Market Street, St Andrews, Fife KY16 9NU
Tel: 01334 472021
e-mail: standrews@visitfife.com

STIRLING (DUMBARTON ROAD)

41 Dumbarton Road, Stirling, Stirlingshire FK8 2QQ
Tel: 08707 200 620
Fax: 01786 450 039
e-mail: stirlingtic@aillst.ossian.net
website: www.visitscottishheartlands.org/

STIRLING (PIRNHALL)

Motorway Service Area Junction 9 M9/M80, Pirnhall,
Stirling, Stirlingshire FK7 8ET
Tel: 08707 200 621
Fax: 01786 810 879
e-mail: info@pirnhall.visitscotland.com
website: www.visitscottishheartlands.org/

STONEHAVEN

66 Allardice Street, Stonehaven, Aberdeenshire AB39
2AA
Tel: 01569 762806

STORNOWAY

26 Cromwell Street, Isle of Lewis, Stornoway HS1 2DD
Tel: 01851 703088
Fax: 01851 705244
e-mail: stornoway@visithebrides.com
website: www.visithebrides.com

STRANRAER

28 Harbour Street, Stranraer,
Dumfries and Galloway DG9 7RA
Tel: 01776 702595
Fax: 01776 889156
e-mail: stranraer@dgtb.visitscotland.com
website: www.visitdumfriesandgalloway.co.uk

STRATHPEFFER

Square Wheels, The Square, Strathpeffer,
Ross-shire IV14 9DW
Tel: 01845 22 55 121
e-mail: info@visitscotland.com
website: www.visithighlands.com

STRONTIAN

Strontian, Acharacle, Argyll and Bute PH36 4HZ
Tel: 01845 22 55 121
e-mail: info@visitscotland.com
website: www.visithighlands.com

TARBERT

Pier Road, Tarbert, Isle of Harris HS3 3DJ
Tel: 01859 502 011
Fax: 01859 502 011
e-mail: tarbert@visithebrides.com
website: www.visithebrides.com

TARBERT (LOCH FYNE)

Harbour Street, Tarbert, Argyll and Bute PA29 6UD
Tel: 08707 200 624
Fax: 01880 820 082
e-mail: info@tarbert.visitscotland.com
website: www.visitscottishheartlands.org/

TARBET (LOCH LOMOND)

Main Street, Tarbet, Loch Lomond,
Argyll and Bute G83 7DE
Tel: 08707 200 623
Fax: 01301 702 224
e-mail: info@tarbet.visitscotland.com
website: www.visitscottishheartlands.org/

THURSO

Riverside, Thurso, Caithness KW14 8BU
Tel: 01845 22 55 121
e-mail: info@visitscotland.com
website: www.visithighlands.com

TOBERMORY

Main Street, Tobermory, Isle of Mull PA75 6NU
Tel: 08707 200 625
Fax: 01688 302145
e-mail: info@tobermory.visitscotland.com
website: www.visitscottishheartlands.org/

TOMINTOUL

The Square, Tomintoul, Aberdeenshire AB37 9ET
Tel: 01807 580285

TYNDRUM

Main Street, Tyndrum, Stirlingshire FK20 8RY
Tel: 08707 200 626
Fax: 01838 400530
e-mail: info@tyndrum.visitscotland.com
website: www.visitscottishheartlands.org/

ULLAPOOL

Argyle Street, Ross-shire, Ullapool IV26 2UB
Tel: 01845 22 55 121
e-mail: info@visitscotland.com
website: www.visithighlands.com

WICK

Norseman Hotel, Riverside, Wick, Caithness KW1 4NL
Tel: 01845 22 55 121
e-mail: info@visitscotland.com
website: www.visithighlands.com

Towns, Villages and Places of Interest

606

618

Y

TRAVEL PUBLISHING ORDER FORM

To order any of our publications just fill in the payment details below and complete the order form. For orders of less than 4 copies please add £1.00 per book for postage and packing. Orders over 4 copies are P & P free.

Name:

Address:

Tel no:

Please Complete Either:

I enclose a cheque for £ _____ made payable to Travel Publishing Ltd

Or:

Card No: Expiry Date:

Signature:

Please either send, telephone, fax or e-mail your order to:
Travel Publishing Ltd, 7a Apollo House, Calleva Park, Aldermaston, Berkshire RG7 8TN
Tel: 0118 981 7777   Fax: 0118 940 8428   e-mail: info@travelpublishing.co.uk

	Price	Quantity		Price	Quantity
HIDDEN PLACES REGIONAL TITLES			**COUNTRY PUBS AND INNS**		
Cornwall	£8.99	....	Cornwall	£5.99	....
Devon	£8.99	....	Devon	£7.99	....
Dorset, Hants & Isle of Wight	£8.99	....	Sussex	£5.99	....
East Anglia	£8.99	....	Wales	£8.99	....
Lake District & Cumbria	£8.99	....	Yorkshire	£7.99	....
Northumberland & Durham	£8.99	....			
Peak District and Derbyshire	£8.99	....	**COUNTRY LIVING RURAL GUIDES**		
Yorkshire	£8.99	....	East Anglia	£10.99	....
			Heart of England	£10.99	....
HIDDEN PLACES NATIONAL TITLES			Ireland	£11.99	....
England	£11.99	....	North East	£10.99	....
Ireland	£11.99	....	North West	£10.99	....
Scotland	£11.99	....	Scotland	£11.99	....
Wales	£11.99	....	South of England	£10.99	....
			South East of England	£10.99	....
HIDDEN INNS TITLES			Wales	£11.99	....
East Anglia	£7.99	....	West Country	£10.99	....
Heart of England	£7.99	....			
South	£7.99	....			
South East	£7.99	....	**TOTAL QUANTITY:**		
West Country	£7.99	....	**POST & PACKING:**		
OTHER TITLES			**TOTAL VALUE:**		
Off the Motorway	£11.99	....			

READER REACTION FORM

The *Travel Publishing* research team would like to receive reader's comments on any visitor attractions or places reviewed in the book and also recommendations for suitable entries to be included in the next edition. This will help ensure that the *Country Living series of Guides* continues to provide its readers with useful information on the more interesting, unusual or unique features of each attraction or place ensuring that their visit to the local area is an enjoyable and stimulating experience. To provide your comments or recommendations would you please complete the forms below and overleaf as indicated and send to:

**The Research Department, Travel Publishing Ltd,
7a Apollo House, Calleva Park, Aldermaston, Reading, RG7 8TN.**

Your Name:

Your Address:

Your Telephone Number:

Please tick as appropriate:

Comments ☐   Recommendation ☐

Name of Establishment:

Address:

Telephone Number:

Name of Contact:

READER REACTION FORM

COMMENT OR REASON FOR RECOMMENDATION:

....

....

....

....

....

....

....

....

....

....

....

....

....

....

....

....

....

....

....

READER REACTION FORM

The *Travel Publishing* research team would like to receive reader's comments on any visitor attractions or places reviewed in the book and also recommendations for suitable entries to be included in the next edition. This will help ensure that the *Country Living series of Guides* continues to provide its readers with useful information on the more interesting, unusual or unique features of each attraction or place ensuring that their visit to the local area is an enjoyable and stimulating experience. To provide your comments or recommendations would you please complete the forms below and overleaf as indicated and send to:

**The Research Department, Travel Publishing Ltd,
7a Apollo House, Calleva Park, Aldermaston, Reading, RG7 8TN.**

Your Name:

Your Address:

Your Telephone Number:

Please tick as appropriate:

Comments ☐   Recommendation ☐

Name of Establishment:

Address:

Telephone Number:

Name of Contact:

READER REACTION FORM

COMMENT OR REASON FOR RECOMMENDATION:

....

....

....

....

....

....

....

....

....

....

....

....

....

....

....

....

....

....

READER REACTION FORM

The *Travel Publishing* research team would like to receive reader's comments on any visitor attractions or places reviewed in the book and also recommendations for suitable entries to be included in the next edition. This will help ensure that the *Country Living series of Guides* continues to provide its readers with useful information on the more interesting, unusual or unique features of each attraction or place ensuring that their visit to the local area is an enjoyable and stimulating experience. To provide your comments or recommendations would you please complete the forms below and overleaf as indicated and send to:

**The Research Department, Travel Publishing Ltd,
7a Apollo House, Calleva Park, Aldermaston, Reading, RG7 8TN.**

Your Name:

Your Address:

Your Telephone Number:

Please tick as appropriate:

Comments ☐   Recommendation ☐

Name of Establishment:

Address:

Telephone Number:

Name of Contact:

READER REACTION FORM

COMMENT OR REASON FOR RECOMMENDATION:

....
....
....
....
....
....
....
....
....
....
....
....
....
....
....
....
....
....
....
....

Index of Advertisers

FOOD AND DRINK

633

PLACES OF INTEREST